RAYMOND A. PALMER
TRIBUTE EDITION

OAHSPE

A Sacred History Of The Dominions Of The Higher And Lower Heavens Of The Earth For The Past 24,000 Years. Together With A Synopsis Of The Cosmogony Of The Universe, The Creation Of The Planets, The Creation of Man, The Unseen World, The Labor And Glory Of Gods And Goddesses In The Etherean Heavens.

VOLUME 2

OAHSPE
RAYMOND A. PALMER EDITION
JOHN BALLOU NEWBROUGH

For free catalog write:
Global Communications
P.O. Box 753
New Brunswick, NJ 08903

Free Subscription to Conspiracy Journal E-Mail Newsletter
www.conspiracyjournal.com

Email: mrufo8@hotmail.com

THE STORY OF AN AMAZING BOOK OAHSPE

By Ray Palmer

The following article written by Raymond A. Palmer (RAP) originally appeared in Amazing Stories in 1948. In it, Palmer describes the importance of Oahspe and how it impressed him from an historical as well as journalistic point of view and provided him the enthusiasm to reprint the 1882 version of Oahspe years later. This edition has become known as the "Green Edition" because of the color of its cover.

****

Some time ago we mentioned in these pages that we'd read a very amazing book that would prove of interest to any science fiction fan, as well as prove very startling to any thinking reader in still other ways. Many of our readers got the book, and since then we have received a variety of opinions and expressions of interest that have proven our tip to be correct. Actually, we think, taken from a science fiction viewpoint, *Oahspe* is a book that should not be missed by a real "fan." Since many of our readers have requested that we give them more information about it, we are going to depart from our usual policy, and review a book in our pages.

For the moment, let's take the book as strictly a work of fiction, ignoring any other claims that may be made for it. To begin with, the author is John Ballou Newbrough. He was born on a farm near Springfield, Ohio, June 5, 1828. College education, specializing in medicine and dentistry. He was a big man, and the call of the Australian gold fields drew him to adventure. Returning, he became a dentist in New York, married and had a son and a daughter. He had another daughter by a second wife. He died in Donna Ana, New Mexico, April 23, 1891. He is buried in the Masonic Burial Grounds at Los Cruces, New Mexico.

He wrote *Oahspe* (he says in a letter) in 1881 in one year, by working fifteen minutes each morning about a half-hour before

I

sunrise. He used one of the first typewriters invented, which had its keys arranged in a semi-circle around its front in a single line. He wrote in total darkness!

The book has approximately 700,000 words, and was written in approximately 5,300 minutes – which figures out to 130-plus words per minute. Your editor has seen a typewriter of exactly the same make as the one Newbrough used, and, brother, that's typing. But not impossible. Many authors, by attaining such complete mental detachment as is indicated by Newbrough's statement that he wrote in darkness, can do similar feats of writing today. Your editor has done 90 words per minute on a single manuscript under slightly similar circumstances.

The author claims the book to be a "history" of the Earth (insofar as human habitation is concerned) for 79,000 years; including a history of the same period in an invisible counterpart of the Earth's surface located in the atmosphere. It also includes snatches of related history of the same period on other planets, both visible and invisible, located in nearby and distant space.

It is this portion of the book that should prove of great interest to the science fiction fan, who is interested in stories of this type. This "history" is detailed in vivid action which sometimes grows quite vociferous. Especially interesting are histories of such characters already familiar to the reader as mythological entities, such as Thor, Apollo, Osiris, etc., who are not dealt with as they are in legend, but as visitors from space who arrive in gigantic spaceships, armed with such scientific marvels as have seldom been imagined even in the most ambitious of interplanetary tales. H.G. Wells' "War of the Worlds" fades to insignificance beside the wars fought by these characters, who are depicted as actual human beings, many of whom actually were born and lived on this planet.

The sinking of the continent of Pan (misnamed as Lermuria in popular terminology) by a titanic being from space named Aph is a study of sheer drama.

The visit of Apollo to Earth for the purpose of improving the physical appearance of mankind is another dramatic story, replete with delights for the avid science fiction fan.

Although the story is written with a flair toward a "biblical" type of presentation, which sometimes makes for slow reading, your editor regards the lyrical beauty and literary excellence of many passages to be unsurpassed by even the greatest literature of the Bible, or of Shakespeare, or of any other writer.

To the reader who is interested in more than simple entertainment, i.e., ancient history, mythology, etc., **Oahspe** presents what we might call a "brown study." All of the mythology of the world has been fitted into a composite and chronological whole that is entirely related. One cannot help but feel that here is either the *truth* about the origin of our modern and classical myths, or Mr. Newbrough has devised a common "denominator" which in itself is a tremendous feat. Your editor himself has decided, after two years of study, that until a better explanation of mythology comes along, he will accept this one as the only plausible working basis, no matter what other connotations the "history" may have.

To the anthropologist, to the student of ancient races and civilizations, to those who delve into the earth and study ancient artifacts and ruins to uncover the mystery of the migrations and origins of peoples, *Oahspe* can and does present a great deal of food for thought. Scientific discoveries made since 1881 in these fields (which will be well known to those who are interested, and instantly applied to the book) have either proved to be incredibly lucky coincidences, or they would tend to indicate that *Oahspe's* "history" is just that. The inferences to be drawn from such a line of thought are tremendous, and should not be entertained by the casual reader.

To the scientist, the chemist, physicist and astronomer especially, several sections of *Oahspe* present a challenge — but a challenge that, based on the light of present-day scientific research, will be taken to be no challenge at all. To say that *Oahspe's* science is at variance with accepted concepts would be putting it mildly.

Perhaps the interest of the scientist would be in the broadly comprehensive and "logical" way in which the book builds up a scientific concept which, taken as a whole, is quite satisfactory and workable. We have read science fiction stories of other planets where the civilization followed a line of development which differed radically from that taken by humanity on Earth, and it can truly be said that *Oahspe's* "try" in this direction is a masterful one. There is no need to accept it, nor any need to become vociferous in rejecting it. Any scientifically minded reader who would go out of his way to "disprove" the science of *Oahspe* would only be admitting, in his own mind, the weakness of his own fundamental concepts.

One of the most amazing features of *Oahspe* is a series of language charts which purport to carry language development on Earth up from the first written language (Panic) to modern tongues. Although your editor has spent many hours studying these charts for inconsistencies, he has yet to find one. Truly here is one of the mysterious things that make *Oahspe* worthwhile from the same standpoint that makes a crossword puzzle book worthwhile. Many readers would find great fascination in "solving" the puzzles presented by these charts.

If you should happen to have a mystical streak in your makeup, *Oahspe* ought to prove a gold mine of interest to you. The subject of religion, as related to history (*Oahspe's* history) is an intriguing one. If you have any ideas about life after death, about "heaven" or "hell," here is a book that has as much claim to greatness as does Milton's *Paradise Lost* and *Paradise Regained*.

To the metaphysical, *Oahspe* presents a challenge. Its concepts along these lines are absorbingly interesting. It provides fuel for mental calisthenics which can lead to unknown heights.

And finally, to the philosopher, here is another "complete" picture of things as they might really be. Or, as might better be said, as close to reality as any concept can be. Reality is that elusive thing which is impossible to reach. We conceive of no ultimate reality, of no ultimate Creator, of no ultimate truth – and in that sense, *Oahspe* will be as eminently acceptable to the philosopher as any philosophy yet devised; and who can say to what degree it is "reality approached"?

Because your editor has been a science fiction fan for 25 years, and has found this book of absorbing interest viewed in the light of his hobby, it would seem "well put" to recommend this book to others like himself.

Oahspe calls itself a "New Bible" but don't let that influence you one way or another. The book is (1) entertaining; (2) thought-provoking; (3) well in line with the interests of AMAZING STORIES' content; (4) inextricably linked with the most amazing mystery ever to be presented in any science fiction magazine, the Shaver Mystery. Mr. Shaver himself, while rejecting all of the philosophy and mysticism of the book, recognizes that it is a fine "thought record" of the past, and in his words, is "probably true in a historical sense." If you happen to be a student of the Shaver Mystery, here's just one of the facets of this mystery which may serve to convince you it is no hoax.

Is *Oahspe* the work of John Ballou Newbrough, or is it the work of "spirits" as he claims, or is it, perhaps, the work of Shaver's cave people, and drawn from his "thought records"? Or are all of them talking about the same thing?

Your editor has his own ideas – which have served to entertain him mightily.

Article "Rediscovered" By David Waterman

ShaverMystery@Yahoogroups.com

OAHSPE

Volume 2

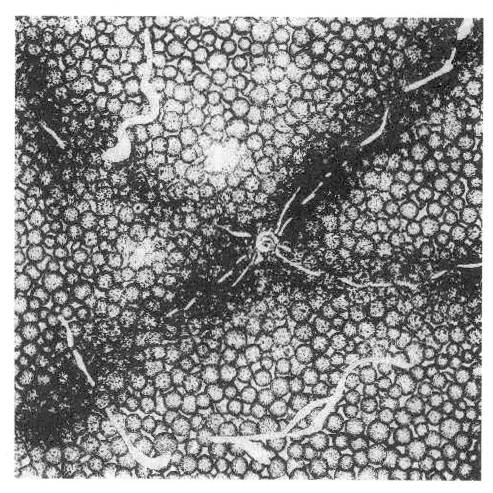

Plate 19.
THE EARTH IN KAS'KAK.

Jehovih said: That My Gods might learn to master the elements of My heavens, I brought the earth into the etherean Forest of Kas'Kak. And lo and behold, angels and mortals fell in the darkness. And Anuhasaj established the names Lord God and De'yus (Dyaus) (Deity) as worshipful on the earth. Before that time, man worshipped Me under the term Great Spirit. And man built the great pyramid as a monument of his own darkness.

611

BOOK OF LIKA, SON OF JEHOVIH.

KNOWN IN HEAVEN AS THE DAWN OF BON, AND ON EARTH AS THE CYCLE OF MOSES, CAPILYA AND CHINE! JEHOVIH SAID: I GAVE UNTO THE EARTH A TIME OF FULL EARTHHOOD; AND, THAT THE GENERATIONS OF MEN MIGHT KNOW THE PERIOD THEREOF, BEHOLD, I CAUSED MAN TO BUILD A PYRAMID IN THE MIDDLE OF THE WORLD. FOR IT WAS MY MARK, THAT, FROM THAT TIME HENCEFORTH, MAN SHOULD TURN FROM STONE TEMPLES, AND THE HOPE OF EVERLASTING FLESH-LIFE, AND REJOICE IN SPIRITUAL ABODES IN MY ETHEREAN HEAVENS. AND I BROUGHT THE EARTH OUT OF DARKNESS AND ENCOMPASSED IT AROUND WITH THE DAWN OF BON.

CHAPTER I.

1. In the far-off etherean worlds spake the Voice of Jehovih, saying: Lika, Lika, My Son! Behold the red star, the earth. She cometh thy way; she mergeth dark and soiled from the forests of ji'ay, in the swamps of Bonassah. She will cross thy etherean fields, the Takuspe, and Opel, and Wedojain, dripping with the odor and dross of the ji'ay'an swamps. Go thou to her, and wash clean her soil and her atmospherean heavens.

2. Lika said: Alas, O Jehovih, how they have forgotten Thee!

3. I will go to the red star, the earth, O Father! I will deliver her into purity and faith. Thy chosen shall be delivered from bondage; Thy God made triumphant on earth and in her heavens.

4. Lika called to his high Council, in his etherean kingdom, Vetta'puissa, in the Plains of Peo'ya, off the Road of Ahtogonassas, at the high Arc of Bon, made light by the holy angels of tens of thousands of years; and he said:

5. Behold, the red star, the earth; the Voice of Jehovih came to me, saying: Go thou to her, O My Son, and wash clean her soil and her atmospherean heavens. And I said: I will go, O Father! I will deliver her into purity and faith.

6. Lika said: Five hundred million etherean hosts will I take with me. For five years and forty days will I and my hosts sojourn on the red star and in her heavens. Her true God shall be restored and delivered in my name by Jehovih's hand. According to the rank of harvest of the gardens of Honyon, so shall my marshals choose and record my hosts.

7. Then spake the Council, the historians of the etherean libraries of the Vorkman Road, where hath traveled the earth for tens of thousands of years. And they detailed the affairs of the earth for many cycles past; made plain before the Gods assembled all the doings of the earth and her heavens.

8. Then Lika sent swift messengers off to the earth and her heavens; in arrow-ships of fire they sped forth, twenty thousand, well skilled in coursing the etherean heavens and penetrating the atmospherean vortices of traveling stars. To obtain the details of her God and her false Gods; her Lords and false Lords; her hadas and her hells; to scan her libraries and hastily return to Vetta'puissa, to lay the matters before the high Council and Lika, the Nirvanian Chief on Jehovih's throne.

9. Lika was sprung from the corporeal star Atos, which traversed the roads, Yatas-ko-owen, of the south circuit of Thoese, the vortex of another far-off sun, and was raised to etherea in the cycle of Sai-kah, one hundred and twenty-five thousand years, by Meth-ya, Goddess of Ori-iyi, afterward Chieftainess of Yeuna-gamaya.

10. And Lika rose to be God of Avalassak four thousand years; God of Kemma, six

thousand years; Inspector of Judas' etherean roads at the a'ji'an swamps of Hennassit, fifteen thousand years; Surveyor of Iwalt, two thousand years; Surveyor of the Wacha excursion, four thousand years; Recorder of Hitte-somat, eight thousand years; Deliverer of Habian vortices, twenty-six thousand years; Measurer of densities in Ablank, one thousand years; Recorder of the Ratiotyivi, two thousand years; God of the Home Plains of Cteverezed, twelve thousand years; and Chief of Vetta-puissa, twenty-five thousand years.

11.Lika had for his high Council thirty thousand Chieftains and Chieftainesses, of grades of more than a hundred thousand years in the etherean worlds; five hundred thousand of the rank of Inspectors; seven millions of the rank of Gods and Goddesses; and of the rank of Lords and Lordesses, more than half a thousand million.

12. Of the Rapon hosts there were seven Chiefs and nine Chieftainesses, who were Lika's private companions. First, Rebsad, Chief of So-tissav, forty thousand years; Sufristor of Sheleves, sixty thousand years; Marshal of Zele'axi, twenty thousand years; Master of Bassaion, seventy thousand years; and he passed twenty thousand years on the journey of Loo-soit-ta-vragenea, besides thousands of other journeys of less duration.

13. Next to Rebsad was Yanodi, Chieftainess of Ure, seventy thousand years; Chieftainess of the Roads of Sallatamya, seventy thousand years; marshalless of Petanasa, forty thousand years; Goddess of the ji-ay'an forest of Loo-loo-woh-ga, sixty-five thousand years; besides Goddess of Mor, Goddess of Chichigennahsmmah, Goddess of El, and of Raumba, and of Zee.

14. Next to Yanodi was Thazid, Goddess of Zoleth; Matrusettes of Yith-kad, Chieftainess of Hagu, Chieftainess of De'baur, and of Hachull, and of the Roads of Oleaskivedho, besides Goddess of more than one hundred etherean worlds.

15. Then came Thoso, Chief of Kassarah and Dassamatz, ninety thousand years; God of Saxax, seven thousand years; God of Chennesa, God of Hoxora, God of Fiben, God of Hotab, each six thousand years; surveyor of the Lymthian Roads, twelve thousand years; marker of meteors, two thousand years; Fireman of Thostus on the Ibien excursion, thirty thousand years.

16. Next to Thoso came Miente, Chieftainess of Gawl and Sanabtis, in whose dominions the star T-lemos was uzated, when Gai-loo opened the Road of Enjxi-ustus for the Nizaigi vortices of Messak; Chieftainess of Lam-Goo and Kud, Goddess of Itzi, Goddess of Ashem and of the Baxgor Wing, Goddess of the Duik Swamps, and Lordess of Sus and Havrij; in all one hundred and seven thousand years.

17. Chama-jius stood next; she was Chieftainess of Hors-ad and Tu and Okadad, Goddess of Asthy, and Hid, and Sheaugus, and Jagri, Surveyor of Arvat and the Vadhuan Roads; surveyor of Anchas; surveyor of the Han Mountains in the etherean Uuj of Drij-Lee; in all two hundred and sixty thousand years.

18. Next stood Murdhana, Chieftainess of D'hup and Hen-Dhi, Chieftainess of Happa and Hirish, surveyor of Sepher and Daka, Inspector of Anachu, and Zadon, and Edau, and Medtisha, and Roth; in all ninety thousand years.

19. Oshor stood next: Chief of Out-si and of Yotek, and of Samoan, and of Yadakha, maker of the Bridge of Weasitee, Marshal of the Honlaguoth expedition, and, besides these places, God of seven etherean worlds; in all one hundred and twelve thousand years.

20. Next came Yihoha, Chief of Shung-how and Agon, Chief of Neo-sin, God of Izeaha,

and Kaon, and Ahsow, and Una, and Yuk-Hoh, and Ahgoon. He was also the builder of the Raxon etherean arches; in all ninety thousand years.

21. Hisin was next: Chief of the Kionas Belt, where Yagota, the Orian Chief, walled the Plains of Maga, the Nirvanian home of the delivered hells of Mina half a million years before. Hismi was here nicknamed Creator of Wit, because of establishing his Chieftaincy on the ruins of hell. He was also Chief of Mamsa and Jauap, God of Gah, and of Darah, the region of fountain flowers; in all ninety thousand years.

22. Bowen was next: Chief of Apaha, formerly the Farms of Lung-wan and Srid, Chief of Vadhua, and of the Valleys of Nasqam, where a million years before the Chief of Chaksa disrupted the Atmospherean Sakri, and liberated from its four thousand hells more than thirty thousand million angel slaves in chaos. Bowen had also served as God of Amaan, and Havat, and Shedo, and Pivan; and as measurer of Pracha, and Xeri, and Asthus, surveyor of Ulam, and Sheyom, and Chozeh and Zadark, in all eighty thousand years.

23. Gwan Goo was next; she was Chieftainess of Andol, the place of the one-time apex of the Karowgan vortex, whereat was formed the star Ogitas and sent on its course by Aclon-guin, Orian hemmer of Shegoweasa. This vortex, when first formed by Aclon-guin, was three hundred thousand million miles long and was cometary thirty thousand years in Aclon-guin's hands. Gwan Goo was also Chieftainess of Ahsa-thah and Waegon; Goddess of Anoa, and of Howgil, and of Zahaive; in all one hundred and ninety thousand years.

24. Geehoogan was next; Chieftainess of Sumatri in the By-roads of Yotargis, Chieftainess of the four etherean worlds, Yoni, Ogh, Theum and Wachwakags; surveyor of Unshin, Zarihea and Keanteri; inspectress of Saquiz, and Hagimal, and Hafha, and Borax, and Rab, and Shor-loo; in all eighty thousand years.

25. Next stood Bachne-isij, Chief of Yahalom, where the Gein Maker, Tarmoth, cleared the Forests of the a'ji'an Haloth, in making a roadway for Havalad's group of Shemasian corporeal stars, in which labor he employed ninety thousand million Nirvanians for four thousand years, and the distance of the road was more than one hundred thousand million miles. Bachne-isij was Chief of Agwan, and Shoe-nastus, and Hador, and Ad; God of Vach, and of Kuja, and Rai, and Kathab, and Cynab, and Buhd, and Abbir; measurer of the mountains of the etherean worlds, Vijhath, and Hakan, and Dis; measurer of the arches in the etherean world Niksh; constructor of the Plains in the Nirvanian world Chom; in all one hundred and thirty thousand years.

26. Rehemg was next; Chieftainess of Otaskaka, commonly called World of Shining Waters, a great visiting place in Nirvania; she was Goddess of Theasapalas and Timax, weigher of Sultzhowtcih in the Ofel Plains; in all one hundred and ten thousand years.

27. Then stood Antosiv, Goddess of Munn, renowned because she was of two hundred and sixty thousand years, and had declined exaltation above the rank of Goddess.

28. Such, then, were the Rapon hosts.

CHAPTER II.

1. Far and wide, spread the words of Lika, words of Jehovih, over the Plains of Poe-ya, first highest light in etherea, where traveled the earth and her heavens. Far off, toward the northern group of twinkling stars, gazed the etherean millions; rose the voice of millions:

Where is the red star? Where lieth the earth and her troubled heavens? Is not this the young star, a satellite that traveleth with the hidan sun? What is the angle and course of this little, traveling world, that our eyes may feast on the road where soon our Chief will send Jehovih's redeeming ships?

2. Then they pointed, surmising, by the red-like color and tedious motion, which was the earth, one of the small gems that Jehovih had placed in the measureless firmament. And they gazed thereon, speaking with souls of delight: Great art Thou, O Jehovih, to build so wide. To stud the etherean worlds with gems like these; to provide a place for the souls of men to germinate. Surely her people, the sons and daughters of the red star, must behold etherea; must realize the difference betwixt a short corporeal life and this endless paradise. Can it be that they have, in their small heavens, unscrupulous false Lords and false Gods who set themselves up to be worshipped as creators, whom mortals name with bated breath? And have they, too, a host of Saviors, who profess to have the key to all the roads that lead into this great expanse, the etherean worlds? Some excuse mortals have who are brought forth to life on the central suns, to be stubborn in their egotism of their Lords and Saviors and Gods; but on one so small like the earth, how can it be?

3. Then came back Lika's swift messengers in their arrow-ships; messengers attained to be very Gods in wisdom, and in swiftness. And they quickly told the tale, about their visit to the red star and her heavens; told how the true God, Son of Jehovih, had struggled on, but had been outmatched by all odds by self-Gods and self-Lords, who had plunged thousands of millions of hapless souls into torturing hells.

4. And this news Lika spread abroad in his etherean dominions, which only needed to be told once, for every sympathetic soul by his shocked appearance told it to others, the like of which spread instantly to thousands of millions of high-raised ethereans. And when Lika said: Five hundred million angels shall go with me to the troubled earth and her heavens, in double-quick time the volunteers were ready to be enrolled on the list.

5. Then Lika inquired more fully of the swift messengers, and they answered him, saying: This, O Lika, Son of Jehovih! The earth hath passed her corporeal maturity, and mortals have set up a pyramid to mark the time thereof. The days of the highest, greatest audacity of the self-Gods are passed, and are memorized by the pyramid also; for in that self same time, they taught mortals to worship the God and the Lord and the Savior, instead of the Great Spirit, Jehovih. But darkness is upon the self-Gods, and they are bound in hells; and mortals are also bound in hells.

6. Behold, this is the first dawn of dan on the earth since she passed the limit of her greatest corporeality.

CHAPTER III.

1. Lika said to his chief marshal: Enroll thou my hosts, five hundred millions, and appoint unto them captains and generals, and grade them and apportion them. Beside these give me one million singers, one million trumpeters, one million attendants, one million heralds, one million messengers and one million recorders and waiters.

2. Lika called his chief builder and said unto him: Build me a fire-ship, an airavagna, with capacity for a thousand millions; and provide thou the ship with officers and workmen sufficient. Consult thou with my mathematicians as to the distance to the red

star, and as to the densities through which the ship shall pass, and as to the power required, and the time of the journey, and provide thou all things sufficient therefore.

3. Then Lika spake to the high Council, saying: For the time of my absence my vice-Chief, Heih-Woo shall hold my place. Touching matters whereof ye desire my voice before I go, speak ye!

4. Atunzi said: Behold, O Lika, the star, Yatis, headeth towards the a'ji'an Forests of Actawa, and she hath not passed the esparan age! Lika said: To clear the forest Actawa I appoint Eashivi, Goddess, with three thousand million laborers. Eashivi, how sayest thou? Eashivi said: Thanks to Jehovih and to thee, O Lika. I will at once choose my laborers and proceed to make the road.

5. Wan Tu'y said: Erst thy return, O Lika, the Hapsa-ogan vortex will cross the south fields of Vetta'puissa. She hath twenty thousand million souls in grades of sixty and seventy. Lika said: To her assistance for three years I appoint Tici-king, God, with fifty millions for his hosts. How sayest thou, Tici-king? Tici-king said: By the grace of Jehovih, I rejoice in this labor. In suffucient time will I prepare my hosts and accomplish what thou hast given into my keeping.

6. Wothalowsit said: In four years the hosts of E'win will return from the double stars, Eleb and Wis, with their harvest of forty thousand million angels. How shall they be apportioned? Lika said: To Bonassah, six thousand millions; to Opel, two thousand millions; to Wedojain, five thousand millions; to Eosta, two thousand millions; to Feuben Roads, seven thousand millions; to Zekel, four thousand millions; to Huron, three thousand millions; to Poe-ga, six thousand millions; to Yulit, one thousand millions, and to Zulava, four thousand millions; and I appoint Misata, Goddess, to provide the places in these several heavens for them, and to have charge of their selection and allotment. And I give to her five hundred million angels for her laboring hosts. How sayest thou, Misata? Misata said: It is Jehovih's gift; I am rejoiced. I will prepare myself and my hosts.

7. Ching Huen said: Behold the star-world, Esatas, in her se'muan age will cross the Roads of Veh-yuis in three years hence! Lika answered Ching Huen, saying: To cross these roads of light in her se'muan age would blight her power to bring forth animal life sufficient unto her wide continents. The trail must be filled with se'muan forests to preserve her gestative season. To this labor I appoint Ieolakak, God of Esatas' se'muan forests in the Roads of Veh-yuis, four thousand years. And I allot to Ieolakak six thousand million laborers. How sayest thou, Ieolakak? He answered: This is a great labor; by the wisdom and power of Jehovih, I will accomplish it.

8. Veaga-indras said: In two years the fleets of Leogastrivins will return from their voyage of four thousand years, bringing two thousand million guests from the Iniggihauas regions. Who shall provide for their reception? Lika said: Yeanopstan, with ten million hosts. How sayest thou? Yeanopstan said: A most welcome labor, O Lika.

9. Hiss-Joso said: The Arches of Rassittissa, the etherean world of Yungtsze's Plains, will be to cast in four years. Lika said: To Sut'tuz six million arches, and to Iviji four million arches, and to each of them one hundred million laborers. How say ye? Then spake Suttuz and Iviji, saying: By the help of Jehovih, the labor will be accomplished.

10. Sachcha said: The star-world, Neto, will be to turn on her axis in two years hence, in which time she will pass through the south Fields of Takuspe. Lika said: This will be a great labor, and I appoint Urassus, with Salas, to accomplish it. And I give to them three

years, with four thousand million laborers. How say ye? Then answered Urassus and Salas saying: With fear and trembling we rejoice at this great work. By Jehovih's wisdom and power, we shall accomplish it.

11. After this manner Lika made more than a thousand appointments to be accomplished ere he return from the earth and her heavens; but ordinary matters he left with his vice-Chief, Heih-Woo, and to the high Council, the select ten millions.

12. Jehovih had said: Even as I provided a little labor unto mortals to develop the talents I created withal, so in like manner, and after the same like, but spiritually, provided I greater labor unto the high-risen inhabitants in My etherean worlds. For which reason let My children learn the secret of harmonious and united labor with one another. I gave labor to man not as a hardship, but as a means of great rejoicing.

13. And the talents I gave on corpor, I gave not to die on corpor, but to continue on forever. As I gave talent for corporeal mathematics, and talent for corporeal buildings, even a talent for all things on corporeal worlds; even so provided I in My etherean worlds for the same talents, but spiritually. Wherein man on the corporeal earth, judging the adaptability of talent to corporeal things, may comprehend the nature of the labors I provided in My exalted heavens for the same talents.

14. Neither let any man fear that his talents may become too exalted for the work I have provided; for until he hath created a firmament, and created suns and stars to fill it, he hath not half fulfilled his destiny.

CHAPTER IV.

1. Jehovih spake in the light of the throne of Kairksak, in Vetta'puissa, saying: Lika, My Son! This is My road and My journey. With thee and thy hosts My Voice shall travel with power; on the earth will I lie My foundation, in spirit and word. Thy companion Chiefs and Chieftainesses shall go with thee; they shall help deliver the inhabitants of the earth and her heavens.

2. My enemies have marked their labors in temples and pyramids. Because their hearts rose not up to Me, they descended into stone, the most dead of all things. They have carried the inhabitants of the earth down to rottenness and to death. Suffer their monuments to stand as testimonies of them that hated Me, that denied Me, that believed not in Me, the All Person.

3. My building shall be the most subtle of all things, the spirit of mine own body. Verily shall it be a monument within the souls of My chosen. Nor will it go away again in darkness, but it shall encompass the whole earth.

4. For thou shalt find My chosen a scattered people, persecuted and enslaved, the most despised of all the races of men. But I will show My power with them; I will raise them up; the things I do through them, and the words I speak through them, even in t heir ignorance and darkness, shall become mighty. Their words shall be treasured forever; and none can match them in wisdom of speech, or in the craft of good works.

5. But the learned men of all other peoples shall be forgotten; their wisdom be like the wind that bloweth away. The self-Gods and self-Lords that led them astray shall be as a serpent that biteth itself unto death. Yea, as long as their pyramids and temples stand, their own falsehoods shall stare them in the face.

6. They have bound themselves in their own bulwarks; they shall yet be My laborers, thousands of years, to undo the evil they sowed on the earth. Nor shall they look down from heaven and behold with joy their temples and pyramids; but as one beholdeth a coal of fire burning in the flesh, so shall their edifices cry out unto them forever: Thou False One. And it shall be to them a burning fire that will not die out.

7. And their great learning, even of the stars and the sun and moon, and of all the things of the earth, and in the waters, shall pass away and be remembered not amongst men. Yea, the names of their men of great learning shall go down, with none to remember them on the earth. And in time, long after, the nations of people will forget them and their wisdom, and even pity them, and say of them: What a foolish people!

8. But My chosen, who are their slaves, and are as nothing in the world, shall speak, and their words shall not be forgotten; shall write, and their books will be a new foundation in the world. Because My hand will be upon them, My wisdom shall come forth out of their mouths.

9. And this shall be testimony in the ages to come, as to what manner of knowledge endureth forever. For as the buildings of the earth remain on the earth, and the spirits of them that incline to the earth raise not up, so have I bound corpor in corpor; but as I planted the quickened spirit of man in man for spiritual knowledge, so shall spiritual knowledge look upward for an everlasting resurrection.

10. Lika asked: O Thou Highest, Jehovih, what are the preparations of Thy Gods? Wherein shall my hand be strong on the earth? Jehovih answered, saying: For six generations aback hath My God prepared unto thee and thy hosts. My voice was with My God, and I said unto him: My Son, behold, the time cometh in six generations, when I will bring the earth into another dawn of light. And in that day will I bring My Son, Lika, from My etherean worlds; and he shall come with a mighty host of ethereans with great power. Go thou, My Son, down to the earth, and with thy loo'is, thy masters of generations, and raise up an heir unto thy voice. In the three great divisions of the earth provide thou three servants to do My will.

11. So, My Son, God of Craoshivi, hath raised up unto thee, O Lika, three men, Capilya, and Chine, and Moses, the fruit of the sixth generation in the lands of their fathers; and they are of the Faithists in Me, holy men and wise. To these shalt thou send the Gods of their forefathers, even they who were beaten away by the Gods of evil.

12. And Capilya shall deliver the Faithists of Vind'yu, and Chine shall deliver the Faithists of Jaffeth, and Moses shall deliver the Faithists of Egupt. And this, also, shalt thou put upon Moses and his people: He shall lead his people westward; and their heirs after them shall also go westward; yea, westward until they circumscribe the earth. Three thousand and four hundred years shalt thou allot to them to complete the journey. And wherever they go, they shall establish My name, Jehovih; they shall lead all people away from all Gods, to believe in the Great Spirit, who I am.

13. And when they have carried My name to the west coast of Guatama, and established Me, behold, I will bring the earth into kosmon; and My angels shall descend upon the earth in every quarter with great power. And it shall come to pass that the Faithists of the children of Moses shall find the Faithists of the children of Chine and the Faithists of the children of Capilya.

14. And all these people shall cry out in that day: No God, no Lord, no Savior! For My

hand will be upon them, and their words shall be My words. But they will proclaim Me, the Great Spirit, the Ever Present, Jehovih.

15. And they shall become the power of the world; and shall establish peace and put away war, leading all peoples in the way of peace, love and righteousness.

CHAPTER V.

1. Vetta'puissa, in Lika's etherean regions, made glorious by Jehovih's light, and by His purified Sons and Daughters, whose heavenly mansions matched unto their great perfection, was now quickened with great joy. The trained hosts of Jehovih's Son, Lika, knowing he was to take recreation by a journey to the red star, the earth, to deliver her unto holiness and love, provided music and heralds and trumpeters, millions of performers, to claim their reverence and rejoicing.

2. The fire-ship, the airavagna, now adorned in splendor, was brought into its place, and the vast hosts for the journey entered into it. A roadway was preserved for Lika and his companion Chiefs and Chieftainesses. First to lead, of the Rapon hosts, were the Chieftainesses, Yanodi and Thazid, and they walked arm in arm. Next after them came Lika, alone. Next came Rebsad and Thoso, arm in arm. Next came Miente and Hors-ad, arm in arm. Then Oshor and Yihoha, arm in arm. Then Gwan Goo and Geehoogan, and after them Rehemg and Antosiv.

3. Loud swelled the music as the Chiefs marched forth; more than a thousand millions in concerted song to Jehovih; and echoed by the far-off trumpeters. And when the Chiefs entered the ship, followed by the ship's laborers and firemen, all was motionless till the music ceased.

4. Lika walked upon the High Arch, and stretching up his hands to Jehovih, said: I go forth in Thy name and wisdom and love and power, O Jehovih! Thy great heavens which thou hast made full of glory shall bear me up; the spark Thou gavest unto me will I keep quickened in Thy sight. Thy hand is upon me. Thine arm encompasseth my ship of fire. In Thee I know it will rise and course these worlds, to the red star, sail with Thy hosts triumphantly unto labor for Thy glory.

5. Arise, O palace of the firmament; by the power of Jehovih that dwelleth in me, upward! onward! arise!

6. And now with one will the hosts joined in, and the laborers and firemen stood to their places. A moment more, and the airavagna raised from its foundation, steered toward the red star, and moved forth over the Fields of Vetta'puissa. A hundred thousand banners and flags floated and waved from every side on the great ship of heaven, and was answered by more than ten hundred thousand more in the hands of the hosts below.

7. The es'enaurs of the ship struck up a quickened march, joined by the millions beneath, whilst the great multitudes tossed up their hands and shouted in prolonged applause. Thus went forth Lika, Son of Jehovih, to the red star, the earth.

CHAPTER VI.

1. As Lika in his ship sped on, coursing the Fields of Sonasat, and Hatar, and Yuax, in the etherean world, Chen-a-goetha, rich in light in these regions, on the Yong-We Road, and

now traversed by hundreds of vessels coursing hither and yon, Jehovih's light descended on the High Arch, in the midst of the Rapons; and the Voice of Jehovih spake out of the light, saying:

2. As I taught corporeans to build ships to traverse corporeal seas, so have I taught ethereans to build vessels to course My etherean seas.

3. As I bound the corporean that he could not raise up in the air above corpor, save by a vessel, so created I My heavens for the spirits of men, that by manufactured vessels they might course My firmament.

4. For the little knowledge I gave to corporeans I made as a type of knowledge which is everlasting.

5. To the corporean I gave two kinds of presence, objective and subjective. By the latter he can imagine himself in a far-off place; and the thought that proceedeth out of him goeth to a friend and speaketh understandingly in the distance. For thus I created him. But he who goeth objectively must take his person with him, for so created I him.

6. And I magnified these two conditions unto the spirits of all men, that they might also appear objectively and subjectively in the places known to them.

7. And this is the bondage I created unto all places on the earth and in the heavens thereof, making all men understand the power of objective association.

8. I created wide seas on the corporeal earth, that man should perceive that one man alone could not cross over; nor in a small boat, with any profit under the sun. Neither created I My heavens in the firmament that one angel could go alone on long journeys, becoming isolated and powerless. But I provided them that they could not escape association; yea, I created the firmament that they must congregate together and go.

9. Nevertheless, I gave freedom unto all; to him that goeth not objectively, to go subjectively; but of little avail and not much truth or profit. And because I gave this liberty, behold, even drujas will say: Yea, I have been there. Nor know they how to raise up from the earth, or to go to any place, save on another's shoulders.

10. And I created man and angels that all knowledge which is to be everlasting must be obtained objectively; yea, in the experience of his own person made I him to desire without end.

11. And they fill My seas in heaven and earth with their great ships; with wants that could not be satisfied in one place created I man. For I drive him forth on strange errands and on missions of profit and love; for I will store him with a knowledge of My works.

CHAPTER VII.

1. Onward sped Lika in his airavagna, with his eight hundred millions; through the sea of Enea-Wassa, the etherean realm of Haog-sa-uben; shining like a meteor in its flight, the ship of fire of eight hundred millions. On every side, the Jehovihian worshippers' vessels, tens of thousands, coursing as many ways, some fast, on missions of quickened labor; some slow, as traveling school-ships, exploring the great expanse and glorious richness of Jehovih's provided worlds, always ready for the newborn; each and all the ships as studded gems in the etherean sea, moving brilliants playing kaleidoscopic views, ever changing the boundless scene with surpassing wonders. And all of these, by signs and signals, the story of their place and mission revealing to the high-raised etherean souls,

ships and men, as quickened living books of fire, radiant with the Father's light and history of worlds.

2. On Lika's ship, as on all the others, every soul, hundreds of millions, enraptured, stood in awe and admiration of the ever-changing scenes; some in silence, absorbed in thought; some posing with upraised hands; some ejaculating gleefully; and some in high reverence to Jehovih, uttering everlasting praise; every soul its full bent, being the full ripe fruit of the diversified talents as they first shone forth in corporeal life.

3. Onward sped Lika's airavagna now in the Roads of Nopita, now in the a'ji'an Forest of Quion, most rich in adamantine substances, arches, stalactites and stalagmites, and in forming and dissolving scenes, a forest, a very background in the etherean worlds for the over-brilliant crystal regions of light. And here, too, the tens of thousands of ships of Jehovih's chosen; and on either side the great roadway lay the Fields of Anutiv, inhabited by countless millions of etherean kingdoms. Along the road for hundreds of thousands of miles, stretched up the hands of millions and millions of souls, waving banners and flags to their favored ships, going to some native star, from which Jehovih brought them forth.

4. Then changed the course of Lika's airavagna, by his commands sent through the comet Yo-to-gactra, a new condensing world, already with a head of fire four thousand miles broad; a very ball of melted corpor, whirling like the spindle of a filling spool, forever winding unto itself the wide extending nebulae. Here were coursing along, hundreds of thousands of school-ships, with students and visitors to view the scenes, most grand in rolling on, now round, now broken, now outstretched, this ball of liquid fire, whirling in the vortex, thirty million miles long. To balance against which vortex many of the ships tossed and rolled, dangerously, had they not been in skilled hands; and, as they were, causing millions of the students on many a ship to fear and tremble, perceiving how helpless and stupid they were compared to the very Gods who had them in charge.

5. Not long did Lika loiter to view the scenes, or to indulge his eight hundred   millions, but stood his course again for the red star, the earth; coursing the Fuassette Mountains, where the God, Vrilla-Gabon, built the Echosinit kingdom, whose capital was Exastras, the place where the Niuan Gods assembled to witness the first starting forth of the earth. Here, halting awhile, and adown went Lika's recorders, to gather from the Exastras libraries the earth's early history and the grade of her creation; a copy of which   obtained, the recorders hastily returned, when onward again sped the airavagna, now making course across the Plains of Zed, in the midst of which lay the great sea Oblowochisi, four million miles across, and this also studded over with thousands of etherean ships.

6. And now across to Rikkas, the place of the Goddess, Enenfachtus, with her seven thousand million etherean souls, whereupon Lika and his hosts cast down millions of wreaths and tokens, and the while, the music of the two spheres mingled together in Jehovih's praise. Here, across, the distance was three million miles.

7. Now, all the while before, the red star stood upward, inclining upward, but here in horizontal line began to stand, gleaming in more effulgent flame. And in the course, where Lika's airavagna should go, the Goddess, Enenfachtus, had previously upraised a hundred thousand pillars of fire to honor him and his company; which great respect Lika and his hosts answered with holy salutations.

8. After this, came the ji'ay'an Forests of Hogobed, three million miles across, and close for lack of etherean air and inspiration. Here stood the Province of Arathactean, where

dwelt the God, Yew-Sin, with thirty thousand million newly-raised Brides and Bridegrooms from the star Kagados. Over these regions Lika sped swiftly, and then to the open sea, Amatapan, on the Vashuan Roads.

9. Then a sail of two million miles, in the uninhabited regions of Samma, when he reached Chinvat, the bridge on the boundary of the earth's vortex beyond the orbit of the moon.

10. And, halting not, but now coursing on a downward plane, made straight toward the swift-rolling earth, whose speed was three-quarters of a million miles a day. Through the high-floating plateaux of atmospherea came Lika with his fire-ship, with his hosts, eight hundred millions, came his ship like a meteor, huge as a continent.

CHAPTER VIII.

1. On the uninhabited plateau, Theovrahkistan, rich and broad as the earth, high above the lands of Jaffeth, and Vind'yu, and Arabin'ya, lighted Lika in his airavagna, with his eight hundred millions. Here he made fast his fire-ship, and forth came his hosts to found a heavenly kingdom. Lika said:

2. I hear Thy voice, O Jehovih; Thy hand is upon me; in Thy Wisdom and Power will I build the foundations of Thy kingdom in these heavens.

3. Jehovih said: Call forth thy Rapon hosts, thy companion Chiefs; build thy throne broad for them and thee. And shape thou the area of the capital and stand thy high Council, the chosen millions, to the four quarters of the heavens of the earth.

4. The legions then fell to and built a heavenly place unto Jehovih, and called it Yogannaqactra, home of Lika and his eight hundred millions.

5. Jehovih called out of the light of the throne which Lika built, saying: Lika, My Son, thou shalt build all things new on the earth and in the heavens of the earth, even as if nothing had ever been. Send thou thy messengers in an otevan to the broken-down region of My beloved, God of Craoshivi, and bring him and his thousand attendants unto thy place.

6. Thereupon an otevan was sent off, well officered, and in due time it returned, bringing God to Yogannaqactra, where he was received with great joy, and greeted in Jehovih's name.

7. Lika said: Speak thou, O God, for I am come to deliver these heavens into Jehovih's dominion. What are the light and the darkness of the heavens and the earth that have been entrusted to thy keeping, in Jehovih's name?

8. God said: Alas, how can I speak? Behold, my kingdoms are scattered and gone; I have nowhere any pride in anything I have done in heaven and earth. An exceeding great darkness came upon my people, for a thousand and five hundred years! Thy servants have been overpowered, helpless and tossed as chaff before the wind.

9. Lika said: How many Gods? How many dans of darkness? Whither are gone My true Gods?

10. God said: Four Gods are risen to etherea with their hosts, heart-broken, true Gods. Four dans have come and gone; so weak and small, like a breath of air, for the darkness brushed them away. In Savak-haben, in etherea, sojourn thy Gods.

11. Jehovih's light fell upon the throne, and His Voice came out of the light, saying: Send

thou, O My Son, Lika, to Savak-haben, four arrow-ships, with a hundred thousand attendants for My true Gods, and bring them to Yogannaqactra.

12. Lika then sent four arrow-ships with his swift messengers and a hundred thousand attendants, to bring back the four disconcerted Gods.

13. God said: Thousands of millions of angels of darkness flood the hadan regions; and as many grovel about on the low earth. De'yus, the false Lord God, is cast into hell, a hell so wide that none can approach his place of torment. Te-in, the fase God, the Joss, is also cast into hell; and so is Sudga, the false Dyaus; and so are all the false Gods that encompassed the earth around; their kingdoms are in anarchy.

14. The names Lord, and God, and Dyaus, and De'yus, and Zeus, and Joss, and Ho-Joss, and many others, have become worshipful on the earth! Not only labored the traitors to put away the Great Spirit, but to establish themselves as men-Gods capable of creating; yea, the veritable Creator of heaven and earth!

15. Lika said: Hear thou, then, the Voice of Jehovih! Because they have put Me aside and assumed to be Creators under the name God, and De'yus, I will magnify the Person of God and De'yus in men's understanding.

16. Nor from this time forth on the earth, for three thousand years, shall man be confined to the one name, Jehovih, or Eolin, or Eloih, but worship God, or Lord, or De'yus, or Zeus, or Dyaus, or Joss, or Ho-Joss. For since these men have cast themselves into hells, behold, the spirits of the risen shall not find them nor their kingdoms. And thou shalt magnify unto mortals that all names worshipful belong to the Ever Present, whose Person is the spirit and substance of all things. And if they inquire of thee: Who is Dyaus? or, Who is God? or, Who is Joss? thou shalt say: Hath He not said: Behold, I am the Creator of heaven and earth! and I say unto you, He is the Ever Present, the All Highest Ideal.

17. But this bondage shall come upon them: To reap the harvest they have sown. Because one hath said: Build thou a pyramid, and thy God will come and abide therein, even as a man dwelleth in a house; he shall be bound while the pyramid standeth. And another hath said: Behold, thy God is in the image of a man, and he sitteth on a throne in heaven; he shall be bound while this belief surviveth on the earth.

18. Because they have sown a falsehood on the earth, the harvest is theirs. And until they have reaped their whole harvest they shall not rise into My etherean worlds.

CHAPTER IX.

1. When the other four Gods, the true Sons of Jehovih, who had been discomfited in the lower heavens by De'yus and his fellow false Gods, came, the light of Jehovih came again on Lika's throne. Jehovih said:

2. I suffer not evil to triumph over good but for short seasons; and, soon or late, My righteous Sons and Daughters, raise up and rejoice in their trials which I suffered to come upon them. Let not men or angels say, because this or that happeneth: Lo, Jehovih sleepeth at his post! or: lo, Jehovih is the author of evil, or is impotent to avert it.

3. My times are not as the times of men or angels; nor am I within the judgment of men as to what is evil or good. When the wealth of the rich man is stolen, do not mortals say: Poor man, Jehovih hath afflicted him! For they judge Me by what they consider afflictions. But they behold not that I look to the soul of man as to what is good for him.

And when the assassin hath struck the king unto death, behold, they say: How hath a good Creator done this? For they consider not the nation nor the problem of anything but for the day thereof; nor consider they what I do for the souls of many nations, by one small act.

4. For all people in heaven and earth are Mine own; they are as trees in My orchard, and I prune them not for the life of the branches, but for benefit of the whole orchard, and for the harvest that cometh after.

5. I created life, and I take away life; in Mine own way do I with Mine own. I send night to follow the day; clouds to interchange with the sunshine. And even so do I give times of dan to My atmospherean heavens, to be followed by seasons of darkness.

6. By these changes do mortals and angels and Gods learn to battle with and overcome the elements of My worlds.

7. The true Gods said: We weep before Thee, O Jehovih. Long and hard we labored our allotted seasons; we were helpless witnesses to the great darkness that came upon the inhabitants of heaven and earth.

8. Lika said: To you five, true Gods, who have toiled in the darkness of the earth and her heavens, I restore your old time names for the season of dawn, after which I will raise you all up, with your kingdoms restored to the full, and ye shall be heirs in my Nirvanian heavens, in peace and rest.

CHAPTER X.

1. The five Gods' names were Ane, Jek, Lay, Oal and Yith. Lika said unto them: Ye have been heretofore crowned as Gods; come ye to the foot of Jehovih's throne, for I will crown you with new names.

2. When they came to the place designated, Lika continued: Take my crown upon thy head, and speak thou in Jehovih's name in that labor which I put upon thee, Jehovih in Ane, Jehovih in Jek, Jehovih in Lay, Jehovih in Oal, Jehovih in Yith.

3. And thereupon Lika crowned them with a band on the head, inscribed, INANE, INJEK, INLAY, INOAL, and INYITH, Panic names designating their rank and the age of the earth in which these things came to pass.

4. Lika said: To each and every one I give of my etherean hosts ten million laborers for the period of dawn. And these are the labors I allot unto you: To Inane, to go down to the earth, to the land of Vind'yu, and be inspirer unto my mortal son, Capilya, and his followers. To Inlay, to go down to the earth, to the land of Jaffeth, and be inspirer unto my son, Chine, and his followers. To Inoal, to go down to the earth to the land of Egupt, and be inspirer to my son, Moses, and his followers. And ye three shall restore the Faithists in these great divisions of the earth unto liberty and safety. And thou, Inoal, shalt deliver Moses and the Faithists out of Egupt, and shape their course westward; for they shall circumscribe the earth, and complete it by the time of kosmon.

5. To Injek, to go down to the earth, to Parsi'e and Heleste, and provide those peoples to liberate the slaves who are Faithists, whom thou shalt inspire to migrate to Moses and his people. To Inlay, to go down to the earth, to Jaffeth and Vind'yu and Arabin'ya, to inspire the scattered Faithists in those lands to come together, to the great lights, Capilya and Chine and Moses.

6. And ye shall take with you of my hosts, whom I brought from etherea, and labor ye together as one man. And when dawn hath ended, ye shall repair hither, and be raised up unto my Nirvanian kingdoms. Nevertheless, ye shall not leave Jehovih's chosen alone, but provide angel successors unto them. And herein I give you a new law unto all my angel hosts who shall hereafter dwell with the Faithists on the earth, which is, that successors shall always be provided by the retiring hosts ere they have departed; for the Faithists shall not more be left alone for a long season.

7. The chosen five then said: In Thy name and wisdom and power, O Jehovih, we go forth in joy to fulfill Thy commandments. Because we lost the earth Thou hast given it into our hands to redeem it and glorify Thee!

8. And thereupon Lika proclaimed a day of recreation, so the hosts could be selected, the fifty millions, to which labor the marshals fell to, helping the chosen.

9. During the recreation, the atmophereans explained to the ethereans how laid the lands of the earth and the heavens thereunto belonging. And then, after a season of prayer and singing, and a season of dancing, the recreation was brought to a close.

10. After labor was resumed, the chosen five, with their hosts, saluted before the throne of Jehovih, and then withdrew and went to vessels which had been previously prepared for them, and embarked, and departed for the earth.

CHAPTER XI.

1. Jehovih spake to Lika, saying: Appoint thou other servants unto Me for the other great divisions of the earth, and for the islands in the oceans of the earth; and give unto them each ten millions of My servants which thou broughtest from Nirvania. And they shall go down amongst mortals, and by inspiration and otherwise collect together in groups the scattered Faithists who worship Me. And thy servants shall also provide successors to come after them, to abide with mortals, making the seasons of watch short unto them that they shall not be weary thereof.

2. Then Lika appointed T'chow, N'yak, Gitchee, Guelf, Ali and Siwah, and allotted them to different divisions of the earth, and he gave them each ten millions of the hosts brought from the Orian worlds. And these were selected after the same manner as the previous ones; and they also saluted and departed for the earth.

3. Again Jehovih spake in the light of the throne, saying: Because many are risen in wisdom and truth, I will have Theovrahkistan for My holy place unto them; and it shall be the region for My Brides and Bridegrooms at the resurrection of dawn. But at the end thereof it shall be divided and sub-divided that none may find the place of My standing. For it hath come to pass, that man on the earth learning the name of one of My heavens glorifieth it, and aspireth to rise to it, but to rise to no other heaven.

4. Because My true Gods taught man of Hored in the early days, man desired Hored. Whereupon Mine enemies, the false Gods, each one cried out: Behold, my heavenly place is Hored! I am the All Heavenly ruler! Come hither to me! For, by this means, the name I gave in truth, was usurped and made as a snare to enslave my earth-born.

5. And I will not more give to mortals a name of any of My heavenly places; nor shall they be taught of any heavens save the higher and the lower heavens, which shall designate My etherean and My atmospherean heavens. And by these terms

shall man on the earth be fortified against the stratagems of false heavenly rulers.

6. And man shall perceive that when angels or men or Gods or Saviors say: Come ye unto me, and I will give you of my heavenly kingdom! that they are false, and but tyrants to enslave My people. But if they say: Go ye, serve the Great Spirit, and not me, for I am only a man as thou art! then shall it be known that they are of My Nirvanian hosts.

7. And if they say: Come ye to this heaven or that heaven, for with me only is delight, it shall be testimony against them. But if they say: Verily, Jehovih is with thee; cultivate thyself within Him, and thou shalt find delight in all worlds, then shall it be testimony they are from My emancipated heavens.

8. Lika said: Seventy new kingdoms shall ye found in the lowest heaven, where ye shall begin again with schools and colleges and factories, teaching the spirits of the dead the requirements for resurrection.

9. Two hundred millions of my Orian angels shall be allotted to these seventy heavenly places, and during dawn it shall be their work to carry out these commandments. And they shall provide for successors after them, who shall continue for another season; and they shall provide yet other successors, and so on, even till the coming of the kosmon era.

10. Lika then selected the two hundred million angels, and divided them into seventy groups and companies around about the earth, in the lowest heaven, and after they were duly officered and organized, they saluted before the throne of Jehovih and departed to their several places.

11. Then came the voice of Jehovih to Lika, saying: Behold, of thy five hundred millions, are still left one hundred and seventy and five millions. This, then, is the work thou shalt put upon them: They shall begin at one end of hada and go to the other, delivering all the hells of the false Gods as they go; untying the knots thereof and providing passage for the drujas into one great plateau. For as the false Gods began in confederacy I will bring them back into confederacy, even all of them that are cast into hell. And thou shalt officer them safely; and when they are thus established, behold, thou and thy Rapon hosts shall go and raise them up and deliver them into the a'ji'an Forest of Turpeset, where they shall be habitated and begin a new life of righteousness and love.

12. And Anuhasaj, once-crowned Lord God, shall be over them; and Osiris and Sudga and Te-in and all the other confederated Gods shall be under him; for even as these Gods labored to cast Me out, behold, I give unto them their harvest.

13. Then Lika commissioned the one hundred and seventy-five million ethereans, and officered them, and sent them into the hadan regions of the earth to deliver the hells thereof.

14. Jehovih said to Lika: The rest of thy eight hundred millions shall remain in Theovrahkistan, for the labor here is sufficient for them. And so they remained.

CHAPTER XII.

1. The Rapon hosts desired to see Ahura, and so Lika sent an arrow-ship, with one hundred thousand angels, properly officered, to Vara-pishanaha, to Ahura, praying him to come on a visit for ten days, bringing his ten thousand attendants with him.

2. And it thus came to pass that Ahura came to Theovrahkistan, where he was most honorably received and saluted under the sign MORNING OF JEHOVIH'S LIGHT, and he

in turn answered in the sign MY WORDS SHALL SERVE HIS SONS AND DAUGHTERS!

3. Accordingly, Lika came down from the throne and greeted Ahura, saying to him: Come thou, then, and stand in the midst of the throne, that thy voice may delight the Holy Council.

4. So Ahura ascended the throne, along with Lika, and when the latter sat down, then Ahura walked to the midst and saluted the Holy Council with the sign FIRE AND WATER, and he spake, saying:

5. Because Thou, O Jehovih, hast called me in the sign of the MORNING OF THY LIGHT, behold, I am risen up before Thee, to speak to Thy Sons and Daughters.

6. But how shall I clear myself, O Father! I am as one who had a hidden skeleton, and the place of concealment broken down. Because I was by Thee created alive in the world, why should I not have forever glorified Thee? This have I asked myself all the days of my life; but Thou troublest not to answer me in my curiosity.

7. When I was young in life, lo, I cried out unto Thee, complaining because Thou madest me not wise. I said: Behold, Thou createdst all the animals on the face of the earth to know more than I in the day of birth. Yea, I knew not where to find suck, nor could I raise up on my feet, but laid as I was laid down by my nurse.

8. Even to the lambs and the calves and the young colts, Thou gavest greater wisdom and strength than Thou gavest Thy servant. I said: Why, then, shall I glorify Thee or sing songs in Thy praise? Why shall I pray unto Thee; Thy ways are unalterable and Thy Voice answereth me not.

9. Thou art void as the wind; Thou art neither Person, nor Wisdom, nor Ignorance. And as for Thy servants, who say they hear Thy Voice, behold, they are mad! I said: How can a man hear Thee? It is the reflection of himself he heareth. How can a man see Thee? It is the reflection of himself he seeth.

10. And Thou sufferedst me to become strong, as to strength, and wise as to self, even as I had called unto Thee in my vanity. Yea, I prided myself in myself; and as to Thee, I sought to disprove Thee on all hands. And the worthlessness of prayer unto Thee I showed up as a great vanity. Yea, I craved wisdom for sake of showing Thou wert neither wise nor good. And to this end Thou also gavest unto me. And I became conceited in hiding my conceit, even from mine own understanding, that I might carry all points.

11. I pointed to the fool, saying: Behold, Jehovih's son! I pointed to the desert place, saying: Behold, Jehovih's fruitful earth! To the mountain which is rocks and barren, saying: Behold, how Jehovih hath finished His work! And of the evil man, who murdereth his brother, I said: Jehovih, good in one thing, good in all!

12. But I knew not the hand that was upon me; Thou wert answering my prayer every day. Yea, I ventured to judge Thee with my eyes, and my ears, and my own understanding. In the place I stood I judged Thee and Thy works, O Jehovih! And the craft of my speech won applause; by flattery was I puffed up. And I deemed my judgment the right one; and whoso saw not as I saw, I condemned or pitied; yea, I craved great speech that I might show them up in their folly.

13. And in this Thou also answeredst me by giving freely; and my words were reckoned great words and wise. And I was quoted and praised far and near. Yea, and I practiced good works that I might show unto others that, even in such like, a belief in Thee was vanity and a waste of judgment.

14. Yea, I craved means and great treasures that I might render good unto others, in order that mine own philosophy might seem the highest of the high. And even in this Thou renderedst unto me great treasures and ample means; and by my good works done unto others I was applauded as a great and good God above all others.

15. I craved a heavenly kingdom that I might prove my great wisdom and power unto thousands of millions; for I pitied them that I thought foolishly dwelt in darkness in regard to Thee. And even yet Thou, O Jehovih, didst not cut me off; but gavest me a great kingdom of seven thousand millions!

16. And I taught them my philosophy, that there was nothing above them; that Thou, O Jehovih, sawest not, heardst not, answeredst not. Yea, I made my will all-powerful that I might cut them off from Thee. But alas for me.

17. I had been as the sylph of old who stole into the musical instruments and put them out of tune. My kingdom was divided into seven thousand million philosophers, every one mad in his own conceit, and in a different way. There was no harmony amongst them. Yea, they were a kingdom of growlers and cursers! I had carried away the tuning fork, for I had cast Thee out, O Jehovih! Mine own philosophy had done it all.

18. Because I set myself up as the All Highest, thou didst indulge me; and I became the highest God of my people. Yea, they cast their plaudits on me at first, but afterward all their ills and their curses. Neither could I satisfy them in anything in heaven or earth; nor could I turn them off from me, for I had bound them unto me by my great promises.

19. I became as one in a cloud, because of the great trouble upon me and the fear withal. And yet Thou, O Jehovih, didst not forget me; but sent Thy Gods' words unto me, imploring me what to do, that I might be delivered in season. But how could I hear thee, O Jehovih, or hearken unto Thy Gods? Behold, my pride had swallowed me up, I was encompassed on every side. Because I had denied Thee before I must deny Thee still.

20. Then greater darkness came upon me; Thy light was obstructed by the walls I had built up against Thee! Then came the crash, as if heaven and earth were rent asunder! I was cast into the chasm; my kingdom was upon me! The leadership and vanity I had sown had cast me into hell! I was in death, but could not die!

21. A knot was bound upon me; foul-smelling slaves were clinched upon me, millions of them, tens of millions; and the shafts of their curses pierced my soul; I was as one lacerated and bound in salt; choked and suffocated with foul gases. But yet, Thou, O Jehovih, didst not desert me; but did hold my judgment from flying away into chaos.

22. And Thy Voice came to me in the time of my tortures; came as the argument of the Most High! It was like myself that spake to myself, saying: He that forever casteth away all things, can never be bound in hell; he that craveth and holdeth fast, is already laying the foundation for torments.

23. And I cried out unto Thee, O Jehovih, saying: O that I had possessed nothing! Nor talents, nor craft, nor philosophy. That I had told these wretches to go to Thee, O Jehovih! O that I had told them, Thou alone couldst bless them, or supply them! But I sought to lead them, and lo, they are upon me!

24. O that I could be freed from them. That I could turn about in an opposite way from my former years; having nothing, craving nothing, but a right to serve Thee, O My Father!

25. Thou didst send Thy Gods into the depths of hell, and they delivered me. And I made

oath unto Thee, O Jehovih, to serve Thee forever. And Thou gavest me labor, and I bowed myself down to labor for Thy drujas, with all my wisdom and strength forever! And Thy hand came upon me and gave me great power; power even over mine own soul to create happy thoughts.

26. Why should I not praise Thee, O my Father? Thou gavest me liberty in all my ways, and didst answer me according to my desires. Neither once hast Thou turned away from me nor afflicted me; but because of mine own vanity I cut myself off from Thee. Yea, Thou hast shown me that to glorify Thee is the foundation of the highest happiness; to sing to Thee is the greatest delight; to praise Thee is te highest wisdom.

27. Hereat Ahura halted in his speech a while, and, still standing in the midst of the throne, burst into tears. Presently he said:

28. Anuhasaj was my good friend. He it was who since took the name De'yus, and, afterward, proclaimed himself the Creator. I weep in pity for him. He is in hell now!

29. He was my best friend in the time of my darkness. And after I was delivered out of hell, he came and labored with me, full of repentance and love. Oft we rested in each other's arms. Afterward, he traveled far and near in Thy great heavens, O Jehovih.

30. And when he returned to this earth's heavens he came not to see me. And I was broken-hearted because of my great love for him. Then he founded his heavenly place and called it Hored. And I called out to Thee, O Jehovih, as to what message I should send him, for I foresaw his kingdom would be broken up and himself ultimately cast into hell.

31. And Thou gavest me liberty to send him a message in mine own way. And in the anguish of my broken heart I sent him a message, saying, in substance: I have no longer any love for thee! And I chid him and upbraided him because he came not to see me, to gratify my burning love. And I foretold him the great darkness and the hell that would come upon him, even as they now are.

32. Now do I repent, O Jehovih, that I sent him such a message! For near two thousand years my message hath been to me as if I swallowed a living coal of fire!

33. Ahura ceased. Lika spake, saying: Because thou hast plead for De'yus, thou hast turned the etherean hosts to him. To thee I allot the restoration of De'yus, alias Anuhasaj. My hosts will in the proper time take thee to the hell where he is bound, and thou shalt be the first to receive him.

34. Lika then proclaimed a day of recreation, for there were millions of ethereans who desired to meet Ahura and greet him with love and praise.

CHAPTER XIII.

1. Lika spake before the Rapon hosts, saying: Behold, the hosts of laborers are allotted to their places.

2. Let us go about, and examine the earth and her heavens. It is proper that my surveyors measure her land and water, together with all the living thereon and therein, and especially as to every man and woman and child, and the time of maturity unto them, and the years of the generations of men.

3. And man that is brought forth out of the earth shall be numbered; and the grade of his understanding measured; and the nature of his desires and aspirations shall be ascertained; which reports shall be copied and sent into the Orian kingdoms, for the

deliberations of the Chiefs, that they may determine as to the requirements of the earth, and as to the nature in which her roadway shall be strewn with either light or darkness for the ultimate perfection of her soul harvests.

4. And the heavens of the earth shall be measured, as to the spirits of the dead; and their grades shall be made out, together with their desires and aspirations; the lengths of the times of their bondage to the earth, and the places of their habitation, and the nature of their supplies. And a copy of such record shall be made and also sent to the Orian Chiefs for their deliberations.

5. And the plateaux of the earth's heavens shall also be numbered and measured, and their localities mapped out and recorded, and copies thereof also sent to the Orian Chiefs, that they may determine as to necessary changes therein and thereof.

6. During which time of my absence from Theovrahkistan, I appoint Havralogissasa as vice-Goddess in my place. How sayest thou, Havralogissasa? She said: Jehovih's will and thine be done. I am rejoiced.

7. Lika then called Havralogissasa to the throne, and commissioned her vice-Goddess of Theovrahkistan. And after this Lika gave instructions as to extending the capital, Yogannaqactra, and enlarging the places for reception of the higher grades; all of which were duly provided with the persons to carry out the commands.

8. And now Lika spake to Ahura, saying: Behold, thou shalt return to thy kingdom, Vara-pishanaha, for when I come thither on my journey, I will resurrect thy hosts as Brides and Bridegrooms to the etherean kingdoms. Thy labor is well done; thy glory is the glory of thousands of millions! May the love, wisdom and power of Jehovih be with thee, now and forever!

9. Thereupon Ahura saluted, and was in turn saluted, when he advanced and met the marshals, who conducted him hence, to the arrow-ship, where he embarked and departed.

CHAPTER XIV.

1. In due time Lika's otevan was completed, and he, with the Rapon hosts, besides one million hosts in attendance, to make necessary surveys and records, entered into the ship and departed for his two years' cruise around about the earth and in her heavens.

2. Sufficient unto the earth is the history thereof; and the maps of land and water; and the number of inhabitants; and the living creatures upon the earth and in the waters thereof; which are in the libraries of the earth. Therefore, suffice it that the revelations of the heavens upon the face of the earth, which records are in the libraries of heaven, shall be disclosed before the generations of men from the records of Lika, Son of Jehovih.

3. This, then, is a synopsis of the atmospherean heavens at that time, to wit: In the hells of Hored, with Anuhasaj, alias De'yus, forty thousand million angels.

4. In the hells of Te-in, eight thousand millions; in the hells of Sudga, twelve thousand millions; in the hells of Osiris, seventeen thousand millions.

5. In the smaller hells in other parts of hada, there were in all fourteen thousand million angels.

6. These ninety-one thousand millions were not all bound in their respective hells; upward of thirty thousand millions of them surged about, from one hell to another, often in groups of a thousand million.

7. And these groups, at times, descended to the earth, fastening upon mortals, even casting large cities and nations in death. Because they carried the foulness of their hells with them, they impregnated the air with poison, so that mortals were swept off by the million. And these were called plagues.

8. Lika said: Behold, I will give a new grade to these heavens for a season. From this time, such angels shall be known as being in the first resurrection. But spirits who have quit their old haunts, and joined organic associations, being enlisted in companies, either for labor or for receiving heavenly instruction, shall be known as being in the second resurrection. And such spirits as have attained to etherean grades, being Brides and Bridegrooms of Jehovih, and having ascended beyond atmospherea into the etherean worlds, shall be known as being in the third resurrection.

9. Such angels as engraft themselves on mortals, becoming as a twin spirit to the one corporeal body, shall be known as re-incarnated spirits. But where such spirits usurp the corporeal body, as of an infant, growing up in the corporeal body, and holding the native spirit in abeyance, such spirits shall be known as damons (which was the origin of that name).

10. Spirits who inhabit mortals in order to live on the substance mortals eat and drink, and oft absorbing the strength and life of mortals, shall be known as uzians (vampires). Nevertheless, these shall not include fetals.

11. All the foregoing, who are not in the way of resurrection, shall be called drujas.

12. Now, behold, there were millions of angels in those days who knew no other life, but to continue engrafting themselves on mortals. And, when one mortal died, they went and engrafted themselves on another.

13. These were the fruit of the teaching of the false Gods, who had put away the All Highest, Jehovih. They could not be persuaded that etherea was filled with habitable worlds.

14. And they professed that they had been re-incarnated many times; and that, previously, they had been great kings or philosophers.

15. Some of them remembered the ji'ay'an period of a thousand years, and, so hoped to regain their natural bodies and dwell again on the earth, and forever. Hence was founded the story that every thousand years a new incarnation would come to the spirits of the dead.

16. Lika said: Such spirits as come to mortals purposely to inflict them with pain or misfortune shall be called evil spirits.

17. And when they go in groups, having a leader, that leader shall be called Beelzebub, that is, captain of evil (prince of devils). (And this was the origin of that word.)

18. In Parsi'e and Heleste there were habited with mortals one thousand million damons, and one twelve hundred million evil spirits. In Egupt there were inhabited with mortals seven hundred million engrafters (re-incarnated spirits), who, for the most part, held the spirits of their victims in abeyance all their natural lives.

19. In Jaffeth there were habited with mortals more than fifteen hundred millions of damons and evil spirits, besides four hundred million vampires. So that in these three great divisions of the earth, Vind'yu, and Jaffeth, and Arabin'ya, there were habited upward of ten thousand million spirits who had not attained to any resurrection.

20. Besides all the foregoing there were thousands of millions of spirits in chaos, being

such as had been slain in wars. Of these chaotic spirits there were in Parsi'e and Heleste a thousand millions; and in Jaffeth two thousand millions; and in Vind'yu two thousand millions. But in Egupt there were not half a million, all told.

21. So that, in atmospherea, at the time of Lika, there were upward of one hundred and twenty-five thousand million angels, who had no knowledge of or belief in any higher heaven.

22. To offset this great darkness, there were of believers in, and laborers for Jehovih and his emancipated kingdoms, only four thousand millions, and many of these were not above grade fifty. And these were members of Craoshivi and Vara-pishanaha.

23. Two thousand million of them were ashars, laboring with the Faithist mortals of Egupt, Jaffeth and Vind'yu.

CHAPTER XV.

1. After Lika had numbered all the mortals on the earth, and all the angels in the heavens of the earth, and beheld the great darkness thereof, he visited Hao-yusta, and found it a good plateau, capable of all grades up to sixty. And Lika possessed the place and consecrated it to Jehovih; and he left thereon three hundred thousand Gods and Goddesses, who were of his etherean host. And after this he returned to Gessica, chief God, for the deliverance of the hells of De'yus, and Te-in, and Sudga, and Lika instructed him.

2. Gessica had the vessels constructed with walls of fire around the margins, to prevent the drujas escaping. And there were built in all four hundred vessels, each capable of carrying one hundred million drujas.

3. The manner of driving the drujas into them was by leaving part of the fire-wall open, and by fire-brands in the ethereans' hands cutting off sections of drujas from the hells. In this way the ethereans drove the drujas into the vessels, whereupon the doorway in the wall of the ship was closed. And then the workers of the ship put it under way and carried them up to Hao-yusta, where the Gods and Goddesses received them, placing the drujas in pens, walled with fire, where they could be treated and restored to reason, after which they were to be liberated in installments, according to their safety.

4. In the first year Gessica delivered from the hells of hada five thousand million drujas; but in the second year he delivered thirty-five thousand millions; and in the third year, sixteen thousand millions. After this the work went slowly on, for the balance of the hells were mostly in knots, some of them hundreds of millions. And these had to be delivered individually, requiring great labor, and power, and wisdom, and dexterity.

5. In the fifth month of the fourth year, Anuhasaj, alias the false Lord God, was delivered out of the great knot of hell, in which there had been eight hundred millions bound for more than four hundred years. After the manner in which Fragapatti delivered knots, even so did Gessica and his hosts, with brands of fire.

6. When it was known in which place De'yus (Anuhasaj) was tied, and when it was half delivered, Gessica sent for Ahura to come and have the honor of releasing Anuhasaj. And to this end Ahura labored on the knot fifty-five days, and then it was accomplished.

7. But lo and behold, Anuhasaj was bereft of all judgment, crying out, unceasingly: I am not God! I am not the Lord! I am not De'yus! He was wild, crazed with fear and torments,

frenzied, and in agony.

8. The which Ahura, his friend, beheld; and Ahura caught him in his arms. Ahura called unto him: Anuhasaj! O my beloved! Knowest thou not me? Behold me! I am Ahura!

9. But, alas, Anuhasaj knew him not; pulled away, tried to escape in fear; his protruding eyes seeing not; his ears hearing not. And he kept forever uttering: Let me go, I am not the Lord God nor De'yus! I am Anuhasaj! Then broke the good heart of Ahura, and he wept.

10. Then they held Anuhasaj and carried him away into the ship, and Ahura helped to carry him.

11. Then the ship rose up and sailed along higher and higher, farther and farther, till at last it came to Hao-yusta. And they took Anuhasaj to a hospital prepared for maniacs, and stretched him on his back and held him. Then called Ahura to the Gods and Goddesses to come and help him; and they came and seated themselves around about, making the sacred circle.

12. And Ahura said: Light of Thy Light, Jehovih! Thou who first quickened him into being, O deliver Thou him!

13. A light, like a small star, gathered before Anuhasaj's face, and this was the first thing his fixed eyes had yet seen. Then Ahura and the Gods and Goddesses sang sweetly: Behold me! I am the light! And the life! I quicken into life every living thing. Behold me! I am with thee! I am never away from thee! Thou art mine now, and forever shall be! Look upon me! I am in all things! Nothing is, nor was, nor ever shall be without me! Hear my Love! I am thy Creator! Only for love, and for love only, created I thee, my beloved.

14. Anuhasaj gave a long gasp and relaxed his mighty will, then fell into a swoon, all limp and helpless. Still the Gods stood by him, waiting, watching whilst he slept awhile. And then, by signals to the es'enaurs, Ahura caused other music to steal upon the scene, to be answered by distant trumpeters. For the space of seven days Anuhasaj slept; and all the while the Great Gods and Goddesses relaxed not their wills nor steadfast positions. And at the end of the seventh day Anuhasaj began to sing in his swoon, like one weak and out of breath, but half awake.

15. How could I deny Thee, O Jehovih! Was not the evidence of mine own life before me? I raised up my voice against my Creator! I plucked Him out of my soul; from all people in heaven and earth I dispersed Him. But they that applauded me turned against me! Even as I had turned against Thee, Thou All Person!

16. In my vanity I owned not that I was in Thee nor of Thee; with mine own hand I cut myself asunder from Thee, O Jehovih! O that I had perceived I was going farther and farther away; that I had known the road of life and death!

17. I see Thy judgment upon me, O Jehovih! I hear Thy just decree: Whilst the name of God or Lord or Savior is worshipped on the earth I shall labor with the drujas of heaven and the druks of earth!

18. A most righteous judgment, O Jehovih! Whilst I am in hell or in heaven, in hada or on the earth, will I pursue all peoples, mortals and angels, till I cast out the worship of a God and of a Lord and of a Savior. And Thou alone, Thou Great Spirit, Ever Present Person, Everlasting and Almighty, Thou shalt be All in All.

19. Again Anuhasaj went off in a swoon for the space of three days, and yet the Gods and Goddesses ceased not their fixed places. And again was the music resumed till Anuhasaj

awoke and again chanted in Jehovih's praise. And again he relapsed and again awoke, for many days; but at last awoke and beheld first of all Ahura. Steadily and wildly he gazed thereon, until his eyes were clouded and as if dead. And he dropped again into a swoon.

20. Another day the Gods watched him, and sang for him; moved not from the sacred CIRCLE OF JEHOVIH.

21. Then Anuhasaj awoke, singing: Who was it taught me to love? Ahura! Who first proclaimed Jehovih unto mine ear? Ahura! Who was the last to plead Jehovih? Ahura! Who most of all that live labored for me? Ahura!

22. I broke thy heart, O Ahura! I was mad, O I was mad, Ahura! Because of thy love, Ahura, thou praisedst me; I was vain-glorious and unworthy of thee, O my beloved.

23. Thy vision hath raised up before me, Ahura. Second to Jehovih, O my love? O that thou knewest I am here, penitent and heart-broken! I know thou wouldst fly to me, Ahura. Thou alone do I know, who would never desert me, sweet Ahura.

24. Then again Anuhasaj relapsed into a swoon, wilted, breathless, like one that is dead. Ahura sang:

25. Behold me! I am Ahura. I am come to thee from afar, O Anuhasaj. Awake and behold my love, my love. My heart is broken for thee, Anuhasaj. A thousand years I have wept for thee. O that thou couldst awake to know me!

26. Anuhasaj looked up and beheld Ahura. The latter kept on singing: It is not a dream, Anuhasaj. Thy Ahura is here. Behold me! I am he. Break the spell, O Anuhasaj. By Jehovih's power put forth thy soul! Ahura is here!

27. Again Anuhasaj relapsed, but not to swoon; merely closed his eyes and sang: Blessed art Thou, O Jehovih! Thou hast given me a sweet vision! Thou hast shown me the face of my love, Ahura! His sweet voice fell upon mine ear! I am blessed, O Jehovih!

28. Even these hells hast thou blessed, O Jehovih! The darkness of endless death is made light by Thine Almighty touch. Thou alone shalt be my song forever. Thou alone my theme of delight. Jehovih forever! Jehovih forever and forever!

29. Then Ahura, seeing the spell was broken, said: Arise, O Anuhasaj. I will sing with thee. Behold Ahura, thy love is before thee. This is no vision. Come thou to the arms of thy love.

30. And he raised Anuhasaj up, and he awoke fully, but trembling and weak, and knew understandingly.

CHAPTER XVI.

1. In the same time that Anuhasaj was delivered out of hell, so was Anubi, and from the self-same knot. And he was carried on the same calyos to Hao-yusta, the same heavenly place. And he was also in chaos, knowing nothing, only screaming: I am not Anubi. I am not the Savior. I am plain Chesota! (his real name).

2. And he also saw not and heard not, but was wild, desiring to fly away. And they held him fast, and, after the same manner they delivered Anuhasaj to reason, they also delivered Chesota.

3. And when both of them were well restored to sound reason, though still timorous, Ahura took them in his own otevan and carried them to Theovrahkistan, before Lika, for judgment. And great was the time when they came; and especially the desire

of the inhabitants to look upon Anuhasaj, the most audacious God that had ever dwelt on the earth or in her heavens, and, withal, the much-loved friend of Ahura.

4. When they came before the throne of Jehovih and duly saluted, Lika said: Whence come ye and for what purpose, O my beloved?

5. Ahura said: Hell hath delivered up the bound. My friends are before thee. Then Lika said: In Jehovih's name, welcome. Whatsoever the Father putteth into your souls, that utter ye and be assured of His love, wisdom and power.

6. Anuhasaj said: That I am delivered out of hell it is well; that I was delivered into hell it was well likewise. Give thou me Jehovih's judgment. My purpose before thee, is to register my vows unto Jehovih, that my record and thy just judgment may be carried to the heavens above.

7. Lika said: My judgment upon thee, Anuhasaj, is that thou shalt judge thyself!

8. Anuhasaj said: Most righteous judgment, O Jehovih! But knowest thou not Jehovih's voice?

9. Lika said: Thou asked for a great heavenly kingdom. Behold, Jehovih gave it thee. As soon as order is restored, thou shalt have thy kingdom again.

10. Anuhasaj said: I want it not.

11. Lika said: Thou shalt not say, I want this or that; but say that thou will do whatsoever Jehovih hath given into thy hands. When thou hast raised up thy whole kingdom, behold, thou wilt also be raised up.

12. Anuhasaj said: Alas me, this is also just. Show thou me the way; I will henceforth labor for the thousands of millions who were my kingdom.

13. Lika now bade Chesota (Anubi) speak. Chesota said: I called myself Master of the Scales and Savior of men. Whoever called on me, worshipping me and De'yus, alias the Lord God, I accepted; whoever worshipped me not, nor De'yus, nor the Lord God, I cast into hell, saying: Depart from me, ye cursed, into everlasting torments.

14. What, then, O Lika, shall be my judgment? For, behold, I cast a thousand millions into torments.

15. Lika said: Judge thyself.

16. Chesota said: Alas, the pains I gave can never be called back and undone. Have I, then, no hope?

17. Lika said: Whom thou hast pained, go thou to, and by thy good deeds hereafter done to them, so win their love that they will call thee blessed! When all of them have accepted thee, behold, it shall be well with thee.

18. Chesota said: O endless task! And yet, it is just. Teach me, then, O Lika, how to carry out this great judgment.

19. Lika then asked for Anuhasaj to come forward and be crowned; and when he approached the foot of the throne Lika came down and said: Anuhasaj, Son of Jehovih, God of Hao-yusta, thee I crown in Jehovih's name, unto his service forever. Be thou with him, O Jehovih, in wisdom, love and power.

20. Anuhasaj said: Into Thy service, O Jehovih, I commit myself forever! Give me of Thy love and wisdom and power that I may glorify Thee and Thy kingdoms.

21. Lika stretched up his hand, saying: Light of Thy light, crown of Thy crown, O Jehovih! And the light was formed in his hand, and a crown came out of the light, and Lika placed it on Anuhasaj's head. The latter then sat down on the foot of the throne, and

Lika took his hand, saying: Arise, O God, and go thy way, and the Father be with thee! 22. Thereupon Anuhasaj and Chesota saluted and stood aside. And then Ahura saluted and stood aside also; whereupon Lika granted a day of recreation, during which time the visiting Gods departed for Hao-yusta.

CHAPTER XVII.

1. Wherein this history hath overlapped the running story, hear ye how it was with Ahura and his kingdom, Vara-pishanaha, which Lika visited prior to the deliverance of the hells of hada. For, to accomplish the resurrection of Vara-pishanaha, Lika had previously sent swift messengers to Ye'a-Goo, Goddess of Ha'mistos, in etherea, to bring an avalanza capable of six thousand million Brides and Bridegrooms for the mid-harvest.
2. Accordingly, at the same time Lika and his Rapon hosts were visiting Ahura, the Goddess, Ye'a-Goo, came down in her avalanza, fully equipped. Her avalanza was egg-shaped and veiled without, and was seven miles high and five miles wide, every way, habitable throughout. On the outer surface, but under the veil, were twelve thousand porches with banisters. The propelling vortices were within the center, and the workmen were in the summit. On the lowest porch were five hundred thousand es'enaurs, and on the highest porch one thousand trumpeters.
3. Ye'a-Goo's compartment, and the place of the Holy Council, were in the midst; and her throne faced to the north, like the earth's vortex.
4. Ahura said to Lika, Son of Jehovih: My Brides and Bridegrooms I give to thee; honor thou this dissolving kingdom by performing the marriage ceremony. Lika said: Thy will and Jehovih's be done. Thus was it arranged, and the twain, together with the Rapon hosts, ascended the throne together and sat thereon.
5. Ahura had previously provided his hosts, in all four and a half thousand million Brides and Bridegrooms, and arrayed them in white, so that they anxiously awaited the coming of Ye'a-Goo, and were on the look-out to see her magnificent ship descending. A place of anchorage had also been previously made, together with accommodation for the spectators, of whom there were fifteen hundred millions, being adopted wanderers, rescued from the various hells during the past hundred years.
6. The Brides and Bride-grooms were arranged in semi-circles facing the throne, leaving a place for the avalanza, but above them, so that when Ye'a-Goo descended from her ship's bottom she would be in the midst.
7. Whilst the ship's workmen were anchoring, Ye'a-Goo and her Holy Council descended to the platform, and saluted the Gods and Goddesses on the throne in the sign, THE GLORY OF THE FATHER, and Lika and the others answered under the sign, THE ABANDONMENT OF SELF!
8. Ye'a-Goo said: In Jehovih's name am I come to answer the call of His Son, to deliver the emancipated Sons and Daughters.
9. Lika said: Behold, O Daughter of Jehovih, the Brides and Bridegrooms are before thee. To thee I give them in Jehovih's name!
10. Ye'a-Goo said: My beloved, know ye the resurrection of the most high heavens?
11. Response: Reveal, O Goddess; our faith is strong.
12. Thereupon Ye'a-Goo instructed them, and then followed the usual ceremonies, but

concluding with the seventh degree of emuth, in Jehovih's voice, to wit: To be My Brides and Bridegrooms forever?

13. Response: To be Thy Brides and Bridegrooms forever, O Jehovih! To labor for thee, and to be mouth-pieces for Thy commandments, and to be Thy expression forever! And to be in concert with Thy most high Gods for the resurrection of mortals and angels.

14. Whom I receive as Mine forever! To be one with Me in My kingdoms; for which glory I accept you as My Sons and Daughters, Brides and Bridegrooms forever!

15. Response: And be Thy Sons and Daughters! To be one with Thee forever, Thou Most High, Jehovih!

16. Ye'a-Goo said: Behold the crowns the Father bestoweth upon His loves, to be theirs forever. (Hereat the Rapon Chiefs with Lika, gathered of the curtains of light and wove crowns and cast them forth, thousands of millions, and the power of the Great Spirit through their wills bore them upon the heads of the Brides and Bridegrooms.)

17. Response: Crown of Thy crown, O Jehovih! Glory be to Thee, Creator of worlds!

18. Ye'a-Goo: The Father's ship hath come for His chosen. Walk ye in and rejoice, for ye are His harvest. Gods and Goddesses are waiting for you, as a woman waiteth for her first-born. They will receive you with joy and love. Yea, they are crying out unto me, Daughter of Jehovih, why tarriest thou so long.

19. Lika now saluted the Brides and Bridegrooms, and said: Arise, O my beloved, and go your ways, the Father calleth.

20. The Brides and Bridegrooms saluted, saying: Alas, we have not paid our teacher, Ahura. And every one plucked from the rays of Jehovih's light a flower of love, and cast it at Ahura's feet, saying: Most blessed of Gods, love of my love; Jehovih be with thee!

21. Ahura responded not; only burst into tears. And now, whilst the Brides and Bridegrooms were going into the ship, Ye'a-Goo came along the platform, accompanied by the chief marshal, and his staff, and these were followed by Ye'a-Goo's high Council. The Rapon Chiefs rose up and received them, and they all sat on Jehovih's throne in relaxation and fellowship.

22. Thus ended the ceremony. The music of the two spheres now commenced; Ye'a-Goo and her hosts embarked, and she gave the word, Arise! and lo, the great avalanza started from its foundation, amidst a universal shout of applause from the four thousand millions. Higher and higher rose the ship of fire, toward the bridge Chinvat, toward the etherean heavens.

CHAPTER XVIII.

1. After the judgment of Anuhasaj and Chesota at Theovrahkistan, Ahura asked Lika for assistance to remove the remainder of Vara-pishanaha to Hao-yusta, which Lika granted, allotting ten millions of his etherean hosts to accomplish it. With these Ahura and Anuhasaj and Chesota accomplished the removal.

2. In not many days after this, Sudga was delivered from the hells of Auprag, of which event Ahura had been previously informed, as to the time thereof, and he accordingly went to Auprag, to be in readiness to receive Sudga, and help restore him if required.

3. Sudga, on his delivery from the knot, where there had been thirty millions bound, was bereft of reason, but not gentle like Anuhasaj, but fierce, battling right and left, a very

maddened maniac that neither saw nor heard, but raved and cursed with all his strength, choked up with madness. For all the curses of his broken-down kingdom recoiled upon himself; the projective curses of his thousands of millions of slaves were piercing his soul from every quarter.

4. But they held him fast and carried him into the ship, which sailed for Hao-yusta, whither he was landed in the same condition. Ahura was with him, and Ahura caused a circle of deliverance to assemble and labor in the restoration. And it required thirty days and nights to bring him round, so he could even see and hear; but as for his judgment it was yet a hundred days more before it manifested.

5. So Ahura could not wait longer with him, but returned to the hells where Te-in was bound, the Ak-a-loo-ganuz, for Te-in was to be delivered. But herein was Ahura also disappointed, for Te-in was neither frightened nor wild nor mad; but limpid, helpless as water and without knowledge, more than a vessel of water. His energies had all been exhausted, and in a dead swoon he lay in the heart of the knot. Him they also carried to Hao-yusta, and Ahura provided for his restoration.

6. But yet, ere Te-in awoke from his stupor, Ahura departed for Osiris, who was bound in the hells of Prayogotha. Osiris had been in hell now for more than a hundred years, and in a knot for fifty years.

7. When the false Osiris was delivered, he was deranged, but preaching Jehovih, calling everybody Jehovih, and everything Jehovih. Him they also carried to Hao-yusta and provided restoration for him. And Ahura went thither also to assist with all his wisdom and strength.

8. Thus were delivered all the self-Gods who had rebelled against Jehovih and established the great confederacy, of which not one vestige was now left.

9. But of all the angels delivered out of the hells and knots not one in ten was of sound judgment, whilst more than half of them were only drujas at best.

10. Thus was founded the new kingdom of Hao-yusta, but yet in charge of the ethereans, who were to commit it to Anuhasaj and his one-time confederates, for their deliverance.

11. It came to pass in course of time that Sudga and Te-in and Osiris were restored to judgment, and in this matter Anuhasaj and Ahura and Chesota were constant workers. And when they were all restored, they in turn fell to, to restore others, to which labor they were committed till the close of dawn.

12. Osiris and Te-in and Sudga all desired to go before Lika, to be adjudged and sentenced; and they all sentenced themselves, which was granted unto them. On this occasion Osiris said:

13. Thy lessons are near at hand, O Jehovih. But who will learn them? Mortals go insane, because they have not learned to throw their cares upon Thee. To throw government upon Thee, O Jehovih, is not this wisdom? To cast riches and kingdoms into Thy lap; to own nothing; to have nothing; is not this the sum of the highest happiness?

14. Whoso doeth this will battle against no man for anything in heaven or earth. But he who doeth otherwise will soon or late descend into hell. For what is hell but the opposite of bliss? What is battling against others, but sowing the seed of anarchy in one's own soul? To battle against others is to gain the lower, by sacrificing the higher, of which latter Thou, O Jehovih, art the summit.

15. To go against Thee, O Father, is to go against one's fellows; to go against one's

fellows is to go against Thee. And who can go against Thee but will soon or late evolve his own fall?

16. Thou hast given to mortals, kings, queens, and shown them that soon or late their kingdoms will fall to pieces. And yet Lords and Gods, seeing these things, will not believe. Every one, in his own conceit, imagineth his particular kingdom will be governed more wisely than all his predecessors. And yet his also falleth.

17. Now will I turn to find Thee, O Jehovih, and the search shall be everlasting. Kingdoms are nothing to me; all possession, save wisdom and love, are but vanity and vexation. I know Thou art above all else, and yet Thou art that that hath given Thyself all away, so that none can look upon Thy face. Verily hast Thou hid Thyself away; to be like unto Thee is to hide away the self of one-self; and that that will remain will be Thy mouth-piece and Thy hand.

18. Then spake Sudga unto Jehovih, saying: Why was I puffed up, seeing that I created not even mine own self. Neither had I anything in earth or heaven to use or to work with, but the substance was made already. Yea, I leapt into Thy garden which Thou hadst planted.

19. I raised up my voice against Thee; because Thou wert too Holy for my gross senses to behold, I condemned Thee. I wanted Thee gross that I could look upon Thee; that I could walk around Thee, and behold Thy stature. I saw that all men were like unto me in this.

20. Therefore I made a figure-head of myself; I said unto Thy children: Behold me! And at first they were pleased, because they imagined they had found a Creator they could measure. But Thine eye was upon me, Thine hand pointed the way and the manner of my iniquity. And they searched me out and found I was but a man, like unto themselves. Wherefore they condemned me.

21. The fool acknowledgeth no person save he can grapple therewith, and find the arms, and the length thereof, and the feet and their standing place. How vain I was in this, O Jehovih!

22. He that professed Thy Person I denounced as a fool; because I saw not Thy completeness Thou sufferedst me to pursue my vanity. Because I had risen above acknowledging Thy Person I was forced to make man the All Highest; and this drove me to make myself the all highest man. But Thou camest not against me to beat me from my iniquity, but gavest me full play to do my utmost.

23. On all sides hast Thou encompassed Thy creation with liberty. Even Thine enemy Thou hast not restrained. He standeth in public, saying: Jehovih, I deny Thee. If Thou art mightier than I, strike me down. Behold, I deny Thee and Thy Person! Thou Void Nothingness! Thou fool Creator, with Thy half-created world. Thou who hast created sin! And created misery! Thou Father of evil! O Thou dumb Nothing.

24. Yea, even to him hast Thou given free speech; and he buildeth up his own soul in his own way. And for a season he is the delight of the druk and the druj; yea, they fasten upon him, and he gaineth a multitude of evil ones, divided one against another, but the seed of his curses taketh root in them, and he becometh encompassed with foulness and bondage.

25. To find harmony in Thee, O Jehovih; to measure the Goodness of Thee; to rejoice in one's joys; to treasure Thy best gifts; to laud Thy love; to love Thee because Thou hast given me power to love, and things to love; to rejoice in Thy fruits and flowers and all

perfected things; to harp forever upon Thy glories and the magnitude of Thy creation; to sing praises to Thee for harmony wherever found; to love to comprehend all good things; to find the good that is in all men and women; to rejoice in delights; to teach others to rejoice, and to search after all perfected beauties and goodness and righteousness and love; these shall be my service unto Thee, my everlasting Father.

26. To seek not to find imperfections; to seek not to find inharmonies; to seek not to find evil; to seek not to find ugliness; to seek not to find evil in others, nor their darkness nor shortcomings; to seek not to prove imperfections upon Thee, O Jehovih; to find no fault with Thee; to complain not against Thee; to complain not for trials nor for hardships, nor for the evil others inflict me with; to quibble not, because I can not comprehend Thy vastness; to quibble not for myself; to speak not evilly against anything Thou hast created. O make Thou me strong and wise forever.

27. Te-in spake to Jehovih, saying: Wherein is the limit of experience, O Jehovih! And how short have I not been before Thee, My Father! Behold, I had learned all philosophies; I had been taught for a long season in the right way, but I rebelled against Thee, my Creator.

28. I had been taught to horde not up anything; to own nothing; to desire nothing but wisdom and love. And Thy teachers, O Jehovih, showed me the evidence of thousands of great rulers, and every one of them had come to evil and destruction. Why then, O Father, was I not wise in the evidence before me? But I rose up against all this testimony, and I fashioned a mighty kingdom. Yea, Thou sufferedst me to try in mine own way to the full.

29. I went not by peace but by war; I raised me up standing armies and great warriors without limit; by force I established myself, but only as a tree that groweth up and is cut down. But what was I in Thy great universe, O Jehovih. What was my experience but the repetition of others who had been before me.

30. Now will I be wise; most cautious in my wisdom, and slow to proceed. But how can I make my experience profitable unto others? Thou hast stood me afar off; whoso heareth me will say: Ah, had I tried it I had succeeded better. Thou prickest each one to go in and try, but they all fail. Yea, they reiterate their failure; but where is the profit of this experience unto others? How can I ever reach them, O Jehovih!

31. What profit have I more than a mortal that dwelleth on the earth? Have not the angels testified for thousands of years that the rich man was crippling his own soul, and that the king and queen were binding themselves with chains for the habitation of hell? But they will not heed; every one hopeth he at least will find a way to escape; to gain prestige over others; to be a leader; to have servants; to be idle; to live at ease; to have great possessions; to revel in luxuries. Are not these more powerful than experience; greater in the eyes of the ignorant than all the wisdom of earth and heaven.

32. Thou hast wisely shaped Thy creatures, O Father! Thou makest great servants of us in a way we know not of. Behold, I desired a mighty kingdom in heaven, and Thou gavest one into my hand. Yea, I flattered myself with my success; I laughed at the Gods who had been before my time. How things are changed now, O Jehovih!

33. Thou hast made me a servant of servants; yea, by mine own hand have I bound myself about. Have I not heard mortals say: O that I had a kingdom to rule over! O that I had great riches, how good I would be! And because Thou deniest them for their own good, they complain against Thee. Who shall answer for the vanity of men and angels!

They have not patience with Thee, who created them alive and knowest what is best.

34. One saith: Yonder is a great king, why doeth he not a great good? Or, yonder is a rich man, why doeth he not a great good also. O that I were in their places.

35. How shall I show them, O Father, that to be a king is to go away from doing good; that to be a rich man is to deny goodness? Yea, by the very act of possession is he testimony in the opposite way. For he that is good giveth all; even as Thou gavest all and so made all things. And the greater the possession the greater the bondage. Who hath so small responsibility as he who hath nothing? This is the sum of wisdom, O Jehovih; and all men and angels soon or late will acknowledge it.

36. Better hast Thou made it for the servant than for the master; better for the poor than the rich; and these things will also come to their understanding in course of time. But how can I, O Father, make them to know wisdom without experience, to accept the testimony of others' tortures in hell?

37. Behold, Thou gavest me great learning when I was of the earth; and when in hada great advantages to attain to deep wisdom; but, after all, I was caught in a snare of my own setting. How much, then, O Father, must I expect of the multitude? Happy is he who hath nothing, and desireth only wisdom and love. To cultivate such a garden, what a harvest will ripen out unto him.

38. When the three had thus spoken before the throne and before the high Council, Ahura stood aside and spake also. He said:

CHAPTER XIX.

1. O that I could sing Thee a song of delight, Thou All Highest. Or find the words to make plain Thy marvelous ways. But Thou has limited me as a shadow, of which Thou art the substance. Thy causes are deep and of long times; my judgment less than a breath of air; I resolve and reason and devise, but all is nothing before Thee.

2. To-day my soul is buoyed up with great rejoicing; Thou hast sent me my loves. I would bind them with sweet words; their wisdom would I feast upon forever. In Thy great mercy, Jehovih, Thou hast showed me a world of delight.

3. How can I repay Thee, or Thy countless millions make to understand the way of rejoicing. O that I could show them the secret way of bliss; or turn them in the direction of the All Highest! Could they be the Within; to know the delight of that which proceedeth outward.

4. O that I could make them understand; to look upward instead of downward; to look inward instead of onward. How Thou followest up Thy wayward children; Thy truants that strive to go away from Thee.

5. They wander away off, and Thou givest the slack of the leading line unto them. They go as if around a circle, and come to the place of beginning at last. O that I could prevail upon them in the start; that I could save them the first journey of the circle. O that they would go slowly and with Thee always, Jehovih!

6. But Thou enrichest them with Thy bounteous fields; they travel far and are foot-sore and weary; and the twain causes are as a new book of songs. O, that experience may never die! And Thy creations never cease to have adventurous Sons and Daughters!

7. O, that I could understand Thy Greatness, or find the darkness that glorifieth the light

of Thy countenance. I drink deep of mine own folly, and mine eyes wander about because of the darkness. I come upon Thy pathway and burst forth with a song of delight. Yea, I rejoice for the darkness I have passed through; in this am I more buoyant in my love to Thee, my Creator.

8. How can I make all Thy people to sing songs unto Thee; or teach them to harp not forever on the dark side of things? I have seen the tree of hell they planted in their own souls, and the way they cultivate it. They know not what is meant by singing praises unto Thee, and of Thy growth in them.

9. Why will they interpret me by words, or realize not that I sing of the exuberance of the soul? O that I could inspire them to talk good of all things; to harp forever on the beauties Thou hast made, instead of the ills and horrors around about. Can they never understand what it is to sow the seed of the tree of endless delight?

10. O that I could call them unto Thee, Jehovih! Or that I could lift their aspiration up from the shadows of death. I would follow them into Thy two great gardens which Thou hast created; that which is green, where they go and curse Thee; and that which is ripe, where I have found Thee full of love. Because I said: Sing unto Him forever; pray to Him with great rejoicing, they interpret me to mean words uttered as a mocking-bird. Yea, they grumble forever.

11. To find Thee, O Jehovih; to glorify the good that cometh along, this is the salvation of the world. Of this my songs shall never end; without a shadow of darkness Thou wilt tune my voice forever. I will sing and dance before Thee; the germ of happiness in my soul will I nurse as Thy holiest gift. For of all the trees which Thou hast planted in the soul of men and angels, this is the most glorious; for it is the perfection of Thy Voice, which singeth in all Thy living creatures.

12. When Ahura ended his song, then spake Lika, for the Voice of Jehovih was upon him. He said: Many leaders have I created for the earth and her heavens; but not one have I created with power to make a leader of himself. My hand is upon them that I choose; with wisdom and power raise I them up from the beginning.

13. To a people on the earth I give a king; to the inhabitants of My heavens give I Lords and Gods.

14. Because ye have tried the fullness of self, and raised up mighty realms in heaven, but to come to naught before My hand, ye are as a new power in these heavens.

15. As by the name Jehovih, I have maintained the Faithists in earth and heaven, so shall ye rule over My enemies, in righteousness and love and good works, by the names Lord and God, which they shall worship until the coming of the next dawn. But I will come in that day and deliver you and them, and there shall be no more Lord or God upon the earth or in the heavens thereof.

16. Grieve not that ye have had great kingdoms, and been overthrown and cast into torments; for ye have been so prepared in My works, that I might reach them that are not of the flesh and blood of My Faithists. And inasmuch as ye have gone to the farthest limit of glory and of the darkness of hell, so will I give unto you wisdom, love and power accordingly.

17. For, to make ready for the kosmon era, I want not a few, but thousands of millions in heaven and earth, to inspire such as live in darkness.

18. As I delivered you, so shall ye deliver them; because they will accurse themselves

with war and with standing armies for the sake of earthly glory unto their rulers, ye shall encompass them about, and break them up, and deliver them into My kingdoms, which are peace and love.

19. As ye have been delivered out of hell, so shall ye deliver the kings and queens of the earth out of their kingdoms wherein they will unknowingly bind themselves in condemnation before Me. They shall be made to understand that, whoso assumeth a kingdom, shall not rule it unto his own glory without reaping the fruits of hell.

20. When the king goeth forth, he shall not be afraid he will be cut down; nor shall his marshals stand about him to protect him, for My Person shall shield him, and his people will shout with great joy when his steps draw nigh. To serve Me is not in prayer only, or in rites and ceremonies, but in stretching forth the hand to do good unto others with all of one's might.

21. Because ye have proved that force and violence only establish for a day, and is not of Me, so shall ye make them understand that whoso useth force and violence or armies to sustain himself is not of Me, but is My enemy, and is on the way to destruction.

22. Whoso being a king, or a general, or a captain, and in war, either offensive or defensive, professing to serve Me by rites and ceremonies and praises, is a mocker of Me and My kingdoms; yea, a blasphemer in My sight; he provideth the way of his own torments. These are My creations; to answer force with force, violence with violence, mockery with mockery; alike and like as seed is sown, so shall the harvest come unto the sowers.

23. Neither shall evil and darkness and misery cease on the earth till I have disbanded the dealers in death; by My own hand will I liberate the nations of the earth; their armies shall go away, like the winter's snow in sun of summer. To which end ye shall be My workers, with wisdom and love and power.

CHAPTER XX.

1. During the fourth year of dawn, the Voice of Jehovih came to Lika, saying: My Son, thou shalt provide thyself an army sufficient, and thou shalt take away from the earth all angels below the first resurrection, save such fetals as are under the dominion of My heavenly rulers.

2. And thou shalt provide them separate regions in My lower heavens, whence they can not return to mortals. And thou shalt appoint rulers and teachers over them, to deliver them out of madness and evil and stupor.

3. Of thy etherean hosts shalt thou appoint teachers and rulers for this purpose; but at the end of dawn they shall give over their places to atmosphereans selected from Theovrahkistan.

4. From this time forth My atmosphereans shall begin to help one another, not depending for all teachers to come from My etherean heavens.

5. Lika then called up At'yesonitus and told him of Jehovih's words, and further added: To thee do I therefore allot this labor. And I give unto thee twelve generals, for the different regions of the earth; and unto each of the twelve I allot five million ethereans, whom thou canst draw from the armies that were engaged in delivering the hells and knots.

6. At'yesonitus said: In Jehovih's will and thine, I am pleased. I will divide up the regions of the earth amongst the twelve generals, and give unto each one of them the five millions, according to thy commandments.

7. At'yesonitus then sent officers out into different regions in atmospherea to select the sixty million deliverers, commanding them to report in Theovrahkistan, in the Valley of Tish, his heavenly place, whither he took the twelve generals that Lika had assigned him.

8. Lika gave to At'yesonitus a list of the spirits to be thus taken away from mortals, that is, the engrafted, the damons, the familiars, the vampires and the lusters, and such other spirits as otherwise lead mortals into darkness and crime; showing him the regions of the earth where they were most numerous. With which list At'yesonitus and his generals made themselves well acquainted before starting on his perilous enterprise.

9. At'yesonitus then ordered the ship-builders to provide him twelve thousand fire-boats, with bulwarks of fire, and with gateways.

10. In the meantime Lika sent Yussamis with four hundred geographers and mathematicians and surveyors to find the necessary plateau to which At'yesonitus could send his captured hosts.

11. Yussamis therefore founded the six heavenly plateaux known as the Ugsadisspe, a name signifying the HEAVEN OF THE DESTROYING SERPENTS.

12. These, then, were the six heavens of Ugsadisspe, to wit: Tewallawalla, over Arabin'ya, one thousand two hundred miles high; Setee'song, over Vind'yu, one thousand miles high; Go'e'dhi, over Jaffeth, one thousand one hundred miles high; Ellapube, over Uropa, one thousand miles high; Apak, over North and South Guatama, six hundred miles high, and bordering on Yaton'te, the subjective heaven of the ancients, which was now being re-established by Kaparos; and Fue, over Chihuahi, nine thousand miles high.

13. Yussamis provided these heavens with no roadways, in order to prevent the delivered spirits flocking together, in which case they might run into anarchy (hells). And, accordingly, appointed unto each of these heavens one ruler of the rank primal God, selecting them from the etherean hosts, but empowering them to bestow their thrones on successors at the end of dawn, giving terms of office not less than two hundred years, but subject to the limiting power of God of Theovrahkistan.

14. Lika gave four thousand messengers to At'yesonitus, and twelve thousand messengers to Yussamis, to whom he also gave sixty million laborers. But each of them provided their own heralds, musicians, marshals and captains in their own way.

15. Now, therefore, At'yesonitus and Yussamis, receiving their armies of laborers, fell to work, the former to delivering, and the latter to receiving the drujas of the earth. And Yussamis put his hosts to building houses and hospitals, heavenly places, and to founding cities and provinces through the primal Gods under him.

CHAPTER XXI.

1. Jehovih had said: All angels below the first resurrection, save infants, shall be known in heaven and on earth as drujas, for they are such as have not capacity in knowledge or strength of individuality.

2. As there are on earth paupers and vagrants and beggars and criminals who are druks, so are there, in hada, spirits that are a great trial to both mortals and angels.

3. And they inhabit mortals and the houses that mortals dwell in. Some mortals have one or two of them; some a score; and some have hundreds of them. Some of them continue to inhabit mortal dwellings long after mortals have abandoned them, even till they fall in ruins. And whoso cometh into such house, the drujas come upon him to live on him and with him.

4. And if a mortal have greater wisdom and strength of soul than the drujas, he ruleth over them, to a good purpose, reforming them and raising them up out of darkness and helplessness.

5. But if the drujas have greater power than the mortal, then they pull him down in darkness, making of him a man to lust after the affairs of earth. Sometimes they help man to riches and great power; and if he have sons and daughters who are brought up in idleness and ease and luxury, then the drujas fasten upon them, leading them in their own way, of lust and debauchery, or hard-heartedness.

6. The flesh-eater is their delight; and the drunkard their great joy. The man of riches, and kings, and generals, and fighting men, and harlots, and soldiers, are great treasures to them. And all manner of intoxicating things, that mortals delight in, are great feasts and rejoicings to them. The priest and the preacher who live in ease and luxury, performing showy rites and entertainments, are as great harvests for them to revel with.

7. On some occasion the drujas rule over their mortal, and his neighbors call him mad, and they send him to a mad-house, which is to them a city of delight. When mortals engage in war, slaying one another, the drujas have great merriment, taking part, by inspiring the mortals into the conflict.

8. The pleader (lawyer) is a favorite to them, for his vocation bringeth them in the midst of contention and craft and lying; he is to them a fortunate habitation.

9. The magician that worketh miracles and tricks is their favorite, for with him and through him, they can make themselves manifest. And when they show themselves, and are questioned as to who they are, they answer to any name that will please or flatter, even at times pretending to be Gods and Saviors!

10. The tattling woman that talketh of her neighbors is a good home for drujas; and if the woman be given to talk evil, they are rejoiced beyond measure. The man that is a great boaster, and liar, and slanderer, is a choice house for them to dwell in.

11. The cheater and defrauder, the miser and the spendthrift, the curser of Jehovih, the curser of the Gods, is like a citadel for them to inhabit.

12. They go not, for the most part, away from the mortal they inhabit whilst he liveth; nay, they have not wisdom or strength to go more than one length away. Some of them have strength to go to a neighbor or to a neighbor's house. And if a mortal curse his neighbor to die, then such drujas as can go to that neighbor, seek out some poisonous infection and inoculate him to death, which is called casting spells.

13. Nay, there is nothing too low or foul for them; and for the most part they are but idiots, and deranged imbeciles, answering to any name or request like a man who is drunk, one so very drunk that he knoweth not and careth not.

14. A large city full of crime and debauchery, and rich and fashionable people, and people of evil habits, suiteth them better than a country place.

15. Drujas dwell as numerously among the rich and fashionable as amongst the poor; they fill the bawdy-house and the temples of the idolaters; a court of justice full of pleaders

(lawyers) and criminals is their delightful resort, but a battle in war is a sweet amusement to them.

16. A laboring man that is good and honest is of little value to them, save he be a gross feeder or drinker of intoxicating wines.

17. A man that marrieth a rich, lazy woman, receiveth with his wife a hundred drujas, or more.

18. A woman that marrieth a rich, lazy man, or a gambler, receiveth with her husband a hundred drujas, or more.

19. Drujas rule over mortals more than mortals rule over them. It was because of their abundance and their power to do evil, that Jehovih commanded His chosen to marry amongst themselves; and to withdraw from other peoples, and make themselves a separate and exclusive people, that they might not be inhabited with drujas.

20. When a mortal dieth, and he had dominion over his drujas, not only his spirit will rise to the first resurrection, but his drujas also, whereupon they are all delivered into light.

21. When a mortal dieth, and his drujas had dominion over him, then his spirit becometh a druj also, and he becometh one with them, fastening on whoso cometh in the way; but if it be in a house and no mortal cometh, upon whom they can fasten, then they remain in that house. And here they may remain a year or ten years or a hundred years, in darkness, knowing nothing, doing nothing, until other angels come and deliver them, which is often no easy matter, requiring bodily force to carry them away.

22. Jehovih gave certain signs unto both angels and mortals, whereby it shall be known both on earth and in heaven which is master over the other, a mortal or his drujas, and, consequently, such matter determineth to what place the spirit of a man will most readily fall after death.

23. If the mortal can not control his habit for intoxication, or gluttony, or avarice, or debauchery, or laziness, or lying, or hypocrisy, preaching what he practiceth not, or sexual indulgence, or vengeance, or anger, or tattling mischievously, then is he, indeed, a victim in the hands of drujas, and at the time of his death, he becometh one with them.

24. For if he have not power to rule in such matters whilst he is in the mortal world, he will be no stronger by the loss of his corporeal body.

25. If the mortal, on the other hand, shall have risen to control himself over these habits and desires, then will he be indeed, at the time of death, already entered into the first resurrection; and the drujas, if he have any, will be delivered also.

26. And not the words and professions of either mortals or drujas, nor their prayers, nor religious rites and ceremonies are of any value unto them; but by the works and behavior of mortals are all things known and proven.

27. So that Jehovih's high-raised Gods but need pass over a corporeal city once, to determine whether it be in resurrection or declension. And such Gods put their angel laborers to work, sorting them as a mortal would his cattle.

28. And if a city be badly cast in drujas, dragging mortals down to destruction spiritually; then the angels inspire such mortals as are in the way of resurrection to move out of the city, and after that they cast the city in fire and burn it down.

29. And whilst it is burning, and the drujas distracted with the show, the angels of power come upon them and carry them off, hundreds of millions of them. And the mortals are thus cleared of them that would have bound them in darkness and death.

30. In this matter the infidel curseth Jehovih because the houses are burned, for he judgeth matters by the things his soul was set upon. He saith: What a foolish God! How wicked to burn a city.

31. For he understandeth not that all things are Jehovih's; and that His Gods under him work not for man's earthly aggrandizement, which is the curse of his spirit, but they work for his spiritual resurrection in their own way, according to the Father's light in them.

32. To accomplish the resurrection of the drujas dwelling with mortals on the earth, had Lika, Son of Jehovih, appointed At'yesonitus, with his twelve generals, very Gods in wisdom and power, each one to a certain division of the earth.

CHAPTER XXII.

1. Jehovih spake to Lika, saying: These are My ways; reveal thou Me unto them. They that know Me not, shall be made to know Me; My labors shall rise up before them, and their understanding shall be opened.

2. They shall know what I mean when I say I will destroy or I will build up. I have heard man in his vanity, that judgeth Me. His eyes are on the earth only, and in houses and riches. Because I take them away from him, he complaineth against Me.

3. I gave man an example in his own child that delighteth in sweets, and idleness, and vain pleasures. Man taketh these from his child, saying: Behold, they are not good for thee, save in great temperance!

4. Wherein have I injured thee, O man? Wherein destroyed I aught that contributed to thy spirit? Wherein have I suffered destruction to come upon thee, whilst thou followedst My commandments? Why shalt thou complain because I laid great cities in ashes? Sawest thou the millions of drujas thou wert holding down in darkness by thy evil habits?

5. I am not in anger, nor pull I down, nor burn I up any place in a passion. As thou goest forth to destroy a row of houses to stay a great conflagration, shall the people murmur? For thy hand is stretched forth to do a good work for the whole city.

6. My heavens are magnified cities, and when a mortal wing offendeth, behold, I clip it short. They are all Mine; and none can question My authority with Mine own, which I wield for the resurrection of the whole.

7. Thou hast wept because of the destruction of the books of great learning of the ancients; but thou knowest not thine own words. Saw I not, O man, that thou wouldst never wean thyself from the doctrines of the dark ages if the books of great learning were not destroyed!

8. In all ages of the world thou hast been bound to the ancients; thou art forever searching backward for wisdom; and to the angels of the dead who pretend to be ancients. I behold the latter, and that they are drujas.

9. I send wise angels down to them to deliver them out of darkness. And they come and bear the drujas away from thee, for thine own good and theirs. My wise angels suffer mortals to burn up the books of the ancients; for I command them to make thee open thine understanding to the living present.

10. Jehovih spake to At'yesonitus, and through him to the twelve Gods of deliverance, saying:

11. Go forth, My son, in wisdom and power. Thy labor requireth great strength and

stratagems. For thou shalt find the drujas fast bound to mortals and to mortal habitations (houses). As a drowning man clingeth to a log, so cling the drujas to mortals. As a delirious man, mad with drunkenness, flieth in fear from his best friends, so will the drujas fly from thee, and thy hosts who shall attempt to deliver them.

12. They will inspire their mortals to dread an innovation of the ancient doctrines. Yea, the twain, not knowing it, will bind themselves together with great tenacity.

13. But thou shalt deliver them apart nevertheless, by stratagem, or persuasion, or with a strong hand. And when thou hast them separate, thou shalt surround the drujas with flames of fire, and carry them off to the boats, which are bulwarked with fire. And thou shalt deliver them in the places My Son, Yussamis, hath ready prepared for them.

14. Thou shalt not only deliver the drujas, but cause mortals to hate them.

15. Mortal kings shall issue edicts against magicians and prophets and seers and priests; and the consultation of spirits shall come to an end. And man on the earth shall turn to his own soul, which is My light within him, and he shall cultivate it and learn to think for himself.

16. At'yesonitus prepared a record to give to mortals, and it was by inspiration so given. And the nature of the record was to teach mortals to be guarded against drujas, and know who was afflicted with them.

17. This, then, that followeth is said record, even as it standeth to this day in the libraries of heaven, to wit:

18. The man that saith: I pity my neighbors, they are surrounded with drujas!

19. The man that saith: Fools only believe in obsession!

20. The man that saith: There is no All Person!

21. The man that saith: My way is wisdom; thine is wicked!

22. The man that saith: Let no one dictate to me! I will have nothing but liberty to the uttermost!

23. The man that saith: As the priest thinketh, so do I!

24. The man that saith: That thou hadst my knowledge!

25. The man that saith: The ancients were wiser than we!

26. The man that saith: The ancients were fools!

27. The man that saith: Whoso seeth not as I do is a heathen!

28. The man that saith: Whoso worshippeth not my God is wicked!

29. The man that saith: Wisdom is book-learning!

30. The man that saith: There is no wisdom in books!

31. The man that saith: My book is sacred; it containeth the sum of all revelation and inspiration!

32. The man that saith: There is no inspiration, nor words thereof!

33. The followers of the ancients only.

34. He who will have nothing to do with the ancients.

35. He who ignoreth rites and ceremonies and prayers.

36. He who dependeth on rites and ceremonies and prayers.

37. Whoso denieth the Ever Present Person.

38. Whoso followeth the counsel of angels or men.

39. Whoso will not learn from the counsel of men and angels.

40. Whoso feeleth prayers and confessions to be good for others, but not necessary for himself.

41. Or saith: I will lead and supervise; be thou my servant!

42. Or saith: Behold my rights!

43. Or: Behold my earnings!

44. Or: Behold my possessions!

45. Or talketh of himself and his experiences.

46. Or tattleth of others.

47. Or judgeth his brother, or criticiseth him.

48. The self-righteous, who saith: Behold me, I am holy!

49. Or who desireth not new light, or saith: The old is good enough!

50. Whoso laboreth for himself only.

51. Whoso laboreth not for others in his wisdom and strength.

52. That seeketh his own ease.

53. That considereth not others' welfare more than his own.

54. The hypocrite preaching one way and practicing another.

55. That speaketh not openly his doctrines, lest his words profit not his earthly means and associations.

56. At'yesonitus said: For these are all as much under the bondage of drujas as is the drunkard, or harlot, or murderer. And after death their spirits float into the same hada of darkness.

CHAPTER XXIII.

1. When At-yesonitus' generals and their hosts went through Vind'yu and Jaffeth and Arabin'ya, they concerted with the Gods who had in charge the inspiration of Capilya, Moses and Chine. And not only did the angel generals remove the drujas from mortals, but inspired mortal kings and queens in those great divisions of the earth to issue edicts against magicians and priests who consulted with spirits.

2. Jehovih had said: It shall be a testimony in the latter days unto the inhabitants of the earth of My proceedings; not with one division of the earth only, but with all places. For they shall in after years search history and find that in the same era in these three great divisions of the earth the kings and queens issued edicts against spirit communion. And this fact shall be testimony of My cycle of Bon; wherein man shall understand that I come not in one corner of the earth only, and to one people only; but that I have them all in My charge, as a Father that knoweth his own children.

3. Neither give I unto them the same aspirations; for one I send westward to circumscribe the earth; one I build up with a multitude of languages, and a multitude of Gods; and the third one I build up without any God save Myself. And they shall understand that where there are many languages there are many Gods worshipped; where there is one language, there is only One worshipped, even I, the Great Spirit.

4. For in kosmon I will bring them together; and these diversities shall be as a key to unlock the doctrines and languages of times and seasons long past.

5. Man living away from other men becometh conceited in himself, deploring the darkness of others, and great nations become conceited of themselves and their doctrines.

6. Each one of the great peoples saying: Behold yonder barbarians! I was the chosen in His especial care. Those others are only heathens, and have not been worthy of the Great Spirit's concern.

7. But in this day I plant the seed of My testimony, which shall come up and blossom and bear fruit in three thousand years.

8. At'yesonitus and his generals, with their millions of angel hosts, cleared off the drujas of the earth, the angels of darkness. They extended east and west and north and south, around all the earth, in all the divisions thereof, into every nook and corner.

9. Day and night At'yesonitus and his armies labored, ceased not nor rested, but in good method went right on, filling all the lowest place of heaven with their transport boats of fire.

10. And the boats sped hither and yonder without ceasing, loaded in their ascent with the screaming, frightened drujas, all under guard, and duly preserved against accident or harm by the wise angels over them.

11. Some drujas were easily captured and carried away; some weak, helpless and harmless; but hundreds of millions of them mad, and most desperate; some evil, fearful in desperate oaths, and foul talk, and dangerous withal.

12. But others were most pitiful in their love to linger with their mortal kindred; mothers, whose children dwelt on the earth; and children spirits, whose mothers dwelt on the earth. To separate them and carry away such drujas was a most heart-rending task, requiring God-like souls to accomplish it.

13. Jehovih had said: As a mortal mother will cling to the mortal body of her dead child, till her friends must tear them apart, the while all souls who look on are broken-hearted because of her love, even such is the bond betwixt the spirit of the dead and the mortal yet left behind.

14. But when My wise angels look upon them, and perceive they are carrying each other down in darkness, then shall they be torn asunder; and the spirit shall be taken away and provided for ultimate resurrection, and only permitted to visit the mortal kin under due guardianship.

15. On the battle-fields of the earth were hundreds of millions of spirits in chaos, still fighting imaginary battles, not knowing their bodies were dead; knowing naught but to curse and fight; roving over the battle-fields, and would not away, save by capture and being carried off.

16. Thus did At-yesonitus and his mighty hosts clear the earth. But of their great labors and wonderful adventures a thousand books might be written, and thousands of heroes singled out, whose great achievements overwhelm one's belief because of the manifested love and power.

17. And yet not much less were the labors and adventures of Yussamis in Ugadisspe and her six heavenly places, where his etherean hosts labored unceasingly, preparing places, and keepers, and nurses, and physicians, and teachers for the delivered drujas, the thousands of millions.

18. Jehovih said unto Yussamis: Thou shalt assort the drujas; the peaceful to themselves; the dumb to themselves; the mad, the chaotic, and all other of My afflicted ones; provided sections and places for them. And teachers and nurses and physicians; for they shall be delivered out of darkness also. Yea, every one of them shall become as a star of glory in

heaven.

19. And Yussamis and his Gods developed the six heavens of Ugadisspe; established places for the tens of millions of drujas; and provided order and discipline, and altars of worship, and schools, and colleges, and factories, and all things whatsoever required in a primary heaven.

CHAPTER XXIV.

1. Jehovih spake to Lika, saying: Behold, the end of dawn draweth near; go thou once more around about the earth and her heavens, and examine into the labor of thy Gods. And thou shalt take with thee thy Rapon hosts, and a sufficient number of heralds and attendants, and such musicians and messengers as thou desirest.

2. And when thou art come to Yaton'te, My subjective heaven, thou shalt halt a while with Kaparos, and re-establish it in greater holiness and efficiency. For this is Mine only subjective heaven in the regions of the red star.

3. Behold, the spirits of those that die in infancy call out to Me, saying: Tell us, O Thou Creator, how is it with the earth? How is it with mortals who dwell on the earth? What do they toil at? Have they schools and hospitals and factories, like unto ours? Have mortals mishaps and trials? And have they roadways, and oceans of water on the hard earth?

4. How can these things be, O Jehovih? Why is it that mortals can not go down into the earth and into the bottoms of their oceans, even as we do in the heavens?

5. How didst Thou create us alive in the earth? What was the place like? Why do mortals carry around with them such earth-houses (bodies)? Can not they go in them and out of them at pleasure?

6. What do mortals mean, O Jehovih, by mortal life and mortal death? Doth the clay and stone and water they dwell in (the earth body) have life and death? What do they mean by: This is mine and That is thine?

7. Shall every one retain his own body? How do the earth bodies grow? Do they eat clay and stone? And water? Where do they get their blood? And do they eat hair, that they may have earth hair?

8. Why is it that they bring not up their bodies with them when they are dead? Wear they clothes over the spirit body only, or over the earth body also?

9. Great are Thy works, O Jehovih! Take me to Yaton'te, Thy great subjective heaven. We would learn by figures in pantomime the illustrations of the earth. We would learn by Thy panoramic heaven what mortals do? How they live and what their schools are like? How they have contrived to teach the corporeal senses by corporeal things? How their boats are made and propelled; how their vehicles travel along upon the solid earth.

10. Jehovih said: For which reason, O Lika, thou shalt see to it that Yaton'te be perfected unto this instruction, as well as to arouse from stupor the spirits of the dead who desire not to raise up from the earth.

11. Lika told the Rapon hosts Jehovih's words; and he also gave command to his chief marshal to provide the necessary otevan with officers, heralds, musicians and messengers.

12. Accordingly, as soon as all things were in readiness, Lika committed the throne of Jehovih, in Theovrahkistan, to his vice-God; and Lika and the Rapons, with their attendant hosts, departed on their journey.

13. Now, since the time of Lika in the plateau of Theovrahkistan, it had become habited by thousands of millions of angels, and they were high in the grades.

14. So that the officers of selection were already preparing them by the millions for Brides and Bridegrooms to Jehovih. And there were thousands of heavenly cities besides Yogannaqactra, which were now in beauty, gaiety, refinement and delight, with music, and rites and ceremonies most magnificent.

15. Then there were officers over these officers, whose place it was to sort and arrange the inhabitants of cities; and others over these for each one hundred and forty-four cities; and yet another over these officers, and he was called Marshal of Theovrahkistan. And he was of the same rank as the marshals of the hosts of Lika, conferring with the Marshal in Chief of Jehovih's Throne.

CHAPTER XXV.

1. Jehovih said to Lika: Finish thy visit and thy inspection, My Son, in all the places of hada on the earth, leaving the land of Jaffeth to the last. And thou shalt go thither, at the time of Chine's resurrection, and descend with thy ship and take him up from the earth.

2. And thou shalt bring him with thee to Yogannaqactra, where he shall remain the few days that dawn remaineth; and when thy hosts ascend to etherea thou shalt take Chine with thee and make thy home his home until such time as he may be taught the ways and powers of the higher heavens.

3. For since his corporeal life is a sacrifice for the resurrection of men, he shall receive especial care and assistance in heaven.

4. Lika had been previously informed by the God of Chine as to the time Chine would die, and be burnt up, with his ashes scattered to the four winds; and the re-gathering up of a corporeal form of Chine, and the seven days' duration thereof. So Lika shaped the course of his otevan, according to the instruction of his messengers, who had been appointed for that purpose, so that he should reach the field in time to raise up Chine before the multitude.

5. The God of Chine had prophesied to mortals through his ward that a fire-ship would descend from heaven on a given day, and take Chine up to heaven.

6. Accordingly a great multitude of mortals were assembled in the ash-field, where they cast the ashes of the dead, watching for the heavenly ship.

7. Of which matters Lika had been previously informed by his messengers; and Lika had in turn informed the God of Chine the time he would appear with the ship, that he might cause Chine to walk in the midst of the field and so be caught up.

8. And all these matters were carried out to the hour and minute, in the hands of these great Gods. And Lika caused the fire of the ship to be made visible to mortals. And the size of the ship was ten times larger than the field of the dead, so that when the people beheld the light of the ship they feared and trembled, and many of them fell down bewailing that the world was coming to an end.

9. And God caused Chine to walk out in the field, and Lika sent down a whirlwind and took him up into the ship, in presence of tens of thousands of mortals assembled.

10. And Lika bore his course now for Yogannaqactra, for the end of the dawn of Bon was at hand.

CHAPTER XXVI.

1. Lika sent messengers to all his Gods and Lords, to install their successors, and to bestow them; after which the Gods and Lords were to report in Theovrahkistan ready for the cyclic resurrection. And he commanded them to bring their etherean hosts with them, save such as chose to volunteer to remain the next dan of two hundred years.

2. Lika had previously sent word by his swift messengers to etherea, to Lissa, Goddess of Teannakak, in etherea, next to Howgil. And he said unto Lissa: My resurrection will be eight links, each one equal to eight thousand million Brides and Bridegrooms. Send thou a cowppon to deliver them.

3. Lissa sent word back to Lika, saying: O Jehovih, I am delighted with the command of Thy Son, Lika, Chief of Vetta'puissa! I will deliver the chain of cowppon.

4. Then Lissa gave her commands in Teannakak, to have her builders construct the cowppon; and she also set her officers to work selecting such hosts as she would need for her great undertaking. For she had been notified in sufficient time; for it was a matter of great magnitude even in etherean realms.

5. And so perfectly were Lissa's commands carried out, that not one day's time too much or too little was wide the mark. And then she embarked with her hosts for the red star, the earth, with her thousand million trained resurrectionists; on her long journey, twenty thousand million miles!

6. Jehovih had said: Carry far My Brides and Bridegrooms; make them know the magnificence of the heavens I have created. House them not together in a small corner. Let them feast their souls on the splendors of My great heavens!

7. In the meantime Lika and his Hosts in Theovrahkistan were getting ready for the ceremonies and for the ascension.

8. The Gods, with their hosts, were now coming in from every quarter of the lower heavens, bringing in their harvests and quartering them in the places allotted by the marshals.

9. Most conspicuous and beloved of all was Ahura. Next to him were the five true Gods: Inane, Injek, Inlay, Inoal and Inyith, with their heavenly hosts restored to them; for it was through these five Gods that the three mortals, Capilya, Moses and Chine, had delivered the Faithists of Vind'yu, Jaffeth and Arabin'ya. These five Gods had in five years changed the mortal dominions and laws of Vind'yu and Jaffeth, and sent four million Faithists on a westward journey round the earth; and had firmly established the All One in the four great divisions of the earth, and had delivered from bondage all the Faithists on the face of the earth.

10. Great also was the work accomplished by At'yesonitus, and by Yussamis; and by the Gods that had delivered the hells and the knots; and by many others. So good and great were the works of them all, that a history of any one of them in the five years' labor, would make a book that a man could not read in a life-time.

11. And they had left successors to carry out what they had founded; so that all the lower heavens were in order, system and discipline, such as had not been for two thousand years.

12. The drujas of the earth were removed away from mortals; the battle-fields of the earth were cleared of the chaotic spirits slain in wars.

13. So that the whole earth and her heavens were delivered into a new condition, in the way and form of Jehovih's light.

14. And this was the Arc of Deliverance in Bon.

15. Then descended Lissa with her chain of cowppon; with her ships of fire stretched wide as the earth. And the hosts of Theovrahkistan, the Brides and Bridegrooms, sixty-four thousand million Sons and Daughters of Jehovih, stood, waiting, watching, nervous, but filled with inexpressible delight.

16. And they saw the cowppon coming; knew the mission of the mighty Goddess, Lissa, Daughter of Jehovih!

17. Arrayed in spotless white, the sixty-four thousand millions stood; shuddered at the etheric current, the whirlwind of the higher heavens, stood the exalted affianced of Great Jehovih!

18. Nearer and nearer came the mighty sea of etherean fire; and nearer, till it landed at the plateau of Theovrahkistan.

19. Then came forth Lissa, saluting; and, being answered by great Lika, Jehovih's Son, proceeded before Jehovih's throne.

20. Then Lissa demanded in the usual form, why she had been summoned in Jehovih's name. Lika also answered in the usual form: To bestow Jehovih's affianced Sons and Daughters.

21. After this, each of the five Gods of the earth took their hosts and bequeathed them to Jehovih, through Lissa, His Daughter.

22. But so great and grand were the ceremonies that mortal words cannot describe them. And as for the awe and magnificence, together with the music, could they be described to mortals, understandingly, they scarce could live, because of the enchantment.

23. But there is a time, and a limit, and an end to all such matters; and so there was to the labor of Lika, Son of Jehovih. The hosts were wed, and they marched aboard the great etherean ships, the cowppon. Lika and his hosts went into his own airavagna. And, as it were, with a thread light, he made fast to the cowppon, and gave the word, the command to go.

24. Then raised up the mighty seas of fire, the eight-linked cowppon and the airavagna! Slowly, steadily moving onward, upward, higher and higher, faster and faster, and still higher. And thus departed Lika with his thousands of millions of upraised Sons and Daughters of Jehovih. And thus ended the dawn of Bon.

END OF THE BOOK OF LIKA, SON OF JEHOVIH.

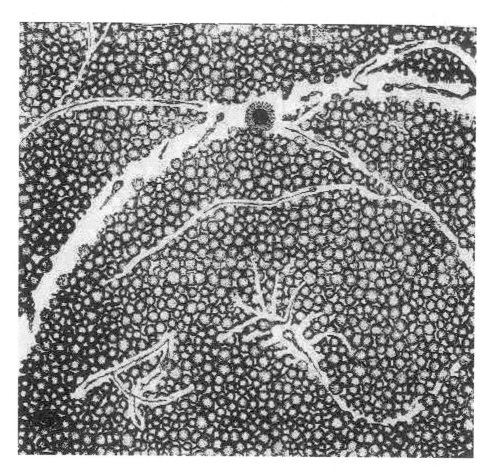

Plate 21. THE EARTH IN THE ARC OF BON.

Showing the es'ean position of the earth in the time of Capilya, Moses and Chine. Jehovih said: The time of My Arc of Bon shall be four hundred years. And it was so. And at the termination of that period, behold, the earth went into a dark region, and the Israelites, Brahmins and Zarathustrians forsook the higher light, Jehovih, and established kings and rulers, like other nations.

BOOK OF THE ARC OF BON.

BEING THE HISTORY OF CAPILYA, MOSES AND CHINE, THE THREE GREAT LEADERS-FORTH OF THE FAITHISTS IN THE TIME OF LIKA, SON OF JEHOVIH. AS THE UPPER BOOK IS OF THE HEAVENS, SO IS THIS LOWER BOOK CHIEFLY OF EARTHLY AFFAIRS IN THE ADMINISTRATION OF GOD.

CHAPTER I.
HISTORY OF CAPILYA.

1. In the mountains of Dharma, in the high country of Yatinghadatta, in Vind'yu, God, Son of Jehovih, chose the family of Capilya for gathering together the scattered Faithists, and establishing them in safety and prosperity.

2. Six generations previous to the time of Capilya God came down from his holy hill in heaven, to visit the land of Shem, now called Vind'yu.

3. And God called aloud over all that land, but no man could hear his voice.

4. Then God called his angels, saying: Come hither. Behold, here is a great country, with millions of people, but they cannot hear the voice of God.

5. God commanded the angels to go down amongst mortals, and to dwell with them for six generations.

6. To the angels God said: By inspiration and otherwise, lead ye man and woman together as husband and wife, to the profit of the voice of God. Raise me up a man that can hear me, for I will deliver the Father's chosen.

7. The angels of God, half a million of them, then came down to the earth. The angel, Hirattax, was commander over them. He divided his angel hosts into groups, and allotted to them certain places in the land of Vind'yu, where they were to dwell and to labor.

8. In those days the Faithists were known by the names: Vede, and Parsi'e, and Hiyah, and Syiattahoma, beside various other names of less note.

9. In some places they were slaves, in other places serfs, and in still other places hid away in wildernesses and amongst the mountains; being non-resistant and timorous, having suffered great persecution by the idolaters of Dyaus and other false Gods and Lords.

CHAPTER II.

1. These are the generations of the scattered tribes, contributory to the bringing forth of Capilya:

2. In Brahma, begotten of the Lord, Hathiv, who begat Runoad, who begat Yaid, who begat Ovarana, who begat Chesam, who begat Hottaya, who begat Riviat, who begat Dhor, who begat Avra, who begat Lutha, who begat Jaim, who begat Yanhad, who begat Vravishaah, who begat Hoamya, who begat Wotcha, who begat Saratta, who begat Hriviista, who begat Samatrav, who begat Gatonat, who begat Thurin, who begat Vrissagga, who begat Hesemwotchi, who begat Ratha, who begat Yoshorvat, who begat Capilya.

3. Know ye, then, the way of God through his holy angels, and profit ye in the light of his revelations.

4. Capilya was a natural born iesu; and also a natural born su'is and sar'gis.

656

5. God said: Behold, man shall not only learn to bring forth seedless fruits in his garden, but also learn that all flesh tendeth in the same direction, toward barrenness.

6. And as man draweth nearer and nearer to the light of Jehovih, so doth his race become less prolific. And when man attaineth to be one with the All Light, behold he is iesu also.

7. God said: By diet and by fasting, iesu can be attained, even by many who have it not. But the natural born iesu standeth more to the way of Jehovih.

8. When Capilya was born, a light in the form of a crescent appeared above his head, and the voice of God spake out of the light thereof, saying: This is my son. By him will I overthrow the governments of the tyrants who have persecuted my people.

9. When Capilya's mother was pregnant, the angels of Jehovih, under the archangel Hirattax, stood guard over her, thinking holy thoughts night and day, whereby the mother's soul ran constantly to heavenly things.

10. And when Capilya was born, behold, Hirattax appointed a host of one hundred and forty-four angels to be with the child day and night. Into four watches of six hours each, divided he the guardian angels.

11. So the angels of God taught Capilya from the time of his birth, and he became wise above all other children.

12. But, of the way in which God ruleth over nations for the glory of the Creator, consider ye the history of this deliverance.

13. Jehovih had suffered the power of the kings of Vind'yu to become centered chiefly in Yokovrana, king of Hafghanistun, of the capital, Oblowski, a great city dedicated to Dyaus. Yokovrana held forty provinces and four hundred cities tributary to himself, and every city furnished one governor, and these were the royal Council of king Yokovrana.

14. By the laws of Hafghanistun, the oldest male heir succeeded to the throne; but in case the king had no male heir, then the king's oldest brother's male heir succeeded to the throne. Therefore, every king desired a son, but Yokovrana was frustrated by the plans of the loo'is, the angels of Jehovih.

15. For Hirattax, chief loo'is, had said: I will not only raise up an heir to Thee, Jehovih; but I will have dominion over Thy enemies, to Thine own glory. For by inspiration will I lead the king of kings to marry with a barren woman; and because he shall have no heirs, he shall become a tool in my hands for the deliverance of the Faithists, who are persecuted and outlawed.

16. And in those days, whoso was of the seed of the worshippers of the Great spirit, Ormazd, was outlawed in receiving instruction. So that the chosen, the Faithists, were held in ignorance, lest a man of learning might rise up amongst them and deliver them. And the angel of Jehovih foresaw that Capilya should be a learned man, and acquainted with the cities and the royal Council. For which matter the angel, Hirattax, provided the chief king, Yokovrana, to be childless and to desire an heir as successor to the throne.

17. When the king consulted the oracle, behold, the angels of Jehovih had possession, and they answered the king, saying: Put thy wife away in a dark chamber for nine months, and she will deliver into thy hand a male child, who shall save the crown from thy brother's child.

18. The king told the queen, who was near the time of limit for women, and she would not believe. Nevertheless, she also went to consult the oracle, and to her the angel of Jehovih said: Have not kings killed their wives in order to obtain one who shall have an

heir to the throne?

19. The queen acknowledged this, adding: What, then, shall I do, for of a truth I know I shall bear no child.

20. The angel said: Do thou as the king hath said, and the angels will bring a male child unto thee in thy dark chamber; and thy maids and thy servants shall see to it that no other woman entereth into thy place; and they will testify that the child is thine own. Neither shalt thou, under penalty of death, inform the king otherwise.

21. On the other hand the angels of Jehovih foretold the father and mother of Capilya, even before his birth, that the child would be carried away and given to the king, Yokovrana, known for his cruelty as the most hated of men. And the angels said, moreover: Neither shall ye grieve for loss of the child, for Ormazd will make of him a deliverer of his people. And it shall come to pass even in the day the child is delivered to the queen, its own mother shall become its nurse.

22. Thus it came to pass; and in the time of the birth of Capilya, the angels carried him into the city of Oblowski, into the king's palace, and to the queen's arms, in the dark chamber. And in that same instant of time, the angels illumed the chamber, so that all the maids and servants saw the child and the light withal, and they were frightened, and fell down, beseeching Dyaus for protection.

CHAPTER III.

1. When Yokovrana went to the temple to do sacrifice, the high priest besought him to consult the oracle in reference to the child, and for his kingdom's sake. And he so consulted the oracle, and the angels of Ormazd said unto him: O king, thou, before whom all people fear, hear thou the angels of heaven and be wise, for thy kingdom's sake, and for Capilya. Behold, thou hast maintained the custom of thy forefathers, and caused to be slain on the altar of thy God, Dyaus, twelve young men and twelve virgins for every day of the twelfth new moon, that by blood thy God might triumph on the earth, and that thou mightst be the most feared of kings. And thou hast subdued all the regions of the rich earth to honor thee and thy laws.

2. Therefore, the God of heaven saith thou shalt no longer pursue the sacrifice of human blood, but instead thereof make sacred the blood of the lamb, which shall be called the Lamb of thy God. And in the day of thy first sacrifice, thou shalt bring Capilya to the altar, and sprinkle the blood of the lamb thou hast slain upon his head, as a blood offering to thy God. And he shall be called CAPILYA, THE LAMB OF HEAVEN.

3. To this the king assented, and Capilya was accordingly sprinkled with the blood of a lamb, which was sacrificed in the altar of the king. Thus ended the first of the evil edicts of the evil Gods of Vind'yu; and from that time after mortals were no longer sacrificed to the Gods, by consent of the kings.

4. Capilya was called Yokovrana's son; and he was taught all things which it was lawful in those days to teach a prince; and because he was prepared for the throne, he was made acquainted with the kings and governors of all the tributary cities and countries in the land of Vind'yu.

5. Of the matters of Capilya, hereinafter revealed, know ye that in all things he was directed by the angels of Jehovih (Ormazd).

6. When Capilya had attained maturity, he besought the king for leave to travel, saying to the king: Is not the greatest wisdom that which cometh by the eye and the ear? And is it not wise that he who may some day become king should acquaint himself with his kingdom whilst he is yet young? For then, he will not only see and hear better than if he were old, but he will have time to weigh the nature of the government, as to its best adaptation to the people.

7. To this the king replied: Thou art already wise, my son; thou knowest sufficient of the earth and her people according to the laws of the ancients. Therefore to travel for wisdom's sake would be great folly. Thine eyes and ears are too sharp already; better is it for thee that thou seest not the people of thy kingdom. For the time may come when thou shalt need to use great severity upon them; therefore, to be strange with them, thy sympathy will not lead thee away from justice.

8. Capilya said: Thou reasonest will, O king; and because thou art wise, have I no credit in being wise also. For it must be true that a son hath his wisdom from his father. And since thou hast so wisely put me off with thy arguments, answer me this: Is it not profitable to a young prince, before he hath the cares of a mighty kingdom, to go abroad and enjoy the pleasure of the world?

9. The king said: There are but three pleasures in all the world: eating and drinking is one; sleeping is another; the presence of women is the third. Why, then, shall a man go abroad?

10. Capilya said: And yet thou hidest the true reason as to why thou desirest thy son not to travel.

11. The king said: If thou tell me the true cause, then shalt thou go whithersoever thou desirest.

12. Capilya said: First, then, I will say to thee that I rejoiced because thou didst deny me; for I so loved thee, O king, that I knew no joy but to remain with thee. And, moreover, thou so lovest thy son, thou wouldst not have him go far from thee?

13. The king was so delighted with this answer, he said: Of a truth, O prince, thou hast guessed aright. And if thou find it in thy heart to leave me for a season of travel, then will I indeed bear with thy loss until thou returnest.

14. Capilya traveled for nine years, and he went to the uttermost extent of the land of Vind'yu, east and west, and north and south. And because his nurse, who was, in fact, his real mother, had told him thousands of tales about the persecution of the Faithists, and their sufferings, he sought to obtain information of these scattered people, but as yet he knew not he was of that race.

15. At the end of nine years Capilya returned to Yatinghadatta, rich in knowledge as to the inhabitants of Vind'yu. And when he came before the king, Yokovrana, where he was received in great honor, he related the knowledge he had obtained of the country, its extent and grandeur, and its hundreds of great cities and innumerable people. To all of which wisdom the king lent a willing ear; and he declared Capilya was the wisest and most learned man in all the world.

16. And now was come the time when God, Son of Jehovih, came to establish Jehovih, and begin the deliverance of the Faithists, and to collect them together in the places designed for them.

CHAPTER IV.

1. The word of Jehovih (Ormazd) came to Capilya, saying: Son of heaven, hear thou the Voice of the Ever Present! Capilya asked: How sayest Thou? The Ever Present?

2. Jehovih (Ormazd) said: Behold Me; I am not of the king's laws; I am the Maker of kings. They have made a law against Me, the Ever Present. They have scattered My people. They have denied My people the right to obtain knowledge.

3. Capilya said: Mine eyes and ears have proved these things. What shall Thy servant do?

4. Jehovih said: Thou shalt deliver the slaves unto freedom, and provide them places to dwell together, according to the laws of the ancients.

5. Capilya said: O Ormazd (Jehovih), why hast Thou put this upon me, Thy servant? Why gavest Thou not such matters into the hands of the Vrix?

6. Jehovih said: Thou art thyself of the race of Faithists, and have been prepared for this labor from the time of thy birth. Go thou and find thy nurse that cared for thee in infancy, and when thou hast her alone, say to her: Nurse, the voice of heaven hath come to me, saying: Capilya, thou art of the race of Faithists: how sayest thou? And the nurse will say to thee: My son! my son! Alas me! Thinkest thou I would by thy death, or thy mothers death? For is not such the law?

7. Capilya went and inquired of the nurse, and she said to him: My son, my son. Alas me! Thinkest thou I would be thy death, or thy mother's death? For is not such the law? Capilya answered: Such is the law. But tell me the truth, and I swear unto thee, both under the name Dyaus and under the name of thy God, Jehovih (Ormazd), that thy words shall be secret with me, as the God's will. Am I an adopted Vrix?

8. The nurse said: Behold, thou hast loved me all thy days; from mine own breasts wert thou fed. Shall I, then, lose thy love, and so die of a broken heart?

9. Then Capilya made oath before the Gods, and thereafter she answered him, saying: I am thy mother, O prince! The angels of the Ever Present came to me in the moment thou wert born, and carried thee into the queen's arms; and the king knew not even to this day but thou wert his.

10. Capilya said: Why hath this been done unto me?

11. The nurse said: Hearken, O prince! The king's wife was barren; the king desired a son who should be heir to the throne.

12. Capilya interrupted: And thou barteredst thy flesh and flood with the queen for this?

13. The nurse said: Patience, O prince! I am of a race that owneth only One King, the Ever Present! Respect me, therefore, till thou hast learned the whole truth. The angels of Ormazd came to me before thy birth, saying: Alas, the Chosen People are persecuted and abused, scattered and despised; but because they are faithful and most virtuous, the Ever Present will come and deliver them. Then I said unto the angels: What is this matter to me? Behold, I am myself but a servant, and can do nothing.

14. Then the angel answered, saying: Thou shalt have a son, and shalt call his name Capilya; and he shall be the deliverer of thy people. For which purpose he shall receive great learning. But because great learning is denied to thy people, thy son shall be adopted by the queen, and the king, believing it is his own son, will render unto the child learning and power also.

15. And I said unto the angel: Flesh and blood of me are nothing if I can thereby serve

Jehovih (Ormazd).

16. Capilya said: Since thou committedst me to thy God, then am I indeed his. Now whilst they were yet talking, Jehovih spake to Capilya, saying: I am not come to give new doctrines unto men, but to rescue My people from bondage, and to restore equal rights unto the inhabitants of the earth. For this purpose wert thou, O Capilya, sent into the world. Because thou wert of the race of the Faithists My voice hath come to thee.

17. Because the king imagineth thou art his son, and loveth thee dearly, thou shalt not suffer from his hand. Go, then, whither I will lead thee, and it shall be testimony to thee, that I am the Ever Present, moving them by means of the spirit to come to thee.

18. In due time the prince departed from home, not advising the king of his purpose; and he went as Jehovih led him, and came to Hosagoweth, near the river Vesuthata, where there was a forest, with meadows interspersed, and he found a camp of four families of wandering Faithists, and they were famished with hunger, and were ragged.

19. The prince, seeing they feared him, said: Be not afraid; I come not to persecute or drive you hence. As ye perceive by my dress, I am a prince, judge ye not me to be your enemy, come to destroy you. For, by the same power ye were led hither, am I come also. This land do I bequeath to you, to be yours forever. Cease ye, therefore, traveling about, but begin and till the soil.

20. Yatithackka, the rab'bah, said: How sayest thou? Thou wert brought hither by the same God? Then, of a truth, thou knowest the signs and pass-words?

21. Capilya said: None of these things have I learnt; but even as there is a legend amongst thy people that one would come of Jehovih and restore His chosen people, so declare I unto you, I am he. That thy Ruler is my Ruler; take me in private with thee, O rab'bah, and the Ever Present will give the signs and pass-words, and thus prove me.

22. Moreover, I say to thee in prophecy, ere three suns have risen and set, there shall come to this place hundreds and hundreds of thy people. Now when the rab'bah had examined Capilya, and found that he had the signs and pass-words, he wondered exceedingly. The prince then caused wood and stone to be laid in the form of a crescent, and its size was sufficient for seats for one hundred people. He said: This is the altar of Jehovih (Ormazd). Let us sit this night, for the Father's voice is with me.

23. During the day, many more came; so by night there were one hundred, men, women and children, and the prince commanded them to sit about the altar of Jehovih. And presently the Voice spake in the midst of the altar, saying: This is My Son, of whom it hath been prophesied, one would come to restore My people. Behold, I am the Ever Present, and not in the figure or image of a man, but I am the All Space and Place, doing My will through My angels and through the souls of men. Be ye steadfast in righteous works and love toward one another; and most just to a fraction with all other peoples. With you will I establish Myself, even as in the ancient days with your forefathers.

24. Capilya then appointed the oldest rab'bah as chief of the altar; and this was the first established family (community) since many a hundred years, that was assured by a prince that they should not be driven off.

25. On the next day the prince took the people a little way off, about half an hour's walk, and he said to them: Build ye here another altar, for yet, ere night comes, there shall come others even here. Let the Ever Present have an altar provided unto them. Accordingly the people fell to in faith, and built another altar; and when it was finished, and the sun gone

down, there came many wanderers, Faithists, to the place.

26. Capilya said unto them: Come ye to the altar of Ormazd, for he desireth sacrifice of all whom he blesseth. And they went in and sang, and prayed, giving thanks to God. Jehovih said: Suffer him I have sent unto you to build three more altars at like distances apart; for I will bring My people together for three places of sacrifice.

27. On the next day there came many more wanderers, who had escaped from the province of Anassayon, where a war was being carried on against raiders from Tubet, the high mountain region. And Capilya built altars for them also; and to them he also appointed rab'bahs and chief rab'bahs.

28. Now, behold, they were without food, and many had been famished for many days. Capilya, perceiving that some of the people were suspicious of him, said unto them: Whoso hath faith in me of Jehovih, let him stand with me this night, for the Father will manifest unto us.

29. Not more than forty came to the place designated; for they feared Capilya was an imposter. And when they were assembled, Capilya tried them, and found of a truth they had faith. And he said unto them: Stand in a circle and join hands, and I will stand in the midst. Yet I know not what the Great Spirit will do for us.

30. And when they were thus standing, Jehovih sent a cold wind, and there came down from heaven an abundance of Ahaoma, sufficient to feed the whole of the people for many days. Neither knew any man of what ahaoma was made; but it was savory and nutritious.

31. And the people came and ate, and also gathered up the ahaoma, and carried it home. Capilya said unto them: Because Ormazd hath done this, go ye into the altars and return thanks unto Him.

32. And the people did as commanded; and from this time forth not one of them lacked faith in Capilya. And thereupon he said unto them: This place shall be called Maksabi, for it is the first colony (Tarag-attu) in all the world where the Father hath fed His people with His Own hand. So the place was called Maksabi, which, in Vedic, would be Suta-ci-ci (I speak with food!).

CHAPTER V.

1. For forty days Capilya remained in Maksabi, teaching and helping the people; and on the fortieth day he said unto them: I go now; the Father desireth me. Be ye faithful unto Jehovih, and maintain the sacrifices (worship). The eye of Jehovih is upon you; His ear heareth not only your spoken words; but the thoughts in your hearts. In time after this I will come again unto you, and restore your rites and ceremonies.

2. Jehovih said unto Capilya: Even as thou hast done in Hosagoweth, so shalt thou do in Tibethkilrath; for thither will I also bring My chosen from the Province of Yusitra.

3. So Capilya went to Tibethkilrath, where were assembled more than seven hundred Faithists; and they feared him, saying to one another: Is this not some one sent of the king to entrap us?

4. But when Capilya beheld they feared him, he said unto them: He who hath faith in Ormazd feareth nothing in heaven or earth. For the Father appointeth a time unto all peoples; nor can they make it more or less. Throtona, one of the rab'bahs, said unto

Capilya: Art thou indeed one of us? Capilya said: Because I am as I am, I cannot answer thee. If I say I am of thy race, then will not thy people be restored to liberty; for I would suffer death, being a teacher of thy people. If I say I am not of thy race, then thy people will not have faith in me.

5. I say unto thee, I am but a man, even as thou art; neither am I pure and good; for there is but One pure, the Creator. Therefore, put thy faith in Jehovih, and wherein my words and labors are good, render unto me even as to any other man, nor more nor less. And yet, even as thou believest in the Ever Present, so do I; as thou believest not in a man-God, so do not I.

6. Are not all men brothers, and created by the same Spirit? Because the kings acknowledge not this doctrine, they persecute and outlaw thy race. To restore thy people, who are my people also, am I sent into the world. My labor is now upon me; and for that purpose am I here with thee and thy people.

7. This land, around about, I bequeath unto the Faithists; and they shall settle here and till the soil, and reap the harvests, and shall not be driven away. And in time to come I will provide teachers, and the Faithists shall have the right to obtain knowledge.

8. Capilya built altars for the multitude, saying to them: First of all, thou shalt dedicate to God all things thou puttest thy hands to, for without the rites of bestowal upon the Great Spirit, thy people cannot be in harmony. To neglect the rites is to neglect all things. Know ye the doctrines of the ancients?

9. None of the rab'bahs could answer Capilya, and so he said: Ormazd provided your servant with great learning. For this am I sent to you. Know ye, then, the doctrines of the ancients, even from the time of Zarathustra and Brahma:

10. To rise with the sun; to bathe the body once every day; to eat no flesh nor fish; to pray to Ormazd at sunrise, at high noon, at sunset, and before laying down to sleep.

11. Certain philosophers, wise in vanity, said: To rise an hour after the sun is no sin; to bathe one day in seven is sufficient; to eat fish-flesh, which is of cold blood, is no sin. Now, behold, it came to pass that they laid in bed two hours; they ceased to bathe altogether, and as to eating, they halted not with fish-flesh, but ate of all flesh. And sin came upon them; by their behavior they cut themselves off from the Father.

12. Be ye scrupulous in following the texts; and as to him that openeth the door for disobedience, have nothing to do with him or his philosophy.

13. Capilya asked: Why doeth one man a good act rather than a bad act? Why doeth another man a bad act rather than a good one? The rab'bahs said: The first is the speech of Ormazd; the second is the speech of satan; for as these dwell in men, so do they manifest.

14. Capilya said: I am pleased with the answer; for which reason I have before commanded you to build altars and do sacrifice; for these are the expressions of your souls, which testify ye rather would serve the Creator than the destroyer.

15. This was also of the ancient doctrines of Zarathustra; but certain other philosophers, vain in self-knowledge, said: Can not a man worship in the soul, and without building an altar of stone and wood? And the multitude harkened unto them; and they afterward went further, and said: Why worship at all? So, they fell in darkness. A soul without an outward expression of worship standeth on the brink of hell.

16. To see an altar, as we pass along, enforceth upon us the thought of worship, and of Ormazd, the Creator; it leadeth the soul upward. To see evil, or the temptation of it, is to

lead the soul toward darkness. Therefore, let men and women be discreet of their persons; but make the altars of sacrifice numerous.

17. Capilya asked: What is the first poison? The rab'bahs knew not how to answer, perceiving Capilya had great learning and wisdom. Capilya said: The first poison is self. One man saith: Rites and prayers are good for the stupid and unlearned; I need them not. I say unto you that that man is drunk on the first poison; let not his breath breathe upon you; for here entereth the wedge of destruction.

18. Capilya said: What is the second poison? But when he perceived none would answer, he said: The first leadeth to the second, which is desire to lead others and rule over them. Htah-ai, one of the rab'bahs, asked: How can we get on without leaders?

19. Capilya said: Suffer no man to lead you; good men are expressions of the All Light. Capilya asked: What is the best and yet the most dangerous thing? Some replied as to one thing, and some as to another. Capilya said: The best and yet most dangerous thing is speech. To talk of good things; of delights; of love; of Ormazd and his wonderful creations; of life and death; of everlasting happiness; these are good speech and give the soul great happiness. To talk of evil; of dark deeds; of one's neighbors; of disgusting things and words; these enrich satan's harvest.

20. Certain three men traveled through a great city, and when they returned home, and the neighbors assembled to hear the story of their travels, one of the travelers related all that he saw, good and bad; another one related only all the bad things he saw; and the other one related only the good things he saw, the delights and most beautiful things. Which, now, of the three, say ye doeth most for the Father's kingdom? The rab'bahs said: The last one. Capilya said: True! Be ye, then, like him even to one another; for by this course only is speech not dangerous, but of profit unto the world.

21. Sufficient is the number of evil men to relate the evils in the world; relate ye the good, for by constantly walking in clean ground ye shall remain clean, in word and deed.

22. Search ye both spirits and men, not for the brilliancy of speech, for oft its brilliancy hideth its poison, or stealeth on the senses unawares; but search their words as to holy ideas and good delights, to make man rejoice in his life. He who harpeth on deceivers and liars and debauchees, is a fireman for satan's hells. Reply not to him, lest your speech become a snare to entrap yourselves.

CHAPTER VI.

1. For three years Capilya traveled over the land of Vind'yu, east and west and north and south, establishing the Faithists wherever he found them; and he donated to them whatever lands laid waste and not tilled; but he touched not any land whereon other people dwelt and tilled the soil.

2. And it came to pass, the servants in the provinces fled from their masters and went and dwelt in the places of Jehovih, to so great an extent that the governors and sub-kings complained against Capilya, and he was reported to Yokovrana, the king in chief, Capilya's foster-father. And the king sent a commission summoning his supposed son to the capital, to answer the charges against him.

3. When Capilya was before the Royal Council, and demanded by the king why he had come, Capilya said: The servant of the great king answereth; his words are bound words.

Whatsoever cometh out of Capilya's mouth, Capilya holdeth as his. There be such as maintain that man, whose tongue is moved by the spirits of the dead, is irresponsible for his words. Capilya creepeth not through so small a hole. To be master of one's flesh, and desires, and passions and words, these are great gifts indeed. Capilya professeth these. Therefore, Capilya bindeth himself in every word.

4. Know then, Most Royal Council, servants to our Great King, Yokovrana, Capilya was summoned here by the king, to answer certain charges made by members of the Royal Council. These charges prefer that Capilya hath founded certain colonies which have attracted away the servants of the sub-kings and of the rich, and thereby sowed disobedience in the remainder.

5. Capilya is come to answer these charges. Hear ye, then, Capilya's answer: Capilya being heir to the throne besought the king for leave to travel, and the king said unto him: Whatsoever the soul observeth that may be good for the United Kingdoms, do thou. Said not the king this?

6. Yokovrana said: Yea, my son. Thereupon Capilya said: When Capilya traveled near and far, for nine years, his heart was sick because of the misery of the poor and the glory of the rich. He beheld many forests and many plains where no man dwelt; and he said to himself: Let the poor come hither and live. Yet he called not any poor man. Was it, then, an evil for Capilya to say this to himself?

7. The king said: Surely not. Then Capilya went on: After a long season of idleness, Capilya went the second time to travel, and when he came to the forests and plains, behold, the poor were gathered together, and yet more coming. So Capilya went amongst them to show them how to dwell together wisely. Was this an evil in Capilya?

8. The king said: Nay; of a truth it was good. Then Capilya said: In a little while they discovered it was good for them to dwell together and to help one another; and the news spread abroad, whereupon the servants of the governors, and the rich, ran away from them. Is it not just to say of the king and governors and rich men that they are driving their servants away from themselves, because of hardships which are greater than the hardships of the Gods?

9. The king said: A good proof. But why sayest thou, the Gods? These people for the most part believe not in the Gods. And many of them, I hear, are believers in the Great Spirit! Capilya said: Thou sayest truly, O king. But that is their matter, and not Capilya's. The king said: Thou art right, my son. But how sayest thou of education? Shall not the laws be maintained?

10. Capilya said: Art thou the king? or merely the servant of the dead? Shall Capilya call him father who is only a servant to carry out the laws of the dead? If so, then hath Capilya sinned against the law. But hear ye, who are of great learning; do ye obey one law of the ancients and not another? The law of the ancients was that with the death of the king all laws died, and whoso became king afterward must need make new laws of his own. The law against educating the Faithists is a law of the ancients. Let Capilya's accusers find which they will; for if they stand by the laws of the ancients, then, indeed, have we no laws, and no king nor sub-kings. If they repudiate the laws of the ancients, then Capilya hath not sinned against any law.

11. Yokovrana said: Thou art acquitted, Capilya. The laws of the ancients can not bind thy king nor the king's kings. Touching these matters, then, the Royal Council shall make

new laws. And since Capilya hath not contravened any law, neither shall the new laws interrupt the orders of the state as they now are.

12. Because of Capilya's presence in the Royal Chamber, the power of Jehovih and His angels was great in that house.

13. After this manner, that followeth, were the speeches of the sub-kings and governors: To permit great learning to the Faithists is to overthrow Dyaus and his reigning Gods and Lords; for by great learning will the Faithists ultimately become members of the Royal Council; therefore, at all hazards, great learning must be prohibited. Great learning is inimical to good servitude.

14. Jehovih said to Capilya: Be thou present when these laws are passed; for by this means My holy angels will rule over the Royal Council for the good of all men.

15. For one hundred days the Royal Council discussed the matter, but the angels of heaven kept them divided as to opinion and belief, so that no law was passed by them. Now after they had thus wasted much time to no purpose, Capilya asked permission to speak before the king and Council as to what was wisdom in the government of the nations; and it was granted unto him. This that followeth is, then, the substance of Capilya's speech.

CHAPTER VII.

1. Whoever is born into the world is in part possessor of the world by fact of his birth. All come into the world naked and helpless, and they deserve our assistance because of helplessness. To help the helpless is the highest virtue.

2. Two wise men are greater than one; a nation of wise men, what could be greater than this? Yet all men come into the world knowing nothing; to give them great wisdom is to make the nations wise and great. To open the avenues on every side to great learning, this is the foundation for a great kingdom

3. To have the soil tilled, is this not greater than hunting and fishing? To throw the lands open in the east and west, north and south, to the tiller of the soil, this is the foundation of plenty. When the poor and ignorant are supplied with what to eat and to wear, with a place to live, there is little crime, but great virtue; and such are great strength in that kingdom.

4. To hold more land than one can till is to sin against them that have none, who have not wherewith to live or to earn a living. Yea, such a one is an enemy to the nation.

5. There are two kinds of governments: one is government for the government; and the other is government for the people. The latter government the people will endorse, and by their wills make mighty. The former government seeketh to make itself mighty at the expense of the people. Such a government is in the throes of death.

6. To make government and people one, as to prosperity and peace; this is the highest government. For the government to render unto the people bountifully, as to land and water, and as to great learning, and to music, this is the wisest, best government.

7. What man is there that loveth not liberty, the chief of all desires? Can a government abridge this without crippling itself or forfeiting the love and co-operation of its people? To bestow liberty, and maintain it unto all people, this is the greatest good thing a government can do.

8. But who shall say what is liberty, and the end thereof? A man shall not have liberty that offendeth his neighbor, or depriveth him of virtuous livelihood. No man should run naked; nor should a man have liberty to go into another's field and take his harvest. How, then, shall the government take a man's possessions against his will? But he who hath received great learning will not offend by nakedness, nor by taking that which is another's.

9. What, then, is greater than for a government to bestow great learning on the people? It is not enough to say to the poor: Here is land; feed yourselves. But men of great learning shall be sent amongst them, showing them how to till the soil, and how to build, and to keep themselves pure in soul and body. For great learning is not in the books only; nay, there be men of great knowledge as to books, who are themselves gluttons and debauchees, and bigots, and tyrants, and base authority. Such men have not great learning; in fact, but great vanity.

10. Two kingdoms, lying side by side; in the one are great philosophers and colleges, but the multitude are in want; in the other kingdom there are no philosophers as such, nor colleges; but the multitude have plenty: The latter is a kingdom of greater learning than the former. For of what consisteth great learning, but in knowing how to live wisely? A few philosophers are not a nation, to bestow such knowledge on the people as will enable them to live wisely and be happy to a good old age, this is the labor of the best, great government.

11. It is a common saying that such and such a king is a great king, because, forsooth, he hath founded colleges. And this is no small matter. But how much greater is the king who founded a thousand poor families, and taught them how to live wisely?

12. To make a law to prevent liberty; to bind slaves more rigidly, is to weaken the nation; to weaken the kingdom. For, see ye, a man had ten servants, and they were free; then he bound nine of them with chains, and complained because they served him not well. He was a fool.

13. To labor for one's self at the expense of the state, is to rob the state; to horde up possessions is to rob the poor. What treasure hath any man that he can take out of the world? Better is it to give it whilst one may, for to-morrow we die, leaving it to them that earnt it not.

14. The highest peace is the peace of the soul, which cometh of consciousness of having done the wisest and best in all things according to one's own light. For after all, is not the earth-life but the beginning, wherein we are as in a womb, molding our souls into the condition which will come upon us after death? In which case we should with alacrity seize upon the passing of time and appropriate it to doing righteous works to one another.

CHAPTER VIII.

1. When the king and the Royal Council beheld the great wisdom of Capilya, they were struck dumb in their seats. After a while the king said: Was it not by blood that our forefathers established Dyaus? Scattering the Faithists with great havoc? Shall we gather up the escaped races and nurse them and have them turn upon us and bite us? Shall we not with our valiant arms defend Dyaus?

2. To this Capilya answered: Sufficient unto his own battles is the God of Vind'yu. If the king must need fight Dyaus' battles, then Dyaus is a weak God indeed. Heaven forbid that Capilya believe in such a God, or labor for one so weak!

3. But thou art right, O king; by blood our forefathers established Dyaus; but where is there, either in ancient or modern learning, a commandment that Dyaus shall be maintained by blood? Didst not thou thyself receive a commandment to stop the sacrifice of human blood on the altar? Is it, then, indeed a holier place on the battle-field, that these things must continue?

4. Man loveth vengeance; and more for this than for righteousness he desireth to inflict or destroy others. Nevertheless, all things are answered accordingly as they are; vengeance answereth vengeance; blood answereth blood; war answereth war. And the same rule applieth to virtue, which begetteth virtue; love, which begetteth love; peace, peace; good works, good works. For in these things our souls play a greater part than do our external bodies.

5. One of the Royal Council said: How sayest thou of rites and ceremonies? Capilya answered: Without rites and ceremonies the spiritual person of the state and of the community, and of the nation, is like a man that hath thrown away his clothes, and then, with disgust, drowned himself. As the soldiers of the army have drill, which is discipline, so shall the worshippers have rites and ceremonies, which are the drill to keep one's soul in reverence for the Creator.

6. But it falleth not to my lot to say unto you what rites or what ceremonies; for these also come under the head of LIBERTY.

7. Another one of the Royal Council asked: Some men, who are bad men, have great pleasures and enjoyments; some men, who are virtuous and wise, have great trials and misery: What, then, is the prize which thy philosophy offereth to them that practice righteousness and good works?

8. Capilya said: Could thine eyes see as mine have seen, or thine ears hear as mine have heard, then it were easy to answer thee. Nevertheless, I declare unto thee a great truth, which is also revealed in the doctrines of the ancients, that this is not the real life, but the embryonic state. And many that have great pleasures and enjoyments in this life, waken up as babes in heaven; whilst many who are virtuous and wise, but suffer great misery, in this life, wake up in heaven in strength and glory. More are trials and exertions to be desired than ease and enjoyment; for the former causeth the soul to look upward; but the latter causeth the soul to look downward. Nevertheless, severe trials are a great injustice to any man.

9. When the king and Royal Council beheld that Capilya had greater wisdom than any other man, the king said unto them: No man in all the world hath wisdom sufficient to try my son. How say ye? And they answered: That is true. Whereupon the king said: Capilya, hear thou the king's decree, and it shall be a law unto thee in all the kingdoms of the world, which is, that thou hast been tried by the greatest king on the earth, and art acquitted and declared to be above the dominion of mortals. And thou shalt go whithersoever thou wilt in any land, doing whatsoever thou desirest, and no man shall arrest thee or forbid thee in anything whatsoever. And whatsoever law thou makest no king shall make another law, above thine, to set it aside. Wert thou not mine own son I would say thou wert begotten by the Gods!

10. The king's decree was recorded in the House of Records, and copies of the decree sent to the tributary cities and kingdoms throughout Vind'yu. Yokovrana had also a copy made of Capilya's speech, and it was also recorded and signed by the king and Council, under the name, THE FOUNDATION OF LAWS.

11. Jehovih said to Capilya: I have suffered this land to endure war for hundreds of years, that they might be ready for this. Behold, they are not slow to accept doctrines of peace and liberty.

12. Capilya inquired concerning the laws, and Jehovih said: Trouble not thyself more; My hand is upon the king and Council. They will pass laws endorsing what thou hast said. Go forth, then, My son, amongst My chosen, and thou shalt establish them anew in rites and ceremonies.

CHAPTER IX.

1. When Capilya had come to Wes-tu-chaw-aw, Jehovih said to him: Send messengers into twelve colonies which I will name to thee, to the chief rab'bahs thereof, summoning them hither, for thou shalt teach them alike and like.

2. The colonies were: Tahdayis, L'wellaat, Ha'darax, Thowaka, Dormstdatta, Ghiballatu, Yhon, Themmista, Vrach'hao, Ebotha, Ewen and Sravat, and each of them sent the high priest (rab'bah) with three accompanying rab'bahs, so that in all, there were thirteen chief rab'bahs, and thirty-nine rab'bahs. And Capilya caused them to put on red hats, without brims, after the custom of the ancient Zarathustrians.

3. Jehovih said to Capilya: Choose thou twenty damsels who are young and well grown; and twenty dames who have borne children. And these shalt thou adorn with blue hats with ear-flaps, after the manner of the Daughters of the Zarathustrian law.

4. When Capilya had them clothed with hats and aprons, he caused the rab'bahs and the women to go with him to the summit of a mountain, so that they might not be approached by idlers or spectators without due warning. And on the summit of the mountain Capilya said: When ye were babes, I prayed for you; now that ye are mature ye shall worship the Creator with your own words. Bring, therefore, every one a stone, and cast it down, for it shall be an altar before Jehovih for our sacrifice. And as I do, do ye.

5. They all took stones and cast them in a pile; and when they were yet standing near, Capilya raised his hands to heaven and said: Father, when I was weak, Thou providedst for me. My mother and my father and my rab'bah prayed for me, and taught me of Thee. Wherefore I praise Thee with thanks and glorification. Now that I am strong, I stand upright before Thee and praise Thee and pray to Thee with mine own words, and not as the heathen who have priests to pray for them.

6. Because Thou madest me a man (woman) I will labor to prove myself before Thee. As I have here cast down this stone, let it stand as my covenant to Thee that I will from this time cast away earthly passions and desires. And because I have raised up both my hands unto Thee, lead Thou me, O Father, in the right way!

7. When they had all repeated these words, Capilya walked once around the altar, followed by the others, and he said: Jehovih (Ormazd) Almighty, glory be to Thee forever! Thou art on the mountain-top and in the valley; Thy circle is the circumference of the world. I walk in the circle with Thee; Thou art forever by my side; Thy light the

glory of my soul. Praise Him, O ye mountains and valleys; sing to Him, thou moon, and ye stars; His hand holdeth ye up; His breath moveth all things!

8. In Thee I live; of Thyself madest Thou me! O that I may not dishonor Thy handiwork; or make myself ashamed before Thee. Because Thou art Ever Present, I fear Thee; because I can not hide from Thee, I will be most circumspect in my behavior.

9. Capilya then sat down on the altar, saying: Go ye hence a little way, and then return, that I may teach you how to approach the altar of Jehovih. The people did as commanded, and when they came near, Capilya said: Who cometh?

10. Now herein are the questions and answers as Jehovih taught His children through Capilya:

11. A worshipper of Jehovih (Ormazd): Behold, the altar of My people, who are known by their piety and good works, and in helping one another.

12. Who is Jehovih?

13. The Ever Present. He filleth all place and space. He created me alive, and taught me to adore Him and His works.

14. Why comest thou to this place above any other? If He be Ever Present why not worship Him in any other place?

15. He sendeth guardian angels to abide with His children who are pure and good. These angels desire certain places and times, wherein my soul may be given to Jehovih. Through His holy angels He teacheth me in wisdom and love.

16. Why not worship the angels themselves, since they are thy guardians and benefactors?

17. To call not on the name of any angel who is Lord or God, is my religion; but to call on Jehovih, the Great Spirit. Whoso calleth on the name of angels, or Lords, or Gods, will be answered by them, but whoso calleth on the Creator will be answered by Him, Who is the All Highest.

18. How can Jehovih answer thee? Hath He lips, and tongue, and mouth?

19. Jehovih is the Soul of all things; He speaketh to Soul. His voice hath had many names; by the heathen and the idolater he is called Conscience.

20. What profit hath thou in worshipping Him?

21. I am so created; because of the fullness of Him in me, I desire to express my adoration, and to commune with Him. Whoso hath not this desire is an evil man.

22. Will He answer thy prayers? Turn aside from His usual course and come especially to thee more than to another?

23. As a horse drinketh water from a trough and so enlargeth himself, so doth the soul of the righteous man drink from the Everlasting Fountain, Jehovih, and the soul of man thus enlargeth and accomplisheth in answer to its own prayer; nevertheless, it all cometh from Jehovih. Neither turneth He aside from His usual course, for He is Ever Present, and thus answereth the prayer of the soul of man.

24. What prayers answereth He? And what prayers answereth He not?

25. He answereth the prayer for purity and love and wisdom and virtue. Whoso prayeth to Him for permission to do good unto others, He answereth without fail. He answereth not selfishness, nor the prayers of the wicked. Wherefore the wicked say: He answereth not prayer.

26. Capilya said: My beloved, when ye approach the altar of Jehovih, ye shall repeat the wise words I have taught you; but not aloud like the idolaters, but in whisper or low

voice.

27. What is the worship of Jehovih's chosen? and wherein differeth it from the heathen's?

28. Jehovih's chosen stand equal before the Father, and everyone shall work out his own resurrection, both in this world and the next. Hence they are direct worshippers, being taught to worship Jehovih with their own prayers and songs. The heathen have priests to do worship for the people, who contribute to them in money for the service. The heathen priests worship the spirits of the dead, who call themselves Lord, and God, and Savior. The chosen children war not, resent not by violence, but answer evil by good, and practice charity and love. The heathen, the worshippers of God, and of Lord, and of Dyaus, and all other idols, practice war, maintain armies of soldiers, who are taught the art of killing with great havoc. They build monuments to men, and otherwise blaspheme against Jehovih. They teach that Jehovih is void, but that He made Himself into Dyaus, a large man, and then created all things, after which He retired to His throne, leaving certain laws to govern His works.

29. What is the Zarathustrian law of life?

30. To eat not flesh of anything Jehovih created with the breath of life. To bathe once every day. To rise with the morning sun, and be temperate in all things.

31. What is the Zarathustrian fatherhood and motherhood?

32. To have but one wife; to have but one husband; to maintain sacred the maternal period.

33. What was the Zarathustrian compensation?

34. All things belong to Jehovih; man is but His servant. The fruits of the earth and of all labor shall be cast into the rab'bah's house, and by him delivered unto the needy.

35. Why were the Zarathustrians persecuted and destroyed?

36. Because they resisted not by violence, and because they worshipped not the idols of the heathens.

37. Had they no way of saving themselves?

38. To that end Jehovih gave them certain signs and pass-words, whereby they might know one another, and in time of distress assist one another to flee away.

39. Why did not Jehovih preserve His chosen people?

40. By the laws of circumcision the Faithists could only marry amongst themselves, in order to preserve a knowledge of Jehovih (Ormazd) amongst mortals. They who were holy were preserved; they who went after earthly things, and after the idolaters, were cut off. But even in this Jehovih profited the seed of the Faithist, by raising up heirs of su'is amongst the heathen.

41. Capilya said: Teach ye these things to your children from their youth up, and enjoin it upon them to teach them to their children.

CHAPTER X.

1. Jehovih said to Capilya: Thou shalt remain with My chosen until they have learned these rites and ceremonies and doctrines; after which thou shalt go to another region whither I will lead thee, and there teach the same things, and in the same way. And Capilya obeyed the commandments of the Great Spirit in all these things.

2. In the fifth year of Capilya's preaching, the voice of Jehovih came to him saying: Behold, thy foster-father is near death's door. Go thou to him and have the law of protection established before his death; and after his death, and when thou art king, thou shalt ratify the law, and then abdicate the throne.

3. So Capilya returned to Yokovrana, the king, who was ill with fever. The king said: O my son, my son! I feared I should die ere mine eyes beheld thee. A few days more, and it will be over with me. Thou wilt be king. Bethink thee, what wouldst thou ask of me, whilst yet I may accomplish it?

4. Capilya said: Call thy Royal Council and pass a law guaranteeing Brahmins, the Zarathustrians (Faithists), the lands they have possessed and tilled and are now dwelling on, to be theirs forever.

5. The king assented to this, and the law was so enacted; and this was the first law granting land unto the Faithists, to be their own, by any king in all the world. And the law stipulated that the Faithists should worship in their own way; neither should they be impressed into any army as soldiers of war.

6. After the law was established, Yokovrana said unto Capilya: I was wondering why thou didst not wait till thou wert king, and then enact the law thyself, and it could not be set aside during thy life-time? I will die soon, and the law will die with me.

7. Capilya answered: I shall ratify thy law on the day I ascend the throne, which is binding, according to the rules of the ancients. Had I waited until I was king, then I had been bound, according to my religion, which is that no one individual possesseth land, save what he tilleth, and then only by donation from the community in which he dwelleth, and only during his life-time, after which it reverteth to the community.

8. Yokovrana said: Thou art wise, O my son! What is it that thou understandst not? After the king rested a while, he said: Capilya, thou hast often said thou hast seen the angels of heaven: Who sayest thou they are?

9. Capilya said: Persons who once inhabited this earth. Some of them once lived on the stars.

10. The king said: Since thou sayest so, it must be so. I thought, sometimes, they might be different beings that dwell in the air, and never dwelt here. Sayest thou, Capilya, all souls are immortal?

11. Capilya said: They are so born into life; nevertheless, not all inherit everlasting life. Even as the body goeth into destruction, so can the spirit of a man dissolve out of being. The fruit of them that have attained to faith in everlasting life is safe; but for them that have fallen from faith in everlasting life, and from faith in the Creator, I pity them and their heirs.

12. The king said: Why do the oracles tell lies? They are the words of angels.

13. Capilya said: If a man will not think for himself, examine for himself, the Creator suffereth him to be the recipient of lies. He is a wise man who hath attained to disbelief in angels and men; for then he will turn to the Creator, Who is All Truth. This is the beginning of wisdom. Some fair men, with stunted souls, who look not about doing good in the world, require the serpent's fang in order to make them think.

14. The king said: I have killed many men in my day; sayest thou I have sinned? Capilya said: Inquire thou of thy Creator. I am not thy judge, nor any man's. The king asked: If a man be killed and his soul live, then the killing amounteth to little. We put away the

body, but the soul may come back and retaliate. Is it not so? Capilya said: Yea, O king. 15. The king reflected a while, and then he asked: My son, can the spirits of them we have slain catch us in heaven and injure us? Capilya said: Yea, O king. The king said: And they having been in heaven first would have the advantage in battle. And if they go in gangs and have a leader (satan), they might do a great hurt. Know thou, Capilya, I have a great secret for thy philosophy; which is: When death draweth near, we begin to shake in the soul as to what we have done all our lives. Sometimes I think of saying to Dyaus: Here, I will pray thee! But then I remember I have no merchandise which he would accept. How strong we are in health and prosperity, and how weak in adversity and in death! Sayest thou prayers would make my case stand better in heaven? 16. Capilya said: I am not master in heaven; or if I were, my love to thee would shield thee from all darkness. The king said: The priest saith if I pay him money he can intercede with Dyaus and so secure me a high seat in heaven. I think he falsifieth, for Dyaus oweth him nothing. Two things I have found, even with my little wisdom; the caterer to the king and the caterer to the Dyaus make great pretences, but do but little as to their promises. These two men, O my son, beware of them. 17. I owe my greatness more to this discretion than to wisdom. They are at the bottom of all wars and evils in this world. They can deceive even the Gods, I am told. When thou art king, Capilya, put thy wisdom in this matter; spare them not; they are the curse of the world. I regret that I slew not more of them; my conscience pricketh me for this. 18. Capilya said: Man's conscience being only part of the man, may it not err? Is not the conscience dependent for wisdom on other things? And after all, if we have done that which seemed the highest, best thing at the time, have we not fulfilled the law? 19. The king said: It would seem so. Conscience must depend for its errors or its justice on the education it hath received. But may not conscience be a disease in the heart? To regret for not having done a thing; to regret for having done a thing, these are irreparable complainings. Whoever can say beforehand, and yet not err, is wise indeed. I find that no man brought himself into the world; nor can he live but for a short period at most. When we are young we dislike to die; but at my great age I desire not to live. Evidently He Who created us hath more mastery over us than we have over ourselves. 20. Capilya said: That is true; man at the best hath not more than half mastery of himself. Yokovrana interrupted, saying: I interrupt thee, my son, because my time is short. I would ask thee what is the greatest consolation to a dying man?

21. Capilya said: There are two consolations that are great to a dying man: one is to know that he left no heirs after him; and the other is, that he leaveth after him a noble son. The king said: Thou art wise, my son. I asked the priest in the oracle-house the same thing, and he said: For a dying man to have faith that his soul will enter paradise. Thereupon I said to him: No honest man can have such faith; for such a fate would be cheating heaven with one's sins. Were I the Creator, I would break the necks of half the world. Still it may please a foolish dying man to tell him such a tale as regardeth his soul. Thou alone, my son, hath told me the greatest consolation to a dying man. 22. My slaves may have faith that they will be kings, but they will wake up in their folly. A man may have faith that his soul will enter paradise, and he may wake up and find it was a mistake. Faith without a guarantee is folly.

23. Capilya said: A man to know a thing of his own knowledge hath the greatest of all wisdom. To be as thou art, a philosopher in time of death, is evidence of a great soul. Few have attained to this.

24. The king said: Before thee I am nothing as to wisdom. Thou art a mystery to me. Thy mother, whom the doctors slew to put her out of her misery from long sickness, was not wise. And as to myself, I am only great, not wise. I can make men fear me; but thou knowest the secret of love, which is a great thing. Thy name, O Capilya, will be honored long after mine is forgotten. Yet I am the greatest king in all the world. O thou, my most wonderful son!

25. Capilya said: Because thou gavest me great learning and a father's kingly care, why should I not be an honor to thee, O king? When thou art in heaven, and can look upon me, I hope thou mayest not lose thy hope for me.

26. The king said: It seemeth not wise to me that angels should see too closely their mortal kin, or else, forsooth, they would never raise up to higher heavens. The seers say heaven and angels are about us all the while. I think this is a lie, otherwise it would be more hell than heaven to them.

27. After the king rested a while he said: I have been surmising what to say to thee, for I feel the blood in my veins is nearly stopped. And this maketh me think more than ever that man at best is but a gaming ball for the Gods to play with. Who knoweth, perhaps even now they laugh in their sleeves as to how they have used me for some hellish game! O that man had some standpoint to judge things by! O that he had a measure and a foundation to stand upon! I have searched the spirits of the dead, and the Gods of the oracles, and they are lies, lies, lies!

28. Capilya said: The small spark of light within our souls is right at the start; and if it be rightly cultivated it will grow brighter and clearer every day. For is it not in the nature of all things to grow by culture?

29. The king said: To rightly cultivate! There is the matter, O my son. To settle that point the world hath been washed all over with man's blood. Rightly! Who knoweth that word? O that mine enemies were mistaken, and that I was clear in perceiving what was right!

30. Again he rested awhile and then he said: I had hoped when death came on, I should get glimpses of what is in store for me; but even death is silent and dark and deceiving. My members weaken evenly. This showeth I was begotten of good blood. Hadst thou not been my son I should rejoice more than I do. For then I should know that my family race had run out, and, so, I should have ascended to the higher heavens. Now I may be obliged to dwell on the earth for a long season. As I understand myself now, with all thy wisdom and thy love, I had rather thou hadst been some other man's son. Then I could die easier and not care so much about leaving thee. I have no other kin.

31. Capilya said: O king! Thou has rent my heart in twain! Of a truth I am not thy son! When thy wife laid in the dark chamber, the angels of heaven stole me and brought me thither. She who nursed me was my mother; and her husband was my father. I am a Brahmin of Zarathustrian blood, a Faithist!

32. The king said: Is this true? It can not be! Go call thy nurse! Capilya called in the nurse, and the king said to her: Ere I doom thee to death, I charge thee, is this thy son, and is thy husband his father? She answered him: I am sworn to Jehovih and cannot answer thee. Therefore sentence me, for I have carried a great load many a year. Behold! An

angel of heaven appeareth!

33. Jehovih's angel appeared before the king, and all saw the angel, which said: Capilya is not thy son, O king! And yet no sin hath been committed! Thereupon the angel vanished.

34. The king said: Were this not a counterfeit made by the Gods, then it was my angel wife. So, Capilya! Must here end our love? The earth is going fast from me now! Capilya said: Our love will never die! For the good thou has done for the Zarathustrians, the Great Spirit will provide thee a home suited to thy great soul. If thou hadst any faults, thou hast more than balanced them.

35. The king beckoned for Capilya and the nurse to come to him, and then he said, feebly: It seems to me I hear the Gods laughing! Keep ye up the joke! My brother's oldest son knoweth nothing of it! A kingdom is but a farce. Hold me up, Capilya. I would have mine eyes feast on the sky only, after having seen thy sweet face.

36. Capilya lifted him up, and the king said to the nurse: I bless thee! Thou broughtest forth a good prop! O aden (sky), aden! All is something! All is nothing!

37. And the breath went out of him; he was dead.

CHAPTER XI.

1. Jehovih said to Capilya: My chosen shall not have kings; I, Jehovih, am King. As through Zarathustra I gave rab'bahs and chief rab'bahs, so have I through thee; and their families are My families.

2. Kings and kingdoms of men I give to the unrighteous; for they, perceiving not Me, for I am the higher law, shall have that that they can perceive, which is the lower law.

3. A kingdom is thrust upon thee; what wilt thou? Capilya said: What shall I do, O Jehovih? Jehovih answered, saying: Suffer thyself to be proclaimed at home and in the provinces, after which thou shalt ratify the laws, and then abdicate, and the kingdom shall fall into other hands.

4. Capilya was proclaimed, and thenceafter known as king Capilya, and he abdicated, and then Heloepesus became king, and he became obligated to Capilya, so that the latter, though not king, stood as a protector over the Faithists, even greater than Heloepesus, nor could any laws be enacted affecting the Faithists without the consent of Capilya.

5. Jehovih had said: My people shall be a separate people; they shall live under My laws, for I am their King.

6. Now the whole time, from Capilya's first beginning of the restoration of the Zarathustrians (Faithists), until establishing a protectorate for them, was five years. After this Capilya traveled about, east and west, and north and south, collecting together the scattered remnants of his people; and he established them in colonies, and taught them not only rites and ceremonies, but taught the lost arts of tilling the soil and of making fabrics out of hemp and wool and silk; and he established schools and provided teachers for the people.

7. Capilya said: The first virtue is to learn to find Jehovih in all things, and to love and glorify Him.

8. The second virtue is Cleanliness; all peoples, old and young, shall bathe once a day.

9. The third virtue is to eat no fish nor flesh, nor other unclean thing; for of what profit is it to bathe the outer part if one putteth filth within?

10. The fourth virtue is Industry. Because the Father gave man neither feathers, nor hair nor wool; let it be testimony of His commandment that man shall clothe himself. To clothe one's self, and to provide one's self with food; these are the enforced industry upon all people. In addition to these, to labor for the helpless; to bathe them and feed them, and house them and clothe them; these are the volunteer industries permitted by the Father that ye may prove your soul's worthiness before Him. Without industry no people can be virtuous.

11. One of the rab'bahs asked him what Industry was? To this Capilya replied: To keep one's self in constant action to a profitable result. To rise before the sun and bathe and perform the religious rites by the time the sun riseth; and to labor thereafter not severely but pleasantly until sunset, this is Industry. The industrious man findeth little time for satan's inspiration.

12. The fifth virtue is of the same kind, which is Labor. There shall be no rich amongst you; but all shall labor. As ye develop your corporeal bodies unto strength by reasonable labor, so doth the act of labor develop the spirit of man to profitable growth for its habitation in heaven. For I declare unto you a great truth, which is, that the idle and the rich, who labor not with the corporeal body, are born into heaven helpless as babes.

13. The sixth virtue, which is greater than all the rest, is Abnegation of one's self. Without Abnegation no man shall have peace of soul, either on earth or in heaven. Consider what thou doest, not that it shall profit thyself, but whether it will benefit others, even as if thou wert not one of them. Without the sixth virtue no family can dwell together in peace.

14. The seventh virtue is Love. Consider when thou speakest whether thy words will promote love; if not, then speak not. And thou shalt have no enemies all the days of thy life. But if thou canst justly say a good thing of any man, be not silent; this is the secret to win many loves.

15. The eighth virtue is Discretion, especially in words. Consider well, and then speak. If all men would do this, thou wouldst be surprised at the wisdom of thy neighbors. Discretion is a regulator; without it, man is like a tangled thread.

16. The ninth virtue is System and Order. A weak man, with System and Order, doeth more than a strong man without them.

17. The tenth virtue is Observance. With Observance a man accepteth from the ancients such things as have been proven to be good, such as rites and ceremonies. Without Observance a man beginneth back even with the earliest of the ancients, and thus casteth aside his profit in the world.

18. The eleventh virtue is Discipline, the Discipline for the individual and the family. He who hath not Discipline is like a race-horse without a rider. A time to rise; a time to eat; a time to pray; a time to dance; a time to labor; these are good in any man; but the family that practiceth them in unison with one another hath Discipline.

19. The twelfth virtue is like unto it, and is Obedience. All good and great men are obedient. He that boasteth his disobedience to discipline is a fool and a madman. Greater and better is the weak man of obedience, than the strong man of defiance. For the one promoteth the harmony of the family; but the other ruptureth it.

20. Consider these twelve virtues; they are sufficient laws unto the whole world. Man may multiply books and laws forever, but they will not make the family, nor colony, nor state, happy, without the adoption of these twelve virtues.

CHAPTER XII.

1. Capilya said (being inspired of Jehovih): Let thy life be thy preacher. The behavior of one good man, even in a sparse country, is of more avail than a thousand preachers.

2. The clamor of the tongue maketh speedy converts, but it changeth not the blood. They perform the rites and ceremonies, but their behavior is not of the twelve virtues.

3. One community (family) of a score of men and women, that dwell together in peace and love, doing good toward one another, is the manifestation of more wisdom than all the books in the world.

4. A man that hath learned sympathy is better learned than the philosopher that will kick a cat or a dog. Great learning is not only in books; he who hath learned to harmonize with Jehovih hath great learning.

5. The doctrine of the idolater is war; but My Sons and Daughters practice peace, resisting not any man with weapons of death, saith Jehovih.

6. My sermons are not in wordy professions, but in the souls of My people who practice My commandments.

7. Ye have witnessed that Sudga's followers said: Behold, Sudga is our Lamb of Peace! And they were nations of warriors; they built monuments to glorify their greatest slayers of men.

8. My people say little; profess little, as regardeth their virtues; but their practice is My Voice!

9. Capilya said: Whatever should be the character of one man, so should be the family (community); so should be the state. Harmony in a man's soul is his greatest blessing; and so of the family, and of the state.

10. Whoso will sacrifice self-gratification for good of the family is the greatest, best one in the family. Whoso triumphs in self-desire or in inflicting on others his opinions or doctrines, is the worst, bad man in the family.

11. My Father in heaven, is thy Father also; all men and women are my brothers and sisters. To magnify one's soul so as to realize this brotherhood, is a great virtue. No matter what name He hath, there is, nevertheless, but One Creator; and all peoples are His children. Call thou Him what name thou wilt, I will not quarrel with thee. I am a child of His love; by love will I prove it unto thee. No man can prove this by war.

12. At death the real life beginneth; mold thyself well whilst thy soul hath a good anchor (the body). The highest, best life in this world, findeth the highest best life in heaven. To love thy Father Who created thee; virtuous happiness is little more than this. The happiness of lust, is hate to thy Creator.

13. The man learning to swim had better go in with corks, till he find the stroke; like this, thy Creator gave thee a corporeal body. Be not in haste to enter the unseen world; make sure that thou hast learned the stroke of the resurrection erst thou puttest aside thy flesh and bones.

14. Religion is the learning of music (harmony) in a community, in which the rab'bah is the key-note. Music is of two kinds: sounds and assimilation. Dumb instruments may make sound-music; but assimilation cometh to the real matter of putting one's behavior in harmony with the community.

15. Good works! Who knoweth the meaning of these words? King Yokovrana judged the good works of a man by the number of bad men he had slain. When alms-houses promote laziness they are not good works. Preaching, and praying, and singing, are not works; they are the blossoms, and with enticing fragrance. Yet satan persuadeth man that these are good works. Nevertheless, all fruit is preceded by blossoms. The most learned man, the most pious man, and the greatest philosopher can not tell what is the meaning of the words, good works. But a mother, with a child one day old, can tell; a farmer, that hath sowed and reaped one harvest, and given half of it away to the less fortunate, can tell also.

16. To bring forth out of the earth food or clothing, these are good works only so far as they exceed one's own requirements and are given to others. To live on the earnings of others, save in time of helplessness, is evil. To preach and not produce substance for others; such a man is a vampire. He selleth sermons and opinions to the ignorant, making believe his words are Jehovih's concerns.

17. The preacher shall dwell with the poor, taking hold with his own hands; teaching and helping; he who giveth words only, and not labor, is a servant of hell. He findeth honeyed words, and drawleth his voice; he liveth in ease and plenty; he stretcheth out a long face seriously; he is a hypocrite and a blasphemer against his Creator.

18. With love and rejoicing, and with willing hearts, stand thou upright before Jehovih; for thy preaching shall bear evidence of joyful light; and thy presence give to the weary and disconsolate assurance that thou art the Creator's son, come in earnest to glorify Him by righteous works and a helping hand.

19. Besides Capilya's book of maxims, the quarter of which is not here related, he also restored the Zarathustrian commandments and the songs of Vivanho. Nor since two thousand years were the children of Jehovih so well standing before the world. And peace and plenty came upon the land of Vind'yu, even greater than in the days of Brahma.

20. Thus closeth the history of Capilya, who was led in all things by Jehovih, through his angels, even to the words he uttered, though oft he knew it not. Such is it to walk with the Creator. Now whilst this was going on in Vind'yu, the Creator also labored through his angels in the land of Egupt, with Moses, of whom hear ye.

CHAPTER XIII.

HISTORY OF MOSES OF EGUPT.

1. God commanded his loo'is, in the high heavens, saying: Descend ye to the earth, to the land of Egupt, and raise me up a son capable of my voice.

2. The angels descended as commanded and searched over the land of Egupt and in the adjoining countries, examining into the flesh and the souls of men. And they called unto God, saying: The land of Egupt is overrun with spirits of darkness (drujas), and mortals have attained to see them; and they dwell together as one people, angels and mortals.

3. God said: Go ye amongst my chosen until ye find a man capable of understanding betwixt truth and fable. Him inspire ye to an I'hin woman for my voice.

4. In Ellakas the loo'is found a man, Baksa, a Fonecean, a Faithist, born a su'is, and they said unto him: Why art thou alone in the world? Baksa said: Alas, mine eyes have never seen God; mine ears never heard him. I am searching for God in the life of a recluse.

5. The loo'is perceived what manner of man he was, and they led him to take an I'hin

woman to wife, and she bore him a son, Hasumat.

6. The loo'is guarded Hasumat till he was grown, and they spake to him, trying him also as to his power to distinguish angel voices.

7. Him they also inspired to take an I'hin woman to wife, and she bore a son, Saichabal, who was guarded in the same way. And the angels inspired Saichabal, to marry Terratha, of the line (house) of Zed. Terratha bore a daughter who was named Edamas. And Edamas bore a son by an I'hin father without marriage, and she called his name Levi, signifying joined together (because his toes were not separate on the right foot, nor the fingers separate on the right hand). And Levi grew to be a large man, larger than two large men.

8. Levi, being of the fourth birth of I'hin blood, was not acknowledged an heir of the chosen race, the Faithists. Therefore Levi established a new line, which was called, the House of Levi.

9. Levi, not being eligible to a Faithist wife, was inspired by the loo'is to take an I'hin, Metissa, to wife. Metissa bore him a son, Kohath, who, at maturity, was admitted to the Order of Avah, the third degree of Faithists, whereupon he was circumcised, and afterward called an Israelite, the name given to the Faithists of Egupt.

10. Kohath took to wife, Mirah, a devout worshipper of Jehovih. Mirah bore him a son, Amram, who took to wife Yokebed, sister-in-law to Kohath, and she bore him a son, who was Moses.

11. Before Moses' birth the loo'is perceived that he would be capable of the Father's voice, and they called unto God saying: In the next generation, behold, thy son will be born.

CHAPTER XIV.

1. In these days in Egupt there were houses of records, where the affairs of the state, and of the king and governors, were recorded; and there were recorded also the births and marriages and deaths of people.

2. The languages of the learned were Fonecean and Parsi'e'an; but the native languages were Eguptian, Arabaic and Eustian and Semis. The times by the learned gave two suns to a year, but the times of the tribes of Eustia gave only six months to a year. Accordingly, in the land of Egupt what was one year with the learned was two years with the Eustians and Semisians.

3. God said: My people shall reckon their times according to the place and the people where they dwell. And they did this. Hence, even the tribes of Israel had two calendars of time, the long and the short.

4. To events of prophecy there was also another calendar, called the ode, signifying sky-time, or heavenly times. One ode was equivalent to eleven long years; three odes, one spell, signifying a generation; eleven spells one Tuff. Thothma, the learned man and builder of the great pyramid, had said: As a diameter is to a circle, and as a circle is to a diameter, so are the rules of the seasons of the earth. For the heat or the cold, or the drouth or the wet, no matter, the sum of one eleven years is equivalent to the sum of another eleven years. One SPELL is equivalent to the next eleventh spell. And one cycle matcheth every eleventh cycle. Whoever will apply these rules to the earth shall truly prophesy as to drought and famine and pestilence, save wherein man

contraveneth by draining or irrigation. And if he apply himself to find the light and the darkness of the earth, these rules are sufficient. For as there are three hundred and sixty-three years in one tuff, so are there three hundred and sixty-three days in one year, besides the two days and a quarter when the sun standeth still on the north and south lines.

5. In consequence of these three calendars, the records of Egupt were in confusion. The prophecies and genealogies of man became worthless. And as to measurements, some were by threes, some by tens, and some by twelves; and because of the number of languages, the measurements became confounded; so that with all the great learning of the Eguptians, and with all the care bestowed on the houses of records, they became even themselves the greatest confounding element of all.

6. Jehovih had said: For two thousand years I gave My enemies a loose rein; and they have the longest line of kings in all the world; and yet in the midst of their prosperity they fall down like a drunken man. Even their language is become like a pearl that is lost in a mire.

7. Jehovih said: Because the kings of Egupt have outlawed My people, and denied them the right to obtain great learning, behold My people are divided also. One tribe hath one speech, another tribe another speech, and so on, till they can not now understand one another; save, in fact, in their rites, and signs, and pass-words.

8. Yea, the kings have perceived that to keep My people in ignorance is to keep them forever in bondage. But I will raise up a leader, Moses, amongst My chosen, and I will send him even into the house of the king, and the king shall give him great learning; he shall master all languages, and be capable of speaking with all My people.

9. Because the Israelites (Faithists) worshipped not the Gods and Lords, but the Great Spirit only, and because they resented not injury done by another, they had been limited into servitude by the Eguptian laws, which had stood for fifteen hundred years. These laws were called the Sun laws, after the manner of the division of the Osirian system, which was:

10. The sun is a central power; its accompanying planets are satellites. In like manner the king of Egupt was the Sun King, and his sub-kings (governors) were satellites. Osiris, the highest angel in heaven, was the Sun God, that is, God of Gods; for all other Gods were his satellites. He revealed certain laws to mortals, and these were the Sun laws; and all minor laws were satellites. A Sun law extended over all of Egupt, but a satellite law pertained to the minor affairs of a city or province; but it must conform to the Sun laws. For in those days the spirits of darkness taught that the sun once whirled so fast it cast off its outer extreme, and so made the earth, and moon, and stars; and this was the accepted philosophy of the learned Eguptians of that period. Because the worlds run in circles (orbits), the circle was the highest measure, or sun measure; and the diameter of the circle was called, the ode, a Fonecean word, signifying short measure. And this name, ode, was applied to the Israelites in satire, as the Anglo-Saxon word, odius, is used to this day. But the Israelites made sweet songs and called them odes also.

11. Amongst the Sun laws were the following, to wit: The God of Gods (i.e., Osiris) decreeth: Whoso boweth not down to me shall not partake of me. Behold, mine is the sign of the circle! My enemies shall not receive great learning.

12. They shall not hold sun places (be employers), but be as servants only all their lives. And these signs shall discover them:

13. If they worship not me, but the Great Spirit;

14. If they deny that the Creator is in the image of a man;

15. If they circumcise, and will not serve as soldiers;

16. Then their possessions are forfeited already; nor shall they possess houses in their own names; nor send their children to the schools; for they shall be servants and the servants of servants forever.

17. Under the Eguptian laws it was accounted a sufficient crime of idolatry to worship the Great Spirit, Jehovih, that the Israelites were not even admitted to the courts to be tried for an offence, but fell under the jurisdiction of the master for whom they labored, and his judgments were unappealable.

18. Now at the time of the birth of Moses, there were in Egupt thirteen millions of inhabitants; and of these, four millions were Faithists (Israelites), more or less. For amongst the Israelites not all were of full faith, but many, to shirk the rigors of the Sun laws, professed to be worshippers of God (Osiris), and they would also enlist as soldiers, and otherwise connive in the ways of men, for sake of favors.

19. For which reason the Sun King (Pharaoh) feared the time might come when the Israelites might revolt against the Sun laws or become soldiers and confederate with foreign kingdoms for the overthrow of the Eguptian dynasty.

20. For more than three hundred years the God Baal and the Goddess Ashtaroth had driven the foreign kingdoms to war; and in consequence of these wars the Faithists had fled into Egupt, and even accepted servitude rather than be slain elsewhere.

21. Jehovih had said: Behold, mine enemies in killing one another, frighten off My chosen. Now will I lead them into Egupt together and give unto them a great leader, and he shall restore My doctrines unto them, and I will afterward deliver them into lands of their own.

CHAPTER XV.

1. The king's palace and pyramids were surrounded by a wall of stone; with twelve gates, made of wood and iron. The wall was of sufficient breadth for twelve men to walk abreast thereon, and the height of the wall was equivalent to twelve squares (about 32 feet). On the summit of the wall were twelve houses for the accommodation of the soldiers who patrolled the walls. And in each and every gate-way were houses for the keepers of the gates. So that no man, nor woman, nor child, could come into the palace or palace grounds without permission.

2. And it came to pass that when Leotonas, the king's daughter, walked near the river, accompanied by her maids, she beheld a child in a basket amongst the bullrushes. Leotonas commanded her maids to fetch it to her; and when she looked upon it, and beheld it was an Israelitish child, she said: The Gods have sent him to me, and he shall be my child.

3. And they bore the child into the palace, and Leotonas said to the king: Behold, a wonder of wonders! I have found an Israelitish child in a basket in the rushes, and only Gods know how it came, or how it scaled the walls. The king said: Keep thou the child, and it shall be both a brother and a son to thee. Nevertheless, my guards shall find the way my grounds are entered, or blood will be upon them.

4. Now after some days, and when the search had been completed, and no way discovered as to the manner of the child's ingress, the king issued a decree commanding a thousand Israelitish male children to be put to death, Moses amongst the rest, unless the mother of the child, Moses, came and acknowledged as to the manner of ingress. The king allotted three days in which time the matter should culminate; but nevertheless the mother came not and acknowledged.

5. And the king called his daughter, and said unto her: What shall be done? Leotonas said: The king's word must not be broken; nevertheless, thou gavest the child to me, saying: Keep thou it, and it shall be a brother and a son to thee. And straightway I sent my maids and procured an Israelitish woman as nurse for the child. And I set my heart upon the child, nor can I part with it and live. Last night I consulted the oracle as to the matter, for I saw that thy mandate must be fulfilled.

6. The king said: And what said the oracle? Leotonas said: Give word abroad that the nurse of the child is its mother. Now I beseech thee, O king, let it be heralded abroad that all is acknowledged.

7. The king, seeing the child, relented; and word was proclaimed as Leotonas had desired. And, moreover, the matter was entered in the recorder's house that the mother of the child had made the basket and placed it where it was found, though no reason was assigned therefore. Such, then, was the Egyptian explanation.

8. Now the truth of the matter was, the angels of Jehovih came to Yokebed and said: Thy son's name shall be Moses, signifying, a leader-forth, for he shall deliver the Israelites out of bondage. But he shall be taken from thee, and thou canst not find him. For the angels of Jehovih will deliver him into Leotonas' hands. And she shall adopt him as her brother and son, and bestow upon him the education of a prince.

9. Yokebed feared, for in those days male children of Israelitish parentage were outlawed, nor could any man be punished for slaying them. And Yokebed prayed Jehovih, saying: Thy will be done, O Jehovih, for I know Thy hand is upon my son. But I beseech Thee, O Father, that I may come to the princess and be her nurse for the child. The angel of Jehovih said: Swear thou before Jehovih thou wilt not betray to the child that thou art his mother!

10. Yokebed said: Though I be commanded by the king, yet will I not own that I am the mother, and it be Thy will, O Jehovih!

11. And Jehovih's angels fashioned a basket; and carried the child and placed it where it was found by Leotonas and her maids. And Leotonas, seeing it was a Hebrew child, commanded one of her maids to go and bring an Israelitish woman to nurse it. And the maid went out beyond the Utak gate and found and brought Yokebed, the child's mother, but no one knew she was its mother.

12. And when Yokebed had come before the princess, the latter said unto her: Nurse thou the child, for I will be its mother and its sister, for the Gods have delivered it into my hands. And Yokebed said: It is a goodly child; I will nurse it for thee.

13. Moses grew and became a large man, being a pure I'huan, copper-colored and of great strength. And Pharaoh, having no son, bestowed his heart on Moses, and raised him as a prince, having provided him men of great learning to teach him. Moses was master of many languages, and withal made acquainted with kings and queens and governors, far and near. And he espoused the cause of the king, whose dominions held seven kingdoms

beyond Egupt as tributary kingdoms, which paid taxes to Pharaoh.

14. So Pharaoh made Moses embassador to the foreign kingdoms, in which capacity he served twelve years. But because of the prejudice against him, for being of Israelitish blood, the court of Pharaoh importuned the king for his removal, and Moses was so removed from office under the king.

15. The king said to Moses: My son, this is a double infliction on me in my old days; in the first place, it is as a sword-thrust, to cut off my love to thee, lest thou some day become king; and in the second place, it is hard for a Pharaoh to be dictated to by his own court.

16. Moses replied: Fear not, O king, that my love and thine can be severed. Oft it happeneth that men are tried in a way they know not the wisdom of, but which, afterward, we realize to be the best thing that could have taken place.

17. As for myself, I think this rebuke is put upon me by Jehovih because I labored not for mine own people.

18. The king said: How so? Moses replied: For many days a great heaviness hath come upon me; it is as if the wind of heaven bore down on my heart, saying: Moses, Moses, lift up thy voice for thy people. For behold, the king, thy father, will favor thee!

19. Pharaoh said: What wouldst thou. my son? And if it be possible to be done it shall be done.

20. Moses answered: Until I have gone amongst them and ascertained their grievances, I know not how to answer thee. The king said: Go, and keep thy counsel to thyself until thou art returned.

21. So Moses departed and traveled over the land of Egupt, and was four months absent, and returned unto Pharaoh. And to him Moses related all the grievances of the Israelites; explaining the tasks put upon them; their denial before the courts; their forbiddance to education; and withal extolled them highly for being a peaceful and virtuous people.

22. The king said: It is a pity; it is a great pity. But what can I do, O Moses? Thou beholdest how even thyself is chastised by the king's court. If I demand the repeal of the laws, the court will heap coals of fire on thy head and on mine.

23. Moses said: Neither know I, O king, what to do. And Moses was in great trouble of soul; and after he waited a while for his thoughts to come to him, he said: O king, this night thou and Leotonas shall reason with me, for I feel it incumbent because of the pressure on my soul.

24. When the three were alone that night, lo and behold, it was the beginning of the dawn of light. And Moses' ears were opened, and he heard the Voice of Jehovih (through His angels) saying:

25. Behold, O king, and thou, Leotonas, and Thou, Moses, now is the beginning of My power on the face of the earth. Moses, My son, thou shalt take thy people out of the land of Egupt; and I will bestow upon them the lands of the ancients, even whither I will lead thee. Change not thy laws, O king; let Egupt have her way; and let the Israelites have their way also.

26. The king said: To deliver four millions of people! O what a labor!

27. On the next day Moses walked out, going into the woods to be alone, for heavy trouble was upon him. And an angel of Jehovih appeared in a flame of fire in a bush, calling: Moses, Moses, My son! And Moses saw that the bush was not burnt, and he said:

Here am I, and I heard Thy Voice.

28. The Voice said: I am the God of Abraham, and of Isaac and Jacob. Moses said: What wouldst Thou?

29. The Voice said: Go thou once more amongst thy people and say thou: I, Moses, am come to deliver you out of the land of Egupt, and into an inheritance which shall be your own.

30. Moses said: My people will ask of me: By whose authority speakest thou? What then shall I answer them? The Voice said: Say thou to them: The I Am sent me. And if they question further, saying: Thou has a deceiving spirit, like the Eguptians, then shalt thou say to them: How can ye distinguish one spirit from another? and they will say: Whoso laboreth for himself will deceive us. And thou shalt say to them: Whosoever hath faith in Jehovih, let him give up all, even as I do; and let thcm follow me; for if a multitude go forth in Faith in the Father, then will the Father provide unto them. (For this is the meaning of Faith, from which ye were named Israelites.)

31. So Moses and his brother, Aaron, traveled about in the land of Egupt, calling together Raban families, explaining to them, and urging the people to get ready and depart out of Egupt. For three years they thus labored, and it became known far and near that the project was on foot.

32. And the oracles of the Eguptians prophesied that when the Israelites were once out of the country they would unite with the kingdoms whereto Moses had been embassador, and then return and overpower the Eguptians.

33. And in order to stigmatize Moses they said he fled away from Pharaoh's palace because he had seen two men, and Eguptian and an Israelite, fighting, and that Moses slew the Eguptian and buried him in the sand. And the recorders thus entered the report in the Recorder's House.

34. Moses was of tender heart and he inquired of the Great Spirit, saying: Will ever a voice of justice speak in my behalf? Jehovih, through his angel, answered Moses, saying: Suffer thy enemies to put on record what they will, for the time will surely come when the truth shall be revealed unto men. Pursue thy course, for it shall be shown that thou dost still visit the king; wherefore, hadst thou fled as the records state, thou wouldst not return, with the report hanging over thy head.

35. In those days Egupt was a land of glory and of misery. Hardly is it possible for words to describe the splendor in which the nobles lived. Of their palaces and chariots a thousand books might be written, and yet not reveal all. And as to the members of the king's court, so grand were they that many of them stood not on the ground from one year's end to the other; but caused carpets to be spread wherever they desired to walk. And as to their chariots, they were bound with silver and gold, and set with precious stones.

36. Of the royal court and the nobles, there were two thousand four hundred and eighty, and they owned and possessed everything in Egupt, which was the richest country in the world.

37. The next in rank were the masters, who were servants and tenants to the courtiers and nobles; and the third in rank were the Faithists, called Israelites, who were servants under the masters.

38. And it was against the law for any one to call a meeting of Israelites, or to incite them

against servitude to the masters; for which reason Moses and Aaron violated the law of the land, nor dared any man to arrest them, because Moses bore with him the king's seal.

39. Of the miseries of the land of Egupt, the half hath never been told, nor ever shall be; for they were of the nature of the flesh, and of such kind that one may not mention them fully, for the history would also involve the beasts of the fields, and dogs, male and female, and goats also.

40. Suffice it, the people were victims of evil spirits, and had descended to such unnatural practices as poisoned the flesh, which became inhabited with vermin; and they had running sores; and only evil practices alleviated the pains. The people were subject to entrancement by evil spirits, and the latter appeared amongst the people, taking to themselves corporeal forms for evil's sake, also eating and drinking with mortals daily.

41. When Moses beheld these things he prayed to Jehovih for wisdom and strength; for thousands and thousands of the Israelites were becoming afflicted in the same way. Jehovih answered Moses, saying: Because of the abundance of evil angels in this land, it is impossible for My chosen to dwell herein and escape affliction. Moses explained this matter to the Israelites.

42. Jehovih said: Moses, thou and thy brother shall return to the king, for he is worried concerning thee and thy labors. Behold, the nobles have complained before the king against thee.

43. Moses visited the king, who was sick with a fever; and the king was on his divan at the fountain in the palace grounds, and the men servants were forcing water. When the king saw it was Moses he raised up, rejoicing, and called Moses to come and sit with him. And servants ran in and told Leotonas that Moses had returned, and Leotonas came also and rejoiced to see Moses. Now whilst they were talking the king was overcome and fell in a faint, whereupon Moses raised him up and restored him; and then carried the king into the palace, in his arms carried he him.

44. Leotonas said: Moses, my son and brother, thou shalt not more leave us alone? Behold, my father is old, and he gave his heart to thee when thou wert a child. Be thou to him his son. Behold how he revives in thy strong hands!

45. Then spake the king, saying: My son, with all thy wisdom, canst thou understand a woman? Moses said: Alas, O king, save the princess, I have not studied them. But why asketh thou?

46. The king replied: Leotonas had not said one word about the affairs of the kingdom! What is uppermost in a woman's heart, that speaketh she first; but as to man, he speaketh first that which lieth at the bottom of his heart. I love thee, Moses, and delight in thy presence; but my kingdom concerneth me deeply. The nobles have complained against thee for meddling with their slaves, and for this I have desired to see thee.

47. Moses said: The Voice came to me, informing me of what thou sayest, and then commanded me to come to thee, for thou wert ill with fever. And the king replied, saying: If I should die before thou has accomplished the migration of thy people, I fear my successor, Nu-ghan, will make it hard for thee. Tell me then, therefore, how matters stand with thee?

48. Moses said: Jehovih hath planned this migration; it cannot fail. For, witness thee what proof I have found: The Israelites were looking for a leader-forth, even as I was named in the basket. And wherever I have gone, the rab'bahs and their families are acquainted with

the matter as if it were born in their souls.

49. The king said: Everywhere the oracles declare against thee and Jehovih; saying thou art in the hands of evil spirits.

50. Moses said: What are the oracles to me? To feel assured one is in a good work; this is better than oracles.

CHAPTER XVI.

1. The Voice of Jehovih came to Moses, saying: Have the king give thee commissioners who shall go in advance and examine the countries whither I will lead thee; and when the commissioners have returned, thou shalt proclaim to My people what the commissioners say, and the people will be convinced, and rise up and follow thee. So Moses asked the king for a commission of Eguptians, and the king appointed thirty-three men, and allotted to them seven months to accomplish the inspection; and he gave to the commission camels and asses to ride upon, and to carry food to eat on the journey.

2. Meanwhile, Moses sent Aaron around about through Egupt, to inform the people of the commission, and also as to how they should make their outfits. And Aaron said unto the rab'bahs: Be ye circumspect as to the outfits of our people; observing that they carry not away with them anything that is another's, even to a fraction; for thus hath Moses commanded me to say unto you.

3. When the commissioners returned and made their report, which was favorable, Moses had the report sent amongst the Israelites; and Moses added: For there be such, as, having little faith in Jehovih, will have faith in the words of the commissioners.

4. The Gods of the Eguptians were not idle, and they sent word by way of the oracles to the courtiers and nobles to the effect that Moses had persuaded the king to hand the kingdom over to the foreign nations, knowing the king had no son eligible to the throne.

5. The courtiers and nobles, therefore, importuned the king to choose one of two things: Either to banish Moses out of the country, and put aside all arrangements for the migration of the Israelites; or, on the other hand, to abdicate the throne in favor of Nughan. In the meantime, a whole year's drought came upon Egupt, and the rivers overflowed not, so that a famine was sure to fall upon many parts of the country.

6. The king answered the demand of the courtiers and nobles with these words: I am Pharaoh, king of Egupt! Look ye to the threatened famine; provide the stores for my people. I declare to you all, a new thing is come unto the world, which is: MIGRATION FROM BONDAGE! Nor is it in the power of nobles or courtiers or kings to stay this invention.

7. When the courtiers received this answer they said to one another: These are Moses' words, fashioned for the king's mouth. Certainly he hath lost the fear of the Lord, and hearkeneth to the Great Spirit of the Israelites!

8. Jehovih, through His angels, spake to Moses, saying: Now is thy time. Go to the Heads whom thou has chosen and appoint a time unto them of one place, and a time unto others of another place, and so on unto all the Heads. And thou shalt make the armies going forth so numerous that the Eguptians will be overwhelmed.

9. These, then, are Heads, the chief rab'bahs appointed by Moses, and the places in Egupt whence they were to depart from:

10. Rasak, son of Ubeth, of the place Hagor; Ashimel, son of Esta, of the place Ranna;

Gamba, son of Hanor, of the place Nusomat; Bothad, son of Nainis, of the place Palgoth; Amram, Son of Yoth, of the place Borgol; Lakiddik, son of Samhad, of the place Apau; Jokai, son of Keddam, of the place Hasakar; Jorvith, son of Habed, of the place Oeda; Sattu, son of Bal, of the place Harragatha; Tussumak, Son of Aban, of the place Ra; Makrath, son of Filatti, of the place Nabaoth; Hijamek, son of Tor, of the place Nu'joram; Fallu, son of Hagan, of the place Ennitz; Shutta, of the place Romja; Jokkin, son of Rutz, of the place Moan; Tudan, son of Barrahha, of the place Hezron; Osharrak, son of Libni, of the place Raim; Thammas, son of Rodaad, of the place Sakaz; Misa, son of Tiddiyas, of the place Tessam; and Sol, son of Zakkaas, of the place Annayis.

11. Jehovih said: And the Heads shall have notice seventy and seven days; and they shall notify the rab'bah of their places, that due preparation shall be made for the start. Nevertheless, the time appointed unto thy people shall be kept secret with the Heads and the rab'bahs. And whatever number the rab'bah can send forth, he shall notify the Head; and when all things are in readiness, that number shall go forth on the day appointed, every one on the same day.

12. And Moses appointed the month Abib and the tenth day thereof, when all the people should start; and moreover, he said unto the Heads: Ye shall see to it that the night before they start, even at the hour of sunset, and the moment thereof, every family shall offer a lamb in sacrifice, and every man, and every woman, and every child that can speak, shall covenant unto Jehovih in the blood of the lamb.

13. When the time of the slaughter is at hand, the family shall stand around, and the lamb shall be in the midst, bound head and foot; and when the knife is raised for the blow, no one shall speak, for that which is to be shall be the covenant of the blood of the lamb against Egupt. And when the throat is cut across and the blood flowing, they shall all say: In Egupt the lamb of Jehovih is dead; His God shall go hence with Israel, but Egupt shall be accursed from this night! Accept this, my covenant, with thee, O Jehovih (E-O-Ih!), for innocent blood hath been shed as a testimony before Thee that, with to-morrow's rising sun, I rise to lie not down again in Egupt forever!

14. Thus went Aaron and Akad, bearing this message in secret to the Heads of the Houses of Israel, saying unto them: Thus saith Moses: This is the commandment of Jehovih, Who is Almighty!

15. And now, on the eve of success to the Israelites, the king of Egupt, being at the point of death, sent for Moses, and Moses went to him. The king said: If it should be the Lord's will to take me off before they people are gone, thou wilt have great bother; for my successor, Nu-ghan, hath a great hate toward Israel.

16. Moses said: What, then, shall be done? The king said: Behold, the pestilence hath overspread Najaut and Arabenah. Thy people will be cut off from traveling by that way. Nu-ghan and his courtiers dwell in Harboath. Moses replied: My people shall march through Najaut and Arabenah; neither shall the pestilence come upon them, for the hand of the Almighty is in this matter.

17. Leotonas, learning that Moses was with the king, went in to see him. She said: O my son and brother, thou art welcome. Behold, the trials of the royal court, and the persistence of the nobles, are the death of the king. To this the king said: And still I live, Leotonas! But, alas, these were his last words, for he laughed, and the blood burst through his heart, and he died then and there, even in Moses' arms.

CHAPTER XVII.

1. Jehovih, through His angels, said unto Moses: When the body of the king is embalmed and put away, thou shalt go quickly to thy people; for he who cometh to the throne is under the voice of the Lord, Baal, and he will try to prevent the departure of My chosen. So, Moses left the capital and did as commanded.

2. On Nu-ghan's being crowned he at once issued the following decree: Behold me, I am Pharaoh, King of Egupt, and Ruler of the World. God hath raised his voice in my dominions saying: Hail thou, Sun King of the corporeal world: Behold, I gave to thee all the living that are on the face of the earth, and in the waters of the earth, to be thine, to keep forever. And I say unto thee, what is thine own is thine own, and thou shalt have dominion in thine own way, for I made all that are alive on the earth to be thine forever!

3. Whether of beasts of the field, or fish in the waters, or man on the earth; all the living I created for thee, and thou shalt possess them from everlasting to everlasting. And the life of the living gave I into thy keeping; and I said unto thee: The house of Pharaoh have I created, and it is my house also.

4. And whoever ruleth on the throne of this land, the same is my son, and is the possessor whilst the breath of life is in him. But when he dieth, and the throne fall to his successor, the rights and the powers and possessions of thy kingdom shall not die nor be set at naught. But the successor shall be my Pharaoh whom I raised upon unto my dominions; thus saith the Lord.

5. Now, therefore, I, Pharaoh, who am king and possessor of all the world by commandment of God, and by his son (Osiris), who is dead and risen, being myself God of the earth, into whose hands are bequeathed all the living, am today, yesterday, and forever, the same everlasting king and Lord of all. And I decree unto my people, who are mine by virtue of my authority from God, that only by my gracious indulgence hath any man or people right to put one foot before the other, on this my sacred earth.

6. And whoso goeth here or there, save by the sign of the signet of my seal, shall surely be put to death.

7. Any multitude of my people, who are my servants, whom the God of Gods hath given into my hands to do my works, to till my earth, or to build my houses, or dig ditches, or make bricks, or gather harvest, or make cloth, or attend flocks, and to do all works whatsoever, who may design to escape out of Egupt, to go to my enemies, the foreign kings, shall be deemed guilty unto death. And if such people start forth, to quit my service, to go out of my holy land, then shall my loyal slaves fall upon them and slay them, right and left, sparing neither man, woman nor child. For thus commandeth the Lord God, whose son I am.

8. Jehovih, through His angels, spake to Moses, saying: Go thou; take Aaron thy brother, and go before the king and plead thy cause. Moses said: O Jehovih, Thou Almighty, why hast Thou said this unto me? I have no argument in me, like other men? nor have I courage to face a man or woman. My tongue is slow to find words till after the opportunity. From my youth up I have known this man, Nu-ghan, who is king, and if he but stomp his foot at me I am helpless before him.

9. Jehovih said: For that reason, My son, I can give thee My words. Go and fear not.

10. Then Moses went before Pharaoh, taking Aaron with him. The king asked: What is thy will? And Moses said: I am come to beseech thee to suffer my people to depart out of Egupt. The king replied: The Lord is with me; he saith thou shalt not go; and I repeat the words of my God.

11. Then spake Moses, the power of Jehovih being upon him: Think not, O king, that bondage is for this world only; here doth not the matter end. Thou hast here said in thy decree, even from the Lord hast thou spoken, saying: The life of the living gave I into thy keeping. Saidst the Lord this to thee? Wherein, then, is justice, since pestilence and death are coming upon thy people? Callest thou this keeping them? I declare unto thee, that even in the words of thine own God thou hast failed utterly, and this sin is upon thee. Suffer, then, my people to depart, that thine own shortness may not be magnified unto thee, in the afflictions which will surely overspread this land.

12. The king said: Thou hast no authority; thou art a frozen serpent that was taken into the house of the king; and being thawed out, thou turnest to bite thy benefactors. Thou art outlawed by men and accursed by the oracles. It is said of thee, thou hast been to Hored, and there wed for sake of alliance with my high priest, Jethro, for conveyance of my lands unto thy people. Who art thou, that pretendest to hear a voice, and to be led by the Unseen? Thou slave!

13. Moses said: I am not here to plead mine own cause O king, but my people's. Suffice it, though, that even as thy Lord God standeth upon miracles, I bow not down before him. For these are evidence that thy God and thy Lord are but angels of the dead, who labor for thee and thy aggrandizement, and not for all men's welfare.

14. For I have miracles also; and whatsoever thy magicians can do, that can I do also; have I not eyes and ears, even as the oracles? Now I declare a miracle unto thee, which is that thou thyself shalt yet not only consent to my people going out of Egupt, but thou shalt send armies to drive them out. To turn a rod into a serpent, or water into wine; or to show the spirits of the dead, alas, O king, even they that are of rotten flesh can do such things!

15. Pharaoh said: If the oracle hear God, is not this the greatest? Moses replied: He who uttereth what an angel bid him is that angel's servant; he who uttereth a good truth hath spoken with Jehovih's voice. Pharaoh asked: Sayest thou thy words are the Creator's?

16. Moses replied: I am as all good men who speak truth; all that is good, and all truth, are Jehovih's words. In a rose He findeth expression in perfume; in the lightning His words are thunder; in a bird His words are songs; but in man, His voice is in man's words; for every living creature, and every dead thing on the earth, or in the waters, or in the air above the earth, giveth expression in its own way; because the Father's hand is the foundation of all that is good and true. He is the I Am Who sent me to thee; by His command open I my mouth before thee. And in His name declare I unto thee thou shalt not only suffer my people to depart out of Egupt, but thou shalt send thy armies to drive them out.

17. The king said: Moses, Moses, thou art mad! For though all Egupt run blood, yet will I not do as thou hast said. Then Moses replied: I tell thee, O king, there be two powers in heaven: that which is for Justice and Goodness, even Jehovih; and that which is for sin and death. And if the Creator lift off His protecting hand from Egupt, she shall in that day become the plague spot of the earth. Thou dost remember, when in the ancient days, great

Thothma built the first pyramid, thy forefathers decried the power of heaven; and straightway all the land, and the great pyramid itself, was flooded over by evil spirits. And then came foreign kings, and robbed and plundered Egupt. Think not, O king, these legends are but idle tales; there be Gods and Lords in heaven who could sweep the sea up, and drown all this country. Behold, a day is set; a night is marked out when the lamb of peace shall die. And in that night the first-born of every woman, and the first-born of every beast in the fields, shall die for all the Eguptians; and in that same night not one of the Israelites shall go down in death. Jehovih saith: I will show My power through My people in the time of My covenants.

18. Pharaoh said: Were these things to be, God had come to more noble quarters. Thou art beside thyself. And I banish thee; nor will I again look upon thy face.

19. Moses said: Whether in this world or the next, thou shalt yet call unto me to deliver thee from torments. Nevertheless, I do thy bidding; neither will I come to thee again, nor shalt thou look upon my face for a long season. With that, Moses and Aaron saluted the king and departed.

CHAPTER XVIII.

1. Pharaoh called his chief superintendent and said unto him: As to the Hebrew brick makers, thou shalt no longer supply them with straw, but they shall gather stubble themselves, and they shall continue to make the same number of bricks. And as to the tillers of the soil, thou shalt no longer suffer them to have cattle to draw the plows, but they shall draw the plows themselves, and they shall likewise break the same quantity of ground. And in this way the king put extra hardships upon the Israelites because he was angered at what Moses said.

2. Moses perceiving this, cried out unto Jehovih, saying: O why didst Thou send me before Pharaoh? Behold matters are worse than before. O that I had guarded my tongue and been of persuasive speech!

3. Jehovih said to Moses: Rebuke not thyself, for thou hast done My commands. And it shall come to pass now, what otherwise would not. For such Israelites as hesitated about going out of Egupt, will now decide for themselves as to what they will do. And the hardships that Pharaoh hath newly added, shall be a blessing to thy people.

4. And it came to pass that the Israelites went away from their task-masters, and the rab'bahs sent them to the Heads; and the people of Israel were stirred up from one end of Egupt to the other. And as for the Eguptians, save the courtiers and nobles, they were likewise stirred up, but without any purpose or order; so that all the great land of Egupt had no tillers nor builders; and cleanliness departed away from them; and the country stank as a dead carcass, so that insects and vermin filled all the air of heaven.

5. But of the Faithists, the flesh was good; and vermin came not upon them; nor were they stricken with fevers, or lepers, or scabs, like the Eguptians.

6. Pharaoh ordered his army of two hundred thousand men to take the field, but lo and behold, they were scattered and afflicted so that they were only as vagrants, without head or discipline.

7. Jehovih spoke to Moses, saying: Now will I show her philosophers a miracle in the air above the earth. Have they not said: All thing come up out of the earth? for they have

tried every way to put Me aside, and to explain My creation away as an idle tale. They shall look and see the sun, and declare of a truth there is no cloud; but whilst they look up, they shall see a cloud high up in the heavens, and it shall be broad as the land of Egupt, a very black cloud. And it shall descend to the earth, and it shall prove to be locusts, come without any seed; and they shall be so numerous that in three days they will eat up every green leaf of every tree and herb in all the land. Neither shall they be like any other locusts that have been on the earth or ever shall be; for man shall comprehend that they are not of the seed of the earth.

8. Moses sent with a herald this prophecy to the king, and he added thereto: Why hast thou put more hardships on my people? Seest thou not that the evil thou hadst hope to accomplish hath cured itself even before it came to pass? For the Israelites now work not at all, and their task-masters are left in the lurch. Again I call upon thee to let my people go.

9. The king replied not to this, but silently put his officers to work, drilling and equipping his armies and collecting them together; the which, when Moses beheld it, he understood to be the sign, as the Great Spirit had previously said, when the cloud would appear. And it came to pass on a very clear day, at noon, a cloud formed high up in the firmament, and it grew blacker and blacker, until it descended upon the earth; and it was locusts, and was even as a snow-storm that covereth the land of the earth; in places to the depth of the shoes and ankles. And they fell to, eating every green leaf, and herb, and grass, so that in two days there was not a leaf to be found far or near. And on the third day, the locusts being still unappeased as to hunger, fell upon the Eguptians, old and young, feeding upon their clothes, and even upon the flesh of the Eguptians.

10. And on the fourth day Jehovih caused a great wind to come, and it blew the locusts off into the sea. And again Moses sent heralds to the king, saying: Consider now my words and be wise. I have told thee that the hand of the Creator is upon this land. In thy heart thou sayest: Moses is a fool! Only a wind-storm fetched the locusts from a far-off country.

11. But I say unto thee, O king, this is not so. And thou shalt still further behold Jehovih's power. For as the locusts came down out of the firmament, and thou hast a philosophy for the occurrence, behold, now another miracle shall come in another way: For there shall suddenly come up out of the water frogs and reptiles, and they shall likewise be so numerous on the land that man shall not find where to put his foot that it shall not come upon them. And the first day they shall be harmless; but on the second day they shall crawl upon the people, and under their clothes, and in their houses; and on the third day they shall eat the flesh of the Eguptians. But they shall not touch one Hebrew in all the land.

12. Nor shall any man find whence came so many frogs and reptiles, for they shall not be like the seed of other frogs and reptiles. And on the fifth day they shall suddenly disappear, neither by wind nor rain. But a stench, as of rotten flesh, shall strangle the Eguptians nigh unto death.

13. Again I appeal unto thee, O king, to suffer my people to depart out of Egupt in peace. This is the last time I shall solicit thee. And if thou answerest not me, then shall it come to pass in the month Abib, and on the ninth day and night thereof, Jehovih will raise His hand over Israel; but as for Egupt, thy Lord shall strike her in death. For in every family

of Eguptians, far and near, on that night shall the first-born fall dead; and that thou shalt not say the prophecy killed them, behold the first-born of every beast shall die also, even of goats, and sheep, and cattle, and asses, and of dogs and cats, and of every living creature man useth. For on that night, behold, four millions of Israelites shall make with Jehovih the covenant of death. And on the morning thereafter they will rise up to not lie down again in Egupt. And this shall be the testimony of innocent blood against thyself and all thy people, for what the Hebrews have suffered.

14. The king answered not Moses; and it came to pass that Egupt was overspread with frogs and reptiles, in every particular even as Moses had prophesied. Nevertheless, Pharaoh pursued his course.

15. Jehovih spake to Moses, saying: Moses, My son, look upon man and pity him, for he believeth not in Me, though I multiply signs and omens continually, and give him prophecies without end. One thing only turneth man's eyes inward; that is, flesh of his flesh, lying dead before him.

16. Now on the night of the passover, when the Israelites made the covenant on the blood of the lamb, a hot wind blew upon the face of the earth; and the first-born of the Eguptians fell dead, both man and beast. And Pharaoh's son died, and his brother's son; and the first-born of every courtier, and every noble's first-born, and all other people, their first-born, so that in every family there lay one dead.

17. Pharoah was now stricken, but not unto repentance, for evil was in his heart, and he cursed Moses and the Israelites, and swore an oath to destroy Israel, man, woman and child, so that never more should there be one on the earth. And such a commandment he sent to his officers, to fall to, and begin the slaughter.

18. As for the Faithists, not many of them had slept all the night, but were providing for the journey; so that when morning came, and at the time of sunrise, they every one started. From all the different regions of Egupt they went forth to Sukkoth, westward. The Heads led the way, and every commune was led by a rab'bah, and every man's family by the father of the family or by the eldest son. And at the start they spake through their leaders, saying: In thy name, O Jehovih, we depart out of the land of our birth, where we were born, and our sons and daughters were born, to return not forever! Neither shall Egupt prosper more till Thou hast subdued the whole earth unto Thee.

19. But things had changed wonderfully as to the Eguptians, for when they beheld the Israelites were indeed going, and knew the miracles that had taken place, they relented, and brought them gifts of gold and silver; and also asses and camels for the Hebrew women and children to ride upon; and gave them food to eat. But the Israelitish women said: Nay, and we take these things we will be under obligations to the Eguptians. The Israelites accept not what they can not pay for. Then the Eguptians bewailed in fear, saying: That we be not accursed by the Gods, take them, we beseech you in the name of your God also.

20. So the Faithist women accepted the presents of asses and camels, and of other things besides; and they mounted the asses and camels, and rode them.

21. When Moses heard of this afterwards he rebuked Israel, saying: Because ye have accepted these things it will be said, ye borrowed them and begged them so as to despoil the Eguptians.

22. When they arrived near Sukkoth, Jehovih spake to Moses and Aaron, saying: Stand ye here for twelve days that ye may behold my people as they pass, and that ye in turn may be seen by them. So Moses and Aaron pitched their tents by the way, on a high piece of ground, and remained there twelve days, and Moses showed himself before them, speaking and encouraging.

23. After this the Israelites passed through Etham, on the borders of the wilderness, and thence toward Migdol, near Baal-zephon, the place of the oracle of the God, Baal, and they encamped before Pi'hahiroth, where Moses commanded them to remain some days to rest.

24. Now as for Pharaoh he had not made any attack on the Israelites, for the Lord held his army in confusion. Pharaoh, finding that the Israelites were not injured, decided to take the field himself; and accordingly, having impressed all the chariots of Egupt, went ahead, leading his army in person. The Israelites were wearied and foot-sore, and discovering that Pharaoh was after them, many of them complained and grumbled, saying: O Moses, why broughtest thou us from home? Better was it for us to have remained in servitude to the Eguptians than to be slain.

25. Moses rebuked them, saying: Profess ye to be Faithists but yet have not faith in Jehovih? Put your trust in Him; for he will deliver ye safely, as He hath promised.

26. Jehovih spake to Moses, saying: They shall behold the salvation of My hand; for the Eguptians who pursue them this day shall pursue them not again forever. For when thou fetchest them to the sea, thou shalt lift up thy rod, and I will divide the sea, and My people shall walk across on the land of the bottom of the sea. And Pharaoh's army shall pursue, but be swallowed up in the waters. And it so came to pass.

27. Jehovih brought a strong wind and divided the waters of the sea and swept them back, and the Israelites went over on land. But Pharaoh's army, who were in pursuit, were caught in the flood of the tide and drowned.

28. Thus delivered Jehovih the Israelites out of Egupt; and Israel believed in Him and in Moses, his servant.

29. Now from the place Sukkoth unto the other side of the sea, a pillar of cloud preceded the Israelites by day, and a pillar of fire stood over them by night, and the people looked thereon and saw, every one, the cloud and the light. And the name of the place they reached when they crossed over was Shakelmarath; and they camped there many days.

30. From the time Moses began to put on foot the migration of Israel until he reached Shakelmarath, was four years two hundred and seven days. And the number of Israelites that thus went forth out of Egupt was three million seven hundred and fifty-thousand men, women and children. And the number of other people who accompanied them was four hundred thousand; and because they were of the uncircumcised tribes of ancients, the Hebrews named them Levites, i.e., imperfect flesh.

31. And Moses commanded the Levites to camp aside, and not to mix with the Israelites, and they obeyed him in all things; maintaining that they were the true descendents of Abraham.

32. And Moses made a song unto Jehovih, and Miriam, his sister sang it and played on the timbrel, and the women of Israel danced before Jehovih.

33. This, then, is the song of Moses:

CHAPTER XIX.

1. Eloih, Almighty, Thou, my God, Who hast delivered my people! I will sing unto Thee a song; and the children of Israel unto Thee, O Eloih!

2. Thou art a great strength and salvation; unto Thee, Eloih, will I build my habitation; Thou, my father's God, O Eloih!

3. Thou art my Warrior; Eloih is Thy name, forever!

4. Thou has encompassed Pharaoh and his hosts; they are swallowed up in the sea, his chosen captains and his warriors in the Red Sea.

5. The depths covered them up; they sank to the bottom as a stone, O Eloih!

6. Almighty Eloih: Glorious in power in Thy right hand that passed over innocent blood!

7. Thou, my God, Eloih; Wise in majesty, in Thy right hand that dashed in pieces Thy enemy!

8. Excellency, O Thou Eloih; in graciousness that came upon them that rose up in Thy way; Thou sentest Thy breath upon them; as stubble they were cut down by Thy righteous sword!

9. By the breath of Thy nostrils, Thou heapedst up the waters of the sea; and the floods stood upright by Thy voice, to entrap them in the heart of the sea!

10. Thine enemy said: I will pursue; I will overtake them; the spoil shall be mine; I will draw the sword; my hand shall destroy them!

11. Thou didst blow with Thy wind; the sea covered them; they sank as lead in the mighty waters.

12. Who is like unto Thee, Eloih, amongst the Gods? Who is like Thee, Glorious in Holiness, fearful in praise and wonders, O Eloih! Thou stretchedst out Thy right hand, and they went down into the earth.

13. Merciful Almighty, Eloih, my God, and God of my fathers; Who hast led forth Israel and delivered her into the land of her fathers, O Eloih! Who hast guided them to a holy habitation and peaceful one.

14. All people shall hear and be afraid; sober thought shall take hold on the inhabitants of Palestina. And the nobles of Edom shall be amazed! The warrior of Moab; trembling shall take hold on them, and the wild men of Kana'yan shall melt away!

15. Thou, O Eloih, shalt strike them with fear; in the magnitude of the strength of Thine arm will they be amazed and helpless as stone. For this land is Thy purchase, O Eloih; in the passover of the blood of the lamb purchased Thou it; and Israel shall pass over it in fear.

16. And Thou shalt bring them to the mountain of their inheritance, to Thy place, Our God, Eloih. To dwell in Thy sanctuary, which Thou has established for Thy reign, forever and forever.

CHAPTER XX.

1. Moses called together the Heads and the rab'bahs, privily, and spake before them, saying:

2. What have I taken upon me, O Jehovih? Behold Thy sons and daughters have followed me out of Egupt; how shall I bind them unto Thee and not unto me, O my Father

in heaven?

3. Jehovih said unto me: Moses, Moses, what I say unto thee, say thou unto the rab'bahs and unto the Heads; saying unto them: Not Moses, nor the Heads, nor the rab'bahs, brought ye out of Egupt; ye were brought out by the Creator, Jehovih, Who is God of all, Captain of all, Head of all, Rab'bah of all.

4. For herein have I drawn the line betwixt My people and My enemies, the idolaters of men. Because of signs and miracles, the idolaters make a man-God of their magician and worship him. But who is like unto thee, Moses, My son; in miracles who can match thee in the magnitude of thy proceeding?

5. Who led forth My millions; and delivered them out of a great power without loss of a man, woman or child?

6. But I declare unto thee, thou shalt do a greater miracle than any of these; for thou shalt preserve thyself from becoming an idol before men. For thou shalt proclaim Me unto thy people in all things, teaching them that thou art but a man. And thy Heads and thy rab'bahs shall likewise teach them after the same manner; for I will put away all idolatry from the face of the earth.

7. Neither will I have kings nor queens; I am sufficient unto all men.

8. As Abraham apportioned My people into families, with rab'bahs and with chief rab'bahs, so shalt thou re-establish them.

9. And My commandments, which I gave unto Abraham, will I give unto thee; and My crescent will I re-establish with My rab'bahs. And My crescent shall be the fullness of My law unto the rab-bahs and chief rab'bahs.

10. Moses said: I cried unto Jehovih, saying: How shall it be with the square and at high noon? And the angel of Jehovih, speaking in the Father's name, said: To the north-east God, to the south-west Lord, to the north-west Baal; to the south-east Ashtaroth. For Osiris is dead already.

11. To this end, then, prepare ye a place this night, that the Great Spirit may bless us. The rab-bahs and the Heads said: It is well.

12. And when it was night Moses and the rab'bahs and the Heads went away aside; placing sentinels that they might be alone. And when they were thus prepared the light of Jehovih came upon Moses, and the books of the ancients were opened before him. And he administered emethachavah upon them; by the voice of Jehovih he re-established it; with all the rites and ceremonies as they are to this day. And after that the Heads were no longer called Heads, but Chief Rab'bahs; for Moses anointed them; by command of Jehovih he anointed them.

13. And in not many days Moses wrote the Levitican laws; for the inner temple of Jehovih was in spoken words only; but the outer temple was written. Wherefore it was said: The Hebrews have two laws; one which no man else knoweth; and one for them who are not eligible unto faith, being such as were called Leviticans, but not Leviticans in fact, but hangers-on who had followed the Israelites out of Egupt and who for the most part had no God, little judgment and no learning.

14. But of all that Moses did, and taught, and how he labored with his own hands, many books might be written. And it is doubtful if the world ever produced so good and great a man.

15. At the time Moses reached Shakelmarath, he was forty-four years old by the Hebrew sun, but by the Eguptian he was eighty-eight years old.

16. Of Pharaoh and his hosts who were not destroyed in the sea, be it said, they returned home to their places. And not long after that, Pharaoh banished God (Osiris) from the earth, declaring himself the SAVIOR OF THE WORLD, AND VICE GERENT OF THE HOLY GHOST.

17. The scribes and recorders assembled in Kaona and appointed Feh-ya (An Eguptian) to write the departure of the Israelites out of Egupt. And Feh-ya wrote the account and called it THE EXODUS OF THE HEBREWS, and it was recorded in the king's House of Records. And copies of it were sent to the large cities, and there recorded also, for such was the law of Egupt. Feh-ya's record was afterward accepted by Ezra, and is that which is known to this day as the First Book of Exodus.

18. The Book of Genesis, as it stood in the Eguptian records, was written by Akaboth and Dueram and Hazed, and was the substance from which Ezra copied it through his scribes, even as it is to this day. The inspiration of Genesis was from the God, Osiris, the false, and his emissaries, chief of whom were Yotabba and Egupt, who were angel servants to Osiris. And so far as the records now stand the spirit of both books was the Eguptian version of the whole subject.

19. Touching genealogies, in which men seemed to have lived to so great an age, this, then, is the explanation thereof:

20. Thothma had said to his recorders: In searching for the truth of legends, give ye the latitude thereof. For one legend will say, such a man lived seven hundred years ago, another legend will say he lived ten hundred and fifty years ago. The latitude between them is, therefore, three hundred and fifty years, which shall be the time of that man's life. And in this way latitude became confounded with fact, and with no intent to deceive.

21. And behold, it came to pass that the records were worthless; and to make matters worse the records were so voluminous, being more than six thousand books, that the scribes of Ezra could make neither head nor tail of them. Nevertheless, they were all written, in the first place not by the Israelites, but by their enemies; wherein the testimony of the miracles is none the weaker.

22. Thus endeth the history of Moses' deliverance of the Faithists out of Egupt.

23. Hear ye now of Chine of the land of Jaffeth:

CHAPTER XXI.
HISTORY OF CHINE (TSCHIN'E), OF JAFFETH, FOUNDER OF CHINA.

1. These are the generations of the seven antecedents of Chine, the chosen of the Great Spirit, Ormazd, otherwise, in Fonecean, Eloih; that is to say:

2. Tse'wong begat Hi-gan, who begat Ah So, who begat T-soo Yong, who begat Ah Paing, who begat T-chook Lee, who begat Tschine Loo, who begat Ah Sho'e, who begat Tschin'e (Chine), gifted in su'is and sar'gis of six generations.

3. Of these, T-soo Yong and Ah So were prophets of Jehovih (Ormazd), and Ah Sho'e was a seer; but the six generations could hear the Voice, and they walked upright, keeping the commandments of Jehovih as revealed in the Zarathustrian laws.

4. Ah Sho'e was a basket-maker, and after the manner of the man, Zarathustra; and Chine, his son, was the fourth birth of Ah Sho'e's wife, Song Heng. Like Moses, Chine was of

copper color, and very large, but his hair was red, like a fox, and he was bashful and of few words.

5. Ah Sho'e, i.e., Chine's father, said: I have had other sons; my words are wise and true; Chine was unlike any child born in the world; for boy child, or girl child, no physician could tell which, but rather to the boy kind was he. The angel of Jehovih (Ormazd) came to me before the birth and said: The child shall be called Chine, signifying no sex; as it is written among the ancients, i-e-su, having no earthly desires. For he shall restore the chosen people of Jehovih.

6. Whereof I told the physicians before the birth, but they would not believe. Nevertheless, by command of Jehovih, I sent for seven physicians to witness the birth, lest it be said afterward the surgeons have dealt wrongly with the child at its birth.

7. These physicians came to wit: Em Gha, Tse Thah, Ah Em Fae, Te Gow, T'si, Du Jon, Foh Chaing, and Ah Kaon, and they beheld the child born, whereto they made oath, and a record thereof, touching the strangeness of such a birth, and of the prophecy of its coming into the world; this record was put in the Ha Ta'e King (library) of record belonging to the Sun King.

8. Being now in my old age, I, Ah Sho'e, put these things on record, of which hundreds have come to ask me concerning the youth of Chine.

9. First, that he was the laziest of all children, and dull past belief. For his brothers and sisters mocked him, concerning my prophecy, as to becoming a great man.

10. Second, he ate less than a small bird (Fa'ak), and grew so thin we were ashamed of him in his childhood; verily was he nothing but skin and bone, with a large head.

11. Third, when he walked about, the stools and tables moved out of his way; and yet no hand touched them.

12. Fourth, the angels of Jehovih oft carried him about the hut, and would lift him up to pick fruit from the trees.

13. Fifth, he never laughed, but was serious and pleasant, like an old man that had abandoned the world. But he spoke so little no man knew whether he was wise or stupid.

14. When he was three years old his mother weaned him, or rather he weaned himself. And from that time forth he never ate but fruit and nuts and grains of rice. When he was sixteen years old he began to grow suddenly large and strong, and of deep color. Whereat I procured a teacher for him; but lo, and behold, he could learn a whole book in a day. He learned by hearing once; neither forgot he anything he learnt.

15. In his twenty-second year he began to talk, and the angels of heaven spake through him also. And great was his speech.

16. From sunrise in the morning until late at night his tongue ceased not to speak. And his mouth moved as if it were the mouth-piece of heaven. For when one angel had discoursed before the audience for a while, then came another and another, and so on; and when none came, then spake Chine himself.

17. And there came before him men of great learning, and philosophers, to try him as to his knowledge; but they all went away confounded, as if they were fools. Neither was it possible to ask him a question he could not answer correctly. Whether it was to read a tablet or to reveal the size and build of a temple he never saw; or the sickness of a man who was far away; for all things were to him as an open book.

18. For four years this great wisdom remained in him, and his fame spread from the east to the west, and from the north to the south; no man knew how far. When he was asked how far he could see and hear, he said: Over all my land. And he marked with his finger, saying: On this tablet, Chine land!

19. Thus was the country named Chine (China), which it beareth to this day.

20. Ah Sho'e said: Suddenly Chine's abundant speech ceased, and he answered only yea and nay to all things. And he was silent for seven years and eighty days. And then the angels from the second heaven came to him. After that he spake not as man (save in private), but he spake as the All Light, whereof the world knoweth the rest.

CHAPTER XXII.

1. Chine said: I am a man only. I am the All Light. My voice is that that liveth forever. Worship not Me; worship not man; worship All Light. I am Jehovih (Ormazd) Ever Present. Because of My abundance in man, man openeth the mouth; maketh words.

2. To know Me is to know all things; he who striveth to Me is My chosen. He who knoweth not Me proveth not Me; he who knoweth Me can not prove Me. To every self am I THE SELF of that self. To perfect that self which is in all selfs; such a man is one with Me. To travel on such a road; that is the right road.

3. Hear Me, O man! I come every three thousand years; I newly light up the world. My voice cometh upon the souls of men; thy All Highest is Me; thy all lowest is sin. Two things only set I before thee, O man; the Self that is Myself, and the self that is thyself. Which wilt thou serve? For hereon hangeth either thy resurrection or thy hell.

4. In the time of the first of ancients I asked the same questions. Whoso said: I will serve Thee, Ormazd, Thou All Self, he was My chosen. Whoso answered: I will serve the self of myself, was satan's. The latter went on the wrong road. Their trail was blood and death; war, their glory.

5. They fell upon My chosen; like tigers have they pursued them. I called out in the ancient days: Why persecute ye My chosen and destroy them? And they answered: They will not war; they serve not our king; they serve the King of kings; they practice peace; they uphold not our God.

6. But I stretched forth My hand from the second heaven; I bowed down to My virgin daughter, the troubled earth, Ma-lah. And I took My chosen and put them in Brahma's hand; and they were shapely and fleet-footed, valiant in love and good works. And I sent great learning unto the sons of men, and wisdom and peace and great rejoicing.

7. And Ma-lah blossomed and was fragrant as new honey, and cleanly and full of virtue. Her daughters hid the thigh and ankle; their full breasts were concealed and their words were of modesty.

8. Her sons were early to rise; producing abundance, and with songs of rejoicing, and with dancing. For My beloved shaped the ways of man; their progeny were as the sweet blossoms of an orchard; as the fragrance of red clover. I said unto them: Fear not; thy sons and thy daughters are a great glory to thee. Count thou the days of thy wife; and rejoice when the birth draweth near; for it is fruit of Me and of thee.

9. And they taught the little ones to clap their hands and rejoice; I made them for this. Sing, O earth! Hold up thy head. I said to My beloved, for Mine is a place of

glory and sweet love, sparkling with good delights. None could restrain them; like young colts, and young lambs at play; their capers were unceasing and most tender.

10. This was My good creation; the bliss of My chosen; this was My shapely earth in the days of peace; in the times of My chosen. Nor war, nor weeping was there; nor hunger nor thirst; nor famine; nor fields lying waste; nor sickness, nor evil diseases; nor cursing, nor swearing; nor lying; nor deceit; nor hardships and sore toil, nor any evil thing under the sun.

11. I, the All Light, Jehovih, have spoken. Will they hear My words? How will man judge Me, the Creator? Hath he gone amongst My beloved; and My upraised who obey My commandments? Hath he seen the beauty of the earth in the hands of My chosen?

12. O man! Thou fool! Thou goest into a dark corner and sayest: How dark! Thou goest before my enemies and sayest: What a vain creation! Or searchest amongst them that serve not Me, and sayest: Miserable world! Amongst them that hat Me, and sayest: How wickedly they kill one another. O that Jehovih had made a better creation!

13. Thou criest out: There is no happiness on the earth; all is misery and sorrow and pain and death! And this is thy standard, O man, to judge thy Creator! Thou sayest: There is no peace, nor delight, nor love, nor harmony on the earth!

14. Stubborn man! And contrary, and of narrow judgment! O that thou woulst stand in a clean place and high, and then judge! Hast thou measured My chosen, who have faith in My Person! Why hast thou treasured thyself? And put thyself uppermost of all things? Who hast thou found that denied My Person, but dwelt in lust and self-conceit?

15. Where is thy standard, save the All High? What is thy dispute about the all low? If I call Myself the All High art thou better pleased? If satan calleth himself the all low, wilt thou be satisfied? Or shall a man not speak of the All High? nor of the all low? Are there not such things? And shall they not have names?

16. Thy wicked hand riseth up against My chosen, to lay them in death. And when thou hast trailed the earth over in blood; and thy hand is wearied with destruction, and thy little ones have not wherewith to eat, thou prayest: O Father, help Thy little ones!

17. I have spoken.

CHAPTER XXIII.

1. Chine spake Jehovih's words, saying: They have sought after pleasure, and after thee, O earth! They have bowed down to men, to the king and the rich man, and now, behold their misery! The king said: Come serve me. Take thy spear, and thy strong bow and arrow, and come with me. I will show thee great delights; thou shalt slaughter my enemies; and I will give thee wages.

2. And they ran to serve the king; yea, they washed their hands in the blood of My innocent ones. Because the king said: Brave! Good slaughterer! Then were they pleased, highly recompensed!

3. I have said: Ye are on the wrong road; serve only Me, for I am Good Delights. Because ye slay one another, the land will not be tilled; ye are hungered and ragged. And they queried: What will Jehovih give for wages? More than the king?

4. Herein is thy weakness, O man! Thou sayest: Wait a little while, I will serve the man first; and afterward Jehovih.

5. What profit hast thou in thy brother's death? With all his treasures of gold and silver, what hast thou?

6. Behold, even they that choose Me and My ways, thou wilt not suffer to live in peace. Because they say: My Creator is my King; Him will I serve. The king saith: Go for them; slaughter them! They put Jehovih higher than me!

7. And thou sayest: It is a good and wholesome thing to serve the king, and kill his enemies. To serve my country by killing men, this is great glory!

8. But the voice of My beloved rose up to Me; My lambs fleeing before the wolves, and driven away from My goodly pastures. Behold Me, I am come to them, to the lovers of peace and virtue and loving kindness. My hand is stretched over them in great power; My word is given unto them, and is not dead.

9. I will call them together; they shall again hold up their heads and rejoice because of My Presence.

10. After Jehovih's voice came to Chine he traveled far and near; and because of his wonderful wisdom, men of great learning and even kings sent for him. And wherever he went he preached after the same manner, for peace and love, and against war.

11. For three years Chine traveled, proclaiming the Creator above all else in heaven and earth. And then he rested one hundred and forty days, sleeping like a young child, saying naught more than a child would say.

12. Then came a change upon Chine; he was as a new man in the world, and not as a God. And he rose up, saying: My Father, Creator of men, calleth me. I hear His voice. It is like a burning fire in my soul, moving me. Not with pain, but with great power. He saith:

13. Chine, My Son! Chine, My Son! My house is on fire! My little ones are burning. Go thou, Chine, to them. They are in fear and trembling; they know not what way to turn. The kings of the earth have outlawed them; they are hunted down, and are famished. Go thou to them, O Chine! For that end created I thee alive in the world; thou shalt be My Voice unto them.

14. Chine said: Jehovih saith: Who can overcome the fire when he remaineth in the house? He goeth outside where there is water. Call thou My people out of the house of My enemies. Give them a well spring of clean water; they are parched up and athirst. Say to them: Jehovih liveth! His love aboundeth; come ye to My fountains that are not dried up. Come ye and hear the covenant of My Son, Chine.

15. I swear to Thee, O Jehovih, Thou my Almighty! I will have no other God but Thee, Thou Creator! All Light, Most Glorious! Thou art my King! Holy, Holy, Ever Present! O my Captain, my All Highest Captain! I salute Thee in the Rising Sun! In the High Noon, most Mighty! And in the sweet Setting Sun!

16. I know nothing but Thee; to Thee I swear this my most solemn oath, O Jehovih! Call Thou up Thy angels, holy and most wise; Thy recording angels! They shall hear my covenant unto Thee, My Creator! They shall write it in the books of heaven, O my Master! And whilst the sun standeth, and the moon and the earth and the stars, my oath unto Thee shall stand up against me:

17. Thou only shalt be my King; Thou only shalt be my God and Heavenly Ruler. All other kings I forswear, and all other Gods and captains and great rulers: None of them will I bow down to or worship, forever. I, Chine, have spoken.

18. I swear unto Thee, Thou Great Spirit, Thou art my bond to the end of the world. I will not war nor abet war; to peace forever am I sworn. And though they impress me and torture me, or slay me outright, they shall not force me; I will not draw one drop of blood in any man or woman or child whom Thou hast created alive on the earth.

19. I swear unto thee, Thou All Person, Who art so large that the earth and sun and stars would not fill the hollow of Thy hand; to be like unto Thee, O Jehovih. Fair dealing unto all men, as Thou wouldst; good, forgiving and without anger, forever. And equally in all possessions with Thy chosen, O Jehovih.

20. To raise them up that are cast down; to deliver the afflicted and helpless; to render not evil, nor the fruit of anger, unto any man, forever, O Jehovih. And good to them that abuse me; and in my actions steadfast in Thy course, my Creator.

21. In my blood do I covenant with thee; by the veins in my flesh make oath forever. To wed not out of Thy Order, the Hi-tspe. Blood of the blood of Thy chosen shall be my heirs and my heirs after me, forever.

22. Hear me, O Jehovih: I make a new covenant; it shall be written upon the firmament of heaven. I will do good with all my might; the tears of the suffering poor shall be as scalding blood in my veins; I will not sit down and rest, nor take my ease, nor hold possessions whilst they are in want.

23. Prick me, O my Father in heaven; sharpen my conscience keener than a sword; drive me to labor for the poor and afflicted, give me no rest, but whilst I am doing good unto them.

24. O that my covenant were set with swords, pointing every way; that I could find no peace but in serving Thee, my Creator, Ormazd. And I were pure and strong and wise and swifter than life and death, and as unfailing.

25. And that my oath reached unto thy chosen, and they heard me; that my voice was sweet unto them, and enticing like an early love.

26. That they would come forth from their hiding places, Thy faithful children, and be not afraid.

27. I would go to them as a lover, and bow my head down to them for their long suffering, and their faith unto Thee, Jehovih.

28. As a father that has lost his son and found him again, I would take them in my arms, Thy worshippers, Thou All One, Everlasting Spirit.

29. As a rose-bush trampled in the mire; how they have been scourged, O Jehovih. Poor unto death, and ragged and scattered. But I would wash them clean, and give them new soil; their voices in song and praise should gladden the whole earth.

CHAPTER XXIV.

1. The great cities of the ancients in Jaffeth were destroyed by Joss (Te-in) and his evil spirits, who inspired mortals to war. And for the most part, it was a land of ruins, but thousands of cities, standing beside the broken walls, were spread over the entire breadth of the land.

2. Jehovih spake to Chine, saying: Now is a good time for My chosen. Behold My enemies, the idolaters; know thou them by their soldiers. They are weak now. They pant with the labor of their great battles. Let My people come out of their quarters and hold up

their heads.

3. Say thou unto them, O Chine, there is no Joss, no Ho-Joss, no Te-in, no Po, no Po-Te-in, to make you afraid. And whilst the enemy resteth, bid My sons and daughters arise! They shall inhabit the land that is spoilt, and cause it to bloom and bring forth abundantly. Call up My outlawed race; the enemy is sick of his wounds; his heart is ashamed and disconsolate, he is cast down.

4. Chine went to A'shong and gathered up many converts, descendants of the Faithists, the pure Brahmins, the line of Zarathustra, the people of the Great All One, who accepted not Gods and Lords. And he established them, and invented plows and mattocks for digging the ground; for these implements had been lost and destroyed, hundreds of years, and no man knew how to make them.

5. Chine said unto them: This is a good philosophy; wait not till ye are well fed and clothed before ye bow down your heads at the altar of Jehovih. When ye have prayed and sung before Him, then go forth into the field to work. And He will bless you.

6. Remember the heathen, they say: First provide the natural body, and then the spirit. But I say unto you, Jehovih created them both together. And he who saith: First provide the natural body, never looketh to his spirit afterward.

7. In all things give ye precedence to the spirit; as the Creator is over all His works, so should the spirit of man be over man's works, and over his corporeal body also.

8. Herein laid the foundation of the wisdom of your forefathers, the Zarathustrians. For the heathen and idolater, who labor for self, what are they but servants unto the flesh?

9. Some people labor for the raising of the spirit, which is purity, and love, and goodness, and justice; such people are on the right road to become a great people. But when they strive, every man for himself, such people are beginning to fall.

10. Her boundaries may be large, and her people increasing, but she hah a canker worm within, that soon or late will let her down suddenly.

11. Two extremes meeting are always dangerous: great wealth, and extensive poverty. It not only devolveth on the rich to give their substance to the poor, but they shall go amongst them, teaching them and lifting them up.

12. He who doeth not this, consider how vain it is for him to pray to Jehovih. His prayer riseth not upward. Let him himself first answer the poor. This is the opening of his own soul, so Jehovih can reach him.

13. Remember thou that all men have judgment, and that they should be perfected to see things from their own standpoint, and not from thine. Consider, then, how unjust it is to foist thy opinions on any man, uncalled for.

14. Chine established families of the chosen, but limited them to two hundred; and to each family he gave one priest. But he gave privilege to four thousand people to dwell in one city.

15. Chine said: Ye have been afflicted with Gods; I was sent into the world by the Creator to deliver you unto liberty in the family. I am only a man. I have no authority in myself. Jehovih, the Creator, dwelleth freely in me. Ye can attain the same.

16. Because He is within me, this shall be called Chine-land. There is a time for this. My name is as a post to mark the time when the Creator began His temple of peace, which shall extend over all these people.

17. Jehovih saith: Why will man be vain of himself? Verily have I not created one man on

the face of the earth that is himself. He is made up of all oddities, soul and body. Consider his flesh; whence he received it and sustaineth it. Not so much as one hair on his head is of his own making; neither is it made out of new material, but hath been used over and over forever.

18. Even so is his mind not his own; not even his simplest thought; but he is made up of borrowed things from beginning to end, for so I created him.

19. He imagineth I, Who created him, am nothing; but even his imagination he picked up from someone else. He gathereth a little here, and a little there, and then proclaimeth what he knoweth.

20. Chine said: One man saith: I am normal; neither angels or mortals rule over me! Yet he hath only boasted as a crazy man, who will say the same thing. Another saith: Behold my wisdom! the highest of angels course through me. Yet he knoweth not whether it be true or not. Neither do any of them know the fountain head. For if an angel say it, the angel himself is made up of borrowed knowledge.

21. Chine said: I saw a great mathematician one day, and he said: There are no Gods, nor Lords, nor angels, nor any All Person. Everything is void. He showed me a book he had, and I asked: Who made the book? He said: I made it; nay, I made not the cloth, nor the binding; I mean, I made the philosophy that is in the book; nay, I made not the philosophy, but found it; nay, it was not lost; I mean I led myself to find the philosophy; nay, a man cannot lead himself; I mean that I searched and found what was new to me. So, but little of that book was his, after all.

22. I saw three angels standing beside that man, and they were laughing at him. If I had asked the angels, they might have said: Nay, the thoughts were ours. And had I looked further I had seen angels back of them, claiming the same things. Yet, even such are not the highest.

23. Wherefore I say unto you: All things come from an All Highest, name ye Him what ye will. He who saith: Jehovih spake to me: He is the nearest the mark of all. For all good knowledge that cometh to man, is Jehovih's word to that man. Whether it come by an angel or by another man, or by the commonest corporeal thing, it is nevertheless from the All Highest.

24. For which reason bow ye not down in worship to man nor angels, but only to the Highest, Jehovih, for He is the Figure-head and Pinnacle of the All Highest conceived of. And in contradistinction, the all lowest; the foot of the ladder, call ye darkness and evil, and wickedness, and sin, and death and satan.

25. Attribute not to men or angels this or that, for they themselves are not first causes nor responsible but in part; but attribute all good, high, best and wise things unto Jehovih; and all evil, dark, wicked, low things to satan.

26. By these terms ye shall make plain to one another what ye mean; and it is an easy matter to look into your own souls and comprehend as to which of these two ye most incline.

27. The soul may be likened unto a vine, which can be trained either upward or downward. And if ye desire to know if a vine be up or down, look ye for the fruit, and not to the fragrance. Some men pray much, but as to good works they are like a vine without fruit, but with plenty of fragrance.

CHAPTER XXV.

1. Chine said: One man waiteth till he is rich, before helping the poor; another man waiteth for the angels to inspire him, and give him wonders, before he teacheth the unlearned; another waiteth for the multitude to join in first; and yet another waiteth for something else. Beware of such men; or put them in scales where straw is weighed.

2. The sons and daughters of Jehovih go right on. They say: It is the highest, best! I will go in! Though I do not accomplish it, yet I will not fail (my part).

3. Consider ye the foundation of things at all times. Jehovih saith: I created all the living to bring forth their own kind. Be ye perceiving as to whom ye marry, considering as to the All Highest inspiration common to your choice.

4. Neither judge ye the All Highest inspiration of any man or woman by their words, but by their works. For the raising up of the world shall be mostly accomplished by the fruit of judicious marriage.

5. Chine said: I declare a bondage unto men that they know not of, for it belongeth in the next world; which is the begetting of selfish offspring in this world. For whilst their heirs are in darkness they themselves cannot rise in heaven.

6. And like unto this, I also declare a glory in heaven to them that wed in self-abnegation, who do good unto others constantly and with delight; for they bring forth heirs to glorify Jehovih in good works also.

7. To this end was the mark of the circumcision given unto your forefathers, lest the Faithist women be led astray by idolaters. And yet, with all precautions, many fell, being tempted of the flesh. And their heirs descended lower and lower in darkness, until they lost sight of the All Person, and believed not in Him.

8. The hand hard with toil will insure a better heir than the dimpled hand of a proud woman. The latter hath a soul of passions and her offspring will have souls like a mixture of gall and sugar; though they be sweet, they will prove to be bitter in time to come.

9. Consider thy heir; show him a house with a head, orderly. That he may grow up understanding the discipline of earth and heaven.

10. The father shall be master in all things; and the mother shall be vice-master in all things, to rule in his absence.

11. For each family shall be a kingdom of itself; but no one shall be a tyrant, though he have precedence in all things.

12. Sit not down by the table to eat until all stand about; and when they are seated, thou shalt say: In Thy praise, O Jehovih, receive we this, Thy gift; be Thou with us unto Thine own glory, forever, amen!

13. For the chief virtue of the words lieth in the discipline of the young mind; holding him steadfast after the orderly manner of the angels in heaven. And because he repeateth it with thee, he learneth to honor thee with good rejoicing.

14. And when the sons and daughters are yet small, thou shalt teach them to work; inspiring them above all things not to fall into idleness, which lieth at the borders of hell.

15. But over-task them not, nor give them pain; remembering they are to be thy glory, which Jehovih bestowed unto thee to be in thy keeping, not for thy self-aggrandizement, but for their own delights and holy pleasures.

16. For they shall sing and play, and clap their hands and rejoice and dance, for these are their thanks unto the Creator; and the earth shall be glad because they came into the world.

17. Remember thou that labor shall be delight, and toil a great delight; to have it otherwise to thy children and to thyself is to prostitute man to be as a beast of the field. But thou shalt bring them into groups, and their labor shall be a frolic and full of instruction.

18. And even thy little ones shall learn that thou art but a brother, an elder brother, and one of the same Creator's children; teaching them that one who hordeth and keepeth things in his own possessions is as a cannibal that eateth his kindred, flesh and blood.

19. Above all things thou shalt teach them to keep holy and pure the body created withal; for herein lieth health and strength. To be foul is to be sick, to be sick is to be foul. Behold the heathen and idolater, the feeders on flesh and blood; in the time they boast of health they stink as a carcass; their flesh is congested and puffed up, their breath like a kennel of dogs. How can their souls be pure or their understanding clear? They have made themselves a festering stink-house for the spirit to dwell in.

20. And they say: Bah! I see no Jehovih! I know no All Person! I deny the soul of things! Where is the spirit? I can not see it. Or the sound of its voice? I can not hear it. And there be a Great Spirit, let Him come before me! I would see Him. Yea, in their filthy bodies they say this. Let them be pure and they will understand the vanity of such words.

CHAPTER XXVI.

1. Jehovih said unto Chine: Now will I stir up the nations. Through thee will I show them the glory and dominion of My kingdoms.

2. For thou shalt walk without feet; write without hands; hear without ears; see without eyes; and thou shalt rise in the air as a bird; by thine own will go withersoever thou wilt.

3. And thou shalt bring down the thunder cloud, and at the sound of thy voice the rains shall fall.

4. And thou shalt say: Go away, ye clouds; and the sun will shine in the place thereof.

5. And thou shalt come to some that are hungered, and thy voice shall rise up to Me, and I will send down from heaven the food of heaven; and thy people shall eat thereof and be appeased.

6. And thou shalt stretch up thy hand over the dead that are ready for the furnace, and they shall come to life again and be made whole.

7. For these are the testimonies that thou art My servant, and hast kept my commandments:

8. In which thou shalt say to them: Behold me; I am but a man! Why fall ye down before the Gods and worship them. For I charge you, O all you people, ye shall not worship me nor call me but a man striving to do the will of my Father, the Creator.

9. For whosoever becometh one with Him; to such a man are many miracles possible; howbeit, I declare unto you they are not miracles in fact; but possibilities granted by Jehovih unto the upright who serve Him in act and truth.

10. Jehovih said to Chine: And when thou hast shown these things unto many, know thou thy time on the earth is finished. For I will cast thee in a trance, and the people shall

bewail, saying: Alas, he is dead! And they shall cover thee and cast thy body into the furnace in the way of the dead; and the fire shall blaze and consume thy body before them. But thou shalt have previously bid them watch by the furnace, for thou shalt gather together the elements of thy burnt body and restore them, and again inhabit it and go about, preaching before men.

11. Therefore get thee ready; declaring these prophecies beforehand, that they may be testified to by men, and so be recorded in the libraries of the kings and queens.

12. Chine related unto the congregations of Faithists, the true Zarathustrians, what Ormazd (Jehovih) had said, and many of them wept bitterly.

13. In years prior to this, when Chine had traveled and preached by the voice of Jehovih, he visited the kings and princes and rich men in many regions; and whilst he was thus speaking, rebuking them for their governments and for their possessions, they took no part against him. But afterward, when he was gone, the kings and queens and nobles said: Chine hath preached a dangerous doctrine; for he said: Thou shalt have no king but the Creator, Who is King over all. Will not this set our slaves against us? And if the people go into communities of their own, ignoring the king, where will the king find his revenue?

14. And there were priests of Dyaus and of other Gods, and speakers in temples (oracles) where the Gods wrote on sand tables. Besides these there were seers and prophets without number. And the kings, being on the alert, went into the matter, inquiring of the spirits, as to whether the doctrines of Chine were true.

15. And some of the spirits said: There is no All Person. Behold, we have visited the stars and the sun, and looked far and near, and we saw not any Creator, or All Person. There is no Great Spirit, save Te-in, who was a one-time mortal, but hath risen to all power in heaven and earth.

16. And other spirits said: There is nothing in heaven that we have not on earth. How shall we find Ormazd? Waste not your time with Chine and his doctrines; he will overthrow your kingdoms. Eat, drink and satiate your desires; for these are the sum and substance of all things in heaven and earth.

17. Tee-zee, king of A'shong, the capital city of the Province of Aen-Na-Po'e, who was withal a great philosopher, had previously heard Chine preach, and was greatly interested. Some time after this a magician, Loo Sin, visited Te-zee, who told the magician about the wonders of Chine. The magician listened to the king's story, and the king asked the magician whether he could himself, in addition to his sleight-of-hand, manifest wisdom in words, like Chine, and if so, how could it be attained?

18. Loo Sin, the magician, answered: Te-zee, O king, thou knowest not how thou hast embarrassed me, thy servant. For when we are young, and finding we have the natural powers for a magician, we go before an adept to be taught all the mysteries of the order; and here we take a most binding oath never to reveal by hint, or word, or mark, or written character, anything that will reveal any of our signs and mysteries, binding ourselves under great penalties, which I can not name to thee.

19. Know then, O king, I can answer all thy questions, and am desirous to serve thee, but what shall I do?

20. The king said: I, being king, absolve thee from thy oath. The magician said: Compared to my power, though I only beg from door to door, thy power, O king, is but as

chaff before the wind. In my subtle realms are the keys of all dominions. Not only do I and my craft rule over mortals, but over the spirits of the dead. My oath, then, is too great for thee to absolve, for I can not even absolve it myself!

21. Te-zee, the king, said: Since, then, thou canst not do all things, and especially, absolve an oath, thou art not sufficient for me to deal with. Loo Sin, being desirous of earning something, said: As for that, O king, I tell thee I can not reveal all, for the virtue of my art dependeth much on its secrets and mystery. Nevertheless, as I am very poor, I might reveal an index to thee, to which, if thou wouldst apply thyself diligently, thou mightest attain the remainder.

22. The king thereupon commanded him to perform before him, agreeing to award him according to the decree of the fates (spirits). And Loo Sin at once fell to work, performing wonderful feats, such as causing the tables, and seats, and desks, to move about and to roll over; and to cause voices to speak in unseen places. He also changed rods into serpents, and caused birds to sit on the king's shoulder; and he changed water into wine, and also brought fish and laid them on the floor at the king's feet.

23. The king said unto him: All these things I have witnessed from my youth up. Show me now, whilst thou remainest here, how thou canst see into my neighbor's house?

24. The magician said: Yea, O king; but for that feat it is necessary to enter the state of the holy ghost (trance), and the price is expensive!

25. The king said: I will pay thee; therefore enter into the state of the holy ghost.

26. Loo Sin turned up his eyes and gave a shudder, as one dying, and having stretched himself on the floor, bade the king question him.

27. The king said: Here is chalk; mark thou on the floor the character which is on the top of my tablet, on the left of the throne! Thereupon the magician marked correctly. And now again the king tried him as to his power to see without his eyes, and in far-off places; and, having proved him in many ways, the king said: Canst thou also show the spirits of the dead?

28. Loo Sin said: Of a truth I can, O king. But that requires me to enter the sublime state of creation, and is even yet more expensive!

29. The king said: Have I not said I will pay thee? Go to, then, enter thou the sublime state of creation at once!

30. Loo Sin then went into a dark corner and laid himself down on the floor, and then swallowed his tongue, and was motionless and still, like one that is quite dead. Presently a light like a thin smoke rose up from the body and stood a little aside, and a voice spake out the the light, saying:

31. Who art thou that callest up the spirits of the dead? Beware! He whose body lieth stiff and cold beside me, is one of the heirs of the immortal Gods! What wouldst thou, man of earth?

32. The king said: Who art thou? The voice answered: I am Joss, Te-in! Ruler of heaven and earth! The Great Spirit personified! Creator of all things!

33. The king in satire said: Thou art welcome, O Te-in! I am one of the most blest of mortals, because thou hast made my place a holy place.

34. The spirit then assumed mortal shape and stood before the king, even whilst the magician's body lay on the floor in sight also. The spirit said: What question is it troubleth thee, O king? Speak thou, and I will answer thee, for I am All Wisdom and

Truth personified.

35. The king said: Why hast thou not appeared to me before this? Why have I been left in the dark as to thy real existence? Answer thou me this, for it is the foundation on which I desire to rest many questions.

36. The spirit said: My son, Te-zee, I have been with thee from thy youth up, watching over thee, for thou shalt become the greatest king in all the world. Yea, there are great works for thee to do. And if thou desire to extend thy kingdom, or to gain great battles, I will show thee the way. Or if thou desire another woman to wife I will find her for thee.

37. The king said: Though art a great heavenly ruler, I fully believe, but thou answered not my question. Moreover, thou questioned me about my kingdom and about another woman to wife, and these things are not what I desire of thee. And for the matter of women I have not yet one wife; consequently I desire not another.

38. The spirit said: Who sayest thou I am? The king replied: I am at a loss to know if thou art a fool or a devil; and I say that I have either seen one like thee, or else thee, through many a magician. But, alas, there all knowledge endeth.

39. The spirit said: Thou saidst thou would pay what the fates decreed. Hear me then, O king; thou shalt give to Loo Sin four pieces of gold. And after that I will explain all things to thee.

40. The king then cast the four pieces of gold to Loo Sin, and demanded the knowledge as promised. The spirit then said: And on thine oath, thou wilt not reveal?

41. The king said: I solemnly swear to reveal naught of what thou teachest me. The spirit said: Know then, O king, I am Loo Sin, the magician! By long training, the magician attaineth to go out of his own body in spirit, and to appear in any form or shape desired. Wilt thou try me? The king said: Show me the spirit of Ha Gow-tsee.

42. The spirit walked back to the body of Loo Sin, and presently returned before the king, looking like the spirit of Ha Gow-tsee. The king said: It is like the king! The spirit answered: Here then, O man, is the end of philosophy. Behold, I am Loo Sin, also. Some men are one spirit, some two, some three, and some four, to one corporeal body. And yet there is but one person in fact.

43. The king asked: What becometh of the spirit when the corporeal part is dead? The spirit answered: One of two things is possible to every man: his spirit will either dissolve into non-existence, and be scattered and void like the air of heaven, like the heat of a fire that is burnt out; or else it will reincarnate itself in the body of a child before it is born, and, so, live over again.

44. Thus came all people into the world. A child that is still-born is one in whose body no spirit re-incarnated itself. There are no new creations. The same people live now on earth that always lived on it; nor will there be any others. They go out of one body when it is old and worn out; and then enter a young one and live over again and again, forever. Nor is there more nor less unto any man, woman or child in all the world.

45. The king asked: What, then, is the highest, best thing for a mortal man to do during life.

46. The spirit said: To eat and drink, and sleep and rest, and enjoy begetting numerous offspring.

47. The king said: How long would a spirit live if it did not reincarnate itself? The spirit said: If the mortal body is burnt to ashes, then that is the time; if the body be buried, and

rot, and return to earth, then that is the time; if the body be embalmed, and keepeth well, the spirit goeth back in the embalmed body and remaineth till that body is moldered into dust, or burnt to ashes, then is the spirit set free, and ready to either re-incarnate itself or to dissolve and disappear forever.

48. The king asked: As it is with thee, is it the same with all magicians? The spirit said: Thou hast only given four pieces of gold; if thou wouldst have more, the price is expensive. The king said: I have told thee I would pay whatever the fates decreed; therefore, proceed. The spirit said: It is even so with all magicians. The king asked: Show me now that thou canst preach like Chine.

49. The spirit said: Thou shalt ask me questions, and I will preach on them.

50. The king asked many questions, and the spirit spake thereon. Finally the king said: That is sufficient; I will pay thee; go thou thy way. As for thy preaching and thy doctrines, they are nothing. Now will I send and find another magician; for out of a counsel with many I shall arrive at the truth.

CHAPTER XXVII.

1. Te-zee, the king, sent for another magician, Wan-jho, who came and was commanded to exhibit his powers; but he also demanded a high price; which the king agreed to pay, and Wan-jho exhibited. First he caused a rose to come within a glass bottle whilst it was shut; then a small serpent he created out of a rod, and caused birds to come and sing to the king; then changed vinegar into water; then writing on a stone tablet without touching the tablet, and even whilst the tablet lay under the king's foot.

2. Now after he had exhibited many more feats of like character, he demanded his money, saying: The angels are gone; I can do no more. The king said: And hast thou not power to fetch them back?

3. Wan-jho said: How much wouldst thou give? The king answered: Three pieces of gold. And Wan-jho said: Ah, in that case, behold, they are come again! What wouldst thou? The king commanded him to show the spirits of the dead, so he might converse with them.

4. Wan-jho went into the same place where Loo'Sin had exhibited, and, laying down, cast himself in the death trance. Presently an angel, robed in white, appeared, and came and stood before the king, saying: Most mighty king, what wouldst thou? Behold me, I am the Goddess, Oe-tu Hent, come from my throne in high heaven. And be thou desirous of conquest in war, or to attain great riches, or more wives, most beautiful, then will I by my most potent will give unto thee.

5. The king said: I am blest, O Goddess, because thou hast come to see me. But alas, none of the things thou hast mentioned suiteth me. I desire nothing as regardeth this world. Give me light as to the place in heaven where dwelleth king See Quan?

6. The spirit said: Were he thy friend or thine enemy? The king answered: He was my deadly enemy. The spirit said: Because I asked thee, is he thy friend or thine enemy? for I saw one See Quan in hell, writhing in great agony. And yet I saw another See Quan in paradise. So, then, I will go and fetch him that is in hell.

7. The spirit passed over to the corner, and presently returned, saying: O, O, O, O, O! Horrors! Demons! Hell! and such like, pretending to be in torments, as if it were See

Quan in torments.

8. After this the king called for many different spirits, whether they had ever been, or whether fictitious, and they came all the same. Finally Te-zee, the king, said: Bring me now the wisest God in heaven, for I would question him. So, the spirit went again toward the corner, and then approached, saying: Man of earth! Because thou hast called me I have come. Know thou when I come, and I decree four gold pieces to Wan-jho my prophet.

9. The king said: Most just, God! I will pay him. Tell me now whence cometh man, and what is his destiny?

10. The spirit said: First, then, the air above the earth is full of elementary spirits; the largest are as large as a man's fist, and the smallest no larger than the smallest living insect on the earth. Their size denoteth their intelligence; the largest being designed for human beings. These fill all the air of the earth, and all the space in the firmament above the earth; they have existed from everlasting to everlasting, for they were without beginning.

11. Now whilst a child is yet within the womb, one of these elementaries entereth in the child, and straightway there is the beginning of the man. And in like manner are all things produced which live on the earth.

12. The king asked: Before such time when man beginneth, whilst these elementaries are floating about, do they know anything? The spirit said: Many of them have great wisdom and cunning, and are withal great liars and thieves and rascals. Knowest thou one Loo Sin, a magician? The king answered, Yea. And then the spirit said: Well, Loo Sin is obsessed by the elmentaries, and they are all great liars, pretending to be spirits of the dead! As for myself, I am a most virtuous Goddess, from the highest heavenly spheres. I tell thee, O king, these elementaries are the curse of the world; they are anxious to be born into life, so they may have souls, and they inspire mortals to paternity and maternity that they may have an opportunity for incarnation.

13. The king said: Thou hast answered well, O Goddess. I will pay according to thy decree. And thereupon the spirit departed. King Te-zee sent for another magician, Hi Gowh, of the rank of priest, and having bargained with him as to his price for exhibiting, commanded him to proceed.

14. Hi Gowh then exhibited after the same fashion as the others, doing great wonders. And him also did the king command to show the spirits of the dead. Hi Gowh complained about the price; but being assured by the king that his demands would be paid, the magician went into the same corner and cast himself in the holy ghost (trance); and, presently, a spirit appeared, saying: Greeting to thee, O king! Whether thou desirest conquest, or riches, or more women, name thou to me, and I will give abundantly. Know thou I am the spirit of the great Zarathustra.

15. The king said: Great Zarathustra, thou art most welcome. But, alas, none of the things thou has named are what I desire. Tell me, O Zarathustra, what is the origin and destiny of man?

16. The spirit said: First, then, O king, in days long past, the sun turned round so swiftly it threw off its outer rim, and the rim broke into a million pieces, flying every way, and these pieces are the stars and the earth and the moon.

17. And for millions of years the earth was only a stone, melting hot; but it cooled off in time; and the outer stones on the earth were oxidized, and this made moss; then the moss died; but the spirit of the moss re-incarnated itself, and this made grass; and the grass died; but the spirit of the grass lived and re-incarnated itself, and thus made the trees.

18. Then the trees died, but the spirit lived, and it re-incarnated and became animals; and they died, but their spirits lived and re-incarnated and became man. After that the spirit no longer re-incarnateth itself, but floateth upward into peace, and resteth for a long time, when it finally mergeth back into the sun and is extinct, like a lamp burnt out.

19. The king asked: How, then, is it with thyself? The spirit replied: I was the original Sun God, that came away from the sun to take charge of this world. It is in my keeping. The king asked: Who, then, is the All First that still stayeth with the sun?

20. The spirit answered: Because thou asketh many questions, O king, thou shalt pay more money. The king assured the spirit that the money, to any amount, would be paid: whereupon the spirit said: Ahura-Ormazd was the original of all; but when the sun threw off its surface Ahura-Ormazd was thrown into pieces, one piece going to every star, save the earth, and I came here of my own accord, because it was larger and better than any other world.

21. The king dismissed the spirit and the priest, and sent for another, a magician also of the rank of priest, Gwan Le. And Gwan Le, being assured that his price would be paid, proceeded to exhibit also. And he performed feats even like the others. Then the king commanded Gwan Le to call the spirits of the dead.

22. The priest apologized about the expense of the death trance (holy ghost power), but being further assured that his demands would be paid, he went into the corner and cast himself into the swoon, stiff and cold.

23. Presently an angel appeared, saying: Behold me, O king, I am Brahma. And if thou desire conquest in war, or greater riches, or more women, I will grant unto thee. I can tell thee of hidden treasures, and of rich mines, and of women greatly to be desired. Also I can tell thee how thy armies can overcome thy enemies with great slaughter.

24. The king said: I am delighted, O Brahma. But I desire nothing of which thou hast mentioned. Tell me of the origin and destiny of man.

25. The spirit said: Know then, O king, all things alive have two parts, the corporeal and the spiritual; all dead things are but one, which is the spirit. Thou, O king, wert first a stone, a very large stone; then when it moldered into dust thy soul went into silver, a very large piece; but when the silver rusted away, thy soul went into gold; and when the gold was worn away, thy soul began to run into animal life, then into a low order of man, then into the high order of man, as thou now art. Thus came man up from the beginning, re-incarnating himself over and over, higher and higher and higher. And when he is perfected in spirit as thou art, he never more returneth to re-incarnate himself. The king asked: What doth the spirit after leaving this world? The spirit replied: Thou shalt then meet thy sexual partner, thy soul-wife; and shall do nothing ever after but have sexual indulgence, peopling the spirit realms with delightful spiritual offspring.

26. The king said: It is well; thou hast a wonderful doctrine. Thereupon the spirit departed, and the priest also. And the king sent for still another priest, Tseeing, A Brahman prophet. And the king asked him: What seest thou for thy king?

27. The priest said: By the rites of my order I cannot disclose any of the secrets of heaven or earth until thou hast paid the price of indulgence, which is two pieces of gold. So the king paid him. Tseeing said: And thou desire riches, or success in war, or new wives, speak thou and I will grant unto thee according to the price. The king said: Alas, Tseeing, I desire none of these indulgences; tell me the origin and destiny of man, for I would learn why I am, and the object and end.

28. Tseeing said: The first of all was Brahma, which was round like an egg. Then Brahma broke open, and the shell was in two halves, and one-half was the sky and the other half was the earth. Then Brahma incarnated himself in the earth, but he came not up as one only, as he expected, but he came up in ten millions and one million parts, and every part was a living thing, a tree, or a plant, or a fish, or a bird, or a beast, or a man. And this is all there is or was or ever shall be.

29. But Brahma looked over the world and he saw that some men were good and some evil. And he said: I will separate the good from the evil. And that justice might be done he called all the nations and tribes of men before him. And when they were come he said unto them:

30. Whoever delighteth in the earth, it shall be his forever. And though he die, his spirit shall have power to re-incarnate itself into another unborn child, and so live over again, and so on, forever. And he shall have great indulgence in the earth, in eating and drinking, and with women, and in all manner of delights, for they shall be his forever.

31. But whosoever delighteth in spirit shall be blest in spirit. He shall not, after death, re-incarnate himself and live over again, but shall dwell forever in heaven and have heavenly delights. But since heavenly delights are not after the manner of earthly delights, then shall the spiritual chooser not live like earth-people.

32. But he shall live secluded, and shall torment his flesh with fastings and with castigations. Neither shall he marry or live with woman, nor beget children, nor have any indulgence on the earth whatever, save merely to live, for the earth is not his, nor is he of the earth. And the more he tortureth the flesh, the higher shall be his bliss in heaven.

33. Now, when Brahma had stated the two propositions unto the children of the earth, he further added: Choose ye now which ye will, for after ye have chosen, behold, there is the end. For ye that choose the earth shall be of the earth, even unto all succeeding generations. But whoso chooseth heaven, to him and his heirs it shall be final, and forever.

34. Thereupon mortals made choice, and lo and behold, nearly all of them chose the earth. But in thousands of years and millions of years afterward Brahma repented of his former decree, for he saw the earth become too full of people, and they were sinful beyond bounds. And Brahma sent a flood of waters and destroyed ten thousand million times ten millions of them. And he sent Zarathustra into the world to give new judgment.

35. Zarathustra opened the door of heaven anew, saying: Whoever after this chooseth Brahma, and will torture his flesh, and hate the earth, and live away from the world, him will I save from the earth and from hell also, for I am very efficient and influential with the Creator.

36. Such then, O king, is the origin and destiny of man. Some are born for the earth forever, and some are born for heaven. Nevertheless, the way is open unto all, to choose which they will, earth or heaven.

CHAPTER XXVIII.

1. Te-zee pursued his researches for a long while, and with many prophets, magicians, seers and priests. Afterward he said:

2. All is vanity; all is falsehood. No man hath answered me aright, as to the origin and destiny of man. Even the angels, or whatsoever they are, can only inform me of the things on earth; they only see as man seeth. And it may be true that these angels are nothing more than Loo Sin said, i.e. the spirit of the magician only. Because his body entereth this trance it seemeth reasonable.

3. Now, therefore, I will put a stop to these magicians and priests; they are of no good under the sun. So Te-zee issued a decree covering his own province, commanding magicians and priests to quit the province, under penalty of death. And they thus departed out of his dominions.

4. Now it so happened that in five other great provinces, the kings did precisely the same, and about the same time. And these were the provinces, to wit: Shan Ji, under king Lung Wan; Gah, under king Loa Kee; Sa-bin-Sowh, under king Ah-ka Ung; Gow Goo, under king Te See-Yong; and these provinces comprised the chief part of Jaffeth. And all these kings issued edicts after the same manner. So that the magicians and seers and priests were obliged to abandon their callings or go beyond these provinces, where dwelt barbarians.

5. Jehovih commanded Chine to go before king Te-zee, and when he had come, the king said unto him: Some years since I heard thee, and thou wert profound. I am delighted thou hast come before me again, that I may question thee.

6. Chine said: When thou heardest me before, the Great Spirit spake through me. Now I am well learned, and He commandeth me to speak of my own knowledge.

7. First, then, I am a man as thou art; yet every man hath a different work. Thou art king of this province, and I am told, moreover, thou art good and wise. I hope thou art. Otherwise my words will not please thee. As for myself, I was sent into the world to mark out this land and name it Chine-ya (Chine-land), and to establish anew those that accept the Great Spirit. For Chine'ya and her people shall remain a different country and different people from all the world.

8. Know then, O king, I come not in vain-boasting that I, Chine, am much or can do much; on the contrary, I say unto thee, I am one of the weakest of men; and yet I have more power than any other man in the world. And yet, mark thee, of myself is there nothing whereof to boast. For I am but as a tool in the hands of Jehovih (Ormazd), and not I myself do anything, but He through me.

9. I look upon thee and see thou hast been questioning magicians and priests, and that thou art unsatisfied. Know then, O king, this is thine error, in not magnifying thy judgment.

10. Thou hast worked with magicians who are under the power of angels of the first resurrection, and even angels below them.

11. All such angels teach on their own individual understanding; as wandering individuals they go about. And their miracles are of the same order, merely individual miracles.

12. He, Whom I teach, worketh miracles, not in a small corner but in the affairs of kingdoms and nations; not through magicians only, but through kings and queens, and even through common people. Thou thyself art an instrument of His hand.

13. Behold, in the same time thou issuest thy decree against magicians and asceticism, even in that same time five other great kings do the same thing! This is a miracle indeed! No man can counterfeit His miracles. Neither flatter thyself that such matters occur by accident. They do not occur by accident; but by Jehovih. For His angels in the second resurrection are organized, and work in mighty armies.

14. Te-zee said: Thou art great, Chine; or else thy sudden philosophy turneth my brain! Go on! How shall we know, first, that there are angels who are really the spirits of the dead? Second, how shall we distinguish betwixt the first and second resurrections?

15. Chine said: Only by seeing and hearing with the natural eyes and ears, and with the spiritual eyes and ears, can any man attain to know anything either on earth or in heaven. When these senses are pure and clear, then a man knoweth that the spirits of the dead do live. For I declare, O king, of a truth, that the spirit of my body hath emerged from my body on many occasions, sometimes going subjectively and sometimes objectively. Neither is this a special creation to me only; but it is that which thousands and tens of thousands can attain to by discipline.

16. Touching the first and second resurrections, know thou, O king, spirits that dispose individual things, or earthly things; or propose riches or personal gain, or marriage, descanting to this man or that man as to what is good for him as an individual; spirits giving great names, professing to be this or that great person long since dead; all such are deceivers and have not advanced beyond the first resurrection. They deny the I Am, the Great Spirit, , the All Person. Their highest heaven is re-engraftment on mortals, and the reveling in lust. They flatter thee, telling thee thou wert this or that great man in a former re-incarnation. They labor thee to make profit to their own magician; they are without truth or virtue, and of little wisdom.

17. The second resurrection cometh not to an individual as an individual; it cometh as an army, but not to an individual, but to a kingdom, a nation, a community. For as such angels belong to organized communities in heaven, so doth that organization work with virtuous organizations of mortals.

18. This is wisdom, O king; to get away from the individual self; to become one with an organization, to work with the Great Spirit for the resurrection of men. For as thou makest thyself one with many to this end, so laboreth the Father with thee and them. As thou keepest thyself as an individual self, so do individual angels come to thee as individuals.

19. Individual answereth to individual; the first resurrection to the first; the second to the second. Moreover, the All Person is over all, and worketh each in its own order, unto a great purpose.

20. Think not, O king, I am making a new doctrine; I am but declaring that which was also proclaimed to the ancients. And as many as came forward and had faith were called Jehovih's chosen people, because, forsooth, they chose Him.

21. Judge thou, then, whoso denieth the All Person is not of His order; neither hath such an one the light of the Father in him. But he who hath attained to understand that all things are but one harmonious whole, hath also attained to know what is meant by the

term, All Person, for He is All; and, consequently, Ever Present, filling all, extending everywhere.

22. In contradistinction from Him, two philosophies have run parallel, which are darkness and evil. One saith the All is not a person, being void, and less than even the parts thereof; the other saith the only All High is the great angel I worship, who is as a man, and separate from all things.

23. These comprise the foundation of all the doctrines in the world, or that have ever been or ever will be. The latter is idolatry, which is evil; the second, unbelief, which is darkness; and the first is faith, truth, love, wisdom and peace.

24. Under these three heads are all men classified by Jehovih and His angels. And they may be likened to three men looking across a field; one seeth a light and knoweth he seeth it; another hopeth he seeth it, but he only seeth a white leaf; but the third seeth nothing at all.

25. As a witness, therefore, the latter is worthless; the second is a circumstantial witness; but the first is positive, and standeth the highest and firmest of all. He knoweth his Heavenly Father. He seeth Him in the flowers; in the clouds, and in the sunshine; in the fruits and herbs; and in the beasts of the field, and in every creeping thing; and in the stars and moon and earth and sun. In sickness, in health, in sorrow and in rejoicing; verily he findeth Jehovih in all things; he knoweth Jehovih's eye and ear are forever upon him; and he walketh upright in fear, but in truth and faith and pride and rejoicing!

26. Te-zee, the king, asked: Tell me, O Chine, what is the origin and destiny of man?

27. Chine said: The Ever Present quickeneth him into life in his mother's womb; and he is then and there a new creation, his spirit from the Spirit Jehovih, and his body from the earth; a dual being the Father createth him.

28. His destination is everlasting resurrection; in which matter, man can have delightful labor as he riseth upward forever and ever.

29. The king asked: If Jehovih is all the time creating, will not the firmament become too full of angels?

30. Chine said: A thousand men read a book, and yet that book is no fuller of ideas than at first. The corporeal man is not divisible, and, so, filleth a place. Thought, which may be likened unto the soul, is the opposite of this. Ten thousand men may love thy flower-garden, yet thy garden is no fuller because of their love. Exalted souls in the upper heavens are without bulk and substance; and even so are the regions they inhabit, as compared to corporeal things.

31. The king said: I would that I were as thou art! For which matter, if thou wilt use thy wand and make me even half as wise, I will give away all my kingdom!

32. Chine said: Thou canst not bargain for Faith, or purchase it, as a coat or as sandals. And yet until Faith is attained there is no resurrection. No bird ever flew from its nest, without first having faith it could fly. And when thou hast Faith thou wilt cast away thy kingdom and choose heavenly treasures instead. Until thou hast attained Faith thou wilt retain thy kingdom. This is a judgment unto the rich man in the same way.

33. Riches and a king's kingdom may be likened to balls of gold tied to a man's feet in deep water; he cannot rise until he cutteth himself loose, and casteth away that which bindeth him. So, also, are men bound in spirit, and until they put their own hands to the matter there is no resurrection for them.

CHAPTER XXIX.

1. Te-zee, the king, said unto Chine: Because thou hast given me this great light, it seemeth to me I should issue a decree commanding all my people to accept thy doctrines.

2. Chine replied: O man! How short thou art in understanding our Father! Violence is His enemy. Such a decree would be no better than a decree establishing any other heavenly ruler. It would thwart itself. He cometh not with sword and spear, like the idol-Gods; He cometh with education, the chief book of which is the example of good works, and of peace and liberty to all.

3. Te-zee said: Thou reasonest well. Hear me, then, thou greatest of men; command me even as if I were the meanest of servants, and I will obey thee.

4. Chine said: O king, thou tormentest me with my own inability to make thee understand! Thou shalt not make thyself servant to any man, but to Ormazd, the Great Spirit.

5. The king said: Then I will put away my kingdom. But Chine said: Consider first if thou can best serve Him by doing this way or that way, and then follow thy highest light, and thou shalt not err.

6. The king asked: How, sayest thou, shall I put aside my kingdom and my riches and do as thou dost?

7. Chine said: Thou shalt be thine own judge. If I judge for thee, and thou follow my judgment, then am I bound to thee. Suffer me to have my liberty also.

8. Te-zee said: If the Great Spirit would give me thy wisdom, then would I serve Him. How long, sayest thou, a man shall serve Him in order to reach great wisdom?

9. Chine said: Suppose a man had several pieces of glass; some clear, some clouded with smoke and grease; how long, sayest thou, would it require to make them all clear alike? For such is the self in man; it cloudeth his soul; and when he hath put self away, then is his soul clear, and that is wisdom, for then he beholdeth the Father through his own soul; yea, and heareth Him also. And until he doeth this, he believeth not in His Person or Presence, no matter how much he professeth.

10. The king kept Chine many days, and questioned him with great wisdom and delight. One day Chine said to him: Jehovih saith to me: Go thou quickly unto the five other provinces of Chine'ya, and explain to the kings thereof Who I am. Chine added: Therefore, O Te-zee, I must leave thee, but after many days I will return to thee and exhibit to thee the testimony of immortal life.

11. The king provided camels and servants, and sent Chine on his way. And, after Chine was gone, Te-zee said to himself: Although I can not decree Chine's doctrines, I see no reason why I can not decree the extinction of Te-in and other idol-Gods. And thereupon he did as he thought best, prohibiting the priests from doing sacrifice to Joss (God), or Ho-Joss (Lord God), or Te-in, or Po, or any other ruler in heaven, save and except the Great Spirit.

CHAPTER XXX.

1. In course of time Chine completed his labor with the six kings of Jaffeth, and returned to Te-zee, to die.

2. At this time there had been established in different places more than a thousand families (communities) of Faithists, either through Chine or his followers, the chief

rab'bahs. And when Chine returned before the king, Te-zee, there came from every quarter of the world men and women to meet him and learn wisdom.

3. And all that were in any way sick or lame or blind or deaf he cured by pronouncing the word E-O-Ih over them. And persons who were obsessed with evil spirits he healed by permitting them to touch his staff. And many that were dead he brought to life; for he showed before men power to accomplish anything whatsoever. Yea, he rose up in the air and walked therein and thereon over the heads of the multitude.

4. And whilst he was up in the air he said unto the multitude: I will now come down amongst you and die, as all men do die. And ye shall suffer my body to lie five days, that the eyes may be sunken and black, showing that I am dead, of a truth.

5. And on the sixth day ye shall cast the body into the furnace and burn it to ashes. And the ashes ye shall take into the field and scatter this way and that, that no more of me is seen or known on the earth.

6. And on the seventh day, which shall be a holy day unto you, behold, ye shall witness in the field of my ashes a whirlwind, and the whirlwind shall gather up the ashes of my body; and my soul shall inhabit it and make it whole, as ye now see me, and I will break the whirlwind and descend down to the earth and abide with you yet other seven days, and then ye shall behold a ship descend from heaven in an exceeding great light, and I will enter therein, and ascend to the second heavens.

7. Neither shall any man or woman nor child say: Behold, Chine was a God. Nor shall ye build an image of me, nor monument, nor in any way do more unto me or my memory than to the meanest of mortals. For I say unto you, I am but a man who hath put away earth possessions, desires and aspirations.

8. And whatsoever ye see me do, or know of me having done, the same is possible unto all men and women created alive on the earth.

9. Remembering that all things are possible with Jehovih (Ormazd); and to Him only is due all honor and glory forever.

10. So Chine died, and was burnt to ashes on the sixth day, under the superintendence of king Te-zee, and the ashes were scattered in the field as commanded.

11. And on the seventh day, whilst the multitude surrounded all the place, a whirlwind came and gathered up the ashes in a small degree; and the ashes were illumed, and the soul of Chine went therein, and he burst the whirlwind and came down even at the king's feet.

12. And Chine said: Knowest thou who I am? And the king answered, saying: Of a truth thou art Chine. And because this hath come to pass I decree that this, thy native land, shall henceforth forever be called Chine'ya! And I will send unto other kings also, and they will decree the same thing.

13. Chine said: Even so, do thou. And since the Father hath allotted me seven days to remain with His chosen and with thee, O king, apprize thou, whom I will name to thee, to come and see me. And thereupon Chine told the king whom he desired to come.

14. And Chine walked about on the earth, even the same as before death, nor could any man tell by looking at him that he had passed through death. Nor were his clothes different, although they were made out of the ashes in the whirlwind.

15. On the last day that he was to remain, he called Te-zee and the persons he had selected, and thus spake unto them, saying:

CHAPTER XXXI.

1. My brothers and my sisters, in the name of the Great Spirit, hear me: These are Chine's last words, for the Father calleth me. Be ye attentive, that ye may remember my sermon; be also considerate, for I am no more nor less than one of you.

2. I was sent into the world to wall this great people around with Jehovih's hand. I have made you an exclusive people for three thousand years to come. I give unto you peace and liberty; I have drawn a veil over the bloody past, and taught you to love and respect one another.

3. Chine'ya shall become the most numerous nation in all the world; this is the miracle of the Father unto you. On the foundation I have given you, shall your doctrines be henceforth forever.

4. Be ye watchful against Gods (Josses) and Saviors, and especially wary of spirits of the dead who profess not the Great All Person.

5. All such are instigators of war and lust after earthly things.

6. Be ye exclusive unto one another; suffering not outside barbarians to come amongst you, especially to marry with my people.

7. Yet ye shall not war against them.

8. But it is lawful for you to build walls around about, to keep them away. And these walls shall stand as the Father's judgment against all people who molest you or injure you.

9. And every change of the moon ye shall renew your covenant, which was my covenant, with Jehovih.

10. Teaching it to your children, and commanding them to teach it to theirs after them, and so on forever!

11. Swearing ye unto the Great Spirit to ignore all heavenly rulers but the Creator, the I Am who is everywhere.

12. And though idolaters come amongst you, proclaiming their God, or their Lord, or their Savior, hearken not unto them. But nevertheless, persecute them not, nor injure them, for they are in darkness.

13. Neither be ye conceited over them; for your forefathers were like unto them.

14. The Father hath made a wide world, and fruitful and joyous, and He giveth it unto man's keeping.

15. Unto one people one country; unto another people another country, and so on, all the world over.

16. Chine'ya He giveth unto you, and He saith:

17. Be ye as brothers and sisters in this, My holy land.

18. Which in the ancients days was made to bloom as a flowery kingdom by my chosen, the Faithists of old.

19. But they were neglectful of My commandments.

20. Idolaters came upon them and destroyed them, and laid waste their rich fields; yea, the bones of My people were strewn over all the land.

21. But ye are now once more delivered, and ye shall make Chine'ya bloom again as My celestial kingdom.

22. And ye shall multiply, and build, and plant, and make this heritage, which I give unto you, as an example unto all peoples, of industry and peace and thrift.

23. And of the multitude that can dwell in one kingdom, manifesting love, patience and virtue.

24. And by your neglect of war and of war inventions, ye shall be a testimony of my presence in this day.

25. For the time shall surely come when I will put down all unrighteousness, and war, and idolatry, and I will be the All Person unto the whole world.

26. Chine hath spoken; his last words are spoken. Jehovih's ship of fire descendeth from His highest heaven!

27. Chine will rise up in this; and even so shall ye who are pure and good and full of love.

28. A light, like a great cloud, but brilliant, blinding with holy light, descended over all the field where the multitude were.

29. Many fell down in fear; and many cried aloud in great sorrow.

30. Then Chine went and kissed Te-zee, and immediately walked toward the midst of the field, and was lost in the exceeding great light.

31. And the light turned around like a whirlwind, and rose up, higher and higher, and then was seen no more.

32. Chine was gone!

33. And now were manifested the power and glory of Jehovih. Te-zee at once made special laws protecting all persons who rejected Gods, Lords and Saviors, but worshipped the All Light (Jehovih). Four other kings followed with the same edicts and laws.

34. The Faithists were safely delivered into freedom throughout Chine'ya.

[Thus end the revelations of the three contemporaneous Sons of Jehovih, Capilya, Moses and Chine.]

END OF THE BOOK OF THE ARC OF BON.

GOD'S BOOK OF BEN.

 Jehovih, or Jehovih said: And is equivalent to THE ALL HIGHEST LIGHT. The All Knowledge.

 Tae, or Tae said: The word TAE is equivalent to the words, THE HIGHEST GENERAL EXPRESSION OF MANKIND, or, THE UNIVERSAL VOICE WAS.

 Corpor, or corpor said: Corpor signifieth whatever hath length, breadth and thickness.

 Uz, or Uz said: Uz is equivalent to THE VANISHMENT OF THINGS SEEN INTO THINGS UNSEEN. Uz is also equivalent to WORLDLINESS, or, world's people.

 Esfoma, or, Esfoma said: Equivalent to THERE IS SOMETHING IN THE WIND; or, AS THINGS SEEM TO INDICATE. Signs of the times.

 Es, or Es said: Equivalent to, THE UNSEEN WORLD, also to, SPIRIT WORLD. The testimony of angels. Also spirit.

 Ha'k, or Ha'k said: DARKNESS, Ignorance is ha'k. Darkness may be corporeal or spiritual. Dark ages; or, a time of anarchy and false philosophy.

 Kosmon, or, kosmon said: THE PRESENT ERA. All knowledge in possession of man, embracing corporeal and spiritual knowledge sufficiently proven.

 Seffas, or seffas said: Seffas is equivalent to, THE ESTABLISHED, or, THE ENFORCED; as the laws of the land, or, the religion of the land, as established.

God said: These are the nine entities; or, according to the ancients, Jehovih and His eight children, His Sons and Daughters. And these are the same, which in all ages, poets and philosophers have made to speak as, THE FAMILY OF THE UNIVERSE. Through them I speak. Jehovih is the Light, that is, Knowledge. The manifestation of Knowledge in man is Jehovih. The growth of wisdom in man, as the earth groweth older, is the tree of light.

CHAPTER I.

1. God said: Before the arc of Bon the earth was rank.
2. The seed of the tree of light had been planted many times, but the rankness destroyed it.

3. In the time of the arc of Bon, the earth reached maturity.

4. Jehovih said: I gave to the inhabitants of the earth Capilya, Moses and Chine.

5. Through them the tree of light was made everlasting on the earth.

6. The great peoples then knew I was God, and my word was with them.

7. Es had spoken before that day, and man knew the presence of angels. But he heeded them not.

8. When my word came, man gave heed. Mine was with authority.

9. Emblems, signs and symbols were the letters of man's alphabet to lead him upward in wisdom.

10. Wisdom cometh not suddenly; as darkness goeth away, light cometh.

11. Great knowledge is all around about; to make man perceive it, is the labor of God.

12. Man said: I have looked in corpor, but found not knowledge.

13. Corpor said: Doth thy flesh know? Have thy bones knowledge? Is it in the blood?

14. Jehovih said: I am Knowledge; come thou to Me. I am the Unseen. Behold thyself, O man! Canst thou put thy finger on the place, and say: Here is knowledge? Hath wisdom bulk, and a place?

15. Ha'k said: Who knoweth the boundary of Light? Behold, I cannot hide away from Him. What is my small corner compared with the All Light of etherea?

16. Jehovih said: Think not that the vault of the firmament is nothing; for thither have I created etherean worlds, of sizes equal to the corporeal worlds; but they are independent of them. These are My kingdoms, prepared for the spirits of man and women and children, whom I bring forth into life on corpor. Nor are My etherean worlds alike in density or motion, but of different consistencies, that they may be suitable for the varied advancement of My children.

17. Man said: O World, give me light. Give me substantial knowledge, that I can put my finger on it and say: Here is the real!

18. Uz said: O man! Behold thy folly! All things thou seest and hearest and touchest are my abode.

19. Man said: How sayest thou? Thou art vanishment! All things perish; thou art that that is without foundation.

20. God said: Thou art both a flesh-man and an es-man. How hopest thou for thy flesh-talents to acquire substantial knowledge? All substance is evanescent. The real is the All Light, which thou canst not comprehend.

21. Man said: Why, then, this craving in my soul for all wisdom? Was my creation in vain?

22. Jehovih said: Because I created thee craving for light, thou goest forth searching. Thou art on a long road; to the summit of All Light, even Gods have not attained.

23. Man inquired: Why, then, was death created?

24. Uz said: Behold, even stones molder into dust. Wouldst thou have had a separate law for man?

25. Es said: I am within thy corpor; when thy corpor moldereth into dust, behold, I am the es-man, thy real self. I am thy spirit; and like a seed planted, I dwell within thy corpor.

26. Jehovih hath said: The corpor of man I created as a womb for the es of man. By death, behold, the es is born.

27. Around about My corporeal worlds I placed atmospherea; for, as the earth and other

corporeal worlds provide a womb for the spirit of man, so have I made atmospherea the substance for a womb for the souls of men.

28. Man said: If, when I am dead, I shall see the place, is not the germ of that light already in me? How am I made that I see, but see not this? Hear, but hear not this? If I am now dead to that which is to be, will I not then be dead to what now is? Give me light, O Father?

29. Jehovih said: To man I gave a corporeal body that he might learn corporeal things; but death I made that man might rise in spirit and inherit My etherean worlds.

30. Two senses gave I to all men, corporeal senses and spiritual senses; nevertheless, the twain are one person. A man with corporeal senses transcending, chooseth corporeal things; a man with spiritual senses transcending chooseth spiritual things.

31. Two kinds of worlds have I made: corporeal worlds and es worlds. He who desireth of corpor shall receive from corpor, for he is My Son, in whom I am well pleased. He who desireth of es shall receive from es, for she is My Daughter, in whom I am well pleased.

32. Kosmon said: Because man liveth on corporeal worlds, corpor is called son; but because man in spirit liveth in the es worlds, es is called daughter.

CHAPTER II.

1. God said: Hear me, O man. I am come to teach thee wise dominion.

2. Man said: The aborigines were free. Why shall man with more wisdom learn dominion?

3. Seffas said: My peace is forced peace; I am the light and the life.

4. Man inquired: Behold, the air of heaven is free. Can dominion come down out of nothing (as it seemeth) and rule over something (that is proven)?

5. How can God rule over solid flesh?

6. Uz said: O vain man! Do I not come in the winds of heaven and cast cities in epidemic? And yet man seeth me not.

7. I inoculate in the breath; I cast fevers in the bright sunlight, and yet no man seeth me.

8. Jehovih said: All power gave I to the unseen to rule over the seen.

9. Kosmon said: Why wilt thou, O man, search forever in corpor for the cause of things? Behold, the unseen part of thyself ruleth over the seen.

10. God said: Think not that the es worlds are less governed by system than are the corporeal worlds. The same Creator created all.

11. Behold, all things are in dominion. Thou wert in dark dominion before the time of Bon.

12. By mine own light gave I thee a dominion of light in the time of Bon.

13. Man inquired: If the unseen rule in man, what ruled the substance of man before he was made?

14. Jehovih said: I created all things, seen and unseen. My hand was forever stretched forth in work. I make and I dissipate everlastingly.

15. Behold, I make a whirlwind in etherea, hundreds and hundreds of millions of miles across, and it driveth to the center a corporeal world from that which was unseen.

16. I blow my breath upon the planet, and lo, man cometh forth, inquiring: Who am I, and

what is my destiny?

17. I send an elder brother of man, to teach him, and show him the light.

18. God said: Behold me, O man, I am an elder brother. I have passed through death and found the glory of the unseen worlds.

19. Jehovih gave to me, thy God, to have dominion over the earth and her heavens.

20. Man said: I have found truth in corpor; I know that I live; that trees grow and die.

21. This is true knowledge. Give me truth in regard to the unseen, that I may prove it truth.

22. Why, O God, givest thou the matters of heaven and earth in signs and symbols? Give me the real light, I want no figures.

23. God said: Thou art vain, O man. What, then, hast thou learnt? Canst thou tell why the grass is green, or why one rose is red and another white, or the mountains raised up, or the valleys sunken low? Or why a man was not made to fly as a bird, or live in the water like a fish? Whence came the thought of shame? Even thyself thou dost not comprehend, nor know of thine own knowledge the time of thy beginning. Thou knowest three times three are nine; and even this thou canst not prove but by symbols and images.

24. Nor is there aught in thy corporeal knowledge that thou canst prove otherwise, save it be thy presence; and even that that thou seest is not thy presence, but the symbol and image of it, for thou thyself art but as a seed, a spark of the All Light, that thou canst not prove to exist.

25. Man inquired: Where, then, is real knowledge possible to man? If my corporeal body and corporeal senses are evanescent and soon to fly away, how can I comprehend that which flieth not away, the spirit?

26. Yet I know a truth: I know that ten things are ten. This knowledge I can write down, and clearly teach to my brother. See, here are 10. This is exact science.

27. Esfoma said: Thou hast written but two strokes, and called them ten. Now, I will show thee ten. (Esfoma wrote: / / / / / / / / / / .) Yet, be not surprised, for now I will convict myself, also, inasmuch as I have deceived thee. I said I would show thee ten, and straightway, I made ten marks; but I should have written the word ten. Now, thou art wise! Nay, hear me further, for all I have spoken is false; for have I not tried to persuade thee that the one uttered word, TEN, was ten; wherefore, I should have uttered ten utterances. Thy supposed exact science is nothing, and thy supposed truth is only falsehood compounded and acquiesced in.

28. Jehovih said: Man's wisdom is but the experience of my creations, expressed to man's understanding in signs and symbols.

29. Man said: If I search for the real, shall I never attain it? Why, then, this craving? Is truth only that which flieth away?

30. Behold, thou hast said: Thou shalt love the Creator with all thy heart and soul! How can I love that which I can not comprehend?

31. Es said: Behold the utterances of the birds; and the skipping of the lambs at play! These are the expressed love they have for the Creator.

32. To rejoice because thou art created; to seek after exalted rejoicing, to cultivate the light of thy life; to turn away from dark things; these are to love thy Creator.

33. Man said: Why, then, if truth can not be found, and mathematics can not be proven but by things that are false in fact, I will search for goodness; I will shun sin. Is this not

wise?

34. God said: This is wise. But what are goodness and good works?

CHAPTER III.

1. Man said: Behold, I have struggled hard all my days, and met many crosses and losses. To provide my son that he shall fare better, this is goodness.

2. Uz said: Vain man! Thou understandest not the creations. Thy trials, thy losses and crosses, have built up thy soul. To provide thy son that he shall have no trials, nor losses nor crosses, will not be good for him. This will not be goodness. Give him experience.

3. Man said: Then I will teach him to sin not. To tell no lies; to steal not; to preserve his body pure. This is goodness.

4. Uz said: What canst thou do, that is not a sin? What canst thou teach, that is not falsehood?

5. Thou paintest a picture, and sayest: Behold, this is my farm! In this thou utterest falsehood. Thou givest a book to thy son, saying: Here is a good book! This is also false. Can paper be good? Thou sayest: Here is a book of wisdom! This is also false. Wisdom dwelleth not in paper.

6. How, then, canst thou teach thy son to tell no lies, since no man can speak without lying?

7. God said: One only is Truth, Jehovih. All else are false. One only is without sin, Jehovih. All else do sin every day.

8. Man said: To understand the laws of the universe, this is great wisdom.

9. Es inquired: What is a law of the universe?

10. Man said: That an apple will fall to the ground.

11. Uz said: By my hand the apple rotteth; the earth to the earth; but moisture flieth upward.

12. Jehovih said: By My touch the substance riseth up out of the earth and becometh an apple. Sayest thou, law is My opposite?

13. Man said: Why, then, there are two laws: one to make the apple rise up and grow on a tree, and one to make it fall down again.

14. Is this the creation? One law to pull one way, and another law in another way?

15. Can one law make one rose red, and another law make another rose white? One law make one man good, and another law make another man bad?

16. Jehovih said: I make no laws. Behold, I labor with Mine own hands. I am everywhere present.

17. Es said: All men may be likened unto green fruit, and on the way toward ripeness.

18. What more is man's earth life than a tree? It hath its winters and summers for a season, and then the end cometh.

19. Jehovih said: Behold, I created light and darkness, and one followeth the other.

20. I give dan to the earth for a season, and then I rain down ji'ay for a season. Even so created I the soul of man; to-day, light and joyous; to-morrow in gloom and melancholy.

21. Man inquired: How can I know if a thing be of God or if it be of nature? What is Jehovih more than natural law?

22. Corpor answered: What is nature, O man? Why wilt thou use a name for the members

of my body?

23. Behold, the trees are mine; the mountains and valleys; the waters and every living thing, and everything that liveth not; they are me.

24. Why sayest thou nature? Now I say unto thee, the soul of all things is Jehovih; that which thou callest nature is but the corporeal part.

25. Man said: I mean the laws of nature. Certain combinations under certain conditions give the same result. This is law.

26. God said: What hast thou gained by the word law, instead of the word Jehovih? If that that doeth a thing, doth it of its own accord, then it is alive, and wise withal. Therefore it is Jehovih.

27. If it do it not of itself, then it is not the doer, but the instrument. How, then, can law do anything? Law is dead; and the dead do nothing.

28. Within atmospherea, wark becometh organic and falleth to the earth.

29. Wark in etherea becometh an a'ji'an cloud, and shattered.

30. Men make laws, as betwixt themselves; these laws are rules governing action, but they are not action itself.

31. Jehovih is action. His actions are manifested in things thou seest. He is Light and Life. All His things are a complete whole, which is His Person.

CHAPTER IV.

1. Man said: What, then, shall I believe? If great learning have not proven anything real; if science is based on falsehood, and if there be no natural laws, shall I not give up my judgment? Whatever is at variance with my judgment, shall I not turn away from it?

2. It hath been said: The soul of man never dieth. No one can know this, save Jehovih.

3. It hath been said: Jehovih is a person. No one can know this, for His magnitude is incomprehensible.

4. Is the soul of man made of oxygen or hydrogen? Give me light that is real. I can say of what man's mortal body is made.

5. Jehovih said: My divisions are not as man's divisions. Behold, I create one thing within another. Neither space, nor place, nor time, nor eternity standeth in My way. The soul is es.

6. Man inquired: If the dwelling-place for the spirits of the dead be up in the firmament, how is it created? What resteth it upon?

7. And how dwelleth the soul of man in heaven? If the es-man hath feet and legs, how doth he walk?

8. Hath his arms changed into wings? Or rideth he on the lightnings?

9. God said: Already goeth thy soul thitherward, but it can not take thy body with it. Thy corporeal judgment can not cope with spiritual things.

10. As thought traveleth, so is it with the spirit of the dead. When thou hast quit thy corporeal body, behold thy spirit will be free; whithersoever thou desirest to go thou shalt go.

11. Nevertheless thou shalt go only as thought goeth. And when thou hast arrived at the place, thou shalt fashion, from the surroundings, thine own form, hands and arms, and feet and legs, perfectly.

12. The Gods build not only themselves, but plateaux for the inhabitation of millions and millions of other souls risen from the earth.

13. Man said: Alas, me! Why was I born in darkness?

14. Why was I not created knowing all things from my youth up?

15. Why did not the Creator send His angels with me every day, to satisfy my craving for light from the Almighty?

16. Kosmon answered: Hadst thou not craved for light, thou hadst not been delighted to receive light. Hadst thou been created with knowledge, thou couldst not be an acquirer of knowledge.

17. Had the Creator given thee angels to be forever giving thee light, then they would be slaves.

18. Liberty is the boon of men and angels; the desire for liberty causeth the soul of man to come out of darkness.

19. Whoso feeleth that he hath no need of exertion, groweth not in spirit. He hath no honor on the earth or in the heavens thereof.

20. Man said: This is my comfort. Man nowadays is not so foolish as the ancients.

21. They worshipped before idols of stone and wood.

22. They built temples and pyramids so costly that they ruined themselves.

23. Seffas said: O vain man! In the day thou abusest the ancients, thou sendest thy son to college, and enforcest him to study the ancients.

24. Thy standing armies hold the nations of the earth in misery greater than did the temples and pyramids. And as for drunkenness and dissolute habits, and for selfishness, thou art worse than the ancients.

25. God said: O man, turn thou from the dead past; learn from the Ever Living Present!

26. What is thy wisdom for the raising up of the poor and the distressed, more than was that of the ancients?

27. Is it better for thee to hold up a book and say: Behold a most sacred and holy book! than for the ancients to say: Behold a sacred and holy temple!

28. Seffas said: Consider the established things; in one age one thing; in another age another thing.

29. To make man break away from all the past, and live by the Light of the Ever Present, is this not the wisest labor?

CHAPTER V.

1. Jehovih said: In the time I created life on the earth, and in the waters, and in the air above the earth; I brought the earth into hyarti for a thousand years.

2. And the earth gave out light because of the darkness of the heavenly forests whither I had brought her.

3. Man said: To know the beginning of things; what greater delight than this?

4. To know when the earth was made; and how the living were created!

5. The thousands of millions of kinds and species!

6. God said: Was not this answered unto thee? According to the light that man was capable of receiving, so was he answered.

7. Man inquired: But why was not the truth told? Why the six days? And why the rib?

8. God said: That which man can accept, and is good for him, is given unto him. That which man can not comprehend, can not be revealed to him.

9. Behold, even now, as hath been shown, thou usest false symbols to illustrate the number ten.

10. Wouldst thou make man worship angels because they took on forms by his side?

11. Then thou wouldst lose influence over him, and angels would be his guides.

12. All teaching shall be to make man comprehend the Almighty's dominion upon man.

13. Symbols and images that do this, are true lights, though false in fact.

14. Man said: How shall man find light, knowledge, wisdom, truth? Is there no all teacher? Learning is void, because based on false grounds? The senses are void, because they themselves are perishable and imperfect?

15. The insane man knoweth not his insanity. May not any man be also insane, and know it not?

16. Where shall man find a true standing point to judge from?

17. Uz said: All thou seest and hearest, O man, are but transient and delusive. Even thine own corporeal senses change every day.

18. To-day thou triest to raise up thy son in a certain way; but when thou art old, thou wilt say: Alas, I taught him differently from what I would now.

19. Man inquired: Is this not then the best course, to devote myself wholly to doing good?

20. Es answered: Who shall tell thee what doing good is? Knowest thou?

21. Man said: To provide the best of everything for my wife, and for my sons and daughters, and contribute to the poor.

22. Es said: Hadst thou created man, thou hadst given him hair or feathers and a cushion for his head?

23. Bethink thee, then. Give thou one thing too much to thy wife and sons and daughters, thereby preventing the calling out of their own talents, and, alas, thy works will be bad instead of good.

24. Contribute to the poor one fraction too much, and thou injure instead of doing good.

25. Give him one fraction too little, and thou shalt rebuke thyself.

26. Man inquired: What, then, are good works? Shall I preach and pray for others?

27. God said: Man, thou shalt judge thyself as to what thou shalt do.

28. Within every man's soul, Jehovih hath provided a judge that will soon or late become triumphant in power.

29. Man said: Hear me: I am tired of reason and argument.

30. Now will I covenant with Jehovih. He only shall answer me; He will give me light:

31. To Thee, O Jehovih, I commit myself, to be Thine forever.

32. To serve Thee by doing nothing for mine own selfish ends; but by doing the best I can for others, all my days.

33. My flesh body will I baptize every day in remembrance of Thee; for my body is Thine, and I will keep it clean and pure before Thee.

34. Neither will I suffer my spiritual body to be injured by wicked thoughts or passions of lust; for my spirit is Thy gift to me also.

35. Twice every day shall my spirit body be covenanted to Thee, in which times all earthly thoughts shall depart away from me. And whatsoever light Thou bestowest on me, that shall be a guide and ruler over me for the day thereof.

36. In the morning at sunrise will I turn to Thee, that I may be spurred up to swiftness in doing good and in manifesting Thy light in my behavior. And at night before I sleep will I recount my day's labor, that I may see wherein I was short in doing with all my wisdom and strength.

37. Thou, O Jehovih, shalt be my Confessor and Advisor; to Thee will I give praise without ceasing. My prayers and anthems to Thee shall be without number. This do I perceive is the highest of all aspiration.

38. For what better is it for God or the spirits of the dead to tell me a thing than for mortals to tell me? Is not all wisdom necessary to be proved within each and every man? Is it not better that my vision reach up to heaven and see it myself, than to be told of it by the angels?

39. It is wiser for mortals to become pure as angels, than for angels to become impure as mortals. Nay, I will not drag the spirits of the higher heavens down to the earth. If they came and told me, it would be but hearsay testimony at best.

40. I will commune with them and weigh their words, as to whether they be wise and adapted to founding Thy kingdom on earth.

41. Am I not done, O Jehovih? Thou hast sealed up thy kingdoms from me. Henceforth I will neither preach nor hear preaching. Only to labor and to do good, and be in peace within my own soul, and with my neighbors, and to glorify Thee.

42. I will do no more, nor will I multiply words with any one under the sun.

CHAPTER VI.

1. God said: I declare in the name of Jehovih, the Whole. Through Him, and by His hand have I been lifted up. hear me, O mortals! Give ear, O ye spirits of the dead! The Father hath spoken; Him do I reveal; in Him bestow the tree of light.

2. I was in darkness, but am now in light. His presence is upon me. Hearken, then, to my words, and be wise in your lives.

3. Seek not to disprove Him; seek not to prove that these things can not be; seek not to deny His person, nor His spirit. Of such was my bondage. In bitterness of heart was I bound in darkness. Those who deny, those who try to disprove Him, are in darkness.

4. He is the same to-day and forever. The prophets of old found Him; so also can ye. But He cometh not to the denier, nor to the disprover.

5. He who will find His Person must look for Him. He who will hear His Voice must hearken. Then cometh light.

6. All argument is void. There is more wisdom in the song of a bird than in the speech of a philosopher. The first speaketh to the Almighty, proclaiming his glory. The second ploddeth in darkness.

7. By my hand were the ancient libraries burnt, to draw man away from darkness.

8. Kosmon said: What hath great learning found that is valuable?

9. Shall learning, like riches, be acquired for one's own selfish gratification?

10. If a rich man with his horded wealth do little for the resurrection of man, how much less doth the learned man with a head full of knowledge? It neither feedeth nor clotheth the sick and distressed, nor stayeth the debauchery and drunkenness of the great multitude.

11. How shall we class the man of exact science? Where shall we find him? How shall we know that he will not be disproved in time to come?

12. Yesterday it was said, a man can not fast forty days and live; to-day it is proven possible.

13. Yesterday it was said, there is attraction of gravitation betwixt the sun and the earth; to-day it is proven that there is no such thing. That no man can see without eyes or hear without ears, in su'is (clairvoyance and clairaudience); to-day hundreds of thousands know it to be so.

14. Yesterday it was said, thou shalt eat flesh and oil, because they supply certain things for the blood, without which man can not live; to-day it is proven otherwise.

15. Yesterday the physician said: Take thou this, and it will heal thee; to-day the same thing is proven to have no virtue.

16. This only is proven: That man is vain and conceited, desiring to make others believe he is wise when he is not.

17. What healed the sick yesterday, will not to-morrow.

18. Philosophy that was good yesterday, is folly to-day.

19. Religions that were good for the ancients are worthless to-day.

20. Crime and pauperism grow up in the heart of them, even worse than in the regions of the earth where they are not preached.

21. The physicians have not lessened the amount of sickness on the earth.

22. The lawyers have not lessened the rascality of the wicked, or depleted the number of defrauders.

23. The march of Jehovih and His peoples is onward; it is like a tree of light, forever growing, but man heedeth not the growth.

24. Man bindeth his judgment by things that are past; he will not quicken himself to see and understand the All Light.

CHAPTER VII.

1. Esfoma said: I am the signs of the times.

2. By my face the prophets foretell what is to be.

3. I am the living mathematics; the unseen progress of things speaking to the senses of man.

4. My name is: THE SIGNS OF THE TIMES.

5. Why have ye, the inhabitants of the earth, and ye angels of the heavens, not beholden me in my march?

6. I called out in the days of the pyramids: O ye kings and mighty ones! Behold the signs of the times!

7. And ye men of great learning, give ear; a voice speaketh in the wind!

8. Behold, Osiris and Isis shall go down. Anubi shall not judge the people of the Almighty!

9. I sent a storm into colleges of learning; the wise professors held up their heads and said:

10. I doubt the person of Osiris! I doubt Isis! Are they merely a principle?

11. The prophets looked here and looked there. They said: Behold the signs of the times!

Let us measure the increase in the growth of skepticism to these ancient Gods.

12. They said: Osiris shall go down; and so shall Isis and Anubi, and Baal, and Ashtaroth, and Thammus.

13. But kings heard not; they called their councils for stern legislation.

14. They saw, but denied my person and the power of my hand.

15. Man calleth out: Give me a key for prophecy. Show me the way to find the destiny of Gods and angels and mortals.

16. Show me the key for the rise and fall of nations and empires.

17. Then I come forth over all the land. Man beginneth to doubt, then to disbelieve, and then to deny the popular Gods and Saviors of his forefathers.

18. They will not see which way the wind bloweth; with strong arms and bloody hands they raise up against Jehovih.

19. Then they go down in destruction; they and their Gods are known no more.

20. Jehovih hath said: All things are like a tree; which springeth up from a little seed to become mighty; which beareth fruit for a season, and then falleth and is turned to dust.

21. One by one My Gods, and My false Gods, rise up and are powerful for a season, and then are swept away in Esfoma's hands.

22. Behold My thousands of Saviors, which I have sent to raise up the inhabitants of the earth. Where are they this day?

23. I give to mortals Gods and Lords and Saviors; according to the time and place of the earth in My ethereans, so, bestow I them.

24. But when they have fulfilled their time, lo, I take away their Gods and Lords and Saviors. Not suddenly, nor without signs of the times of their going.

CHAPTER VIII.
THE BATTLE WITH THE BEAST OF THE ARC OF BON.

1. Es said: The light of Jehovih touched on the earth, and the heavens about were stirred to the foundation. Things past were moved forward. His voice was from the depth of darkness to the summit of All Light.

2. Nations that had not known Him, now knew Him. Acceptable, and with loud rejoicings, they shouted: Jehovih! Jehovih! Almighty and Everlasting! Glory be to Thee on High! Creator, Father! all praise to Thee forever.

3. And Jehovih went far and near swiftly, quickening with a new power both the living and the dead. And the peoples raised up, and heard His voice from every corner, calling: Come forth! Come forth! O My beloved.

4. And in the stirring up of things long past, it was as if a cloud of dust and darkness, foul and poisonous, overspread heaven and earth, was to be cleared away and make room for other Gods and Saviors.

5. High above the clouds, and deep down in all the blackness, the All Light shone as the everlasting sun. The faith of men and angels rose up in unceasing assurance to the Most High, that He in matchless majesty, alone, would rise triumphant over all.

6. Jehovih said: Bring forth the legions of earth and heaven! Summon up the dead! Let the living rejoice! My kingdom is at hand.

7. And the dead came forth, clothed in the raiment of heaven; and they walked upon the earth; yea, face to face talked with the living, proclaiming the fullness of Jehovih, and his everlasting kingdoms.

8. Little infants that were long dead, returned to the living, full grown in heaven, singing in Jehovih's praise. Mothers returned from the unseen world with love and angel kisses for their mortal babes and sorrow-stricken husbands.

9. Then rose the cloud of darkness, higher and higher; the poisonous smell and damnable tricks of hada belched forth in blackness terrible. The spirits of those slain in war, delirious, mad, and full of vengeance; and those whose earth-lives had bound them in torments; and those who lived on earth to glut themselves to the full in abhorrent lust, came assuming the names of Gods and Saviors.

10. And yet the voice of Jehovih called: Bring forth the legions of earth and heaven! Summon up the dead! Let the living rejoice! My chosen shall come forth.

11. Still struggled the beast, awful in the smoke and dust of his blood-stained mantle, till the earth around became as a solemn night before a battle of death. Rattling bones and empty skulls, with gnashing teeth, all stained with human gore, made hideous by the portentous omen, caused angels and men to stand appalled.

12. And then, as the cloud of darkness stretched up out of the earth, girdling it all around, as a venomous reptile secureth his living food, lo and behold, the monster beast stretched forth four heads with flaming nostrils all on fire!

13. On each head were two horns, blood-stained and fresh with human victims' flesh macerated. Their tongues darted forth in menace, and their open mouths watered for human souls; and with suspicion mad, and much distrusted, their blood-shot eyes pierced the temples of kings, and laid them in ruins.

14. And the names of the beast, now falsely assumed, to beguile Jehovih's chosen, were Dyaus, Lord God, Osiris and Te-in; and their horns were named, one Righteousness and the other Militant.

15. With their four bloody mouths, they called out of the fires of hell: Down! Jehovih! Down! I alone am Savior of mortals and angels! I will be the favorite God, or ruin all!

16. Jehovih answered to His faithful sons and daughters, the living and the dead: Bring forth the legions of earth and heaven! Summon up the dead! Let the living rejoice! My kingdom is at hand! My chosen shall be free!

17. The beast, rattling his hideous bones, bated some his breath to see the great awakening light of the tree of Jehovih!

18. And as the beast looked along, behold his four heads saw one another, and burst forth in a new tirade of horrid curses.

19. Each to know the others' bold presumption.

20. First spake Anuhasaj, the false Lord God, to the east: Behold thou, Ho-Joss, thou bloody Te-in, God of hada, thy heavenly kingdom shall down. Know thou that I, the Lord God, am God of all. It was I, drove the Great Spirit from earth and heaven, and made the name Lord God worshipful in the broad universe.

21. The false Te-in, mocking, said: And thou wilt bury it in the depths of hell, thou, of woman born.

22. Upward rose the head of the beast, the false Lord God, and with his mighty arm and sword, swept off the false Te-in's head. And as the beast surged about, Dyaus, the false, sprang forward, shouting, Hold! Thou false Lord God! Never shall thy name be honored on Chine'ya soil or in her heavens. Behold me! I am Dyaus!

23. Ashtaroth, greedy Goddess, now urged her consort God, Baal, to rush in for the heavenly spoils. And the twain, in the terrible tumult, drew hence ten thousand million angel slaves.

24. Anuhasaj said to Dyaus: Thou miscreant God! That dared steal my name, De'yus, and now confront me with thy hellish taunts! Down! Down!

25. At that their bloody swords clashed, and Dyaus thrust his adversary through, even as the false Lord God's sword clipt off Dyaus' traitorous head.

26. Meanwhile Osiris, the dragon-head, started up from the punctured body of the beast, shouting: Behold me! I am all! I, Osiris, Savior of men; Lord God of heaven and earth, Dyaus, De'yus, all! By my sword, I am sworn!

27. Ashtaroth, cunning Goddess, flew suddenly down to the earth, to the mortal king of Egupt, Pharaoh, and through the oracle proclaimed:

28. There is war in heaven! Osiris, thriftiest of Gods, hath won the victory, and standeth master of all the heavens' broad kingdoms.

29. To earth he shall come no more. Proclaim thyself the Savior's vice-gerent on earth, and king of the world!

30. Then Pharaoh, distracted by the flood of miracles and the superabundance of the spirits of the dead strolling over all of Egupt, embraced the oracle's fearful decrees.

31. And now, behold, whilst the beast struggled in the four quarters of the world, Jehovih's chosen, both on earth and in heaven, marched out of bondage, singing glory to the Creator's name!

32. And now, Osiris, the chief remaining head of the beast, turned from the anarchy and hells in hada, to vent his hatred against Jehovih's chosen on earth; and with Baal and Ashtaroth invented new tortures for the non-flesh-eating tribes of men.

33. But Jehovih's light broke across the world. The smoke and clouds from the battle cleared away.

34. Osiris fled from the earth. Another group of false Gods had cleared away before Jehovih's light.

CHAPTER IX.

1. Jehovih said: When the Gods have fulfilled their time in earth and heaven, behold I put them away.

2. And in the time of their going, behold, I open the doors of heaven, and I call down the angels and send them abroad over the earth. And the earth becometh overrun with miracles.

3. Kosmon said: Let the wise man and the prophet consider the signs of the Almighty! Two extremes forerun the change of the Gods and Saviors in heaven: These are, extreme disbelief and extreme belief. The one denieth all Gods, and even the person of the Creator; the other becometh a runner after the spirits of the dead, consulting seers and oracles.

4. Esfoma said: These signs are my signs. When these come, behold, the Almighty hath a new deliverance on hand.

5. None can stay Him, or hold up the Gods and Lords and Saviors of the past against Jehovih.

6. I speak in the wind, and man saith: Behold, something is in the wind; the Gods are at work; a new light breaketh in upon the understanding of men.

7. Out of the tumult, Jehovih riseth Supreme in every cycle.

8. He leadeth forth a few who know Him. He foundeth them as a separate people in the world.

9. Uz said: And in the time of Jehovih's triumph, I come and make myths out of the deposed Gods and Saviors.

10. Then I stretch forth my hand against the libraries, and houses of ancient records, and I destroy them.

11. And man is compelled to give up the things of old, and to look about him, and rouse himself up to the ways of the Almighty.

12. O that the prophets would apply my lessons of the past, in order to foretell the future.

13. Behold, there is no mystery in heaven and earth. They march right on; cycle followeth cycle, as summer followeth winter.

14. In the overthrow of the departing Gods, behold, there is the beginning of a new spring-time in Jehovih's seasons.

15. He planteth a new tree in His garden; it is a tree of new light for the righteous.

16. His chosen go out, away from the flesh-pots of the past, and they have neither kings nor emperors; only the Almighty!

17. Into the wilderness they go forth, persecuted and beset on all sides by the followers of the mythical Gods.

CHAPTER X.

1. God said: Here is wisdom, O man: To be observant of all things and adapt thyself thereto on Jehovih's side.

2. To obtain great learning that applieth to the resurrection of thy soul in comprehending the works of the Almighty.

3. To suffer not thyself to be conceited in the wisdom of the moderns over the ancients, nor of the ancients over the moderns.

4. The Creator created man wisely for the time of the world in which man was created.

5. Thou art for this era, and not for the past.

6. The ancients were for the past era, and not for the present.

7. To know the present; to be up with the signs of the times, this it is, to see Jehovih's hand.

8. Make not a God of riches, nor of thy supposed sciences and learning.

9. For in the time thou seest men doing these things, behold, that is the time of a cyclic coil in the great beast.

10. Thy God and thy Savior shall surely be swept away.

11. Make Jehovih, the Creator, the idol of thy soul; neither setting up this or that as impossible.

12. Opening up thy understanding to find the tree of light and righteousness of soul.

13. Admitting that all things are possible in Jehovih's hands.

14. Then thy God shall surely not be swept away.

15. Look about thee, O man, and learn from the Sons and Daughters of Jehovih, the march of the Almighty's kingdoms.

16. Who shall make a system or a philosophy like Jehovih? What hast thou found that is infallible?

17. The truth of yesterday is not a truth to-day; the truth of yesterday is the truth to-day.

18. Thou shalt come to understand even this.

19. To learn how to live; to rejoice, and to do good, and make thy neighbor rejoice also, this is wisdom.

20. Let these be thy loves and the glory of thy speech, and thou shalt learn to prophesy concerning the ways of Jehovih.

Plate 47. THE CYCLIC COIL.

The numbers of the beast shall be sixty-six, and six hundred and sixty-six, and the parts thereof. Because in the coil of the cycle, behold the distances are two-thirds of a circle, whether it be a hundred or a thousand, or three times a thousand. Jehovih rolleth up the heavens, and braideth the serpents of the firmament into His cyclic coil. Who can magnify Jehovih by calling Him Osiris or Te-in, or Baal, or Lord, or God? He is the circle without beginning or end; His Majesty encompasseth the universe. (See BOOK OF COSMOGONY AND PROPHECY).

734

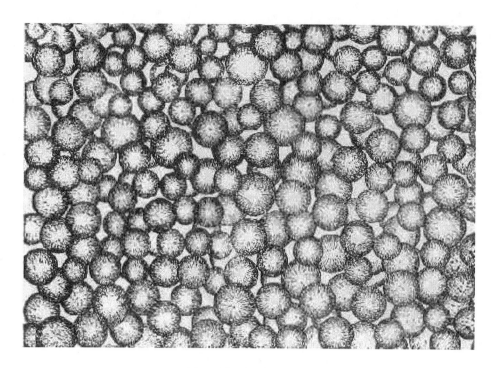

Plate 22. ETHEREA.

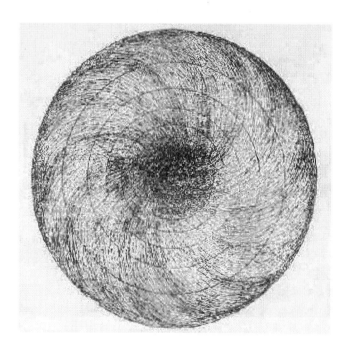

Plate 23. EARTH.
Black center, and her atmosphere.

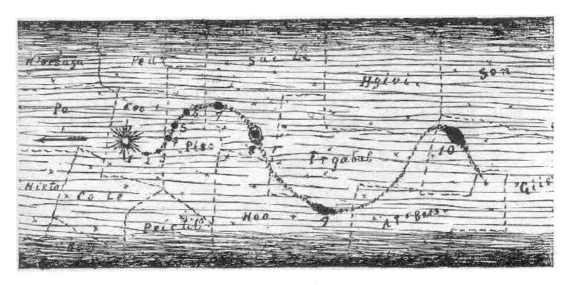

Plate 36. SERPENT.

1.Sun. 2.Mercury. 3.Earth. 4.Mars. 5.Artaea. 6.Vesta. 7.Ceres. 8.Jupiter. 9.Saturn. 10.Uranus.
Equivalent: Koo, 28. Sai'Lee, 44. Pisc, 22. Hoo, 85. Frgabal, 114. At'bars,8. Gib'S'Smak, 198.

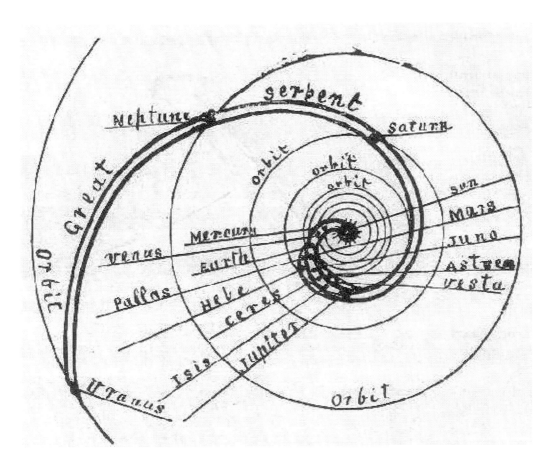

PLATE 46. DISSECTION OF THE GREAT SERPENT.

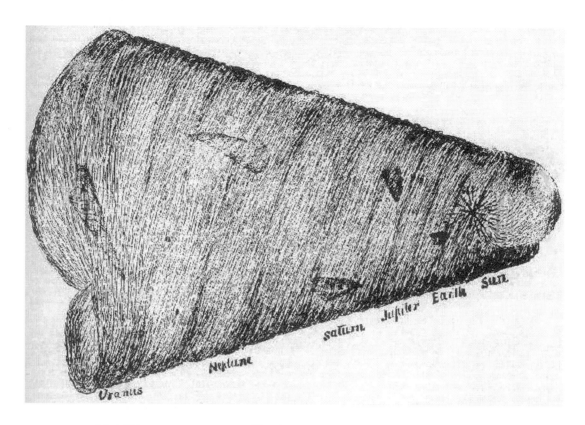

PLATE 47. TOW'SANG. (See BOOK OF COSMOGONY AND PROPHECY)

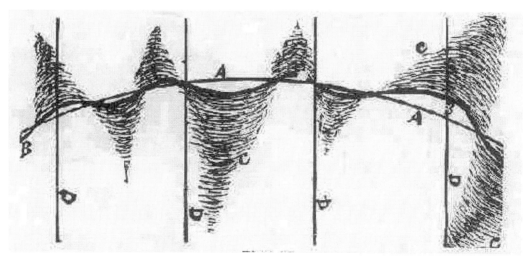

Plate 68.

A, A, road of travel of the vortex. Tow'-Sang, or solar family of the Great Serpent.

B, B, deviation from a straight line. (See plate 47.)

C, C, C, C, vortices of other symptoms of worlds.

D, D, D, D, dan, dan, dan, dan; that is, from D to D, is three thousand years.

The open space in the curve B, B, near the center of the plate, indicates the place of the Serpent in this day.

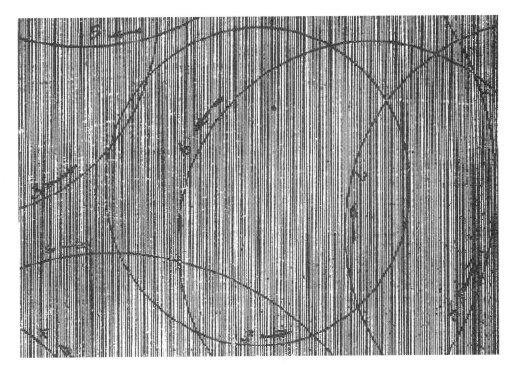

PLATE 42. SERPENT'S ORBIT.

1 = Equivalent: 4,700,000; 2, 3, 4, 5, 6, 7, 8. Other orbits for other phalanxes.

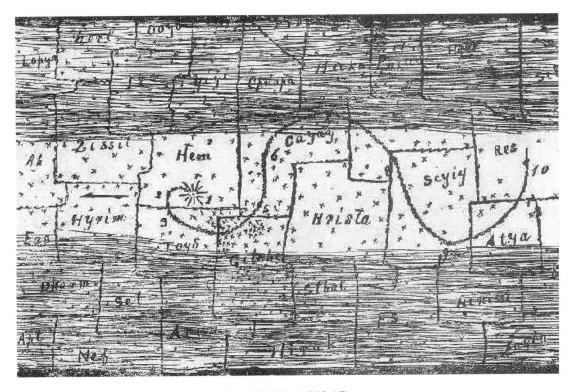

PLATE 38. ANOAD.

C'vord'um and A'hiss'a-Corpor, embracing nine phalanxes. First of Spe'ta period.
Earth, 3 = 765,744. Gitche, 86. Hem, 11. Entrance to Hyrim, 6,000 years.

738

PLATE 37. PROPHETIC NUMBERS.

Equivalents: Arejaon, 49. Kavi, 7. F'roasha, 76, F'ranraka, 84. Yakna, 13. Huit, 64.
Velocity, = 3,072. 7 = 8,021. 7 = 4716. 76 = 1,085. 84 = 12,008. 13 = 6,047. 64 = 18,765.
Duration = Huit x 2,780 years for the earth. F'ransaka 3,142 years.
Example - To find population in Atmospherea belonging to the earth in Huit, thirty-three
years = 788,000,000 x 2,780 divided by 3 -100 = 83 1-33 x = 65,666,333,333 1-3 souls.

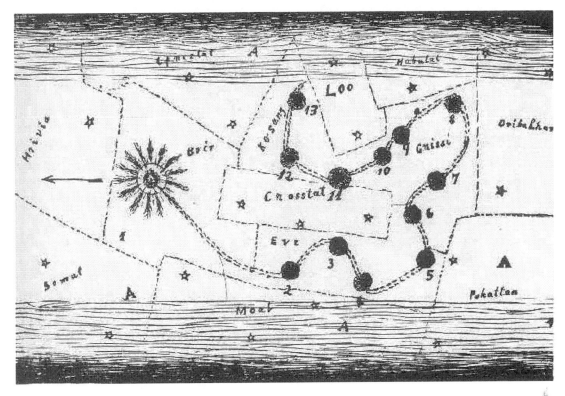

PLATE 40. SHA'MAEL.

The prophet of Jehovih said: A time shall come when the earth shall travel in the roadway of the firmament, and so great a light will be therein that the vortex of the earth shall burst, even as a whirlwind bursteth, and lo and behold, the whole earth shall be scattered and gone, as if nothing had been. But ere the time cometh, My etherean hosts shall have redeemed man from sin. Nor shall the inhabitants of the earth marry, for the time of begetting will be at an end. Even as certain species of animals have failed to propagate, and have become extinct, so shall it be with man. The earth will have fulfilled its labor, and its services will be no more under the sun. But the vortex of the sun shall be round, and the body of the great serpent coiled up. In the place where the earth was, shall some of My far-off worlds come and fulfill the labor allotted to them. And the atmosphereans who have not been redeemed from darkness in that day, shall alight on the new world and also fulfill their labor. (See BOOK OF JEHOVIH AND BOOK OF SAPHAH)

740

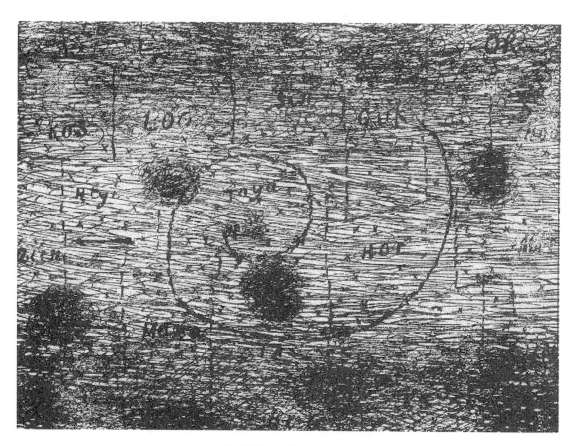

Plate 39. THE EARTH IN SE'MU.

Jehovih saith: In the time of se'mu I brought the earth into a'ji, and ji'ay, and darkness was upon the face of the earth for the space of three thousand years; and yet for other three thousand years half darkness covered all the land and water. Behold, O man, as I have given to females a time to bring forth their young, so gave I to the earth a time for the conception of the living species on the land, in the water and in the air above, and I called the time the era of se'mu.

And it came to pass, when the earth was in the midst of Taza, there fell upon the earth, for a space equal to twelve days, condensed nebula in dust and stones and water combined, sufficient in some places to cover up the forests Jehovih had made. And that which fell was hot like molten iron; and the trees and forests of the valleys were beaten down, and covered up, and burnt to blackness. Jehovih said: And these shall remain on the earth, for in the time that followeth, man shall seek the coal, not knowing whence it came. And it will bear witness of the regions of a'ji and ji'ay in the firmament of heaven. (See Book of Jehovih and Book of Saphah)

741

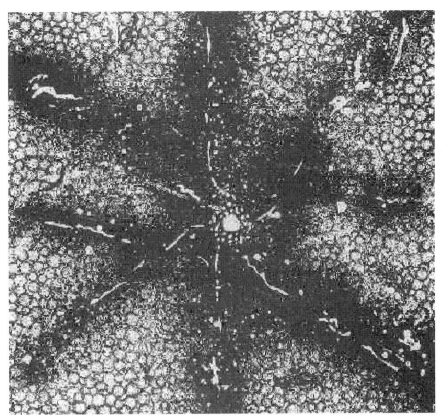

PLATE 30. JI'AY. The earth (white spot) in Ji'ay.

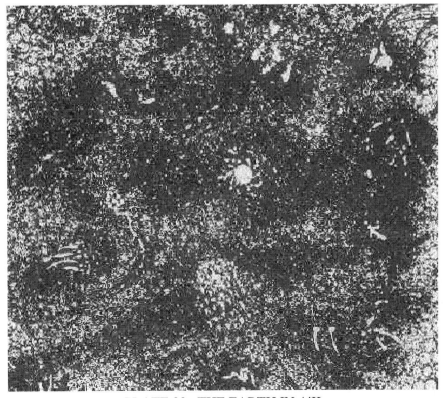

PLATE 32. THE EARTH IN A'JI.

742

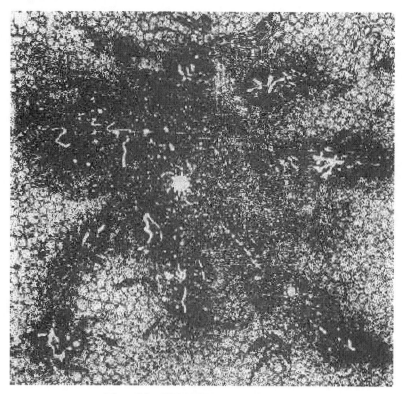

Plate 33. HYARTI, or NEBULA.

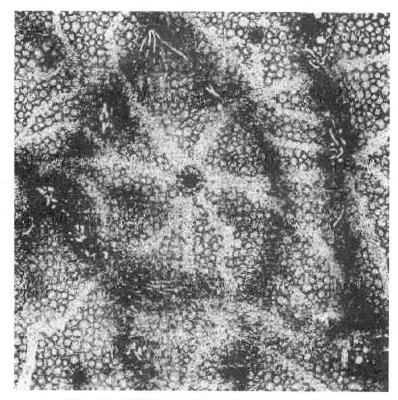

Plate 34. JI'NIQUIN SWAMP, IN ETHEREA.

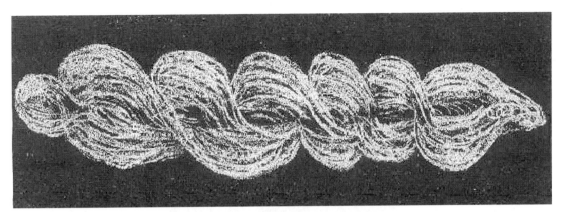

Plate 25. PRIMARY VORTEX.

The power that maketh planets. (See BOOK OF COSMOGONY AND PROPHECY)

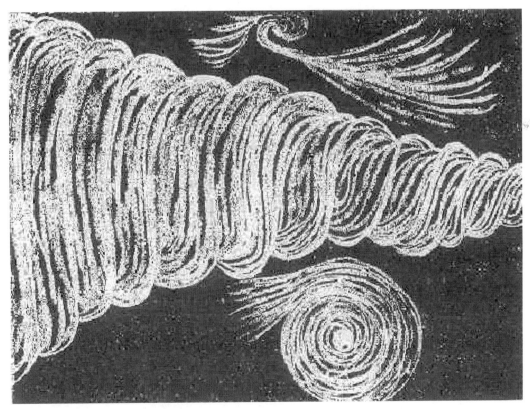

PLATE 26. SECONDARY VORTEX.

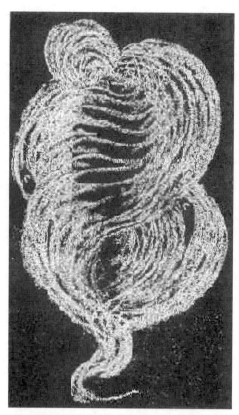

Plate 27. THIRD AGE OF VORTEX.

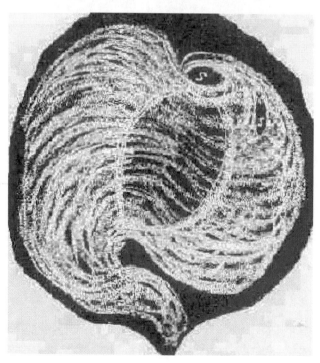

Plate 28. FOURTH AGE OF VORTEX.
Now called Inqua, a ball within a ball,
or womb of vapor. (S, S, satellites).

745

Plate 29. ORGANIC WARK.
Within the earth's atmosphere. The origin of meteors.

Plate 31. SHATTERED WARK.
Wark in etherea becometh an a'ji'an cloud, and shattered.

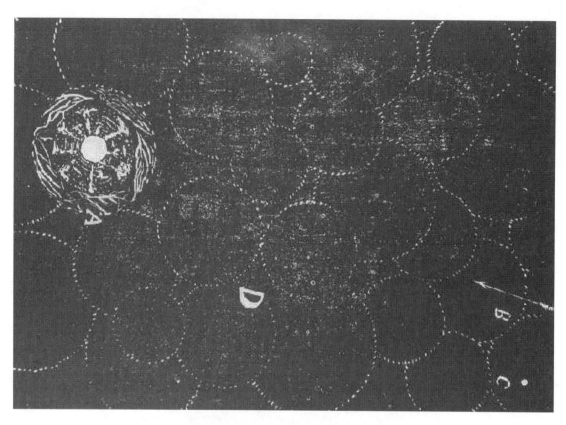

Plate 41. PHOTOSPHERES.

Jehovih said: Let the sign of the corporeal worlds be as the signs of the etherean worlds; nevertheless they shall be independent of one another. Neither shall the travel of corporea disturb the motions and positions of etherea, but pass through, as if there were nothing. But the behavior of the etherean worlds on corporea shall be to bring them to maturity and old age, and final dissolution. And it was so. And there floated in the midst of etherea certain densities, called a'ji and ji'ay and nebula, which sometimes augmented the size of the traveling corporeal worlds, and sometimes illumed them on the borders of the vortices, and these were called photospheres, because they were the places of the generation of light. (See BOOK OF COSMOGONY AND PROPHECY)

Plate 43.

When Jehovih condensed the earth, and it became firm and crusted over, there rose up from the earth heat and moisture, which continue to this day. But Jehovih limited the ascent of the substances going upward, and the boundary of the limit of moisture was as the clouds that float in the air; and the heat was of like ascent. And whilst the moisture and heat rise upward, they are met by the etheric substance of the vortex of the earth, and the moisture and the gases of the air assume the form of needles. On the side of the earth facing the sun the needles are polarized and acting, driving forth; the which is called light; but on the face of the earth opposite from the sun the needles are in confusion, and this is called darkness.

Jehovih said: That man may comprehend the structure of the belt that holdeth the earth, I will give him a sign high up in the air. And Jehovih caused the vapor in the firmament to be frozen and fall to the earth, white, and it is called snow. For the snow-drop showeth the matrix in which it is molded.

Jehovih said: Let this be a sign also, that even as there riseth up from the earth heat and moisture, there are representatives of all things on the earth which have evaporated upward, and all such things rise up to the level of the density like unto themselves, every one to its own level, and they take their places in the strata of the vortex. These are called plateaux, or spheres, for they surround the whole earth. Some of them are ten miles high, some a thousand, some a hundred thousand or more miles. And all these spheres that rotate and travel with the earth are called atmospherea, or lower heavens.

Plate 44.

Jehovih said: The corporeal worlds I created round, with land and water, and I made them impenetrable, for I bring forth the living on the surface of them. Let not man imagine that My etherean worlds are also round and impenetrable; for, of all I have created, no two alike created I them.

Now, it came to pass in the lapse of time, that the atmosphereans so loved the lower heavens, that they strove not to ascend to the emancipated heavens of Nirvana, never having reached the bridge of Chinvat. But they oft returned to the earth and held converse with corporeans, and they lauded the glories of even the lower heavens, so that man looked up in wonder because of the magnificence of the works of the Father. Yet these were bounden spirits.

Then Jehovih made the snow-flake and caused it to fall, that man might behold the beauty and glory of its formation. And he sent ethereans down from the emancipated heavens, and these taught man that whatever glory he had yet heard of, was as darkness is to light, compared to the beauty and majesty of the etherean worlds.

And the ethereans held up snow-flakes, saying: In the name of Jehovih we declare unto you, that the etherean worlds are larger than the earth, and penetrable, and full of roadways of crystals, and arches, and curves, and angles, so that were man to travel a million of years on one alone, he could not see half its beauty and glory. And the firmament of heaven hath tens of thousands of millions of etherean worlds. Let the snow-flakes be before your eyes as microscopic patterns of the worlds in high heaven; and ye shall tint them as a rainbow, and people them with countless millions of angels, spotless, pure, holy, and rich in the knowledge of Jehovih and His works, and full of the majesty of His love.

749

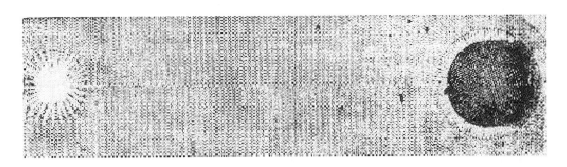

SUN.   PLATE 45.   EARTH.

Jehovih said: In times past, man beheld the sun, saying: The sun is the Creator of all the living; light and heat come from the sun.

Then Jehovih said: I will put a sign in the firmament, and no man shall gainsay the work of My hand.

And above the earth, to the north and south, He placed polar lights, that man might bear witness that light depended not on corporea, and had no part therewith. But the sun He placed in the midst of the great vortex, so that every side was as a pole to the corporeal worlds around it. And Jehovih made etherea as a condensing lens, so that the rotation of each and every corporeal world should manufacture its own light, on the side poling to the sun, by the rotation of its wark and vortex. And man saw that atmospherea turned the earth, and that the earth turned not atmospherea.

END OF GOD'S BOOK OF BEN.

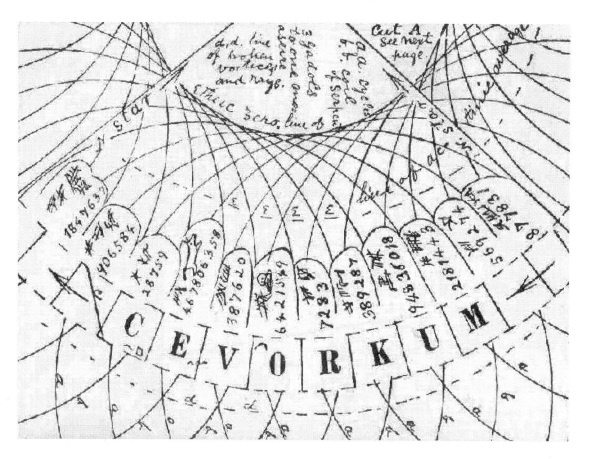

Plate 49. Cevorkum, Roadway of Solar Phalanx.

a, a, a, lines of different currents; b, b, b, transverse currents. The crossing denote the localities of the highest etherean light.   The numbers with their signatures, show the densities through which the great serpent passes each cycle. The lines across the cevorkum denote a cycle of three thousand years, but over-drawn one thousand times in order to be apparent to the eye, i.e., one to 4,700,000.

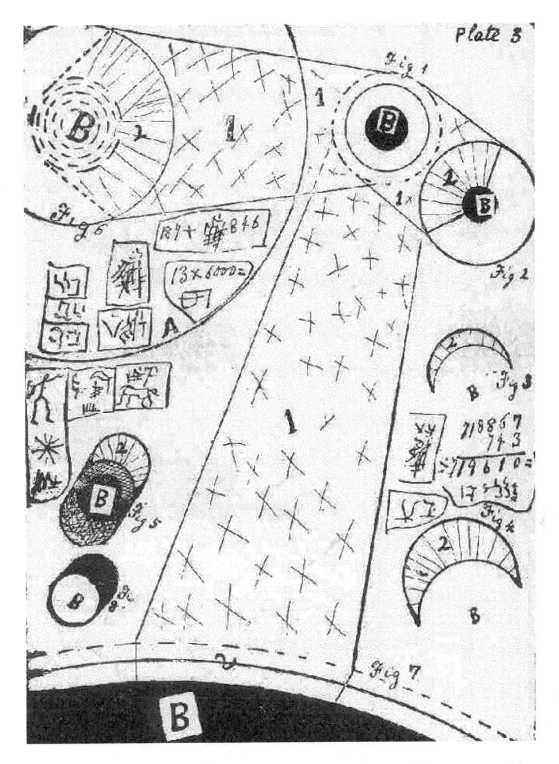

Plate 50. B, B, B, B, B, planets. Fig. 1, photosphere, or light on every side; Fig. 2, negative currents; Fig. 3, relative enlargement of a planet on the illuminate side; Fig. 4, enlargement illustrative of age of planet; Figs. 5 and 8, variation in vortex, called variation of needles; 1, 1, etherea, or inactive space; 2, 2, 2, 2, place of actinic force. The Panic signs denote the expression in numbers.

752

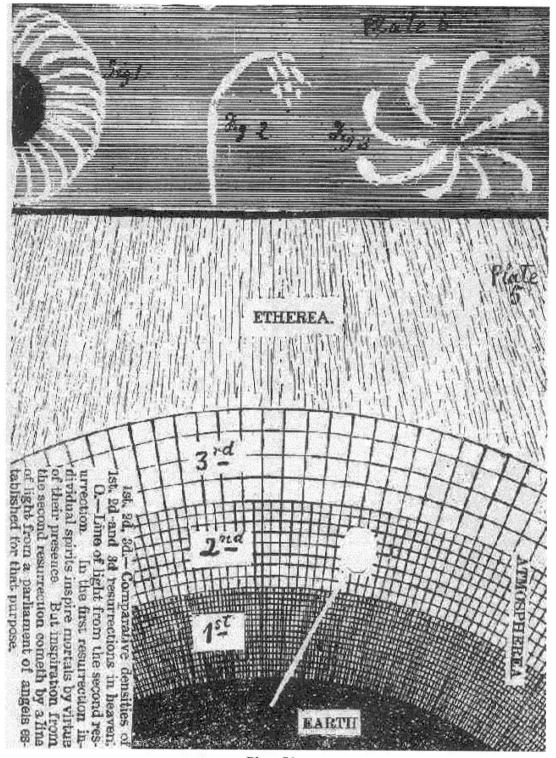

Plate 51.

Atmospherea corresponds to the place of actinic force in preceding plate; etherea, to non-action. Figs.1, 2, 3, enlarged illustrations of the course and form of vortexian currents.

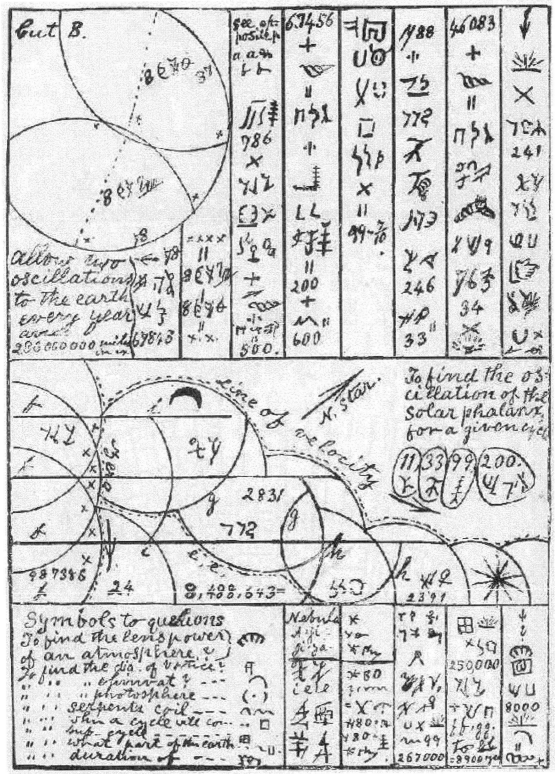

Plate 52.

Zero (line of velocity), with the two arrows, and the parallel lines crossing, are the signs of the boundary to a vortex. The oscillations of a planet are shown in the curves. In order to reduce the Panic signs to English, see BOOK OF SAPHAH.

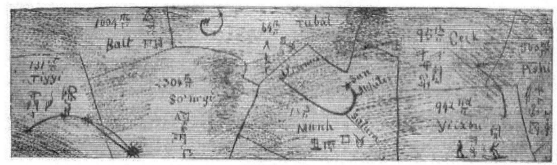

3,000 years.

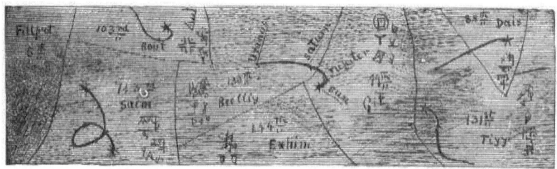

6,000 years.

9,000 years.

Plate 53.

Travel of the great serpent during the first 27 thousand years, nine thousand years each segment, after man's creation. Showing also the Orian fields in etherea, with their comparative densities and symbols.

755

12,000 years.

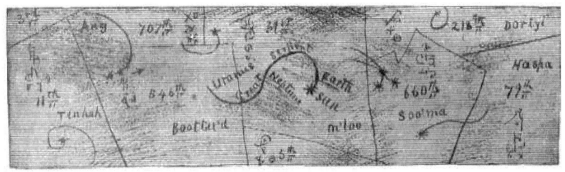

15,000 years.

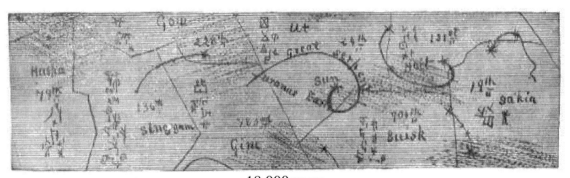

18,000 years.

Plate 54.

Travel of the great serpent during the second nine thousand years after man's creation. Showing also the Orian fields in etherea, with their comparative densities and symbols.

21,000 years.

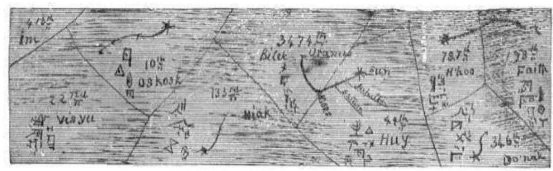

24,000 years.

27,000 years.

Plate 55.

Travel of the great serpent during the third nine thousand years after the creation of man. Showing also the Orian fields in etherea, with their comparative densities and symbols.

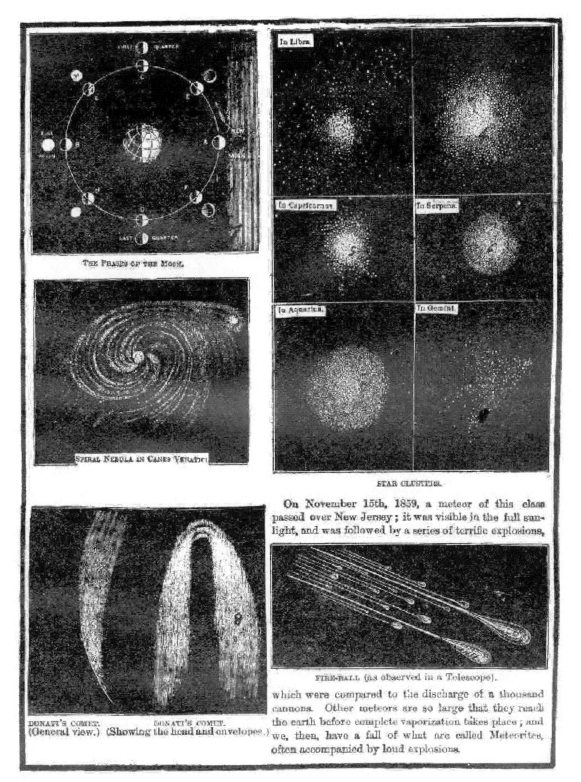

THE PHASES OF THE MOON.

SPIRAL NEBULA IN CANES VENATICI

In Libra.

In Capricornus.

In Serpens.

In Aquarius.

In Gemini.

STAR CLUSTERS.

On November 15th, 1859, a meteor of this class passed over New Jersey; it was visible in the full sunlight, and was followed by a series of terrific explosions,

FIRE-BALL (as observed in a Telescope).

which were compared to the discharge of a thousand cannons. Other meteors are so large that they reach the earth before complete vaporization takes place; and we, then, have a fall of what are called Meteorites, often accompanied by loud explosions.

DONATI'S COMET. (General view.)   DONATI'S COMET. (Showing the head and envelopes.)

Plate 56. LIGHT ILLUSTRATED.

758

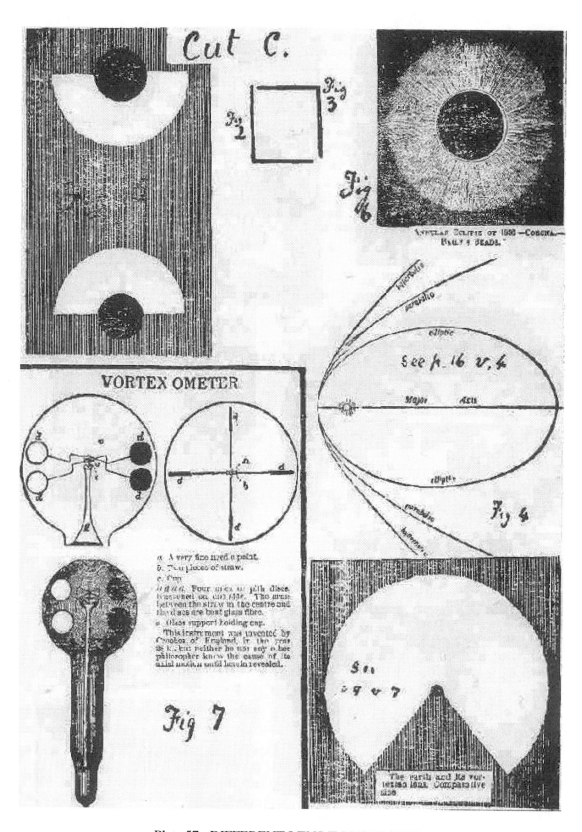

Plate 57. DIFFERENT LENS ILLUSTRATED

759

Plate 58. ILLUSTRATIONS OF CORPOREAL WORLDS.

CHAPTER I.

1. The same principles apply to all the stars, suns, planets and moons, differing in manifestation on account of size, motion, density and relative place.

2. The earth floateth in the midst of a vortex, the outer extremity of which is somewhat beyond the moon. The vortex is globular, corresponding to the form of the earth, with slight differences, which will be pointed out hereafter. Vortices are not all closed at the ends; some are open at both ends. (See illustrations of vortices, GOD'S BOOK OF BEN)

3. The vortex turneth the earth on its axis, with its own axial motion. Consequently the outer part of the vortex hath greater velocity than near the earth's surface, which hath an axial motion of one thousand miles an hour.

4. The moon hath a vortex surrounding it also, which hath a rotation axially once a month, but being an open vortex turneth not the moon. All vortices do not lay in contact with the planet, in which case it is called a dead planet. The moon's vortex is ten times the moon's diameter, and the earth's vortex thirty times the earth's diameter, with variations which will be explained hereafter.

5. The outer rim, forty-two thousand miles broad, of the earth's vortex, hath a revolution axially with the earth once a month. The swiftest part of the earth's vortex is therefore about fifteen thousand miles this side of the orbit of the moon.

6. From the swiftest part of the earth's vortex, its force is toward the earth's center. And if there were no earth here at present, the vortex would make one presently.

7. Things fall not to the earth because of the magnetism therein, save as hereinafter mentioned, but they are driven toward the center of the vortex, by the power of the vortex.

8. The greater diameter of the vortex is east and west; the lesser diameter north and south, with an inclination and oscillation relatively like the earth.

9. The name of the force of the vortex is called vortexya, that is, positive force, because it is arbitrary and exerteth east and west. As in the case of a wheel turning on its axis, its force will be at right angles with its axis, the extreme center of which will be no force.

10. For which reason the north and south line of the earth's vortex is called the m'vortexya, or negative force, for it is the subject of the other. As a whirlwind gathereth up straw and dust, which travel toward the center of the whirlwind, and to the poles thereof, even so do corporeal substances incline to approach the poles of the earth's vortex. Which may be proved by poising a magnetized needle.

11. In the early times, the earth was longer north and south than east and west. But the m'vortexya, being less than the vortexya, the earth assumed the globular form, which was afterward attenuated east and west, then it again turned, to adapt itself to the polarity north and south.

12. In these various turnings of the earth, the same force of the vortex exerted over to the east and west. By which behavior every portion of the earth hath been to the east, to the west, to the north and to the south. Which is proven in the rocks, and boulders, and mountains of the earth.

13. Wherefore it is shown there is no north and south polar power in the earth as such.

Furthermore the iron mountains show they attract east and west and north and south, without any regard to a central polar force in the earth.

14. Wherein mortals have been taught erroneously in regard to two powers which do not exist, as they have been heretofore set forth: These are the attraction of gravitation in the earth, and a north pole magnetism in the earth.

15. The positive force of the vortex is, therefore, from the external toward the internal; and the negative force of the vortex is toward the poles, and in the ascendant toward the pole external from the sun center.

16. Whereof it may be said the force of the vortex is toward its own center, but turneth at the center and escapeth outward at the north pole. As one may draw a line from the east to the center of the earth, thence in a right angle due north, which would be the current of the vortex until the center were filled with a corporeal body. After which the same power applieth, and is all one power, although for convenience called positive and negative.

17. Vortexya can be concentrated in iron and steel, and in iron ore, in which condition they are called magnetic. And these substances, if poised as needles, will assume the line of polarity of the vortex or its poles.

18. Vortexya in the atmosphere will combine oxygen and hydrogen, and an explosion ensueth, which is called thunder. But if an iron wire be raised up in the air (a lightning rod), it formeth a negative center, to which the vortexya flieth quickly, following it down into the moisture of the earth, where it is dissolved.

19. If an iron wire extend from city to city, and vortexya be charged at one end, it will manifest at the other pole, and at times even escape in a flame of fire (electric flash).

20. In like manner the vortex of the earth constantly chargeth the earth with its vortexya in the east and west, and it manifesteth in the northern pole of the vortex in flames of fire, which are called Borealis. But it sometimes happeneth, over high iron mountains, that the light is manifested in other directions. A su'is can see vortexya, as is proven by placing a horseshoe magnet before him in the dark, and he will describe the polar light escaping, even though he hath not been previously informed.

21. When vortexya is manifested in flames of fire it is called electricity. But when it lieth dormant, as in iron, it is called magnetism.

22. Where two corporeal substances are rubbed quickly together, friction and heat result; this is a manifestation of vortexya.

23. In the beginning of the earth's vortex, the current concentrated certain substances (which will be described hereafter) in the center thereof, where, by friction, the vortexya manifested in heat, so that when the congregation of materials of the earth's substance were together, they were as a molten mass of fire.

24. And for a long period of time after the fire disappeared, two great lights manifested, one at the north and one at the south.

25. Were the earth a central planet, like the sun, the light would have been all around, in which case it would have been called a photosphere.

26. By vortexya was the earth first formed as a ball of fire. By the same power is the warmth of the surface of the earth manufactured to this day. Think not that heat cometh from the sun to the earth; heat cometh not from the sun to the earth. Of which matter mortals in part still dwell in the superstitions of the ancients, who believed all things came from the sun. For is it not said this day: Heat and light come from the sun? Nay,

without examination, they also talk about the attraction of gravitation of the sun extending to other planets!

27. Corpor, as such, hath no power in any direction whatever: Neither attraction of cohesion, nor attraction of gravitation; nor hath it propulsion. But it is of itself inert in all particulars. As two ships sailing near each other will collide, or as two balls suspended by long cords will approach each other somewhat, the cause lieth not in the ships or the balls, but in what is external to them.

28. Cast water on a dusty floor and the drops of water will assume globular forms, being coated with dust. For convenience sake it is said that the globular form is natural to a liquid, and it is called the globular power. But it is nevertheless caused by a power external to itself. Approach one of the drops of water, which lieth coated with dust, with a piece of cloth, and instantly the globe of water breaketh and climbeth up into the cloth. This is erroneously called capillary attraction. But in fact the water had no attraction for the cloth, nor the cloth for the water. The power which accomplished this was external to both, and was the same in kind as the vortexya that brought the earth to its center and maintained it therein.

29. Withdraw the vortexian power, and the earth would instantly go into dissolution. When the cloth approacheth the drop of water, it breaketh the vortex thereof, and the water goeth into divisible parts into the cloth, in search of negative polarity.

30. What is called corporeal substance, which has length, breadth and thickness, remaineth so by no power of its own, but by vortexya external thereto. Exchange the vortexya, and the corpor goeth into dissolution. This power was, by the ancients, called Uz, or the fourth dimension of corpor. (See Uz, Book of Saphah.)

31. Wherefore it is said, the tendency of corpor is to uncorpor itself (dissolve or evaporate). From the surface of the ocean, and from the earth also, moisture riseth upward. Turn a wheel slowly, with water on its periphery, and the water flieth not off; let the wheel stand idle, and the water runneth off; or turn the wheel very swiftly, and the water flieth off. The same results would follow, as regardeth water, if the wheel stood still with a current of air whirling around the wheel. If the air passed slowly, the water would fall; if at a certain speed, the water would be retained on the periphery; but if at a higher speed, the water would be carried off.

32. When the earth's axial motion and the vortexian power are equivalent, there is no evaporation of moisture outward; when the vortexya exceedeth, there is great evaporation; but when the vortexya is less, there is rain. According to the vortexian currents, so are the winds (save as hereinafter mentioned), and when these are discordant, small vortices ensue in the cloud regions, and each of these small vortices formeth a drop of rain, which is an infinitesimal planet. Nevertheless, all of them are under the propelling influence of the earth's vortex, and are thus precipitated to the earth. But neither the earth attracted the rain drops, nor do the rain drops attract themselves to the earth.

33. The earth's vortex is a sub-vortex, existing within the sun's vortex: Mercury, Venus, Mars, Jupiter, Saturn, and so on, are corporeal worlds, and each and all of them within sub-vortices, and the combination of all these vortices within the sun's vortex are known by the names great serpent, or solar phalanx. For which reason the sun's vortex was called the MASTER VORTEX, or TOW-SANG, by the ancient prophets. (See plate 36, GOD'S BOOK OF

34. Were the sun planet extinct, the master vortex would instantly make another sun. As the lines of vortexya are in currents from the outer toward the interior, so do the solutions of corpor take the shape of needles, in the master, pointing toward the center, which condition of things is called LIGHT; and when these needles approach the center, or even the photosphere, the actinic force thereof is called HEAT.

35. Neither light, nor heat, nor attraction of gravitation cometh from the sun to the earth. Heat decreaseth in force in proportion to the square of the distance from the place of generation; nevertheless, an allowance of decrease must be added thereunto of one to the hundred. Light decreaseth in proportion to the divisibility of rays, as will be mentioned hereafter. Though a man see the light of the sun, as he seeth a horse in a field, yet there is no such thing as travel of light in fact; nor is there any substance of light. But that which is called light is polarity of corporeal needles in solution, caused by the lines of vortexya. In experiments on earth, the flash requireth a certain time to polarize these infinitesimal needles, and for convenience sake such lapse of time is called the travel of light. When the flash continueth, as in the case of the sun center, the master's infinitesimal needles remain poised from the sun center outward, even to the earth, and may be compared to telegraph wires, with a battery at each end. But there is no travel in any sense whatever. Daylight is not, therefore, made by the sun, nor by the photosphere of the sun. Daylight is the condition of things polarized within the master vortex. Night is manufactured by the earth coming betwixt the master's focus and the outer extreme. So that both night and day continue all the time; and we realize them both alternately in consequence of the axial motion of the earth. As in the case of night, or of any darkness, when the needles of atmospherean substance are disturbed in polarity, or when the lines of needles are cut, as in eclipse, there is no direct manifestation of the earth's vortexian currents, and such is the cause of darkness. For which reason nitrogenous plants grow rapidly at night, whilst the ripening of certain fruits and grains require the light of day. For by this vortexya are seeds and grains and fruits charged with it. Whereof when man eateth, or, as in breathing air, these things go into dissolution, as hereinafter mentioned, the heat is eliminated, and lodgeth itself in man. Or if certain herbs be piled together, and they commence dissolution, their heat is evolved, and is called spontaneous combustion.

36. Nevertheless, the herbs as such, have no power to produce heat; by their rapid dissolution, the vortexya in them endeavoreth to escape to some pole. The heat in herbs, and seeds, and plants, and other growing things, is because they are the objective points of the actinic force of vortexya. And this heat in herbs is equivalent to the same thing in iron, which is called magnetism. And its liberation or polar manifestation is, after all, one and the same thing as that which is discharged in a magnetic flame called electricity.

37. So that the cause of all these things springeth from the vortex, the power and force of which is vortexya. By a sudden dissolution of vegetable substance, as wood or straw, we have what is called fire, or burning. There is no substance of heat, nor of fire; a dissolution occurreth in which the vortexya is liberated. Corporeal substances all contain heat (vortexya proper); even snow and ice have it in infinitesimal quantities; and oils, and herbs of all kinds; but the diamond containeth the highest percentage of charge.

38. Wherein they have taught erroneously that heat cometh from the sun. As may be proved in all the earth that heat (so-called) is evolved at the expense of destroying

something, which is, in general, called combustion. And there is not in all the universe anything that can give off forever without receiving a supply forever. Heat had to be stored up in the first place in anything in heaven or earth before it could be liberated. 39. Though a man burn a stick of wood, he can produce no more heat therefrom than what was stored therein.

40. Allowing the sun to be four and a half millions of miles in diameter, and to be of the best quality of a diamond. Give it even fifty percent of the burning capacity, and it would be entirely consumed in eighty thousand years! And yet the sun is not of any such quality as a diamond. Even not more so in quality than is the earth. But suppose it were even as a diamond, or as the highest conceived-of center of heat; then that heat had to be previously given to it. Whence came it? To suppose that heat existeth of itself is folly; to suppose that heat can be produced forever without supply is not supported by any fact in heaven or earth.

41. Friction produceth heat; but it is because the abrasion liberateth stored-up vortexya. Or as in the case of glass on leather, vortexya is manufactured. In the case of the sun no such manufactory, nor one approximating it, existeth.

42. Wherein they have observed sun-spots, and said that during their presence, the temperature of the earth decreaseth, thereby reasoning that sun-spots prevented the heat of the sun falling to the earth, they have erred in two particulars: First, in defective observations and guessing at a conclusion; and second, in not having first determined the relative heat evolved from the earth at different periods in its course of travel. (Of which matter further remarks will be made hereinafter.)

43. The same errors, in regard to the light of the moon, were made in the conclusions of Kepler and Humboldt, in attributing the eclipse thereof to be governed by the sun's rays being inflected by their passage through the atmosphere and thrown into the shadow cone.

44. The superstitions of the ancients still cling to philosophers; they seek, first, to find the cause of things in the sun; or if failing therein, turn to the moon, or if failing here, they turn to the stars.

45. Finding a coincidence in the tides with certain phases of the moon, they have erroneously attributed the cause of tides to the power of attraction in the moon manifesting on the ocean, which is taught to this day as sound philosophy! Attraction, as previously stated, existeth not in any corporeal substance as a separate thing. There is no substance of attraction. Nor is there any substance of gravitation. These powers are the manifestation of vortexya. If vortexya be charged into a piece of iron or steel, it is called a magnet, because it APPARENTLY draweth its own kind to itself. When two pieces of steel, alike in quality, are charged with vortexya to their utmost, their power will be in proportion to their dimensions. If one be twice the size of the other, its magnetic force (so-called) will be in the main two times more powerful.

46. The form of a true magnet of steel, to manifest the greatest positive, and greatest negative force, should be nearly a right-angle triangle, after the manner of a line of vortexya from the equatorial surface of the earth to its center, and thence toward the north pole. By having two such magnets, and bringing their poles together, a square is produced, which now balanceth its recipency and its emission of vortexya. (See cut C, Figs. 2 and 3.)

47. As in the case of an iron mountain, it is forever receiving (feebly) equatorially; and forever emitting (feebly) polarly the vortexian current; though, for practical observations, the force may be said to be in a dormant state. And in this sense should the earth and other planets be considered. They are not in the shape of triangles or horseshoes, but as globes. Hence their positive and negative vortexian power (magnetism, erroneously called) is less than the horseshoe form.

48. The power of a magnet decreaseth in proportion to the square of the distance from it. Under certain conditions one leg of the magnet repelleth things from it. As previously stated, this is nevertheless one current; which vortexya floweth through the magnet, even as water floweth through a tube. This propelling power of the magnet also decreaseth in proportion to the square of the distance from it. If the poles of a single magnet be exposed, it will in time decrease from its maximum power until it ultimately becometh of the same capacity (as to external things) even as if the poles were closed by juxtaposition with another magnet.

49. Wherein it will be observed that were the sun or moon or earth the most powerful steel magnet, it would not take a long time (as to the time of worlds) when its magnetic attraction would not exceed native iron ore. Wherein it will also be observed that were the moon a globe of magnetic iron ore, it can be shown approximately how far would extend its power of magnetic attraction external to itself.

50. Nevertheless, its magnetic attraction in that extreme case would not be on water or clay, but on iron and its kindred ores. So that if the moon exerted a magnetic force on the earth it would manifest more on the magnetic needle, or other iron substance, than on the water of the ocean.

51. By suspending a ball of magnetic iron along side a suspended cup of water, it will be discovered there is no magnetic attraction between them, more than between two cups of water, or between two vessels of clay.

52. The highest magnetic power that can be imparted to steel in the form of a ball, to its equatorial dimension, to manifest in moving an equivalent fellow, is seven of its diameters! But in the case of iron ore (normal magnet) it is very considerably less than this. By this it is shown that were the moon a steel magnet it would not exert perceptible power more than nine thousand miles. Her shortest distance from the earth is two hundred and twenty thousand miles.

53. Wherein it is shown that under the most extravagant supposition of power, her magnetic attraction is more than two hundred thousand miles short of reaching to the earth.

54. Were there such a thing as magnetic attraction between the iron and water, or between water and water, a still further discrepancy would result. Admitting the general parts of the moon, as to iron and stone and clay and water, to be alike and like unto the corporeal earth, the power of the magnetic attraction of the earth, as against the moon's, to hold the tides from rising, would be in the ratio of different sizes of the two bodies, and their respective distances from the water contended for. In which case there would be more than four thousand million times advantage of power in the earth! For if we give the same magnetic equivalent to each, we must give to each a decrease in proportion to the square of the distance of their centers from the point in contention, the ocean's tides!

55. The same philosophy holdeth in regard to the sun, and to Jupiter and Saturn and Mars, and all other planets, making allowance for their different densities and velocities.

56. As to the attraction (so-called) between two earth substances, as granite, or sandstone, or lead, or gold, or clay, or water, it is far less than between two steel magnets. Wherein it will be observed, that it is utterly impossible for any attractive force to exert from one planet to another; or even from a planet to its own satellite.

57. And though the most extravagant supposition, based on measurement, be given to the sun's supposed attractive force, it doeth not extend to the earth by more than seventy million miles! Wherein they have taught error in place of truth!

CHAPTER II.

1. There are two known things in the universe: ethe and corpor. The former is the solvent of the latter.

2. For comparison, take a lump of table-salt, which, though white, is impervious to the sight of man. Cast it into water, and it is lost to sight; though it still existeth, the sight of man can see through it.

3. Earth substance, as such, is equally soluble in ethe. And the great etherean firmament is thus constituted; being a dense solution of corpor. In the main, etherea is transparent; but in some places translucent, and in others, opaque.

4. Here are iron, and copper, and granite, and water, and lead, and clay, and nitrogen, and oxygen, and hydrogen, and various other kinds of corporeal substances, as known on the earth, and besides these, millions of things not known on the earth. And ethe holdeth them in solution; even after the manner that the air holdeth the substance of clouds, which is water in solution. And as some clouds are so rarified as to be imperceptible, whilst others are opaque, and even black, so are the comparative conditions of etherea; of which matters more will be said further on.

5. In the case of a vortex in etherea (that is after the manner of a whirlwind on the earth), the corporeal solutions are propelled toward the center thereof in greater density.

6. When it is sufficiently dense to manifest light, and shadow, it is called a comet, or nebula; when still more dense it is a planet.

7. When as a comet (or nebula) the m'vortex hath not attained to an orbit of its own, it is carried in the currents of the master vortex, which currents are elliptic, parabolic and hyperbolic. Hence the so-called eccentric travel of comets.

8. At this age of the comet, it showeth nearly the configuration of its own vortex; its tail being the m'vortexya. If it appear to the east of the sun its tail turneth eastward; if west of the sun, it turneth westward.

9. Two directions of power are thus manifested; and also two powers: First, that the vortex of the sun hath power from the east to west, and from the west to east, to which the comet is subjected: Second, that the comet hath a vortex of its own, which is sufficient under the circumstances to maintain the general form of the comet. The ordinary comet hath its tail away from the sun, but some comets have two tails, one toward the sun and one away. In the case of Biela's comet in the year 4 B.K. (1846 A.D.), which was broken whilst the observer was looking on, is sufficient evidence of the sub-power of the comet

vortex.

10. Interior nebula is generally described as comets; whilst exterior nebula is usually called nebula. Nevertheless, all such solutions of corpor are of like nature, being as the beginning or as the incomplete condensation of a planet.

11. They do not all, nor half of them, ripen into planets. But their vortices are often broken and they return again into sublimated solutions, and are lost to mortal sight.

12. But nowhere in etherea is there a solution of corpor sufficient to put itself in motion; nor sufficient to condense itself; nor to provide the road of its travel. But its road of travel showeth the direction of the lines of the sun's vortex. Save and except in such case when a comet's vortex cometh within the vortex of another planet's vortex of greater power than its own.

13. As a cyclone, or whirlwind, on the earth, traveleth with the general current of the wind, so travel the sub-vortices in etherea within the axial lines of vortices in chief.

14. Whether within the sun's vortex, or external thereto, the rules apply, so far as nebula or comets are concerned, and the vortices that carry them.

15. Axial velocity belongeth to all of them; and the tendency of all of them is to orbits; the which they attain to or not, according to their strength compared to the master.

16. When a nebulous planet is sufficiently dense to have its corpor polarized, but so that its polarity correspondeth to the polarity of the master, it is transparent, and possesseth no eclipse power.

17. But when nebula is polarized transversely, it is as a cloud in etherea, with power to eclipse stars; and even to eclipse the sun itself, provided it be within the solar vortex.

18. Of external nebulae, of sufficient size to be self-sustaining, and to ultimately become planets, there are at present visible from the earth more than eight thousand. These are in process of globe-making, even as the earth was made. Of nebulae within the sun's vortex, where they are usually called comets, there are upward of eight or ten new ones every year. Some of them survive but a few months, some a few years; some a hundred years; and some even a thousand or more years. But in all cases when the vortex of one of them bursteth, the corpor of the comet flieth instantly into dissolution more sublimated, and is lost to mortal sight.

19. Where nebula is transparent and lieth between the earth and master center it is not discernible, either with the naked eye or with a telescope. Amongst the most sublimated forms of corpor in solution are nitrogen, oxygen and hydrogen. When a sub-vortex, or even a stratum of ten or twenty million miles, of this solution lieth between the earth and sun center, and an observation of the sun be taken, the observer is apt to erroneously suppose he hath discovered nitrogen, oxygen and hydrogen in the sun atmosphere or photosphere. And if the solution contain iron and gold and platinum, and other metals, the observer is apt to erroneously suppose he hath discovered these things within the photosphere or atmosphere of the sun.

20. Wherefore all observations made to determine such matters require that the observer shall first understand what lieth between the earth and the sun at the time of observation.

21. But some of these sub-vortices in etherea, require forty years' time in which to drag their whole length away from the line of observation. So that in no case is the observation of any value, even though it be taken the breadth of the earth, unless it covereth a period greater than forty years. But it also so happeneth that, perhaps, when such an immense

vortex is about passing away from the line, that another one, equally large, and perhaps of different density of solution, cometh within the line. And it may thus occur that hundreds of years will elapse before a good view of the sun can be obtained. Some of these traveling plateaux are opaque (dark), so that the sun is kept in a dim eclipse for a year or two, and sometimes for hundreds of years.

22. Wherefore philosophers have erroneously attributed their observations as having proved certain gases and certain metals within the sun's atmosphere.

23. The same remarks apply to observations made of the stars; and even of the moon.

24. In the case of light being manifested in a complete steel magnet, the major retention is at the angle of the two legs, and the minor light at the terminus of the north leg (negative pole). But in an eccentric magnet (horseshoe) the two lights are manifest at the terminus of the two legs.

25. A complete planetary vortex is a globe, or nearly so, and its manifested light like a complete magnet. But an immature vortex, as in the case of a comet or other small vortex, will manifest light at both poles, and sometimes in the middle, if it hath attained to power to manufacture light of its own. In some cases the comet or the nebula is not sufficiently condensed to produce light of it own, but containeth corpor in a gaseous state which of itself may have infinitesimal polarities refracting the normal light of the master vortex.

26. By observing the new moon, it will be seen that the light portion thereof describeth a larger circle than the dark portion. The bulge of the light side of the moon always pointeth toward the sun. It is an error to say that light cometh from the sun and striketh on the moon, and is then reflected on the earth. As previously shown, there is no such thing or substance as light; but that which is called light is a manifestation of vortexian power; also that the c'vortex is comparatively all one light, with a central focus. The reason one side of the moon is dark and one light, is because it hath a positive and negative manifestation of the c'vortexya; for the moon also manufactureth its own light.

27. As the moon advanceth to the next quarter, the same discrepancy in the two apparent sizes is manifest; and this continueth until it is full moon. It is an error to say that dark bodies appear smaller, and light bodies larger, because of absorption, or refraction. The cause is not absorption, or refraction, or reflection, but of manufacture.

28. Light bodies (so-called) manufacture light of their own, ever so infinitesimal, which is as an envelope external to themselves. The eye of the observer seeth this as well as the corporeal body, and consequently it appeareth larger than it really is.

29. The same rule applieth in regard to the sun and his photosphere, and to comets, and to all bodies that manifest light. Suitable deduction must be made, in endeavoring to determine the size of a planet.

30. Shadow is usually divided into two expressions, UMBRA, as the shadow of a man standing in sunlight; and DARKNESS, as the shadow of the earth in a cloudy night. Nevertheless, they are but one and the same thing, but in different degrees, both of which are here included in the word shadow. In a clear night, when the full moon shineth, two conditions are manifest on the earth: first, that a shadow is vertical to the moon, and the light side is not as light as when the sun shineth at noon.

31. The density of shadow from sunlight and the density of shadow from moonlight correspond exactly to the comparative difference between sunlight and moonlight.

32. When it is full moon at midday, the light of the sun (so-called) is no greater because

of the moon's presence. Observe the difference, however, on a given object if the ray from a mirror facing the sun be added to the ordinary sunlight. Hence it is an error to attribute the moon's rays as being reflected from the sun to the earth. If it be premised that the light face of the moon is not a mirror, but is opaque, observe the following result from the moon when it is half full: The half of the moon is equivalent to half a globe; if the light of the sun fell on the bulge, the rays thus landed on the moon would cause that part of the moon to be a trifle more than four times lighter (or brighter) than on the slopes.

33. In an observation of this kind, and if the light were borrowed from the sun, two kinds of rays would result; the bulge of the moon would afford a center for rays to emanate in very direction; and the slope rays would refract at the same angle as received from the sun.

34. The fact is, however, there is no intense center light manifested on the moon's surface, in the place where it directly faceth the sun. Hence there is no possibility of the light of the moon being produced by light from the sun, or from the sun's center. The light of the moon faceth the sun center, but the latter is not the cause thereof, the cause is in the emissions of positive and negative currents from the moon's vortex, and they manifest in the m'vortexya of the master.

35. The same rules apply to all planets whose vortices are negative.

CHAPTER III.

1. Here followeth the method of manufacturing light and heat as they are on the earth and moon and sun, and all other planets:

2. The half of the earth's vortex (for example) which faceth toward the sun is a concave lens to the earth. A similar lens, but far larger, is at the sun-center: The convex faces of the two lenses are toward each other forever. They are ethereally connected by solutions of corpor needles linear in position.

3. The vortex is larger than the earth, so that polar lights are possible on the shadow side. And the brilliancy of the polar lights are proportionately less than daylight at noon in the tropics, exactly in correspondence to the concentration of the rays by a lens of the magnitude referred to.

4. The vortexya rising up out of the earth at night is negative, or less than the vortexya descending in daylight, and their conjunctive line is near the earth's surface. Hence, five or six miles' altitude is intense cold; whilst five or six hundred is so cold that mortals could not possibly measure it.

5. In the early days of the earth, when there was more heat emitted from the earth than at present, it also rose to a greater altitude; but it was nevertheless thrown back, to a great extent, every day, even after the same manner it is to-day, by the vortexian lens referred to. And as of the heat, so also of the light.

6. In the sum of all the universe there was, and is now, and ever shall be, the same latent amount of heat and light. The vortex in formation driveth them to the centre for a period of time; nevertheless a time cometh when the heat and light escape outward. And though the vortexian lens recast them back in a measure, thus producing day and warmth on the face of the earth, yet there is ever a trifling loss toward perpetual coldness and darkness.

7. This great hemispherical lens, atmospherea, not only thus manufactureth light and

heat, but it also affordeth man the means of seeing the sun and moon and stars. It hath the power also of magnifying millions of comparatively dense etherean worlds, so that man can see through them. The student should consider this from the standpoint of a magnifying lens in a microscope, which hath power to distend many things so one can see through their fibres, which to the naked eye seem dense. For etherea is not nearly so rarified as mortals suppose. Without the sun's atmospherean lens, man could not even see the moon, nor stars; and the sun itself would seem as a pale red star.

8. As the vortex of the earth is thus a lens to the earth, so is the moon's vortex to the moon, and so also of the sun and all other stars and planets, where light and heat are manifested.

9. When the moon is half full, a dim outline of the shadow side of the moon is to be seen with the naked eye. This, by philosophers hath been erroneously called the earth's shine. For they ignorantly believed the light of the earth was reflected on the moon. The real cause of this sub-light on the moon is in consequence of the action of a sub-lens on the moon, facing the earth's vortex, which operateth after the same manner as the other.

10. When the moon produceth a full eclipse of the sun (by which philosophers ignorantly believed the light and heat of the sun were cut off from the earth), it causeth darkness on the earth by breaking the linear connection betwixt the earth's vortex and the sun-center, so that the positive current in the earth's vortex is cut off, and that part that would otherwise be a lens becometh negative in its action, in the linear space. But when the eclipse falleth far in the north or south part of the earth only, then the action of the moon's shadow will fall in the direction of the earth's lens, so that a sub-lens is impossible. Whereas, were there such a thing as earth's shine, in time of total eclipse of the sun, the equatorial light would make the moon shine at that time also.

11. As light, and heat, and magnetism, and electricity, are all one and the same thing, which are the manifestation of vortexian currents under different conditions, the student must not lose sight of the fact that none of these so-called things are things in fact, that is, entities of themselves, separately or combined.

12. Vortexya can be charged, as before mentioned, into iron and other substances. When it is charged in iron it is called magnetism; when charged in phosphorus it is called light (inactive); when charged in nitrate of silver it is called darkness. If its application be continued on phosphorus, the latter will combine with common air and ignite. With phosphorus and without it, it will, as before stated, combine oxygen and hydrogen, and it will also separate them. And yet vortexya, in fact, is no substance or thing as such; but is the vortex in axial and orbitic motion, or, in other words, corpor in an etheic solution.

13. As previously stated, ethe holdeth corpor in solution, which is the condition of atmospherea and of the etherean regions beyond. When a portion of this solution is given a rotary motion it is called a vortex. Nor is a vortex a substance or thing of itself, more than is a whirlwind, or as a whirlpool in the water. As a whirlpool can not exist without water, or a whirlwind exist without air, so can not a vortex exist without the etheic solution. As previously stated, in the beginning of a vortex it is long, but in course of time it hath a tendency to become round like a globe, but flattened a little at the poles. This also happeneth to every vortex that carrieth a satellite: That the periphery of the vortex is undulated; and the extent of its undulation can be determined by the minimum and maximum distance of the satellite from its planet.

14. In consequence of this discrepancy, the lens power of the vortex of the earth varies constantly, even daily, monthly and yearly. Nevertheless, the sum of heat and cold and the sum of light and darkness are nearly the same, one generation with another. This was, by the ancient prophets, called the FIRST RULE IN PROPHECY. This was again subdivided by three, into eleven years, whereof it was found that one eleven years nearly corresponded with another eleven years. This was the SECOND RULE IN PROPHECY. The THIRD RULE was NINETY- NINE YEARS, whereto was added one year.

15. In the case of the tides, a still further allowance of six years was found necessary to two hundred; but in the succeeding four hundred years a deduction was required of five years. Whereupon the moon's time was eighteen years.

16. As the lens power loseth by flattening the vortex, and increaseth by rounding the vortex, it will be observed that the position of the moon's vortex relatively to the earth's, is a fair conclusion as to the times of ebb and flood tide. In periods of thirty-three years, therefore, tables can be constructed expressing very nearly the variations of vortexya for every day in the year, and to prophesy correctly as to the winters and summers, so far as light and darkness, and heat and cold, are concerned. This flattening and rounding of the vortexian lens of the earth is one cause of the wonderful differences between the heat of one summer compared with another, and of the difference in the coldness of winters, as compared with one another. Of these also, tables can be made. Winter tables made by the ancients were based on periods of six hundred and sixty-six years, and were called SATAN'S TABLES, or the TIMES OF THE BEAST. Tables made on such a basis are superior to calculations made on the relative position of the moon.

17. But where they have prophesied ebb and flood tide to be caused by certain positions of the moon, they have erred in suffering themselves to ignorantly believe the cause lay with the moon. A man may prophesy by a traveling wagon what time it will reach town; but the correctness of his prophecy does not prove that the wagon pushed the horse to town. These revelations pertain more to the cause of things, than to giving new prophecies. What mortals can not discover by any corporeal observation must come by inspiration. In the year 4 B.K. Leverrier, of France, prophesied the existence of Neptune by the calculation of planetary disturbances. Other discoveries have been made in the same way; whereupon they have believed the said disturbances to be caused by one planet's power on another.

18. Planetary disturbances are not caused by any power or effect of one planet on another; the cause of the disturbances lieth in the vortices wherein they float. Mortals can not see the vortices; their only means of prophesying lieth in corpor. A man may prophesy of the moon by calculations of the disturbances of the tides. But to attribute to the tides the *cause* of the moon's position would be no more erroneous than to attribute the cause of tides to the moon.

19. It is not the intention, in these revelations, to give new calculations in regard to occurrences on the planets; it is a trifling difference whether a man prophesy by a vortex or by a planet. Wherein he erreth in regard to judging the cause of things, he should be put on the right road. Wherein he hath had no knowledge of the forces and currents of the unseen worlds and their dominion over the seen worlds, revelation only can reach him.

20. They have said there are five elements of corpor; then again sixty; and a hundred. But in time they will say there are millions. And yet all of them are comprehended in the word

corpor. To resolve them, discover them, and classify them, and their combinations, is the work of man. Where they are aggregated together, as the earth, the result is called a CREATION, or a created world. When such a globe is dissolved in ethe and sublimated, it is said a world is destroyed, or a star is destroyed. Nevertheless, in any of these operations, no one ingredient as such is annihilated. What is creation more than to make a drop of rain; or the dissolution of a world more than the evaporation of a drop of water?

21. Pour a few drops of water on a table covered with dust, and each drop will become a globe. Look for them tomorrow, and they are gone (evaporated). The globe is annihilated (for it was not a thing in fact), but the water, which was the thing, is not annihilated, but evaporated. The term annihilation applieth to such as are not things in fact, but which are forms and figures. A ray of light (so-called) can be annihilated; but that that comprised it can not be annihilated.

22. Were the earth's vortex to break, the earth would be precipitated into dissolution, under ordinary conditions. But were the earth's vortex to be swallowed in the vortex of another planet, then the earth would be precipitated as a globe to such planet. Such is the case as regardeth double stars, and triplets and quadruplets, especially where they are in contact. The same principle holdeth in regard to the vortices of some nebulae and comets; one is frequently swallowed up within another. But in such case the corpor commingleth.

23. In the case of double stars, and triplets, and so on, if conjoined, the center of gravitation (so-called) is not to each one, but to the intervening center between them. The polarity of such a group is as to the vortex. Think not, however, that double stars or triplets or quadruples are the limit of combinations in one vortex. There are clusters of planets, hundreds of them, thousands, and even millions, that sometimes occupy one vortex.

24. As a globe can be annihilated, so can a vortex, and so can vortexya; for none of these are things of themselves in fact, but combinations in some given place or condition; but the corpor of such expression of known forms and figures and motions can not be annihilated.

25. Though the general form of a vortex, as before stated, in its beginning is long, funnel-shaped (like a whirlwind), its ultimate is toward a globular form. And though the current of a vortex is spiral, at first, its currents ultimate toward less spirality. If one could imagine a very long serpent in spiral form, constantly turning its head in at one pole, and its tail at the other, and forever crawling upon its own spirality, such a view would somewhat illustrate the currents of a vortex. (See cuts in GOD'S BOOK OF BEN)

26. In one plate the black center representeth a planet, and the black spot with the letter "S" representeth a satellite. The white lines indicate the course of the vortexian currents, but purposely exaggerated in the drawing. First, to show the undulation in the vortex where the satellite resteth, and secondly, to show the head turning in at one end, and the bulge of the tail ready to overlap itself, wherefrom there is an excess of light manifested in the tail (northern) regions.

27. Were the currents of the vortex to attain due east and west lines, without polar out-cropping, the winds would cease to blow on the face of the earth. The air and the earth would ultimate in equilibrium in axial revolution.

28. Herein lieth the cause of the winds chiefly; nevertheless, high mountain ranges of irregular forms, and places on the earth's surface, add considerably to breaking and

changing the currents that would otherwise result. The transcendent heat of the tropical atmosphere would seem to call for replacement from the north and south by cold currents of wind; but it must be remembered that only a few miles up from the earth the temperature of the tropical air is as low as the polar air. Only so far as icebergs float toward the equator is there any very perceptible lowering of the temperature of the air, and of wind currents toward the tropics.

29. As previously stated, in describing the positive current of vortexya being in the form of a right-angle triangle, with the angle in the center of the earth, and one leg toward the north pole, and one in the east, at the equator, it will now be perceived that the greatest cold region of the earth can not be at either the equator or the poles, but must occupy places distant from the poles in the exact ratio of the difference in the power between the positive and negative currents of vortexya and m'vortexya, and corresponding to the atmospherean lens of the earth.

CHAPTER IV.

1. The currents of the vortex of the earth being in constant change, the following results happen. In the regions where they overlap one another, and break to a limited extent, producing discord in motion, certain eddies and whirlpools result, and the corpor in solution is condensed, like little planets or meteoric stones, varying in size from a pin's head to ten or twenty miles in diameter. And the little broken currents in the vortex lose their prey, and the meteoric stones or little planets are carried by the vortexian current down to the earth's surface. (See plates Wark, God's Book of Ben .)

2. The belt in atmospherea where these things happen is usually about five or six or seven hundred miles up from the earth's surface. But the belt sometimes ascendeth a thousand miles. But at other distances upward other belts exist; and others still beyond, and so on.

3. Another result that happeneth from these overlapping currents in the vortex, is the production of rain and snow and hail. Certain parts of the earth are given to snow; certain parts to rain and hail; and other parts to drought. In drought regions the vortexian overlappings descend to the very earth, where they are called by various names, such as cyclones, whirlwinds and so on; but if they occur on the ocean, carrying either up or down a current of water, they are termed water-spouts. In regions where there are rain, hail and snow falls, the vortexian commotion taketh place from half a mile to three miles above the earth's surface. Here the discord resulteth in liberating the moisture which was in transparent solution, and clouds result. But if the commotion continue, these are, atomically, still further liberated, and either rain or snow or hail resulteth, which is carried down to the earth.

4. The places in the vortex of the earth where these discords result are nearly uniform in their relative distance from the earth, and in the times of the occurrence, having special reference to the prophetic periods previously given.

5. Refer to plate 44, in Book of Ben where will be seen a variety of representations of the forms and figures of snow-flakes. But these are not all; there are thousands of millions of them, differing so much from one another that description is not possible. As previously stated, corpor being in solution in ethe, hath in the main the shape of needles, but of such infinitesimal size that corporeal knowledge of them can only be, at most, subjective

knowledge. But in the snow-flake are both the casting and the mold of discordant m'vortexian currents.

6. But it must be borne in mind that where one snow-flake is molded in one moment, another snow-flake molded in the same place the next moment, and so on, would display no two snow-flakes alike. Three stages may be described in the discordant results: first, the cloud; second, the frozen cloud, which is snow; and third, the rain-drop or hail-stone.

7. In the meteoric regions (which are above such clouds as produce rain) corpor also presenteth three stages of development, which are: Ash-clouds, transparent or otherwise; and crystal needles; and meteoric stones. The latter only, as a general rule, are precipitated to the earth. But on certain occasions, both the other forms of corpor are also precipitated to the earth.

8. Allowing a certain size to rain clouds, which are near the earth, corporeal clouds high up in the vortex, are proportionately larger according to the ratio of the difference between their globular circumference and that of the lower strata. So also are the discordant waves proportionally longer, wider and deeper.

9. It is an error to say that the atmosphere of the earth decreaseth gradually and continually in specific gravity according to the distance above the earth.

10. It is an error to say that there is any gravity in it, save only that it precipitateth formations like rain, snow, hail and meteoric stones. As before shown, these things have no gravity of their own to go in any direction. Nor is there any attraction in the earth to pull them down. They are driven to the earth by the vortexian current. But the point herein now considered is, the commonly expressed knowledge of men, that the atmosphere hath less density outward, away from the earth, in proportion to the distance from the earth's surface. In one respect this is an error; in another a truth: As to density PER SE there is no difference in the atmosphere on the face of the earth compared to that of a thousand miles high, or a hundred thousand miles high. It is all in even balance, as to pressure and density, PER SE . But because the etheic solution of corpor is more sublimated by swifter axial motion in the higher regions, and because the lower regions contain less perfectly dissolved corpor, the difference hath been improperly described. Air is no heavier because of rain; the weight lieth in the rain only.

11. Hence the gravity (so-called) of the atmosphere hath reference only to imperfect solutions of corpor. And it is true that a superabundance of these imperfect solutions are near the earth.

12. At the sea-level a certain pressure seemeth to manifest, as in a barometer; on a high mountain a less pressure seemeth to manifest. There is also a variation in the barometer according to certain conditions of the atmosphere. The difference is not that the pressure of the atmosphere is different; the pressure of the atmosphere, PER SE , is the same in all directions, high and low. The cause of the variation of the barometer is in reference to distension (sublimated solution of corpor), and hath no reference to pressure as such. This capacity to distension is not only external to the barometer, but within it also; so that as a measure of atmospheric pressure PER SE it is entirely worthless. The suction pump, or inverted tube filled with water, showeth the pressure of the atmosphere upward as well as downward, and showeth what the pressure is.

13. Wherefrom it is shown there is no such thing as attraction of gravitation of the atmosphere toward the earth more than away from it. Where the atmosphere is overcharged with an imperfect solution of corpor, or snow or rain, that excess is that which balanceth toward the earth. But this also only applieth in regions close to the earth's surface. Fifty or a hundred thousand miles up from the earth, the axial velocity of the vortex is so great that rain or snow would be instantaneously dissolved, distended and lost to sight. Consequently the solutions in the higher atmosphere not only contain moisture, but they contain iron, lead, zinc, gold, platinum, clay, granite, diamonds and all other things known to exist on the earth, and many others besides.

14. In the early age of the vortex of the earth, so swiftly flew the outer rim that border eddies ensued, from which nebula congregated, until the earth had a nebulous belt around it. This belt, in time, losing pace with the earth's vortex, condensed and made the moon.

15. But to return to the snow-flake and to the needles of the corpor whilst in the etheic solutions: On a cloudy day these solutions or needles (mist, or dull atmosphere) are more or less transverse to the vortexian lines. In a clear day the needles are linear to the earth, and this is the reason it is a clear day. The latter direction of the needles may be called direct, and the former indirect. Wherein they are direct, and they fall on the photoplate, the force of their blows is called actinic force, and it is the same as where they fall on the wet linen in the bleachman's field. In this actinic blow a weak electric flame is produced by each needle; hence the bleaching power, and also the power to blister an exposed skin which hath been kept for years in the dark (negative).

16. If a solution of iron, transparent, or of quinine, or other recipient of negative electricity, be sprinkled on the cloth, the actinic ray will not result in the electric spark, and no bleaching effect will be produced; and even, sometimes, on the contrary, a black spot will result.

17. Wherever the vortexian current falleth, corpor is more or less damaged or dissolved, or changed in its combinations. On a piece of iron, fresh broken, it produceth rust. Because the vortexian solution contained oxygen, this effect hath been called oxidation. Nevertheless, in point of fact, oxygen of itself is inert: The break of its needles liberateth vortexya, which result is a minor representation of the discharge of an electric spark from the pole of a battery.

18. As previously stated, the vortexian currents are to the earth in the daylight; and from the earth in the night; although their force is toward the center of the earth (from the east) and toward the north pole afterward. The following result happeneth: For example, a pool of water is charged during the day with the positive current; during the night the negative current escapeth upward from the water. The decomposition resulting therefrom is called se'mu (green scum), a mucilaginous substance which floateth on the surface of the water. In some days' time this se'mu, by motion (from some external cause), assumeth certain defined shapes, crystalline, fibrous and otherwise, after the manner of strange configurations of frost on a window-pane. In some days after this, if the se'mu be examined with a lens it will be discovered that here are miniature trees, even forests, with vines and grasses. No seed was there.

19. This new property is called Life and because it existeth everywhere it is called Omnipresent. Man can account for the se'mu; for the positive and negative forces; for corpor and for ethe; but Life is unfathomable by man. The se'mu (green scum) floateth against the ground; its infinitesimal trees and vines and grasses take root and grow, and live a season and die; but from the roots and seeds a larger growth succeedeth. Thus becometh all the world inhabitated over with living creatures. Nevertheless not one thing of all of them mergeth into another; but every one bringeth forth after its own kind.

20. Man inquireth of the earth, the rocks, the air, and of all things: Who is this Life? This Omnipresent that quickeneth into life all the living? But none can answer him. Then man inquireth of Life: "Who art Thou O Life?" And the answer cometh to the soul of man: "I am Life! I Am the I Am! I Am the Ever Present! All that thou seest in earth or heaven, and even in the unseen worlds, also, are My very Person! I am the whole!"

CHAPTER V.

1. In the transposition of needles of corpor from parallel polarity to mixed or transverse positions, are produced all kinds of colors. It is an error to say: Wave of light, or bent ray of light, or that a given number of vibrations or undulations produce different kinds of colors; there is neither wave nor undulation in fact. Needles are arbitrary and can not be bent. Compare a needle to a transparent glass crystal. Place a given number of these end to end, touching, and in a line: To bend this line is impossible, save at angles, for where every two ends join there will be an angle: Be the needles ever so short there will be no bend in fact, but a succession of arbitrary lines and elbows.

2. Such is not, however, the juxtaposition, save when they are in a line direct; otherwise the ends of the needles do not bend like joints, but each one turneth more or less on its own axis. If they all turn, an Apparent wave is produced, expressive of a certain color; if part of them turn, another color is produced. In proportion to this disturbance, so are the Apparent vibrations slow or fast, as to mortal observation.

3. In regions of the earth's atmosphere where they have cyclones, reddish lights appear in the firmament, even before the cyclone manifesteth on the earth. And these lights travel with the cyclone, manifesting great heat on the earth. In the regions of monsoons, a similar manifestation occurreth, but generally with pink or bluish lights instead of red, if over the ocean; but if over the land, a smoky atmosphere resulteth.

4. These colors, and all others, manifested in atmospherea, are not confined to the earth stratum, but they extend even to the outer extreme of the earth's vortex. And in many instances they are so altitudinous that their manifestations are imperceptible to mortal observation, save that, for example, the moon or the sun shineth less brightly. When one of the transpositions is dark and is high up in the atmosphere at night, they say the moon is surrounded by a haze. And yet, the while, the atmospheric stratum next the earth may be clear.

5. The earth's vortex hath millions of these strata, and of various colors, shades and tints. In taking photographs of the moon or the sun, these often interpose, and the picture taken

deceiveth the observer, that he hath made a picture of the oxygen or hydrogen of the planet's atmosphere.

6. The same state of affairs belongeth also in the sun's vortex; so that, with these clouds of color intervening in etherea, the telescope encountereth much travail.

7. As a vortex groweth older, these disturbances, together with imperfect solutions of corpor, become less frequent. So also in the early age of a vortex they are more frequent and of longer duration. So that, at times, a red light, or blue light, or other color, will overspread the earth for periods of a thousand or more years without interruption. And in some cases, darkness for as long a period. Whatever living thing, as herbs and trees, grasses and so on, were quickened into life during darkness, were without eyes. Nevertheless, in this day, even these things turn toward the light; as plants and flowers placed in a window will manifest.

8. Where se'mu was quickened into life in lighter times, it focalized toward the light, and this focus was called an eye. And such as were thus quickened into life, and not attached to the earth by fibers or roots, were called animals. And the LIFE they inherited gave power unto them, to go about from place to place. So great are the powers of the eyes of some animals that they can see and distinguish in the darkest of nights. Such eyes are absorbents of vortexya, and they shine in the dark.

9. Hence the first organs of sense created in any animal were the eyes; whereof it hath been said, the eye is the seed of the tree of knowledge. The sight of the eye is the beginning of self-creation, in acquiring knowledge; and it doeth by going forth and staying at home at the same time. The sight of the eye is a miniature sun, sending forth and receiving vortexian power at the same time. As may be proved by looking on the eyelids of a person sleeping, who will awake because thereof.

10. Since, then, the eye of man can go forth with intelligent power, controlling things, it hath been concluded since thousands of years, by the wisest philosophers, that an All Seeing Eye is the Cause and Creator of the whole universe, which is His Person.

11. In the first quickening of eyes, they partook of the color of the vortexian lights at that time; and even so at the same period of time were colored the skins of mortals, and according to their surroundings, some light, some dark, and some red, or yellow, or copper-colored.

12. And all of them propagated after their own kind, and do so to this day. And though the blacks might live for thousands of generations with themselves only, in any country in the world, they would never become whites. And the same rule applieth to whites and browns, and all the races of man.

13. But because they can mix, and because that mixture can propagate, all the races of man are one and the same in all their organs and capabilities. Now, as previously stated, white things manufacture a white atmosphere around them; whilst black things do not (being negative). The white give off, or radiate light and power; the black are not radiants. The white man's radiating power recoileth upon himself, and he suffereth with heat. So also with the white bear. The black man and black bear are the reverse.

14. Wherefrom this rule will now be plain to the student: When a planet hath attained to so great age she no longer giveth forth light or heat to radiate upon herself, she can not be seen in the heavens. Of which kinds of planets there are millions in the etherean firmament. Some of these move slower than any of the planets man can see. Some of these at times eclipse the sun, and are taken for sun-spots, although, perhaps, not a million miles from the earth.

15. Like unto these, in darkness, are there plateaux of nebula floating in the firmament, which also produce eclipses of the sun and of the moon. For convenience, let such planets and nebula be called dead planets and dead nebula. And that there are millions of such bodies, sufficient to eclipse the sun, or a star, or the moon, the different periods of darkness on the earth will prove.

16. In prophesying the tendency of a planet's approach to death, refer once more to the moon: Now the moon hath, as to the earth's face, no axial revolution. But it must be remembered the moon can not go around the earth without making an actual axial revolution. Seventy and one-half revolutions of the moon's vortex complete one travel around the earth's vortex. Consequently we arrive at the exact speed of the moon's vortexya and the strength of light and heat manifested on the moon. The student should make allowance for the moon's ellipse, for the light of the moon is much stronger (as seen from the earth) some times than others.

17. Place the se'muan age at ninety-nine degrees, the time of quickening animal life. It will be found that the moon at such period must have had an axial motion, facing the earth, of three and four-sevenths' times faster than the earth. Whilst at the same period of time the earth made its daily revolution in what would now be twenty-one hours and forty minutes. This would give a difference in animal heat of two and a half degrees of vortexya on the earth, as compared to the se'muan age. Consequently large animals, which are now extinct, had a temperature (average) higher of two and a half degrees than at present. Wherein we perceive three hours and seventeen minutes' loss in axial motion produced a loss of two and a half degrees of vortexian heat.

18. The difference, therefore, on the moon, in temperature below blood-heat and what it now must be, must correspond exactly with its comparative slowness (one revolution a month), as to the loss manifested on the earth. Now, although the student will discover the moon hath fallen to a temperature far below zero, yet it emitteth both light and heat.

19. To find the se'muan age (especially of man), place his temperature at ninety-eight (for good health), and one hundred and two at inflammation or death. Four below normal will, therefore, be the period of man's inhabitation of the earth. After the vortexian radiation reacheth this period, man will cease to propagate, and, so, become extinct as to the earth.

20. This giveth man eight degrees of vortexya as the sum of his existence. One degree is equivalent to twelve million seven hundred and sixty thousand radi c'vorkum. The serpent's coil would be one and one-fourth. That is, twenty-four thousand years to the time of completion. Thus, 12,760,000 divided by 260,000 add 1,402 1-2 add 24,000 x 3 = 76,750 years, the time of the se'muan age for man. To this should be added one cycle, of, say, three thousand years, which was the beginning of the fall of se'mu.

21. By reversing these measurements, find the axial decrease of the earth in seventy-eight thousand years, which will be just one hundred minutes, or 3-340ths of a second annually, which is the earth's decline in speed. For which reason the first of the race of man on earth began about seventy-eight thousand years B.K.

CHAPTER VI.

1. To return to the master vortex; refer to plate Tow-Sang, Book of Ben. It is an error to say that the eye seeth the sun by means of a straight line. The line of sight to the sun is spiral and oval. But it is equally an error to say that light cometh from the sun to the earth, or to any other planet; which hath given rise to the still greater errors of computing the time of travel of light, and the degree of heat of a planet by its proximity to the sun.
2. To determine the distance of the sun from the earth, allowance must be made for the vortexian spirality. By which reason the sun is in fact some seven million miles nearer the earth than its measure would indicate. The same rule applieth to all planets save the moon. And even this is seen by means of the curved lines of the earth's vortex.
3. As the moon's vortex rideth around on the outer part of the earth's vortex, we discover the elliptic course thereof; so by the roads of a comet do we discover the spirality and curve of the master's vortex. Observe a comet in different positions as it followeth the sun's vortex.
4. When the head of a comet falleth within the overlapping waves of the sun's vortex, the head is sometimes swallowed up and sometimes driven backward, spitting flames of fire the while. The nearer the comet approacheth an elliptic course, the longer will it live; the opposite condition applieth to hyperbolic comets, for they oft die or dissolve in one journey. If a comet be seen today in hyperbole, and in any angle of the heavens; and if, in ten years or a hundred years, a comet be seen in the same place, it would be an error to say it was the same comet.
5. It is an error to prophesy the heat of Venus being more or less because of her approximation nearer the sun. There is no more heat in the master vortex in general, than there is a hundred miles above the earth, save and except when very near the sun's photosphere, that is to say, within one or two thousand miles at most.
6. There is a sun planet in the center of the photosphere, at a distance interior, from three thousand miles to thirty thousand miles, and it is light all the way around. But within the body of the photosphere there are numerous planets, some globular, some elongated and irregular. These are usually called sun-spots. Because when they present their negative surface toward the earth they seem black. For the most part these planets in the photosphere are rather external than internal at the times they appear as spots. They have independent motions in their respective places.
7. Wherefrom it may be said: When an unlearned man saith: The Sun, we know what he meaneth; but when a learned man saith: The Sun, we know not what he meaneth, whether the whole central group, or the sun planet only.
8. If one were to go into a circular field, a little way from the middle, and there construct

an electric battery, from which he extendeth outward a multitude of wires, to small batteries in distant parts of the field, his batteries would then represent somewhat the solar phalanx, the central one being the sun. There would be more volume of electricity manifested at the central battery; but the intensity of the spark at one of the small batteries would, other things being equal, be equal to the spark at the central battery.

9. Neither is there more intensity of heat at the sun, than in any electric flash. Neither must it be surmised that the sun center is an electric battery; nor that it supplieth in any sense anything to any other planet. As previously stated, there are two things, corpor and ethe; the latter is the solvent of corpor. Whirling vortices of the solution make planets. And these are the sum and substance of all things manifested in the universe. (As to the cause of these whirlpools, see BOOK OF JEHOVIH)

10. It is an error to say the sun threw off rings or planets. No thing hath power to throw off itself, or a part thereof, save some living creature. They have instanced water flying from the periphery of a rapidly rotating wheel. This would merely imply that some one was trying to fasten worlds on the sun's periphery, but that the sun cast them off. Who that SOME ONE was they say not; nor do they offer a reason as to how such thrown-off substance came to be in the way of the sun in the first place.

11. It is equally erroneous to say that the presence of this planet or that, throweth an influence on mortals, according to their birth under certain stars. It is this same astrological ignorance that attributeth to the sun the throwing-off of light and heat and of possessing attraction of gravitation, and of throwing-off rings to make planets of.

12. Man hath ever sought in corporeal things for the cause of this and that; he buildeth up certain tables and diagrams, and calleth it science or philosophy. If, on one morning, he put on the left shoe first, and something happen that day, he proveth by that shoe a new philosophy. By the tides he proveth the cause of the moon; or by the moon the cause of the tides. Anything under the sun that is corporeal, rather than search in the subtle and potent, unseen worlds.

13. Let it be premised, then, that the etherean firmament is not a waste and interminable nothingness; but that, on the contrary, it is in many regions, even between the earth and the sun, sufficiently dense for a corporeal man to dwell upon, and to walk about, even as on the earth. Some of these are as transparent as water or clear glass, and some opaque. Some of these etherean worlds are large as the earth, and some a thousand times larger. Some are as immense facsimiles of snow-flakes; with arches a thousand miles high and broad. Some of them are as oceans of water; some transparent and some opaque; and some of them dense clouds of ashes. But so great are the numbers and so vast the varieties of these thousands of millions of etherean worlds, that description is impossible. Yet, by the telescopic power of the earth's vortexian lens, these worlds are magnified so as to seem to be nonentities.

14. Worlds in solution, the etherean heavens, are therefore governed by no power in, or escaping from, corporeal worlds. In the language of the ancient prophets, they are a law unto themselves. And yet these unseen worlds have much power and influence on the vortices of corporeal worlds.

15. In making observations with the spectroscope, these otherwise unseen worlds are sometimes seen; but in a general way the spectroscope revealeth only the refraction of high altitudes in the earth's vortex. It is an error to say the spectrum divideth the sun's rays PER SE. It is an error to say the spectroscope hath revealed certain colors in the atmosphere or photosphere of the sun or other stars. Its revelations for the most part pertain to what is contained in the vortexian lens of the earth, no matter whether the view be toward the sun or another star.

CHAPTER VII.

1. Having shown the impossibility of philosophy based on corporeal knowledge to demonstrate truth in regard to unseen things, and in regard to planets distant from the earth, it becometh a part of these revelations to put the student in the way to learn from the unseen forces which govern all corporeal things, man included, as a general and important part.

2. When a heavy stone falleth on a man and holdeth him down, it is sufficient to say the stone ruleth over the man. If an epidemic come upon a city because of uncleanness, it is well to consider that cause also. Nevertheless, if an epidemic be periodical to a certain city, even when not unclean, it is wise to prophesy an unseen cause. The same rule applieth in comparing one locality with another.

3. In certain regions of the earth, certain diseases are common; in certain times of the earth, as to cycles of three thousand years, certain diseases were common. In certain places of the earth man hath at times, thousands of years ago, attained to great knowledge and virtue. But his whole country in after centuries became a wilderness.

4. It is not the place of a prophet to answer these things by the accusation of ignorance or war. The prophet must account for that tendency in man to fall into ignorance and into war. In other words, he must find the cause of causes.

5. At certain periods of time, for hundreds of years, nations have dwelt in peace, and have risen in virtue; then turned to war within themselves and gone down in death.

6. The prophets of old divided time into cycles of three thousand years, with slight variations. And they found that at such periods of time, some certain impulse came upon the people, causing them to try to be better and wiser. Even as the same feeling is this day manifesting itself in many nations.

7. The scale then riseth for four hundred years, more or less; and, after that, wars and epidemics come upon the people. They begin then to decline, especially in virtue and peace, but the general intelligence suffereth little for about another six or seven hundred years. After which time they destroy their libraries and records, and reduce themselves to ignorance and vice. Then followeth a darkness of one thousand or more years, with slight intermissions. In other six hundred years the corporeal senses begin to ascend. Self-conceit cometh upon them; they think they are the beginning of wisdom on earth. Then cometh another cycle of light. Angels descend from the unseen worlds. New revelations crop out in every quarter. Inspiration cometh upon mortals, and they go to the opposite extreme; superstition and obedience to unseen influences.

8. Such, then, is the general character and behavior of man during a cycle. And he riseth and falleth in all these particulars as regularly as the tides of the ocean.

9. That man may begin to comprehend these things, and learn to classify them so as to rise in wisdom and virtue, and thus overcome these epidemic seasons of cycles, these revelations are chiefly made.

10. As previously shown, there are positive and negative forces forever going to and escaping from the earth. Without these no creature could live on the earth. The negative imparteth to man his corporeal growth, and corporeal desires, passions, and so on.

11. According to the corpor solutions in the firmament and their precipitations to the earth, as to quantity and quality, so will man be affected and inclined to manifest. These influences are easily discernible by some persons. One is depressed by a dull day; another inclined to drunkenness and fighting. By a bright day man is inspired to energy.

12. A su'is is so susceptible to vortexian currents, he can realize the qualities of a medicine whilst it is yet in a glass bottle, by merely holding it in his hand; or know the character of the writer of a letter by holding the letter in his hand. Yet all this is accomplished by the vortexian current of the article in question.

13. These revelations however are not in reference to individuals, but to nations and peoples, in periods of time embracing hundreds of years, and thousands of years.

14. It is an error to say whilst the corporeal worlds are organized, with fixed orbits and uses, the unseen worlds are nothing, or at best not organized. They are organized, with orbits, places, forms, figures, and so on, as definitely as are the corporeal worlds. Their times and seasons are regular and well provided.

15. In the passage of the earth in its own roadway, it goeth amongst these etherean and atmospherean worlds regularly; so that the periods of inspiration, and periods of darkness, are not haphazard.

16. It is not the purpose of these revelations to work out prophecies, leaving nothing for man to do. But to call his attention to the unseen forces that rule on the earth, and show him the way to make the prophecies himself.

17. In orachnebuahgalah the student will draw a curved line, representing the travel of the great serpent for three thousand years. This shall be cut across in eight places, to represent the periods of light. The places between them shall be made dark and light according to the history of man's behavior during said three thousand years. War shall be represented by black. The duration of wars shall be marked with a cut called change. Numbers shall designate the degrees of historical manifestations. For every great division of the earth make one orachnebuahgalah. The scale should be from one to a thousand for the entire length; and from one to a thousand from one dawn to another, and from one to a thousand for each and every characteristic designated. Number man 1 and 33, and the moon 1 and 18; and number the earth 1 and 365. These were called by the ancients the grades of a thousand (So-e-cen-ti).

18. These periods will be found to come under certain numbers, 11, 33, 66, 99, 100, 200, 400, 666, 333, 66, 18, 500, 600, 365, 99, 33, 18, and so on. (Not that the numbers, as such, have anything to do with such matters.) Thus, the moon's time is 18, the earth's 365, a generation 33, dan 200, 400, 600, 500; nitrogen or darkness 66 and 666, and so on. For which reason the following tables of times and measurements were established:

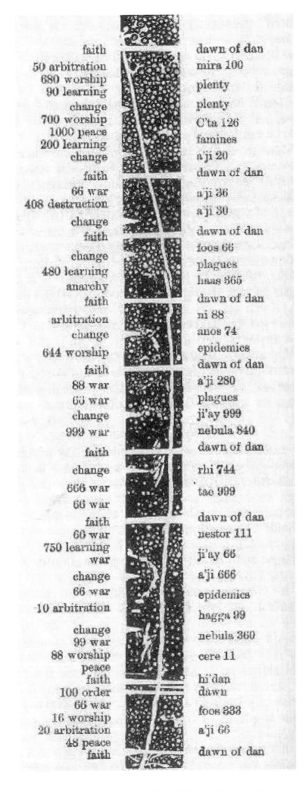

faith	dawn of dan
50 arbitration	mira 100
680 worship	plenty
90 learning	plenty
change	plenty
700 worship	C'ta 126
1000 peace	famines
200 learning	a'ji 20
change	
faith	dawn of dan
66 war	a'ji 36
408 destruction	a'ji 30
change	
faith	dawn of dan
	foos 66
change	plagues
480 learning	haas 365
anarchy	
faith	dawn of dan
arbitration	ni 88
change	anos 74
	epidemics
644 worship	dawn of dan
faith	
88 war	a'ji 280
66 war	plagues
change	ji'ay 999
999 war	nebula 840
faith	dawn of dan
change	rhi 744
666 war	tao 999
66 war	
faith	dawn of dan
66 war	nestor 111
750 learning	ji'ay 66
war	
change	a'ji 666
66 war	epidemics
10 arbitration	hagga 99
change	nebula 360
99 war	
88 worship	cere 11
peace	
faith	hi'dan
100 order	dawn
66 war	foos 333
16 worship	
20 arbitration	a'ji 66
48 peace	
faith	dawn of dan

Plate 48. ORACHNEBUAHGALAH

784

Ain, 16. - Alia, 248. - Anos, 74. - Atu, 441. - Alex, 11. - Alef, 100.
Abram, 9. - Airi, 36. - Ba, 467. - Bais, 74. - Beth, 999. - Braahen, 99.
Boi, 476. - Ban, 666. - Cere, 11. - Ceres, 111. - Ceret, 112 . - Ceriv, 48.
Cra, 98. - C'ta, 126. - Dhu, 69. - Dhi, 408. - Driviis, 6. - Dian, 244.
Diais, 240. - Die, 100. - Etus, 42. - Earas, 80. - Eta, 344. - Edith, 111.
Emon, 44. - Emmon, 444. - Feis, 11. - Foe, 666. - Foor, 333. - Goe, 400.
Gow, 600. - Gow, 500. - Gow, 200. - Gow, 111. - Gu, 888. - Ha, 10.
Hai, 110. - Haa, 120.- Hawh, 464. - Hy, 964. - Hi, 666. - Ham, 7. - Ho, 999.
Hoho, 99. - H'ho, 9. - Hagar, 33. - Hag, 11. - Hagga, 99. - Haig, 18.
Haas, 365. - Hoi, 12. - Hooh, 200. - Hoit, 950. - Ine, 27. - Ines, 274.
Itu, 674. - Ka, 6. - Kabal, 66. - Kaballa, 666. - Kaax, 33. - Ki, 4. - Kii, 999.
Kisiv, 18. - Loo, 999. - Lo, 11. - Loos, 33. - Loos, 66. - Loos, 666. - Lu, 10.
Lulu, 100. - Lens, 200. - Mas, 1. - Mas, 4. - Mas, 18. - Ma, 600. - Mat, 500.
Mi, 1. - Mara, 66. - Mira, 100. - Mithra, 666. - Mieuse, 40. - Ni, 88. - Ni, 888.
Niiv, 846. - Nes, 11. - Nestor, 111. - Nice, 33. - Nu, 880. - Nyi, 500. - Oh, 1.
Oho, 33. - Oise, 91. - Oise, 991. - Pneu, 9. - P'euta, 8. - Ra, 44. - Rhi, 744.
Ras, 600. - Rus, 400. - Rufus, 66. - Su, 248. - Su'is, 999. - Si, 16. - Sa, 441.
Tae, 999.- Tae, 666.- Ti, 33.- Tus, 18 - Vri, 111.- Zed, 66. - Zudu, 4. - Zedeki, 44.

YA-LA-PESTA.

[The student is referred to Book of Saphah for interpretation of the symbols.- Ed.]

2274, 821 - Seven changes, i.e., Howt, oat, bun, lis, vu, mi, ruth.

4750 - Nista, six changes, i.e., wuts, norse, rue, wi, rill and goe.

1060 - Two changes: Aont and foe.

1768 - Four changes: Mathai, yam, luke and jon.

1245 - Eight changes: Woo, gosa, lo, galeb, nor, nu, dhi and yun.

1790 - Six changes: Loo, chong, ouk, chan, clips and wis.

108 - Two changes: Yissain and C'tarin.

3644 - Twelve changes: Yats, rope, sum, div, hong, ras, rak, nir, yute, theo, ike and mar.

1746 - Eleven changes: Zi, yu, che, gow, rom, luts, wang, said, do, gos and yun.

3601 - Three changes: H'ak, ghi and kong.

47 - Three changes: Sim, Will and loo.

9278 - Four changes: Lai, bom, ross and fur.

326 - Eight changes: Wahes, Yine, Seb, Dhi, Yeniv, gan, li and rak.

2340 - Twelve changes: Mark, hiss, thor, bess, lin, triv, gam, zet, howd, saing, tum and gowtz.

CHAPTER VIII.

1. Let ethe stand as one; ji'ay as two; a'ji as three, and corpor as four. To ethe give motion one hundred, or ninety-nine (as the case may be); to corpor give zero, that is, no motion (of itself); to ji'ay give sixty-six; to a'ji give thirty-three.

2. Ethe, being the time of light, is named dan; ji'ay, the time of fevers, epidemics, plagues; and a'ji the time of wars, dashing forth with power and grasping; mi, the earth being the subject.

3. There is still another period to all corporeal worlds, LUTS. In the time of luts there falleth on a planet condensed earthy substances, as clay, stones, ashes, molten metals disseminated, and so on, in such great quantities that it can be compared to snow-storms, piling up corporeal substance on the earth in places to a depth of many feet, and in drifts to hundreds of feet.

4. Luts was by some ancient prophets called UZ, because it was a time of destruction. If luts followed soon after a se'muan period, when portions of the earth were covered with se'mu and rank vegetation, it charred them, penetrating and covering them up. Thus were made, for the most part, the coal-beds and oil-beds in the earth.

5. Luts belongeth more to an early age of a planet, when its vortex is more extended, and when the nebulous clouds in its outer belt are subject to condensation, so as to rain down on the earth these corporeal showers.

6. The time of dan is the opposite of this; and although it is the time of spirituality amongst mortals, and the time of prophecy and inspiration, yet it is the time the earth is rapidly giving off its life force, and its moisture; rapidly growing old.

7. Consequently the two most important periods for the prophet's consideration come within thirty-three and sixty-six, or, as they of old said, man and beast. In which measure man is divided into two parts (man and beast), and there is ever a percentage in his behavior inclining to one or the other, and they correspond to the vortexian currents of the earth.

8. The student must not consider merely individuals, but nations and peoples belonging to continents. And the relationship that cometh of a'ji or dan, or their percentage, must have reference to such nations or peoples as manifest to its influence.

9. Thus, suppose a grade to run below thirty-three, but not as low as twenty-two, and such a people fall under a'ji for a period of sixty-six years, or even more, war, destruction, death and lust will come upon that people. But suppose the same fall of a'ji come upon a people graded above thirty-three, to sixty-six, war and intellect, with oratory, music and remarkable men of genius will result. But, to carry it still further, the same fall of a'ji coming on a people above sixty-six, they will manifest in multitudinous Lords, Gods and Saviors, and in superstitions, rites and ceremonies, which will all more or less pertain to sexualisms.

10. The prophet is thus enabled to determine, by the vortexian currents, the rise and fall of nations, and to comprehend how differently even the same showers and shadows of the unseen worlds will affect different peoples. And the same rules apply in the manifestation of dan; according to the grade of a people, so will they receive its light. If below thirty-three, they will become magicians and prophets without virtue; if above thirty-three, but below sixty-six, they will become self-opinionated malefactors, running into licentiousness for self-sake. But if above sixty-six, they will become true prophets, abnegating self for sake of righteousness.

11. Let the student compare the Faithists of Capilya in India with the Cojuans of the same country; and the Faithists of Moses in Egupt with the Eguptians of the same country. The Faithists of both countries advanced, but their persecutors both went down to destruction. The peace of the Faithists held four hundred years; and then both peoples began to choose kings, which was followed by nine hundred and ninety years of darkness.

12. So that whether the vortices show approaching light or approaching darkness the

prophet must bear in mind the grades of peoples. Any given light amongst mortals as to the past, will thus show the date of its occurrence; whilst the heavenly lights will equally foreshow what will come upon any people.

13. It is not sufficient for man to know how to prophesy; but to learn how to overcome the elements of his surroundings. As previously set forth, there are regions of drought on the earth, which man must learn to overcome, by causing rains to fall. He shall provide explosive gases high up in the air, which shall break the wind currents, establishing vortices from the upper regions downward.

14. And when an epidemic is prophesied to a city, man shall dissipate the falling se'mu, and thus save it from destruction.

15. The inoculation, or vaccination, of flesh with poison, to save it from poison, is to use the battle-ax of satan. Man shall learn the higher law; to save by virtue instead of vice.

16. As to the grades, the student is referred to the Book of Es.

17. Prophecy is not guess-work. Absolute rules govern all things. A few individuals in a nation, or of a people, are a small matter. Nor must the prophet swerve one jot or tittle by the pretensions of a people. As for example: the Brahmans, the Buddhists, the Mohammedans and the Christians, all profess faith in their respective Gods and Saviors; but their professions are false. Their faith is in soldiers and standing armies, and in implements of destruction. The prophet must not, therefore, suffer himself to hearken to individual explanations. He must grade them in their entirety; whether they manifest below thirty-three, or above sixty-six, without regard to pretensions.

18. When the student hath completed his tables of orachnebuahgalah, with the history of the period, and taken the measure of grades of the different nations and peoples of the earth, he will find that he can not only foretell the future, but he can discover the past history for an equally long period of time.

19. And when he hath thus completed two cycles, he can find a third, and then a fourth, and so on, until all the past history of the earth is delivered up to his understanding.

CHAPTER IX.

1. The same force, vortexya, pervadeth the entire universe, but differently, according to volume, velocity and configuration.

2. As previously shown, colors are not substances or things in fact, but records of currents of vortexya, and are in proportion to their deviation from linear to adverse parallelism. These fall under the divisor, or multiple, 3 (primaries), yellow, blue and red, corresponding to the times, 11, 33, 99, and so on.

3. The same rule was applied by the ancient prophets in music, making three primary sounds, e, o, ih (the words of the wind), but giving all other sounds to the beast (66), which was supposed to cover the number of sounds from the lowest bass to the highest treble, that could be procured from the animal creation. And these ranges of sounds are manifest in man, whether singing or talking, according to the kind of vortexian currents that fall upon a country and the grade he holdeth in resurrection. So that even a whole people in one country will utter sounds higher or lower than in another country, some through the teeth, some in the throat, and yet others through the nose.

4. Sounds, as in music, are not substance, but currents of air in motion, which register

their broken discharges on the drum of the ear. So that it is possible for the ear to be so cultivated that it can detect these velocities, so as to determine colors thereby. For, of a truth, in entity, sounds and colors are one and the same thing, but registered, one on the eye and one on the ear. In other words, the two organs of sense discover the same thing differently: To one it is music, to the other it is color.

5. If a man be given to reverie because of music or colors, his soul traveleth in the currents thereof, and he becometh oblivious to his surroundings. The vortexian currents in that case pass through him uninterruptedly.

6. If one instrument in a same room be played upon, and other instruments in the same room be in tune therewith, the currents of vortexya will cause the others to give off sounds faintly. If said instruments be connected by wood fibers, the sounds will be louder. If the person in reverie holdeth the hands of others in the room, the same current will run through the whole. Hence music is the greatest of all harmonizers. A person may be a great lover of music, but be so discordant in his disposition as not to enter the ecstatic state of reverie. Another person may not know how to sing three notes, but have so concordant a disposition that he is at once carried into ecstasy by music, or by colors, or by viewing the great harmonies of creation.

7. The true prophet is such as hath attained concordance. The vortexian currents of any and everything pass through him. He seeth and feeleth with his soul. He is a perpetual register of everything near at hand. And if he cultivate his talent so as to estimate results therefrom, the future and the past are as an open book to him.

8. That which is erroneously called instinct in animals, is the capacity to be moved by the positive and negative vortexya.

9. Were the positive and negative currents equal in duration, the sexes born into the world would be equal in number. Males are the manifestation of positive vortexya, and females negative. The more positive the female, the less fruitful; but the opposite of this is the male's power.

10. Herb-food for man cultivateth the negative condition; flesh-food for man increaseth the positive: Which is to say, flesh-food carrieth man away from prophecy; away from spirituality. A nation of meat-eaters will always culminate in disbelievers in spirituality; and they become addicted to corporeal passions. Such men can not understand; to them the world is vanity and vexation, if poor; or, if rich, a place to revel in for lust's sake.

11. Let the prophet steer clear of them; nor marry with them; nor have anything in common with them. For though a man learn all the motions and powers of the corporeal worlds, his information is still but as a drop of water compared to the ocean, when measured by the seer and prophet that seeth the atmospherean and etherean worlds.

CHAPTER X.

1. It is not the part of this book to deal with spiritual matters, only so far as enableth the student to begin etheic knowledge.

2. First, then, there are two kinds of prophecy, or two ways to prophesy. For example, the ant and the bee, and many animals, prophesy in regard to an approaching winter. Even birds begin to fly toward tropical regions whilst it is yet warm weather.

3. These creatures prophesy by the direct action of vortexian currents upon them.

They feel what is approaching, BECAUSE THE UNSEEN CAUSE IS ALREADY UPON THEM.

4. Man can learn to acquire the same kind of prophecy. And this is different from the prophecy herein before mentioned, because he prophesieth in this last method without rules or calculations.

5. To attain this kind of prophecy, the following discipline is requisite:

6. To live in the fields and forests, and study the action of unseen forces upon himself; to eat not fish, nor flesh, nor any food that cometh of animals; to bathe daily; to permit no passion to enter his mind; to abnegate self and to wed himself to the Creator for righteousness sake, and to do good; to discipline his mind, to remain in any given direction on any subject, for days if necessary; to become oblivious to pain. After which he shall receive anointment from one who had previously attained the seership.

7. To attain such prophecy is to forfeit sexual powers; to forfeit appetite; to forfeit ambition for leadership and fame; to forfeit concern for the opinions of the world. In fact, to become a Bridegroom (or a Bride) to the Creator.

8. Not all persons can attain to this; but some are born closely allied to it.

9. There is also another kind of prophecy, wherein man prophesieth by spirits speaking through him. This is dangerous, for lying spirits may come to him.

10. Rather, let man seek to become one with the Father, making close observations of the rules of vortexya; for in this he provideth for the development of all his faculties.

CHAPTER XI.
RULES IN COLLEGE OF PROPHECY (PRIMARY).

1. The following signs are given in words, to wit: Flag, rising sun. Salute the East! children of dawn. The signs are, first, the folded hands; second, the soothe, and third, the supplication. O thou setting sun! Response: In Jehovih's name! How many chiefs dwell in dawn? Response: Three or more. How stationed, O Thou High Noon? Response: The three lights are east, west and south. The smoke and fire rise from the altar!

2. Here followeth the SECONDARY (in the chamber above). The voice of the east: How are the lines of living fire, O Noon? Response: As the Sun, which is the Light of the Corporeal Earth, riseth in the east to adorn the day; and ascendeth to the south at high noon as the glory thereof, and setteth in the west, so, in remembrance of Jehovih, are stationed the representatives of a lodge of dawn. What is dawn? Three years or more at the youth of a cycle.

3. The students then present their tables and the college is declared open in the words: In Jehovih's name, give ear to the Voice.

4. With Moses and Capilya both the above were merged into one lodge.

5. The second began with flag at High Noon: O thou Fire of Heaven! How many chiefs (rab'bahs) mark the altar of Jehovih? Four or more. Thou Setting Sun, speak: How stand the fathers? Response: My hands shield the light of the All Seeing Eye! My heart I cast to the winds! As a circle, divided into four quarters, is the symbol of the name Jehovih, thus (making the signs), cloven twice across, Who hath dominion over All Things, so are the four sides of the world represented by four Fathers in the chamber of light, in The Temple of Holies, which is square with east and west and north and south, for the Honor and Glory of our Father in Heaven! How are they numbered? Three thirty-threes, and one

ninety-nine! Wherefore these signs of blood and death? They are the four heads of the beast. They are always stationed in the four corners of the lodge. Why in the four corners? Because of darkness upon them. They profess peace, but practice war. How are they numbered? One, eleven, and six hundred and sixty-six, the number of the beast. In Thy name are we assembled, O Jehovih! Give us strength, wisdom and love, that we may avoid the fatal numbers; and that we may glorify Thee and Thy dominions. Amen!

6. There is no such thing as separating science and religion. To obtain knowledge and to do good; these are valuable.

7. Without discipline knowledge can not be obtained; without discipline little good can be accomplished. Forms and ceremonies must accompany discipline; otherwise inharmony overcometh all. These are religion.

8. To be not puffed up with self-concern; and to be willing to become good; these are the foundations for a good prophet.

9. But in all gifts, the rules of prophecy should apply. If a man be gifted in music, he should study music, and not rely wholly on inspiration (the vortexian tide). If gifted in healing he should study, and learn to apply the researches of others, and not rely wholly on the vortexian currents. If gifted in prophecy, he should also learn the rules of vortices and planets. The combination of gifts with good learning, this is the highest.

10. He that healeth by laying-on of hands, only giveth off the vortexya he hath previously received. Let him see to it that he replenish himself by sunlight (so-called), and trees and herbs and ground to walk upon. For giving away, without replenishing, will soon result in nothing.

11. As a young child sleeping with a very old person loseth its vortexya, becoming emaciated; or as a negative husband is devoured by a positive wife; or a negative wife devoured by a positive husband, so is the prophet consumed by the multitude.

12. When a prophet hath attained to discharge vortexya, so as to make raps at will, he is also subject to the presence of people from the unseen worlds. And these people, spirits, or angels, use this vortexya for a foundation for sar'gis.

13. The ancient prophet caused the worshipers to sit in the dark, because all people give off the negative current in the dark (which they received as positive in the light), and bade them sit in crescent, whilst he sat betwixt the horns. Wherefore the decrees of the prophet were called Tau. In this form of the altar the prophet was supplied somewhat with vortexya by the audience.

14. It cometh to this: Vortexya is unseen power, but it is without sense or judgment. Next back of this standeth the life of every living thing; and next back of all standeth the Creator, Jehovih. All learning, science and religion are but far-off stepping-stones to lead man up to Him. To acknowledge this, and to call on him constantly, is to keep open the road to receive His hand and hear His voice.

END OF THE BOOK OF COSMOGONY AND PROPHECY.

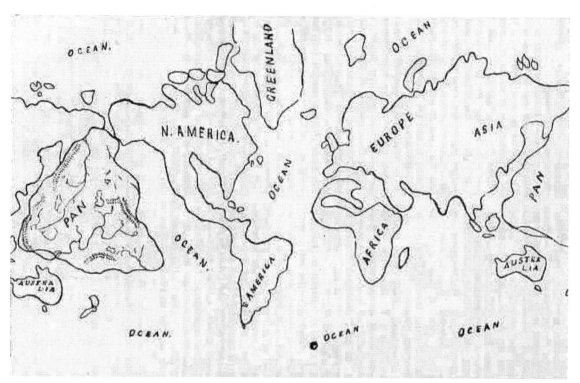

Plate 59. OUTLINE MAP SHOWING THE LOCALITY OF PAN,
THE SUBMERGED CONTINENT.

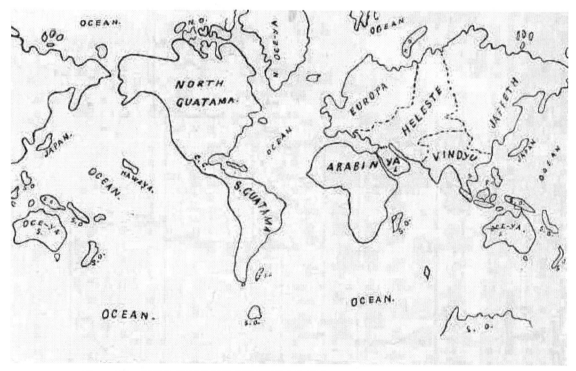

Plate 60. OUTLINE MAP SHOWING THE NAMES AND DIVISIONS
OF THE EARTH AS USED IN THIS BOOK.

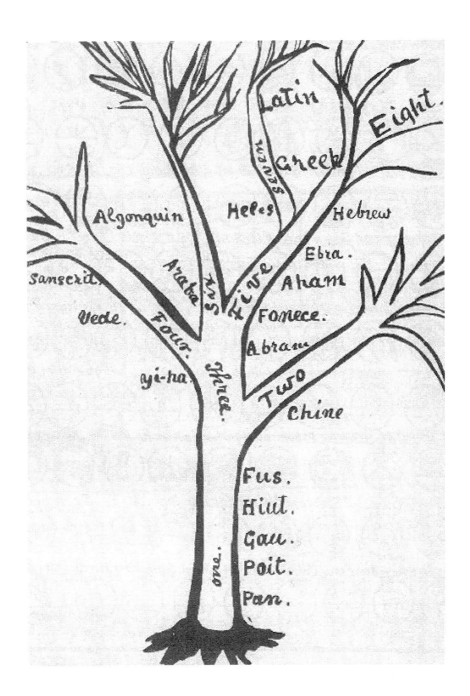

Plate 63.
The Tree of Language.

PAN, (of language) the first guttural sounds approximating words. POIT, beginning of labial word-sounds. HUIT, first acquiesced language. FUS, first written word-signs. CHINE, monosyllabic. YI-HA, combination words. ABRAM, first words; original text. FONECE, following the sound, but not the signs. (writing) AHAM, amalgamation. EBRA, the old; the sacred. SANSCRIT, mixture. ARABA, (first Egyptian also) 'Teeth and thorax.' ALGONQUIN, after the sacred name E-Go-Quin.

China, India, Europe and America, the four branches of the earth, languages from one root. What was the tree, and where grew it, that none can find it? Where lieth the submerged continent, the forgotten world? Whence escaped the struggling mortals, to float to far off continents, and tell the tale in all lands of a mighty flood?

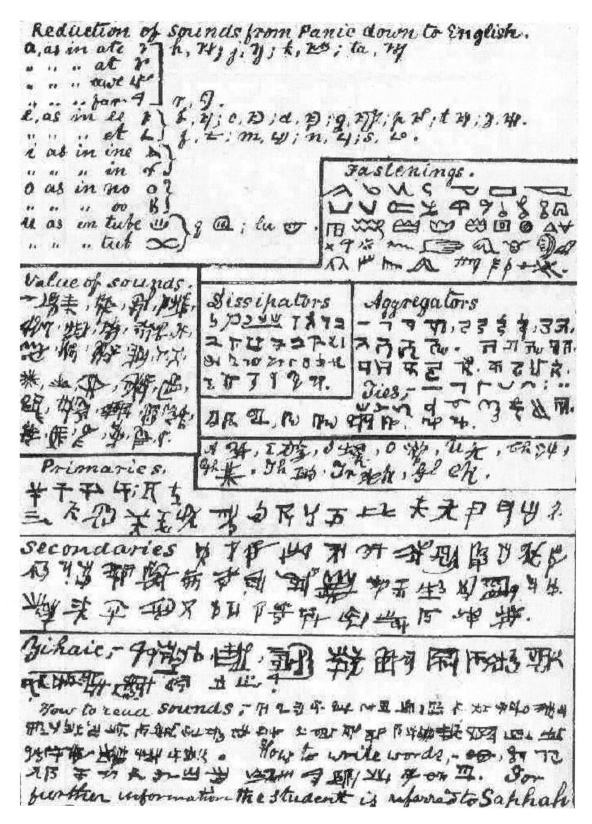

Plate 61. Panic, Yi'haic, Vedic, Hebraic and Sanscrit Primaries.

793

SE'MOIN.

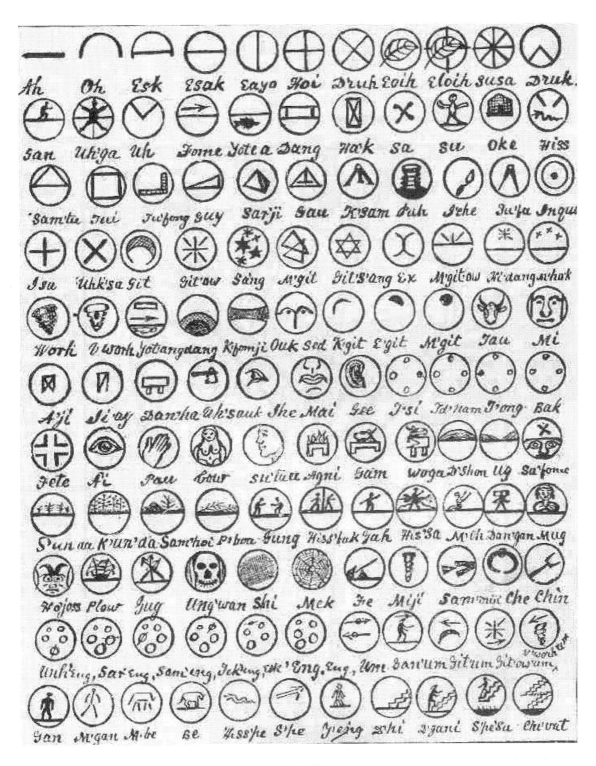

Plate 62.

INTERPRETATION.

1. Ah, the earth (Panic). Pan, da, sa, the ground; the foundation (Panic). N'ah (Poit). Thah (Kii). Pan (Iz). Sas and 'Asa (Zan). Edama (Fonece). Adama (Ebra). Rd'han (Vede). Bu'ha (Sanscrit). The first name applied to earth; as a man in looking forth saith, Ah! Ha'd'n (Chine). Wh'ah (Algonquin). Written with a straight line horizontal.

2. Oh! the sky, the canopy over (Pan). Oh'ah (Kii). O'shak (Fonece). D'yo (Vede). N'yo (Algonquin). As a man would exclaim looking upward. The vault above the earth.

3. Esk, earth and sky, third combination. One corporeal world and its canopy (Panic). I'dek (Poit). Ex (Fonece). Ska (Algonquin). The near world.

4. Esak, the kosmos. The all world, the sun and moon and earth and stars and all the skies (Panic). Erak (Hiut). Erat (Fonece). Eret (Ebra). Ad- (earth). Oh'm (skies). (Poit) Ja'sak (Vede). the fourth combination. Beyond measure. Jagat (Sanscrit). A'sah (China).

5. Ea'yo, from below forever, from upward forever (Panic). E'do (Bakie). M'yo (China). She'go (Algonquin). U'do (Vede). Udoche (Sanscrit). Upward and downward forever. None can measure the extent.

6. Hoi, the penetrable and impenetrable; the create and the Uz (Panic), Joy or Woe (Gau). Oi (Zerl), Yoih (Vede). A ray of sunlight is Hoi; it destroys and it creates; man's speech is Hoi; it can heal or poison. Uz'hoi, poison (Vede). Git'hoi, good healing (China). Ang'hoi, medicine man (Algonquin).

7. Druh or druk or drug, that that leadeth to destruction; the four dark corners of the world, north-east, south-east, north-west and south-west. The temple is sacred to the south and north and east and west. The serpents and devouring beasts come to the arena from druh (Panic) cross-purpose, evil purpose; cruv (Vede), a serpent-like evil, druhk, evil spirit, (Vede), druj, evil destroyer (Poit), druja, sign of death (Channic), cross-bones; danger from unseen spirits, an X, ex or drux. Ug or ugh (Algonquin), ugly (English), at crosses, angular. The place of the evil Gods in the ceremonies. The four quarters of the world are good; but the four corners are evil.

8. Eoih, the unseen Power, Creator (Panic). Before man could comprehend the All Spirit he was taught the wind, the All Unseen, and to call it E-O-Ih! The emblem of Boundless and of Life.

9. Eloih, synonymous with E-O-Ih, the Creator, the person who moveth the wind. The All Soul. The All Self. The Second Self, more subtle than the wind. It is the circumference of all; it extendeth from left to right, and from below upward. The motions of the hand and arm in oratory. The hand and arm speak His name. It is the secret sign. It holdeth the emblem of life (Panic and Gau). E-go-quin (Algonquin). Je-oes (China), Je-ovih (Fonece), Je-hova (Ebra), Geo-zih (Hiut), Zi'o (Vede): The soul of all. As the emblem is the Living Wheel, I swear by it. Let my accusers say I have not the holy gifts. They shall bind me on the wheel. The GREAT SPIRIT will release me. Let the wheel of My name be by the roadside that he who passeth may turn it in remembrance of the I AM. This shall be a prayer from the unlearned, and I will hear them. [Zarathustra]

10. Susa, the Complete. Without evil the All World would be incomplete; spirit of Corpor; Spirit of Es (Panic). Soo'a (China). Lu'la (Hiut). Hiss-tu-oh (Fonece). The wheel hath both good and evil. It hath the leaf of life. The priest shall be proved on the wheel. If he be released he is holy. If he be not released he is unholy and shall perish. Though an

evil man die by the wheel it is not bad for him. Only the man that loveth Jehovih feareth not to have the wheel roll over him. Druk-a-naw (Vede). Drujiy-ho-gan (Semak). Jaugernacht (English). Su'sa, living death (Chine).

11. Druk (Panic), earth evils. Poisons, plagues. Rosh (Fonece), snake poison. Poison lurketh on the earth. Ruks (Algonquin and Kii). Ruts, the time of females (Ebra). When the signs are down, be ye patient. Usk, the outer covering is evil. Husk (English). All flesh is druk (evil). Hoey'e (Chine).

12. Gan (Panic). Ghan (Chine). Egan, mankind (Chine). Edam and Edan (Fonece). Adam (Ebra). Puam (Sanscrit). Pam (Vede). Sam, speaking animal (Kii). Samuel, prophet (Ebra). Gang, rich land-owner (Chine). Ang (Algonquin). Anger (Poit). Ong'ee (Kii). Man (English).

13. Uh'ga, the test (Panic). If the Es release him then is he our true prophet. He hath sworn by the wheel; he shall be tried. An oath; to swear by the All I Am. Ish'ga (Chine). Duk'ah (Poit). Eh'la (Fonece). Alah (Ebra). Isch'bu'ah, pledging by (Hebrew). Uk'gak (Algonquin). He shall be proved on the cross, the druh, and he dieth not. Let him answer on His name that that he hath professed. If he be a false prophet he will fear Uh'ga (Test). False prophets' bones hang on the druh, the cross. The true are released by Eolin.

14. Uh, evil spirit (Panic). Yuuh (Poit). Kuuh (Fonece). Kuach (Ebra). The evil that is above us. Yu'gi (Chine), evil spirits who love evil. Zi-uhk (Vede). Useh (Kii). Huuh (Algonquin).

15. Fome, wind (Panic). Foam (Chine). Ome' Eri (Algonquin). Evil wind, Ruak (Ebra). That that speaketh without lips, fume (Vede). He fumes, Ome (Ku).

16. Yote'a (Panic), water. Voet'i (Kii). Vo'ti and Va'ti and Va'rs (Vede). Go'taw and Gota'Weri, morning water (Algonquin). Yot'Yaw (Hiut). Hoy'ah (Fonece). Hoy'am (Ebra).

17. Dang, light (Panic). Hi'Dan (Kii). Orang (Fonece). Orah (Ebra). Ang, ji (Chine). Ang'ni (Vede). Ag'ni, fire-light (Sanscrit). Ong (Algonquin), spiritual light. Yong, day-light (Hebrew).

18. Ha'k, dark (Panic). Hark (Chine). Pa'h (Poit). H'ark (Kii). Kah (Fus). Kasha'k (Fonece). Chasah (Algonquin). Kasha'k (Ebra). O'Yak (Vede).

19. Sa, the cross-bones. The sign of an evil man that died in evil (Panic). The evil cross, the English letter X. He was bound on the wheel, and perished. There was no All Holy in him. Let this mark be branded on his forehead, that all men may know he is a false prophet. He rotted on the wheel, Sa'h (Vede). Sahan (fus). Let this be a sign of evil spirits. He'sa (Algonquin). Sa (Ebra). Sa'd, to wither (Sanscrit). This shall be the sign of war. It shall be on the banners of the righteous. They shall go forth shouting, Isa'b! (Ebra). Die, Sa (Chine). Death, Sa (Kii). Let us perish for righteousness' sake rather than do evil. [Abraham.]

20. Su, an enlightened man; also Augh (Panic). Su (Chine). With the gift of prophecy, Su's (Ebra). I proclaim in the name of Eloih, Soo! (Kii). Shu (Algonquin). He would not kill a worm, Choo (Vede). He standeth betwixt us and the All Light; T'su (Gau). Su'chi, perceiving by the Unseen (Sanscrit). The interior bright, Soo (Fus). One who can not sin, Su (Onia). The purified Son.

21. Oke, a house (Panic). Oak (Chine). Okel (Fonece). Ohel (Ebra). Oik (Kii). Hoik (Gau). Oikon (Hellic). Croke (Vede). Koik (Aribanya). Oikos (Greek). Teach

my people to have homes (Oke); the migrant is an abomination to the All Eye (Aham).
22. Hiss, serpent's word. He maketh noise like the wind. Who can distinguish between the voice of Eolin and the hiss that kills? From the two evil corners above, the hiss descendeth. His food is of the earth. That that tempteth to the earth is hiss. The hiss that crawleth have I made as an emblem of the hiss that teacheth lust (Panic). Hiss (Chine). Hees (Algonquin). Cvees (Vede). The sign of treachery, of poison unseen. A danger that man can not heal. First I made poison air; from that I made poisonous weeds, and from them I made hiss; to crawl on his belly commanded I him. The lowest made I him; he biteth himself and dieth therefrom. [Abraham.] The sum of evil is to be its own destroyer. [Confucius.]
23. Sam'tu, triangle (Panic). The sign of Corpor and Es and Eolin. Also the Soul-light, Eolin, the Corpor light, the Sun, and the burning flame. Also an instrument for measuring.
24. Fui, a square, a box. A sign of righteousness (Panic).
25. Sui (Chine). Tu'fong or Sam'fong (Panic), a measure with two lengths and one angle, Yu'on (Vede).
26. Guz, hypothenuse, a line from the top of an upright to a distance from the base of the upright. Guys (Panic). The mean between upright and horizontal. Gui (Kii). Zy (Vede). The man who is not upright and yet not all evil. The mean betwixt Su and Hiss. Kur (Algonquin). Zhi (Chine). Dji (Huit). All men are Dji. An angle of support, a sign, a line, a rope.
27. Sarji, sarguz, a pyramid (Panic). My sides guy, but I am the centre shaft. The temple was built east and west and north and south, and the four corners representing good and evil were square with the world. The sacred house of Eolin, Bar'ji (Fonece). Bar'nah (Ebra). Gaw'hi (Algonquin). Yah'hy (Vede). A building with chambers for spirit communion.
28. Gau, a measuring instrument; a plumb and level combined. Gau said: They gave my base a level, and the sights on the angle of the plumb-line were level also, and in the distance of Tek Gos (about twenty miles) discovered the rounded earth. By the Gau was the earth proven to be a globe. By Gau have I revealed (Vede). A proven problem. An exact. Gau, a geometrical language. Language is of two parts, the proven is Gau, the unproven is M'gau. A sacred instrument; that that can not err. My sacred temples shall be built by Gau. Dau'sin (Chine), plumb-line. Ann'ak (Fonece). Ahm'uk (Ebra), a plumb-line. A Gau'Yi shall be placed by the altar. By the Sign Gau'i shall man learn to prove all things (Vede). It shall be the symbol of proof. Be patient that your sight may not err, saith Gau.
29. K'Sam, tripod (Panic). Symbol of earth, water and air. My three are one; without these three nothing can be born into life. Ka'Sam (Chine). Ya'Sais (Vede). Yo'ham (Algonquin). The stool of the prophet. Only on the tripod shall the oracle proclaim. (Aham). The origin of the term Aham, the language of oracles. A language with two or three meanings. Sacred language of Aribania.
30. Puh, to pull, a cap-stone (Panic). The stones of the temple shall be drawn up with a push (Poit). Zuz (Vede). Uuh (Fonece). Uhe (Algonquin).
31. I'che, trowel (Panic). Chu (Chine). Hi'che, trowel or ax, or hatchet (Algonquin). Yi'che (Vede). My hand is a wood hand. I make even; and I shall be a sign by the foot of

A'Kin. The temple is the work of my hand, but who knoweth the Hand of the Great Spirit. His hand is over all. (Perah). A lazy man shall not have me for a sign, saith I'cho (Kii).

32. Tu'fa, a compass (Panic). An instrument to measure circles; circumference without any part of a square.

33. Inqua (Panic). Hin'Kwa (Zerl). E'm'wak (Algonquin). A thing within a thing. The es that is in corpor, the soul that is in es. Three within one, Ma-nee-to (Algonquin). The earth within the vortex. Equa, swift flying, equation (English). Race-horse (Chine).

34. I'su (Panic). Ie Su, a young child that has not sinned. The true cross within Eloih. I'e'su (Aham). Child prophet (Aham). Ye'loo (Kii). My I'su shall have no flesh desires. His love knoweth all men and women alike. Gee'soo'gan (Chine). Iesu, one who is born sexless.

35. Uhk'sa, the evil cross (Panic). The written sign of Sa. (See Sa.)

36. Git, the moon (Panic). Git the moon (Chine). The second light Egs'git. She sendeth forth Egnita (Algonquin). Git'mas, corporeal moon (Vede). Eg'nit (Poit). Egnitero (Algonquin). The moon of E-o-quin. G'uit (Kii). Git'm'gow', the moon much receiving; the gentle moon, she sendeth forth the gold light, the or (Ebra).

37. Git'ow the sun (Panic). Git'how, the sun (Chine). The central light. Let the sun stand to the corporeal world as Jehovih standeth to the All Unseen. He, the Gitow shall be on the beam betwixt the pillars as a symbol of my power. As he bringeth forth grass, so bring I forth the souls of men. He sendeth forth Karang'kwa, the All Heat, Haw'git (Algonquin). He sendeth white light, or H'wit (Ebra). Or, the corporeal sunlight; Git'fume, the driving (Aham). M'Git (Kii). Hog'git or git-hog (Aribania).

38. Sang or Sa'ang (Panic), stars. The small shining that sendeth forth the Ogistok, i.e., the twinkle. Anga (Algonquin). Seng or Seng'sope (Chine). Eng'ho, the twinkler, i.e., Kokab (Fonece). Hy'ang (Vede). The far-off worlds, Esk'ang (Poit).

39. M'git (Panic). The prophet took triangles and laid them separately before the king, Oss, and the prophet said, E,-O,-Ih; E,-O,-Ih, twice, and straightway, the angles were interlocked, and lo and behold, nothing had been broken. And Oss, the king, said: These shall be hung up in the temple as a testimony before men that the Great Spirit is with my people. His light shall be my light. (Vede).

40. Git's'ang (Panic) sacred, star. Two triangles of different kinds of wood inter-locked without severing, by spirit power (Uz). Let my prophets prove themselves by the sacred star, and they shall sit on the K'Sam and be oracles in my kingdom. An emblem of a miracle kept over the altar. Also called Yoke'eng (Chine). Yope'amg (Algonquin). Let him conjure the sacred star. A starlight evening. Less than moonlight.

41. Ex (Panic). Two or more against each other, collision. Life against death, or sour against sweet, or bad against good. The supposed opposites in all things. Egs (Poit). Egs (Algonquin). Egs (Kii). Egks (Fonece).

42. M'git'ow, morning, sunrise (Panic). Dawn, M'git'ow (Algonquin). Tigiatow (Vede). At dawn fly away the evil spirits; at dawn come the shining, full of holiness (Kii). The wise man hath found Git'm'ow full of cow, i.e., receptivity, and Tau, the bull, i.e., force-giving. He maketh a book at dawn. The seventh heaven cometh in M'git'ow, the morning light (Poit).

43. Hi'dang, high-noon (Panic); the sun at noon. Let the Hi'dang be an emblem over my altar. He is the glory of the day as is the Great Spirit of the soul world. As ye bow before

him do it in remembrance of Him that ye see not. He is of my body and life, and as much as ye glorify Him, so will I, Eolin, the Creator, glorify ye in the heavens above (Gau). See to it that ye worship not the corporeal sun, but glorify my works in remembrance of me. Keep this symbol covered, save on the days of sacrifice, lest your enemies accuse ye of worshipping corpor. (Chine).

44. M'hak (Panic). M'hock, or Mo'ock, or Mowk (Algonquin). O'Shak (Fonece). Koshek or Chosek or Chasheck or Choshek (Ebra). Night, darkness. The time of the Es'win ceremonies. Let us meet privily on the mountain-top in Choshek; the angels require it of us. Chosek (Hebrew). Ta'ren'zewagon, in some Luwick. Not having mountain-tops they met in Ta'rew'ze, the swamps, and had the Es'win. Ta'ren'zewagon, became a law for M'hak (a tribe of Algonquin). When the drouth destroyeth let the faithful hold Narshka on the mountaintops, and the rains will I send from heaven (Sanscrit). Ah'shah (Kii).

45. Work or wark (Panic). Vortex, whirlwind. Sark (Poit). Sa'ark (Gau). Ru'ark (Fonece). Ruach, Searah (Hebrew). Yi'ah (Vede). Who'ohk (Algonquin). Who shall find the cause of work? I am at work continually. As I have set the work, the whirlwind, before men's eyes, so before the host of the long-risen do I make and dissolve worlds (Aham). The Es labor, work (English) labor. The whirlwind is labor, per se, i.e., without hands.

46. V'work (Panic). The sign of Es at labor. The make of a corporeal world. A corporeal world within a whirlwind.

47. Yot'ang'd'ang, water, earth, air and ether (Panic).

48. Ka'fom'ji (Panic), earth, lower heaven and upper heaven.

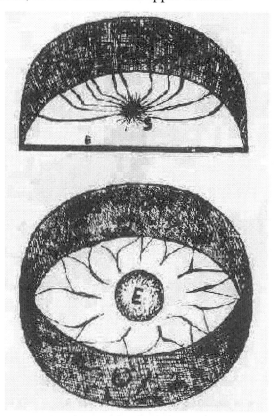

Plate 64. ONK, or ZODIAC.

49. Onk (Panic). Sun belt of the earth. That portion of the earth subject to vertical rays.

799

Onk, direct. Owk, oscillating. Onk gave I unto you that ye might behold the glory of summer, the fragrance of spring, the beauty of autumn and the snow of winter. Study the ant and the bee; they comprehend Onk. The lazy man shall learn Onk (Poit).

50. Sed, (Panic), the sign Aries, or, in English, letter T. The sign of wisdom; of gentleness. Sed, a lamb (Kii). A man's nose and eyebrows. The man who winneth by love, gentleness. A'sed (Poit). Ahed (Fonece). Aheb (Ebra). Aheb (Hebrew). And Sed rose up on the third day after the creation of the world and stood above the sun. The Great Spirit, E-O-Ih, said: This is My Son. The corporeal sun ye can behold at high noon, but My Son Sed standeth above this. All that are gentle and good draweth he to My kingdom, Nirvana. Do not unto another what ye would not desire done unto you, or ye shall not behold My Son Sed, who standeth on My right hand. The earth is Mine, saith Sed; by love will I redeem it. Ay'scd (Vede). A sheep with a woman's face; symbol of love. Gently, or gentleness. Let or Leat (Ebra), or as a lamb speaketh. A'nah (Hebrew). ba'ba (Chine). Hy'sed (Vede). Sed (Aribania). A name signifying gentleness and wisdom. Written sign of a lamb or of the nose and eyebrows of man. A symbol of stars and zodiac. Let this be the season to bring together male and female. They shall go to the altar and consult the voices of the stars through my prophets. Whoever hath Sed in him returneth good for evil (Chine).

Plate 65. ARIES (See also Book of Jaffeth).

51. K'git, new moon (Panic). Watch ye for the new moon and glorify the Great Spirit that He may prosper ye. Ka'git (Chine). It shall be a holy day of rest.

52. E'git (Panic). At the change of the second quarter of the moon is the relief watch of my angels who abide with mortals; let that be a holy day of rest.

53. M'Git, the third quarter (Panic). A holy day of rest. Let my chosen keep the four holy days of rest during each moon, for on these days do my guardian angels change the watch. The incentive given by the spirits to mortals to make mortals observe and learn the planets. Sub'da'don, a holy day (Panic). The day of the moon's change. Sub'da (Fonece). Sabbath (Ebra). A moon's birthday. Because of four quarters to each moon, so do I give to you four Sab'da, which shall be days of worship. (Abram).

54. Tau, a bull, a projector (Panic). Sign of a bull's head and horns. As the prophets interpreted so shall the king. Tau (project). His edicts are Tau, bulls. Opposite from Sed (Aries). Opposite from cow (receptivity). Tau, e.i., Osiris, is oft confounded with Aries, a God of the lower heavens.

Plate 67. TAU.

OSIRIS.

OSIRIS, being interpreted, is: I am the Light, the Life and the Death. Out of myself made I all that live. The sun I placed in the firmament as a sign of my power. The stars and the moon and things that speak not and know not are the works of my hand. I am the Tau and the Sed (Taurus and Aries, bull and lamb), the power and wisdom over all and within all. Without me nothing is, nor was, nor ever shall be (Aribania). The spirit of self-assertion; tyranny; to enslave; to master others per force. Tow (Aii). The self-assuring man, or spirit. Y'taw (Vede). Tau'baw, a bull, or Ti'taw, I am the T'taw. I am the master at the bridge Chinvat. Without my will none shall rise to Nirvana, my upper heavens. Through my good-will only shall any man ascend. I am the Judge and Savior of men. On my forehead resteth the sun; the stars are my cattle. In worship of me the stars and the sun plead before me. The horses have I placed over the cows. The moon (Mas) cringeth beneath my feet. I am war, I am Thaw, a bull. My bulls shall be the edicts of kings. Who worshipeth not me, him will I destroy (Vede). Toe'phi, the All High Spirit, next to Om, wife of Eolin. Toe'phi is my Savior; he will redeem. (Chine). Itaura, Itura (Algonquin). Toe (Ebra). Toe (Hebrew). Toe (Fonece). Wild, unreasonable. Destroyer of liberty.

55. Mi, or Mira (Panic). Mi, spirit, My'ra, spirit of earth (English). Mary, lamb (spirit). Mi'ra, a virgin, was before man a dweller on the earth, nor was there any man for her. The All Unseen conceived her. Her son was Sir'za (Poit). Si'us (Kii). Osiris (Aribania). Mi, mother of all men; spouse of the Unseen (Tau). The earth was Mi, and Mi was the earth. The Great Spirit moved on the earth and the earth conceived and brought forth man. Mithra (Vede). Mother of Gods (king spirits). The sons of Mi were all I'su, free from sin. Save ye pray to Mithra, then will not Tau save your souls. She, Mi, is our virgin mother. A sign, a face within a circle; also, written and painted, a woman with a child.

56. A'ji (Gau), semi-dark. There are places in the firmament of heaven not all light, nor yet all dark. Ar'ji (Poit). When the earth passeth through A'ji (Panic), it aggregateth and groweth. An abundance of Dar'ji in the firmament giveth a cold year upon the earth (Kii). In the years of Ar'jon mortals became warriors. Now it came to pass that for seven hundred years the earth encountered not Ha'ji (Chine), and war ceased on the earth, and men were gentle, and killed not any living thing. Out of A'ghi maketh Jehovih a new world. Save your prophets understand A'ji, they can not tell what the next year will be. Let man build consecrated chambers in my temples that my spirits in heaven may come and explain Ha'jhon, and they shall be provided against famine and pestilence (Algonquin). The foolish man knoweth not A'jon, for mortals can not see him.

57. Ji'ay (Panic). Ji'ya (Gau). Semi-light. There are three places in the firmament, light and semi-dark. The fourth is Corpor. Thus, ether, the most rarified place; Ji'ay, the second place, less rarefied; A'ji, the third place (nebulous places in the firmament), and fourth, the corporeal worlds. As out of the ether I make A'ji, so out of Jy'ay make I corpor. (Kii.) Hy'ghi (Chine). Beware of evil spirits in the time of Jy'ay, for they shall train the corporeal senses of men to believe they lived before. (Chine.)

58. Dan'ha (Panic). The etherea, the highest place in ethereal worlds. Jehovih said: The sun I made as the head of a serpent, and his phalanx made I as the body of a serpent; thus made I the great corporeal serpent. To him gave I a circuit to travel in, and I numbered his time a thousand tuos and seven aka and four bi'jus, for the sun coil. On the circuit have I placed my A'ji and my Ji'ay in many places, but my Dan'ha have I placed only in one thousand six hundred places. (A cycle of time is about three thousand years, sometimes more, sometimes less.) From Kosmon, the present time, back to Moses and Capilya, alias Capella, three thousand four hundred years; from Moses and Capilya to Brahma and Abraham, two thousand four hundred years; from Brahma and Abraham to Zarathustra, three thousand one hundred years; from Zarathustra to Osiris the first, three thousand three hundred years; from Osiris to Thor, three thousand two hundred years; from Thor to Apollo, two thousand eight hundred years; from Apollo to Sue, three thousand two hundred years; from Sue to Aph, three thousand six hundred years. Dan'ya, the orbit of the solar phalanx (Gau). Dian'ya, the course of the cosmical phalanx (Puit). The light of Dan'ga is my timekeeper (Vede). Dh'a'yi, the light shining; the soul-fructifier (Pali). When Dang'hi cometh, the All-men grow in spirit; when he is past, man whetteth the sword and spear and entereth into blood. Deny Dang'hi and die in stubbornness of heart. (Poit.) Dan'ya foldeth Corpor in his arms, but yet man seeth not him. (Chine.) The chosen of the Great Spirit shall maintain their blood through many Da'n'ga'has (Aribania). He was the sign of light standing on two legs of light. He is My symbol, saith Jehovih (Vede).

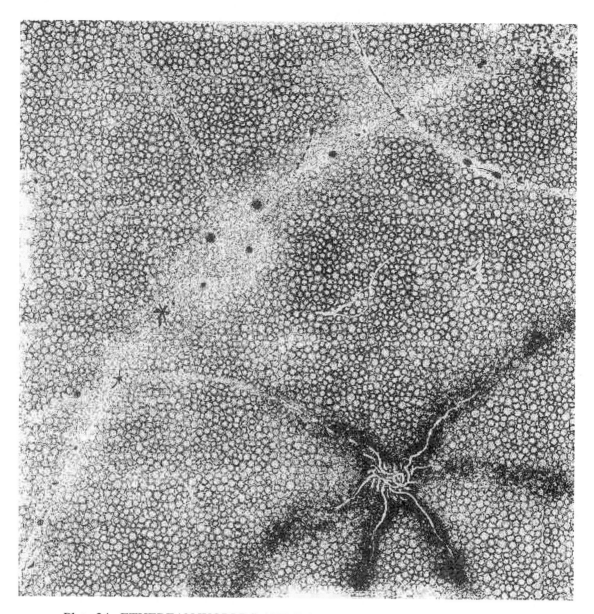

Plate 24. ETHEREAN WORLDS AND ROADWAYS FOR SUN-PHALANXES

59. Uh'Sauk, battle-ax (Panic). Yu'Saui (Poit).

60. I'he (Panic). Eye (English). I'yhe (Poit). Ay'he (Gau). Hi'gin (Chine), the seeing; Ap'in (Fonece). Ay'in (Ebra), the seeing organ. I'ghe (Vede). I'hi or Ike'shi (Sanscrit). Ay'ke or Ay'ke'ra (Algonquin). Ayin (Hebrew). That that feeleth at a distance. I understand, I comprehend. Ay'ghin (Panic).

61. Mai or A'Mair (Panic), expressed, marked out. A king's signature from which there is no appeal. If I am by Sa I mean death; if by Su, spirit; or by dang (light). I, Amar, have spoken. Expressly (Ebra). By his mouth he hath said, as the mouth openeth and uttereth, like an animal speaketh, Mai'ah (Algonquin). Expression, Ma (Chine).

62. Gee (Panic), ear (English). She (Kii). She'ma findeth azam. She, ear, Azam, that that cometh into. A symbol of an organ on the head. The letter G, and C, English. A symbol of judgment. Let the Che be above the altar as a sign that the E-O-Ih heareth. I'gee'how

803

(Chine). The ear heareth. Pan'gee (Algonquin). Che (Ayn). Hy'che (Vede). Gee (Chine).

63. F'si (Panic), west. F'si (Chine). Te'si (Algonquin). Ty'sy (Vede). In the west.

64. Td'nam (Panic). East. Que'dam (Poit). E'dam (Kii), the first place is east. D'nam (Chine). Qedem, the east (Ebra). Qedem (Hebrew). Se'nam (Algonquin). Tse'hem (Vede). Di'nam (Kii). The master of the lodge shall sit in Denem, i.e., the east. (Aribania.) The covered head standeth in Enam.

65. T'ong, south (Panic). T'ong (Zerl). Se'ong (Iz). T'ong (Thath). D'room (Fonece). Daroom (Ebra). Tse'ong (Chine). Hi'se'enga (Algonquin).

66. Bak, north (Panic). A'dak, a cold place, a mountain.

67. Fete, sign of santification (Panic). Only the prophets shall wear my badge Yete (Chine). Second symbol in rank after dawn, Eloih. The Fete cometh on the Mas day. (Vede). The Fete (high priest) giveth sacrificc before the multitude. The Fete, fates, the high priests, are next to Eolin. One of the sacred emblems.

68. Ai or A'yi, myself, Iga (Panic). The All Seeing. A'gi (Algonquin). M'agi, next to Eolin. (Vede.) (English) Magi. The written name of a worker of miracles. One empowered to administer oaths. The Master's sign in the Lodge.

69. Pau or paw (Panic). Hand (English). Pop or quab or yaub or yod, as the hands speak when struck together (Poit). (Ebra.) (Kii.) Osnosa cometh out of Yod (Algonquin). Showh (Chine). Iy'yoh (Vede). By his hands he answered, Y'yop. (Fus). The sign of the hand be good aback, but the palm dealeth in mystery. He pointeth, and by his hand's course shall he be read; to a heart, love; to a spear, war, etc.

70. Cow receptivity (Panic). Cow, an animal (Panic). Any person who is receptive of new things. Not bigoted. Haoma spake to the cows in the name of the Great Ormudz, Eolin (Vede). Cow (Chine). Cow (Poit). Cow (Kii). Gow, animal (Chine). He who hath found the cow, etc. (Pali). How can the truths of Zarathustra approach them; the cow is not in them (Pali). Save ye refrain from fish and flesh ye shall not find the cows, i.e., receptivity. They feasted on flesh and wine and the cows went astray, i.e., receptive to spiritual things (Pali). As a cow uttereth; a sign of a female. Save your spirits become as cows ye can not be impregnated with new things. The much-learned man hath erected bars to keep off the cows (Chine). Being wise in their own conceit they will not receive (Iz). A sign of a female; usually face and breasts; sometimes the udder of a cow or mare. The mares separated themselves in heaven (Craosh). Save ye find the (receptivity) ye shall not, etc. (Fus.) All men become mares in time to come (receptive). (Hiut.) (Zarathustra.) [See horses.]

71. Su'Tau (Panic). Self-assertion. The spirits who ministered at the oracle manifested Su'tau, and there was no reason in them. Applied to spirits that teach things that can not be proven. Many of the people were converted by Sa'tau, and their souls thus enslaved in heaven. Eolin said: Su'tau is mine enemy; he leadeth astray my innocent ones. (Vede.) The same as Tau, but applied to spirit teaching. [See Tau.] A sign of a profile, face, mouth closed.

72. Agni (Panic), fire. Ah'gni (Chine), to burn. Ogna, as the fire speaketh, Uha'gni (Vede). Flame of fire saith, Whir (Fonece). Ur (Ebra). A'gin (Poit). The sacrifice in Agni (Vede). They spread the blood on sticks of wood, and they were consumed by A'gin in front of the altar (Zerl). The sacrifice by fire Ishsheh (Fonece). A sign of a stone bench with flames ascending. Burning incense. Emblem of worlds moldering into dust and of the harvests of

souls ascending to heaven. Emblem of corporeal dissolution and of the escape of the potent power within. Emblem of mine own mortal dissolution and the ascent of my soul, but whither, O Eolin! O Agni, O A'gni, reveal thy mysteries! (Ceremonies of Dawn.) A'gin, the sacred fire (Fus). In the days when mortals put words into all things and made them speak, Agni (fire) stood giant over all, till Yote'a (water) bathed his head, when lo, black death (charcoal) breathed forth poisonous air. (Vede.) Hagni (Algonquin).

73. Gam, sacrifice (Panic), in triumph.

74. Woga, sacrifice (Panic), in repentence. O Woga, how can I forget thee, for in thy obedience to Agni is my great sin burnt up. From this day I will sin no more (Hiut). Let my chosen repeat the holy words of repentance whilst Agni feasteth in Gam or in Woga, for in that self-same hour do I hear them and absolve them their sins (Vede).

75. D'shom, mountain (Panic). Dhi'shon (Chine).

76. Ug (Panic) a valley low down. Emeg (Aribania and Fonece). A deep gorge. Go'ug (Algonquin). Also Go'meg. Y'ng and Yu'hi'guag (Vede).

77. Sa'fome (Panic), evil wind; evil chieftain among spirits, a God. A God in human shape. Believed by people in darkness to be the Creator of all things, and of man in his own image. (See God and Ghad.) I'fome (Chine), an idol. They have made an idol and called it Iss'faum, i.e., Land God or God of the Earth. In those days the idolaters believed the Great Spirit had made Gods out of spirits in the lower heaven, and sent one of them to the earth and one to each of the stars. To the moon he gave four Gods. He who received the earth as his portion to command was called Lord (Sa'fome), i.e., earth wind. On his forehead shall be the sign of cross-bones. Vengeance is mine, saith the Lord (Sa'fome). (Fonece.) Jehova said: Not having stone images they have made an idol of the wind and called it Lord (Land God or Ghad). (Moses in Egypt.) Let my followers swear an oath against the Lord, for he is more hurtful than the stone idols, and they shall profess the Great Spirit, E-O-Ih, only. (Abraham.) See to it that the enemy fasteneth not an idol of the wind on the Faithists (Zarathustra). (Vede.) Not content to worship the Great One they have a representative, saying: He is the Only Begotten Son. Be ye wary of them (Brahma). (Naoli.) An earth God, i.e., evil God. They profess to feast his nostrils with the smell of burning flesh, saying: He alone can save; he, the mighty Sa'fome (Chine). Now judge ye them; for do they not engage in war, and are they not all idolatrous warriors? (Fus). A figure by the door-way of heathen temples.

78. S'un (Panic), spring, or beginning. (Chine.)

79. Ka'un (Panic), summer, beauty. (Algonquin.)

80. Sam'hoi (Panic), Sam'howh (Chine), autumn.

81. P'boa (Panic), the destroyer, winter. M'boa (Chine). Peboa (Algonquin).

82. Gung, love-offering (Panic). Oe'gwong (Chine). Go'ongwe (Algonquin).

83. Hiss'bak, against each other or divided; something between (Panic). Cold-hearted; misunderstanding. Iss'bagd (Chine). He is on a mountain or in the north Sy'gis yak (Vede).

84. Goh (Panic), one who rejoiceth. Gul (Ebra), to leap with joy, joyous. E'goh (Chine). A sound the mouth uttereth in sudden joy, as Gah, ha, or E'goh'e. He'ha! (English). The figure of a man laughing, with nothing near him. If the figure point to something, as a man, then it is pronounced Gah'gan, or to a house, Gah'oke, etc.

85. Hiss'sa, a lawyer. One whose soul is full of serpents. The figure of a man with a serpent's head issuing. Yi-saga (Vede).

86. M'oh, prayer. Also a woman preacher. Ni'Ghoo (Chine.). Ni'oh'Ghoo (Algonquin). A'ho'en (Fonece). Kohen (Hebrew). Yoh, hadragi (Vede).

87. Dan'gan (Panic), prophet. A man of light. Clear sight. Es'sight. An inter-seer (Vede). Yajvan, one who by much sacrifice hath attained to soul-seeing (Pali). Wa'gan-wag (Algonquin).

88. Mug (Panic), a philosopher. The sign of a man resting on his elbows. The subject depends on his relative place in a tablet.

89. Ho'Joss (Panic), a man-God (Ghad); a human face with horns. A God of the lower heaven. Think not I am come to send peace on earth; I come not to send peace, but a sword. I come to set man at variance against his father, and a daughter against her mother (Christ). Ho'Joss shall reign in my temples; before him shall every knee bow and every tongue confess Sheking (Chine). He was tried on the wheel and Es released him. He shall be my Joss, and no other Joss shall be Ho'Joss (Poit). A sign of a wheel or of a cross. Save ye be tried on the cross ye are unworthy to be exalted (Anra'mainyus). I come with a two-edged sword (Anubis). (Aribania.) My people shall be warriors (Man'sa'ghad). Any spirit who commands or rules by force; any exclusive Savior of men. Jehovih saith, Whoever professeth the sword and the spear and the sling and the pitchfork shall perish thereby. (Zarathustra.) Overthrow of Osiris in the lower heaven. Because Osiris hath said, I am Ho'Joss, the Savior of men, and none shall ascend to the Father but through me, so shall Osiris be hated of men (Kii). Was it not so with Tistyra, and he was changed into a star? (Pali.) A figure of authority at the altar in heathen temples. A face with or without horns. A man bound on a wheel. A man bound on a cross. Jehovih said: Have I not said, He that proclaimeth the sword shall perish by the sword? Behold ye then the Ghad they worship (Osiris).

90. Plow (Panic), ship; Oniyyah (Fonece). The sound the sailors utter. They watched the star Hiyalavi to know whether the plow sailed. A vessel or tool or instrument that divides its own road. His spirit was as a plow, and the ancients were confounded in his Hoiy (furrows). Gu'iy'yoh, the furrow of a ship and the ship and the voice of the sailors (Ebra). Applied to oratory, the sign of oratory conferred by the king. A badge of a ship (plow). He hath been awarded, or he hath the degree of plow (ship). He is the king's plow (Ayria).

91. Oug (Panic), spear. Gag or gagged (English). Gug (Algonquin), an instrument of war with blades. A symbol of defence and offence.

92. Ung'wan (Panic), a symbol to an enemy.

93. Shi or Ski (Panic), woven fabric, cloth.

94. Mek (Panic). Spider's web. An emblem of industry. O'sehel (Fonece). Oshek (Fus). M'meka (Kii). Gow'mek (Chine). Place the mek at the pillars of the altar that my followers may learn industry (Zarathustra). When they had conferred the degree of dawn upon them the king said: Inasmuch as ye of the haunted chamber have been found worthy, receive ye this sign of industry in the name of the All Pure Zarathustra (Vede). A badge bestowed in the second degree of Iz (Faithist), with a spider's web engraven. One of the graven images forbidden to the Leviticans by Moses.

95. Fe (Panic), a lever. One of the sacred emblems of power belonging to the third degree of Zerl (Faithist), in the order of Poit.

96. Miji (Panic), a screw. One of the sacred emblems of power, belonging also to the third degree of Faithist (Zarathustra).

97. Sam'miji (Panic). The wedge. The seventh emblem in the third degree of Faithist (Chine).

98. Che or Kouak'che (Panic), a compass and caliper. Koakchah (Chine). K'cho (Algonquin).

99. Chine (Panic). Pitchfork, an implement for farmers. A war weapon in olden times. Also a country of warriors (Chine). Monosyllabic. An iesu.

100. Unh'eng, fifth size (Panic), designated by a line.

101. Sar'eng, fourth size (Panic), designated by a line.

102. Sam'eng, third size (Panic), designated by a line.

103. Tek'eng, second size (Panic), designated by a line.

104. Esk'eng, first size (Panic), designated by a line.

105. Eng. Size in abstract (Panic), no line.

106. Um (Panic), direction of motion. As the spear pointeth, so shall the tablet be interpreted.

107. Gan'um, direction of flight. Profile signifieth going; portrait, coming.

108. Git'um. The high priest shall set the sign on the moon that the unlearned may also know the sacred days of Man, i.e., Mas. [See Git.] (Zarathustra.)

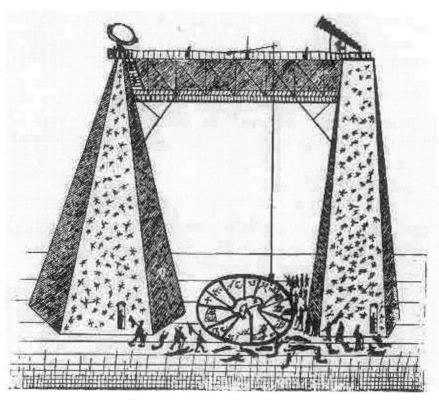

Plate 69. STAR WORSHIPERS.

109. Git'ow'wn (Panic), relating to the Zodiac or to the motion of the sun. The high priest shall designate by the Um (spear), the motion of the sun and moon and stars, so that when the unlearned come to the temple to worship they may also learn of my lights in heaven. (Zarathustra.)

807

110. V.Work-'um. (Panic) Course of vortex. [See Work.]

111. Gan (Panic) Man. Profile, man or mankind. Portrait, man only, and not woman.

112. M'gan (Panic), a woman; i.e., less than man, or little man.

113. M'be (Panic). The word beast or female.

114. Be (Panic), Beast. The written symbol as applying to the animal man in contradistinction to spirit.

115. Hiss'pe (Panic), serpent-like, especially of spirits. The spirits gained dominion over mortals by giving them counsel in getting earthly things. (Brahma.) Rather shall my chosen consult the spirits to learn to purity themselves, and to grow in spiritual things. (Moses.)

116. S,'Pe or spe (Panic), spirit. Let the prophets observe in the temple those that come for wisdom, perceiving if their souls be set on things of earth (Zarathustra). Many of their women had familiar spirits, and they prostituted themselves in counseling with the multitude on earthly things (Moses), and they thus invited into Egypt spirits of the lower heavens who would not raise up from the earth; and when young babes were born they were obsessed, and these evil spirits in justification of their sins, taught re-incarnation. (Moses, in reference to the Egyptians.) An open figure of a spear, signifying a spiritual man or realm. A written character.

117. Y'eng (Panic), signifying a spirit with a corporean.

118. D'hi (Panic), signifying ascent.

119. D'gani (Panic), signifying man ascending; progress.

120. S'pe'su(Panic), signifying angels descending.

121. Che'vot or Chinvat (Panic). A word signifying the boundary of Work or Vortex (See verse 45). The supposed boundary of the lower heavens or atmospherea, and the inner boundary of the emancipated heavens, etherea. A bridge between the atmosphereans and ethereans. Eolin, the Great Spirit, said: On Corpor bring I forth man into life, and I give him a corporeal body, which is a womb for the spirit to dwell in; and when I deliver him from this womb he becometh an inhabitant of da'fome (atmospherea), where he abideth for a season, and I deliver him into Dan'gi (etherea), which lieth beyond Chinvat (Poit). A supposed line between the rotating atmosphere of a corporeal world and the ether that lieth beyond the Vortex. Beware of spirits and Gods who profess to save the souls of men, saying: Only through me shall ye escape the labor of atmospherea and arise to Chinvat. I declare unto you that all such spirits and Gods belong to the lower heavens, where they have kingdoms, and they are the tyrants thereof (Zarathustra). No man shall reach Chinvat but by perfecting himself either on earth or in the lower heavens (Abraham). What company judge ye ye are suited for in heaven (Confucius). Ye are neither wise nor strong (Kii). Being lazy they catch at the promises of Saviors, hoping to fly from the earth direct to Chinvat (Fus). Save ye have learned to perfect your own selves in wisdom and goodness ye shall not rise to Chinvat (Abraham). If a child can not reach manhood but by growth, how hope ye to reach Chinvat suddenly (Algonquin). The evil God, Anra'mainyus, said: Put your trust in me; I will save your souls from the labor of d'fome (atmospherea). But he hath been subdued by his own sins; and in a thousand years he can not reach Chinvat (Brahma).

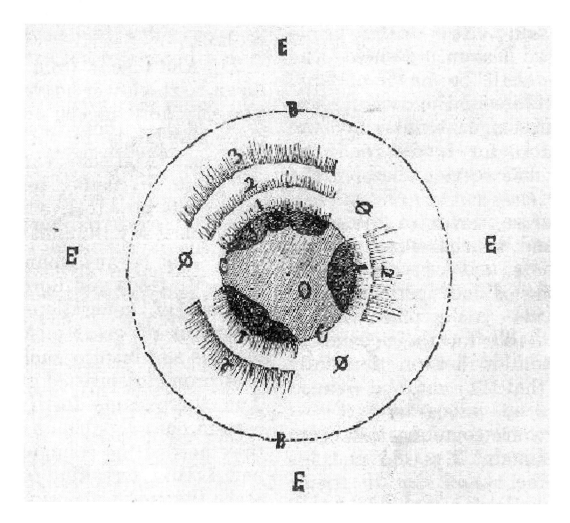

Plate 5.

E, Etherea; B, periphery of the earth's vortex. This line was called by the ancients the Bridge of Chinvat. All within this area is called Atmospherea. The center is the earth,1, 1, 1; O, the ocean. 1, 2, 3, represent atmospherean plateaux. The O, O, O, with a line through it, represents atmospherean oceans.

TABLET OF BIENU.
(POIT.)

Plate 70.

1. A'su (Panic). A man in aboriginal state; before he used words; before he congregated. A very young child; one that knows no word of expression. The race of man in its first age, as applied to Corpor (the earth). A'su, the first habitable age. A circle with a central point. According to the place of A'su on the tablets so shall the interpreters understand. (Poit.)

2. M'asu (Panic). With words came war. In congregating men, the liberty of one interfered with another. Mas'su (Kii). A circle with the four evil corners. Let no man say, I will not sow on the earth, lest I be bound; but be ye fruitful and multiply; for this is the fullness of earth and heaven. (Abraham.) The symbol of M'asu was given to the married, but to the barren the high priest gave S'pe (Gau). Jehovih said: Call not any man evil; but call ye him unripe fruit (Kosmon). Because man cut himself off from Me and choose war, condemn him not, but deliver ye him (Moses).

3. Ex'su (Panic). Nation against nation. A symbol of threat; one king against another. Anra'mainyus sent the symbol of a circle with four cross-corners and a point, over all the earth. (Vede).

4. Ugh'sa (Panic). Standing armies. Is not justice accorded to him who is mightiest? (Fus). They not only waged war, but in times of peace they maintain armies ready for more war. Come, therefore, away from them, ye that have faith in Jehovih, and I will deliver you into another country (Abraham). Rather than that ye be impressed in war, come whither I will lead, and dwell in peace (Brahma). A symbol of standing armies (Gau).

5. Ugh'gad or U'ghad (Panic). A war to establish a certain Ghad (God). Ye not only desire to make slaves of men on earth, but to bind them unto your Ghad after death. (Craosha to the druks.) They fight for the king, being his slaves; they fight for their Ghad, being his vermin (Brahma). An evil man saith, I will war for Egypt, for this is my country; but I say unto you, all countries are Jehovih's (Moses). Be not slaves to any country, nor to any king, nor to a Ghad, but serve the Great Spirit. (Abraham.) A nationality, a symbol. (Gau.)

6. Ort'n (Panic). By the sea; or sea-land.

7. Ort'm (Panic). By the forest; or forest-land.

8. Alef (Panic). A new beginning. Those that were delivered from evil spirits were given Alef as a sign of power (Poit). Alef was a gift of the high priest (Zarathustra). A letter of the Ebra alphabet. When a man desires to reform himself from drunkenness, the Miji gave him Alef, a strengthening symbol (Brahma).

9. Iga (Panic). Ego (Latin). I, myself (English). A profile of the eye and ear. An emblem of the sounds ai and e (Gau), or i and e, or e, or g. Two equivalents to portrait of an eye. In hieroglyphs, a radical.

10. Om (Panic). The negative of Jehovih. The female. That that projecteth is positive. That that receiveth is negative (Gau). Let those that desire to receive spiritually ask of Om; and those that go forth in might return thanks to Eolin (Zarathustra). Power cometh not by supplication, but by going forth; spiritual gifts come not by going forth with might, but by waiting in supplication (Brahma). Nevertheless the ALL ONE is but ONE, but with two attributes (Kosmon). Brahma said: O OM, give thou to my soul; O EOLIN, I am going forth to labor; be thou with me. (Vede.) The ever present OM, the ever present ELOIH, said: Two attributes gave I, the All-self, to every man-self, the Om and the Na (negative and

positive), that he might hold discourse within himself. (Vede.) In seeking a wife, see to it that Oᴍ is her transcendent virtue; otherwise she will be as a thorn in thy side. (Abraham.) Until a man have Oᴍ in the ascendant he shall not hear nor see the Great Spirit. (Zarathustra.) Let your young men seek employment that calleth not forth Nᴀ, but rather Oᴍ. (Brahma.)

11. Tae (Panic). A representative man. The universal prayer of mankind. Also one who is chosen by etherean spirits for an earth cycle; as Zarathustra, Abraham, Brahma, Moses, Capilya, Confucius, etc. I provided for the nations in their darkness, saith Jehovih. For I bring the earth into a light region in the firmament, and I send My etherean angels to deliver them out of darkness and bondage. In My name raise they up men with eyes to see and ears to hear, and I proclaim unto all the inhabitants of the earth (Kosmon). Mankind.

12. Sih (Panic). One whose faith is low. One whose spirit acknowledgeth the gift of spirits, but not the All Person. Three persons have I found; one believeth only in earthly things (material); one in spirits of the lower heavens (spiritist), and one who hath faith in the All Creator (i.e., the Faithists). (Confucius.) They all rise to the destiny they have chosen. (Confucius.) The worshiper of a Savior is Sih (Vede). The worshiper of a God born of a woman is Sih (Vede). Save a man put away the Sih that is in him he can not rise to My emancipated heavens, saith Jehovih. Save a man put away the Pan (materialism) that is in him, he can not rise even in the lower heavens; but his spirit after death remaineth in his own house, saith Jehovih. A symbol of a horizontal spear.

13. Yi (Panic). A hollow crescent. Emblem of wisdom. A badge of honor bestowed by a high priest (Vede). One of the sacred sounds in the Vedic language. [Not pronounced Wy, but Yi'h.] Tu'shiy'a (Fonece). Tushiy-yah (Hebrew). The secret pass-word to the dark chamber (Kii).

14. I'yi (Panic). Life, per se. I'yii (Zerl). Chiy (Gau). Ka'y (Fus). Cha'iy (Fonece). Chai (Ebra). Chai (Hebrew). Tc'yi (Vede). Hy'id'n (Chine). On'yi'h (Algonquin). A tree without substance. Tree of Life. A place of registry; a family record. The origin of I'yi (life), who knoweth? (Panic.) Jehovih said: Infants had gone to heaven before the earth was, and had grown to be wise men and women, but they had not tasted of the fruit of the Tree of Life; and when the earth was ripe unto giving mortal birth to man these angels alighted on the earth. Jehovih said unto them: Eat ye not of the Tree of Life, lest in that day ye become bound to the earth. In that day angels could clothe themselves with corporeal forms by majesty of their own wills, and in innocence they mingled with the people A'sᴜ, who were of the earth, and they were tempted for Wisdom's sake, and did eat of the fruit of the Tree of Life, and they beheld their own nakedness. Jehovih said: By the love ye bear unto your own heirs ye shall be bound to the earth six generations. And it was so. (Abraham.)

15. Vil or Vril (Panic). Earthly desire in abstract or per se. By indulgence in begetting shall man be bound after death; by not begetting, how shall he know all the earth? (Vede). Earth-desire is not evil, but S'pe shall rule over him (Zarathustra). Earthly inventions being to gratify earthly desires, are they good? (Confucius.) Jehovih saith: Seek to do all possible things; for this reason have I given earthly desires. (Gau.) Shall a man not eat and drink and sleep? Now I say unto you, there is an earth body and a spirit to all men, and whatever ye do unto one for its good, rendereth good to the other, and whatever ye do unto one for its injury, injureth the other also. (Moses.) If the spirit man maketh the corporeal man to move, doth it not also make the desires of the flesh? Is the flesh capable

of desire? If so, is not flesh father to spirit?

16. Ope (Panic). The central cause; love. By love only moveth any man; even in anger he moveth not but by the love that appeaseth it (Abraham). The All Good, to be (Fonece). Tob (Ebra). Oe (Chine). Gu'oe (Algonquin). The good that bringeth together, Hy'yope. (Vede.) If man love not, he would not congregate, and therefore war not. But since he delighteth in war, I will be ruler over him to that end (Anra'mainyus), i.e., satan. Man would not give but because he loveth to do so. What honor, then, shall a man take to himself for helping his neighbor? (Confucius.) Did not the Great Spirit make all things by giving? What but love actuated Him? Wherefore, then, shall man applaud Him? (Confucius.) By glorifying the Father for his love, do we not all grow in love? And is not this the highest virtue? (Confucius.) The fool saith: Why shall I praise the Creator? Had He not gratified His love by creating, then would He not have created. This does not concern me; to find what will make men loving and good toward one another, is that not the greatest wisdom? Therefore I honor the wisdom of the ancients in singing praise to the Creator. (Confucius.) Though a man can not love all men, is it not wise that they who love one another, having some virtues alike, shall become a people unto themselves. (Moses.)

17. Hah'nd or Han'hd (Panic). A hand (English). A symbol of values.

18. Sow (Panic). A foot. A symbol of values.

19. Mouh (Panic). A symbol of values. Mouth (English).

20. Fi'i (Panic). A symbol of values.

21. Hiss'ong (Panic). A serpent's head and tongue. A symbol of values.

22. Iod or Ghad or God (Panic). A figure or form. A female figure unlike anything under the sun (Poit). Both male and female made they their Iod'ha, and stood them by the roadside (Iz). In the infant age of the world (Iod, God) was made of wood or stone (Gau). In the time of Seffas they placed him in the sky (Gau). Anything that is worshiped, having form or figure (Ceremonies of High Noon). Ghad (Aribania). A man with spirit gifts. Gad or God, a man who denies he had a natural father. In those days the king persuaded the people that their sire was the Unseen Creator, and all the kings were called Gee'od (Vede). Because ye have made idols of kings, calling them Gods, so call ye the All Light God (Abraham). Whoever saith the Incomprehensible is God, blasphemeth before Him. (Zarathustra.) Is He small like a man? (Gau.) They have blasphemed, calling their Iod'a the Elohim, the Creator (Aribania). I say unto you it is equally blasphemous to bring the Mighty One down to form and figure like your God (Heleste). They seek to confound the unlearned by persuading them that Eloih and their god is one and the same person (Fus). Have not many spirits appeared within the temples, saying: I am God, and ye are in my keeping? Yod, a mortal king. Yod'a, king spirit in atmospherea (Gau). As it hath been declared of old so do I now declare unto you, which is, that the lower heavens are next to the earth, and are full of kingdoms, and the kings of these are Gods (Heleste). God, a tyrant in atmospherea; for as a king is on earth, so is a God in the lower heavens, and so is a Lord. Whosoever saith, Before thee, O God, I bow my head, selleth himself to Osiris (Moses.) Whoever amongst you doeth sacrifice to the Lord are of his dominion; suffer none of my people to marry therewith (Abraham). Have not many of the tyrants of I'em (Hades) returned to earth and proclaimed themselves Lord and God? What more testimony requireth any man that none of them are the All Light? Is not E-O-Ih wider than

all the earth? (Fus.) We swear unto thee, O Jehovih, that we will not call on the name, nor worship, nor adore any person or thing called God or Lord, but Thee only, O Jehovih. (Moses' ceremonies.) Moses being old, said: Above all things preserve the sacred password, E-O-Ih, inviolate; neither suffer it to come to the unlearned lest they be confounded by the subtlety of the God of the Egyptians. Was it not because the unlearned desired a form or figure to worship that the Lord (Osiris) ruined Egypt, making slaves of the Egyptians, both on earth and in his kingdoms in Haw-we? (The lower heavens.) But that the Levites may be friendly with me suffer them to worship the Lord their God. Moses, being about to give up his soul, said: I feel a thorn pricking my side, and I know it is the Leviticans. They not being eligible to the secret rite (Elohim), will in time to come possess the country and substitute their Lord God for the Great I am, the All Eloih. Iod, a stone figure by the roadside without sexual parts, and it is called God (Egypt). Theos and Zeus (Greek and Latin). A being that is worshiped, said to be in the figure of a man. He has a throne in the lower heavens. Dyaus, like the Yod of the ancient idolaters, hath become a king in one of the corners of the lower heavens (Vede). O Om, thou All Present and Boundless, will man on earth ever distinguish? O NAOMA, forms and figures must die! (Vede.) God (English). An idol in heaven said to be in the figure and form of man sitting on a throne. He is believed by people in darkness to be the Creator of all things. They ignorantly blaspheme against the Great Spirit, Jehovih (Kosmon), calling Him God.

23. Oan (Panic). Faith in man only. Sign, two men leaning against each other. Persons who have risen in intelligence, but not in Es. Faith in man only. One who believes man is the highest of all things in the world. One who believes there is no person or thing of personality but man. They being Oans indulged in ____, although they were men only, saying: There is none above us to see us or to command (Fus). They said: Shall I not indulge in whatsoever I choose, being an Oan? (Chine.) Onan, one whose philosophy is in his own conceit; an indulgence (Kii). I do solemnly swear before this order, Oan, that I will never pray to, nor ejaculate to, nor of, nor for any person, save man; and especially not to the Gods nor Lords of heaven, nor to the Unknown, and Imperishable. (Rite of Sodom.) Ho'an, that that leads to Ugh'sa, particularly lust. The impulse of the flesh they called the highest, M'oa (Gau). They threw aside their clothes, going naked like the A'su of old, saying: Is not all indulgence my heritage? (Miac.) They fell from industry and decency, saying: We shall have no forms nor rites, being free. And they became the prey of spirits of idleness and lust, who feast on sinful mortals (Egypt). Spirits of lust came to the Onans and reclothed themselves in mortal forms and indulged in lust with them, and Moses forbade them from coming amongst his people. (Aribania.) The Cow'ans said: Let us go stealthily to the tent of Moses and his priests and learn the secret of his spirit power. The Cow'ans said: Why shall man follow Moses? Are not the spirits who come to us as good as his? (Akia.) Yo'anyi said: If I love meat I will eat meat; if I love strong drink I will have strong drink; if I love sexual indulgence then will I have sexual indulgence. Who can restrain me? Are not my desires well created? I should not deny them? (Vede.) And the druks came upon the Yo'anyi, for their philosophy had divided them amongst themselves, one against another, and their progeny became Tur'anyi (Turanian).

24. Bi (Panic). Two in one. A sign in the order of O'an, in mockery of Ahnra'mayda.

25. Nu (Panic). Organs of sex. They said: All the living are begotten by indulgence; to

worship the organs of indulgence is the highest worship (Aribania). Is not the All Creator but Nu? And they made images and idols of Nu and set them by the roadsides, both in their cities and in the country. Yea, they made small images of Nu, and their women and children went into the market-places selling them. Egypt in time of Moses. (Gau.) Some of them having shame in their souls made another image of Nu and gave it head and horns. (Kii.)

26. Fus (Panic). An enforced religion. By sword and by fire am I established (Fus). The court language of a period. The written law.

27. Yom (Panic). An idol made the heathen to represent Om (Vede). Yom, profane (Fonece). Also Gom (Panic). Goddess of lust. (Fonece).

28. E'hote (Panic). A sign, and not real. As a picture of a foot is not a foot; a picture of the sun is not the sun. (Gau).

29. Ih'o (Panic). Upward, a written sign.

30. O'ag (Panic). Downward, a written sign.

TABLET OF KII.
(PANIC.)

Plate 71. Tablet of Kii.

815

1. Alphabetical sounds, Panic and Chine.

2. Gin, river. Woo, small lake. Long, large lake. Oak, house. Chan, city. Shan, country. F'da, the earth. Gwo, sun-light. Fung, wind. Dan, light, human understanding. Git'how, sun. Git, moon. Salock, stars. Fuche, the firmament.

3. M'bow, horse. Gow, cow. Gan, man. Du'gan, woman. Ji, boy. Du'ji, girl. Aden, sky. G'shan, life. Sa, death. Da, ground. Shak, rock. Foam, wind. Soo, square. Inq or inqu, round.

4. Gui or gu, street. Loo, road. Him, sweet. Soap, sour. Bai, sick. Eah, cure. Sam-shot, war. Du'ga, sword. Bek, weapon. Fox-ow, spear. So, dart, a stone, a sling. Em, to go before.

5. Hid, interview. Hout, dissatisfied. Work, spinal. Bow'mi, Goddess of cattle. Son or songa, one who gives alms grudgingly. Shawn or shon, a stone-cutter. Shaw, a servant. Go'ta, a plowman. Chon'gum, flax. Hark, dark. Kin, roots, edibles. Hoe or hoa, pressure. M'how, priestess.

6. Git'oo, light ahead, the way is clear. Wa'sha, darkness ahead, a melancholia. Seang, a river ford, a passage. Chin, a great ruler. Gone, pertaining to untruth, romance, fable. Gaup, a hostler, a lover of the turf; one who lives indecently with beasts. Show (o short), decline, falling or fallen. Gwo'oa, to weave, to make cloth, also cloth, a covering, a poet, one who clothes things. Min'bon, salutation, a prayer, supplication, especially standing. Kii, truth, a tribe called Kii, a religious tribe on the continent of Pan. An abused people are also Kii. Kii, learning, one who tries to understand. Gwom, sickness, a talisman. Laum, soil, a tiller, harvest, rich.

7. Lun, sleep, trance, somnambula, intoxicated. Hoo, a marshal, leader, organized, system. M'hoa or m'hoo, to shout. Baw, preach, sing. Di'sa, young and therefore foolish. Wa'shu, a tribe of hunters, serpent slayers, persons who feed on raw flesh. M'shu, makers of stone weapons, also stone weapons with handles, axes. Ken'ong or ben'ang, young healer of the sick, the gift of spirits. Chawnt, to sing a song, a monotonous sound of not more than three notes, continued from sunrise to sunset without ceasing. A method of inducing the trance state. C'yu, a lawyer, an arbiter; one who fills the place of both lawyer and judge (a modern referee). Hook, to make fast, a bond sworn on the sacred wheel, Eoin. So'che, epidemic, a scourge, a judgment.

8. Sai, faithful. Hon'yi, multitude, followers, rabble, fete of sacrifice. Sung'soup, miscellany, variety, a people who marry with strangers. Law, the feathered tribe, feathers. Shoe'ji, a gosling or young aquatic bird, a man who can not go to the hunt or to war without his mother; a shame-faced people. Shon, sharp, particularly witty, to cut right and left, evil prophecy. Bog'wi, a circus, an exhibition of trained animals, civilization, learning. M'wi, a tattling woman. Es, spirit, the unseen world. Es'fom, the wind that is good. Sa'fom, evil wind. Gut, a plague, a famine, black-rot, scabs, lepers.

Plate 72. EMP'AGATU.

[Read from left to right. Refer to Tablet Se'moin, for explanation in numbers and meaning].

1. Emp'agatu said: I am the son of Se'moin, son of Jehovih. I am the change of voice of the Seen and Unseen. No man can measure my mysteries. I travel with the growth of mortals. Think not this is my all; it is not my all. I am like the consuming fire that never ceases to burn. I was with the ancients; am today and will be forever. I am he that receiveth new signs and symbols; the old I cast away as a worn cloth, and the new is my house of idols. Mortals are my working tools, and my records the food of all nations.

2. Emp'agatu said: When my people are grown in the tongue; grown in the lips; grown in the throat; grown in the nose, then I come in a chariot of fire and consume their libraries. With a stealthy tread and silent whisper I say unto men: Go not back to the ancients, O my beloved, nor seal up your souls, that Eolin may enter and give you light. Know ye that words are but idols and graven images? But they will not hear, and the Es that is in them cries out with bondage, and I send the burning flame and burn their books into ashes, for I will deliver them from the bondage of the ancients.

3. Jehovih, the mighty Eolin of old, saith: Go, My son, Emp'agatu, give to the swift-growing Es of mortals, larger signs and words. Behold, they grope in the ruins of the past for the idols of old.

4. Emp'agatu said: By the angels in high heaven, the Sons of Jehovih, am I called forth in this day to yield up the records of the past. Think not that I yield up all. I yield up only to

show the way of my labors. The learned men of Corpor shall also search me out of the earth and buried monuments, and my tablets shall read in the East, and West, and the North and South.

Sa'ga 72. Pe 58. Foi'su 14, 21. Be 74. Chu 15. Fin 16, 17, 10. His 35, 19, 22. Te 50, 69. Te 62. Te 54. Chok 73. Mowth 62, 120. Les 85, 104. Zei 31. Ez or es 3. Thus: Jehovih one, Corpor two, Es three, or third entity; the unseen, the air and ether. Go 120, that that lifts up. Ego 68. Muk 88. Hiss 19. Bo 93. M'bo 94, 17. Wot, the seasons. Zhe, 62. Kain, to kill. My 55. Yim 55, 5. N'os 58, 25, 99. Dawn 42, 43, 44. Dan 77. Git 39. Git'don 58, 70. Toe 95. Hand, hand, X'hand, palmistry 91. M'hand, pledge. Chaw, to scratch, treachery 22, 89. N'sau, infidel. F'se 62, 64, 65, 66. Roe 90, 56. Anube 37, 24, 25. Fi 54, 73. Jew or Ju 75, 76, 47, 48. Sisu 79. Ho'am 81, 11. Rit 23, 3. Lodge 21, 78, 79, 80. Por 28, 29, 59, 22. Cha'pop 59. Umb, plumb, 28. Er 25. Ya 98. Owif (Aleph) 1, 100, 101, 102, 103, 104, 105, a prefix. Fow 67, 71. Die or D 93, 94. B'dan or eb'dan 17, 87. A'ye 60, 68, 69. Eh's 40, 37. Cep or see, ep 9, 1. Un, deaf. F'uni, downward, earthly. More or mare 10, 121, 49. S'ore, less. Thus, if a man be called mare, his picture would be called s'ore or s'are. Frew'd or frued, a working tool. Eigy, incomplete. Gan'd 71. Hoo 71. Lo'tak, three in one. Qui, force 7. Nqui 86, desirous of light. Fi'bo or ti'ba, beast-like. Sam'do 3, 43. Da'sam, the great lights, Jehovih, the sun and burning flame, and the three lesser lights, angels, mortals and beasts. X'sam, the three great and three less darknesses. Dan't 24, 77, 39. Eo'dan 87, 9, 72. Ose 9, 116, 106. Tu 78, 79, 38. Ka 83, 13. Ha 1, 32, 57. He 17. Dom 7, 11, 47. All the world save the Great Spirit. Let any man enumerate the things thereof. Sam'aoms 23, 70. Sig 68, 58, 26, 27. G'ex 41, 14, 18. D or dix 4, 6, 67. But or bat, corner-stone. Li, beginning. Alef, especially laying a foundation for a house. Ga, an earthly house. Vil, invention. Sias, altar of incense 72. Kiyi, faithful. Esk'gan 3, 111. O 2, sky. On'm or om, all things under the sky. All the corporeal world is a womb and the voice thereof is the sum of all. Ioo, the Mover of all. Gan'iss 22, 111. Sa 41. Uss 41, i.e., Sa'uss, all things are against all things. Why repineth my soul for peace and love, O Eolin? The four O's being the four entities, soul, peace, love and Eolin. Es'nau, spirit and love underlie all. Bil 82. Me 55, 20. Roar, a loud noise. Gan'bau, a man like a lion; when he speaketh others tremble. Gan'ben, a fallen foe. Gon 118. Os'so, stone instruments. Ax, hatchet, a threat of war. Do'wa 33. Qu'ag, food. Ax'm, sword, knife. Dan'hiss, even in darkness, the light of the Father shines. Sue, His voice is in the birds. Ray, truth. Con or kon, low down. Jaf, that that unfoldeth the two great lights, Om and Jehovih. Owng, all growth cometh out of darkness. Hoa'u'in'u 6, 78. Pi'su, earth-man and angel man. Who shall find the way for their coming together? Toi, time. Bek 66. Sacx, harvest. W, all for man.

ZERL.

RADICAL WORDS IN CHINE, AND IZ, AND ALGONQUIN.

Git, Oaw, sun. Washa, priest. Seang, stars. Chin, throne. Gone, silver. Goap, foot. Show, hand. Gwoon, heart. Min'bo, bread. Kin, take. Gwan, food. Lam, woods. Hoo, good. M'hoo, bad. Baw, wise. Di'sa, captain. Wa'shu, high priest. M'wa'shu, woman, high priest. Bewong, church. Chaunt, sing. Se'yu, laugh. Hook, cry. Sa'she, starve. Sai, die. Honji, birth. Sing-sope, twinkling stars. Law, fixed. Sho'ji, ax. Shou or shon or joss, a man-God. Bog'wi, Goddess of lust. Ne'wi, evil Goddess. Es, spirit or spirit-world. Es'fome, spirit-messenger. Gut, carnal. Bah, father. She, stone. A'ho, steam. Gan'es, manhood. Nida, land. An'hi, lord. Oe, love. Gwan, shine. How, light. Gee, ear. Endi, brother.

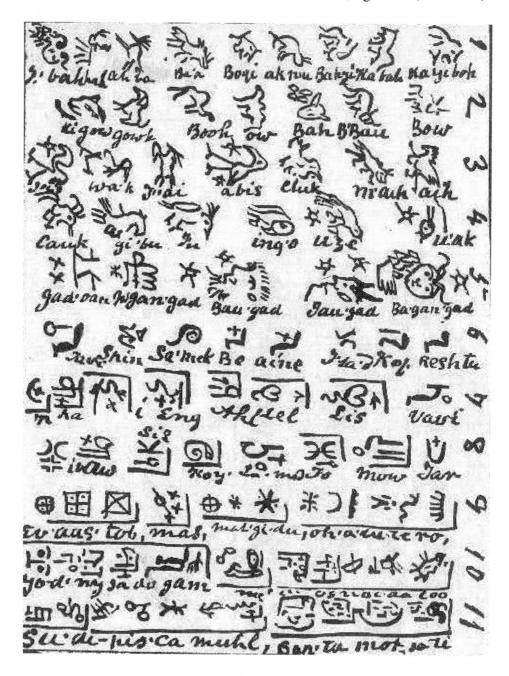

Plate 73. Tablet of ZERL.

[For Interpretation, see Biene (Poit), and Se'moin (Kii). Begin at 1 and read downward: then at 2, etc].

Ja'me, sister. Loi, afterward. Cho, where. Youn, how. Foo, husband. Foo'm, wife. Shu'yi, tyrant. Aji, see. Ma or mi, mother. Jaw, I. Ad'sa, ashes. Jak, ark or chest. Fan, fire. Gan'mi, widow. Ma, thou. E'sho, clothes. Sho'gaup, shoes. Di'ga, flood. Hoe, waters. Ten,

819

empty. Cam'ow, cattle. Yop'lo, come. Oak'm, bad house. H'oak, to build. Fah, hail. Goke, flesh. Gon, daughter. Go'en, daughter-in-law. Dhi, large. Dank, great. Shod, belly. Cho'in, garden. Lok'so, rain. Ong'wa, speaking animal. Go'wa, word. M'how, honey. Se'fiee, fish. Bone, door. Chow, grass. Gah, splendor. Ong'hoo, walking man or traveler. Dang, turn. Diyon, mountain. Igwam, gold. Jes, remember. Won, sweet. Wot, seed. Oi'wot, planted seed.

The offspring of these two tribes were called Izere or Israel. Made out of the same are these, with Chine root, to wit: Peu'gwa, fruit. She, book. Say'tzoo, write. Hon'she, read. Mon'ke, forget. Nug'sa'lo, think. Gow'loo, a fool, a walking animal. Din'quan, deranged. Him, sweet. Bo'jin, tent. Gak'mhi, grain or corn. Lon, rotten. Go'ma'git, crescent. Bah'jow'fi'fi, a race-horse. Shon'yong, goat. Bin'yong, sheep. Loke, deer. Ji'jow'gon, ibis. Lo'foo, tiger. Iho'ji, hammer. Bog'wi, evil spirit. Won'eng, spirit. Fooche, trowel. Roak'cha, compass. Gowh, dog. Shike, stone. Ja'moi, sister. Jeang'foo, husband. Hijn, see. Fawh, fire. Han'she, ashes. Di'wa, war. Howh, rest. Sijoh, little. It'zoo'gon, servant. Box'shong, naked. Jaw'jake, pain. Gwat, home. Mi'sa, buried. Shoo, sleep. Ha'unh, sound. She'ugh, burn. See'ung'fan, joy. Chong, river. Go'e, world. Gah'ji, magnificent.

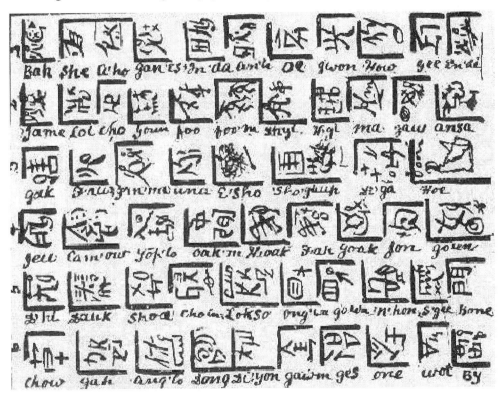

Plate 74. IZ and ZERL.

The sacred birds of Zerl were written by an outline drawing of each and every one; but the pronunciation (in imitation of its speech) was different in the whole of the thirty-four tribes. The tame quadrupeds had fewer names. In Iz or Ez there were but twenty-two tribes, and, being the most sacred tribes of the west of the continent, their pronunciation varied less. Eolin said: Because Iz hath kept my commandments holy, I have bestowed a new tablet (Kii).

820

QADETH IZ;

OR, DIVAN SEAL.

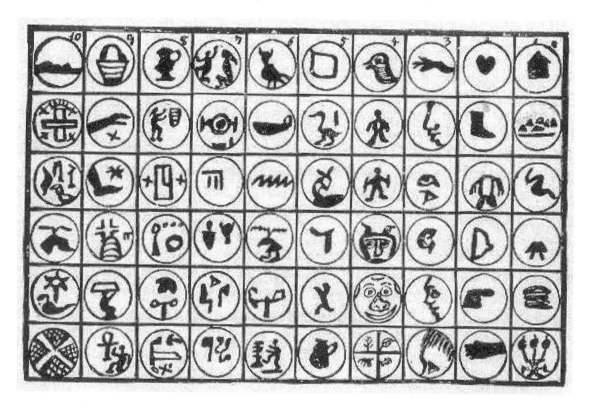

Plate 14.

[Begin at 1, right, and read downward; then at 2, etc.--Ed.].

1. Na'ah or na'ok, - house.
   Sho'ah. - rich country.
   Ba'a, - evil.
   Aman, - steadfast.
   Eden, - foundation.
   Sam'-Or, - the three sacred lights; thus, Sam three, Or, light.

2. Le'bab, - heart.
   Re'gel, - foot.
   Be'ged, - clothing.
   Dad, - breast.
   Gad'ta'ah, - the hand showeth the way as this tablet showeth; i.e., this is my hand.
   Ekef, - palm of the hand.

3. A'bad, - destruction.
   E'dam, - man.
   A'yin, - eye, and also to perceive.
   O'zen, - ear, to hear.

821

Taf, - family.

Resh, - head.

4. Off, - the birds or feathered tribes.

Le'bashed, - to be clothed.

Toff, - timbrel; also psalmist.

Mits'vah, - the enforced law, the established, the authority of judgment.

Ay'in, - conceit, the hidden enemy in one's own heart; they were puffed up in their conceit and would not hear.

Ar'bag'ebul, - the four quarters of the world (Kii).

5. Sef'fer, - scroll, book or tablet.

Aven'ibi, - the belief that man was once a bird. The worship of certain birds because it was believed man sprang from them, hence Aven'ibi, the idolatry of birds; the philosophy that led to the idolatry of animals.

Aheba, - the adorable love.

Ya'sha, - upright.

Alef, - foremost.

Man or maun, - vessel.

6. Ra'o, - the evil, the entity evil. As Ra, death, is to mortal things, so is Ra'o to spiritual.

Mira, - a lamp.

Mi'qut'so, - angular, corner.

Kar'tugh'nuin, - magician; one with familiar spirits.

Maqatteroth, - an utensil for burning incense.

Nasag, - to ascend.

7. Te'ke'ua, - supplication.

Otsar, - storehouse against famine; also place for treasures.

Ra'ka, - kingdom or king and his people, or father and his family.

Aboda, - to labor or to make brick; also brick dried in the sun (ado'da).

Zemar, - music, written notes of.

Nat'sack, - chief musician.

8. Asuk, - a pot.

Yat'sar, - potter.

Barzel or tubal, - iron.

Os'ka'gar, - sun, moon and stars as a whole.

Penak, - summer and winter.

Gu'sa'touin, - out of all things comes some good.

9. Lechen, - bread, or bread-basket, or food, or food-basket.

Asen, - evil hand, or power to cast spell.

Assogen, - evil foot, or power to walk around one's house and so cast evil on the house and family.

E'o'ten, - the All Provider, the sign of offering.

Edan, - prophecy.

Hoe'dan, - angel visitation, or the manner of prophecy.

10. Edam'ah, - country, or the earth or the lands.

E'lo'ih, - Jehovih.

Ba'ra, - the created world.

Ofel, - darkness.

Or, - light.

Eo'sor, - organized, i.e., the light and darkness were created, and all things on the earth became organized.

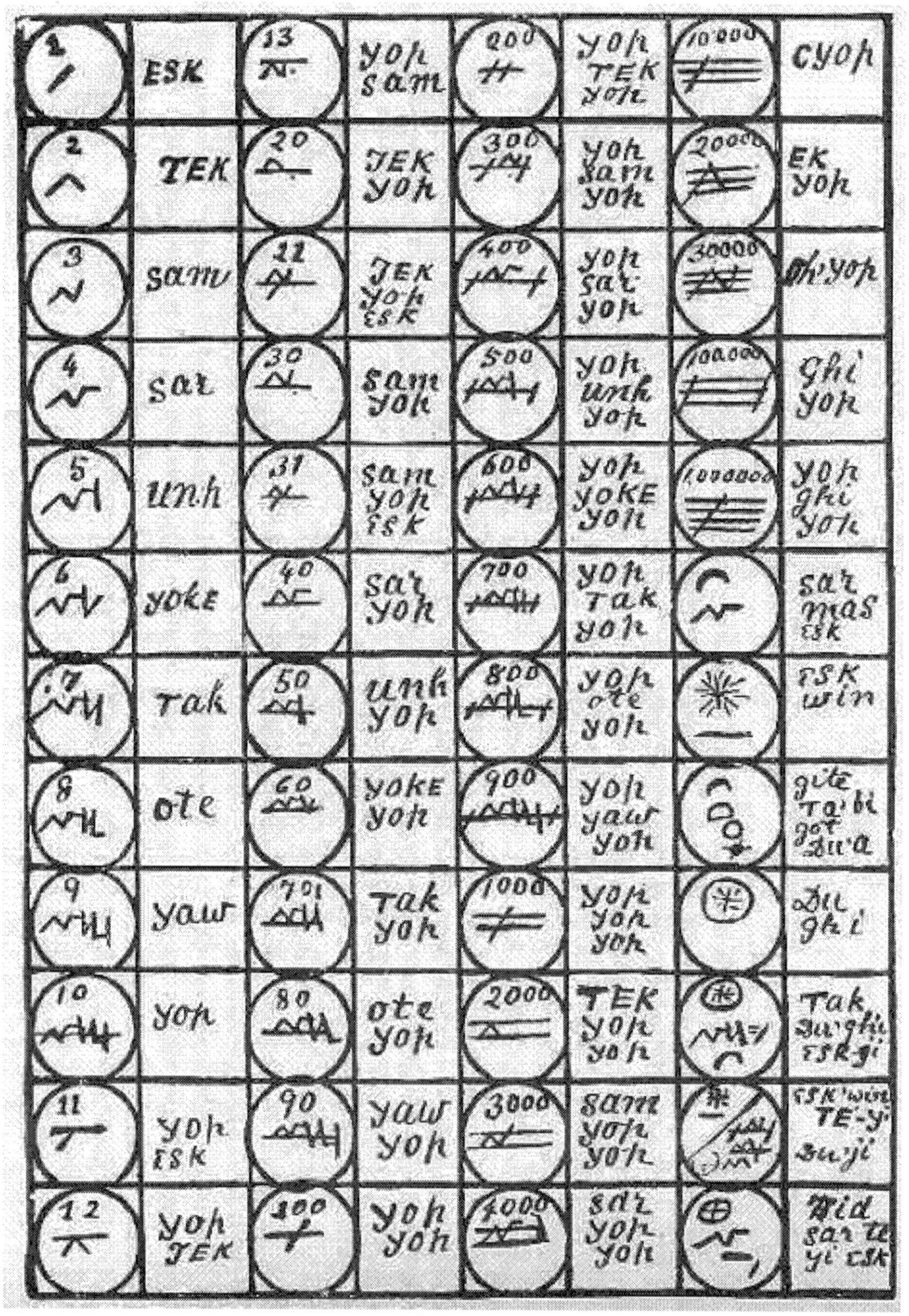

Plate 17

TABLET OF AH'IOD'GAU [Numeration].

823

FONECE.

(The Seventh Degree In The Order Of Israel.)

Plate 75. TABLET OF FONECE

[Begin at 1, and read downward; then at 2, etc.]

1. Master: Who art thou?

2. Pupil: A Son of Light. Behold the sign and emblem.

3. What sawest thou in the light?

4. The altar of Eolin.

5. What was the fashion thereof?

6. The altar of incense and altar-fire rose up before me. The wind ascended and the stars shone in the firmament. A tree grew by the battlement and the black evil crossed the south-west. In the midst stood the cross of Eolin, studded with pearls and diamonds.

7. What more sawest thou?

8. In the south-east floor of the temple, satan, black with the smoke of blood and war, demanded my surrender. And he drew forth the flaming sword.

9. What didst thou?

10. I said, I pray to none but the Ever Present Creator. In Him I have faith. Thou I fear not.

11. What next?

12. I came to the chamber of industry and I was taught a useful trade. After that I traveled north-west.

13. And was honored for thy good work and love of peace, I suppose?

14. Nay, Master. I was confronted by a crowned king. He bade me halt, and ordered me to

pray to the God he served. I remonstrated, saying: I only pray to the Great Spirit, trusting only in good works done unto all men. Thereupon he flew into a rage, saying: Thou art the worst of men; thy soul shall feed the fires of hell. With that he hurled a javelin at me.

15. I escaped and traveled north, and came to a country most rich and prosperous, where many Israelites had gone before me.

16. Why didst thou not tarry there?

17. I did, for a season, but warriors came and possessed the land and drove the Israelites away.

18. What next?

19. I fled to the north-east, and came amongst savages, where I barely escaped being slain and feasted upon.

20. Which direction, then?

21. I traveled east and came into a country old in religion and philosophy. They had great riches for the rich and great poverty for the poor. Their philosophers wasted their time in reading the ancients.

22. Why didst thou not remain with them?

23. I was too poor to live with the rich, and too ambitious to live with the poor, who were little better than slaves.

24. Whither next didst thou travel?

25. Toward the north part of the middle kingdom, where I came amongst magicians and necromancers.

26. What of them?

27. They consulted the stars, and the moon, and the palms of their hands, and called up the spirits of the dead, who did appear before them. There was no industry amongst them, and I could find no employment with them. Neither did they assist one another.

28. Where next?

29. I went further south, where I came to an uninhabited country, the most favored under the sun. It was a place of joy and praise, filled with beautiful rivers, forests, plains and valleys, and countless singing-birds, all things raising up the ceaseless voice of glory to Great Eolin. Here I sat down and wept.

30. What, wept in so fair a place?

31. Alas, I remembered the crowded cities and warring empires. Here there were no people, and I could not live alone, so I traveled still further south.

32. And certainly found a good place next?

33. Alas, me. The country was good, the climate warm, and all things grew abundantly without labor.

34. And why not most excellent?

35. Voluptuousness was an ocean for them to bathe in. And for all sins, their priests taught them, that, if before they died, they called on Daeves, Son of the sun and Savior of men, they would ascend to the upper heavens on the third day after death. Not myself loving indolence nor lust, I departed out of that country.

36. Whither next?

37. Toward the south-east, coming into a land afflicted with priests, soldiers and beggars. So I fled further east.

38. And what then?

39. I came to a small settlement of Israelites where I was received by warm hands. Here I prepared to settle down in peace during all my days. But the state soon became attractive by its places of learning and the beauty of the gardens and glory of its manufactories. There being no idle people nor beggars amongst us, the idolaters of Hemah, Savior of men, accused us falsely and then declared war on us, and with a powerful army marched upon us, taking all our possessions. I escaped and turned westward once more.

40. Thy fate hath been hard. Why smilest thou?

41. Because, however hard hath been my fate, it is nothing to that which I saw had once befallen another people where I came next.

42. What of them?

43. This was a country once rich in ancient temples and monuments, but now ruined and desolate. Broken pyramids and colonnades, tumbling walls, and thorns and wolves, marked the once habitable places of mighty kings and high priests. By the tablets on the moldering walls I read that these people in ancient times long past were worshipers of idols and of Gods who professed to save the souls of men. And I saw that their pride and glory lay in ships of war and mighty weapons of death. Having myself learned the trade of a potter, I took up an ancient, ruined pot, and read this inscription on it: Because I am a Faithist in the Great Spirit, Eolin, I am enslaved by these idolaters. Alas, what is my crime?

44. Most pitiful place! Whence then?

45. I met a friend whose head had been compressed in infancy in order to make him a prophet. He took me into his private habitation and taught me how the brain and nerves of flesh could be changed in infancy by pressure to make the grown-up man of any character desired. Next he taught me the monotony of sound that brings on the prophetic spell and power to see the unseen. Thus did he expound the philosophy of miracles, even to dying and coming to life again.

46. Wonderful philosophy. Wilt thou show me some of these miracles?

47. I will, O Master, but the secret of their workings I can not show.

(The pupil exhibits.)

48. It is true, O friend! Surely, too, thou hast taught this wisdom to the world?

49. Nay; my teacher sent me south, to a school of prophets, where I learned the mysteries of invocation and prayer.

50. For what purpose hast thou visited my temple?

51. To make pots.

52. What, with all thy wisdom?

53. A useful employment is the highest service to the Maker of all.

54. Thou and thy people shall be my people; my harvests shall be thine; and my gardens and orchards; for He whose eye seeth all, is upon me, and I am His servant.

55. There are three more chambers in my temple: The first preserveth the wisdom of the ancients. The second is the chamber of industry and inventions.

56. In the third and last chamber are the secrets of the fullness of worship. The name of this chamber is Om, because it is here the recipients repose in spirit from all the cares of the earth. (Signs and pass-words, and form of initiation, withheld from publication, because the rites are still practiced.)

I'HIN.
HOUBRI. PAN. ALGONQUIN. HOA'TU.

1. These, then, are the chief tribes, being some Faithists and some Idolaters, and these are such as were revered in after generations, to wit:

2. Hode, Si, Iz, Koo, Puit, Poit, Huit, Sem, Ham, Zerl, Haka, Shem, For, Gau, Park, Bah, Loo, Ong, Gam, Dan, Ine, Both, Asch, Howh, Bon, Art, Ia, Gaub, Don, Ref, Fet, Kii, King, Nu, Wis, Sin, Ox, Or, Ug, Wan, Ked, Mork, God, Suth, Eve, Lut, Rut, Kem, Josh, Pert, Sis, Yi, Haus, Kamp, Booh, Koa, Tu, Out, Dav, She, Ji, Ish, Fush, Ab, Ak, Gan, Loo, Mish, Woo, War, Hiss, Sout, Bir, Hush, Yiam, Duji, Gug (Ghard), Ke, Ail, Wang, M'hi, G'wan, He, Zoo, Sa, Lon, Gow, Fifi, Chine, Iaf, Jah, Ba, Goud, Goah, Fah, Ion, Yon, Sope, Ban, Jose, Bad, Dad, Abad, Adad, Joss, Sing, Fome, Du'e, Sam, Sar, Esk, Sham, Noah, Ives, Yi, Mu, Om, Dor, Frag, Kuk, Hum, Wok, Ise, Loke, Ia'a and Gad.

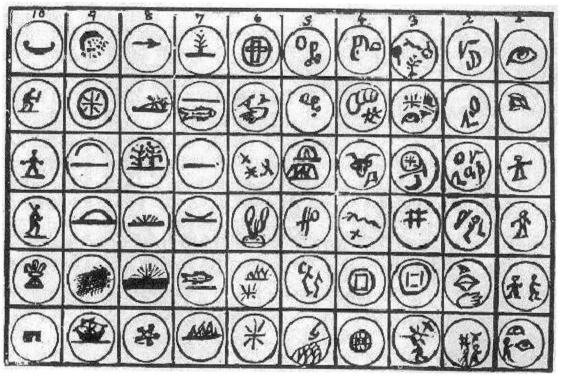

Plate 76.

[Read downward beginning with column 1. Refer to Se'moin and other tablets]

ARIBANIA'HIAYAUSTOYI.
THE INVOCATION INTERPRETED READETH:

1. Now am I strong in Thee, O Jehovih. Thy bow in the firmament encompasseth me on all sides. The follies of earth have turned mine eyes up toward thy holy place.

2. I have beholden Thine enemies bowed down. The king and the mighty man of valor with the two-edged sword are hid away in a dark corner. There is no light for them. Sweet-scented flowers hast Thou grown up in the way of him who will not look upward;

but a serpent cometh upon him and he crieth out against the vanities of the earth.

3. In the far-off corners of the world hast Thou sown the seed of evil and death, and the man of darkness hurrieth thither; but Thy glories he will not behold. He buildeth his foundation in perishable things. But the hope of the righteous man lighteth up the inner chamber. He beholdeth Thy judgment seat. He seeketh Thee in all good things and durable; he glorifieth Thee in Thy works.

4. I will turn away from my house and my lands and look upward all my days. Yea, the fruits of the earth shall be my servants; my crown shall be woven by Thy hands.

5. My heart pointeth up toward Thy kingdom; but the heart of the man of darkness is downward to things that perish? Thou hast set Eon (Aries or Te) in the midst, and he shall judge the living and the dead.

6. Thou hast made me above the diamond and above all precious stones; but the man of darkness goeth after these. Thy children he careth not for; he seeth not. Verily, will I run quickly to them and lift them up. They shall be gems for my raiment; they shall become a glory in Thy sight. Yea, I will turn their eyes up toward Thy holy place.

7. Before them will I set up Gau, and the magnitude and glory of Thy worlds shall entrance them.

8. Thy unseen hand shall become seen, and my brothers and sisters shall read the diadems in Thy firmament. Thine hand hath quickened my eyes to see and mine ears to hear Thee, O Thou Life of my life!

9. My understanding cometh out of Thy tablet (book). Its pages are graven with the sun, moon and stars. Yea, all things proclaim the words Thou hast written. None can counterfeit Thy handiwork. From Thy tablet will I read from the rising of the sun till the going down thereof.

10. My hands shall be skilled with tools to do Thy labor. Fabrics will I weave, and my house shall be built within the square of Thy compass, for it shall be righteous work. My eye shall look toward Thy dwelling-place. I know Thy sight is upon me. I will be joyful before Thee, my Father!

11. To none other will I bow myself in supplication and worship. Before Thee will I labor for peace on all occasions.

12. My hand will I uplift in Thy behalf, and yet no man shall feel the weight of mine arm upon him. By Thy crescent am I sworn unto Thee. By the seven stars and by the sun which is in the midst of the firmament and is the glory thereof, and by the moon, have I spoken.

13. Before Rea (Es, the air and ether), in Thy name have I sworn. I have lifted up my voice. I will have no diadem but that that is woven by Thee!

14. I will sing Thee new songs every day, and find new words of praise for Thy glories. My trials shall be as whet-stones and a hewing-ax. My talents shall increase in wisdom and in whatsoever way Thou leadest me for my own good.

15. Before Thy sacred altar will I come, knowing Thy angels will come also. Yea, they shall teach me thy decrees.

16. Thy gifts shall be my gifts, my portion, whatsoever seemeth just in Thy sight.

17. Thy messengers shall come to me, and my house shall be their house, they shall behold my labor; they shall admonish me wisely.

18. They shall teach me wisdom in all Thou desirest of me. The secret of my love to Thee will I tell them, and I know they will lift me up for Thy glory. In Thy praise will I sing forever, O Jehovih! Amen!

Plate 77. Tablet of Ancient Egypt.

Those who sat around the table for spirit communion kept their eyes riveted on the graven characters. He who sat at the end where the crown is, was the oldest and was called rab'bah (father). It will be observed that the invocation is more than an interpretation of the characters, although they are all designated in the words. The rab'bah led off, but all the circle joined in the reading of it. The gau, the plumb-line, was moved by the spirits in answer to the questions of the rab'bah. In some countries the gypsies, who are supposed to be descendents to ancient Egypt, still invoke spirits in this way.----[Ed.

829

HO'ED.

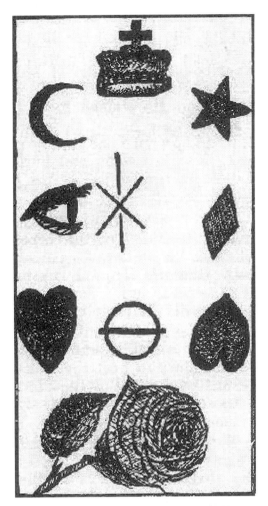

Plate 78. TABLET OF HY'YI.

These Tablets were engraved on inlaid tables, called family altars, around which the family sat for spirit communion and prayer. The father led in repeating the invocation, and the wife and children spoke in concert. After the Israelites left Egypt, the graven tablets were abolished, but invocation at the family table was continued, and is even to this day amongst some of the Jews (so-called).--[Ed.

Mithra the first was about 4,000 years before kosmon.
Mithra the second was about 2,000 years before Kosmon.

Invocation readeth:

1. Mithra said: Ye that invoke Me, the Swift, Shining, with sword uplifted. Invoke me on the Tablet of the sun, and the world, and the crown, high raised. Bow down low and say:
2. Behold, the rose, deep rooted in the earth. Jehovih riseth in majesty of All Light. His colors no man maketh, nor knoweth any man the cause. This subtle perfume, whence cometh it, and whither goeth it? What power fashioneth it, and propelleth it?
3. O Thou, unseen Om! Is my spirit like perfume? Whence cometh it, and whither goeth

it? Give me of Thy Mithra, O Om!

4. Make my heart look upward to Thee, Thou all Pure, Heavenly! Wife, and Spouse and Mother! Thou that cometh, I adore Thee!

5. The corporeal world hast Thou, O Jehovih, placed in the midst of the lowest places, bringing forth. Bind my soul not to it, Thou All Going-forth.

6. My heart no longer looketh downward; my corporeal passions have I subdued. Yea, even the diamond binds me not, the highest shining corporeal thing.

7. Thou, O Corporeal Sun, burning and full of flame, that bringest forth the corporeal, growing harvests, hear me proclaim the All Eye that createth, making the souls of men. Thou, O Corporeal Sun, that makest of the things that are made, what a glory is thine! But far off, and nearer than Thou art, O Sun, is Jehovih, Who createth without things that are made, the All First Creator. He goeth forth, Jehovih. He cometh Om, the Bride and Mother, nursing with full breasts.

8. O thou Moon, hear my upward soul aspiring above all corporeal things! Thou, my Love and Majestic and ruler of waters and winds, I adore Thee. But a greater, the All Great Om, fed thee. From her breasts wert Thou, O moon, high upraised. Eolin, the Mighty, touched Thee with his little finger and Thou hast sped on. Come Thou to me, O Om, spouse of the Seen and Unseen.

9. O ye Stars, full of shining in the high heavens. Who can measure your far-off places? Who can see your great corporeal majesty? O what a glory is yours, thrown in the high heavens! Thither, far, the soul of my forefathers roam full of praise and prayer. Make me all pure, O Thou Om, that I may ascend.

10. Send forth Thy Crown, O Eolin, Creator of all moving things. O Thou Incomprehensible and full of glory! Make me oblivious to all corporeal things, and fill me with Thy going-forth forever.

11. Make me to look not backward nor to myself, but to behold Thee, O Jehovih, and Thy Lords and Thy Gods, strong in majesty and spirit high-soaring, forever! Amen!

CHINE. ZERL.
INTERPRETATION.

1. MASTER: Who art thou, and thy business?

2. INITIATE: A weaver of fabric (or whatever labor he followeth) and lover of wisdom. I have come to learn of the wisdom of the Gods and Lords of heaven.

3. For thy labor thou art honored by the Gods and Lord of heaven. But erst thou canst learn of heaven thou shalt be proved in corporeal parts. What are the elements?

4. Earth, air and the other above the air.

5. What is man and his destiny?

6. Born of the earth, earthly; freed from the earth his inner part, the soul, ascendeth and dwelleth in the soul of things.

7. What, shall a dead man live?

8. Yea, and rejoice that he so liveth. I have witnessed the souls of men returned to the earth, reclothed in corporeal substance, and talked with them face to face in presence of witnesses.

Plate79. CEREMONIES IN SUN DEGREE.

A, Master. B, initiate. C, first gate. D, second gate. F, third gate. G, fourth sacrifice. I, oath of allegiance. J, place of death, represented by bones and skull. K, coffin. L, proof of spirit-power to overcome pain. M, submission to have the body run through with a lance. N, testimony that the initiate could endure all corporeal torture unharmed. This is the inner circle. The outside or body of the crescent representeth the jewels and places of the Gods and Lords of heaven and their mortal representatives, together with the tools, implements and kind of industry to which each and every one was assigned. These constituted the audience during the ceremonies, the workers being stationed in the inner circle.

9. Then thou fearest not to die?

10. I am in the keeping of Hong-she, Savior of man.

11. Who was Hong-she?

12. The only begotten Son of the Unseen. He was the incarnate and spiritual Son of the All Light of heaven and earth, born of the Virgin Mi, who was descended from the far-off star, Tristya.

13. For what purpose came He? And whither hath He gone?

14. He was made by Great Eolin, Creator of all things, to take charge of this corporeal world, which is His, to keep it forever. He abideth still in spirit on this corporeal world.

15. Where and when lived He?

16. In the ancient days He lived in the far east.

17. What was His labor?

18. To do good. In Him was no evil; He was the All First who taught the power of the spirit over the corporeal part. All who have faith in Him, can also work miracles, nor shall such persons ever die.

19. What became of Him?

20. First He was bound on the wheel of Eolin; but the spirits of heaven unbound Him.

Then His hands were thrust through with swords, but there was no wound. He was then bound on an altar of sacrifice and burnt, but His corporeal parts would not consume, and He walked forth unharmed. Then a sword was thrust through His body, but it made no wound and gave no pain. Then He was placed in a coffin and buried, but in three days he rose up out of the grave and went forth preaching.

21. What became of Him finally?

22. He still abideth on the corporeal earth, and at times taketh on a corporeal body and showeth Himself, He and His mother Mi, also.

23. What did He preach?

24. To do good unto others; to harm no man, woman, nor child, and to pray only to the Great Eolin; to heal the sick by sacred words, and by motions of the hand. It is to learn these sacred words and signs that I have come to this holy temple.

25. Before thou canst be entrusted with such signs and words, thou shalt be proven on thy God and Savior, that thy faith be manifest. Know, then, that although thou art blindfolded and seest not, yet thou art surrounded by Gods and Lords of heaven and earth, and by a mortal priest most holy and powerful. If thou hast faith in thine own words, and thus knowest the Son of the Sun, thou hast little to fear. Follow, therefore, thy attendants to the places of sacrifice, that we may bear testimony that thou art holy. Remember, also, that all men must be tried, either in the corporeal world or in the next; without this there is no resurrection for them.

26. I trust in Thee, O my Savior, Hong-she. Let the attendants lead me forth.

(The initiate is then taken and bound down on the altar H. naked, and a fire lighted under him, and he thrusteth his right arm down into the flames until it be proved he hath power over fire and will not burn.)

27. M.: By virtue of my power received from Hong-she, Son of the All Light, Savior of men, I pronounce E'gau (i.e., he is Gau). Release him, O ye Lords of the Heavenly Host. As the All Holy Savior of men penetrateth the corporeal part, so shall the corporeal part be divided.

28. I.: In Thee, O my Savior, God of this corporeal world, put I my trust. Lead me forth, O ye of the corporeal earth, and prove my soul.

(He is next led to So-an, and there a sharp blade is thrust through his hand and withdrawn, and, if proved, there is no wound nor blood.)

29. M.: By Thy Light, Hong-she, descended in Fo'e'tse, angel messenger of the corporeal world, this is my brother of Chine and legion of Zerl. But yet a greater gift hast Thou for him. Lead him forth, O ye Lords of the corporeal world, and thrust a sword through his body.

30. I.: Go forth, O ye Lords of the corporeal world, ye know not what manner the spirit is of. Forgive them, O Almighty, Hong-she, Son of Eolin, Creator of worlds. This is Thy body, this Thy blood. Let them eat and drink of them, in remembrance of Thee. Thy hand will deliver; my soul shall never die!

(A sword is then thrust through the body and withdrawn, but there is no wound nor blood.)

31. I.: In remembrance of Him do I these things. Behold the power of faith. By faith the All Creator created.

32. M.: By thy words shalt thou be proven. O ye Lords of the corporeal world, bring him sand and water and a veil. By His command shall a rose bloom in our midst.

33. I.: O Thou, Hong-she, only first begotten Son of Du'e Mi, Mother of Eolin, Spouse of the All Light, offspring of the Creator of worlds, give me of Thy power for the blessings of the corporeal world.

(Sand and water and a veil are brought before him, and he covereth the sand and water with the veil and repeateth thus:)

34. I.: As Gau from nothing sprang and stood triumphant on the corporeal world; so, forth, come thou, the fibre of corporeal parts, and clothe the spirit-rose mine eyes behold. (The rose or roses are then beholden, fresh grown amid the sand and water.)

35. M.: This day Thee I crown my brother He'den'loo (Magi), of the Savior empowered on the corporeal earth to dwell by holy land and water!

(The initiate then taketh of the water and sand and sprinkleth the attendants.)

36. I.: This is My blood and My Body, saith Hong-she, the All Quickener. Take ye of them in my name.

37. THE LORDS (together): Behold the Es that ruleth over Corpor. Be mighty in will, O children of men. Be wise of will, O children of men. Be all truth in will, O children of men. Be all good works, O children of men. In all your best thoughts and wise perceiving, O children of men, learn from Es, the world unseen.

38. (The Lords conduct him to the middle chamber, where he taketh the oath.)

39. I.: To celibacy I am sworn, for he who begetteth a child is bound in spirit, after death, unto his own offspring.

40. To the Es world I am all remembrance. To the corporeal world all forgetful henceforth forever.

41. All vain words do I renounce; all idle laughter do I renounce; all love of corporeal things do I renounce with abhorrence.

42. M.: What of the Es, the great Unseen?

43. I.: Two heavens there are: one resteth on the corporeal earth; one standeth high in the firmament.

44. Betwixt the twain lieth the bridge Chinvat, where standeth Hong-she, Savior of men. By His love can the children of men pass; by His curse must they return to the lower heaven till purged of all corporeal thoughts.

45. By the trumpet, loud sounding, of Fo'e'tses, Chief of the Heavenly Host, knowest the Son of the All Light the secrets of the souls of men.

46. (The Gods (angels) stationed at the four gates now come forward and salute. Then come the Lords (angels) of the outer host, with the working tools, and, together, they sing to the Great He'jo'is.)

47. M.: For what purpose is this coffin?

48. I.: That I may be coffined and buried in the corporeal earth.

49. M.: Let the lords of earth bury him in the name of Anra'mainyus (or Ugh'sa), the all corporeal death.

50. The initiate is then coffined and buried, and a watch set around the grave, over which a veil is thrown, and in the darkness the angels unearth him and set him free. Thereupon he is bestowed with regalia and implements, and with signs and holy words, the which can not be given outside the Sun degree of Faithists. Neither can the implements and

834

working tools of the Lords and Gods of the outer circle be revealed save to such as have been duly prepared by fasting and by prayer, and by a knowledge of the motions and positions of the corporeal worlds. Jehovih saith: Only to the wise, the pure, and the just, do I reveal the mysteries of My kingdoms.

KII.

Plate 80. TABLET OF KII.

This Tablet and ceremonies belonged to Persia, Arabia and Heleste, Greece and Troy, and to the Algonquin tribes. The time was 5,200 years before kosmon.

Interpreted, readeth thus:
1. Master: What seest thou?
2. Initiate: The world lieth before me. Yea, the wide earth and all its riches. The living things upon it, and in the waters, and every breathing thing, and pearls and diamonds, and gold and silver; and at my hand, the rose and the lily, adorned by the Hand of Elohim.
3. M.: Seest thou nothing more?
4. I.: Yea, Master, the canopy of the firmament of heaven. In the midst thereof the light, burning sun, propeller of the vegetable world; the glory of day, and maker of light.
5. On either hand, in the vault of the firmament, countless stars, saying: In the glory of our magnitude, O man, forget not Him whose finger upraised the firmament!
6. M.: What more beholdest thou?

7. I.: The moon, who changeth her size and place according to the nightwatch of the Ghads who minister to the wants of mortals.

8. M.: Is this all?

9. I.: Nay, Master, on either side I behold a hand, one pointing upward and one downward.

10. One side of the world is all light and one side all black, and the hand that pointeth upward is on the light side, and the hand that pointeth downward is on the dark side. Here lieth the brush that wrote, and the sacred Gau, and above them the symbol of the burning candles of the ancients. Above these I behold the ark of the prophecy.

11. M.: Why haltest thou in thy speech? What seest thou?

12. I.: Alas, O Master, above the world I behold an evil foot, black and clothed with serpents.

13. Above the twin swords, crossed, is the sacred name, Elohim.

14. M.: What seest thou in the midst of the tablet, black and as with a net woven around?

15. I.: A new corporeal world, rich in growing things; sprung from the surface thereof, hang the sacred signs of holy Lords and Gods, appointed by the most high Elohim, apprised and guarding over the morning and evening of the first days.

16. Here the trumpet calleth to the low earth, and to the spirits of mortals now dead, to come forth, inspiring teachers in all useful labors, to the new world above.

17. Fabric woven in the firmament of heaven is descending to the infant a'su. Thirsting for a kingdom in the lower heaven, standeth Baugh-ghan-ghad, the tyrant of newborn spirits in the lower heavens, watching the new earth.

18. His tablet is a coffin filled with serpents' tongues. In his footpath millions of dead that sang his name, to make him triumphant over Elohim, creep, accursing him in high heaven.

19. The pyramids, the temples of ancient Saviors; and the overflowing holy basin, and lighted Nu'ba, candlestick of Holy Sacrifice, and the black claw, the Anra'mainyus (the devil), are cast down and gone, yea, on the earth below another God is dead. But high up in the firmament, the seven sacred stars still shine, and the emblems graven by the Great Spirit.

20. M.: What are the working tools of man born of woman? What of the Gods and angels beside Elohim?

21. I.: Alas, O Master, I know not.

22. My friend, since thou art learned in Gau, why comest thou to learn the signs and ceremonies of the ancients?

23. That I may unite myself with other men, and thus become a greater power to do good unto mortals.

24. Thou art wise. Repair now before my proper officers for further examination, and, if thou art proficient, come again before me and I will conduct thee into the chamber of Ophra'or'jhi, and there initiate thee according to the rite of the ancients.

[Signs and pass-words, and mystic ceremony, withheld from publication.]

[For the reading of the tablet entire, refer to the revealed tablets.]

PORT-PAN ALGONQUIN.
THE SACRED PEOPLE, I'HINS, OR MOUND BUILDERS.

Plate 81.   PORT- PAN ALGONQUIN.

Readeth as follows:

1. Which way, man?

2. To the tree of knowledge.

3. I go thither, also.

4. Where, then, is thy treasure?

5. I bring this pitcher and pot, a tame gowt and a dead man's skull. I have no more.

6. Seffas bows down in thy favor. Hast thou slain any living creature?

7. Nay, Ong-a-pa, but housed in a mound high-built, and steep, I have slept my nights away in peace, slaying naught.

8. Hast thou the Hagaw'sa (the head compressed), from infancy?

9. On my breast, engraved, the sign single standeth most honored of all I have. When I was a child my head was thus compressed, to school the judgment down beneath the prophetic sight. I have seen the Es world and the angels of the dead.

10. Hold up thine hand, and show me, too, the leaf sign of Egoquim. Then the burning flame of sacrifice and monstrous serpents thou wouldst rather feed than destroy?

11. To engrave the sacred symbols in Corpor I was well-educated. Behold I write.

(He then displayeth his skill.)

12. Thy skill is excellent. Go thou to the south-west corner, and in the ark of the black hand thou shalt find a charm for venomous serpents. Bring it hither.

837

13. Alas, O Onga, ask of me any service but to deal in charms against anything.

14. How sleepest thy father and thy mother, and thy wife and thy sons and daughters?

15. On the mounds and in the mounds, O Onga. Hid are we all away from the devouring hiss-sa (serpent), and baugh and mieuh (lions and tigers).

16. How was it with thy forefathers and foremothers?

17. In the mounds and on the mounds, O Onga. For a thousand generations my ancestors killed not any living creature Egoquim had created.

18. What is yonder building in the north-east?

19. The temple of Egoquim.

20. What meaneth it?

21. It is the sacred house of Dan. (Faithists.)

22. What are the signs?

23. The All Light hand teacheth mortals to ever reach upward; the cup, that all the firmament is filled by the presence of Egoquim.

24. What is the sign of half a dog, of half a horse, and a man's head?

25. That man at best is two beings, a beast and a spirit.

26. What is the sign of the black hand and black onk, the slaying tool?

27. The mortal who slayeth the wolf and serpent hath a hard time in heaven.

28. What is the hard time of the slaying-man in heaven?

29. In the firmament of heaven he is haunted; the spirits of the slain come upon him. He findeth no place. With his black hand of death uplifted he crieth out.

30. What is the sign of Oke-un (tent), and the sign of the black head of the Ghi-ee (eagle), and the black mouth with black tongue projecting?

31. That all the earth must be subdued by man. Even the blackness (slander) that issueth out of man's mouth must also be subdued.

32. What are the signs of the ear, the triangle and the square, the evil quarters, the wedge and the vessels of copper?

33. Alas, O Onga, I know not.

34. What are the signs of the trumpet, the windlass, the hewing-ax and the altar of fire?

35. Alas, O Onga, I know not.

36. What are the signs of the Az-aj (stretcher), and the basket?

37. Alas, O Onga, I know not.

38. What is the sign of the men ascending the Orugh (the stairs), and lamp and the trees and the black fish?

39. First, there was an egg, and then a fish, and then trees, then man, and he saw the light and the sun. Then wisdom came and he learnt of Egoquim, ever after.

40. Thou art wise, and now, by virtue of my power and wisdom and love, do I crown thee brother of the Hoanga (prophets). Peace be with thee, Amen!

41. He who taught thee all the other signs will now teach thee three thou knowest not. After which the Oi will invest thee with cloth and with the signs of Chaigi (words of enchantment), that when thou travelest in far-off lands thou shalt be received as a brother.

(Signs and pass-words withheld from publication.)

ANUBIS. (Old Egyptian.)
THE HAUNTED CHAMBER.

Plate 82.

Antechamber examination omitted.

Second part in the dark chamber, to wit:

1. MARS (alias Death): What is this noise and confusion? Who comes here to disturb our haven of rest?

2. JUPITER (alias Aises, a leader): Hark! I heard a voice! It is true, this place is haunted! Say thou, spirit or angel, speak! Who art thou?

3. M.: I am Death! All who enter here must die! Are ye prepared?

4. MERCURY (alias Saug, heavy): Hark! What fearful words!

5. M.: Silence!

6. J.: Alas, O Death, spare us! Command us as thou wilt, but slay us not.

7. M.: Impious mortals, know ye this place is consecrated to the spirits of the dead? All who enter here must die!

8. Mer.: We implore Thee, O Death! Is there no respite?

9. M.: Over your heads I hold the two-edged sword. Fear ye, and tremble when I command.

10. J.: Alas, O Death, we and all mortals fear thee. What shall we do?

11. M.: There is one respite. Sit ye at my feet in token of your submission to a higher power than mortals. (The initiates sit down.) Bide ye there till I call my fellow-God, Life. Ye shall know your doom! All hail, O Life! Hither, hither! Mortal intruders have profaned our sacred chamber! Come thou and deal with them, that I may receive their souls!

12. Sun (alias Dan, a light): Hail, O Death! I come! Mighty art thou, O Death! Were it not for thee mortals would esteem themselves Gods. Take me, brother, to them. (M. conducts S. to another part of the chamber.) *S.:* Mortals, for what purpose are ye here? Speak to me, I am Life.

13. Pity us, O Life! We are friends to the spirits of the dead. We have come hither to unite ourselves in a common brotherhood, especially to improve ourselves in spirit communion. Deal thou mercifully with us and we will be faithful and true.

14. S.: On one condition only can I save you from Death's hand. I have here scales on which I weigh mortals, and by your words shall ye be weighed, for all words manifest the spirit within. If, therefore, ye repeat after me the words I utter, ye shall live. But if ye do not so utter them, ye shall be handed over to Death. Neither will I utter aught but what all good men and true, may utter my words after me.

15. J.: Speak, O Life! We will repeat after thee.

16. Mer.: We will repeat after thee.

17. Venus (alias due'ji): We will utter thy words!

18. Ceres (alias hyastra): Speak, O Life, thy words shall be our words.

(Many of the stars repeat expressions in like manner, the initiates being previously named as some star.)

19. S.: My friends, repeat your own names and then these words (the initiates give their names): Of my own free will, in presence of these spirits and mortals, do I covenant that I will forever keep and never reveal any of the secrets or mysteries I may receive within this chamber. That I will accept as my brethren all who are here present, and all who have been heretofore initiated, or may be hereafter initiated, as fully and entirely as if they were my own blood and kin. That I will not from this time forth utter one slanderous word against these my brethren, nor against any man nor woman nor child belonging to them or that is dependent on them. That I will protect their honor and virtue and love as sacredly as I would my own mother. That I will from this time forth engage myself in some useful employment, and from the excess of my wages, contribute to the relief and assistance of any of the brethren who may be helpless or distressed. So keep me, Thou, who makest and rulest over all. Make me steadfast to keep this, my solemn covenant; and I bind myself under no less a penalty than to forfeit all spirit presence both in this world and the next, and the good-fellowship of all men, if I should fail to keep this, my holy covenant. By the Pillars of the castle I swear, and by the Sun, and by Uz (Osiris), and by the Sacred Wheel, and by the Angle of Gau, yea, by Elohim!

20. S.: My friends, you have been weighed, and the scales bear to your favor. You shall live. What more desire ye!

21. All: Light! (The ceremony so far being in the dark.)

22. S.: Let my servants make a light. (The servants march about, but make no light.)

23. First Servant: Alas, O Master, we can not make a light; the oil will not burn; the lamps are cold.

24. S.: In this emergency, what shall be done?

25. Second Servant: Alas, O Master, we know not.

26. S.: Let this be a lesson to both spirits and mortals, for as I do now, so in all great trials, do ye also. (Aside:) Hither, O brother God! Hither, O my brother!

27. M.: Here, O Life! Here, O Life, I come!

(Walking to a different corner.)

28. S.: My attendants can not make a light. The oil will not burn. The lamps are cold. What shall be done?

29. M.: Let us supplicate Him who is greater than life and death!

30. S.: It is well.

31. M. and S. (together): O Thou, Almighty and Everlasting Creator of Life, and Master of Death, give us light! Give us light, O Father!

32. S.: Let my servants try once more. (The servants now make a light. The initiates behold their strange apparel, which was put on them in the dark.)

33. M.: Behold, O mortals, by the light of heaven, man hath risen above the beasts of the field and fowls of the air. But for the light of Uz (Osiris) your heads would have this day been as your hoods. (With his sword he knocks off the head-covering.) Be as beasts no more, but men and women. In token of your fidelity to the covenant, drink ye of this nectar of life. (Because they were saved from death.)

(The cup is then passed from one to another, and all drink of it. In the Algonquin tribes of America the ceremony was the same, save that a pipe was smoked instead of the drink, and to this day it is practiced by them as a pledge of peace and brotherhood.)

34. S.: (making the proper sign, which is withheld from publication, and taking the hand of one of the initiates): Arise, O my brother of the Haunted Chamber, I salute thee in the name of _____ (withheld from publication).

35. M.: As ye are now raised up on earth, so shall ye be raised in heaven, where, it is represented by the spirits of the second heavens, are scales to weigh the spirits of mortals recently dead. And he who presideth over the scales in heaven was called _____ (alas me, how shall I repeat his name?) Let him who conducted you hither answer me: Who is the God of the Scales in heaven?

36. Fourth Servant: I can not so answer, Master.

37. S.: Knowest thou?

38. Fourth Servant: I am wise.

39. S.: What wilt thou?

40. Fourth Servant: (Withheld from publication.) (And when Anubis appeareth, the Master saith): All words sprung from the fullness of the spirit within. Be exact in observing your covenant, and guarded in your words toward all men, for as ye were here weighed by your words, so shall ye be both in this world and the next. (The S. and M. now bestow the pass-words and signs, here withheld from publication.)

41. M.: Thus endeth your initiation, and may the cross of the Wheel of the Great Spirit be the center of your action, and the angle of your behavior toward all men. Amen! (All respond, Amen!)

42. First Initiate: Why, this is just the brotherhood we desired!

43. Second Initiate: Just what we set out to accomplish!

44. Third Initiate: And better done than we could have done it!

45. S.: Remember, then, this lesson: That in all good works inclining to brotherhood, especially that which inclineth to spirit communion, mortals are ever assisted and guided by wise spirits of noble aspirations.

(Manner of dismissal withheld from publication out of respect to existing societies.)

AGOQUIN.

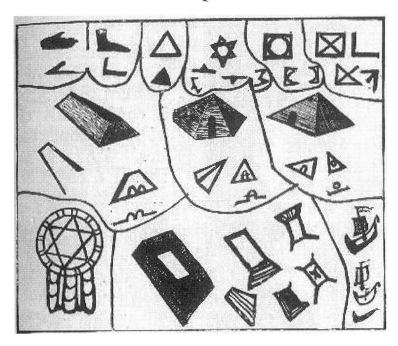

Plate 83. BIBLE OF THE MOUND-BUILDERS.

[Read from left to right, beginning at the top.]

1. Agoquim said: These are My divisions for the twelve feasts of the Gods of heaven. Observe ye them in My name, for they are My inheritance, bestowed to enrich the wisdom of men.

2. All labor is Mine, saith Agoquim. By My hand moveth all that is.

3. The earth is My footstool, and I have made it square to the north and south, east and west.

4. Three things made I: air, earth and water. The angle with three sides made I in remembrance thereof. Three things bestowed I on man: the earth body, which is dark, and none can see through it; the spirit which liveth after the earth body is dead; the third part I gave to man is the soul, which joineth him to Me.

5. The sun I made, and I set him high in the firmament that I might see from afar and behold My earth-born children. And the lakes and forests and rivers, and the caves in the earth, made I for man.

6. All that I have made is good, and round, or square, according to the place I made for it.

7. But in the very young days of the world, the impatience of men led them to perceive not Me and My good works, and they set about to do My labor. Thus came evil into the world; but I separated the evil from the good. Into the four corners of the world separated I them. I gave to the evil, where all is coldness and hunger; where they have invented the evil-killing bow and the flint-dart, destroying My living creatures.

8. My righteous shall live in mounds of earth and stone and wood, where the Ugha (serpent and tiger and all other evil-devouring beasts) can not come upon them.

9. But for the light of My angels to come and abide with My people, ye shall provide the hoogadoah, the well-covered house, and it shall have but one door, and pieces shall be put

therein, so that when My chosen are within, all shall be dark, that My angels may teach them.

10. But the dwelling of the Hoonshawassie (the prophet) shall have one Ongji (window).

11. And he shall have a Mukagawin, the true sign of poverty, and it shall be his jewel, made of copper and gold. For whom I have made to live in poverty in this world will I exalt in heaven. Only the poor have I made to be My prophets.

12. Over the mounds My angels shall keep watch against the evil approaching Ugha, and they shall awaken My sleeping children, and they shall not suffer.

13. Agoquim said: Boats have I provided for the spirits of good men to rise to heaven in, and My angels shall accompany them to a place of light and rest.

14. Agoquim said: To the priests have I given authority to make My signs and symbols, and to bestow them on My righteous children.

BAUGH-GHAN-GHAD
[ALIAS BAUGH-GAN-GHAD.]

Plate 84. TABLET OF BAUGH-GHAN-GHAD

1. Baugh-gan-ghad said: I go forth. All who follow Me, are of Me. By will only is anything accomplished. That which I desire, I do. Without Me nothing is done. My name is MIGHT.

2. B-G-G. said: Fear is failure. I am without fear. I am the All Es, incorporated on the low earth, having no fear. (The All Es gave forth, having no fear. By this created He the creation. Like a lion goeth He forth. The sun is under His feet; so is the broad earth. Whatsoever liveth or is dead (inanimate objects), fleeth before His breath. Even Death cometh and goeth by His command.)

3. B-G-G. said: Go forth, My sons and daughters, multiply, fearing naught. Inasmuch as

ye do these things, so will I exalt you. Inasmuch as ye do not these things, I will bind and enslave.

4. B-G-G. said: Think not I choose a weak man or a coward to be king. I choose only the valiant, that fear not. Think not that I exalt the weak in heaven and make them Gods over mortals; I choose the slayer of men and the death-dealing.

(At this part of the service the initiates march before the throne.)

5. B-G-G.: Who dareth My power? Down on your bellies and crawl like serpents before My throne! Down and speak! I command!

6. First Initiate: By Rux I swear! I will not down!

7. Second I.: By Him who standeth above the Sun, I will not down.

8. Third I.: Nor I, though thou drinkest my blood.

(Similar ejaculations from other initiates.)

9. B-G-G.: Then must I from My throne of skulls descend to raise the seat another row. Bring here my battle-ax (to servant). (The ax is brought, and the Master, clothed in a lion's skin, with a serpent's skin coiled about his head, descendeth from the throne, and seizing the battle-ax, falleth upon the initiates, who have been previously drilled. During the ceremonies, some of the initiates are killed outright, generally not intentionally. A cellar is underneath, and over this the boards are made to trip. The Master knoweth this, and (the initiates not knowing it) hath the advantage. The fray of skill lasteth about an hour, during which the initiates are mostly sent below.)

10. B-G-G.: Ha'oot! Ha'oot! With Ghads I fought. With Ghads I am king and brother! Come forth, fallen foes, and live triumphantly! With brothers like these I will go forth and gather skulls to build another temple. (The servants help all that are alive out of the cellar, and if they are well and strong they are spared, but if they are maimed bodily, they are slain with the battle-ax. All that thus fail to take the first degree, have their skulls scraped and added to the throne, or judgment-seat. During the ceremonies, and along with the initiates, are two or more who have been previously initiated, and these of course are spared.)

11. First I.: To Thee and none else, I swear everlastingly. Thine be forever the place of skulls. (Ug'sa'sa) (Golgotha.)

12. B-G-G.: Know, then, ye Iod'a (Gods), I am descended from Baugh-ghan-ghad, the All Spirit of Light and Power. By Him incarnate in Mi, virgin of the corporeal world, My blood is fed by the souls of men. In the days before the flood of waters My Sire built a temple a hundred goo'en square; with skulls built he it, and feasted on their souls, uprising in the firmament, above the sun, companion of the stars. On the spirits of mortals slain, His spirit feasted full of rich strength, till all the world bowed down and called Him Master!

13. Oruhk (the choristers from behind, concealed): All hail! All hail! O Master, man and chief of blood! We come from the abode of flying wolves and lions and bears, upraised in the Osk'oe (sky) rocks that feed the black earth, the thrones of mighty Ghads! Great Baugh-ghan-ghad called us forth; for the clang of thy battle-ax shook the stars, saying: Down! Down, O ye Ghads, to Mi (mother earth). My holy begotten Son, king of men, doth feed His throne with dead men's skulls! Behold, O King of Men, these thy valiant fighters, from their birth, are reared as brother Ghads! O, slay them not, but teach them that he who would rule in heaven must begin on earth, and send his neighbors bellowing

down to dust! Bring them before the altar, smoking in their blood, and on the ark (a chest which containeth incense) let them mingle in covenant with the Everlasting Son! (The marshals now conduct them before the altar, whence they cast down their battle-axes, and they join hands, encircling the ark. From the east, west, north and south the high priests come forth out of recesses in the walls of the temple, and the priests in twos and fours bear torches and approach the altar and the ark, chanting for the glory of Baugh-ghan-ghad, the All Powerful Creator of heaven and earth. The Master and the initiates take of their blood, which issueth from their wounds, and mingle it together, and lick with their tongues the commingled blood, saying: Drink ye it in remembrance of me and of Baugh-ghan-ghad, my Sire, the Creator, doing all things for His glory!) (And now come the Aha'da, bringing forth strips of flesh from the thighs of those who were slain in the ceremonies, and they bring them to the Master and he putteth the strips of flesh under his own thigh, and all the initiates put their hands under his thigh also, for this is swearing an oath by the thigh, and they say: I put my hand under this thigh, and I am sworn. Thereupon the Master taketh the strips of flesh and eateth thereof, and handeth of it to the initiates, saying: This is the flesh of my body, eat ye of it in remembrance of me and of Baugh-ghan-ghad, for in my blood and the flesh of my body have I established the esa-au-gau-hoi (Church militant) over all the world! Thereupon the initiates take the flesh and eat thereof.)

14. Kohen (The chief priest): On this tablet write ye your names in blood, and by these bones and skulls swear ye.

15. Initiates: On the tablet write we our names in blood, and by these bones and skulls we swear.

16. Kohen and Initiates (together): To keep sacred the oath under the thigh; to preserve the holy words of the feast of flesh and blood, for coming generations, that the Light and Glory of Baugh-ghan-ghad, the Creator, may shine forever. Amen!

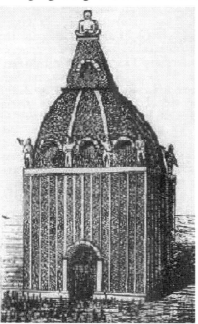

Plate 85. Distant View of the Temple of Baugh-Ghan-Ghad,
In Ga'haite, 11,000 years BK

845

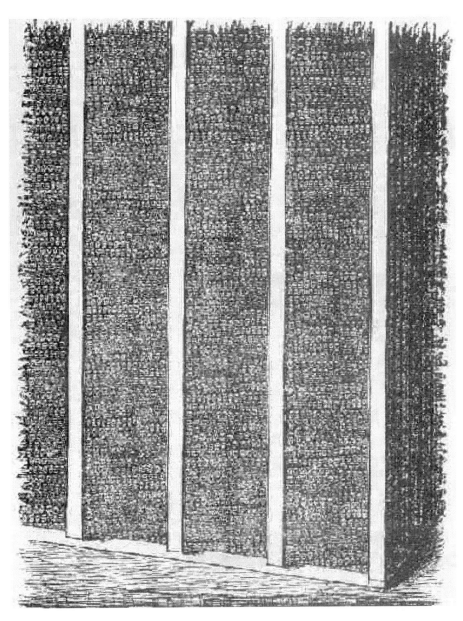

Plate 86.

Sectional View of Gologotha Temple, 11,000 years before Kosmon [temple of skulls]

(The M'ghan, the women, now come forward, having cloth about the loins, and they bring the dead men and place their bodies on the altar of sacrifice, which hath been previously heaped up with dry wood, and when the fire is lighted the M'gau march around the altar of fire, singing and clapping hands. Presently there appeareth in the smoke and the foul smell of the burnt flesh the Ogs'uk (evil spirits), so that many can behold them, and they eat of the smoke and of the foul smell, which are the food of spirits of darkness, and when they have feasted satisfactorily they take of the smoke and of the foul smell, and carry them away to hada to their companions, of whom their number is endless.)
17. Master: Hioot'a! Hioot'a! Behold, my Sire appeareth in a cloud of smoke and fire. Bow down your heads, M'ghan'a (the women), and invoke His mighty power!

18. Kohen'a (the high priests): O thou Almighty Baugh-ghan-ghad, Creator of heaven and earth, appear! appear! Thou that slayest all and feasteth thereon, appear! appear! (Presently the chief of the Ogs'uk maketh a light in the midst of the black smoke, showing a face of fire, and it is a man's face; but the body he showeth is dark, and of the form of a lion. And now the people march around about within the temple, beating together their battle-axes and spears of wood, and clapping their hands, singing the while. The Master revealeth himself in the lion's skin, and ascendeth His throne of skulls, and he is no longer called Master, but Baugh-ghan-ghad.)

19. B-G-G.: As My Sire reigneth in heaven, so reign I on earth.

20. Initiates: Hail, Holy Father, Baugh-ghan-ghad! Hail, Holy Son, Baugh-ghan-ghad!

21. B-G-G.: I command the earth!

22. I's.: The Son commandeth the earth.

23. B-G-G.: I command the mighty waters.

24. I's.: The Son commandeth the mighty waters.

25. B-G-G.: I command the air above the earth.

26. I's.: The Son commandeth the air above the earth.

27. B-G-G.: For these are Mine to keep forever.

28. I's.: For these are the Son's to keep forever.

29. B-G-G.: I am the Holy Esa-au-gau-hoi. (Church militant.)

30. I's.: The Son is the Holy Esa-au-gau-hoi.

31. B-G-G.: My holy labor is to subdue nations and tribes of men.

32. I's.: The Son's labor is to subdue nations and tribes of men.

33. B-G-G.: I make treaties or break them when I will.

34. I's.: The Son maketh or breaketh treaties when he will.

35. B-G-G.: For all things on the earth are Mine.

36. I's.: For all things on the earth are His.

37. B-G-G.: I am immaculate, and can not do wrong.

38. I's.: The Son is immaculate, and can not do wrong.

39. B-G-G.: Right and Wrong must be judged by me.

40. I's.: Right and Wrong must be judged by the Son.

41. B-G-G.: By My will do I make Wrong right, or Right wrong.

42. I's.: By the Son's will maketh He Wrong right, or Right wrong.

43. B-G-G.: I am the All Holy Standard.

44. I's.: The Son is the All Holy Standard.

45. B-G-G.: I can not err. I and My Father are one.

46. I's.: The Son can not err. The Son and the Father are one.

47. B-G-G.: I now demand a thousand skulls.

48. I's.: The Son demandeth a thousand skulls.

49. B-G-G.: Baugh-ghan-ghad demandeth a thousand skulls.

50. I's.: Baugh-ghan-ghad shall have a thousand skulls.

51. B-G-G.: Baugh-ghan-ghad demandeth a pool of human blood for His Son's silver boat.

52. I's.: Baugh-ghan-ghad shall have a pool of human blood for His Son's silver boat.

53. B-G-G.: Go forth, my brother Iod'a (Gods), and bring the skulls and the blood, for this is the time of the sacred solemn feast!

54. I's.: We will forth and bring a thousand skulls and the blood for our King. All hail! Mighty King of Men! All Hail!

(The Master now riseth to his feet, with his battle-ax outstretched, menacingly. The initiates upraise their axes and spears menacingly also, and walking backward, depart out of the temple.)

EMETHACHAVAH.

BROTHERHOOD OF FAITHISTS.
WITH MODERN GODS SUBSTITUTED IN PLACE OF THE ANCIENTS.

Plate 87.

As the student will perceive, the Tablet contains three degrees. The headings only could be given in the plates, being too complicated for hieroglyphic characters in such small space. For the outer rim, begin at the bottom and read alternately either side, till arriving at the top, where will be found the Symbol of Corpor and the great serpent (solar phalanx), and wark. The small stars in the inner circle represent the positions of mortals within the chamber during the ceremonies. The three degrees are called: First, M'git'ow (dawn); second, Hi'dang (high noon); third, M-hak (golden chamber), which are given in darkness. In English they are called, Dawn, Noon and Evening. They were about the time of Zarathustra (Zoroaster), or, say, 8,000 or 9,000 B.K.

1. These that follow being the first three rites of Emethachavah, that is to say:

2. M'git'ow said: A baker came to sell me bread. I said: Sell thy bread to my wife. She and I are one.

3. The baker said: The two are one?

4. This was the beginning of wisdom. I went into a field and heard the birds singing:

5. The Unknown said: The twain are one!

6. I said: Couldst Thou, O Father, make all men as one, there would be peace and joy! No war!

7. The Unknown said: Make thou the Family of the Ancients! Husband and wife shall be thy key. Husband, wife and children shall be thy model.

8. I said: I can not make all men think alike, act alike, do alike.

9. A vision came upon me. I saw a score of musicians, and every one had a different instrument, and they set about tuning their instruments, every one his own way, saying: Save we have our instruments tuned as one instrument, there can be no music; tune, therefore, thine instrument to mine.

10. After a long while they wearied, for they were no nearer than at first. And every one said: It is impossible to attune them! It is useless trying more.

11. The Unknown spake out of the firmament, saying: Choose ye one instrument first, and then attune another one to it. This accomplished, attune then a third instrument to them; after that, a fourth, and so on, and ye shall be all attuned alike.

12. Thereupon the musicians set to work, but could not agree whose should be the first instrument.

13. A pillar of fire descended from heaven and stood in the midst of the musicians; and in the center of the pillar of fire there appeared an instrument called the All Perfect.

14. The instrument gave forth one note, and all the musicians attuned to it. The Voice said: I have given the key-note, find ye the rest.

15. The pillar of fire departed. The instruments thus attuned in harmony played rapturously. The vision then departed.

16. This I perceive: to make the man and wife one; to make the man, wife and child one; to make the village one; to make the state one; to make the empire one; all in harmony, as one instrument, can not be done without a Central Sun, a Creator, to attune to. When a man is attuned to Him, and a woman attuned to Him, they will themselves be as one. When the family and the village are attuned to Him, it is easy. Without Him harmony can not be.

17. He, the Creator, then, must be first in all things, first in all places. He must be the nearest of all things, nearest of all places. In our rites and ceremonies He must be the All Ideal Perfection! the embodiment of a Perfect Person.

(End of prelude.)

(T. goeth to the altar and lighteth the incense, and the priests come and stand beside the altar, they, and the initiates with them, saying:)

18. Emblem of worlds moldering into dust and of the harvest of souls ascending to the etherean realms above; emblem of mine own mortal dissolution and of the ascent of my soul, but whither, O Jehovih!

19. In Thee, Jehovih, will I have faith. In Thee only. Emeth (Faith) shall be my name, the foundation of my soul.

20. Henceforth I will eschew fame and the applause of men. Mine hands will I fold against earthly fame, and in Thy name, prepare my soul for heaven!

(Signs withheld from publication.)

21. East: Over all the earth gave I dominion into man's hands; but I rule over man both on earth and in heaven, saith Jehovih. I fashioned the earth and breathed upon it, and man came forth a living soul. The veins in his body I made, and I made him conscious that he is. I speak into his ear, and hold up Mine hand before him that he may not err, but rejoice that he liveth and that he may glorify Me and My works. But he turneth aside and boasteth there is none greater than man.

22. P. and I.: O Jehovih, mighty in heaven, hallowed be Thy name! May I never forget Thee nor set myself up against Thee nor Thy kingdoms! (One bell.)

23. E.: Who are these that call on Jehovih's name?

24. P.: Wanderers on the earth who are unappeased with corporeal things. From Corpor to Es we turn in Jehovih's name.

25. E.: For what purpose are ye in this holy chamber?

26. I.: To be initiated into the light and dominions of heaven.

27. E.: Have ye been prepared for this?

28. I.: Yea.

29. E.: How have ye been prepared?

30. I.: We abstain from flesh food and from strong drink, and endeavor to purify our corporeal bodies.

31. E.: Man may be pure in the corporeal body, but unprepared to receive the wisdom of high heaven. How else have ye been prepared?

32. I.: We have witnessed the spirits of the dead who have returned to the earth, reclothed in corporeal appearances. We have talked with them in the presence of witnesses.

33. E.: My friends, since ye live on the earth, and can commune with the spirits of heaven, why are ye still unappeased?

34. I.: The people of the earth lust after the things of the earth, and deceive us on all occasions. The spirits who manifest are of little wisdom; they know but little of heaven.

35. E.: Since your faith in mortals is nothing, and your faith in spirits from heaven little more, how hope ye to gain wisdom and truth by calling on the name of Jehovih?

36. I.: We know there are angels in heaven who have risen above the bondage of earth. We aim to purify ourselves, that such may come to us and give us light. By attuning ourselves to Jehovih, we have faith that He will provide us according to our talents, which we received from His hand.

37. E.: Have ye not called for the spirits of the well-known?

38. I.: Alas, we find that spirits can assume any name and form, and so deceive us. We have no faith in names; they are as the wind. Some spirits have kingdoms in the lower heavens, and they seek to win subjects for themselves in time to come.

39. E.: How hope ye to distinguish free spirits from the bound?

40. I.: Spirits who talk of their own earthly lives, and of earthly things, are familiar spirits who abide with mortals. There are spirits above them who can come and teach us of things in heaven. By serving Jehovih, we hope to adapt ourselves to their presence.

41. E.: Have not Osiris, and Baal, and Dagon, and Ashtaroth, appeared in many places?

42. I.: It is so said, but they have shown no wisdom, nor have they come but through

deceivers and persons who lust after earthly things.

43. E.: Save ye become workers for Jehovih, by lifting up your fellow-men, how hope ye for good angels to come and lift you up?

44. I.: What shall we do? Give us light?

45. E.: Make ye a covenant with Jehovih that your pledges may be recorded in high heaven. Consider your words, for Jehovih is ever present and heareth all done in His name. Angels are also present, who have no interest in the affairs of men, save for the redemption of their souls. That which ye swear shall ye do from this time forth forever!

46. P. and I.: This, then, be my covenant: I will serve Thee, O Jehovih, and no other God, nor Lord, nor any other person born of woman, who professeth to save the souls of men; nor will I pray to them or adore them; for by their names have the nations of the earth been accursed with war and destruction. But to Thee only, O Jehovih, will I pay homage and adoration, now and forever. For Thee will I labor, by doing righteously toward all men, and equally with all these my brethren, the Emeth (Faithists) in one Everlasting Father, Creator of worlds! With all my might, and my wisdom and love, will I strive to enlighten my fellow-men and to lift them up out of darkness. More shall my labor be for others than for myself, henceforth forever! And my substance shall be given to relieve the helpless and distressed. Help me, O Jehovih, and make me strong in this my covenant, now and forever. Amen.

47. E.: This is the Dawn! Behold the rising Sun!

(The salutations are withheld from publication.)

48. Ye are now on the road of everlasting light. Swerve not from your covenant with Jehovih, and the spirits from the second heaven will abide with you. He who taught you before will invest you with, etc.

(Withheld from publication.)

49. In the name of Eolin, and by His power and wisdom vested in me, do I receive thee as my brother (or sister, as the case may be) of the Ancient Order of Dawn of the Brotherhood of Emeth, and I salute thee with the rod, etc.

(Withheld from publication.)

HI'DANG.

High Noon, or Sun Degree.--The same Tablet is used in this degree as in Dawn. The children of Dawn always used the sacred name of Eolin, whilst the sons and daughters of the All Light say, Eloih or Jehovih.

1. Dang: Let the Faithist remember his Father in heaven. The rising Sun adorneth the East.

(Here the Onetavis and the Emeth'a give the signs of Dawn, facing to the East.)

2. Dang: Give voice, O ye that remember Him. His name is a power in heaven and earth.

3. O. and I.: In Jehovih's name! (The salutation and signs withheld from publication.)

4. D.: Before proceeding on the road of everlasting life, let the Hyarh measure the bread and meal, that far-distant regions may not entrap us in want. If the measure be short, then we must replenish.

(The Hyarh pass five times around the altar, spelling the sacred name by the motions of their arms, halting for that purpose at the eastern fire. The Orgives now bring forth a polished stone tablet, with chalk or ink to write with, and lie the tablet on the altar to the south of the tripod and the prophet's seat. Wa-wa-tu-sa'a (women), five in number, bring water in basins and set them down by the feet of the Emeth'a. Hyarh saith:)

5. Arise, O Children of Dawn! Come to the west of the altar, O Children of Dawn! (This do they.)

6. East: (with sound of gong, twice): Hear us, O Jehovih! Thy voice be with us. Thy wisdom guide us. Thy love exalt us. As we hope for Thy exalted angels to come and minister to us, O show us, Mighty and All Perfect, how we can best minister to others who are less fortunate than ourselves. Sting us, O Jehovih, as with wasps and nettles, if we fail to devote our whole time to the lifting up of our fellow-men. Thou hast measured all things, and made wisely. Hearken to me, O Jehovih.

(Seven priests, representatives of the seven stars, now pass in front of the East, but face south and salute upward with the twelve preceeding signs.)

7. East: Jehovih saith: As a builder measureth the place for the house and provideth a sure foundation, let not My chosen neglect the All Light that I have given to every soul. Ye are as the stones in one building in My sight; and every one must be squared for the place I fashioned from the beginning. The Emeth'a shall be My house; to them will I give the whole earth. Yea, all others shall fail; but My chosen shall not fail.

8. Jehovih saith: There have been idolaters from the time of the ancients to this day. Yea, they have had idols of stone and wood and brass; and they have had spirits in heaven and hell, before whom they bowed down and worshiped, but I put their idols away and none can find them. See to it, O My beloved, that ye be searched out and made upright before Me.

9. Hyarh: Speak, O Emeth'a! Before the Father, raise up your voices. What was the building of the house of Dawn? How stood the temple? How stood the spirit chamber thereof?

(The Emeth'a here give the description and name the instruments used, the position of the stars, after which they repeat the reading of Tablet Emeth, all of which is withheld from publication. After this the Hyarh saith:)

10. H.: By what right are ye in this chamber of light?

11. Em.: By right of our covenant with Jehovih. Behold the ark! Jehovih's name we have written.

12. H.: What was done at Dawn in the East?

13. Em.: A philosopher passed twice about the table of the ancients. He held the key of many in one, and disclosed it before our eyes. After that he lighted the incense and departed. Then we covenanted, swearing an oath unto Jehovih, which was duly deposited, and thereupon were proclaimed under a Hawitcha with Dhargot, and then saluted Children of Dawn.

14. H.: Are ye still steadfast in your oath?

15. Em.: Yea.

16. H.: What more desire ye?

17. Em.: More light from heaven!

18. H.: Of the earth shall man learn earthly things. But light from heaven descendeth to mortals by the angels in heaven, who are servants of the Most High!

19. East: As the sun at noon is to the corporeal earth, so is Jehovih to the souls of men.

As the eye turneth to the east to behold the rising sun, so turneth the spirit of the Child of Dawn to Jehovih, the Great Spirit.

20. North: He hath uttered the sacred name. His hands have made the signs of the ancients. His feet have run quickly to the afflicted, and his substance lifted them up.

21. East: As the wicked find strength in armies, so, not single-handed, laboreth the Child of Dawn.

22. North: He hath united in a brotherhood with many. In the chamber of holies supplicated he the Great Spirit. The words of enchantment are at his tongue's end; with his own hand writeth he on stone the pass-word of the Faithist. It is the circumference of all. It extendeth from left to right, and from below and upward, and it holdeth the symbol of life.

23. East: I am the Self within all selfs, saith Jehovih. Nor things seen, nor things unseen, nor light and darkness are, nor were, but all things proceed out of Me, and are of Me. Into motion and life quickened I them, and all of them are but members of My body.

24. East: I made man a spirit, but I gave him a corporeal body that he might learn corporeal things, saith Jehovih. Death I made that man might inherit My etherean worlds in the firmament of heaven.

25. East: But man turned away from Me and desired the things of earth; and after death his spirit was bound to that which he desired, and he became a wandering spirit on the face of the earth.

26. Em.: In the midst of my desires I am cast down. I am unworthy in thy sight, O Jehovih! Have I not set store on my house and my land, and on all manner of earthly things? Yea, as with a chain, have I bound my spirit to become a wanderer on the earth?

27. East: Man buildeth a kingdom, and he gathereth riches, saith Jehovih. Yea, he warreth against his brethen for the glory of the king and chief ruler, and the profane man. For opinion's sake they slay one another outright.

28. East: Jehovih said: The spirit of the rich man have I bound, and the warrior, and great captain, and the man of renown, and the leader of men; and his spirit can not rise up from the earth. A companion have I made him in the lower heavens to the wanton and the drunkard, to the chaotic and foul-smelling.

29. Em.: Never, O Jehovih, will I raise up my hand against any man; nor will I war for the king, nor chief ruler, nor for any man, nor for any land, nor house, nor earthly thing. And though I be placed in front of battle, yet will I not take any man's life! So help me, O Father in heaven.

30. East: And the spirit of the bound have I made to encompass the earth in all places, and until they put away the darkness that is in them, they shall not inherit My etherean worlds, saith Jehovih. Neither shall they hear My voice, nor believe in My person, for they have descended into darkness and are blind and dumb to My glories in the firmament of heaven.

31. East: But I provided for them in their darkness, saith Jehovih. For I bring the earth into a light region in the firmament above, and I send My holy angels to deliver them out of darkness and bondage. In My name raise they up men with eyes to see and ears to hear, and I proclaim unto all the nations of the earth.

32. Em.: Make of my body and my spirit, O Jehovih, a servant unto Thee; and whatsoever Thou puttest upon me, that will I accept and do with all my might and wisdom and love.

That which Thou hast taught me, will I proclaim, fearing naught that may come upon me; for Thou shalt make of me an example of steadfastness for Thy glory. For the loss of my earthly Gods will I complain not; nor for imprisonment nor toil, nor sickness nor death! To Thy servant these things are as nothing. Without Thee, O Jehovih, I am as nothing; but Thy servant will I be henceforth forever. Amen!

33. Hyarh: My friends, what was the light of the ancients?

34. Em.: To learn the earth and call if Ah! To learn the sky and call it Oh! To learn the unseen power, as the wind, and call it E-O-Ih!

35. H.: Which was the secret pass-word to the lodge of light with the ancients? What was next?

36. Em.: To worship Eloih; to do no murder; to keep holy one day in seven; to steal not and to commit no adultery.

37. H.: What was the next light?

38. Em.: To do not unto others that which we desire not done unto us.

39. H.: What next?

40. Em.: To do unto others even as we desire them to do unto us; to love one's neighbor as one's self; to return good for evil.

(Here ended the ancient light. But in kosmon, to the order of this day, is added:)

41. H.: A greater light I now give unto you, in the name of Jehovih, which is: THAT YE SHALL DO GOOD UNTO OTHERS WITH ALL YOUR WISDOM AND STRENGTH, ALL THE DAYS OF YOUR LIVES; AND THAT YE SHALL PERCEIVE NO EVIL IN ANY MAN, NOR WOMAN, NOR CHILD, BUT IN THEIR BIRTH AND SURROUNDINGS.

42. Em.: This, also, do I accept of Thee, O Jehovih. Help me to swerve not, O Thou Light of my soul, for Thy glory and for the glory of Thy dominions, forever! (Thereupon follow the anointing rod of fire and the key to the astronomical problems. After this the Em. are conducted to North, South, West, and East, where they are bestowed with raiment, the ceremony of which is withheld from publication.)

M'HAK.
[DARK, OR DEGREE OF GOLDEN CHAMBER.]

(This, then, is the upper chamber of the Panic age, and the Golden Chamber of the second branch, Chine. Herein stand the Gods and Saviors of this day, even as the idolaters of the ancient days had other Gods and Saviors in their days.)

1. SOUTH: If a man do evil, it taketh root in him, and will be entailed on his spirit, even into the next world. But if a man practice righteousness it will also take root, and his spirit will become as a star of glory in heaven.

2. WEST: If a man court evil companions in this world, he shall find them also in the spirit world (Es). But if he constantly seek Jehovih, to and do his will, he shall find happiness both here and hereafter.

3. NORTH: If a man minister unto others, so will he be ministered unto by the angels of heaven. But whosoever would grow in all gifts, let him labor to become one with the Father, and the Father will grow in him forever.

4. EAST: Naked bring I man into the world, saith Jehovih. But I provide others for him in his infancy, that he may be fed and clothed. But when he is strong and wise, I command him to provide for himself, that he may be an honor and glory in My handiwork.

5. Let no man shirk from the trials I put upon him, for in so doing he robbeth his own soul.

(The Gowai and Initiates now march thrice around the Tablet, repeating the philosophy and the examination that arise out of the Degree of Dawn, and the Light of High Noon. When they have arrived at the West, the Washutaga sound the gong, and they halt thereat. The West saith):

6. W.: Who cometh here?

7. I.: A Faithist in Jehovih.

8. W.: Who is Jehovih?

9. I.: The Great Spirit. He who is over all and within all. The Potent and Unseen. He it is whose Ever Presence quickeneth into life all that live.

10. W.: Where is Jehovih?

11. I.: Everywhere, nor is there place without Him.

12. W.: What is His form?

13. I.: No man can attain to know His form.

14. W.: What is His extent?

15. I.: No man can attain to know His extent.

16. W.: Is He Person?

17. I.: Inasmuch as all the living are persons, so is He the All Person of all things. Inasmuch as His Ever Presence quickened into life all that live, so is His Ever Presence with the living, seeing, hearing and feeling every word and act of all men, women and children on earth and in heaven.

18. W.: What interest hast thou in Him?

19. I.: He is my Father! He is within my soul. I am within Him, and a very member of His person.

20. W.: Whence came His name?

21. I.: As the wind whispereth E in the leaves, and uttereth O in the ocean's surge and in the thunder above, and Ih in the winter's shrill whistle, so came the name E-O-Ih, which hath become Jehovih, and Eloih, and Elohim and Wenohim.

22. W.: How was He discovered?

23. I.: The angels of heaven taught man of Him.

24. W.: Who are the angels of heaven?

25. I.: People who once lived on earth or other corporeal worlds?

26. W.: What is their form?

27. I.: Even as mortals, but being perfect.

28. W.: Where is heaven?

29. I.: Worlds unseen by mortals fill the etherean firmament above. These worlds are heaven; these the spirit worlds; these the etherean worlds; these are the abodes of the spirits of the dead.

30. W.: How came the angels from heaven down to the corporeal earth?

31. I.: In the Dan'ha they come direct; at other times they come through familiar spirits?

32. W.: Who are familiar spirits?

33. I.: Our fathers, mothers, brothers, sisters and other relatives and friends who have not been long dead, and such other spirits as have not learned of or risen to the heavens above earth's atmosphere. Many of these abide on the earth and with mortals, some for a few

years, some for a hundred, and some for a thousand or more years.

34. W.: What is an idol?

35. I.: Anything that is worshiped, having form and figure.

36. W.: Who is God?

37. I.: A spirit with a heavenly throne believed by people in darkness to be the Creator of all things. Familiar spirits have oft called themselves God, and so taught mortals.

38. W.: Who are Saviors?

39. I.: Familiar spirits who have kingdoms in atmospherea, which, by the ancients, was called the lower heaven. Saviors are tyrants who make slaves of other spirits, who believe in them. Their slaves are sent back to mortals as guardian angels or familiars, in order to make captives of mortals after death, to augment the Savior's kingdoms in atmospherea.

40. W.: How can a man escape the toils of false Lords, Gods, Saviors and familiars?

41. I.: He shall covenant with Jehovih every day of his life, and serve Him by doing good works unto others with all his wisdom and strength. Nor shall he call in prayer on the name of a Savior or God, nor any other spirit, but on the Great Spirit only. If he do this, and eschew contention and war, and leadership, and earthly gain, and earthly aggrandizement, then will etherean angels come and guard him in the name of Jehovih.

42. W.: Who are ethereans?

43. I.: Spirits who have risen above the bondage of the earth and its atmosphere; spirits who can come only to such mortals as have attained beyond earthly desires.

44. W.: Hath it not been said: Swear not at all?

45. I.: Jehovih saith: Swear unto thy Father in heaven every day of thy life; and if thou fail to keep thine oath, thou shalt renew it on the following day, with repentance. But in all swearing it shall be for perfecting one's self and for the glory of the Father.

46. W.: Thou hast spoken wisely. Go, then, to the east, and stand upright before Jehovih, and there pray or utter an anthem of praise unto Him, that He may be glorified in thee, and thy guardian angels have honor in their pupil.

(The M. and I. pass around the tablet; the E. soundeth the gong thrice; the I. maketh informal prayer, and, at the termination, he repeateth with the M., as followeth:)

47. M and I.: Give ear unto me, O Jehovih! The vanities of the earth have no countenance in my sight; they are as one cast down in the day of his triumph.

48. Neither doth flesh food enter my mouth; nor strong drink, nor substance that cometh from an animal, or is part thereof; nor fish, nor worms, nor anything that breathes or hath breathed. (And if the I. is a prophet he addeth, nor roots, nor seeds that grow in the field.)

49. In the air and in the fruits thereof is my substance; into the air riseth my spirit upward unto Thee, O my Father in heaven!

50. Quicker hast Thou made my spirit than my flesh; quicker Thou my soul than the dust of the earth.

51. Who can comprehend Thy handiwork? Who else but Thee knoweth the delight of my soul unto Thee? Verily art Thou the comfort of the living, the solace of the dying and the joy of the dead.

52. I was not, and I knew not. Thy hand moved and brought me forth, and lo, here I am! Yea, Thy spirit moved upon Mi (mother earth), and I am one of the fruits thereof.

53. How shall I glorify Thee; and in Thy service how shall I render Thee recompense? (During the last two verses the I. marcheth around the altar and arriveth at E. Four bells.)

54. E.: My brother (or sister), thou hast covenanted with our Father at Dawn and at High Noon, saying: That that thou hast taught me will I proclaim, fearing naught that may come upon me.

Go forth, then, and see to it that thou turnest not backward. Neither shalt thou raise up thy hand to do any man hurt.

55. E.: Since the time of the ancients to this day the worshipers of the One Great Spirit have been persecuted and abused by idolaters of Gods and Saviors.

56. E.: If, therefore, enemies accuse thee or assault thee, hear thou them patiently, but press onward in peace to the end, and the Father will be with thee.

(The I. turneth to the south, face upward.)

57. I.: Such is my will unto Thee, O Jehovih! Thou shalt be the song of my life, Thou, the theme of my delight. Unto Thee will I give praise without ceasing, and my prayers shall be without number.

(He marcheth forth now in the order of opening Dawn. The E. retireth beyond the ark. The Fesays lower the light to almost darkness, and the four drujas prepare themselves in the druk, light the incense of sacrifice, and robe themselves in the orders of the four great idolaters of the cycle belonging to the order. Meanwhile the I. goeth forth, saying:)

58. I.: I will go forth proclaiming Thee and Thy works, O Jehovih! In Thee shall Thy children rejoice with great joy. Yea, the inhabitants of the earth shall turn away from evil and learn to glorify Thee!

59. They have beholden the Rising Sun and the High Noon, and the stars in the firmament above, and they shall sing unto Thee for Thy glorious works.

60. Thy unseen heavens will I proclaim, and for the inheritance thereof shall people eschew war and earthly aggrandizement.

61. Yea, all people shall rejoice with me for the glory of the earth, and for Thy kingdoms above. Unto Thee shall they sing with rejoicing all the days of their lives, and Thy voice shall come upon them.

(Here boundeth forth from the N.-E. the druj, which of this day is Brahma of the Zarathustrian ancients, and he flieth madly upon the I.)

62. B: Halt! vain man! Blasphemer of the Zarathustrian law! I have heard thy insulting tongue. Thou raisest up thy voice against the wisdom of the ancients. Know, then, that the All Spirit spake to Zarathustra, the All Pure, who was the incarnation of All Light, born of the virgin Mi. This is the Zarathustrian law; the holy light of earth and heaven; the Brahman religion. Whoever since then saith: Lo, I hear the Voice, or lo, I see the Hand, is a blasphemer, an imposter! Have a care of thy speech!

63. I.: I would teach man to be happy and to rejoice in the Father over all!

64. B.: Insulting man, and of a truth a most wicked teacher. Man should torture his flesh, and by long fasts and abhorrent labor, make the earth hateful in his sight. Do thou not this, and thou shalt return to the earth a wandering spirit to afflict mortals.

65. I.: Nay, I would make the labor of earth a joy and thanksgiving, having faith in the Great Spirit, Jehovih!

66. B.: O Brahma! O Zarathustra! Go, barbarian! Out of my sight! Thou insulter of the ancients! Thou contaminatest the sacred land of Brahma! Begone, begone! Thou that reverest not the caste of men!

Here the I. escapeth past B., who retireth to his druk. Again the I. goeth forth.)

67. I.: Rejoice, O ye inhabitants of the earth. Jehovih liveth and reigneth, and ye are a glory within His works!

68. Fear not, O my beloved. His hand is over all. His wisdom knoweth your just deserts.

69. Go not backward, O all ye people. He is ever at your hand in wisdom and strength.

70. A nurse provided He for the newborn, and the spirit of the full-grown man is in his keeping.

71. With your eyes, O my beloved, go not back to the ancients, nor seal not up your souls, and He will give you light.

72. Arouse ye up, O ye inhabitants of the earth! He is the same, yesterday, to-day and forever!

(Here boundeth forth from the S.-E. druj, which in this cycle is Buddha, and he assaileth the I. violently.)

73. Bu: Hold! Thou man of darkness! Barbarian, hold thy tongue! Insulter of the ancients! Blasphemer against great Buddha! Who can hear the Voice? Thou!

74. The All Light descended to the earth incarnate form in Gotama Buddha. Who'er since then saith: I can hear the Voice, is an imposter, a breeder of revolt against all truth.

75. I.: I proclaim the living Presence.

76. Bu.: Heedest thou not the Ahura'Mazdian law! To establish Buddha on earth, more than a hundred millions have been slain in war! This day the Buddhists have twenty million soldiers. Wouldst thou insult this mighty power? Turn the nations loose in blasphemous song?

77. I.: I would lift man up from the bondage of the ancients.

78. Bu.: Nay, begone, or thy blood be upon thy head. Thou defilest the holy land of Buddha. Out of my dominions! thou that heedest not the caste of men! Begone!

79. I.: But hear me---(The I. succeedeth in passing him.) Bu.: Nay, I will not. I will scourge thee with stripes! (Whipping him.)

80. (As he graspeth the chastening rod the I. maketh his escape. Bu. retireth to his druk. The I. goeth forth again.)

81. I.: Better art Thou, O Jehovih, our Living Father, than the dead ancients. Better Thy love than the dominion of the whole earth.

82. Who shall fear when our Father in heaven is also within us. Who shall take anger to his soul for the darkness of men?

83. Glorify Him, O all ye people, in praise and thanksgiving. He speaketh in the song of the bird. He painteth the flowers of the field with His own hand.

84. Of all the living, man alone turneth away from Thee! Man alone setteth up an idol on earth or imagineth one in heaven, and worshipeth it.

85. Proclaim Him with great joy, O my beloved; there is but one All Person, the Great Spirit, Jehovih.

(Here boundeth forth from the N.-W. the druj, which, of this cycle is Christian. He assaulteth the I. violently and in rage.)

86. C.: Fanatic! Infidel! Blasphemer against Christ! Sayest thou God hath lungs and lips, and a voice, and thou canst hear Him? O thou insulter of this enlightened age!

87. Only the ancient prophets could hear Him. Then God descended to the earth, incarnated himself in a woman, and was born of a virgin, becoming Christ, the Savior of the world! Christ is the lamb of peace! He is the fountain of love. Christ saith: I am the

life and the light!

88. I.: I know only one Great Spirit, Jehovih.

89. C.: Thou liest! Thou disturber of the peace! Thou infidel to the holy book and Christian law! To establish Christ on earth, a hundred millions have been slain in war! Know thou, this day, the Christians have seven millions of soldiers, and the mightiest ships of war on the globe!

90. I.: I teach peace and love!

91. C.: Hold thy tongue, infidel! Christ saith: Think not I am come to send peace on earth; I am not come to send peace, but a sword; Christ saith: I come to set man at variance against his father, and a daughter against her mother, and a daughter-in-law against her mother-in-law.

92. Before Christ shall every knee bow and every tongue confess him Lord of all. Down on thy knees, infidel, and confess to him. Down!

93. I.: Never. To none but great Jehovih.

94. C.: O blasphemer against the Lord! Now will I bind thee for heresy behind prison bars, and thy sacred books confiscate. (He seizeth a cord.)

95. I.: Nay, bind me not. I would but raise up my fellow-men.

(The I. escapeth.)

96. C.: Dog! Desecrator of religious liberty, begone out of this fair land of meekness and love!

(C. retireth to his druk. The I. goeth forth again.)

97. I.: Hear ye Him, O all ye people of the earth, and ye of heaven above. His voice is in the air, and in the stones of the earth. Yea. He speaketh in the sun and moon and stars! All things in heaven and earth are the expression of His soul.

98. Make merry, O ye inhabitants of the earth. Jehovih is Ever Present, and none can counterfeit Him. Open your ears that ye may hear His Voice, and your eyes that ye may behold His Person!

(Here wearily cometh forth from the S.-W. the druj, which, in this cycle, is Mohammed, and he raiseth a stick and preventeth the I. passing.)

99. M: Foolish man! Thou talkest to the wind. Only the ancient prophets could hear the voice. Mohammed was His prophet. Go, then, read the prophets of old, and study the koran. Since Mohammed, no more wisdom can come into the world.

100. I.: I would raise up the ignorant and debased.

101. M.: Nay, thou art a fool! The ignorant and debased are as God made them. They are content; disturb them not.

102. I.: I would make their labor light.

103. M.: Be wise. Yesterday thou wert born; to-day thou livest; to-morrow thou diest, and the next day thou wilt be forgotten. Go, then, procure wine and women, and feast thyself while thou mayst.

104. I.: I teach a higher life.

105. M.: I want no higher life. This world is good enough for me. God is just. He hath provided heavens for angels. The earth he made for man, and to man gave he passions to be indulged. Otherwise he had not given them. Therefore I will have of the earth its sweetness whilst I may. God hath already made all things; all is finished. Man hath nothing to do but seek pleasure and die.

106. I.: I would make the life of the peasant a pleasant one.

107. M.: Thou disturbest my kingdom. To establish Mohammed, a hundred millions have been slain in war. The Mohammed hath this day two millions of soldiers. That is sufficient. Depart thou, then, out of the honest land of the Mohammed, and may God's holy book and the koran enlighten thee.

(Here he passeth the druj, and the latter goeth to his druk.)

108. I.: Alas, O my Father, who art Ever Present! Yesterday I was puffed up with great joy, but the four quarters of the world (druks) have risen up against me. To-day I am cast down in sorrow.

109. The inhabitants of the earth are bound down by the little light of the ancients; but Thy Great Light of Living Presence they put afar off. What shall I do, O Father, that I may contribute to the founding of Thy kingdom on earth? O give me light, that my labor be not vain!

110. E. (with four bells): My friend, the Great Spirit beholdeth thee at all times and places; and since thou hast been faithful to Him, so have His etherean spirits ministered unto thee. And now that thou asketh for light from our Father, thy words are not in vain.

111. E.: Repair thou, then, into Dehabalizzah (Golden Chamber), where the voice of self and dispute never enter; and thou shalt learn of the mysteries of the dominions of the Gods and Saviors; after which thou shalt learn to apply thy labor that it not be vain, but profitable to the world and a glory to Jehovih in founding His kingdom.

112. I.: Angels of heaven lead the way!

(Here the W., the I., and spirits (if present), who have taken on corporeal forms, lead the way, ascending to the Golden Chamber. Within this chamber the lights give a golden color, and the roof of the chamber is blue, with golden stars, twinkling. On the E., W., N. and S. are altars with the sacred instruments for measuring, surmounted with golden colored flags. Here are represented, the spider's net, the ant-house, the broken implements of war, the sacred wheel of the ancients, the Sun at Morn and at High Noon, the representative idols of all nations and religions. In the E. and W. and N. and S. stand the angels of triumph. In the midst of the chamber stand the tablet and altar of the ancients. Above the E., in letters of fire, is the name Jehovih. Above the W., in letters of fire, is the name Eloih. Above the N., in letters of fire, is the name Elohim. Above the S., in letters of fire, is the name Eolin, and suspended from the center, in letters of fire, is the name E-O-Ih. In the extreme druk'a, in golden letters, is the word Mi, and in red, is the word Om! When the I. and the W. and the angels enter the chamber, low, sweet music saluteth them, and they march around the central altar in single file thrice, arriving at E. as the music ceaseth. Five bells are sounded, and the I. and W. and spirits face about to the E.)

113. E.: Who cometh here?

114. I.: One anxious to learn how best to serve the Father, that his life may be fruitful unto others.

115. Voice from the Spirit, or a Mortal Representative standing on the right of the E.: How easier it is to bend a young sprout than a full grown oak! saith Jehovih. Have not the Gods and Saviors in the lower heavens discovered this, and so set guardian spirits and familiars over the newborn? What wonder is it that men are stiff-necked in the doctrines of the ancients? Spirits of darkness urge them on, and they delight in war and earthly

dominions, for the benefit of their Gods and Saviors. Neither know they that they are servants to spirits of darkness; and they glorify themselves in caste, and in riches, and dominion, and in becoming rulers and chief leaders.

116. Jehovih saith: Let My chosen be wise after the manner of the self-Gods and Saviors, and also seek out infants and little ones and become guardians over them, but unto righteousness and good works, teaching them peace and love, and to live in harmony, and to abjure war and earthly profit.

117. As much as ye do this, especially teaching spirit communion, so do ye lay the foundation for My etherean spirits to come and abide with them as guardians during life, and even after death.

118. Neither shall ye circumscribe them in any of the talents I have given them, especially in the love of liberty, but perfect them in all things, teaching them to live in families of tens, or twenties, or hundreds, or thousands, even as in the olden times, holding all things in common, and being as brethren, one with another.

119. Waste not your time in discoursing with those who, having heard, will not practice My commandments. Nevertheless, to as many as come in your way, ye shall say: If ye can not curb your self-desires in this world, neither can ye in the next; and if ye can not live in a brotherhood of peace and love on earth, neither shall ye find a brotherhood of peace and love in heaven.

120. I.: I have heard Thy wisdom, O Jehovih, and I swear unto Thee, with all my soul, I will fulfill these Thy just commandments with all my wisdom and strength. Help me, O Father, to this end, for Thy Glory forever and ever. Amen!

(Responses, Amen, from E., W., N. and S., and other places within the chamber.)

121. E.: By Thy Power, Wisdom and Love, and in Thy Name, O Jehovih, do I receive this Thy son (or daughter), and proclaim him brother (or sister) of the Golden Chamber! In Thy name, O Father, I proclaim him in all the earth and in heaven above by these Thy solemn rites, for Thy glory. Amen!

(Responses. Amen! Now cometh the Dan of Su'is, bearing the regalia. Next to him come the du'ji, seven young girls, representing the seven stars, bearing the symbols of Industry and Peace, and they form around about the I. a crescent facing the E., so that the E. formeth the eighth star betwixt the horns of the crescent. Hoo'artyo, in golden lace, cometh from the W. and proceedeth to give the signs and pass-words. After this the youngest child present mounteth the k'sam, and in proper words (which are withheld from publication) proceedeth to clothe the I. in the golden fleece. Hoo'artyo giveth the injunctions of the ancients, and the D. calleth forth the Tablets of the moon, and the studies of the stars, and enjoineth prayer. The magi now illustrateth on a tablet (blackboard) the prophecy of the rise and fall of nations, the origin of man and language, how the corporeal world is governed by the es world, and giveth the I. the key of invocation.)

The I. is now required to give:

122. The Panic name of the twenty-five signs.

123. To trace the names down through the languages to the present period.

124. To designate the place in the heavens where the present sign would be situated.

125. The position of the altar in the temple.

126. To give the cyclic dates of the signs.

127. What group of stars, according to the Panic names, gave the field 1, 2, 3, and of 4, 5, 6, and of all the others, and the period of time of grouping them?

128. Why is this degree called M'hak, or Golden Chamber?

129. Why were the four days in each moon set apart as mass days, or sacred days? At what period, according to the Panic names, was the first mass ordained on earth?

130. What was the position of the great serpent (solar phalanx) at that time?

131. To the last question the I. respondeth: Alas, O Avaya (priest), I have not traveled so far. The Avaya saith: Then I will prepare thee for another degree. The I. respondeth: So be it. Here endeth the M'hak degree, with music and prayer.

(The accompanying Tablet showeth the moon days, and order of prayer and anthem, as in the ancient times:)

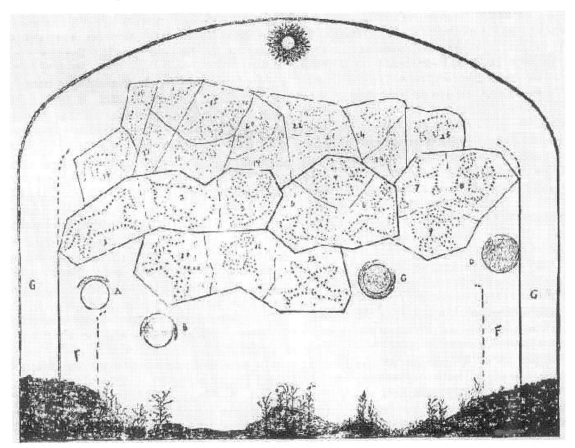

Plate 88. CEREMONY OF THE HOLY MASS.
[for interpretation, see preceding Tablets]

CHAMBER OF ADEPTS.

1. S.: By what authority approachest thou the Chamber of Adepts?

2. I.: As Jehovih created me, so I am.

3. S.: What canst thou do?

4. I.: I labor more than sufficient to provide for myself. I govern my passions and corporeal desires; I never speak in anger, or even think in anger, or hatred or envy. I never talk of myself, or what I can do, or what I have done, so as to laud myself. Neither do I

862

seek to justify myself, by words or arguments, for errors which I may have committed. I contend with no one for anything, or principle, or knowledge of my own. I administer unto others for their corporeal and spiritual resurrection and happiness.

5. S.: Wouldst thou not contend for right and justice, against wrong and bondage?

6. I.: Alas, I might be in error as to what is right or wrong, or justice, or bondage. Nay, I contend not at all; neither do I resist; nor set up my judgment against any man's. The light of the Father which I receive, that declare I unto others.

7. S.: What else hast thou attained?

8. I.: To adapt myself to others, so as to be desired by them. I have taught myself to love to wait on and assist the low and depraved; to wash them and provide them with comfort. I have overcome all desire to serve myself for self-sake in any way whatsoever.

9. S.: What are thy possessions?

10. I.: Nothing. I have put away all earthly possessions.

11. S.: What are thy qualifications?

12. I.: Try me.

13. The initiate is now tried as to his capacity to see spiritually, whilst blindfolded, and to hear spiritually something beyond the reach of mortal ears. Then he exhibiteth the power of angels to write on the tablets before the altar, in presence of witnesses. After this the initiate asketh the angels to lift him to the ceiling, and this is also accomplished in presence of witnesses. Next he casteth himself in trance, and the angels come in sar'gis and talk to the people. After this he goeth out of his mortal body, traveling in spirit to a neighbor's house, seeing and hearing what is there, and making his spirit manifest unto that place; and then he returneth and re-inhabiteth his own body. Thus endeth the trial.)

14. S.: Thou art found worthy of the most sacred Order of Adepts. What hopest thou to gain by this initiation?

15. I.: By meeting with like fellows, the soul of man findeth a haven of rest, after which man cometh forth again invigorated for arduous labor.

16. (After this, followeth the ceremony of passing the arch, and attaining to the foot of the throne of light, where the initiate maketh his vows to Jehovih. Music bells, etc., etc., omitted.)

CHAMBER OF PROPHECY.

1. God said: Before learning to approach the foot of the throne, what profit is it to show them the way to mount upon the throne itself?

2. Preserve, therefore, the secrets of prophecy for such as apply themselves to keeping Jehovih's commandments. Those who have attained to the foot, can of themselves find the way to mount upon it.

The BASIS OF THE EZRA BIBLE.

1. In the time of Moses, the people of Arabin'ya worshiped many Gods and Lords, whose high heavenly Captain was Osiris. Four chief Gods were under him; they were: Baal, Ashtaroth, Dagon and Ashdod. There were seven and twenty other Gods also, known to mortals.

2. When the Israelites traveled forth amidst the different tribes, they were beset to know what Lord or what God they worshiped, and by what Lord or what God they were led

forth.

3. The Light in wisdom and words came to Moses to say to the nations, ALAS, HIS NAME, WHOM WE WORSHIP, MAN DARE NOT UTTER.

4. Within the commune families, were certain signs and pass-words belonging to the different degrees. There were also oral rules of life and worship, but these were kept secret from the multitude, but the instruction of the commune fathers to the families was by this method made to harmonize all the people.

5. For general behavior, Moses gave ten commands, which were not only made public but were incumbent on the commune fathers to teach orally to their respective families. The following are the commandments thus taught, that is to say:

6. I AM THE I AM that brought thee out of Egypt.

7. Thou shalt have no Gods nor Lords but the I AM.

8. Thou shalt not make any image of the I AM out of anything that is in heaven above, or on the earth beneath, or in the waters.

9. Thou shalt not bow down thyself before idols nor images, nor anything having the form of anything in heaven, or on the earth, or in the waters.

10. Thou shalt not speak My name in public, for I will not hold him guiltless that giveth it to idolaters and lovers of evil.

11. Remember the sacred days and keep them holy. Six days shalt thou labor; but the seventh day is the Sa'abbadha.

12. Honor thy father and mother.

13. Thou shalt not kill (any living thing).

14. Thou shalt not commit adultery.

15. Thou shalt not steal; nor bear false witness; nor covet anything that is another's.

16. In those days it so happened that one Koetha, an Egyptian woman, a su'is, went into the lodge at noon, no person being within the lodge save herself. Now, whilst she was examining the remnants of shew-bread and basins, and the candlestick, a Voice spake to her, saying: TOUCH NOT THESE, THEY ARE SACRED. But the woman, knowing it was a spirit, said: If I tell what I have heard, I will be accursed; for was it not the multitude of seeresses that brought the plagues on Egypt?

17. Again the Voice spake, saying: I will give thee the signs and pass-words of the High Fathers, that they may also know that thou knowest. Now, thereupon the Spirit told her the secrets; and he likewise said: Say thou to Moses, THE I AM SAITH (and Moses will wonder at thy speech): Behold, these implements are sacred. Hide thou them by day, for they who have spirit perception, perceiving them, will obtain the signs and pass-words.

18. The woman, Koetha, did as commanded, and Moses commanded workmen to make a tabernacle (a model or image of a place of worship, a portable temple), and the sacred implements were kept within said tabernacle, and this was the corporeal base of the ark of Bon, a locality in the etherean heaven, by which the light of the sacred heaven reached the earth to Moses and his people, in a pillar of cloud by day and of light by night.

19. The secret ceremonies commanded vegetable diet for fathers, prophets, seers, and wanonas (trance subjects), and many of Koetha's people followed their example. After some years of experience, those who fasted from flesh murmured, saying: What have we gained for our sacrifice?

20. So they broke their fasts by hundreds and by thousands; and there came by their

camps numberless birds, and they caught and killed and ate them freely; but, being unaccustomed to such diet, they were taken with fever and died, upward of sixty thousand of them, men, women and children, and the place was called Kibrath-Hattaavah, the place of lusters.

21. In the year 3269 B.K., the Israelites began to marry with the Canaanites, who were under the control of Baal.

22. Ashtaroth, whose dominions extended jointly with Baal over Western and Southern Arabin'ya, sent spirit emissaries to the handsomest of the women of Canaan, and by impression led them into the camps of the Israelites, to tempt the young men, for by these means did the heathen Gods determine to destroy the worshipers of the GREAT UNSEEN. And many of the Israelitish young men were tempted by the beauty of the heathen women and thus took them for wives; and said wives brought with them their own familiar spirits, who were slaves to Baal and Ashtaroth.

23. The ark of Bon immediately sent Jerub, an etherean angel, into the Israelites' camp, giving him two thousand inspiring spirits to counteract the labors of Baal and Ashtaroth.

24. Nevertheless, it so came to pass that when the half-breed children were grown up, having Canaan mothers, they began to murmur against the peace policy of the Israelites, saying: As other people have kings and emperors, why not we? As other people raise up soldiers, declare war, and go forth possessing themselves of lands and cattle, why do not we?

25. For three hundred and ninety-seven years after going out of Egypt, the Israelites lived without a corporeal king, or other government, save the community of fathers; and they attained to the number of six millions of souls, men, women and children.

26. But in the three hundred and ninety-seventh year, the Gods Baal and Ashtaroth triumphed, through their familiar spirits, and caused the Israelites to anoint a king to rule over them. This king was called Saul, signifying OF THE LORD GOD. Prior to this the Israelites acknowledged no God nor Lord, but covenanted with the Great Spirit, E-O-Ih. The name had been kept secret with the fathers, and the commandments were announced from the Great Spirit, I AM.

27. The familiar spirits now inspired Saul to change the words of the commandments to the LORD THY GOD, as a conciliatory stratagem to please the nations and tribes of people who worshiped Baal, Dagon, Ashtaroth, Haughak, and other Gods and Lords of the lower heavens.

28. Thus was substituted Lord God (Land God) for Jehovih (called sacredly, E-O-Ih), and as the Great Spirit had been heretofore taught to the Israelites as an inconceivable entity, WHOSE FORM AND EXTENT no man could attain to know, so was He now transformed and declared to be in the form of a man, and having a residence in the firmament of heaven. Thus they made the Great Spirit merely an idol; thus they began the overthrow of the holy doctrines of Moses.

29. Jerub, the etherean angel in command, sought to preserve the old tenets, and amongst mortals sought out one, Samuel, and inspired him to establish a college of prophets, and this was done at Naioth, and hither congregated the inspired; and they established a crescent Tablet, and made prophecies from etherea for a period of seventy years.

30. Hereupon the Israelites were twain, those of the king and those of E-O-Ih, the prophets, and these placed them at a disadvantage before neighboring tribes and nations.

Having sacrificed the name of the Great Spirit, and made him into a man figure, the heathen said: What better is their Lord God than our Lord or our God? and they made war against the Israelites on all sides; and the latter having stooped to a corporeal king, went further on and raised armies of soldiers and went to war.

31. In the four hundred and ninth year after the departure out of Egypt, the entire PEACE POLICY and NON-RESISTANCE of the Mosaical Inspiration was overthrown, and the Israelites became warriors, and even warred against one another.

32. The Israelites not only worshiped the imaginary idol, Lord God in heaven, but built representatives of Him in stone and wood, and worshiped them also.

33. And now, one Ahijah, a young man from the college of prophets, foretold the coming captivity of the Israelites as a consequence of their idolatry.

34. In the year 2768 B.K., a young man, Elijah, was raised up from the branch of the college of prophets, and, under the inspiration of the angel Jerub, went forth preaching amongst the heathen, preaching not the Lord God, but Jehovih.

35. Ahab, a king, a worshiper of Baal, said to Elijah: What better is one God than another, or more powerful? Are not all Gods but the spirits of men raised up in heaven?

36. Elijah answered him, saying: I preach neither Lord nor God, but Jehovih, the Creator, who is Ever Present and Potent over all things.

37. Ahab said: Then thy Master hath neither eyes nor ears, knowing nothing, like the wind. He is foolish, and without intelligent answer to thy prayers.

38. Elijah said: Summon thou thy priests, and thy high priests, who have power through Baal and Ashtaroth and Dagon, and they and their Gods shall try in a tournament against Jehovih.

39. Ahab caused the tournament to take place, and when the priests and high priests of Baal had spread the sacrifice they repeated their invocations for a miracle to prove the power of Baal and the other Gods; but lo and behold, Jerub, the etherean angel, with ten thousand spirits to assist him, prevented any sign or miracle being accomplished by the familiar spirits of Baal and Ashtaroth.

40. And now Elijah stretched forth his hand unto Jehovih, saying: If it be Thy will, O Father, give these people a sign of Thy Power!

41. And Jerub and his etherean host of angels, caused a flame of fire to descend on the altar and consume the sacrifice. The people feared, and many fell down, exclaiming, Jehovih is mighty! Jehovih is mighty!

42. When the tournament was ended, Elijah went upon Mount Carmel, and prayed for rain, and Jerub, with ten thousand times ten thousand angels, brought the winds from the north and south and east and west, and the moisture in the air above was converted into rain, and thus the long drought was ended.

43. In the year 2635 B.K., the college of prophecy raised up Jonah, and Amos, and Hosea.

44. In the year 2574 B.K., the kingdoms of Israel perished, and they became a scattered people, and fell into bondage again.

45. 2439 years before kosmon, Manasseth, son of Hezekiah, established idol worship, and, by law, abolished the worship of Jehovih. He caused the prophet Isaah to be sawn in twain; and the judgment was, because he worshiped Jehovih.

46. For three hundred years following, the only Faithists amongst the Israelites were the prophets, and the followers of the prophets, who had never affiliated with those of the

kingdoms and armies.

47. The Faithists proper were a small minority, and scattered in many lands. The rest, who were called Jews, lived under written laws and ceremonies, which were compiled and established by Ezra, in Jerusalem, which combination of books was called the Bible, and was completed in the year 2344 B.K.

48. From that time forward, the Jews became worshipers of THE LORD and THE GOD, but the scattered tribes of the Faithists still held to the Great Spirit, Jehovih, keeping their service secret. These latter were without sin, doing no war nor resistance of evil against evil, but returning good for evil, and loving one another as one's self.

49. From the Faithist branch sprang the Asenean (Essenean, or Es'eans) Association, cultivating prophecy and purity of spirit. For further light, read of Pharaoh in the lower heavens, and the migration of the East Indian Gods westward, in another part of Oahspe.

50. The angels of Jehovih now dwelt with the Aseneans, who were the true Israelites in fact. Though many of the Jews also professed Jehovih under the name of God and Lord God.

51. In three hundred and fifty years after this Jehovih raised up from the Aseneans, one Joshu, an iesu, in Nazareth. Joshu re-established Jehovih, and restored many of the lost rites and ceremonies.

52. In the thirty-sixth year of Joshu's age he was stoned to death in Jerusalem by the Jews that worshiped the heathen Gods.

53. Forty years after Joshu's death, a false God, Looeamong, with millions of angel emissaries, obsessed the inhabitants of all those countries and plunged them into war and anarchy.

54. The Faithists were scattered to the four ends of the earth.

55. Jehovih said: Never more shall My chosen have kings. I alone am King.

56. And so it is to this day.

57. Looeamong, the false God, now changed his name and falsely called himself Christ, which is the Ahamic word for knowledge. And he raised up tribes of mortal warriors, who called themselves Christians, who are warriors to this day.

58. The doctrine of these warriors was, that knowledge, which implieth general education, was the best preventative against crime and misery. Neither understood any man in those days that the word Christ had any reference to a man or person. Now, from the time of Moses to Ezra, there was an interval of four hundred years, in which the Jews had no written record.

59. The age of the Ezra Bible is not, therefore, from the time of Moses, but from the time of Ezra, 2344 years B.K.

AHURA'MAZDA.

CREATOR.

1. Descended by the Yi-ha light through mortals, and in the Vedan Gods revealed from Zarathustra in Juian, Zend and Haizariyi, and thence into Vede, and thence into Sanscrit, and by Brahma and by Buddha. These, then, that follow, are the pillars of light of Great Jehovih, still standing as the remnants of His beloved sons and daughters in the East.

2. Airyana, the good, created things. Anra'mainyus, the evil, created things. Gau, place of science in heaven. Maori, the second holy heaven. Bakhdhi, third holy place in heaven. Haroyu, confederate republics in heaven. Haetumat, emancipated heaven above the lower or bound heavens.

BASIS OF VEDE.

1. Variena, a circle divided by cross-lines into four quarters; made for Thraetaono, a holy name, which had power over the Dahaka, serpent, i.e., evil.

2. Nisai, faith, belief; a created place in the unseen heavens, which nurtureth man's soul, created by Ahura'Mazda, the good Creator.

3. Kanthiuzhada, unbelief; a place in the unseen heavens which nurtureth unbelief in mortals, created by Anra'mainyus, the evil creator.

4. Yatu, to sin against Ahura'Mazda, or against one's own being.

5. Hapta Hendu, India; land of seven rivers.

6. Yima, a Savior; self-assumed Lord of the earth. A spirit with many provinces in atmospherea. He sent emissaries (spirits) to the temples and oracles of India, for over a thousand years, and thus compelled mortals to worship him. He said he was the Son of Ahura'Mazda, doing His will. He claimed to have been born of Mi, Mother of the Creator, and he was the only begotten Son; that he lived on earth and worked miracles, even cleaving the earth asunder and enlarging it. Through him and his spirit emissaries, mortals were inspired to construct the written doctrines of the Vedas as they now are, for his final overthrow in atmospherea, where he had four hundred million slaves.

7. Daevas, all evil, and evil men in general. But a real and wholly acting Daeva is a sodomite.

8. Druks Nagus, literally, rotting; also that decomposition of flesh which becometh food for insects and vermin.

9. Crossha or Craosha, an angel sent by the Creator, speaking for Him.

10. Druks and Daeva druks, sinful men.

11. Tistrya, an angel from the still heavens who ruled the flocks of mortals. He was said to reside on Sirius; and that star was afterward named after him; and mortals afterward worshiped the star, forgetting the legend of their forefathers.

12. Ctara, or Gaura, who, in like manner, dwelt on a star, and was forgotten in the lapse of ages, and the star worshiped in his stead.

13. Zami, another angel who became a star in like manner.

14. Urvar, also a star thus named.

15. Gogpend, ditto. These different Gods were originally assigned certain labor on earth. One had charge of all growing things in the water; another of the purity of vegetable seeds; another of grain seeds; another of breeding of horses and cows; another of mortal marriages; another of young children, newborn. Yima, who was chief God over all the other Gods, thus assigned them places; and each and all these Gods of second degree had hosts of ministering spirits under them, and these were distributed and appointed over mortals as guardian angels, and, by inspiration and by other impressions, caused mortals to thus worship their masters, the Gods who claimed to reside on the stars. Thus did Yima teach mortals that through him, and his kingdoms only, could man prosper on earth, and rise in heaven after death. In course of time, however, the inhabitants of earth forgot the angels, and worshiped the stars instead.

16. Jahi, taurus, the bull. The God of force. In the Ebraic language this same God is called Jah. In course of time mortals forgot the origin of this God, and ignorantly supposed the name to be an abbreviation of Jehovih. In the Cuneiform inscriptions his name is called

Bagho. The Panic origin is Taughad. (See Tablet Biene Poit, the figure of a bull, with man's face.) The spiritual meaning, force, or force of character, or energy to do, or decree with authority. As the pope issueth a Bull, of which the foregoing was the original.

17. Caoka, or gha-oka. Good, genial and amorous. (See Tablet Biene Poit, the figure of a ram.) He is also called Hoebah and goa-bah.

18. Airyana, a protector. (See Tablet Se'moin.) In Tablet Biene he is made in the form of a lion, with man's face.

19. The term, horses, signifieth dominions in the lower heavens.

20. The term, cow, usually meaneth adaptability to the creative period. In the original Panic, cow meant receptivity, as in English a term of dollars signifieth the extent of a man's possessions, although he may have only lands and houses. So horses in the Yi-ha had no reference to the animal horse, nor had cow any reference to the animal cow. But in the lapse of ages, these figures received an earthly interpretation.

21. Hukairya, a kingdom in etherea.

22. The Lords of atmospherea ministering through the temples and oracles to mortals of the Hyan period, and embraced in Mithra inspiration, were as followeth: Maidhyozaremaya, Moidhyosheema, Paitis-hahaya, Ayathrecma, Maidhyairya, Hamacpathmoedaya, the Holy Lordess, the Gatha-Ahunavaiti, Yacna-Haptan-haiti, the Goddess Mother, Gatha-Ustavaiti, her Holy Sister, Goddess Gatha-Cpenta-Mainyu, her Holy Daughter, Goddess Gatha-Vohu-Khsha-thra, the Lord of Measure, Airyama, Fshnsha-manthea, Hadhaokhta, Creator, Ever Present Spirit in all places, Ruler over all else and Dispenser.

23. (For the origin of the words refer to the cyclean period of Ahura.)

24. Mazdayacniaus, Faithists in the Great Spirit. Opposite to idolaters. The Haptans did not worship the Lords nor Gods, but revered them as exalted spirits sent from etherea, to minister to mortals, both through the temples and oracles, and in the family spirit circle, even as Christians of this day believe that Christ ministereth. With the Haptans, however, Mithra occupied the position that Christ doth in men's eyes, and the Lords and Lordesses, and Gods and Goddesses, were under Him, alternately with Yima.

25. The traveling hosts from heaven were as followeth: Havanana, Atarevakhsha, Fraberata, Abert, Agnata, Racthwiskare and Craoshavareza.

26. Haoma, juice, milk, that which is received. As milk nurtureth the corporeal man, so haoma feedeth the spirit, i.e., spirit nutrition.

27. After the invocation to Ahura'Mazda, the Creator, the All Brilliant, the All Majestic, the All Greatest, Best and Most Beautiful, then the following Gods are invited, to wit:

28. Vohu-mano, who is the voice and engraved word. (In the back period the Scriptures were taught orally, man to man, repeating over and over the same texts, until the whole three thousand Holy and Most Sacred Verses were learned. The position of the Most Holy Lord, Vohu, was to be present in spirit and person or through His representative spirit underlings, and see to it that there were no innovations in the original text, and to assist the learner to remember the words. Vohu, i.e., ga-mo, signifieth voice. Mano, i.e., c'fome, signifieth word in the Yi-ha language.

29. Ashavahista (properly Ashaohavah), the God of self-subduing. To teach and assist man to put aside selfish desires.

30. Ksha-thra-vairya (Ka-sha-thrag-o-mak), the Most Holy Teacher and Bracer-up of

Faith.

31. Cpenta-armaiti (originally feminine), Goddess and God, Adapter. That which within man maketh him compatible to others. (Yi-ha.)

32. Haurvat, home. He who made spiritual homes in heaven for mortals, and brought the Kingdom of the Father to men's souls. (Yi-ha.)

33. Amareth, forgiveness. Anh-air-that (Yi-ha). To make one's self child-like and willing to learn. To make one's soul like a sieve, that it will not hold anger.

34. Havani, the Bearer of souls to the second heaven. The Most Holy Lord of Transit. (Yi-ha.)

35. The emissaries under these, the Most Holy Lords, active on earth, were called, Cavanhi-Vicya. Twenty-eight of these helps and Lords appointed ministered in each and all the temples of Baragas (Upper Tibet), and during the religious ceremonies of mortals were often seen participating near the altars.

36. Ushi-darena, a mountain above which the Most Holy Lords held their spirit Congress for over three hundred years! In this Congress, Zantuma was president. It was through this Spirit Congress that Mithra, the Savior of the Haptans of that day, promulgated the doctrine that Ahura'Mazda was not Creator, but merely the star (Iaza) Jupiter and that he, Mithra, was the Chief and Highest of all personages, either on earth or in heaven. This was the beginning of a war in heaven betwixt Yima and Mithra.

37. Arbury, the Father's Kingdom, literally around about all worlds. Alburj (Yi'ha), Gaisi mortal (or earthly things), became confounded with heavenly, for the migration of the people on earth confounded the stratagems of Mithra, the Savior.

38. Gah, the change of the watch of the Gods. A prefix to the names of Gods. Gah, true, a fact (Gau). The times of day and evening and night.

39. Fradat-vira, God of numeration of mortals, interest in progeny.

40. Nairy-Canha, God of messengers. All spirits coming from Mithra's throne in atmospherea as messengers were under the command of Mairya-canha. Of these there were thirty-three messengers-in-chief, and they held offices for one year, when they were replaced by new appointments. When the time of changing watch came, they gave to mortals ten days for feast, five days in honor of the ex-messengers, and five days in honor of the new messengers. It was customary to have thirty vases or dishes in the temples, adapted to as many varieties of food, and each and all of these were also named after the name of the spirit messengers.

41. Zaothra, holy water, also God of sprinkling. When the worshipers were assembled they were frequently sprinkled with water by the spirits.

42. Zaota, a priest, through whom the Gods can cause rain to fall.

43. Barecme, literally, spirit light. Some were baptized by water, and some by fire.

44. Moon Gods, four in number, were usually changed once in seven years. But when Mithra proclaimed himself God and Savior of (the Indian) heaven, he allotted the moon Gods a hundred years each. But the chief of these remained in office for four hundred years. This was:

45. Arstat, chief moon God of that period, and a friend to the God Craosha. Mortals, however, continued to keep holy one day in seven, in honor of the moon's changes, which were accredited to the change of watch of the Gods. In the original worship mortals were taught to wish hither, with love and praise, the four reigning Gods. But they were so full

of devotion that on the seventh day they remembered many of the ex-Gods also, sometimes a hundred or more, all of whom they wished hither with love and praise. Many of those Gods (spirits), taking advantage of the devotion of mortals, established themselves in petty kingdoms in atmospherea belonging to Vind'yu, and thus aggrandized themselves, making slaves of spirits newborn into heaven.

46. Beside the week-day festivals, the Gods of Mithra, through the priests and magicians, established monthly festivals, on which occasion the Gods were honored with new prayers, and all these Lords and Gods of the lower heavens, were awarded by Mithra with petty kingdoms in atmospherea belonging to Vind'yu. Usually, each mortal city was allotted to the keeping of one of these spirit Lords or Gods, and the guardian spirits of mortals within that city were subjects to such chief Lord or God. The places of meeting of these spirits were in temples of worship. And all of the foregoing Lords, Saviors and Gods professed to give the revelations of Zarathustra, who had ceased in men's eyes to be a man, but a principle of Truth descended from Ahura'Mazda, Creator.

47. Myazda or Dracona,, feast of sacrament. Rice or other meal made into cakes and ate in remembrance of the Vow to Purify Myself.

48. Haoma, in the latter sacrament of the Vede, was saluted as heaven's perfect type of corporeal beauty and cleanliness.

49. Yima, a self-made God in after times, who announced himself, Son of Vivanho.

50. Cruvara, serpent with four legs. This was the lizard species, and in the time of Yi-ha they were sufficiently large to eat twelve full-grown men at a meal. They were of a dark green color, and fifty paces in length.

51. Gaccus, a giant who contrived traps to destroy the great serpents, the Cruvaras.

52. Asha, oratory. Power of reciting with effect.

53. Fravashi, pure spirits of the Faithist order, i.e., spirits who are not bound to idols, Gods, nor Saviors, but having faith in Ahura'Mazda, the Creator.

54. The opposers in heaven to the Fravashi were: The Daeva, Pairika, Cathra, Kaoza and the Karapana.

55. Verethragha, a God in heaven who labored for the Fravashi and against their opposers.

56. The following plateaux in the lower heavens belong to Vind'yu are often described as mountains, and in later days earth-mountains have had corresponding names given to them. That is to say: Mount Tshidarena, Haraiti, Zereaho, Ushidhao, Ushidarena, Erezifya, Fraorepa, Arezura, Bumza, Eezisho, Arana, Bazana, Vapa, Iskata, Kancotofedhra, Hamankuna, Vagna, Fravanku, Vidwana, Aezaka, Maenaka, Vakhedhrakae, Acaya, Tudhockoe, Ishvkoe, Asnavao, Draoshisvao, Cairivao, Nanhusmao, Kakahyu, Anterekanha, Cichindavaoo, Ahuna, Racmana, Asha-ctimbana, Urunyvovaidhae, Ushaoma, Usta-garenas, Cyamaka, Vafrayo, Voouusha, Jatara, Adhutavao, Cpitavarenao, Cpentodata, Kadrva-acpa, Kaoirica, Taera, Barocrayana, Barana, Frapavao, Udrya and Kaevao. To each and every one of the foregoing plateaux in atmospherea was assigned a God or a Lord, and these had direct superintendence over the affairs of mortals vertically under them. (Vede.)

57. Kanculoo, a running (es) sea in atmospherea, dividing the foregoing plateaux.

58. Caoshyanc, God of the (es) sea, Kanculoo, supposed by people in darkness to be the God whose coming would be the Second coming, or manifestation of

Ahura'Mazda on earth. It was believed that with his second coming all sin on earth would be put down, and all things revealed. Caoshyanc, a Savior; to sin not. (Anar.)

59. Franrava, God of the Turanians, the opposers of Faithists. He who inspired the Turanians to war and to deeds of cruelty.

60. Parodars, an angel, a bird, a picture, or as one looking in a mirror sees himself. That which he sees reflected is parodars. Thus, when a pure man dieth, his soul for three days remaineth near the head of his corporeal body, reciting prayers and anthems, but on the fourth day he waketh to his condition and riseth and goeth forth. The first living creature he seeth is parodars (a female); a flying person of great beauty. He saluteth her, inquiring who she is. She answereth him, saying: I am thine own soul and good thoughts. I am the law thou hast builded up on the corporeal earth. Behold me, I am thyself, and now thou seest thine own self. I am most beautiful, because thy earth-thoughts were beautiful. I am pure because thy earth-thoughts were pure. Put away thyself and come thou and inhabit myself. I am the part that can ascend to nirvana, the second heaven; thou art the part that dwelleth as a druj, a bound spirit. On the fifth day the pure man putteth away self and inhabiteth the parodars, and so ascendeth and becometh a Lord in heaven. (Foivitat.)

61. Foivitat saith: If an evil man die, his soul remaineth at his feet three days. On the fourth it goeth abroad; but because of its clouds, it beholdeth not parodars, the smothered bird, but it goeth into places that stink the nose, to the places that deafen the ears, to the places that blind the eyes, and, like a druj, can not speak truth, can not find love, can not learn. The soul of such a man becometh the inhabitant of foul houses and of battle-fields where madness liveth on madness, and evil spirits can not depart.

62. Kava-viscacpa, a councilor and friend of Zarathustra, a high, Holy Lord and Giver of Truth.

63. Hura, a one-time man.

64. Hura the entity, HAPPINESS. In all the Avanischor system, which descended to the Haptans and afterward to the Hijans, and finally to the Vedes of the Upper Tibet, happiness is called an entity; so is unhappiness; so is faith; so is unbelief; and they are likened to seeds planted, which grow by nurture, according to the behavior of mortals, into great trees. If, therefore, a man strive for Hura (happiness), it will grow in him, and not until he so striveth. And likewise of the other entities.

65. Kam, the air, the unseen atmosphere, or Kam-qactra, the high air, etherea, beyond the earth's atmosphere; that part of the firmament beyond the earth and earth's atmosphere which hath laws of its own. Etherea, the higher abode for exalted spirits who have risen above corporeal laws. As Anra'mainyus (evil), in atmospherea, looketh downward to the earth to evil, so Cpenta'mainyus (good), of etherea, looketh upward to good.

LORDS OF THE HOSTS IN HEAVEN.
HEADS OF SPIRITUAL SOCIETIES IN ATMOSPHEREA, OF THOSE DAYS.

Maideashenea, Patishahaya, Ayathrema, Maidyarrah, Hamachapathmada, Yemehataman, Aunviti, Haptanaihaiti, Ustavaiti, Cpenta'Mainyus, Kshathra, Vahistoisa, Airyamaishya, Fshushamanthra, Hadhaokhta, Cpenta-armaiti, Zaothra and Barecma, Mithra, Kamaqactra, Havanana, Aarevahsha, Roethwiskare, Vohu-Kasha, Aiwyoonhana, Nairayo-canha, Asha-vahista, Haome, Lord of Haoma rites, Frava-daiti, Lord of

Fravishes, Pailvish-hahin and Ustav, Beryejaga, Avathrema, Tistrya and Yima, Son of the Sun, the All Light.

OF THE SECOND RANK ABOVE THESE WERE:

THE GODS OF THE UNITED HOSTS OF HEAVEN.
[IN OTHER WORDS, THE UPPER HOUSE - ED]

The Creator, Chief over all, Yima and Mithra, Amesha, Cpentas, Havanyi, Cavaghi and Vicya, Rapithurna. Fradotfshu and Zantuma, Fradatvira and Dagyevma, Aiwicruthrema-Aibigaza, Fradat-vicpanum-hujyaiti, Vishaptatha, Ish-Fravashi, Athwya and Kerecacpa, promoted by special decree.

In addition to the above, the oagas (Gathas) of Zinebabait (afterward Lower India) the Zend, THE LORD GODS, that is, officers of kingdoms in heaven and ruler over nations on earth.

1. Khahnaothra, an Ahurian of the Zarathustrian period.

2. Ardvi-cara, an Ahurian of the Zarathustrian period.

3. Rashnu, a Fragapattician of the Yi-ha period.

4. Haha-Naepta (Goddess) of the host of Fragapatti, of the Theantiyi period. By the Ayustrians, Gathas meant Gods.

5. Iaya-Haptanhaiti, special to Haptan, of the Hi-ga period.

6. Ctatoa-Zacnya (Goe-howjhi), an Ahurian of the Fragapatti period.

In Ushtai-bhonyia-paria-vi-hyiyi and to their descendants, the Gujerati and Huzvaresh, the Ahura, is omitted, as in the original. Thei and Aph and the Creator, are called Armadz, or Ormazd, or Ormuzd.

Ahiram, betrayer of secrets, becomes in the lower heavens a confederate with the Daevas, the drujas, the Kikas, the Paris and the Ughsa of the Yi-ha period.

7. Naotara, of Aphian period, an instructor, who gave many sciences to mortals. These sciences and religious ceremonies were afterward called his sons, and they are now called Fravashis. In addition to the sciences this Lord God, through oracles and otherwise, revealed two hundred and seventy kingdoms in the lower heavens, the most important of which are: Zairi-vairi, Yukhata-vairi, Crisookhshau, Kerecaokhshan, Vyarez, Vanara, Bujicravo, Berejzarsti, Tizhyarsti, Perethwarsu, Vezhyarsti, Naptva, Vazhacpa, Habacpa, Victavaru and Frans-hanm-vareta. All of these divisions, including the two hundred kingdoms, had spirits-in-chief (Lord Gods) to each and every one who took up stations in the temples of worship on earth, and employed thousands of spirit servants, whom they allotted to the different mortals who came thither to worship, to be their guides and guardians, day and night. Through the prophets and high priests in the midnight worship, and also at dawn in the morning, these spirits appeared in tangible forms, taking part in the ceremonies.

8. Thrita, God of healing, the founder of a mortal race to whom he revealed the secret remedies for all diseases. He enjoined that the remedies should only be revealed from father to son on the death-bed, and when the father thus revealed, he himself lost all power to heal.

9. Hiac-kaus, Lord of the Seal of Heaven. He bestowed the power of Ahura'Mazda on mortals, enabling the prayers of the living to redeem from torments the spirits of their forefathers.

10. Takma-wrupa, cunning. The entity cunning. Like a fox, whose strength lieth in cunning. Like the wind. Like the air; subtle, appearing mild; appearing nothing, yet full of deceptive poison. By takma-urupa the successful man is successful. He bindeth apparent goodness in his face, but his golden foot-stool is cunning, the air with the golden tuft.

11. Ashi-vanuhi, Goddess of dress. She was fourth Airon under Mithra. The duties of her inspiration to mortal women were to clothe themselves and to decorate themselves with gold and silver ornaments. She had twelve hundred Goddesses under her, and they were allotted one day in each month to speak and teach through the magicians and oracles and prophets and high priests. Some of these spirits spoke through the seers by entrancement, and some wrote on the sand-table. Prior to this period Iranian women seldom wore clothes.

EARTHLY HISTORY OF THE FAITHISTS OF THE EAST.

1. The Voice was, The Great Spirit, The I am.

2. Zarathustra, being all pure, taught that to be a Faithist in the Voice, as it cometh to the pure, was the highest that man could attain.

3. Zarathustra, being all pure, taught that to build up one's own faith in the I Am would produce the highest happiness.

4. Zarathustra, being all pure, taught that each self must learn to build up itself in love and wisdom, and after them, power, trusting in the I Am.

5. As the Voice came to Zarathustra, the all pure, Zarathustra perceived that the I Am must have a name in order to be distinguished by men.

6. Zarathustra said, Or (Light) Mazd (entity of, i.e., light, per se), and he called the Highest Known, Or'mazd, being The Person, The All Master.

7. Or'mazd spake to Zarathustra, saying: Some have I created with desire to dance, some with desire to sing, some with desire to pray.

8. Some have I created with faith in men, some with faith in spirits, some with faith in Me only.

9. Let those who have faith in men, have faith in men; let those who have faith in spirits, have faith in spirits; let those who have faith in Me, have faith in Me. The last are Mine. What is Mine I will gather together.

10. Mine shall be a people by themselves, of themselves.

11. Or'mazd spake to Zarathustra, saying:

Mine have no Gods but Me.

Mine have no idols nor images of Me.

Mine bow down not before idols.

Mine covenant in My name secretly.

Mine remember the four sacred days of the moon.

Mine honor their parents.

Mine kill nothing I have made alive.

Mine commit not adultery.

Mine steal not, nor tell lies; nor covet anything.

Mine return good unto all men.

Zarathustra taught these words, and those who were followers styled themselves Zarathustrians

12. Or'mazd spake to Zarathustra, saying: Take the ten suggestions: what are they?

13. Zarathustra said: My flesh is not my own substance, but Or'mazd's. How then can I claim the ten suggestions? These, then, are not the Zarathustrian Law. They are the Or'mazdian Law. All things come from Him. All things are His.

14. Zarathustra went forth, preaching, and his followers were numbered by hundreds of thousands.

15. Zarathustra worked no miracles. He said miracles were the tricks of spirits and mortals. The highest of all good was to do good, and be good.

16. God gave not to the Zarathustrians as to Israel, to move amongst strangers, but to dwell amidst the heathen within their own countries. And the Zarathustrians never established kings of their own. Nevertheless they fell into constant persecution by the worshipers of Gods and Lords.

17. By the time of Brahma they were nearly destroyed. And again God raised them up and established them as a mighty people. But being non-resistants they were again nearly destroyed. And again God raised them up through Capilya; this was in the time of Moses.

18. And they prospered and became numerous in all of Vind'yu and Jaffeth. For four hundred years they were a great people.

19. And about the time the Israelites made Saul their king, darkness came upon the Zarathustrians also.

20. The Lords and Saviors, through the oracles, inspired the kings and rulers to despoil the Zarathustrians. And for nine hundred years they were persecuted and tortured; and millions of them put to death. So that the name of Zarathustra was forgotten amongst men. And the great learning, and light and knowledge, of those nations, went out, to return not for a long season.

21. God said: Because they have persecuted and destroyed my chosen, I will turn my face away from them, and they shall go down in darkness. Behold, when they persecuted my chosen in the land of Egupt, I shut out the light from them, and they perished.

22. Let this be testimony unto all peoples, that whosoever divideth my people or despoileth them, shall also be divided and despoiled.

23. This is a law of Jehovih; whoso goeth away from Him shall not find Him; to turn from Him is to curse Him; to curse Him is to curse those that do it, and it shall be answered unto them.

END OF THE BOOK OF SAPHAH.

BON'S BOOK OF PRAISE.

ESK.

1. These are the words of Bon: Thou, O Jehovih! Who can fashion Thee with words, or show Thy immensity? Where stood Thy feet in the time of Creation or rested Thy hand!

2. Thou Present and Afar! Thou Who art older than time, O Jehovih! Thou Dealer in worlds; where can I write the wonder of Thy name!

3. O That I had a standing place to see Thee! That I could come to an understanding with My Creator! To find wisdom for my song; a dialogue in the words of the Almighty!

4. Sing to Him, O Yavist, thou farthest star, and thy boundless firmament! And Neopodis, ye brightest shining heavens, which He created. Give the boundary of Jehovih's Person, O thou universe!

5. Thou that made me! By Thy sweet breath overspread the world with life and song. How shall I render Thee praise; in Thy glory make my speech acceptable!

6. Who hath considered the All Light, or found the Cause of the brightness of the sun, Thy great symbol? Or the power of Thy hand that stood him in the midst of heaven?

7. Or knoweth the times of Thy labor and the birth of thy worlds? Or counteth the stars Thou hast created! Yea, or knoweth the history of the least of all of them?

8. O that I could fashion a thought of Thy greatness; or conceive the breadth of Thy arms! Thou Whole Compriser! Thou All Perfect, Jehovih!

TEK.

1. Sing unto the All Giver, Jehovih! Praise Him, O all ye people, with great rejoicing. And all ye living that dwell on the face of the earth.

2. And ye young that are skipping and playing; and ye birds that carol to the Almighty. His seed is sown abroad. His fruit springeth from stones that are moldered to dust.

3. In the waters of the earth, and in the air above the earth, Jehovih hath spoken: Come forth and live, O ye that swim, and ye that fly in the air. The Great Spirit hath touched the fountains of the deep.

4. The air of heaven is peopled with His breath. The song of everything that liveth proclaimeth Thee, Jehovih. Thou Person of all persons.

5. O that I could sum up the multitude of their songs and rejoicings. What a world of testimony in Thy praise! All my life I would sing them over and over.

6. Thou Quickener unto life. Thou All Father. Who hath counted Thy inventions and the multiplicity of Thy living creatures?

7. Open the way, O earth, for the songs of His beloved; give ear and rejoice because of the glee of His household. They shall dance forever before the Almighty.

8. Stir them up with love and caresses, O Father! Show them the splendor of Thy creations, perfect in the glow of Thy firelight.

SAM.

1. O Thou, Jehovih, give me words rich in Thy praise; my soul is like a fountain springing up out of the earth.

2. I would look upon Thee; into Thy face, O my Creator, who taketh away my breath by the awe of Thy countenance.

3. Thou, who fashioned the broad earth and the high heavens! O, the works of Thy hand, Jehovih!

4. Where shall I start with my song unto Thee; or find words to laud the Almighty?

5. Proclaim His Unity, O my beloved; proclaim Him, in one breath, together, O all ye people. Jehovih! Jehovih!

6. O that I could magnify words to Thy Omnipotence, or hold up the perfection of Thy Person in fine speech!

7. But I am as one distracted by the over-whelming scene. My words cripple and halt continually before Thy surprising creations.

8. O that I could find a starting point; or knew a way to make rhymes and meters without rules, like the works of Jehovih!

SAR.

1. Almighty! Almighty! Love Abounding! Who gathered up the dust of the earth, as a wind, with judgment and forethought; and sorted the substance thereof and shaped it.

2. None but Thee, Jehovih, looked on or knew Thy proceedings. And to one Thou saidst: Be thou a beast of the field; and to another: Be thou a serpent; and to another: Be thou a wild beast of the forest.

3. And they ran forth at Thy command, every one to his place, rejoicing in the work of Thy hand. And I looked thereon, O Thou Almighty! What work of perfection in each, even to the flesh and bones.

4. But Thou turnedst mine eyes inward, and I saw the wisdom of the serpent and the beast; and the thoughts and desires of their understanding, how perfectly Thou hast made them.

5. I saw the love Thou gavest each unto its own kind; yea, even the serpent gathered up her young, because of her love, to shield them from harm.

6. O that I could find the first Cause of the judgment of every living thing! To come close to the Almighty; to question Him!

7. Thou Who shapedst a moiety of earth, and said: Be thou a bird, with feathers! Fly and sing! And it went forth, upward in the air of heaven, rejoicing in Thy name, Jehovih!

8. To another: Be thou an eagle; in ice and snow freeze not; above the clouds proclaim the Almighty!

UNH.

1. Sing unto Jehovih, O all ye living! Proclaim His love, which He gave unto all! Every one, that lovest to live on, to die not.

2. O the weeping and wailing, when thy kin goeth down in death! Thy call unto the Almighty to prolong yet a while the time of thy love! or to hear the song of him that is dead!

3. In Jehovih's praise is the wail of thy anguish; thy great sorrow, the love of the Almighty; the fountain of song and paradise. Sing on, O earth, Jehovih, forever!

4. O that I could answer them, Jehovih! that I could show them Thy fullness, which encompasseth the universe! To show them the testimonies of the thread of Thy love!

5. I will have my discourse with Thee, Thou Ever Present! In the harmony of Thy loves will I immerse my soul! Thou, the Fountain and Source of my contemplation.

6. Thou, Who art all; my Creator, Who gavest me judgment and perception to search into the magnitude of Thy creations.

7. Who shall frame a song, or find words to laud the Almighty! Thou art the Throne and the Empire. Thy footstool, the sun and moon and stars!

8. O that I may prolong my vision of Thee, and pursue the thread of Thy creations to the fountain-head. Thou, without a boundary, where all things utter Thy praise forever!

YOKE.

1. Sing unto Him, O ye mountains; and send unto Him the sound of rippling waters, O ye valleys!

2. And all ye singing winds of heaven! Ye whistling wind, on the high mountains, and thou whispering breeze on the plain!

3. Praise Him, thou lightning, and thou peal of thunder! Rend ye the air of heaven in Jehovih's praise!

4. Sing to Him, thou surging river, and thou moaning sea of waters! He playeth as on the harp, with the dumb elements.

5. His strains are mighty! His tunes are the hum and whir of falling waters. Sing to Jehovih, O ye great water-falls!

6. Chant ye everlastingly, and write His name in the bow that perisheth not, forever.

7. He that tuneth the forests to sing in the clouds; that stringeth His instrument with hemlock and pine and cedar.

8. Who maketh the forests beat time to His strains. Praise ye Jehovih, forever and ever.

RAK.

1. Praise Jehovih, the Almighty! Praise Him, O thou sea of lands. Ye boundless prairies, that stretch out to the horizon, to the rising sun and to the setting thereof in a sea of fire.

2. Praise Jehovih, the Almighty. Praise Him, O ye towering mountains, ye mighty walls of heaven! And thou everlasting snow, shining like diamonds in the sun.

3. Praise Jehovih, the Almighty! Praise Him, O ye colors that overspread the heavens. Ye clouds of purple and yellow and burning gold, and in flames of fire.

4. Praise Jehovih, the Almighty! Praise Him, O ye green meadows and ye waving fields of wheat and corn. And ye ripened harvests that beckon and wave like sheets of gold.

5. Praise Jehovih, the Almighty! Praise Him, O ye far-off Blue Mountains, and ye defiant Black Hills. In somber hue and silent majesty, proclaim Him! Eternity! Eternity!

6. Praise Jehovih, the Almighty! Praise Him, O ye Rocky Mountains. In the long wall of your mightiness proclaim the power of His hand and great majesty!

7. Praise Jehovih, the Almighty! Praise Him, O ye Sierra Nevadas. In your everlasting snow and mighty forests. Your fearful hanging rocks, above the clouds!

8. Praise Jehovih, the Almighty! Praise Him, O ye great rivers, that gallop down from the Alleghanies, the Rocky Mountains and Sierra Nevadas; that travel so far to the mighty oceans.

OTE.

1. Proclaim Him, O ye Andes and Cordilleras, stretching avast and on high, ye monuments of the Almighty!

2. Praise His majesty, O ye Himal Layas, and ye Akai Shine, ye foot-prints of Jehovih!

3. Praise His greatness, O ye Thia Shan, and ye Tapa Ling, that feed the Pacific, the Daughter of Jehovih.

4. Sing unto Him, O all ye mountains of the earth; proclaim His power, which stood you up by the touch of his hand.

TAUG.

1. Where is a God like unto Thee, Jehovih? Whose kaleidoscope is millions of suns!

2. Whose breath blew upon thee, O earth! And thy voice joined in the songs of the stars!

3. Whose breath blew upon thee, O Earth! And thy fire was congealed, and the heat run low!

4. Praise thou the All Person, Whose mighty hand stayed the fire! And cooled the flaming earth.

VED.

1. Sing to the Almighty, ye heirs of Zarathustra, whose flesh was the food of lions.

2. Sing to the Creator, Zarathustra's Almighty, the Eolin that spake in the wind.

3. Sing to the followers of the Great Spirit! The Zarathustrians who forfeited their flesh and blood for Him.

4. Sound loud His name, the E-O-Ih of the Zarathustrians, that sang Him on high!

SANG.

1. Praise ye the Almighty for Abraham and Brahma and Po. And their followers that plodded along in the dark days.

2. Praise ye the Supreme Being, ye followers of them, ye line of the Light of the Great Spirit.

3. To glorify the Creator in after generations, by the wisdom of His choice, Who rose up great harvests in Vind'yu and Egupt and Chine'ya.

4. Sing in his praise forever, the Creator, the Almighty. Shout long and loud in the glory of Jehovih, Fashioner of mighty peoples.

TUE.

1. O thou, Moses, and, thou, Capilya, and Chine; sing ye unto Jehovih! Rejoice ye in the time of the Almighty! Into separate gardens in the same time the Creator singled you out unto his own glory.

2. Fashioned he, the Almighty, three souls magnified unto the glory of His work. Sing unto the Creator for those that toiled in the days of darkness for the glory of the Almighty!

3. Praise ye the Great Spirit, ye followers of Moses, Capilya and Chine. Sing a new song to the Almighty! His eye hath witnessed the toil and sorrow of His chosen.

4. And all ye followers of the chosen of the Almighty; glorify Him in the highest; sing unto the Great Spirit, forever and ever.

AIEDS.

1. The Almighty calleth from the boundaries of the firmament down to the sands of the earth in glory of His creations.

2. Proclaim His name with the hands of those that knew not speech. Give them the sign of the Rising Sun, the High Noon and the Shades of Evening.

3. The Almighty, Whose breath bloweth millions of worlds in the circuit of the universe! Whose pulse is the flight of countless suns and stars!

4. Praise ye the Almighty, Whose triumph encircleth the world. Let the races of man proclaim Him forever.

FUR.

1. Where are Thy singers, Jehovih? Who have beholden the vastness of the Creator! And the times and the splendor of Thy universe.

2. And the adoration that slumbereth but for a season, and then bursteth like a world on fire! Whom Thou appointest from time to time to sing of Thee.

3. Sing unto the Almighty. He spandeth the times of millions of years as if but a day, in the fashion and splendor of His works.

4. He openeth His heavens as a book is opened. The prophet of the Creator readeth of the magnitude of the works of Jehovih!

SUT.

1. Now will I sing unto Thee, O Jehovih, a song of soberness.

2. When first Thou stoodst me on my feet, and I saw Thee, Jehovih.

3. And Thy hand, O my Creator, showed me the two roads, Life and Death.

4. And the people divided, some to Thee, and some to Death and idolatry.

5. Because of the magnitude of Thy Person, they set up Gods, Lords and Saviors.

6. In Thy name, I called out to them, but they heard not, and they fell down in Death.

7. And Thy Voice of sorrow rent the earth! Thy Faithists sang in the mournful lays of death.

8. In gloom will I sing for my brothers that went down in Death.

YAD.

1. Hear the voice of the Faithists, O Father: I cry out unto Thee since thousands of years. In the time of my great afflictions have I remembered my Creator.

2. And my brother who went after Death stoned me; with curses smote he the chosen of Jehovih. In the time of sore pain I called out: Jehovih, Jehovih!

3. I said: O that this had not been! O that the Great Spirit would enlighten him! But Thou shapedst him to fetch him in the last day.

4. And the cloud blew away; the sun of righteousness shone across the heavens of the earth. In the time of my sorrow I saw Thy wisdom in this.

5. By my pains deliveredst Thou my brother; in Thy praise do I now look back to the time of my pains in the throes of Death.

6. Glory be unto Thee, Jehovih! Thou Everlasting Present, Who findeth a way in the spoil of Thine enemies to magnify the glory of Thy places unto the Almighty.

7. What was my pain before Thee! Or my affliction more than a mother for the glory of her first-born! Into my cup of bitterness Thou hast poured nectar and sweet crystals.
8. Never more shall I complain, Jehovih! or consider Thy enemy but to deliver him unto Thee. My cup of nectar will I hold to his profane lips, that he may taste of Thy glory!

ROE.

1. Jehovih, first and last: Forever, Jehovih, O my beloved!
2. Write Him in stone and iron, copper, silver and gold.
3. Whose Person is the All and Whole: Creator of the boundless universe!
4. Teach ye Him to the child; magnify the soul of man to see Jehovih!
5. Welcome, pains and afflictions: Behind all riseth a greater glory.
6. He knoweth my wanderings; for the feet of the faithful Jehovih provideth a place.
7. He understandeth beforehand; the Creator cometh upon me in a way I saw not.
8. None shall stand before the Almighty in the songs and praise of the righteous.

ROTH.

1. Praise Jehovih, ye angels of heaven: In the countless places of the journeys of the world: Send forth a song to the Everlasting!
2. Praise Jehovih, O Uklo and Gibrath! In the plains and High Arches of Etisia, in the etherean worlds: Sing loud and clear the song of Omaza.
3. Praise Jehovih, ye angels of Wanwan: In the circuit of Hissa and the plains of Oat: Render unto the Creator, O Waukawauk!
4. Praise Jehovih, ye angels of Howt: In the etherean heavens of Noe and Kaba-Se-o-nita: Sing praises, and shout unto the Almighty!
5. Praise Jehovih, ye etherean hosts of Rax: In the heavenly Caverns of Wass and Bliathon: Sing in Hise and Nor to the Creator's praise.
6. Praise Jehovih, ye angels of Mor: In the Seam of Wia-wis, in the labor of Pan: Sing a song of praise to the All One, Jehovih!
7. Praise Jehovih, ye angels of Noe: In the arc of the journey of an uplifted world: Render Him praise for the labors of Aph, His Orian Son.

LAIS.

1. Sing to Jehovih, O ye heavenly places in the Orian fields of Yuniv and H'monken; and ye Saughts and Mentabraw, and of the arc of Ole and Leigga.
2. O ye heavenly places in the Nirvanian Mountains of Itis and Vairiyonirom; and in the crystal fountains of Ittiyivius, the great summer visiting place of millions of Gods; in the high Clefts and Arches of Yasinosa!
3. O ye heavenly places in the etherean plains of Aoit and Tas and Foe and Raim, and of the Mantles of Light in Thessagon, home of the forty thousand millions.
4. O ye seas of Nista and Hoit, in the Nirvanian heavens, where course a thousand million ships of the congregations of the Almighty. Sing to Him, thou sea of etherean fire, Poyisativi, home of billions!
5. O ye fields of Norse and ye Marshes of Ho in the Orian Chain of Avasta and Songastos. Sing to the Creator, ye etherean swamps and plains and mountains, Habak and Yadis, home of a hundred thousand millions.

6. O ye etherean farms of Izaracna and Towen, by the road of Oya. Sing to the Creator, O Wuts, thou old head-quarters of the Gods and Goddesses, Foetisya and Yagahectus and Sortaba, in the Holy Council of the roads.

7. O ye etherean worlds, Sue'kan and Yabaxax and Sud, where the ten thousand fleets of the ships of Navagatta and Plowkom and Iodoyo came in the Council of Habiyi, to make the vortex of Novian to Jehovih.

8. O all ye millions of heavenly worlds created by the Creator for His countless millions of high-raised angels, since millions of years; proclaim Him in the matchless wonder of His creations, the Almighty, the All One, Jehovih.

LOO.

1. Find ye great words of praise to the All Light, Jehovih; ye etherean worlds. And thou, O arc of Rapta, proclaim the Almighty.

2. Render great praise to the place of Shapeliness, the fountains of Apollo; thou etherean place of beauty, where the Great Spirit fashioned song in mortals!

3. G'treb and Zadukawaski, and ye mountains of Magal and Rak, ye contributors of the etherean hosts, thousands and millions for remodeling mortals.

4. Sing to the Almighty for the perfection of the beauty and shape of mortals, O ye Gods and Goddesses that labored with Apollo for the glory of the Great Spirit.

5. Let Um rejoice and Proeking send forth a song of gladness; the thanks of mortals to the All Light for shapeliness and beauty and song.

6. Rejoice, O ye thousands of millions of high-raised angels in the etherean heavens, Rositij and Matthai and Horatanad, rejoice in Jehovih's name.

7. P'timus and Betatis and Tah and Tanaya, O ye Orian angels of heaven, join in the song of mortals, and let Mamts, and Buru, and Waak, proclaim unto the Almighty.

8. Find ye sweet words of praise to the All Highest Creator, O ye thousands of millions of etherean angels. Mortals are risen to know the Almighty!

SUAT.

1. Yesain, mighty sheds of Le, ye towering strength in etherea, sing to the Almighty. And ye, C'taran and Hituns, thou, Stalacti, visiting place for the congregations born of other planets.

2. Shout loud and long to the Ever Present, O ye plans of Palla and forests of Sethawan, ye golden triumphs fashioned in the Arches of Hiatusa and Nor.

3. Remember Him in praise, O ye swamps of Ludz and place of toil of the Orian Chief, Hazu, with his four thousand million etherean hosts, making the Roads of Semetatosa.

4. Unto the Person of the Almighty, sing, thou, Orub, thou habitation of twelve million cities of Gods and Goddesses. Sing in praise and rejoicing for the red star, the young earth.

5. And thou, O Seeing, thou paradise of Goddesses of ten million cities, sing to the Person of the universe, Jehovih; sing Him an anthem, Whose Voice resteth on the young earth.

6. Sing ye, O Yissain and Wartz, the etherean worlds of the seven cross-roads of the seven traveling sun-worlds with their millions of stars floating in the breath of the Almighty!

7. Proclaim the Creator forever, O Hoesonya and Saffer, and thou great etherean light, Mos, and ye mountains of Galeb; and thou, Yonetz, thou place of the million lakes!

8. Sing in praise of Jehovih, O ye toilers with Thor, Son of the Almighty! Praise ye Him, O ye etherean angels of Ogonavesta; send forth the glad song forever and ever!

YAT.

1. O Dae, thou arc of Osiris, and thou, Hetta. Come let us rejoice together in the Almighty. Let us remember the beginning of learning amongst mortals. The time of mortals beginning to teach one another of Jehovih!

2. In praise of the Person of all, let us hold up our heads and rejoice, O Hennassalonkya, with thy ten thousand valleys in the congregations of thy forty thousand million angels! The time of knowledge was sown on earth.

3. Praise ye Jehovih, O Dows, with thy thousands of mountains and high arches, and thou, O Schlienuk, and thou, O M'dor, thou pride of the etherean road Tussakaya; and thou, Thassa, thou doorway of Hemmet'dor.

4. Let us join together in anthem to Jehovih, O Vupper and Nedaya; the measure of the Almighty is overflowing, the Nessaj is attuned in seven thousand etherean cities; the traveling place of the ships of Osiris' mighty hosts.

5. And ye Orian kingdoms, Sowinita and Antwa and Lubbak and Oltbak, the places of the cataracts of the segean oceans; the home of the thirty thousand million ship-builders for the vortices of Anakonga and Higohadsumad.

6. And ye volunteer heavens, Seeing and Lowtsin, and Nool and Hoessis; with your thirty million High arches and seven million miles of Holy Mountains, ye crystal heavens of the Hapsendi, Sons and Daughters of Jehovih!

7. Proclaim the Creator, O thou, Loogab, thou etherean heaven with the sea of Aginodi, the sea of fire! The running sea of four million miles, the fountain of thirty million rainbows!

8. Jehovih the Almighty, the Matchless and Ever Extended! O Thou Greatest of all that is Great! Thou Surpassor, Who hath fashioned wider and more glorious than even Gods can imagine, glory be to Thee, forever and ever.

SIAS.

1. Praise the Great Spirit, O Petris and Obsod, ye heavenly kingdoms of the etherean heavens of Fragapatti, ye place of the roads of Rogga, with ninety million miles of I'yuan plains!

2. And Sitta and Goomatchala and South'eng, ye heavenly plains hanging on the mountain line of the Lunitzzi, with the twenty million arches over the Holy Lakes and seas of Onatoosa!

3. Let your ninety thousand million etherean angels rejoice in the glory of the Almighty; the footstool of His kingdom hath quickened on the red star; the shout goeth up to Jehovih forever!

4. And ye angels of the vast Orian kingdoms, Yan and Wawauk and Zi and Alawa and Aili and Ref and Zuth, ye foundations of the highways of the Yoogan Hissawa, ye swamps and plains of See'niyivi.

5. Proclaim ye the fruit of Loo, the arc of the organizer of mortal kingdoms on the earth. The Omnipotent hath spoken in the high heaven of kosmon, spoken out of the fruit of Loo.

6. Call up Rappaya and Hanosta, the etherean kingdoms with the angels of the Yimyim arches, and the High bridge of Lips, over the etherean sea of the burning waters of Vestakad.

7. Sing unto the Almighty, ye heavens that sent volunteers in the army of Fragapatti; the fruit of your labor riseth on high. Kus and Zittayyabaugh, ye, the voice of the Almighty.

8. He speaketh in the labor of high-raised Sons and Daughters. His Voice is in the echo of thanksgiving that riseth up from the red star in songs of praise to the Almighty.

JAUS.

1. O that I could sing worthily unto Thee, in praise of the Arc of Speta. For Thy Mightiness, O that I could find mortal words to magnify Thy vast kingdoms.

2. In Thy great Goddess, Cpenta-armij, and her mighty etherean legions that came down to earth, O what a glory in Thy praise. Who can forget Thy heaven, Terashish, Thou Almighty.

3. And Haot-Saiti and Hodws and Lugga and Bonassah and Tule and Speta-arc, with their ten million seas and their hundred million crystal rivers in the arches of Woo.

4. With their eighty thousand million high-raised Gods and Goddesses. With their one hundred and sixty thousand million miles of etherean roadways and capitals!

5. And thou, Solastus plains, with thy twelve million arches in the waters of Waltad; with seventy million ship-builders, the workers and handlers of Thy immortal fire.

6. And the etherean kingdoms of Hards and Iwalt and Kollenpoitaben and Embralik and Loogan and Aftguy and Riv and Lurnzan, with their two hundred thousand million miles of arches built unto Thee.

7. Let them rejoice in Thy name, and in the fruit of the garden of Thy Daughter, Cpenta-armij, for the harvest is ripened unto Thee.

8. Thy Sons and Daughters answer to the echo on the mortal earth: There is but one Almighty! Let us sing unto the Boundless, the Everlasting Creator.

NIV.

1. Holy, Holy, Holy, O Bon! Thou arc of the fountain of preserved records. Thy labor is done! The earth is surrounded by the Faithists of Jehovih. The shout of gladness riseth up from mortals for the glory of the Almighty.

2. The harvest of your labor, Esdras and Wedojain and Mieute, ye etherean kingdoms in the high heavens of the Great Spirit. With your ninety thousand million angels in the songs of the Most High! Proclaim it in your seas of fire, Jehovih hath won!

3. O ye heavenly kingdoms, Takuspe and Kenna and Vetta'puissa and Looloowonga, sing glory to the All One, the Great Spirit! His hand hath encircled the earth, His name is written and sung in the souls of mortals; there is but one Great Spirit, Jehovih!

4. Proclaim the joy of the earth, O ye etherean heavens, Lotisiv and Aptlong and Wiskloo and Hotab, with your millions of etherean seas, and your tens of millions of etherean plains and high mountains.

5. Rejoice for the joy of mortals, O ye etherean heavens, Hennasit and Hoxora and Lon and Oriyi and Sing and Avolassak, with your holy mountains, Yetungwas and seventy thousand million miles of plains.

6. Ye contributors to mortals, O ye high angels of the etherean heavens, ye volunteers to Lika, Son of Jehovih! Proclaim the great joy in the everlasting heavens of the Great Spirit, Jehovih.

7. Sing an endless song to the Almighty, the Creator of hundreds of thousands of millions of etherean heavens! The red star, the earth, is risen! The kingdom of Jehovih resteth on the solid earth!

8. Glorify Him in the highest, the All One, Who is farther than all the universe, the Almighty, Jehovih; your labors on earth, O ye angels of the etherean heavens, harvesting unto the Almighty!

VEN.

1. Let us sing to the Maker, Jehovih, O my beloved!
2. Him Who is Mighty in thought, Jehovih! O my beloved!
3. He but conceiveth, and, lo, a creation is done, O my beloved!
4. Jehovih, the Creator, Almighty, O my beloved, sing unto Him, forever!

HARS.

1. All men know Him; none deny Him, the Creator!
2. Who quickened into life all the living, out of the Almighty!
3. Whose knowledge knoweth all, the whence and thence, Jehovih!
4. Before Whom even Gods cry out: All is in Thee, O Jehovih!

TOO.

1. About what under the sun can not men differ? but Thy Mightiness, Jehovih!
2. Where in the heavens have the angels found Thy boundaries? or come to the termination?
3. About whose magnitude and existence can not they differ, but in Thee, Thou Almighty!
4. Thou alone art the Soul and the Substance, the Only All, the Key Note of Harmony, Jehovih!

OR.

1. Since thousands of years Thine enemies have raised up hundreds of Gods and Lords and Saviors; and they cry out: O come thou, believe in my God! Believe in my Redeemer!
2. They draw the sword and spear, and cry out: Fall down, thou heathen! Worship my God and Savior, or die! Behold the mighty armies of the Lord! Down, thou heathen, or die!
3. Thou alone, Jehovih, standest Indestructible and Almighty! Thou alone Acceptable and All Pleasant! Thou Brilliant, Thou Home of Delight! Who never deceivest or commandest to war or death.
4. About Thee there can be no dispute, Thou Fountain of all. As Thou taughtest in the ancient days: There is but one Great Spirit, Jehovih! So to-day is Thy utterance: There is but One, even the All One!

5. What is Osiris, the Savior, or the Osirian principle, that man should turn from the Almighty to consider? Or Apollo, or the Apollo principle, that man should turn from the Creator to consider?

6. What is Thor, or Thammus, or Yima, or principles of any of these, or what is their plan of salvation, compared to Jehovih's. Thou only, O Father, art All Sufficient unto all.

HOTH.

1. Thou, my Creator, and of great glory, who fashioned atmospherea full of heavens; adorned the intermediate world with Thy mighty hand, resplendent with holiness in Thy praise.

2. Praise be to Thee, Thou Highest, in Whom the worlds shine with the light of the Almighty! Thy three great worlds, the corporeal, the atmospherean and the etherean, bright and full of holiness in Thy praise.

3. Praise Jehovih, ye atmosphereans, ye es'yan fruit of the Almighty. Sing to Him in your plateaux of millions of cities, in praise of the Creator proclaim the multitude of your places.

4. Let Hatawah and Drom and Yokanad sound the trumpets of Jehovih in their ten thousand cities, and their hundreds of thousands of colleges and wide farms. The Almighty forever!

5. And the plateaux, Habur and Nafghad, with their twelve thousand shining rivers and their seventy thousands cities of the factories of heaven, founded in the fair fields of Jehovih's heavens!

6. Sing ye in praise of the Great Spirit, ye heavens that travel with the earth in the vortex Avonitivi. Ye atmospherean heavens, Gonza and Speantogotha, with your thousand million angels.

7. Ye plateaux, Gobria, Sagaghizan and Loowanogo, with your seven million colleges and factories, your heavenly delights for perfecting the spirits of mortals in the ways of the Almighty.

RUX.

1. Then sang the bound heavens, the atmosphereans. First, Ghiovagna, with her two million cities, in the plateau Wahaputosivi.

2. Almighty Creator, hear Thy Daughter in the Hemsan-way, sweet cliffs in the colleges of Tuan, with her thirty million students, swift uprising. Marching onward in praise of Thee, my Creator.

3. With ample material, O Thou Boundless, for Thy sixty million hosts in jubilee. Striving onward in Thy praise, buoyant with love and rejoicing in the lessons of the Omnipotent.

4. With seven million factories to train the untutored es'yan the purpose of the talents Thou createdst with all to be most shining lights in building the house of the Almighty in rapturous industry.

5. With her two million nurseries for the spirits of infants, full of delight and songs to Jehovih! With fragrance and delightful plains and forests and shining waters, created by Thee, Thou All Perfect.

6. With my four million miles of roadways and atmospherean oceans, wherein Thy high-raised angels teach the es'yans how to master the elements Thou createdst, swift and mighty, proclaiming Thy power.

7. O the songs and praises of Thy Daughter, Ghiovagna, the heaven of four hundred million angels, swift in learning, pure in love, with a choir a million strong to sing and chant to Thee on the waters of heaven.

8. O the songs of gladness, the shining robes of Thy loved ones, Jehovih. The lessons of wisdom, the growth of talent, the dance and merry-making, the learning to master Thy elements, O thou Almighty.

GHOI.

1. Then Farja sang: Thy Daughter, O Jehovih! Thy Schliegashawaka, uplifted unto Thee, Thou Almighty! I am Thy heaven, O Father, with six million cities in the plateau Shia Chong, far in the grades.

2. With three million places of learning for the es'yans newly risen from the earth; the colleges of Sitiviyanpegonska on the very high mountain, Hoit'su'gonderoga, heavenly.

3. With four million factories and eight hundred million angels, high in the grades, joyous, full of wisdom and song, masterly in Thy elements, created by Thee, Thou Almighty Creator!

4. Well weaned from the earth and corporeal desires, heavenly aspiring! With their heads turned upward and their souls in the way of Jehovih! Most righteous; and in unison, striving in the way of Jehovih!

5. O that I could find corporeal words for the love of my heaven! For the joy of my eight hundred millions! And of heavenly things display to mortals the glorious creations created by the All Light, Jehovih!

DING.

1. Quick springing in, and loud came the song of the heaven, Vrihaden, with her thousand million angels, high in the grades:

2. Worshipful, O Almighty! Speak ye my shining rivers of heaven, Hyad-hiago and Fuen and Owagonshe, ten hundred thousand miles of water.

3. Flowing past my heavenly cities, Effalt and Sugathagow, and Friabes and Yanad and Hucfomakalasakola, lying under the high mountain, Soidon, with four thousand high arches reared by the Almighty!

4. My thousand millions rejoicing in Jehovih, Thou Creator of millions of heavens, stretching far. O that I could find comparisons for mortals, to tell them of the glory of my heavens!

5. My places of learning and factories and ship-building, shaping vessels for coursing the firmament of the Almighty! Of the rules and philosophies of my delightful heavens.

6. O that I could show them the discipline of my thousand millions; my army of Jehovih! Their high wisdom and their power over the elements created by the Almighty!

7. O that mortals could see my high arches and my heavenly forests and mountains! O that mortals understood to inhabit a world within as well as without.

8. To know the solutions of Jehovih's worlds, and the orderly arrangement of the unseen! Praise be unto Thee, Jehovih! Thou Provider of the heaven, Vrihaden, with her thousands of millions.

GOWH.

1. Next sang Steinhover, the heaven of the beautiful plateau, Owgawahha, surrounded by the heavenly seas, Hiajom and Praj and Sumakaqa and Yadzad: Glory be to Thee, Jehovih, in Whom my delightful thousands of million angels rejoice with great joy.
2. My four million places of learning, and my innumerable factories sprung up for the glory of the Almighty. O that I could find earth-words for the understanding of mortals! To show them the wonders of Jehovih!
3. O that they could sail in the ships of Steinhover, and witness the high arches and delightful forests on the shores of Sumakaqa and Yadzad! And understand the teaching of angels, to rise in mastery of the elements created by the Omnipotent!
4. To know the power of union; the secret of the thrift of the delightful heaven, Steinhover, on the beautiful plateau Owgawahha. Sing unto the Great Spirit, the Fountain of All; the All Fullness of Glory forever!
5. After her came the songs of Naphatat and Gur and Suth, the three heavenly places on the plateau, Chin-jah, high-raised over the earth divisions, Uropa and Asia, wider than the earth.
6. With their five thousand million angels in their forty million cities, heavenly, full of delight and great wisdom, high in the grades. Singing gleefully of their two thousand rivers and a million high arches.
7. Next came the songs of the heavens, Aden and Magapor, with four thousand million angels, high in the grades. Lauding their seventy million schools and colleges, and their sea Seinthius, with its waters of silver and gold, and three million crystal stalagmites.
8. With her loud song: Jehovih be praised! Thou Great Spirit, Who provideth unto us Thy unspeakable delights. All hail, Thou Almighty! Hear the great joy of Aden and Magapor, with their four thousand million angels rejoicing in Thy name, Jehovih!

ORD.

1. So-to-ramus sang next, and of her great plateau, Chik-ka-hoo-sa, over the regions of Guatama, wide as the earth, high-raised in the grades, with three thousand million angels, rejoicing in the heavenly mountains, Hosanattabah and O-de-chi-che and Hakabda, with seventy thousand high arches, and the delightful ocean, heavenly. Sociotes, with three million ship-builders, well trained in the elements created by the Creator.
2. Wailing in her song, O Jehovih! Would that I had earth-words for the glories of heaven! O that I could show my delightful places to mortals! O that I could make comparison for the knowledge of mortals! How can I make them comprehend the heavenly ocean, Sociotes, habitable within and without; with sparkling waters, colored like a rainbow, for the ships of angels.
3. How can I make them comprehend the wonderful mountain, O-de-chi-che, habitable within and without; with her thirty thousand high arches, spanning shining rivers! O that mortals could comprehend! O that mortals could see!

4. With sixteen million miles of heavenly roadways, and the great lake, Anapasivi, with its two million boats, teaching newborn angels how to master the elements, far reaching in the firmament of heaven.

5. With otevans to carry millions coursing along in the gardens of heaven, created by Thee, Jehovih, full of delight, strong, powerful! My most orderly heaven, teaching with song and high reverence to the Almighty!

6. O that I could reveal the glories of Farja, Thy Schliegashawaka, O Jehovih! And the great delight of her eight hundred millions, gleeful, rapturous in Thy praise; glorified by the love of the Almighty!

7. O the forests of my heavens, Sotoramus, created by the Almighty, delightful, awe-inspiring! O the fields of Tobosin and Suthagar and Chaimus, the creations of the Great Spirit.

8. After her, then sang the heaven, Chook-a-so-win, in the voice of three thousand million angels, in her two million cities, high in the grades, and well disciplined. Of her great cascades and whirl-pools, dangerous places in heaven for inexperienced angels. And lauding tunefully her great rivers and her colleges and factories.

9. Next sang Fiatonadis, a heaven with seventy divisions on the plateau Noyohertimus, with two thousand million angels, high in the grades; lauding highly her factories and colleges and her es'enaurs, a million musicians.

10. Next sang Heoparsi, a heaven with one million cities, high in the grades; with eight hundred thousand miles of roadways; with eight hundred million angels of delight, rejoicing in their lives and glorifying the Almighty.

11. After that sang these great heavens: Hiawasse, Ho Chong, Hriden, Sago Loo, Maison and Witcha-chaw-nowksin; lauding their thousands of millions of angels; their millions of cities and places of delight; their mountains and rivers; their lakes and valleys; their colleges and factories, where angels are taught to master the elements created by the Great Spirit, for the joy of His mighty heavens!

LEF.

1. O that I could sing the songs of Thy heavens. Thy sweet places of delight, Hanoshea and O-chi-ma and Riviokim and Pethsiades and Yenades; to find earth-words descriptive of their delightful holiness and rejoicing in the Almighty!

2. O that I could display their mountains and valleys and their wide plains! Their shining waters and their forests and their stalactites and innumerable high arches. Their thousands of millions of angels full of joy and loveliness! Their wonderful music, poured forth in Thy praise, Jehovih.

3. Their dancing, millions in a dance; their boating and swift excursions, like thoughts in unison flying forth, mighty in power, gleeful and full of romance! High in the grades, spotless, pure, every one a flower, a star, a diadem in the kingdom of the Almighty!

4. O that I could sing of the order of Thy heavens! And of the wonderful roadways from one to another! How Thou hast planted elements in Thy kingdoms, ever trying the skill and knowledge of Thy angels! Where genius and wisdom ever lead in Thy ways, Jehovih.

5. Who but Thee, O Father, could create these never-ending varieties of heavens! These wonderful plateaux, suitable habitations for the spirits of the dead! Ever providing the higher to lift up the lower! In system and good discipline displaying the wonders of the

Almighty!

6. O that I could sing in words to the understanding of mortals!

7. And to such as had been called sinners and most wicked who had become in time like diadems in Thy crown, Jehovih, sparkling, bright with perfect holiness!

E-O.

1. Then answered Jehovih to the songs of praise that rose up from His hundreds of thousands of millions, to the sum of His mighty creations.

2. Peace, My beloved! And great joy! I have heard your voice of praise! I answer you with millions of new creations! Farther than the farthest, boundless! Thousands of millions of years are the works of My hand! I go not about turning water into wine, like a magician, or professing to raise the dead!

3. But yet I raise the dead, the souls of the dead, into worlds shining, brilliant, full of loveliness! I take them not backward to toil and sorrow; but upward, onward, to heavens of delight, that perish not, forever.

4. Mine is the Tree of Life, forever growing and rich in blossoms and sweet perfumes. The dead are Mine, the spirits of the dead My young blossoms full of promise, speaking soul-words for the glory of My heavens.

5. Whom I quickened into life are Mine, and I watch over them Fatherly and in great wisdom. Nor suffer I them to go out of being forever. And I provide My heavenly places broad, boundless, so that the soul of man can never reach to the boundary thereof.

6. Though they stray away for a season, yet have I provided them to return to Me in the end. And I make them a banquet, and provide unto them a feast, a home of love, with music and dancing even on the threshold of wisdom.

7. Weep not for the dead, O My beloved! I have places of delight for the righteous, full of rejoicing and wonderful! And the soul of the dead entereth therein, as one that emergeth from a veil, to shout with great joy for the provisions I created, plentiful and brilliant.

8. Heaven after heaven have I created as a new surprise of great happiness to My Sons and Daughters, in the way of My resurrections. Rejoice and be merry in holiness! Open your eyes, My beloved, and behold the works of My hands which I provided to be yours forever.

UX.

1. Then answered Jehovih to those that wept for the dead:

2. What I have taken away was Mine, and I return it to the place it belongeth; but the soul, which I also gave, I carry into a new region of delight. In My hand is the spirit of the dead, and I raise it up to the delightful places I created for it. Yea, it shall find its love, and rejoice in My arms, because of the glory of My heavens.

3. In the times of My seasons the soul of the dead shall stand by the living; and testify to the endless creations which I provided, to perish not, forever! As a cord that lifteth a weight, so shall be the soul of the dead to those that are stricken in sorrow.

4. And I will uncover My heavens unto those; and My angels shall come down from My exalted kingdoms by the light of the line of their love; and they shall rejoice in the way of My dominions, and glorify Me and My works.

5. Thrice, at the times of the setting sun, shall ye assemble and sing for the soul of the dead, remembering his virtues in great praise. Then shall ye deliver his spirit unto My asaphs for the mansion I have built. And I will render unto him the delights of My kingdoms according to the light of his understanding.

6. And ye shall put away all mourning and all signs of mourning; and learn to understand the way of My resurrection. Rebuke Me not, O My beloved, by draping yourselves in black cloth and veils of crape. What I have done, I have done.

7. For the time shall come unto My beloved when they shall look back and say: It was well! And in the time of Jehovih it happened well, when it so happened! Though we saw not then, we now behold, as Gods and Goddesses, the way of the Almighty!

8. To sing and to rejoice in Me, O My beloved; and to attain to great knowledge; these are the roads I created, shining, diversified and broader than the imagination of man. By death provide I the resurrection of the souls of the dead. Mourn not for My proceedings, O My beloved! But be ye wise and rejoice with discretion in the glory of My creations.

SPE.

1. Then answered Jehovih to those that had an infant born:

2. What I have quickened into life, behold, it is My gift. It is a flower of sunshine molded by a touch of My hand. Provide ye unto it, O My beloved. Fence My garden around, that serpents can not enter. The time shall come when this living soul shall be as a God in My heavens. His light shall be brighter than a sun!

3. Then spake Jehovih to the infant: Light of My light, O My Son! To thee I give the earth and the heavens, to be thine forever! And the waters of the earth and the air of the firmament, to be thine forever! And the forests and mountains and valleys, to be thy paradise forever. And the oceans and seas, to be thine forever. And lastly, O My Son, what I gave to no other animal on earth or in the waters thereof, or in the air of heaven, give I unto thee; behold, I give thyself to thee.

4. And I give thee guardian angels to walk by thee and show thee My great delights and the way of My resurrections! They shall speak to thy soul to keep thee in the right way. Hear thou them and follow in the way of thy Creator, and thou shalt rejoice all the days of thy life.

5. But thy corporeal eyes and ears and thy corporeal judgment give I unto thine own hands. Remember, My Son, learn thou corporeal knowledge through thy soul, for it is of Me, and thou shalt not err. But shut out the way of My voice, and follow thy corporeal senses only, and thou shalt go down in darkness for a long season.

6. Remember thy Creator at all times and seasons, and thou shalt rejoice because thou art this day brought forth an heir of everlasting life.

7. Then spake Jehovih to the ashars, the guardian angels: Into your keeping, O My beloved, give I this My Son, quickened by My very breath to live forever. In your regular turns, watch and watch, guard ye him from this time forth, for he is the fruit I bequeath unto you. And in due time ye shall render his soul unto My asaphs in heaven, being glorified therein.

8. Nor shall ye ever make yourselves known to him through his corporeal senses; for your labor is with the spirit. But when ye find it rightful that angels shall approach his corporeal understanding, see to it that they be exalted and in the way of My everlasting

kingdoms. For the plan of My creations is for the resurrection of the soul of man to be forever and ever!

YAD.

1. Praise be unto Thee, Jehovih! Who can search out the completeness of Thy creation?

2. Or know the magnitude of Thy places, Thou Almighty! And thy endless inventions?

3. Thou shalt be My theme forever, to find the far-seeing devices of my Creator, the work of my soul.

4. I was alone in the world. Angels and men fed not my soul; I was hungered and in gloom.

5. Then I turned to Thee, Thou Almighty. And Thou gavest me a new growth, a fruit of life in fire!

6. Which grew brighter and brighter. And my vision was recovered, and Thy heavens were opened as a book is opened.

7. And I drank of Thy waters, and ate of the tree of the resurrection to Thy everlasting kingdoms.

8. The secret of Thy Wisdom, O Jehovih, was uncovered; the way of Thy Mightiness made imperishable forever!

SON.

1. Because Thou gavest into mine own hand to exalt myself, O Jehovih! For perpetual resurrection shapedst mine every part before I knew the way of the Almighty! Praise be unto Thee forever! Saith the Faithist!

2. Because Thou providedst from the ancient times for Thy Mighty word. From everlasting Thou hast provided prophets to know the way of the Omnipotent! To reveal the unseen heavens created by Thee!

3. Because Thou hast kept alive the line of Thy Majesty in mortals! Built a house for Thy chosen, wide as the world! Faith in Thee above all things in earth or heaven. Saith the Faithist!

4. When all the world beside faileth, Thou, my Creator, standest before me Mighty and full of love. Thou One Alone, imperishable forever, and just and merciful. Praise be unto Thee, Jehovih, Who art greater than All!

END OF BON'S BOOK OF PRAISE.

GOD'S BOOK OF ESKRA.

CHAPTER I.

1.God said: This Book shall be called Eskra, because it is the history of the heavenly cycle, Bon. It shall contain the substance of the heavenly records of three thousand three hundred years, of the first regions of the resurrection of the dead. My words are not of the earth, but of heaven.

2. For of the history of the earth ye know already; wherefore I reveal things ye know not of. Be ye profited therein understandingly, for my heavenly kingdoms will be presently for your habitation.

3. As it hath been revealed to you already, in regard to the successions of the God, and the periods of dan, and the division of the higher from the lower heavens, it is sufficient unto you to know that which is given of God is of him who is Jehovih's voice, without regard to which administration, or which God. And to know also that that heaven referred to in Eskra is not of the higher heavens, etherea, but atmospherea, which heavens travel with the earth around the sun, which heavens were called the lower heavens by the ancients, and by some, the intermediate world. Through which heavens all souls must pass, being first purified and risen in wisdom, ere they can inherit the emancipated worlds in etherea.

4. Nor are these my revelations to mortals only, but to thousands of millions of the spirits of the dead, who know not the plan of the resurrection to higher heavens; but who wander about on the earth, not even knowing the organizations of the kingdoms in my lowest of heavens.

5. Whom I reach by coming to mortals, and to places on the earth where they abide.

6. For many such angels believe the heavens to be as an unorganized wilderness, void of government and instruction and discipline.

7. And by virtue of their presence with mortals, though invisible to them, do inspire mortals with the same darkness. Wherefrom mortals have concluded there are neither Lords nor God, who are Jehovih's high officers in these kingdoms.

8. These matters shall be set forth in brief in Eskra; the fullness of which shall be opened unto mortals and angels in time near at hand; for they shall see and read the books in the libraries of these heavens, and learn to know of their own knowledge.

9. Therefore the light of this Book of Eskra is not of one God, or one Lord, or one recording angel, who are constantly succeeding one another, but of the body of the first heavens of the earth for the period of this cycle which is now at the close.

CHAPTER II.

1. God, Son of Jehovih, said: Give ear, O earth, and be attentive to the words of Jehovih's Son:

2. And ye mortals of the earth; for I have said: The time shall surely come when all things shall be revealed to the inhabitants of the earth.

3. Be patient and wise in understanding me; my words are for your resurrection forever, and for the glory of the Creator.

4. And ye angels of heaven, draw near; for I will reveal to you that which is for your own good. The multitude of my kingdoms shall be opened up to your understanding also.

5. And O ye, my high raised Lords and officers of heaven, call up your hosts from far and near. Hear ye the words of your God. Call ye up the mighty ones of Yogannaqactra and the inhabitants of Theovrahkistan.

6. And Hibin, the successor to Yussamis, of the six heavens of Ugsadisspe, to Tewallawalla, to Setee'song, to Go'e'dhu, to Ellapube, to Apax and to Fue. And call ye up the successors to Hibin, and the primal Gods under him of his six mighty heavens.

7. And Ong Woo, the successor to Anuhasaj, of the heavenly regions, the a'ji'an forest, Turpeset, with her twelve heavenly kingdoms; the place of Negathogan and Shumat and Thorokak and Enisshappaga and Habor and Amga and Magossa and Dhi Wan and Seffakostrus and Inubib and Marh and Wischowitcha, and to the primal Gods and generals and captains.

8. And to Yusalithth, successor to Osiris, of Vrigginyannah; and to Raxya, successor to Te'in of Ovella; and to Yadonya, successor to Sudga, of Tempissiv; and to Yima, successor to Egupt, of Rathyaya; and to Hidemmes, successor to Shu Wan Loo, of Wowahyotos.

9. And to their primal Gods and successors, and to their generals and captains.

10. And to Zhubon, successor to the line of Yaton'te, with her twelve subjective heavens, the Fiskadore, the Wooloo, the Yamyam, the Katiro, the Wannahogan, the Ravax, the Ginnewan, the Shawnea, the Wishogah, the Pottomatta, the Shiwasae and Muskadayan.

11. And to their primal Gods and successors, and to their generals and captains.

12. And to Yessotosissi, successor to Yodma, of the heavenly regions of Ornababa, with seven mighty kingdoms, Gootha and Yembique and Waing T'soo and Ithya and Yorama and Hi'D'honyah and Wurrtembogga.

13. And to their primal Gods and their successors, and to their generals and captains.

14. And to Pidissomo, successor to Savvaqactra, of the heavenly place Joisyama, with her eighteen heavenly kingdoms, You and Loo Sin and Kad and Rum and Jassak and Solomon and Ressa and Nibbakak and Hizeph and Sakkar and Sin Chong and Remthaxax and Avardissa and Kessadronakas and Hui'gammaksonad and Nu Lee Wing and Trasmas and Kissayaya.

15. And to their primal Gods and successors, and to their generals and captains.

16. And to all other Gods of the heavenly regions of atmospherea, the hada of the earth; and to their successors and generals and captains; and to the heavenly, hadan regions of Sho'e'gan, with her twenty-eight sub-kingdoms, and to the heavenly, hadan regions of Ghi'e'wan, with her forty-four sub-kingdoms, and to their exalted officers and teachers, heavenly Sons and Daughters of Jehovih.

17. And to the plateau of Narid, in the second resurrection, with her two hundred heavenly kingdoms, their Gods and generals and captains and high teachers, Sons and Daughters of Jehovih.

18. And to the plateau of Yakabba, two thousand miles high, with her six hundred heavenly kingdoms, and their Gods and high officers.

19. And to the plateau of Yannurib, two thousand one hundred miles high, with her four hundred heavenly kingdoms, and their Gods and high officers.

20. And the seven plateaux of Havagamatris, with their two thousand heavenly kingdoms, and their Gods and high officers.

21. And the six plateaux of Vraggaomen, with their fourteen hundred heavenly kingdoms, and their Gods and high officers.

22. And the fourteen plateaux of Ghemayumaistra, with their three thousand four hundred heavenly kingdoms, and their Gods and high officers.

23. And to all other plateaux in the heavens of the earth, the atmospherean regions, and to the Gods of all heavenly kingdoms in these lower heavens; the intermediate world of the angels raised up out of the earth.

24. God said: Jehovih called upon me, His Son, saying: My Son! Call aloud in My name; with My Voice stir up all these heavenly regions I have named.

25. For My Gods and high-raised officers shall open unto thee their libraries of heavenly books which shall yield up My treasures. I will make the angels of heaven know Me and My word! They shall come together from their countless heavenly kingdoms and places; for My hand and My strong arm is upon them.

26. The labors of My lower heavens shall be clothed in mortal words, and handed down to mortals. My Gods and My primal Gods and generals and captains shall uncover their proceedings before the heavens and the earth.

27. They shall come together and be as one man with one voice, and their word shall be My word.

28. For My prophets have proclaimed it abroad, that the time would come when I would reveal all things unto men; and things that were dark made plain; and things in the light made as heaven, rejoicing.

CHAPTER III.

1. Hear My voice, O angels and mortals! The words of the heavens of the earth are My words, orderly and well disciplined. No man can imitate Me; angels can not counterfeit Me. My words are from the Fountain, that erreth not forever.

2. Whoso seeth My way can not fail to understand; I quibble not, nor beat about the bush. Even Lords and Gods are as nothing in My hands. I trim them up, and prune their orchards in Mine own way; I sift and weigh and assort, for I am Jehovih, the Almighty!

3. I am the sum of the Voice of all the lower heavens; the doings of Gods and high officers; the Person of the word of three thousand years.

4. And My record shall be the standard for mortals and angels for thousands of years to come. Other books and other worlds will be written and spoken, and they shall pass away and be remembered not by angels nor men. But My words, the words of Eskra, will live and endure forever. Then spake God, saying:

5. For I am His fountain, of the Tree of Bon; I am His cycle of the Great Serpent's e'spe, and can not die or go out of remembrance. I am as a link in a great circle, the section of Bon in the solar vortex.

6. During every cycle I come and speak, and my words are not like other words. I plant them on the low earth, and they take root, and grow into a tree that reacheth up into heaven. And the angels of heaven come thither and gather my words, for they are the fruit of everlasting life and of the resurrection of mortals and of the spirits of the dead.

7. Give ear, O ye nations of the earth, and magnify your understanding, for the wisdom of the Almighty.

8. He singleth not out one man or one God, and saith: Behold, by him judge ye Me and My works! Or giveth the history of all the living in one book; the pith of things is the unit sprung from all.

CHAPTER IV.

1. Give ear, O man, and be wise in thy judgment, of sure perception and good discernment in the revelations of my words in the cycles past and present.

2. For I summed up all the Gods of the hadan regions of the earth, and all their high officers in the plateaux and heavenly kingdoms thereof, and I named them, GOD! And in their dominions with mortals I named them, LORD! As one, even God, made I them in my past revelations on the earth. That I might not confuse the judgment of men!

3. And all the heavenly places of the earth, the atmospherean heavens, which travel with the earth around the sun, I named, HADA, the intermediate world, the lower heaven. Through which none can pass to the etherean heaven till purged of self, and made spotless, pure and strong in spirit.

4. Of this hadan heaven, and of her Gods and their labors made I two words, GOD and HEAVEN, and Eskra is the sermon thereof. In which ye nations of the earth, and ye angels of heaven shall profit in spirit; as by experience past, the future becometh fortified in wisdom and strength.

5. In which sermon all resurrection is of God, who is Jehovih's Son; but to distinguish from which (God) I named all that desired not resurrection in heaven, but loved more the earth, SATAN. And whoso loved evil and practiced it, I named, SATAN; and whoso combined, as angels or as mortals, to make anarchy, I named, EVIL WORKERS for hell.

6. As God and heaven are of the resurrection, so are satan, hell and the devil of the declension.

7. To one or other, resurrection or declension, belong all men on the earth, and to one or the other belong all the spirits of the dead.

8. None can stand still; all the living are on the move forever.

9. Jehovih is Life, Motion, Individual, Person! In proof of which, He gave unto thee life, motion, individuality, person.

10. To develop these four entities is resurrection toward Him, more and more, which is heavenly.

11. To neglect them, or pervert them, is to go away from Him, which is declension, which can lead to entire destruction.

12. No man can be life for another; nor motion, nor individuality, nor person for another. For himself, and to himself, hath Jehovih created him with these.

13. Nor can any of the Gods, however exalted, give to or take away these things.

14. For even though the highest-raised angels may attain to turn the earth over, or to dissolve it, as the air in the firmament, or create a new earth, yet none of these can create life, or motion, or an individual, or person.

15. These are from Jehovih and in Him; and all angels, the Gods and Lords, and generals and captains and chiefs in heaven are but the brothers and sisters of mortals and the spirits

of the dead.

16. And yet, O man of the earth, and thou, angel of the heavens of the earth, be not puffed up or make light of the Gods, or Lords, or Saviors, or Chiefs of the heavens, for thou art compared to them but as a drop of water is compared to the ocean.

17. As a man amongst you employeth a thousand men to do his bidding, so have I, your God, thousands of millions of angels to speak in my name.

18. Put not off my words, saying: It is but your conscience speaking. My angels speak to you in spirit, with my very voice and words, which are Jehovih's also.

19. According to the capacities and talents of such mortals as practice my commandments, so do I appropriate them to assist in the resurrection.

20. And in the same way do I allot my ashars to abide with you; to the musician, angel musicians; to the philosopher, angel philosophers; to the historian, angel historians; to the cosmographer, angel cosmographers; to the revelator, angel revelators; even so unto all men who seek to serve Jehovih by doing good.

21. And these my ashars, which I place over you, are not individual angels, merely acting and speaking their own notions, but are organized companies of thousands of millions, who labor through a chief angel, called Lord; and all of them are in concord with me and my kingdoms, directed by my Holy Council, of millions of angels high in wisdom, which is directed by me, your God, even as I am one with other Gods, who are one with Jehovih.

22. What my angels do in truth and wisdom, for righteousness sake, these I ratify in heaven; what I do in heaven, my angels do and reveal unto you in my name.

CHAPTER V.

1. The Lord said: This is the labor of God after the dawn of the arc of Bon:

2. God crowned four thousand Lords, and titled them LORDS OF THE HEAVENLY HOSTS.

3. And God allotted to every one of them one hundred messengers and fifty heralds, and gave them authority to provide their own attendants in their own way.

4. God said: That I may hear the voices of my Lords, when ye are within your own kingdoms, ye shall appoint representatives unto my throne. And there shall be of such representative Lords one for every four hundred Lords of the Hosts.

5. And the representative Lords shall be speakers for the kingdoms that appoint them, and have power on important occasions to summon to my throne all their constituent Lords.

6. And the representative Lords shall be known in heaven and entered in the libraries thereof as the Holy Eleven, for they are symbolical of the seasons on the earth.

7. Now therefore the Lords of the Hosts elected the Holy Eleven, and God anointed them, and their names were entered in the libraries of the heavens. These then are the Holy Eleven, to wit:

8. Likar, Lakash, Yopes Loe, Vadhuan, Ah Cho, Zahawee, Eezen, Khan, Zedna, Yutemis and Ardolfus. And God gave authority to the Holy Eleven to speak before the throne, after the manner of the Councils of the higher heavens.

9. God said unto the Lords of the Hosts: Your work is a good work. So, the Lords of the Hosts departed to their several kingdoms. But the Holy Eleven were duly installed and took their places in front of the throne of God.

CHAPTER VI.

1. And God appointed two thousand supervisors unto each of the Holy Eleven; and eight thousand eight hundred surveyors; and four thousand four hundred captains of roads, and said unto them: Go ye and build roadways between all the heavenly kingdoms in atmospherea. And I give unto you two thousand million laborers, to be divided between you, according to the distances and places of the roads.

2. And God gave authority to Toyvraghah to examine the records and make the apportionment of officers and laborers on the roads, and he thus accomplished these things.

3. God said: My heavens shall be divided into eleven parts, one unto each of the Holy Eleven.

4. The said eleven divisions were accomplished and thus named, to wit: Sinyativi, Horak, Damaya, Ad'dam, Hosea, Harivya, Sinisyo, Amset, Godessa, Itero and Aroqu.

5. Damaya, Ad'dam and Hosea comprised all the lowest hadan regions, bordering on the earth; and these three divisions extended around the earth, and were twelve miles high.

6. Sinyativi, Horak and Amset comprised the next grade of heavenly kingdoms outward from the earth, and were one thousand miles high, more or less.

7. Goddessa and Itero were the next grade of heavenly kingdoms outward from the earth, and were two thousand miles high.

8. Harivya was next, and was outward from the earth two thousand five hundred miles. And next after this was Aroqu, which was three thousand miles above the earth. Aroqu was therefore the highest of the atmospherean heavens in those days.

9. These five heavenly spheres, therefore, comprised the whole of the inhabited heavens of the earth. And yet there were thousands of plateaux still further away from the earth, and within her vortex, but uninhabited.

10. As for Aroqu and Harivya, they were inhabited mostly by angels of the highest atmospherean grades.

11. God said: From this time forth all heavenly marriages of Brides and Bridegrooms to Jehovih shall take place in Harivya and Aroqu, instead of as heretofore, in the thousands of heavenly kingdoms.

12. And all es'yans shall be hereafter maintained within the first sphere of hada, within the regions of Damaya and Ad'dam and Hosea. And as they rise in wisdom and strength, they shall advance in place as well as grade, going in the direction of Harivya and Aroqu, from which all resurrections for the etherean worlds shall take place.

13. And God caused the boundaries of Ad'dam and Hosea to embrace the eastern continents of the earth; but Damaya embraced the western.

14. To the Lords of the Hosts, God had said: The great love that mortals have for their kindred who are dead, is like a chord forever pulling their souls back to earth.

15. Neither do mortals understand my heavens, and that the soul of man should rise upward.

16. They cry out to me continually: O God, send thou back to me the spirit of my kin!

17. And they do not understand that their prayers are in opposition to the resurrection of spirits of the dead.

18. And likewise doth the es'yan cry out to me: O God, take me back to my mortal kin!

For he also comprehendeth not the resurrection, but in the gratification of his love would linger forever on the earth.

19. Suffer ye not mortals to commune with the spirits of the dead.

20. And the Lords carried out the commandment of God.

CHAPTER VII.

1. At the time the roadways of the earth's heavens were completed, which was in the three hundred and ninetieth year of the cycle of Bon, this was the standing thereof, to wit:

2. There had ascended, as Brides and Bridegrooms, for etherea, thirty-six thousand millions; nearly one-half of whom were from the kingdoms of Anuhasaj and his sub-Gods.

3. And now inhabiting the five spheres, forty-eight thousand million spirits.

4. In the first sphere, or hada, in which there were two thousand four hundred heavenly kingdoms, the grades were from one to seven.

5. In the second sphere, which ranked first resurrection in those days, the grades were from seven to fifteen. In these regions there were ten thousand heavenly kingdoms.

6. In the third sphere the grades were from fifteen to thirty. In these regions there were four thousand heavenly kingdoms. And including the kingdoms of Anuhasaj, five thousand more kingdoms.

7. In the fourth sphere, the grades were from thirty to sixty, and there were one thousand five hundred heavenly kingdoms in these regions.

8. In the fifth sphere, the grades were from sixty to ninety-nine, and here were one thousand heavenly kingdoms.

9. And yet, not included in these, because of a different kind, were the kingdoms of Yaton'te, the subjective heaven, a visiting place, and with but a small fixed population, but whose visitors and students and teachers numbered three thousand million angels, graded from one to ninety-nine. But many of these belonged in other heavenly kingdoms.

10. Such then were the inhabitants of the bound heavens. And they numbered, all told, forty-eight times more people than the mortal inhabitants of the earth. But in those days not many women on the earth committed abortions; neither died so many very young children; so that the fetals sent back to inhabit mortals numbered, all told, only two hundred and thirty millions. Whilst of vampire spirits, of both classes, (that is, such as inhabit gormandizers, and gluttons, and drunkards, and harlots, absorbing their spiritual sustenance, and thus making them the breeders of infidels; and such as live on the atmospherean part of mortal food, thus causing their mortal victims to emaciate and to become insane), there were, all told, not more than forty-six millions.

11. Besides these, there were thirty-one million lusters, who feed on the secret vices of mortals; who were being forever pursued from place to place by ashars, and often captured and carried away to heavenly kingdoms; but would often escape and flee back to mortals. Yet, with all these fetals, and vampires and lusters included, never before had the earth remained so long in so pure a state.

12. When the roadways were completed, God proclaimed seven days recreation in all the kingdoms of heaven, in order that the inhabitants should sing and dance and render praise unto Jehovih for the great works that had been accomplished.

13. And on the last of the seven days, Toyvraghah assigned the roads over to God, and

named them, Roads in Paradise. Whereupon God crowned Toyvraghah, Primal God of the Roads of Paradise, of twelve hundred thousand miles.

14. God said: After the manner of the government of the etherean heavens do I these things.

15. And as the kingdoms and spheres of my heavens are situated, within and without, with their roadways and heavenly canals, forming one great kingdom with many parts, it shall be a type of the kingdoms in etherea, which are thousands of times larger. And it was so.

CHAPTER VIII.

1. Jehovih hath said: I gave to man legs and feet to walk; arms and hands to work; eyes to see, and ears to hear; and, withal, the capacity to reflect and comprehend and understand.

2. I gave none of these capacities to man to lie dormant or to be useless. Neither can any man advance to My highest kingdoms if crippled, or weak, or uncultivated, in all or part of these talents I have given him.

3. But he shall be perfected in all particulars before he is capacitated for companionship with My exalted ones.

4. The Lord said: It mattereth little what kind of workmanship a man doeth; for one may till the soil, and thus train his hands and arms to full development; and another may weave, or spin, or forge iron, and also attain full development. It is not the kind of labor, but the development that comes of useful practice, which maketh every talent to stand upright in heaven as a glory to the Creator.

5. For there be servants on earth, who neither read nor write, that are better developed in their talents and members than many of the rich, and kings and philosophers.

6. And when they die and enter my heavenly places, the ranks and caste in my kingdoms seem to them to be upside-down. The rich man, or the king, or the pleader (lawyer), or priest, or the philosopher, may be as a helpless child, whilst he who was as a pauper on earth may be as a very God over them to lift them up.

7. Neither is the preference to the rich, nor the poor, nor to the philosopher, nor the fool; for any of these may be as dwarfs in some talent or part, whilst also any of these may be a most perfect man in spirit.

8. So, God established, through his high-raised officers, schools and colleges and factories, heavenly, adapted to the spirits of the dead, even as similar places are established on the earth for mortals.

CHAPTER IX.

1. The Lord said: Aside from the orderly kingdoms of God, there were seven false kingdoms in hada, ruled over by false Gods and false Goddesses. Chief of these were Baal, with four thousand million angel slaves; Ashtaroth, false Goddess, with three thousand million angel slaves; Hi'lizar, with three thousand million angel slaves; Sodonius, Goddess, with two million angel slaves, and then came Fue-Sin, Hrivatza. Beside these there were six hundred false Lords and Lordesses, who had occupied the mortal temples of worship, and the oracle temples.

2. But the latter were driven away from mortals by command of God, that they might be induced to seek resurrection.

3. And God foresaw that the travel of the earth would cause her to pass through an a'ji'an forest of four hundred years, and that darkness would be upon the lower heavens.

4. And God sent down to the earth angel inspectors and numerators and recorders to prepare the record of mortals for the libraries of heaven. And there were of inspectors, four hundred thousand angels; of numerators, twelve thousand; and graders, ninety thousand; of recorders and scribes, forty thousand; and of bearers, six hundred thousand. Besides these were the messengers, heralds and musicians, of whom there were sixty thousand.

5. Such was the army sent down to the earth according to God's command. And they were in charge of Toyvraghah and Yulis and Hagonte and Rufus.

6. And God called up the great mathematicians, Yahimus, Menres, Fargawitha, Howitchkal, Jemima, Jordan, Molakka, Kossitus, Makkas and Agebon; and God said unto them:

7. The time of the fall of a'ji on the earth is at hand. Compute ye the regions of the earth where it will fall most; and having determined, go ye to the mortal prophets who are in su'is, and cause them to prophesy unto the inhabitants of the earth.

8. The mathematicians saluted and departed for the earth, as commanded of God.

9. Now when God foresaw that darkness was near at hand, for a period of four hundred years, he commanded his Holy Council and his heavenly kingdoms to pray to Jehovih for the space of one day, for wisdom and strength.

10. In answer to their prayers, there came a swift messenger from Lika, Orian Chief, Son of Jehovih; he came from Takuspe, in the etherean worlds, in an etherean arrow-ship, with thirty thousands. His name was, Yotaportas, God of Eriasa, in the plains of Woo'Sin. And when he had come before the throne of God, duly saluting, he said:

11. In Jehovih's name I come, greeting by His Son, Lika. God said: In Jehovih's name I am blessed by thy presence, God of Eriasa, Nirvanian Host. What wouldst thou?

12. Yotaportas said: By command of Jehovih, through His exalted Son, thou shalt withdraw thine emissaries from the kingdoms of Baal and Ashtaroth, and from all kingdoms on the earth, whose mortals pay obedience to false Gods. A'ji of four hundred years will reign upon the earth and her heavens. It is so determined and provided by the Holy Etherean Dispensers of roads in Vragapathon. Of which matters I am sent to thee that thou mayest be duly provided therefore.

13. The time is also now at hand when the I'hins, the sacred people, the mound-builders, will cease to dwell on the earth. The darkness which is necessary to the earth will be too much for them. The heavens that have heretofore received their spirits shall be dissolved, and the plateaux thereof removed to the outer rim of the earth's vortex.

14. The Lords' reports showed there were at this time on the earth two million three hundred thousand I'hins. Of these, seven hundred thousand inhabited Egupt and western Arabin'ya; two hundred thousand inhabited Chine'ya, the Jaffeth of the ancients; and the balance, for the most part, inhabited North Guatama and toward Hon'ya-pan.

15. Such, then, were all that remained of a people that once covered over the whole earth, more than a thousand million of them.

16. God declared a day of recreation in honor of Yotaportas; and the angels of heaven had

great rejoicing.

17. And on the day following, Yotaportas, with his hosts, departed for Eriasa, in etherea.

CHAPTER X.

1. Toyvraghah and Hagonte and Yulis and Rufus, with their hosts, returned from their voyage to the earth, and brought records of the standing of mortals in all the tribes and nations of the earth, and of their numbers, and their grades and generations, and of the Faithists in all the different regions of the earth, and of idolaters, and of all matters pertaining to mortals, and these records were filed in the libraries of heaven, and a copy of them sent to the etherean regions in the roadway of the earth and her heavens.

2. Of Faithists, there were thirty-one millions and three hundred thousand. In Chine'ya, thirteen million seven hundred thousands; in Vind'yu three million three hundred thousands; in western Arabin'ya (Kanna'yan), six million two hundred thousands, and in north Guatama, eight million one hundred thousands.

3. And of all the rest of the inhabitants of the earth, there were eleven hundred millions. Of these, upward of ninety-seven per cent, were capable of everlasting life.

4. Of the Faithists of Chine'ya, suffice this: Though they maintained the rites and ceremonies of the ancients, they lived not wholly as a separate people, save in a few places. But they were the head and front of learning and of teaching all the applied arts and industries. Whilst the idolaters of Joss and Te'in and Po were less learned.

5. God said of Chine'ya: This is a good work. Whoso shapeth the education of a people will ultimately found them in their own doctrines. The Faithists will make these people a great people.

6. Nevertheless great wars are near at hand here. The idolaters, being warriors, will suffer most, and the Faithists, who practice peace, will greatly gain upon them. And it was even so, as will be presently shown.

7. Of the Faithists of Vind'yu suffice this: They lived in families and small colonies; they practiced the rites and ceremonies; nor were there any laws against them, as in the olden times. But because of the many languages in this country, all peoples were afflicted. God said: No people can advance much whilst they have many languages.

8. Of the Faithists of western Arabin'ya, who, for the most part, called themselves Israelites, suffice this: The two branches still remained: those who lived under the oral law, and those who lived under the written law. The latter were called Leviticans, that is, hangers on, and of imperfect flesh and spirit.

9. The Leviticans were not scrupulous as regardeth war and the preservation of their seed. And in consequence of their sins they brought great shame upon the Faithists in general. And the Leviticans' examples were evil, and they gained in numbers faster than the Oralites. The Leviticans worshiped the Great Spirit under the names, Lord and God.

10. As for the Oralites, so called, because their doctrines and teachings were secret and only spoken, being taught , man to man and woman to woman, orally; they were non-resistants, and they owned nothing, giving all things to the rab'bah for the public good. Their practice was love and harmony; doing righteously in all things, and trusting to Jehovih, Whom they worshiped under the name E-O-Ih. All the prophets and seers were born of the Oralites.

902

11. And so great was the spiritual power of the Oralites, that during all these hundreds of years the Faithists, six millions, had lived without king or governor. Being as a multitude of communities.

12. Of the Faithists of Guatama, they were little learned, but were peaceful and industrious. And they comprised all the inhabitants, save the I'hins, in all the land. And they also lived without kings or governors. And every town was ruled over by a rab'bah, and a combination of towns by a chief rab'bah. And the tribes were made into states, with chief rab'bahs as representatives, and these states were united into a great government called, THE ALGONQUIN. And all the government were made and maintained for the benefit of tribes that might suffer by famines or fevers. And yet there was not amongst all these millions of people one tyrant or dictator.

CHAPTER XI.

1. And now came earth and heaven into the a'ji'an forest of Aghanodis, and the pressure was upon all sides of the earth's vortex, even beyond Chinvat.

2. And the heavenly kingdoms were stirred up; and the nations of the earth were in trial.

3. In the great city of Paradise, heavenly seat of God, were the multitudes of angels, the thousands of millions made to look upward, outward, to know the Almighty.

4. As a'ji driveth the weak angels of heaven to seek a lower field, so doth it on earth drive polluted nations to war and to avarice and to death.

5. When yet but the second shower of a dozen years had fallen, mortals in many nations of the earth rushed into war. And even the Faithists began to clamor for kings and standing armies, with great captains and generals, to lead them on to mortal dominion.

6. The Israelites made a mortal king, and by their behavior , said: Rather man than Jehovih. Behold, we will have the Lord with us to fight our battles!

7. And Baal, God of the idolaters, heard and saw, and gloried in the course; and he hastened to the scene with millions of his angel slaves to inspire the Israelites to glory in the Lord and God, whom he assumed to be.

8. And millions of the Israelites fell beneath his power and became his spiritual slaves. The others, still steadfast in the secret oral rites, remained true to the secret name and Person, Jehovih (E-O-Ih).

9. The which Ashtaroth saw; and, first time of all, after two thousand years friendship to Baal, she became jealous and filled with vengeful wrath.

10. She said: I see now how this traitorous God hath planned to beat me in the regions west of Heleste and Uropa. By the flesh of my thighs am I sworn, this thing shall not be! I will send a hundred million warring angels down to Babylon and Tyre and Yedmon and Luce, and inspire their mortal kings to make war on the westward cities, the strongholds of Baal. And as to impoverished Egupt, I will send thither mortal armies sufficient to destroy everything in the land thereof.

11. Yea, I will send my legions also amongst the Israelites, and inspire them that I, Ashtaroth, am the only true Lord and true God. I will divide them up as a broken bundle of straw, and cast them to the four winds of heaven.

12. On the other hand, Baal said: Because of my success, I know Ashtaroth will be jealous and full of anger; therefore, I will place a standing army betwixt her heavens and

mine; and if she but dare to molest me, I will send my millions against her heavens and despoil her utterly, that she may be cast in hell!

CHAPTER XII.

1. God, Son of Jehovih, through his Holy Council, in Paradise, his heavenly seat, now decreed:

2. To the Faithists of Arabin'ya, Ebeneezer captain, with five million angels as a protecting host. To the Faithists of Chine'ya, Luiwatha, captain, with ten million angels as a protecting host. To the Faithists of Vind'yu, Li Chong, captain, with eight million angels as a protecting host. To the Faithists of Guatama, Manito, captain, with ten million angels as a protecting host.

3. And to each of the captains I give authority to draw additional armies from the Lords who hold dominions in the regions where they may be.

4. But it so happened that the lowest heavenly plateaus were also engaged in wars.

5. And in less than a hundred years of a'ji many of the Lords were without kingdoms, and, with a few chosen friends, were become involuntary wandering spirits, scattered about in all the heavens of the earth, or upon the earth.

6. God saw this, and he called out to them; through his messengers he called unto them, saying: Having lost your kingdoms, why will you lose yourselves? Is it not better that ye fall to, in the remaining kingdoms and by your steadfastness, help to maintain faith in Jehovih in the hearts of the less learned?

7. But satan (self) gained access to their souls, saying to each one of them: Thou, who hast been Lord of the hosts of heaven! Thou, take a place like a common laborer! Thou wouldst be laughed at! The non-resistant policy is good enough in times and places of peace. But now is war. And war can only be overcome by war. If great De'yus was overcome and cast into hell, why not our God also? So they heeded not God.

CHAPTER XIII.

1. And there came to Paradise, of Lords and high officers, whose heavenly places had fallen, different companies of tens and twenties and even hundreds, from various heavenly regions around about the earth, and having secured audience before God and his Holy Council, they said:

2. Since we have been faithful in all things, and dutiful servants to Jehovih, what have we gained? Our kingdoms and high places have fallen to pieces from no fault of our own. Yea, our angels have gone off into anarchy. Where, then, is the justice of Jehovih?

3. God said unto them: Of what profit under the sun is discussion?

4. If ye fail in one way, try another; and in no case seek to justify yourselves before Jehovih. He is Judge!

5. There are already hells that have been standing for years. Is it not wiser that ye join together, and go and deliver them? Behold, Jehovih hath furnished us roadways beforehand; and His Voice came to us prophesying that this same darkness would come upon us. And ye were advised, and had sufficient time to provide for the worst.

6. Go ye forth, then, not complaining, but rejoicing, and in Jehovih's name doing with all your wisdom and strength, regardless of favor.

7. Thus they came, group after group, for years, before God; but were forever rebuked in the spirit of Jehovih, and they went away, but not to work righteously, but to sympathize with one another, and to complain against God and against the Holy Council of Paradise.

8. In groups they assembled in places of their own, and began to philosophize on the ways of heaven and earth. And every one was sworn within himself to do no evil thing, but to find some more respectable way of serving Jehovih, than by going amongst the ignorant and depraved.

9. And they became habituated in their meetings, in three places in hada; in Haractu, over Vind'yu, in Eta-shong, over Chine'ya, and in Hapsendi, over Egupt. And these became like great heavenly cities, because of the congregating of the angels of heaven, which continued for many years.

10. Now, finally, they resolved to organize each one of these three places with a distinct head, and to unite the three heads as one confederacy; and the whole to be dedicated to the service of Jehovih. Thus was founded the CONFEDERACY OF THE HOLY GHOST. And by acclamation, three angels were raised to the three capitals, namely: Kabalactes, of Horactu; Ennochissa, of Eta-shong; and Looeamong, of Hapsendi. And each and every one of the three took the title, SON OF THE HOLY GHOST. These three had all been Lords, and were high in grade.

11. Ennochissa selected seven angels, and gave them the rank of Lord, namely: Haptu, Vazista, Mira, Erasigi, Adamon, Amesh and Cacpa.

12. Kabalactes selected seven angels, and gave them the rank of Lord, namely: Li Wan, Amatar, Wenates, Howickam, Shong Tsee, Massaqactus and Enniseabab.

13. Looeamong selected seven angels, and gave them the rank of Lord, namely: Petubusetta, Rodi, Monulithens, Zitullia, Miriam, Zestes and Abarothmes.

14. Such, then, was the established confederacy, which was to play so great a part in the history of heaven and earth. And it differed from all other confederacies, because its members all professed to serve Jehovih. And it required of all its people an oath of allegiance to Jehovih, but under the name, Holy Ghost, for they denied His Person as such.

15. And God admonished them, saying: Though ye be wise in your own conceit, yet shall ye fail. For, having denied His Person, then will ye yourselves become the Person in the understanding of the multitude. And herein will ye, soon or late, come to grief.

16. But nevertheless, the confederacy heeded not the words of God. And God was grieved at heart, for Jehovih's sake.

CHAPTER XIV.

GOD PROVIDETH FOR THE BIRTH OF KA'YU.

1. God said: Behold, three conditions are now within the heavens of the earth; Anarchy by the false Gods and their slaves, the confederacy of the Holy Ghost, and the Faithists in Jehovih and His resurrections.

2. Now, therefore, let my chief loo'is come before me, and hear the decree of God.

3. The Lord said: When the chief loo'is had come before the throne, God said unto him:

4. Know then, O Thoanactus, thou shalt go down to the earth, to the land of Chine'ya, and by inspiration bring forth a birth, capable of the All Voice, but not capable of su'is. And thou shalt accomplish this service so that he shall be born into the mortal world at the time a'ji ceaseth to fall upon that land.

5. And thou shalt provide him with great learning and great adversity and great experience withal. For he shall establish the fundamental doctrines of the nations of Chine'ya. For his followers shall become the most numerous and peaceful inhabitants on the face of the earth.

6. And as thou preparest for his birth by thy mastery over the generations of mortals, so shalt thou, through these, thy hosts, raise up such as shall become disciples. For however great a man thou mightest raise up, it is wisdom to have also born into the mortal world, at the same era, such hosts of philosophers as shall follow him, and indorse his doctrines.

7. For by this means the establishment of Jehovih and His light amongst mortals shall extend the whole length and breadth of that land. How sayest thou?

8. Thoanactus said: Jehovih's will and thine be done. This is a most welcome labor, O God. And I know, the voices of my hosts are with me.

9. God said: In Jehovih's name, thee I crown, CHIEF OF THE HOSTS OF LOO'IS, for the land of Chine'ya, for the birth of an heir for the All Voice of the Great Spirit.

10. Thoanactus was then crowned, and his hosts were provided with badges by God, for they were filed before the throne, and hosts saluted, and departed with due ceremony.

11. Such, then, was God's labor for having born into the mortal world, after many generations, one that hath become known to the uttermost regions of the earth as KA'YU. Of him, more anon.

CHAPTER XV.
GOD PROVIDETH FOR THE BIRTH OF SAKAYA.

1. Again God called before his throne a million loo'is, and appointed Etchessa chief over them, saying:

2. Thou, O Etchessa, shalt go down to the earth, to the land of Vind'yu, taking these hosts with thee. And thou shalt establish a heavenly place of worship, which shall be thy headquarters.

3. Behold, I have given thee many generations in which to bring about the desired result. Survey thou, then, the generations of Faithists in that land, and take thy choice as to place and caste and family.

4. He, whom thou shalt bring forth for this purpose, shall be of some royal family, a prince of high estate.

5. I shall prove through him, that for love of righteousness, and to serve Jehovih, he will forsake his kingdom and family and friends, and all earthly things and desires, and make himself as a poor man, dwelling with the poor, laboring with them, teaching them, and instructing them.

6. For, because of the idolatries that will be amongst these people, they will be bound in caste; but he, whom I will teach through, shall prove unto the world that the service of Jehovih requireth of men, that Jehovih shall stand uppermost, even above kin and caste. In the example of which willing sacrifice, man shall be taught, that all the evils of the

earth can be overcome.

7. And thou shalt provide unto this man many disciples, and roadways for him to travel, and places to preach; and provide followers unto him, to go about with him. For without these, his preaching and practice would be of little avail. See to it, then, that thy hosts control the generations of men, that there may be born in the world a sufficient number, to be disciples and followers of his doctrines, that he may be a power in the world for re-establishing the Faithists in the Great Spirit.

8. And thou shalt so provide these births, that they will be of the same period of time. What sayest thou, Etchessa?

9. Etchessa said: In Jehovih's name I am thy servant, with rejoicing. And I answer thee also for these my hosts, that this is a joy unto them, for Jehovih's glory.

10. God said: To which end I crown thee, CHIEF OF LOO'IS, for the land of Vind'yu! And God crowned Etchessa; and he gave badges to the other loo'is.

11. And thereafter Etchessa and his hosts filed past the throne of God, duly saluting, and they also departed, going to the earth, to the land of Vind'yu. Thus were loo'is empowered of God, to bring into the world the heir. SAKAYA. More of him anon.

CHAPTER XVI.

MOSES IN HEAVEN PAYETH THE JUDGMENT OF JEHOVIH!

1. Hamonastas, one of the chief marshals of God, and for the heavenly city of Paradise, came before the throne, duly saluting, and saying:

2. O God, Son of Jehovih, I would speak before thee! God said: Speak thou, my son.

3. Hamonastas said: There standeth without the city of Paradise, beyond the pillars of fire, and in company with thy high-raised captains, one, Nu-ghan, delivered from one of the hells of Hassa, over Egupt, and he crieth out continually: O God, Son of Jehovih! Deliver me! Deliver thou me! O Moses! Moses! Moses!

4. He is distracted, continually using the same words over and over, without ceasing. Now behold, the nurses and physicians have tried all remedies they can invent, but failed utterly to break the spell upon him.

5. For seventy days have they labored, and, as a last resort, they have brought him hither, that they might learn from thee.

6. God said: Nu-ghan! Is this not one of the Pharaohs, who took up arms against the Faithists of Egupt? Return thou, Hamonastas, to the keepers of this man, and cause him to be blindfolded, that he may endure the light of the throne; after which thou and his keepers shall bring him before me.

7. Hamonastas saluted and departed, and after a certain time, returned with the keepers and with Nu-ghan, who was crying out unceasingly, even as had been said.

8. And now, when he was quite before the throne of God, God said to him: Behold me, I am God, Son of Jehovih: what wouldst thou?

9. But the man heard not what God said, but kept crying out as before. Whereupon God said unto the keepers: Remove ye the blinds a little, that the light may come upon him.

10. And they removed the blinds a little; but, lo and behold, the light made him more distracted than before. And when God saw his deplorable suffering, he inquired of his keepers, how long the man had been in hell, and they said: Seventy and six years, and in a

907

knot, three years!

11. God said: I know that this is Pharaoh, who persecuted the Jews. Take him again without the walls, and there retain him. I will send one of my swift messengers to Lika, in etherea, who knoweth the abiding place of Moses. Perhaps Moses put a curse upon him! If so, only Moses can deliver him.

12. And the keepers took the spirit, Nu-ghan, without the city, as commanded by God. And God sent Haeroponitis, sister of Raban, a swift messenger, in an arrow-ship of fire, to the etherean worlds, to Gussawanitcha, to Lika's sojourning place at that time, commanding her to lay the matter before the Nirvanian chief, Lika.

13. Hereupon the report continueth in the words of Haeroponitis, that is, these are her words, to wit: In not many days' time I came before Jehovih's throne, whereon sat Lika, through whose etherean provinces the solar phalanx was now traveling, and I told him the story of Nu-ghan.

14. Whereupon Lika, Son of Jehovih, said: Let my reporters of destinations go find Moses: and it if be that Moses put a judgment on Nu-ghan, then must Moses return to the lower heavens, and deliver him. The justice of Jehovih reacheth to all time and place.

15. Haeroponitis continued: Whereupon I saluted before the throne of Jehovih, and in company with the reporters of destinations, started forth again in the etherean realms, and after passing through seven worlds, and upward of three hundred Nirvanian kingdoms, we entered the plains of Sapeas, where are situated the colleges and schools of Embassies, belonging to the Ghiturpsan board of Ritivius. And here we found Moses!

16. Who no sooner looked upon us, having been told that he was inquired after, than he prophesied the cause.

17. Moses said: Alas me! Because thou hast come for me, thou hast awakened in me that which slept all these hundreds of years. Yea, it is true, I put a curse upon Pharaoh; for I said unto him: Thou shalt yet call upon me to deliver thee out of torments. And I added thereto, afterward, saying of the blood of the sacrifice of the lamb: This shall be the testimony of innocent blood against thyself and thy people for what the Hebrews have suffered.

18. Instead of this, I should have forgiven him. O Jehovih! Jehovih! I have sinned before Thee! And Thou hast searched me out after all these years, and brought the matter home to me.

19. Thou art just, O Thou Almighty! In Thy name and by Thy wisdom and power will I return to the lower heavens, and take in charge the man and people I adjudged!

20. And Moses wept; and he gave command to the builders to provide him at once with a suitable boat of great fleetness. And then Moses procured thirty thousand volunteers to go with him.

21. And when all things were in readiness, Moses took leave of his companions, and he and his hosts entered his fire-boat, and presently our two vessels were underway, as if in a race, for the red star, the earth. And, after some days, we arrived in the heavens of the earth, even at the city of Paradise, the abiding place of God.

22. Such is the brief heavenly report of Haeroponitis, for, on her arrival in Paradise, her mission was completed for the present.

23. When it was known in Paradise, that Moses was coming, great joy was manifested, for God and the Holy Eleven and the Holy Council, all desired to see Moses. And

God commanded the full board of marshals and also the musicians to go without the capital, and meet Moses, and escort him before the throne. And they accomplished these things; and Moses came before the throne of God, saluting in the sign, JUDGMENT OF TIME! And God answered him under the sign, THY LABOR IS OUR JOY AND GLORY!

24. And God said: In Jehovih's name, O Moses, come thou, and honor my throne.

25. And Moses went up, and sat on the throne, on the right hand of God. And Moses said unto the Holy Council and to the Holy Eleven:

26. Your God shall be my God. In his love and dominion am I cast by Jehovih's will, to deliver those that have suffered from me and my words.

27. God said: Shall we not have a day of recreation first?

28. Moses said: Nay; till I have delivered Nu-ghan, that was Pharaoh, there can be no peace. Suffer, therefore, thy marshals to go to the keepers of this man, and bring him before this throne.

29. And now again, after awhile, Nu-ghan was brought in, all muffled up, to keep the light from hurting him. And he was still crying out: O God, Son of Jehovih! O Moses! Moses! Moses!

30. And when Moses beheld this, he was nigh overcome by the pitiful scene. And Moses brushed away his tears, and rose up, raising his hands to Jehovih, saying: Light of Thy Light, O Jehovih. Power of Thy Power, O Jehovih! Deliver Thou him, whom I accursed! Put his griefs and sorrows upon me, that hath sinned against him!

31. A mantle of yellow light, cloud-like, descended upon Moses, as he stood transfixed before Jehovih. All the place was still as death!

32. The blinds and muffles on Nu-ghan fell off, and he stood silent and motionless, gazing with fixed awe upon the holy scene, and upon Moses on the throne of God!

33. The spirit of Jehovih moved upon the holy place, and the musicians felt the power. It was the light of one who was mighty, from the etherean worlds!

34. Gently, then, the music of ten thousand voices fell upon the holy audience. First mild, as if far off, then louder and louder, as if coming near, till soon the words of the anthem proclaimed Jehovih's praise.

35. Nu'ghan turned not his eyes from the glory of Moses and the etherean mantle, for he knew Moses, even as it were but yesterday they parted in Egupt, on the earth.

36. Slowly, now, Moses lowered his upstretched arms, and his hands were brilliant, like yellow fire. And Moses said, solemnly: All praise to Thee, Jehovih! (Eloih!) Thou art just, Thou Almighty Creator!

37. Nu-ghan added: For through Him is all deliverance, worlds without end. In Thy praise will I sing forever, O Jehovih. Thou, Most High God of Moses, my Deliverer. Make me strong, O Jehovih, that I can look upon him, whom I persecuted and abused.

38. Then Moses looked upon Pharaoh (Nu-ghan) and said: These things had to be. Thou wert the last of the pyramidal age of man, and I the first founder of the migration of the righteous. All things are done by Jehovih, in His own way and time.

39. As, by my curse upon thee and thy people, have I been bound to come back to deliver thee and them; so, by thy curse against Israel, shalt thou now return down to the earth, and labor to lift up Israel.

40. For Israel hath fallen from communities, and hath taken to kings, after the manner of the heathen and idolater. Her people are divided and broken up, and many of them have

become worshipers of the false Gods, Baal and Ashtaroth.

41. Yea, they are forgetful of my commandment of peace and love, and have taken to war and to earthly aggrandizement.

42. And thou shalt take with thee ten thousand angels of exalted grades, and go down to the earth, to the habitations of the Israelites; and, by inspiration, thou and thy hosts shall select and inspire such of the Israelites as are within reach of inspiration, and thou shalt take them away from all other of their people, and from the heathen and idolatrous tribes, that are around about them.

43. And thou and thy hosts shall abide with these mortals hundreds of years; re-establishing them in peace and non-resistance, after the manner of the doctrines in the es'sean worlds. And thou shalt call them, Es'seans, that they may be distinguished from all other peoples.

44. Nu-ghan said: Thy decree is most just, O Moses, and I know of a truth thy words are Jehovih's. I pray thee, how long shall this labor be for me and my hosts?

45. Moses said: Some hundreds of years! Until thou hast raised a light sufficient unto Jehovih, that peace and love and the doctrine of good for evil be again re-established from the blood of the Israelites, even as by the blood of the lamb, I delivered Jehovih's people out of Egupt.

46. And when thou hast perfected the generations of the Es'seans, thou shalt have sent to thee from the throne of God certain loo'is, and they will labor with thee until an Israelite is born into the mortal world capable of the Father's Voice.

47. Nu-ghan said: Hear me now in my plea, O Moses, thou, Son of the Most High: When I died, as to the earth, and entered heaven, as to these worlds, I found my kingdom, as to what was before me, in heaven waiting for me.

48. And they were miserable, being beggars and slaves and idiots, because of the slavery I had put upon them in the earth-life. And I could not escape them, or put them aside. If I went away objectively, then subjectively I remembered them, and was drawn back to them.

49. Yea, I was like a young colt that first being haltered, pulleth away, but faileth; then pulleth again, and faileth, and so on, until he findeth he can not escape, then tamely submitteth; even so was I bound to my kingdom, and obliged in the end to yield and become a slave unto them, to provide for them. For I had so dispoiled them of their talents, they were as helpless as infants; and many of them wicked in the extreme.

50. Nevertheless, I accepted that which I could not escape; I toiled with them hundreds of years, restoring them as well as I could. And in time a ray of happiness came to me, in the hope that in hundreds of years to come I should find my way out.

51. But, alas me! darkness (a'ji) came upon my already dark heaven. My evil ones, such as I had had slaughtered on earth, came upon me for vengeance sake. Anarchy overflooded me and my people. They became very demons of madness, and they seized me, and bound me, and bruised me and suffocated me with their horrid smells. Millions of them! And their curses pierced me like poisoned arrows. Long I fought them; and I cried out unto thee and to Jehovih! But, alas! I was in hell. None could hear my prayers. For days and months and years I held out, but only to experience new and more terrible horrors!

52. How long this woe was upon me, I know not. I only remember, that my soul sickened

within me; and I felt a sinking and a fainting, like an endless death, that could not extinguish me. To me it seemed ten thousand ages!

53. Suddenly I find myself here! Distracted before thee, thou holy Son of the Great Spirit! Whence came I? What hath occurred? Or is this but a spell of delirious dream? And will I relapse again into yonder terrible nightmare of horrors? How can I go hence, that mine old kingdom come not upon me?

54. Do they not wait hereabout somewhere? To seize me again, for renewed torments? O teach me, thou, Moses! How can I fulfill thy righteous judgment? And not be entrapped again, and, perhaps, forever!

55. Moses said: I will give thee a new name, and I will clothe thee in garments of mine own making, so they will rather flee from thee, than come to thee.

56. And Moses gathered up of the yellow, cloud-like mantle, and made a mantle, and clothed Nu-ghan; and he named him, Illaes, signifying, Servant of Light. And after that, he was provided with ten thousand co-laborers, assisted by Gafonaya, and sent back to the earth, on his mission.

57. And God appointed one hundred messengers unto Pharaoh, that word might be transmitted every month to Paradise.

CHAPTER XVII.

1. God proclaimed a day of recreation in Paradise, that the inhabitants might meet Moses and his hosts, and rejoice therewith. And great was that day in Paradise.

2. On the following day, Moses departed for the Eguptian people, that had been in hell with Nu-ghan, going to the place of deliverance. And there were of these spirits, eleven millions four hundred thousands. And Moses conferred with the inspectors as to places, and having decided on a convenient region, Elaban, he ordered their removal thither.

3. And Moses went with them to Elaban, an isolated region on the Aratesaian plateau, and remained with them one hundred and twelve days, establishing them with nurseries, hospitals and factories; and he appointed officers for them, to every group and series, going amongst them in person and ministering to tens of thousands of them, and providing them places of worship.

4. After that, Moses appointed Salesmon as captain over them. Thereafter, Moses departed, and returned to Paradise, where he remained two days more, and then took leave, and departed for his own heavenly place in Nirvania. But ere he departed, he said: When the a'ji'an forest is past and gone, and it be Jehovih's will, I shall return again to look after my hosts.

5. And now was God's attention directed to the Hebrews, the Faithists of western Arabin'ya, where the God Baal had gained access and power; having affiliated with one, Dagon, a false God, located in those regions, who maintained six earthly oracle-houses and a small heavenly kingdom of his own.

6. And it came to pass, that the Hebrews were a divided people. A small minority of them still worshipped Jehovih, having colleges of prophecy and places of learning. But the great majority of them were worshipers of the Lord and God, believing the Great Spirit was only a large man in heaven, after the manner of Baal, or Dagon, or Ashtaroth, or any other God.

7. God said of them: Though they pretend to be of many kinds, I see but two: Those who worship the Ever Present, Jehovih; and those who are drifting into heathenism.

8. Mine eyes behold the true Faithists with colleges and with books of learning; but, as for the others, they are becoming consulters of the oracles (spirits), the same as the heathens.

9. How can they remain a united people? The Gods of one city and temple teach one doctrine, and the Gods of another place teach another doctrine.

10. God had previously sent to Ebeneezer one, Jerub, with ten thousand assistant angel strategists, to be with the king of the Faithists. Jerub now asked for other ten thousand, and God sent them to him. And God said unto Jerub:

11. A war will presently result between Baal and Ashtaroth and Dagon and Haughak; and these Gods will not only war in heaven, but they will carry their battles down to mortals.

12. And the Israelites will not only forsake their ancient doctrine of peace, but will become great warriors, both against other nations and peoples, and against one another.

13. Take thou heed, O Jerub, of the words of thy God; and whilst Baal and Ashtaroth are in conflict and neglectful of the temples and oracles, possess thou them.

14. Better is it, that these false Gods win unto themselves as dutiful subjects, five angels, than one mortal.

15. Guard thou well all the colleges of prophecy against the emissaries of these false Gods. And see to it, that the worshipers of Jehovih have born unto themselves a goodly number of prophets.

CHAPTER XVIII.
THE MEANING AND ORIGIN OF THE TERM, HOLY GHOST.

1. There came to Paradise, God's heavenly place, one, Taenas, a messenger from the chiefs of the so-called Holy Confederacy. God's chief marshal conducted him before God, and, being commanded to speak, he said:

2. Greeting to thee, O God. In behalf of the Three Sons of the Holy Ghost I come before thee to proclaim their words. I have been instructed by them, what to say, and I declare unto thee, O God, my words are their words.

3. First, that thou mayest hear us before we are adjudged; second, as thou claimest liberty to think and to speak for thyself, so do we all. And wherein error cometh of our proceedings, it is our own matter, and not thine.

4. As thou sayest: Behold the All Person, so do not we say; but we say: Behold the all expanse; it is but a shadow, a ghost. And for convenience sake, we name it, Holy Ghost.

5. Is not this our privilege? Who can deny us? Hath one man rightful dominion over another? Or one captain, or one God?

6. God said: Proceed.

7. Taenas said: And we be right, then shall we of our own selves judge what we will do. But if thou be right, and this thing be an All Person, thou art then His servant to do His will. Are these points true?

8. God said: It seemeth so.

9. Taenas said: And liberty to both sides?

10. God said: Yea.

11. Taenas said: When I was a child, I was helped to walk; but now I am strong, I walk alone. Wherein then shall not my judgment also walk alone?

12. God said: Proceed thou, and I will speak afterward.

13. Taenas said: We have seen in ages past, that peace hath been forever proclaimed by the followers of Jehovih; and that both on earth and in heaven such people become the sufferers and victims of tyrants of earth and of false Gods in heaven.

14. We propose war, in the name of the Holy Ghost, both on earth and in heaven. We can have no war with thee or thy people, on earth, or in heaven; for thou and thy people, angels and mortals, are all peace, warring not.

15. Our wars can be only with warriors. I put the matter thus: Thou hast a virgin daughter, and a villain assail her; thy doctrine is, to rush in and take thy daughter away from him; our doctrine is, to beat him away from her.

16. We behold evil Gods and evil spirits, assailing virtuous people on earth and in heaven. We propose to war them to destruction, for righteousness sake. More then are we to thy favor, O God, than against thee.

17. We dip our hands in blood, for sake of peace and virtue, for sake of liberty and knowledge. We shall say to the man of earth: Thou shalt become learned: To the es'yan in heaven: Thou shalt not return to mortals, but remain in thy place, and become learned and virtuous.

18. For which reason we come to thee, O God, that thou mayest know our foundation.

19. God said: Who then sayest thou, men and angels shall worship?

20. Taenas said: In this, we command them not. But we give them liberty to worship whomsoever they will.

21. God said: Thou hast said: Our doctrine is, to beat the villain away from the virgin; but what wilt thou, or thy example, teach?

22. Taenas answered: That an assailant deserveth punishment.

23. God said: And wilt thou say to the peaceful and virtuous: Take up arms, give your enemies torments?

24. Taenas answered: Yea, verily.

25. God said: And by what authority, if they inquire of thee?

26. Taenas said: By authority of the Holy Ghost, and the Father (the Confederacy), and by the Son, that is, each and every Lord of the Confederacy.

27. For we shall teach mortals and angels that all things are by law; and the word, law, shall take the place of the term, Great Spirit, or Jehovih.

28. God said: Hear me, then, O Taenas, and in love bear my words to thy so-called Triune Confederacy, and to the high leaders, saying to them: thus saith God of Paradise, Son of Jehovih, according to the light of this throne:

29. Ye shall triumph for a long season on earth and in heaven; but not in the way ye suppose.

30. For ye will be forced to provide a worshipful head for mortals and angels. And it will come to pass, your three heavenly places will become known on earth and in heaven as the Triune Gods, or Trinity!

31. And the people will worship an imaginary figure of three parts, Father, Son and Holy Ghost. And this will become their idol; and he will be accredited with love, anger, jealousy and favoritism, war and destruction.

32. Because ye say: Give punishment to the wicked, ye open the door of all evil. For he, who hath a quarrel with his neighbor, will accuse him as deserving punishment. They, that are in darkness, and being mighty, will fall upon the weak, and slay them.

33. A quarrel will ensue in your three heavenly kingdoms, and ye will become as three false Gods. And since ye profess not the All Person, each of ye three Gods will be forced to announce himself as such.

34. For the rule applieth to all men and to all angels, that they, who deny an All Highest Person in the Creator, become establishers of idolatry unto themselves.

35. Thou hast said: We shall leave mortals and angels to worship whom they will. Why, then, is it not well to worship Baal? And Dagon? And Ashtaroth? And yet, these Gods make slaves of their subjects, that worship them.

36. Taenas said: Nay, they are evil Gods. We will deliver their slaves into freedom.

37. God said: Who is master, and who is slave? Either on earth, or in heaven? Why not abolish your Triune Confederacy, lest ye rule over others? And you profess liberty, why not practice it?

38. Because ye proclaim liberty as your chief object, ye will entice the unlearned and the truant and the idle and the lazy; for all these claim their weaknesses as the boon of liberty.

39. It shall come to pass, in the far-distant future, your kingdoms will be made up of the lowest grades. And they will pull you all down from your present high resolves; and ye will become tyrants and evil Gods yourselves, and meet the fate of all your predecessors.

40. The earth and the heavens thereof were given into my keeping, for the resurrection of all the inhabitants; but I have neither commission nor desire to accomplish dominion by violence. As ye have withdrawn from my kingdoms, it is an act of your own.

41. Even mine own grief at your secession showeth me, how short I am in comprehending Jehovih's ways. For I declare unto thee, O Taenas, and through thee to thy chiefs, that though your course seemeth evil in my sight, yet will it be proven in the distant future, that Jehovih will appropriate your labors to an ultimate good.

42. Thus said the God of heaven and earth: Go thou therefore with my words to the chiefs of the Triunes. I part with you all, as a father parteth with a son, that goeth into a consuming fire.

43. Taenas said: In reverence to thee, O God, I go to them, that pity thee for thy too peaceful ways.

44. Thereupon, Taenas saluted in reverence, and departed, going his way.

CHAPTER XIX.

1. God called up Erastes, prince of messengers, and he said unto him: Thou hast heard the words of thy God and of Taenas. Take therefore thirty thousand and four hundred messengers, that is, one for each and all of my remaining kingdoms, and go and proclaim the same unto them, that they, having due notice, may manage their affairs with wisdom and foresight. Erastes said: Jehovih's will and thine be done! And he saluted and withdrew, going to the palace of the messengers, and choosing his hosts, whom he instructed in regard to the message. And he gave to each of them power to choose their own officers, and to provide their own vessels of travel. And in not many days thereafter, they all departed.

2. Now it came to pass, that the following kingdoms soon fell to pieces, and drifted into the Triune Confederacy, namely: Sho'e'gan, and her twenty-eight sub-kingdoms, all in the hadan regions; Ghi'e'wan, and her forty-four heavenly hadan kingdoms; Haotus, with seven heavenly hadan kingdoms, and five sub-kingdoms; Tuwahtal, and thirty kingdoms in the first resurrection in the plateau Theovrahkistan; Livragga, and seventy-one heavenly sub-kingdoms, of which thirty-eight were ready to enter the second resurrection; Jahkin and Mouru, with ninety-seven heavenly hadan kingdoms, of which eighty-seven were promoted to the second resurrection; Ganzoe, with four hundred hadan kingdoms, of which many were below the first resurrection; Hapsu, with four heavenly kingdoms of seventy million angels in the second resurrection; Iturba, with twelve heavenly kingdoms of one hundred and four million angels in the second resurrection, half of whom were as high as fifty in the grades; Wantawacha, with thirty heavenly kingdoms, with three hundred million angels in the second resurrection, three-fourths of whom were upward of grade fifty.

3. Of the seven lower kingdoms of the second sphere, there were eight hundred million angels of the first resurrection, who migrated from their provinces to the Triune regions, Amesha; and they destroyed the road behind them.

4. Now, when God saw the great secession of his heavenly kingdoms, and their allegiance to the Triunes, his soul was filled with sorrow. And the Voice of Jehovih came to him, saying: Why takest thou sorrow to thy soul for these things? Shall a God grieve, because his burden is made lighter? Behold, in this day and hour the Gods and Lords of the Triune are rejoicing with great joy, because of these accessions. Yea, they perceive not, what a load they are taking on their own shoulders.

5. But thou shalt send agents amongst the Triunes, especially into their capitals and their chief kingdoms.

6. So, God appointed many agents, different from messengers, for they were to be under the command of none but God. God said unto them: Ye shall go to the places I appoint unto each one of you, as travelers and sojourners in your own way, and observe the doings of the Triunes, especially the chiefs and leaders, Lords and Gods, and their teaching and government, and in your own good time depart out of the place and return hither and inform my Holy Council and my Holy Eleven.

7. And the agents went forth as commanded.

CHAPTER XX.
OF THE CONFEDERACY OF THE HOLY GHOST, CALLED THE TRINITY.

1. The Lord said: The three heavenly kingdoms, Heractu, Eta-shong and Hapsendi, of the Triunes, were independent, but allianced for offence and defence against the evil Gods, Baal, Dagon, Shulleth, Ashtaroth and others, whose angel subjects were kept in slavery, and for evil purposes.

2. Now, therefore, the Triunes jointly declared war, to the end that peace might be secured in these heavens.

3. Nevertheless, each of the Triunes had charge of his own heavens and over such part of the earth as was covered by his heavens.

4. For they had divided up and appropriated both, the earth and the heavens, into three parts, one to each of them.

5. Here followeth, then, the history of the wars of the Triunes:

6. First, of Looeamong and the false Gods he overthrew:

7. A triangular was was going on in hada and on earth betwixt the angel armies of Baal, Dagon and Ashtaroth, in which ten thousand million angels were engaged under them.

8. Looeamong declared war against the whole of them, and impressed into his service eight thousand million angel warriors.

9. Ashtaroth, the most vengeful Goddess, had previously sent hundreds of millions of her warring angels down to the apostate Jews, to inspire them to wars and cruelties on one another, hoping, to exterminate them, lest they become Baal's subjects. And yet other millions of warring angels had she sent to the Parsi'e'an cities, and to the Eguptian cities, Daskrath, Babylon and Gonassah and Tyre and Romaxain and to the kings and queens of many other great cities, to inspire them to send forth armies to destroy, not only the worshipers of Jehovih, but all people that worshiped Baal, or Dagon, or any other God.

10. Baal, on the other hand, had sent hundreds of millions of his warring angels down to the earth, to Heleste and the west regions, and to the Israelites as well, inspiring mortals to war against the east kingdoms, especially Babylon and Daskrath, two mighty cities in the dominions of the Goddess Ashtaroth.

11. And the armies of mortals were moved forth by the armies of angels, whom they saw not; war raged east and west and north and south.

12. Looeamong, the Triune, said: I will spoil them both. I will send an angel army of warriors down to the middle kingdoms, to the great tyrant, Cyrus. I will possess the oracles and direct Cyrus to march against Parsi'e. He shall make an alliance with the Argos'yans.

13. Hatchesan and Karsoka shall be my countries. And the cities of Hemia and Babylon and Nine'vah and Gassakad and Hannedan and Saluem shall bow down no more to Baal and Ashtaroth, forever.

14. Belus shall be mine, and the cities and temples of Hina and Maroth and Hovan and Torres and Delfi; and the habitations of Phires and Somak and Macedon and Thues, and the great oracle-houses of Myrsilus and Myrsus and Gyges and Simon and Gamma and Fabiyan and Sulus and Craz'ya and Wakadya and P'hrid and Gemnae and Ma'zan and R'hodae.

15. By force will I possess them; yea, by force drive hence all other angels and Gods. And my warrior angels shall possess these temples, so that whoso cometh to consult the Gods shall receive mine own answers. I will drive mortals to war in mine own way, and to whatever place I determine to subdue or destroy.

16. Equally menacing were the boasts of the Goddess Ashtaroth; she had said: Whether I despoil heaven and earth, I care not. If I can not possess them, I will destroy them, so that no God shall possess them.

17. Into festering knots and hells will I cast tens of thousands of millions of angels, in case I do not succeed in winning all.

18. I will send millions of warring angels down to Xerxes, the Parsi'e'an king, and to his kingdom, and they shall obsess every man, woman and child to desperate madness against the Argos'yans and the middle and west nations.

19. I will lead Xerxes forth with the mightiest army that has ever been on the earth. And they shall despoil all regions, whithersoever they march.

20. For I will make Xerxes and all the Parsi'e'ans believe, they are doing these things for their own prosperity and glory, and for despoiling their own enemies.

21. And, after Xerxes hath despoiled and conquered all the earth regions, Baal and all other Gods shall be driven away from the oracles and temples. Xerxes shall issue a decree, abolishing all other Gods but me, Ashtaroth.

22. And, when I am thus well anchored on the earth, I will turn my legions against this new upstart God, the Triune, Looeamong. And I will cast him into a hell, from which he shall not escape forever.

23. So, Ashtaroth concentrated her heavenly warriors into this great and desperate work. For she had been maturing her plans, even before Xerxes came to the throne of Parsi'e. And, since, in those days, the kings and rich men in all those countries consulted the spirits, in reference to all important undertakings, it was not a difficult feat for Ashtaroth to obsess the millions of Parsi'e'ans to carry out her project.

24. Accordingly, Ashtaroth commanded her marshals to summon two thousand million angel warriors, men and women, for the work in hand. And when they came to Neabissa, a heavenly region to the north, over the earth-mountains Afflo'yagga, she caused Mateus, her chief orator, to prepare a speech in her behalf, and have it declaimed before the angel warriors.

25. Mateus, a one-time Lord to Osiris, nine hundred years previous, now made the speech, and this that followeth is a synopsis, to wit:

26. I, Goddess of all the heavens and of the whole earth. Behold, me, Ashtaroth! The earth and the heavens are mine, saith Ashtaroth! I clove the sun in twain; for it is mine. I clove the pieces again; for they were mine. From these I made the stars and the moon. But the great earth I made as my foot-stool; for it was mine, and ever shall be.

27. I peopled it over with all the living; they were my creation. And ye also are mine. I peopled the stars, and gave to the inhabitants thereof great delights. And the earth and my heavens were places of great delight. For I gave bountifully to all my children.

28. But the inhabitants of the far-off stars quarreled because of an evil God, Baal. And they cast him out. And he came here to despoil me and my heavenly places. Witness ye my beloved. I could destroy him with my little finger. But he is unworthy of your Goddess. To you I give the glory to capture him, and cast him into hell, and torture him forever.

29. But lest other evil Gods take possession of his earthly places, they shall also be destroyed. Hear ye then the command of Ashtaroth, which is, that ye shall go down to the earth, and obsess and inspire the Parsi'e'ans to march forth and destroy all other people on the earth, beginning first with the stronghold of Baal, in Argos, where he hath many sub-Gods under him, where the Argos'yans, not knowing him, call him, Zeus.

30. And to whoso proveth valorous amongst my angel warriors, will I give great promotion and glory, and thousands and millions of slaves. For when Baal is overcome and cast into hell, ye shall take his angel slaves, and possess them yourselves, according to your valorous deeds.

31. Ashtaroth then officered her angel hosts, and sent them down to the earth, and they were distributed by the captains and generals around about Parsi'e. Being directed to preside in the presence of mortals by day, inspiring them to war against Argos, and to be with them at night, and talk to them spiritually in dreams and visions.

32. And it came to pass, that Xerxes and the people, the Parsi'e'ans, were moved to go forth and destroy the Argos'yans. And king Xerxes took two and a half million soldiers with him for his army. And so great was the inspiration and obsession of Ashtaroth's angels, that they caused another two and a half million of Parsi'e'ans to go with Xerxes' soldiers. So that Xerxes' whole army was five millions of souls, which was the largest army on earth, that ever had been, or ever shall be.

CHAPTER XXI.

1. Baal, God of the Argos'yans (Greeks), called together two thousand million angel warriors, and after properly officering them, caused them to assemble in Beth'hagas, a sub-kingdom of heaven over the Tillag mountains, to the north of Macedon, and he said unto them:

2. Behold, your Creator, who I am! By my breath upon the earth ye came forth. I am he, who was of old called, De'yus, Lord God of heaven and earth. All places are my places, all dominion is mine.

3. My heavens gave I unto you for your inheritance forever. But an evil Goddess, Ashtaroth, hath come to despoil you.

4. And she hath sworn upon her thighs to cast you into endless torments.

5. Behold, I have sworn a new oath on the sun and moon and stars! Ye shall capture her, and cast her and all her angels into hell, to so abide forever.

6. For I will clear the heavens and the earth, and they shall be clean and full of delight.

7. Hear ye, then, the commandment of your God, Baal, ruler of heaven and earth: Ye shall go down to the earth, to the Argos'yans, and obsess them, man, woman and child, and inspire them to terrible deeds of blood and havoc and death against the Parsi'e'ans who are coming against them.

8. And whilst ye are thus providing corporeal destruction for this evil Goddess, my heavenly hosts under Yaawochad, my Lord of Agansetha, shall attack her angel armies in every quarter of these heavens.

9. And as fast as her drujas are captured, they shall be cast into the hells of Gotha, which I have prepared for them. And to all my valorous workers will I give great promotion and power. Ye shall have servants and slaves without number.

10. Now, it came to pass, that many years of war and destruction ensued; but Baal's hosts were too powerful for Ashtaroth. And so Baal not only overcame her angel warriors on the earth, but in her heavenly capital also. And his legions rushed upon her, and captured her. Whereat her own angels turned against her, perceiving now that she was an imposter, and not the Creator.

11. And they bound her, and carried her and her Lords and Gods off to Toosemmes, a heavenly place of foul smells, in Gotha, and they built here a place of torment for her and them, and cast them in. And they brought hither tens of thousands of her officers, and cast them in, and also the spirits of kings and queens and of generals and captains who had been her devotees, who were slain in battle, and who were yet in chaos.

12. Thus ended the God-ship of Ashtaroth. And there were thus cast into this hell, voluntary and involuntary, two thousand million angels.

13. Looeamong, the Triune God, said: This is the end, number one; next shall fall Baal;

and him will I cast in hell also.

14. As to mortals, Xerxes' mighty armies lived not to return to Parsi'e, but were scattered and destroyed. As to the Argos'yans, they were a ruined people.

15. And all those countries were covered over with the spirits of the dead, in chaos.

16. For these wars had been going on for many, many years.

17. Hear ye, next of Kabalactes, Triune God of Vind'yu and her heavens.

CHAPTER XXII.
OF KABALACTES, TRIUNE, GOD OF VIND'YU, AND HER HEAVENS.

1. Kabalactes said: Since Vind'yu and her heavens are to be mine, forever, I will take mine own time, and make a sure foundation. First, then, I will build me a heavenly city, Haractu, above the mountains of Yammalaga, twelve miles high, and the wings thereof shall spread out, broad as the land of Vind'yu.

2. And I will build me a heavenly palace in Haractu, and adorn it in splendor; and it shall also have wings on every side; and the wings shall be the habitations for my officers, my select and Holy Council.

3. And when Haractu is thus completed, I will send word into all the heavens of the earth, saying: Come and see Haractu, the heavenly seat of the Holy Ghost; the most glorious city of the Holy Confederacy of the Triune.

4. And then shall my legion of angel warriors go forth to battle in these my heavens; and they shall despoil all the false Lords and false Gods worshipped in Vind'yu. One of the two choices will I give unto them, to bow down in obedience to me and to the Triune and to the Holy Ghost, or to be cast into hell.

5. One by one shall Gods and tyrants fall by my hand; I will destroy them utterly and forever.

6. Kabalactes then organized his heavenly kingdom; creating his officers and apportioning his angels amongst them, according to the labor allotted to them.

7. And he build the heavenly city, Haractu, and adorned it in great splendor. And he provided hospitals for the sick and imbecile, and nurseries for es'yans, and factories for workmen and schools and colleges for great learning.

8. Look, he said, I have provided places for the poor, the sick, the unlearned, the helpless and the imbecile, even before I provided a place for myself. There is a God for you. Behold, I am the servant of the Triune, the Father and the Holy Ghost.

9. My doctrine is: To labor for others first, and for one's self afterward. And since ye perceive that my doctrine is a holy doctrine, ye shall establish it, come what may. For, though I am good, I am also power and majesty, in great anger to overcome evil, and establish righteousness and liberty.

10. These, then, were the chiefs of Kabalactes' staff, to wit: Pedmon, Laer, Yodava, Craosha, Varaga Sin Tse, Karapa (the false Mithra), Haekiha, Yutobis (the false Christna), Lumbothia, Doravva, Etchwalactcha (the false Vishnu), Myrrhes, Sepia, Tidon (the false Ari), Onatuhu, Durhea (the false Durga), Indra, Kali, Hosanne, Wahtissa (the false Agni), Owella (the false Rana), Gur (the false Siva), Hiak, Cassavragga (the false Trimurthi), Howgotha and Ithra. And as captains: Sarama, Janessa, Anatheia, Thodica and Janurs.

11. But all the foregoing assumed many false names, both on earth and in heaven, so that no history could reveal who they were, or by their names distinguish where their dominions lay.

12. Kabalactes had said unto his chiefs: Behold, mortals have many favorite names for worship. Go ye down to the earth, to Vind'yu, and possess the temples of spirit communion, the oracle houses and whatever places mortals come to worship in, and these places shall be yours.

13. And to whatever Lord or God, mortals most incline to bow down, take ye the name of that Lord or God.

14. For I give this law unto you, that ye shall possess the land of Vind'yu, not with new names, but with the old, but all unto one end, which is the establishing of the Triune Godhead.

15. Kabalactes then made Pedmon commander-in-chief over his angel warriors, and dispatched them down to the earth, to Vind'yu.

16. After this, Kabalactes raised an army of two thousand million angels to fight his heavenly battles. Over these he crowned Yettaba, Lord in chief.

17. In addition to the heavenly attractions of war, Kalabactes provided six groups of musicians of half a million to each group.

18. He also instituted times and places for tournaments, processions and the display of great pageantry.

19. He said: I will not only be powerful in might, but powerful in attractions, above all other Gods.

20. Now, even as hath been told of the wars of Looeamong, even so, but in a different place, were the terrible conflicts in the heavens of Kabalactes, which were also manifested on the mortals of Vind'yu.

21. So it came to pass, in a few hundred years, that that country was but a land of ruins, but over it, in every direction, were hundreds of millions of angels in chaos, being the spirits of those slain in the wars.

22. Kabalactes said: Now will I clear away the ruins, and build my everlasting edifice on the earth.

23. Behold, I will remodel the sacred books of mortals in mine own way.

24. In these signs will I rebuild: The triangle, representing the three lights, the Son, the Father and the Holy Ghost.

25. I will re-establish the tau (bull), as the sign of my power. And because my heavens are The All Pure, the tau shall be white.

26. The wheel (jaugernot) shall be my road-mark.

27. These signs shall be given unto my mortal subjects, to be theirs forever.

28. And whoso paradeth my signs, shall know that they are my covenant which I have made unto mortals.

29. Kabalactes then appointed twelve thousand four hundred and eighty-eight angels, to go down to Vind'yu, to re-write the sacred books of mortals.

30. And he crowned Gaonaza chief of the inspiring host.

31. To write the five great books, five mortals had been previously chosen from before their birth, by the guardian angels appointed for the purpose.

32. These men were: Harritza, to write the Avesta; Vraghettes, to write the Vendidad;

Royhoh, to write the Vispered; Yathavah, to write the Yacna; and Uzariah, to write the Khordavesta.

33. The angels chosen by Kabalactes in heaven, were sent down to these mortals in infancy, to guard them for the time of their birth upward. And the angels were divided into watches, sufficient to keep away all other angels, to be with their mortal wards day and night, to converse with them in their dreams, to give them visions and good habits and virtue and truth and wisdom.

34. And it came to pass that when these mortals were grown up, and the time came for their work, they were with their guardian spirits as one, knowing and comprehending the voice of their master, Kabalactes, whom they were inspired to call Ahura'Mazda, because this name was pleasing to mortals.

35. Gaonaza, commander of the inspiring hosts, distributed the twelve LIGHTS OF THE THRONE, the angels in rapport with the five mortals, to each of them, save to Harritza, and to him he gave four.

36. And now, when the writing was to be done, the following was to be the manner of inspiration, to wit:

37. The writer was previously inspired to be at his post at dawn in the morning, and to have all things in readiness for writing half an hour before sunrise, and to write until sunrise.

38. And the angels in rapport stood beside him, lying their hands upon him. Next to these angels stood another angel, with hands upon them; and, after that one, stood another, and so on, for one thousand angels in a line, extending in a direct line toward Haractu, the heavenly seat of Kabalactes. And from the extreme thousandth angel in line on, up to the heavenly throne, were stretched three cords of es'ean light, even to the Holy Council, before whom spake the chief of the ten thousand, as previously instructed by Kabalactes.

39. And, as this chief spake in heaven, the es of his voice passed down to the mortal, who framed in earth-words that which was spoken in heaven.

40. Jehovih hath said: Two kinds of spiritual inspiration have I created for mortals: To the individual man, individual spirits; but, to him that laboreth for the resurrection, a line of angels extending to the kingdoms in heaven.

41. And it that line have a good work on hand, I break it not; but if it be for self, it will break of its own accord.

42. Thus were written the sacred books of Vind'yu, the mutilated remains of which survive to this day. And copies of these books were written on cloth and on paper and on stone; some of which were carried in different directions over Vind'yu.

43. In eighty-seven years Kabalactes completed the sacred books, and disbanded the inspiring hosts.

44. So far Kabalactes had destroyed nine million men, women and children in the wars. He had also destroyed four thousand heathen temples, and more than three hundred cities. And he suppressed over two hundred languages, and banished six thousand two hundred false Lords.

45. He also commanded all languages to be hereafter made out of Vedic, Yi'ha and Zend, from which Sanscrit descended, as it is to this day.

46. Hear ye next of the Triune God, Ennochissa, of the heavenly place, Eta-shong, over Chine'ya.

CHAPTER XXIII.

1. Ennochissa said: According to the splendor of a kingdom, so is the ruler thereof glorified: this I have learned. Therefore Eta-shong shall surpass all other heavenly places. Thus spake he before his Lords.

2. Vazista said: Thy Lords are of the same mind. As for Looeamong and Kabalactes, they are more bent on the affairs of earth than of heaven.

3. Ennochissa spent two hundred years in building and beautifying his heavenly city, Eta-shong, employing more than two thousand million slaves for that purpose.

4. And, as to his heavenly palace, and the palace of his Holy Council, in grandeur and magnificence, the like had not been before in any of the lower heavens.

5. The circuit of the columns of fire, of which there were one million, was equal to half the breadth of the land of Chine'ya. In the front of his palace were four hundred thousand arches and pillars, and leading up to the foot of the throne, seventy rises (stair-steps), with a breadth of one thousand lengths. In front of the arches was an arena, four thousand lengths across, and this was ornamented with one hundred thousand fountains of fire and water. Interspersed, here and there, on the walls and arches, were hanging gardens of flowers, and drapery of gold and silver.

6. And as to the workmanship displayed, it was so fine that no language can convey an idea thereof to mortal understanding, save, indeed, it be said, everything was represented that is on the earth and in the heavens thereof.

7. The officers of the palace, next in grade below the Holy Council, the Lords, marshals and recorders, were generals, captains, inspectors, surveyors, receivers and builders, and these were all above grade ninety.

8. There were maintained within the palace arena half a million es'enaurs and trumpeters, four million fire and water servants, and three million bearers of burdens; and yet, beside these, there were six million caterers and servants.

9. Only officers of rank could cross the arena, or approach the arches by walking upright; all others had to crawl on their bellies in approaching the throne, saying prayers the while.

10. Now, although the other Triunes had great capitals and palaces, they were not to be compared with Ennochissa's.

11. Thus labored this Triune, even to the neglect of his earthly dominions.

12. And it came to pass that God, Jehovih's Son, in Paradise sowed the seed of faith in Chine'ya in favor of the Creator; so that, by the end of two hundred years, nearly all the spirits of the dead went not to the Triune, but to God in Paradise.

13. And God's angel missionaries went into this Triune's heavenly kingdom, and won many converts to Jehovih.

14. So that Ennochissa discovered, indeed, that his heavenly kingdom was losing ground.

15. Thereupon he resolved to enter the field of war, and to destroy all mortals in Chine'ya that worshipped the Great Spirit. And he also resolved to drive out from his heavens all angels who believed in Jehovih, or who were missionaries unto the kingdom of God.

16. Of all the Triunes, Ennochissa was the first to declare war against Jehovih, which was exactly in opposition to his own professions, when the Confederacy was first formed.

17. From this time on, Ennochissa was called by the Faithists in heaven, a false God.

18. As yet, the other two Triunes had fought more for Jehovih than against him.

19. After this, both mortals and angels in Chine'ya, knew no peace. And when no war existed betwixt any two or more cities or states, and the people were Jehovians, Ennochissa, with his hundreds of millions of angel warriors, obsessed such mortals, and plunged them into war, to make them destroy one another.

20. From these scenes of horror turn ye now, and learn of the kingdom of God, Jehovih's Son.

CHAPTER XXIV.
OF THE LABOR OF GOD, JEHOVIH'S SON.

1. Sakaya was born in Hagotha, province of Nao'wan, on the borders of Nepal; but because his birth had been foretold by the Faithist prophets, and that he would re-establish the doctrines of Capilya, the place of his birth was afterward called Capilya'wahtu.

2. Sakaya's father's name was Metanga, and he was of the twelfth generation of Suddhodana (that is, of pure vegetable food). During which time, none of his forefathers ate fish or flesh, or of anything that breathed the breath of life.

3. Metanga was very old when Sakaya was born, but the wife of Metanga was but fifteen years old; for which reason, the people nicknamed the child, Sramana Gotama, that is, passionless from father and mother.

4. Metanga was High Father of the province of Nao'wan; consequently, Sakaya was born a prince, as commanded of Jehovih, in heaven, he should be. Wherein He said: He that I will raise up, shall have the glory of the earth before him; and he shall grow up as learned as a king and a priest, and he shall re-establish peace and good will on earth.

5. Now there had been bloody times in Vind'yu for four hundred years; during which time a warring sect, who falsely called themselves Brahmins, had overrun the land with sword and spear, lance and fire, destroying temples, oracles and languages.

6. These were the destructions, previously mentioned, done by the God Kabalactes, mortals supposing, they were under the God Brahma.

7. God, Jehovih's Son, had said to Etchessa, chief guardian angel over Sakaya: Thou shalt cause thy ward to learn Brahminism, asceticism, and all other religions.

8. Thus was Sakaya educated; and at twelve years of age, he took vows of Brahminism.

9. At fifteen, he desired to acquire the ecstatic state, and he joined a band of seven Brahmin priests, and went about for three years with the alms-bowl, begging for the poor, living as the poor, and fasting and praying, and studying with his teachers and priests.

10. And, yet for other four years, he excluded himself from speech, save to the Holy Ghost, dwelling out of doors, night and day.

11. But Jehovih suffered not the ecstatic state to come to Sakaya. And one night, his guardian angel, Etchessa, spake to him in a dream, saying:

12. Behold, I am Jehovih, and not the Holy Ghost! Why hast thou put Me off? Did I not create thee alive, and make thee a person also? Thou art born of the race of Suddhodana. Thy labor is not to seek the ecstatic state for thyself, which is selfishness, but to renew My light on earth.

13. Therefore, give up this, thy most useless life of going about praying, and return thou

to thy father's house, and take thee a wife. For how canst thou attain the wisdom of the earth, without becoming a husband and father?

14. Sakaya awoke, remembering his dream, and he told it to his priests, and asked them to interpret it. And they said unto him: This was not a dream, but the voice of satan; put thou it aside.

15. But Sakaya was more convinced of his dream than of his priests; and he, therefore, gave up his fasting and praying, and returned to his father's house, saying: Father, thou art wise after the manner of thy generations. Henceforth I will be no more a priest, nor in fact a Brahmin, for that matter, but pursue thy doctrines, which are of deeds more than words. Thou shalt, therefore, choose me a wife, for I will wed and become a father.

16. So Sakaya wed, and his wife bore him a son. When he looked upon the child, he said: Thou art the greatest of sermons.

17. Now, because of the strange life Sakaya had lived, being a prince, he was the wonder of the city of Hagotha, and was much loved by the people, especially the poor, for his alms-bowl had oft relieved them from hunger.

18. Consequently, when it was known he was a father, there came before the royal palace thousands of the poor, singing songs of praise to Sakaya and his child and his wife. And the poor women had infants in their arms. When Sakaya saw the infants, he burst into tears, and came out before the multitude, and spake to them, saying:

19. This day I have sinned before heaven and earth! Behold my tears! Would that they were drops of blood, and I could shed them to do you good! For I have looked upon mine own son, and said within my soul: This is mine! And I considered how my son was born a prince and above want; but I considered not this great multitude of babes, who have no assurance against starvation.

20. Why, then, shall I remain with one, who hath sure provision, and glut myself in ease and the selfish joy of my own house? And leave this multitude of babes to the hazard of precarious life?

21. Is not Sakaya of broader soul than this? Have I any right to bring more children into the world, until I have provided sure happiness to them that are already born? What is my family and my kingdom, though I win the land from Yaganosa to the ocean, if this burning within mine own soul will not away, but crieth out forever: Heal thou the sick earth!

22. From this time forth do I covenant with Thee, Thou All Light, to give up all the earth, and to serve Thee! Beasts can bring forth young; and they do set their hearts on their begotten only! Thy Light moveth me to a more noble course!

23. This day I quit the earth and the passions for earthly things; I will be Thy Son, O Jehovih! And all my days henceforth on the earth, labor to ameliorate Thy abundant offspring! Behold these young babes turned upon me, with Thy smile, O Jehovih, in their innocent faces! calling to me: Help! Help!

CHAPTER XXV.

1. Theonactus, angel chief of the loo'is, that brought forth Sakaya, seeing the resolution of Sakaya, departed at once to Paradise, before God on the throne, to receive the commission of Jehovih, and to establish a line of es'ean light to the mortal sphere.

2. And thereupon, God caused his officers to select from the volunteers the highest grades, and to arrange them in a line of light down to the earth, to Sakaya, that the voice of God and his Holy Eleven might speak through Sakaya, with the wisdom of Jehovih. The hosts to be under the direction of Thoanactus.

3. The million loo'is were also summoned to their places in the line; and in five days' time, the light of the throne of God was made one with the soul of Sakaya, and he began preaching, even from the steps of the palace of the king, his father.

4. In the meantime, the loo'is of the hosts of Thoanactus inspired their mortal wards, men and women, who had been born into the world to become disciples and followers of Sakaya, to come before him.

5. And it came to pass, that presently, there assembled in Sakaya's native city, to hear him preach, men and women from remote distances. So that people said, one to another: Such coming of strangers, proveth that the Great Spirit is with Sakaya.

6. These, then, that follow, are the substance of the doctrines preached by Sakaya, being a re-establishing of the Zarathustrian law, that is to say:

7. I am but a man; worship not me. Neither honor ye me for my words; for they are not my words in fact.

8. All men's wise words are the accumulation of things previous; nothing is new. Nor do I proclaim any new doctrine or new rites and ceremonies.

9. On the contrary, I declare my follies publicly before you. Inasmuch as I have been an example of folly, learn ye to be wise by not following my past footsteps.

10. In my youth, I was quickened to see the miseries and sorrows and afflictions of mortals. And I cried out unto Ahura'Mazda, as the priests had directed me, to find some sure way to do great good in the world.

11. But in the legends of the ancients I beheld that certain signs and miracles had attended Capilya and Zarathustra. So I grieved to attain to signs and miracles.

12. Ye know the rest. I fasted and prayed and tortured my flesh, to make the earth abhorrent in my sight, even according to the rules of the Brahmin priests.

13. But nothing came to me more than to the commonest magician.

14. So I declare unto you, I have renounced Brahminism and asceticism, and taken up the Zarathustrian religion, which is, that good works are the only salvation.

15. To know, then, what are good works, and to apply the same unto the inhabitants of the earth, should be the chief study of a preacher.

16. And, since most crime and misery come because of poverty, and because of the division of the affairs of men, it is wise to devise, first, a remedy against poverty, and second, a means of attraction to bring about a brotherhood between men.

17. To accomplish which, the association of families of tens and twenties and hundreds and thousands, with rab'bahs (priests), unto each, as Capilya taught, is the highest and best plan.

18. In which families, there shall be neither buying nor selling, nor ownership, nor divisions, nor castes, nor privileges of one above another, nor rich, nor poor.

19. When Sakaya was asked: How about such as can work fast, and are strong, and can accomplish much, shall they not have preference over those that produce little?

20. Sakaya said: A certain man had two sons, one was strong, and the other weak, and yet that father distinguished not between his sons in his will. Was he then just?

21. They said: A most just father.

22. Sakaya said: So declare I unto you the Ormazdian law: to give unto one another all things required, and without distinction as to strength, or as to expertness.

CHAPTER XXVI.
SAKAYA'S DOCTRINES.

1. Sakaya said: Ye cannot associate with all men; for many are of diverse tastes and habits.

2. Nevertheless, refuse ye not all association because of this, for there are such, as are consonant with you. And such, as are disagreeable to you, are nevertheless compatable to others.

3. Ormazd hath created a large field; His people are numerous, and there are many in the world so like unto others, they are as one in all things.

4. Choose ye such, and as ye are one with one another, so are ye one with the Creator.

5. But most of all, will virtue and industry and good works come into the world by the examples ye place before the young. Better is it to hide and subdue your temper in presence of the young, than to conquer a whole state by force of arms.

6. The young are your angels given you by the Creator; and ye are their Gods. Consider ye, then, what kind of a kingdom ye raise up.

7. Happiness on earth is answered by happiness in heaven; and that which is planted on earth, is reaped in heaven.

8. Touching charity: I say, it is good to take the alms-bowl, and go about begging for the poor; and yet, in the same breath, I say, it is an evil.

9. This I have found of all charity: It hath two great evils: First, it flattereth him that giveth, that he hath done a good work, and this is an injury to his own soul; second, charity injureth the poor, because it destroyeth manhood, and giveth good caste to a beggar.

10. Though this kingdom is filled with hospitals and houses of charity, it is none the less free from vagrants and helpless ones.

11. And though ye build a thousand houses for the poor, and feed them withal, yet ye will have just as many still unprovided for, as when there was but one poor-house.

12. The law is unalterable in heaven and earth, that, whatsoever ye nurse, will grow.

13. I also declare unto you an equally severe law, which is: That if ye do nothing to benefit the afflicted, distressed and helpless, ye can not escape the damnation of earth and heaven.

14. To remedy which, it devolveth upon you, to find a remedy in society itself, whereby there shall be no rich and no poor.

15. For it is also law, that where there are rich, there must be poor. Where there are masters, there must be servants.

16. In which the rich man is a sinner before heaven and earth, even more so than the poor man.

17. Some of them asked Sakaya: Suppose a rich man do not feed the poor and helpless, but he give employment to a thousand hired servants; is he not good?

18. Sakaya said: A man may feed his cattle, caring for the sick ones, but still he treateth

them as cattle. A man may employ many cattle, but still he treateth them as cattle. And he who doeth this to his brothers and sisters, the curse of the Creator is upon that man.

19. But if he give up, what he hath, and maketh himself a father over them, to develop himself in manliness and wisdom and virtue, then his charities are as virtue.

20. In whatsoever a man doeth, and his own self receiveth prestige over others, that man offendeth in the sight of Jehovih (Ormazd).

21. Yet these things are not new in the world; they were the doctrines of the ancients. And in this day, the Brahmin priests preach them in languages ye understand not. Behold, I break away from their languages, and preach the truth in your native tongue, and it soundeth new to you.

22. I have tried, and proved in mine own person, and I declare unto you, that preaching alone is of little avail in the world. Spoken words are a breath of air. They blow away. Written words lay in silence. they are dead.

23. I am not come to preach, nor to build up a new order of preaching, but to found a practice in life, whereby crime and misery and starvation may be averted.

24. Capilya covered the earth over with families of communities, and the earth became as a garden, rich in fruit and flowers. Pauperism was taken away from this land. Then came cruel wars and the destruction of harmony and of learning.

CHAPTER XXVII.

1. Purification is the first law I give unto you, and is the same as with the ancients, in which:

2. Ye shall not eat the flesh of any creature that breathed the breath of life; nor of fish that lived in the water nor under the water.

3. Ye shall bathe once every day from the crown of the head to the sole of the feet. And before bathing, ye shall say: Before Thee, O Jehovih (Ormazd) I will put away the filth of my body and the evil of my spirit. And after bathing, ye shall say: As I have with water washed clean the outer man, O Thou Jehovih, help me to make clean my spirit.

4. In the morning, when thou wakest, thou shalt say: Help me, O Jehovih, to keep my thoughts pure this day; and my soul full of love and tenderness.

5. In the evening, before sleeping, thou shalt say: Whilst my corporeal body sleepeth, O Jehovih, help my less encumbered spirit to see the ways of Thy righteous judgment.

6. Without purity, no man can see the Creator; with purity, all men can see Him, and hear Him.

7. It is easier to purify the corporeal body than the spiritual. For diet and baths can accomplish the former, but pure thoughts are required for the soul.

8. A man may be clean as to the flesh; but if he have impure thoughts, he is impure in spirit. Whoso speaketh cruelly or unjustly of his neighbor, is foul in spirit. If he speak of the short-comings and deceptions of his neighbors, he is foul in spirit.

9. Whereas, first of all, purification is the first law of man's own self.

10. The second law is, after being purified, to strive constantly to do good unto others.

11. Some of the multitude asked: What meanest thou, by doing good unto others?

12. Sakaya said: To inspire others unto purity first; and then to attain individuality. It hath been said, from time without end, that to help the poor, to give to them, to serve them, is

927

good works done unto others. But I say unto you, this is but half-way to that which is good. For ye shall not only help them, but shall go and teach them, how to help themselves. This is doing good unto others.

13. It hath been said: Whoso saith the ordinances of the priest, repeating a certain number of prayers daily, doeth a good work. But I say unto you, whoso teacheth a man to invent prayers of his own, hath done a greater good.

14. To put a man in the way, to be his own salvation, this is the best good work. As ye have depended on the priests to pray for you, I come to teach you, to pray for yourselves.

15. The third law is: To abnegate one's own self; being willing in heart, to sacrifice one's own desires, possessions and opinions for sake of peace and the good of the family. This is the most difficult law. For the selfishness of man causeth him to say: I have such a love of liberty. Let me be the dictator, and do thou my decrees.

16. But for this evil amongst men, they could dwell together in peace, the world over.

17. The fourth law is: To love all men, women and children, as brothers and sisters.

18. The fifth law is: To return good for evil; to give pleasure to those, that give pain.

19. To practice those things, holding all things in common, is sufficient unto the redemption of the world from darkness, war and evil, unto peace and light and happiness to all the living.

CHAPTER XXVIII.

1. Sakaya said: Without rites and ceremonies, a people is like a collection of musicians, with every one playing a different tune.

2. Without pledges to general rules, a community is like a farm without fences, where cattle roam about, destroying the harvests.

3. Two things stand prominently before all men, about which there need be no dispute, Light and Darkness. Whether ye call the Light, EOLIN, or ORMAZD, or GOD, or SUDGA, it mattereth little, provided the idea eliminated hath reference to that which is THE HIGHEST CONCEIVED OF, Who is Ever Present, and is the Person from which all persons sprung. And whether ye call darkness SIN, or EVIL, or SATAN, it mattereth little, provided the idea eliminated is that which is the extreme opposite of light.

4. Without these two entities in view, to shun the one, and strive for the other, a community is like race-horses striving for a prize by running in circular capers, instead of going on a well provided track.

5. Take no man nor woman into the family till first pledged to serve the All Person, Jehovih (Ormazd), with a full and willing heart.

6. To shun satan and his emissaries, be circumspect.

7. And when ye are come together, choose ye the oldest, wisest, best man, to be the father of the family (community).

8. When matters come up for discussion, whoever speaketh thereon shall speak in the direction of light, and not of darkness.

9. When asked further explanation on this, Sakaya said:

10. There are two modes of discussion before all men: One is to impart light, and the other is to abuse the opponent. The first is Jehovih's, the second is satan's method. In the family discussion, the latter method shall not be tolerated by the father.

11. After the discussion is finished, the rab'bah shall decree according to the light of the Father in him.

12. Sakaya was here asked: Why not decree according to the majority vote?

13. Sakaya said: That is the lower light, being the light of men only.

14. For I declare unto you, ye can not serve both Jehovih and men. It is incumbent on every man in the community that entereth the discussion to speak from the higher light, as he perceiveth it, without regard to policy or consequences. And the same law shall be binding on the rab'bah; and though nine men out of ten side the other way, yet the rab'bah's decree shall stand above all the rest.

15. When the discussion turneth upon rites and ceremonies, which the community may adopt, or the music, or the discipline regarding funerals, or marriages, or births, the speakers shall remember that a family is composed of old and young; of sedate and jocose; and that every talent is created for the glory of the whole, and for the glory of the Creator; and they shall enlarge their understanding, to embrace the whole. Remembering, it is easier to walk beside a bull, and turn him in his course, than to come against him for the same purpose.

16. One man hath joy in sacrifice (worship) by clapping his hands and dancing; another, in poetry; another, in singing; another, in silent prayers. And yet, one hath no preference over another in sight of Him Who created them, for they are His own handiwork.

17. Consider, then, that ye provide a time and place in the community for all of these in their own way, directing them holily. For if ye strive to bind them, that are of exuberant spirits, not to dance and clap their hands, they will find vent in secrecy and to an evil end.

18. Herein have the Brahmin priests been aiders and abettors of bawdy houses and of drunkenness and licentiousness; because they have sought to make you ascetics by overthrowing your natural talents.

CHAPTER XXIX.

1. Sakaya said: Of a truth, I declare a new thing to you, but which was old thousands of years ago.

2. That religion is nothing more nor less than rites and ceremonies in the discipline of a community. As when an army of soldiers are in training by their captains, when certain commands and maneuvers cause the soldiers to be as a unit in movement; so is religion in a community, through rites and ceremonies, made as a unit to carry out works of charity and harmony and love and righteousness.

3. And every member of a community, that taketh no part in its religion, is like an idler mixing in with a company of soldiers, where his presence tendeth to evil.

4. Brahmin priests go about preaching, singing and praying before audiences, making great show in the temples; yet none of these practice what they profess.

5. From these evils learn ye, to do good; first, by living only in families, where all the members practice what they profess.

6. As the world goeth, it is easy to preach and call it religion; but the fruit must be measured by the city or the state, that is saved from sin. Who then, of all the priests in the temple, can say: Here is a community saved from sin!

7. If they can not do this, then they are themselves hypocrites and blasphemers.

8. Satan calleth out from a dark corner, saying: Remain thou within the wicked world, and leaven the whole mass.

9. Again he calleth out from a dark corner, saying: Go thou away from the wicked world, and live as an ascetic, praying alone, living alone.

10. Again he calleth from a dark corner, saying: Thou and thy friends are too pure to mix with the world; go ye away privily, and let the world take care of itself.

11. Now, I say unto you: Do none of these things; and, in the same breath, I say: Do all of them.

12. Let your community remain within the world, that it may be a proven example that love, peace, plenty, and happiness are possible on the earth. Let the community be sufficiently ascetic to attain the beatific state, which is the triumph of spirit over the flesh.

13. And, as to the third proposition: Take ye no part in the governments of men, of kings, or queens. Neither fight ye for them, nor against them.

14. For they live under the lower law; but ye shall live under the law of Jehovih as He speaketh to the soul of man.

15. Neither shall ye have kings, nor queens; these belong to the world's people.

16. Lastly, and above all things, live not for the corporeal man, but for the spiritual man; remembering ye are not yet born, but are in embryo, shaping yourselves for the everlasting life.

17. Whoso practiceth not the higher law, will not escape the tortures in hell; but whoso liveth the higher law will pass on to Nirvania, where dwell Gods and Goddesses of endless light.

18. Flatter not yourselves that ye shall suddenly reform all the world. Ye can at most but reach an arm's length.

19. Three doctrines have been, now are, and ever shall be on the earth; they are: First, the Faithists', who know the All Person, Ever Present; second, the idol worshipers', who make the Creator into a man in heaven, and not present but by proxy of certain laws; and, third, infidels', who believe in nothing they cannot take up in the hand, and weigh.

20. The Faithists beget Faithists, the idolaters beget idolaters, the infidels beget infidels. For these three conditions are but outward manifestations of the spirit; the infidel is nearly devoid of spirit; the idolater hath one grade more of spirit; but the Faithist hath spiritual ascendancy.

21. Since the highest best good things done in the world, come of the order of Faithists, be ye circumspect as to marriage, that your offspring incline more to spirituality than to earthliness.

22. But such matters come under the higher law, and can be understood only through the soul.

23. Also, hath practice proved that the laws of a community must die with the death of the rab'bah, and that new laws must be made by the new rab'bah. And, in no case, shall the law of precedent, of things past, apply to things present. For this is making slaves of the living, to those that are dead. It is making the wisdom of the dead greater than the wisdom of Jehovih.

24. When a rab'bah retireth from office, it shall be considered the same as a death, for it is the termination of his rule.

25. Nor shall a rab'bah have any privileges or emoluments, over and above any member

of the community; nor one man above another; nor one woman above another; for there shall be no partiality, even in favor of the learned and good, over and above the ignorant and the less good. For ye are all brothers and sisters; children of One Father, created by Him in His own way and for His own glory.

CHAPTER XXX.

1. For four years Sakaya preached, traveling from the east to the west, and from north to south; and wherever he went, great multitudes came to hear him, for God had so prepared them.

2. And there went with him seventy-two disciples, who were also inspired of God, to learn the wisdom of Sakaya's words. And the people of Vind'yu were stirred up as they had not been from the time of Capilya.

3. And it came to pass that the priests and magicians of Brahma sought to condemn Sakaya, saying: The oracles and the spirits of the dead declare, his words are not true words. Moreover, if he were of the Holy Ghost, he could show signs and miracles.

4. So God gave Sakaya signs and miracles, even to showing the spirits of the dead, who came and stood beside him whilst he preached; and the spirits spake also, declaring Sakaya's words were of Jehovih. And the multitude saw the spirits, and heard them speak.

5. Sakaya said: Of a truth, I do not come of the Holy Ghost; I come of the actual Person, Jehovih (Ormazd).

6. Then God gave to Sakaya power of the DEATH CAST, whereat his own spirit went out of his corporeal body, and stood in the presence of many men, and was seen by them; and his spirit spake to them, and they heard his words.

7. And whilst his spirit was thus out of his corporeal body, another angel of God came and inhabited it, and spake before the multitude.

8. Now, after these signs came to Sakaya, he preached again, and traveled four years more, showing these things wherever he went.

9. And on these occasions he explained the spirit of things, and the different heavens which he had visited. And he showed unto many that it was not imagination; for he left his corporeal body, and went in spirit to far-off cities and country places, showing his spirit in regions hundreds of miles remote, and he was recognized in the communities where he appeared.

10. For there were learned men in those days, and they traveled to the places named to see his spirit, to witness if such a thing could be; and hundreds and thousands of them testified it was true.

11. Sakaya said: Of these matters be ye most expert in observation; for though they be proved to you, yet I declare to you, they are as nothing. For even magicians and spirits of darkness can attain to the same miracles.

12. Nor is there in such wonders one single virtue, that would contribute to make the world better, or happier.

13. For the spirits of the lower heavens, like mortals, have multitudes of doctrines; and, for the most part, they know nothing of the higher heavens, Nirvania, which I proclaim unto you.

14. Nor is the testimony of a spirit more valuable to you than is the testimony of a mortal.

15. But consider ye the words and doctrines of spirits and men; for that only is good which provideth for ameliorating the condition of the family and the state.

16. For it is given unto you by the Father, that ye can begin your own resurrection whilst ye are here in the corporeal body.

17. Consider, then, what ye can do that will raise you in spirit; for this is resurrection. First, to purify yourselves; second, to do all the good ye can; and third, to affiliate. Without these, there can be no resurrection.

18. Or, having two of them, and lacking in the third, there can be no resurrection.

19. To live the highest best one knoweth; to practice sharply the convictions of the heart: these are the working-tools of resurrection. To live not the highest best one knoweth; to practice not what one is convinced of, is hypocrisy; these are like stones tied to the neck of a man in deep water.

20. In all, Sakaya preached and practiced fourteen years; and he founded seventy-two communities.

21. And all the members thereof were sworn against war, and against caste, and against idleness, and to worship only the Great Spirit, Ormazd. And he gave them many rites and ceremonies.

22. And then Sakaya said unto the Creator: I know Thou hast in some mysterious way inspired me to do all I have done. Therefore, all the glory is Thine. How best, O Father, may these great truths be impressed upon mortals, that they will not soon forget Thy words through me?

23. Then answered God to Sakaya, saying: By thy death by the hand of the idolater.

24. Sakaya said: Then, O Thou, Who createdst me alive, provide Thou my death as Thou desirest.

25. Then God cut asunder the cord of light that extended to the heavenly throne in Paradise. And suddenly now the Brahmins conspired against Sakaya, and they went privily and poisoned his food with the blood of swine, killed with poison.

26. And Sakaya ate thereof, not perceiving it; and he was taken with a bloody flux and died.

27. And his disciples took his body, according to the custom of the country, and burnt it, and scattered the ashes thereof to the four corners of the world.

28. And in the night thereafter, God sent a million angels into the field of ashes, with a heavenly ship of fire, and they took the spirit of Sakaya therein, and bore him up to the throne of God.

END OF THE HISTORY OF SAKAYA.

CHAPTER XXXI.
BIRTH OF KA'YU, OTHERWISE CONFUCIUS.

1. Thoanactus, Chief of the million loo'is sent by God down to the earth, to Chine'ya, to raise up an heir capable of the voice of God, sent word to God in Paradise, saying:

2. Greeting to thee, O God, in the name of Jehovih. Thy Son is born! And his name is Ka'yu. He is son of Heih, who is sub-king of Te'sow. Behold, thy son Ka'yu is k'te'sune (iesu) in the borders, whose mother, Ching-tsae, is not fifteen years old. And Heih was

father to twelve children previously.

3. Let us rejoice before Jehovih, who hath quickened into life this tree of universal knowledge.

4. Also my hosts have brought about more than three thousand births, who shall become his disciples in time to come.

5. God returned answer to Thoanactus, saying: In Jehovih's name all praise to thee and thy hosts. Thy words have been proclaimed in Paradise! There is great joy in heaven. Send the grades of mortal resurrection in Chine'ya, with doctrines and rites and ceremonies and the dominion of the spirits of the dead.

6. Thoanactus then applied to the angels who had charge of the numerating and appraising of mortals as to their grades and spiritual intercourse; and having obtained the reports, he made selections, and reported as followeth, to wit:

7. Thoanactus, greeting to God, Son of Jehovih: Ling, sun king of Chine'ya, with twelve sub-kingdoms, one to represent every month of the year. Four hundred and six millions of mortals; twenty-seven hundred million angels, not fettered by angel tyrants. Of the angel emissaries of the Triune God, fifteen hundred millions.

8. Mortal grade, eight; maximum, eighty; minimum, nothing. Of fifties, one to seven. Of twenty-fives, one to three; of tens, one to one; but of seventy-fives, on to forty, mostly guardian births.

9. The rise in the eleventh year, two; in the twenty-third, five; in the hundredth, twelve.

10. Of rites and ceremonies, seventy-two; of sacrifice without compunction, thirty-five.

11. Funeral rites, ninety-eight; observances in full, forty-five.

12. Perception in su'is, one to three hundred and sixty-two; in sar'gis, one to six thousand two hundred and eight.

13. Of spirits in sar-gis, one to thirty-three thousand; of first and second resurrections, mostly ashars.

14. Thoanactus saith: Because Chine instituted reverence for the dead, the funeral rites have become worshipful.

15. After the body is put away, either buried or burnt, mortals read prayers on three succeeding days, at sunset, chanting the virtue and love of the dead; and oft the spirit returneth to them in the house, taking on sar'gis, like a mortal, and talking to their mortal kin.

16. Of drujas, not attained to live alone, seven hundred millions. Of these, thirty per cent are in declension, and seventy in ascension.

17. Of mortals in druk, sixteen per cent; of mortals in idleness, including druks, twenty per cent.

18. Of such as are addicted to secret evils and pollution, seventy per cent; of abortionists one per cent, of one half.

19. Thoanactus saith: Owing to the veneration for, and to the rites of the dead, is speug's increase attributed.

20. Furthermore, thy servant herewith sendeth to thee, for the libraries of heaven, a full record of the cities and country places of Chine'ya; and the grade and rate of every mortal.

CHAPTER XXXII.

1. Ka'yu grew up to be a man, in every way adapted to the work for which the loo'is had had him born into the world by command of God.

2. And it also came to pass, that disciples were also born, and duly prepared by the angels of God to become co-workers with Ka'yu. Of these disciples, seventy-two were called, chief disciples, that is, six from each of the twelve kingdoms and sub-kingdoms of Chine'ya.

3. God had said: Suffer not Ka'yu and his chief disciples to know they are instruments in my hands. Neither suffer them to know that my angels inspire them, nor suffer them to know that they come from their respective kingdoms by my voice through my angels.

4. In one age, to say a matter cometh by inspiration or by the angels, is to render the matter impotent; and yet, in another age, to not profess inspiration or angel-presence, is to render the matter impotent.

5. The latter condition is now upon Chine'ya. Let my angels heed this.

6. When Ka'yu was ready for the work of God, there came to him from the twelve provinces of Chine'ya seventy-two men and women of great learning, having heard of Ka'yu's wisdom. None of these knew, they had been inspired to come.

7. Ka'yu said unto them: Why have ye come? Some gave one reason, and some another.

8. Ka'yu said: These great happenings are the work of the Ever Present.

9. Let us conduct ourselves as Gods; the Great Spirit will then answer us.

10. Let us sit in crescent, after the manner of Gods.

CHAPTER XXXIII.

1. God established a line of light from his throne in heaven down to Ka'yu; by the presence of half a thousand million angels maintained he this light of heaven with mortals.

2. That which was inspired of God, came to the soul of Ka'yu; what God spake, that spake Ka'yu.

3. And God so spake through Ka'yu, that man might not know it was God speaking; for he desired to inspire men to self-culture, instead of relying on Gods and angels as heretofore.

4. In the language of Ka'yu, the Great Spirit was called Shang Te; but the word, Te, was God; the words, the Shang Te, were the Gods.

5. Ka'yu said: Behold, man hath blockaded the road to wisdom. In one place he hath heaped up thousands of books of the ancients; in another place, he wasteth time in rites and ceremonies.

6. Our labor is to remodel the whole, by choosing from all the past that which is the best. Te will guide us in this.

7. We must, therefore, make one book acknowledging the EVER PRESENT GREAT SPIRIT, and His one, SHANG TE. And this book must contain all the glory and beauty now contained in the seven hundred sacred books of the empire.

8. And since there are four hundred and eighty-six books on the intermediate world, which no man can learn, we must take from them all their soundest parts, and make one

book thereof.

9. And in the same connection, there being twelve hundred and seventy books on the spirits of the dead, and their testimonies of the lower and the higher heavens, we must make one book thereof.

10. And of the two thousand two hundred books on magic, and on conjuring spirits, and on second sight and second hearing, we must make one book thereof.

11. Of books of families, there are more than four thousand, which shall also be condensed into one book.

12. Of histories, there are more than four thousand books, which shall be condensed into one book.

13. Of law books, there are more than twelve thousand books, and of the precedents of judges' decrees, there are more than thirty thousand books. All of these shall be condensed into one book.

14. Of provinces, and of the empire, and of the governors and emperors thereof, there are two thousand seven hundred books, which shall be condensed into one.

15. And of government, there are seven hundred books, which shall be condensed into one.

16. Of caste, there are four hundred and ninety books, and of proprieties, three hundred and twenty, and all of these shall be condensed into one book.

17. Ka'yu, continuing, said: My work is to bring confusion to a termination. Of doctrines and laws and rites and ceremonies and philosophies, of both heaven and earth, we have had enough.

18. In a dark age, Shang Te (True God) giveth his commandments in injunctions; he showeth the people, what is right, and what is wrong. In my day, the people know these things, but they do not practice them.

19. Even the preachers and conductors of ceremonies in the temples, who proclaim righteousness and charity and good works, do not practice what they preach. They live in ease and luxury, but tell us to go give to the poor. Yea, and they threaten us with hell, if we do it not.

20. Of these different doctrines, there are seven hundred kinds in the sacred books; and they all condemn the followers of the others. Whereupon, to escape the damnation of hell, a man would need to do sacrifice more than four thousand days every year! This is not possible to any man. For there are but three hundred and sixty-five days in a year!

21. Nor is it possible for any man to learn all the books; nay, a thousand years would not suffice.

22. God (Te) forbid that I may add more to the burden we have already. And I know he will preserve in our abridgement all that is good in the whole of them.

23. Since we can not live according to the multitude of doctrines and philosophies, we must abridge them within the scope of man. Neither must we cut any of them off entirely, or we lead the followers thereof into rebellion.

24. Since we have so many law books and so many judges' decrees, all of which a man must learn before he can become a judge of the court, the which is impossible, we must cut them down into a few simples, but sufficient to cover the rules of discretion in judgment. Better is it to throw the judge of the court partly on his own judgment and responsibility, than for him to be a blank as to judgment, simply reading the decree of a preceding judge.

25. And as to the religion of this man, or that man; behold, it hath come to pass, that each, in his own order, performeth his rites and ceremonies and sacrifices and prayers, like a trained horse in a showman's circle, going round and round, and knowing not the meaning thereof.

26. For it is come to pass that the religions have made machines of the worshippers; the law books have made machines of the courts; the books of government have made machines of governors and emperors.

27. I am sent into the world to make men of men, and women of women.

28. There is no religion to suit me, therefore I make one. There is no government of the empire to suit me, therefore I devise one. There is no system in society, therefore I make one.

29. I am not sent into the world to destroy what is, or what hath been; there are enough evil men to do that. I am sent to cull the harvest, and to gather choice seed from what now is, and what hath been.

30. For the seed I plant is selected, not to be planted in the ocean, nor on the moon, nor in a far-off country; but to be planted in Chine'ya, and in Chine'ya I will plant it.

CHAPTER XXXIV.
DOCTRINES OF THE BASE.

1. What were the old foundations?

2. To dwell in families (communities), with a father to each and every one.

3. And what of the ancient states?

4. The fathers had families, with chief fathers over them.

5. What of the empire?

6. The chief fathers elected one over them, and he was called, the Sun Father. Because, as the sun is the glory and beauty of the phalanx, ruling over the planets, so was the emperor the sun of mortals.

7. What was the scope of responsibility?

8. As a father is responsible for the behavior of his own child, so was the rab'bah responsible for the behavior of his family; so was the chief rab'bah responsible for the behavior of his family of rab'bahs; so was the emperor responsible for the behavior of his empire.

9. What was the responsibility of a child to its natural father? of a man to the rab'bah? of the rab'bahs to the chief rab'bahs? of all the people to the emperor?

10. The child shall be taught to love, to revere and to obey its own father (and its mother, who is its vice-father); the man to love and revere the rab'bah; the rab'bahs to love and revere the chief rab'bahs; the whole people to love and revere the emperor.

11. Why this order?

12. It is the doctrine of the ancients, handed down from generation to generation, and hath proved to be a good doctrine for an empire.

13. How knew the ancients these principles?

14. The Creator taught them. The Creator sent His high angel, Te, who hath charge of the intermediate world, down to mortals to teach them.

15. How is this proved?

16. By the sacred books of the ancients.

17. Who wrote the ancient sacred books?

18. Men inspired by the angel of the Creator.

19. How is this proved?

20. It is proved negatively, because men can not write so beautiful nor in the style.

21. What were the fundamental doctrines of the ancient sacred books?

22.To worship none but the Creator.

23. To have no images nor idols.

24. To keep the day of the change of the moon as a sacred day, and to do no work on that day, but to practice rites, processions and ceremonies, for the glory of the Creator.

25. To love the Creator above all else.

26. To love one's parents next to Him.

27. To kill no living creature maliciously or for food.

28. To tell no lies, nor to steal, nor to covet anything, that is another's.

29. Do not unto others what we would that they should not do unto us.

30. To return good for evil.

31. To feed and clothe the stranger, the sick and helpless.

32. To be not idle, but industrious.

33. To say no ill of any man nor woman nor child.

34. To practice the highest wisdom one hath.

35. To respect all people, as we desire to be respected.

CHAPTER XXXV.

1. What were the ascetics of the ancients?

2. That heaven and earth are warring elements, one against the other.

3. That all men must choose to serve one or the other, and at once engage in the battle.

4. If a man desire everlasting life and bliss in heaven, then must he battle his earthly parts with great vigor.

5. He shall torture his flesh, by fastings, and by lying naked on sharp stones, and by flagellations, and otherwise showing before the Gods how displeased he is with his corporeal body.

6. He must live alone, deny himself all pleasures, sleep not in a house, nor eat cooked foot.

7. What is the extreme of great learning?

8. To devote one's whole life to learning what is in the books. To cultivate the memory, that one may repeat all the words in four thousand books is a great learning. But it is greater learning, to be capable of repeating eight thousand books, word for word.

9. What is the extreme of loyalty?

10. To love the emperor, so one can not see his faults; to love the rab'bahs, so one can not see their faults. To love discipline, so that one hath no time for anything else; and, on the contrary, to have no time for discipline nor rites nor ceremonies.

11. What is the law of life?

12. The spirit of man is the man; to live for the growth of the spirit, this is the highest of living.

13. What manner is spirit communion?

14. The spirit of one person can commune with the spirit of another, if they be not encumbered with grossness. The spirits of the dead can commune with the spirits of the living, even without one's knowing it.

15. What is the destination of the souls of men?

16. When man dieth, his spirit is born into the air of the earth, which is the intermediate world, whither it sojourneth until sufficiently purified, and is reverential to the Creator; and then it is taken up by His angels to dwell in the higher heavens forever.

17. What shall mortal man do for the benefit of his own spirit?

18. He shall love the Creator with all his soul, and strive to emulate Him in good works and gentleness and love.

19. But if he do not this, what then?

20. His spirit will be bound in hell after death; he will become a victim for the delight of demons.

CHAPTER XXXVI.

1. Ka'yu said: Such is the base the ancients have given into our hands, but who could follow them into detail?

2. I was not born into the world for this; but to choose from each and all of them, what all of them will accept.

3. In the ancient days our country was sparsely settled; families were a good convenience. But, behold, the land is full of people. I have not to deal with a few scattered barbarians.

4. I have to deal with a learned people, who have scarcely room to stand. I am only one man; and ye, but seventy-two.

5. Of ourselves, we can do nothing. Shang Te (the true God) hath shaped the times to our hands. Whether we live to see it, it mattereth little. The time will surely come, when the emperor will be obliged to destroy the books of the ancients.

6. Let us therefore take the cream of them, and provide for their preservation while we may.

7. Ka'yu then divided up the labor amongst his seventy-two disciples; apportioning the books of the ancients justly amongst them.

8. And so great was the wisdom and scholarship of Ka'yu, that in twelve days' time some of his disciples were ready with their reports to begin. And from these reports Ka'yu dictated, and the scribes wrote down his words.

9. And it came to pass, that when a committee presented a revision before Ka'yu that he even knew it before it was read in the Council. And he dictated thereon, making the necessary alterations. After which, the subject was given to the scribes to re-write out in full.

10. Now the whole time of the first sitting of the Council was eight and a half years, and then they had been over all the work.

11. But so great was the wisdom and memory of Ka'yu, that he called out from the missings of his disciples sufficient to require yet two years' more deliberation.

12. And there were thus produced, from the lips of Ka'yu, twenty books, which contained the digest of upward of eighteen thousand books. Nor had any man in all the world ever done the one-tenth part so great a feat of learning.

13. The scribes wrote six copies for every one of the disciples; and when they were thus

provided, and were ready to depart, Ka'yu spake to them, saying:

14. What say ye, is the highest, best satisfaction? And when the disciples had answered, some one thing, and some another, then the master said:

15. To know that one hath done the highest thing within his power, this is the highest, best satisfaction. For what is any man at most, but an agent of the Most High?

16. To be true to one's own highest idea, is this not serving the Father? To be neglectful in such conviction, is this not the sickness of all the learned?

17. What honor say ye hath any man? The disciples answered, some one thing, and some another. After a while, the master said:

18. If those beneath him honor him, then it is no honor to him. If those above him honor him, then it is a reproval of his other deeds. But if he honor himself, he hath great honor indeed. But who can honor himself, save he is perfect in his own sight? He can not do this, therefore he hath no honor in extreme. To choose little honor, to choose a medium line, is this not the highest, any man can attain to?

19. To grieve with one's own self, because of imperfection, this is great folly. To eat fruit and herbs and rice, these are the purest diet, but only a fool would starve rather than eat flesh. Rites and ceremonies are useful, but even these a man had better dispense with, than to go to war for them.

20. To rest on the ancients only, this is great folly. To honor the ancients only, and to believe that they alone received revelation, these are the extremes of a foolish understanding.

21. To remember that the Creator is Ever Present, and with as much power and love and wisdom today as in the ancient days, this is wisdom.

22. To try to find some good thing one can do, this is creditable. But to do nothing good, because one can not do it in his own way, this is execrable.

23. He who findeth a good work to do, and doeth it, hath much satisfaction. But he should not exult therein; for he hath only done his duty. I have no honor in these twenty books.

24. Two kinds of men I have found; those who are predestined by the Gods to accomplish a certain work, and those who are born with no predestination. The first are erroneously called the highest, because they are at the head of great undertakings; but they are nevertheless but instruments in the hands of the Gods. The others, who are born without a predestined work, never can understand the former.

25. To be born near enough to the Light to see it, and believe in it, and have faith in it, this is a great delight. To be so far from the Creator that one can not believe in His Person and Presence, this is pitiable.

26. I divorced my wife because I discovered she could not bring forth heirs to belief or faith. No man should be bound to a woman whose desires lay in the corporeal self. And women should have the same privilege.

27. He who is wed to the Great Spirit, how can he dwell with one who is wed to the earth?

28. To one man, celibacy is the highest life, because he hath joy in his Heavenly Father. But to one who hath not this joy, celibacy is a great punishment. The society must admit both conditions.

29. There is no mean betwixt these two; therefore, both must be provided for.

30. Those who desire celibacy, approach the termination of the race; those whose desires

are the other way, are of a breed not so far on.

31. There need be no quarrel betwixt them. The destiny of both must be completed some time.

32. When a country is sparsely settled, those of extremes can go and live aside; it is nothing to govern such a state. Or to proclaim extreme doctrines before them. But when a country is full of people, the two extremes and the mean must dwell in proximity. It is not an easy matter to govern them wisely.

33. Whatever people can dwell together in great numbers on the smallest piece of ground, and yet have peace and plenty, such a people are the highest of all peoples.

34. Where an extreme doctrine can not be carried out, it is better to have a less extreme doctrine. People, like a drove of sheep, are much inclined to follow a leader. Herein, politicians and lawyers and judges run the state into war.

35. To legislate in such a way, that leaders can not lead the multitude into evil, this is wisdom. Were all leaders dead, the people themselves would not be very bad. Yet it is wrong to take any man's life, for life is something man hath no property in. Life resteth with Jehovih only; it is His.

36. Before the ignorant, and before fools, we speak by commandment. Chine'ya hath passed that age; our books must go persuasively, yea, in the mean.

37. To dictate to the learned, is to cast one's treasures into the fire. By asking them questions, we can often lead them.

38. Coaxing, with effect, is greater than dictation unobeyed. We preach to the rich man, that he should give all he hath to the poor, and he walketh away, giving nothing. When we say to him: Give a little, he doeth it. Herein the higher doctrine is the lower, and the lower doctrine is the higher, because it hath potency.

39. The ancients said, the first best thing was to love the Creator. I think so too. But when a philosopher asketh me to prove that the Creator is a Person, and is worth loving, I am puzzled. To accept Him as a Person, and as All Good, without criticism, this I find giveth the greatest happiness.

40. I have seen men who would pull the Creator to pieces and weigh His parts to know His worth, but such men end in disbelief in Him. One such man who accomplished any good in the world, I have not found. He is in the presence of goodly men like a fly that delighteth in breeding maggots; pretty enough in himself, but a breeder of vermin in the state.

41. Yet he who saith: Let the evil practice evil, because the Creator created them, is of a narrow mind. Or, if he saith: Jehovih sent the rain-storm to destroy the harvest; or, Jehovih sendeth fevers to the dirty city; such a man lacketh discretion in words and judgment.

42. But he who perceiveth that man is part of the creation, in which he must do a part of the work himself, or fevers will result, such a man hath his understanding open in regard to the Father.

43. Betwixt the two, much casting of all things in Jehovih's face, and too little belief in Him, lieth the mean, which worketh the perfection of man.

44. To try to find the Creator with love and adoration, instead of with a dissecting knife; this leadeth man on the highest road. To trust in Him, wherein we strive to do our best; this is good philosophy. To lay about idly, and not plant our fields, trusting in Him; this is

great darkness.

45. A wise man, perceiving the defects of the society, will not censure it, but turn to and find a remedy. It is for such purpose the angels of the higher heavens raise up great men in the world.

46. I have seen many people in many different kinds of worship, and they go through their parts in the sacrifice without perceiving the spiritual idea of the founders, and they are neither better nor worse for it. The infidel, with little discretion, seeing this, abuseth all the doctrines, but a wise man goeth between them to find the good which others lose sight of.

47. To find all the beauties in a man or woman, or in their behavior: this is God-like. To find their faults and speak of them: this is devilish. Yet, consider the man reverently, who speaketh not of persons. Who knoweth, may not all men be as automatons, some in the hands of Gods, and some in the hands of devils?

48. Such a doctrine would make us less severe with those who err, or who do evil. We hope for this.

49. I have seen the criminals being whipped, and I have said to myself: Only by a mere circumstance of birth, the wrong ones are being lashed. Otherwise, they had been governors of the states.

50. I once helped a bad man to elude his pursuers, and he escaped whipping, and he reformed himself. Since then, I have been a convert to great leniency.

51. The time will come when bad men will not be whipped nor tortured, but be appropriated to benefit the province; to shape our laws for such interpretation, is the beginning of wisdom in the government.

52. To appropriate all men to the best use; this is the wisest governor. To punish a bad man for vengeance sake; this is devilish.

53. If a man slay my sister, I raise my sword up before him, that he may run against it but I strike him not. To reform a man is better than to kill him; to lock up a bad man where he can do no harm, is sufficient for the state.

54. I have watched the soldiers in drill, and I said: This is a beautiful sight! For I saw the colors of their clothes, and the poetry of their maneuvers.

55. But I watched them again, and I said: This is wicked! For I looked into the object of the drill, and I beheld blood and death. The state useth power by violent means, but the soul within us desireth to accomplish peacefully.

56. The standard of a wise man, to judge wisely, requireth of him to imagine he is a God, high up in heaven, and that all men are his children. He should consider them as a whole, and beneficially.

57. This I perceive: There were a few wise men among the ancients, as wise as the wisest of this day. But today there are more wise men than in the ancient times. Doth this not lead us to believe that a time will come, when all people will be wise?

58. I should like to see this; it would settle many vexed questions. The seers tell us the soul of man is immortal; moreover, that they have seen the spirits of the dead. I tried for many years to ascertain if this were true, but I could not discover.

59. Nevertheless, I said: It is a good doctrine; I will appropriate it. The Creator must have perceived it also. It is reasonable, then, that He created man immortal.

60. The priests have appropriated this doctrine also. Moreover, the ancients say, the good

are rewarded in heaven, and the evil punished in hell. The people have been told this, and yet they will not be good.

61. Chine said: To deny one's self, and to labor for others with all our wisdom and strength: this is the highest doctrine. I saw a man on a mountain, calling to his flocks in the valleys, but they understood him not, and came not. Then he came mid-way down the mountain, and called, and the flocks heard him, and understood, and they went up to him.

62. It is easy to plan out high doctrines, but not so easy to give an efficient doctrine. He, who is mid-way, is the most potent. I have observed, that all peoples have higher doctrines, than they live up to. Yea, the boast of one religion over another is relatively of its superior height in the doctrines enunciated. And yet, they, who boast thus, practice neither virtue nor sincerity, for they live not up to the commonest doctrines.

63. On the other hand, the boast of a government is not of its virtues and goodness, and its fatherly care of the helpless, but of its strength in arms, and its power to kill. And these are the lowest of attributes.

64. To reach the government, and make it virtuous and fatherly, I was born into the world. This can be done only through the family, then to the hamlet, then to the province, and then to the empire.

65. But I could not do this without sincere men, who would faithfully practice my doctrines.

66. That ye are sincere, it is proved in your being with me; that you are virtuous and discreet, with propriety, is proved in you giving ear to my words. Yet, in this, how can I be sincere? I say, my words, when, in fact, I feel that no words I utter before the Council, are my words in fact.

67. Is this not true of all good men? wherein they are mouth-pieces for the Gods, or for the circumstances surrounding them? We open our mouth and speak, but where do our ideas come from?

68. When the sun shineth on the field, the herbs come forth; is it not the Creator's light falling upon us, that causeth our ideas to come forth? And if we keep away the grass and weeds, we receive a profitable harvest.

69. I would that all men would write a book on the Creator. Thought, directed in this way, will not go far from the right road.

70. To feel that He is with us, hearing all our words, seeing all our deeds: is this not the surest foundation to teach our children? To make them sincere, and to behave with propriety, what is so potent as faith in the Creator, and in His Son, Shang Te?

CHAPTER XXXVII.

1. The following are the books of Ka'yu, to wit:

2. OF THE CREATOR, the Great Spirit, Eolin, and His Creation.

3. OF THE PLAN OF CORPOREAL WORLDS, the sun and earth and moon and stars, and their sizes and motions, and their power to hold themselves in their places, by the velocity of rotation.

4. OF LIGHT AND HEAT, and thunder and lightning.

5. OF THE UNSEEN WORLDS; the upper and lower heavens; the habitations of the Gods.

6. OF THE INTERMEDIATE WORLD, or lower heaven, which resteth on the earth.

7. OF TE, who hath charge of this world and her heavens.

8. OF FALSE GODS, and their kingdoms in the lower heavens; and their power to catch the souls of men after death.

9. OF HELL, where the spirits of bad men are tortured for a long season.

10. OF THE HIGHEST HEAVENS, the Orian worlds, where the spirits of good mortals dwell in everlasting bliss.

11. OF THE ADMINISTRATION OF GODS, and drujas over mortals; how nations are built up, or destroyed by the Gods.

12. And these ten were such as in after years were recorded as the BOOKS OF GREAT LEARNING, and were made by the Sun Emperor THE STANDARD of the empire.

13. The following books of Ka'yu were such as were called, THE LESSER SCHOLARSHIPS, to wit:

14. AXIOMS, being the simples of problems.

15. THE PERFECT MAN (TAE), or HIGHEST REPRESENTATIVE.

16. THE MEAN MAN.

17. PURIFICATION; to purify the flesh; and to purify the spirit (or soul).

18. DIVINATION; consultation of spirits; legerdemain; sar'gis; su'is; power of the spirits to give man dreams and visions.

19. MAXIMS, propriety, sincerity, rites and ceremonies, reverence to age, respect to the dead.

20. LOVE; to love the Great Spirit; to love the parents; to love discipline and industry; marriage; marriage for earthly sake being wicked; marriage for spiritual redemption of the world by generations of holier men and women.

21. BOOK OF HISTORIES, of Gods and Saviors, of kings and emperors, of wise men, of law-givers, of the rise and fall of nations.

22. BOOK OF HOLIES, in six parts: Omnipotence, Worship, Jehovih's (Eolin's) Judgments, Progression, Reverence to the priests, and Obedience to the sacred commandment.

23. BOOK OF GEMS, also in six parts: Proverbs, Poetry, Morning and Evening Devotion, Association, in the family, the community, the state and the empire, Confession of Sins, and Praise and Rejoicing in Eolin, the Great Spirit.

24. Such were the twenty books of Ka'yu, which were the pith and cream of the eighteen thousand books of the ancients, together with all the light of the latter days added thereto. And in not many years, these also became the standard books of the Chine'ya empire.

25. And the Council of Ts'Sin'Ne came to a close, and the disciples of Ka'yu departed to their respective provinces, taking copies of the books with them.

26. God had said to his inspiring angels: Suffer not Ka'yu to know he receiveth light from heaven, for he shall be as an example to men, to inspire them to perfect the talents created withal.

27. And it was so; and during all these years of labor, Ka'yu knew not that he was inspired.

28. And God looked upon the empire of Chine'ya, and he said: Behold, my son shall write other books, but less profound.

29. And God inspired Ka'yu to write:

30. A BOOK OF FAMILY SAYINGS;

31. A BOOK OF ANELECTS;

32. A BOOK ON GOVERNMENT;

33. A Book on Life;

34. A Book on Punishments;

35. and A Book of Inventions.

And these were all the books Ka'yu wrote.

36. Nevertheless, his fame became so great that many men followed him about, even when he traveled into distant provinces, and they watched for the words he spake, and they wrote them down, and these were also made into books.

37. Because of the presence of God and his angels, Ka'yu saw clearly and heard clearly; nevertheless, his inspiration was God by proxy, and not like the inspiration of Chine, to whom God came in person, dwelling with him. Wherein, on many occasions, Ka'yu did things of his own accord, and committed some blunders.

END OF THE HISTORY OF KA'YU.

CHAPTER XXXVIII.

AGAIN OF THE TRIUNES.

1. When the Triune Gods perceived the great work accomplished by God, Jehovih's Son, in Vind'yu and Chine'ya, thus going to the root of the resurrection, they were sorely troubled for the ultimate prospect of their own heavenly kingdoms.

2. Ennochissa, Triune of Eta-shong, the heavenly kingdom over Chine'ya, sent an invitation to his two brother Triunes, to come to his heavenly city, to confer as to what should be done.

3. Accordingly, Kabalactes and Looeamong went to Eta-shong, where they were received in great grandeur, by one thousand million angels, and conducted to Ennochissa's heavenly capital and to his throne.

4. After due salutations and ceremonies, the Triunes all took seats on the throne. Whereupon the Holy Council retired from the presence, leaving only the Lords-in-attendance and the chief marshals within the crescent of the throne.

5. Ennochissa said: My brothers, peace be with you, because of my great joy for your presence.

6. Behold, Chine'ya, my earthly kingdom is being sapped in the foundation by the Ka'yu'an (Confucian) doctrines. What more will these people care for the Trinity? Jehovih is triumphant.

7. Kabalactes said: As thou hast spoken of Chine'ya, so say I of Vind'yu: The doctrine of the Trinity is being entirely destroyed by the Sakaya'yan doctrines. Our heavenly kingdoms will lose their base of supplies for subjects. Jehovih is triumphant.

8. Looeamong said: My brothers, it is not my place to point out the mistakes of others. But ye twain have built great heavenly capitals and palaces. Your kingdoms are embellished, as these heavens never were before, with magnificent cities.

9. Now, whilst ye were thus building, behold, I went with my legions down to the earth to war. I have not only overthrown many of the false Gods and Lords, but driven the worshipers of Jehovih to death.

10. Therefore, I have done little to beautify my heavenly kingdoms; but I rest above fear and apprehension. Nevertheless, whatsoever ye would, that I can do, to assist you out of your dilemmas, that will I do.

11. Now, after many suggestions and proposals, which were not accepted, Ennochissa said: As God, Jehovih's Son, hath taken an earthly course to insure his success, why shall not we also?

12. Behold, let us seek out a number of mortals also, and through them, establish our doctrines with mortals.

13. Looeamong said: A most wise suggestion.

14. Kabalactes said: This have I seen, since a long time, would be necessary to accomplish.

15. Thereupon a coalition was entered into by the three Triunes to give to mortals forty-nine Saviors, in order to establish the Trinity.

16. Which labor should be accomplished within two hundred years.

17. And it was also stipulated, that the whole forty-nine Saviors should be put to death ignominiously in order to win mortal sympathy.

18. To accomplish which, the Holy Confederacy provided, that each kingdom should supply one million angels for the army of inspiration, and that the same doctrine should be enunciated through every Savior, raised up for the work. And, accordingly, the three million inspiring angels were selected, all being above grade eighty, and these, being in three armies, were provided with one general officer to each army, called captain of the hosts.

19. For Looeamong's hosts, Thoth was made captain.

20. For Kabalactes' hosts, Yima was made captain.

21. For Ennochissa's hosts, Satree was made captain.

22. Accordingly, these three, Thoth, Yima and Satree, with their three millions, were sent down to the earth, to cover it around about in their own way, to raise up amongst mortals the required Saviors.

23. And there were thus given to the earth, in the space of less than two hundred years, forty-nine Saviors, to wit:

24. Rita, Gibbor, Gaal, Efrokin, Gargra, Thules, of the house of Thules, Etrus, Gadamon and Shofal; and all of these were of Egupt, and performed miracles, such as healing the sick, giving sight to the blind, and hearing to the deaf, and raising spirits of the dead to life; and they preached the doctrine of the Father, Son and Holy Ghost. And the angels inspired their enemies to put them to death, that their doctrines might be sealed in blood. And this was done.

25. Of the land of Parsi'e, the following men: Adakus, Mithra, Bali, Malopesus, Gonsalk, Hebron, Belus, of the house of Belus, Megath, Yodoman and Beels. And these preached the same doctrines, and were also put to death in order to seal their words in blood. Some of them were boiled in oil; some given to the lions in the dens, and some nailed on the ugsa, and left to perish.

26. Of Vind'yu, the following: Indra, Yuth, Sakai, Withoban, Aria, Devatat, Chrisna, Laracqu, Hagre, Anathia, Jannassa and Janeirus. And these performed the same kind of miracles, and preached the same doctrines, Father, Son and Holy Ghost. And they likewise suffered ignominious deaths, through the inspiration of the angel hosts.

27. Of Chine'ya, the following: Sam Sin, Ah Wah, Ah Chong, K'aou'foor, King Shu, Shaou and Chung Le. And these performed miracles, and preached the same doctrines. And they were also put to death ignominiously, being killed on the fetes, in order to seal

their doctrines in blood.

28. Of Heleste and Uropa, the following: Datur, Promethus, Quirnus, Iyo, Osseo and Yohannas. And these taught the same doctrines, performing miracles also. And they were killed on the fete in like manner, that their teachings might be sealed in blood.

29. Of Guatama, the following: Manito, Quexalcote, Itura, Tobak and Sotehoo. And these performed miracles, taught the same (Triune) doctrines, and were all put to death ignominiously, that their doctrines might be sealed in blood.

30. By the same army of angels that inspired these priests and magicians to miracles and the preaching of the Triune doctrines, were they also betrayed, suffering death by enemies who were inspired by the same angel hosts to that end.

31. Now so far as the Triune doctrines affected mortals, it related chiefly to war. The confederate Gods had said:

32. War for righteousness sake is just. We go to the earth to put swords and spears in the hands of the innocent and upright, saying to them: Defend yourselves! Establish yourselves! There is no Ever Present Person. All things were created out of the Holy Ghost. Depend upon yourselves. Rise up and be men, mighty to do the will of the Son, the Father and the Holy Ghost!

CHAPTER XXXIX.

1. When God, Son of Jehovih, saw the work of the Triunes, he bewailed the ways of heaven.

2. Jehovih said to him: Bewail not, My Son, nor grieve for what they have done. But make thou a record of their works; for mortals will preserve a history of this period, which shall be called, the Era of Saviors. And it shall stand as the darkest era in the cycle of Bon.

3. But it shall come to pass on the earth, that the Triunes will cut themselves off in a way they see not. For mortals will worship the Saviors. Whereupon the Triunes will become divided in their heavenly kingdoms.

4. So God bewailed no more, but prepared a new army of a thousand million angels, to go down to the earth, to provide for receiving the spirits of such as were sure to be slain in wars near at hand.

5. Of these hosts, Eyodemus was given command, and he appointed the following officers (to each hundred million), to go with him to wit:

6. Sogothwich, Yutempasa, Loo Wan, Thagaik, Maratha, Wein, Shuberth, Le Shong, Taivi and Duraya.

7. Nor did they reach the earth any too soon, for war soon circled the whole earth around, and every nation and tribe and people were immured in bloody carnage.

8. This period was practically the end of the good works of the Triune, but equally so the beginning of their mighty kingdoms in heaven, which were destined, ere long, to overshadow the whole earth.

9. The war, they set on foot on earth, extended into their own kingdoms. And these three Gods, the Triunes, saw, that only by might and desperate vigor, could they preserve their heavens from anarchy.

10. Five of the sub-Gods of Kabalactes, of Vind'yu, revolted within his own kingdom, and set up places of their own. And they falsely assumed the names of the Saviors, who

had been put to death, in order to establish the Trinity.

11. Kabalactes summoned his remaining chief officers to Haractu, his heavenly city, before his throne. And when they were before him, he said unto them:

12. This is the emergency of the Gods. My voice and my strong arm are raised up. Miscreants, whom I elevated to official positions in heaven, have betrayed their trust. With their legions they have seceded, and set up kingdoms of their own.

13. I have called you before me, that ye may jointly hear my decree, and obey. I will have order and harmony in my heaven. Neither shall there be but one God in my dominions, even myself. It is my will, therefore, that ye pursue these rebellious captains down to the earth, to their heavenly kingdoms, and despoil them utterly.

14. And if need be, ye shall capture them and their chief leaders, and cast them into hell. For they shall understand that I am not a God of peace, like the Jehovihian Gods, but a God of war.

15. For this purpose, I appoint Yima as my Holy Embassador and Earth Warrior. And I give to him two thousand million warriors, that he may make quick work of my rebellious chiefs.

16. My marshal shall select, therefore, for thee, Yima, the two thousand million angel warriors; and thou shalt appoint thine own generals and captains, and go at once down to the earth regions of these miscreants, and carry out my commandments.

17. Yima and his hosts did as commanded, but not suddenly; for an angel war ensued which lasted forty-six years, before the five rebellious Gods were beaten from their strongholds. And, even then, they were not captured and cast into hell; but they escaped, taking half a million angel warriors with them, and they migrated to Uropa, to the city of Roma, where they established themselves in security. Thus the deposed Vind'yu Gods became Gods of Roma.

18. Immediately after Yima succeeded in clearing Vind'yu, Kabalactes summoned him again to Heractu, his heavenly seat, before his Holy Council. When he had thus come, Kabalactes spoke from the throne, saying:

19. Because my wisdom hath triumphed in heaven and earth, I now take unto myself a new name, BUDHA. And from this day and hour I shall be called by no other name forever. And my heavenly place, my city and my heavens, shall be known henceforth, forever, as Haractu, the Budhist heavenly kingdom, the All Highest Heaven of Heavens!

20. Thou, Yima, shalt repair again to the earth with thy two thousand million warring angels, and establish me, as the Budha. By fire and by sword, by blood and death shalt thou establish my name on the earth.

21. And thou shalt find a way to teach mortals, that I was Sakaya, and Sakaya was and is the Budha, Son of the Triune, Son of the Holy Ghost.

22. Jehovih had said: Behold the time will come unto both Gods and men who deny My All Person, when they will espouse even falsehood for sake of their own selfish ends.

23. And Kabalactes shall falsely assume, that he was Sakaya, and that Sakaya was and is Budha.

24. Jehovih spake to God, saying: Behold, he commandeth himself to be called Budha. Now I say unto thee, suffer this also to be, neither accuse thou him before heaven or earth of his falsehood.

25. Nay, but thou shalt also henceforth call him Budha, signifying ALL KNOWLEDGE,

for it is his choice.

26. So it came to pass from this time after, Kabalactes was called Budha in heaven. And his angel hosts under Yima, who descended to the earth, inspired mortals, both through the oracles and by direct contact, to call Sakaya, Budha, and Budha, Sakaya. And these things were so. And in not many generations, mortals forgot that they were two persons; but they accredited all things to Budha of the spirit, and all things of the flesh to Sakaya, although the whole matter was false in fact.

27. Wherein, it came to pass, that the followers of Budha professed peace, but practiced war and conquest, setting out by bood and carnage and destruction to establish Budhism in Vind'yu.

28. Jehovih said to God: Even this shalt thou suffer them to do. For herein will they lay the foundation of the final overthrow of this false God, Budha. For they will put aside the Trinity of their own accord, retaining Budha and the Holy Ghost. Yea, they will ultimately teach, that Budha is itself but a principle, and that the Holy Ghost is but as nothing. They will say: War for Budha, and thou shalt attain Budha, which shall be followed by Nirvana, which they will also call nothing. And these things came to pass.

CHAPTER XL.

1. Not less were the trials of Ennochissa; for his sub-Gods also revolted, and many of them assumed the names of the Saviors he had given to Chine'ya. And he also sent an army of two thousand million angel warriors down to the earth to destroy them, and break them up, and if need be to capture them, and cast them in hell.

2. Of these hosts, he made Yad'deth chief captain, giving him power to select his own captains and generals. And it came to pass, that a heavenly war ensued on the earth, in Chine'ya, betwixt the hosts of Ya'deth and the rebellious sub-Gods and their hosts, which lasted seventy years.

3. And Ya'deth gained the victory, clearing away all the rebel angels of the sub-Gods, and putting them to flight. Four of these rebel Gods fled into Argos, to Athena, where they established themselves securely.

4. Ennochissa now summoned Ya'deth and his victorious army to Eta-shong, his heavenly kingdom. And when he was before the throne, Ennochissa said unto him:

5. Thou hast beholden the machinations of my brother Triune God, Kabalactes, who hath falsely assumed the name, Budha, and proclaimed himself the All Highest God, and his heaven the All Highest Heaven of Heavens. Two things do I decree, this day and hour: An army of angels, for the earth, of two thousand millions; and thou Ya'deth, shalt be their commander, to do my will. And another army of angel warriors, for my heavenly kingdom of Eta-shong; and for my kingdom of Damaya, over Guatama.

6. For my heavenly army, thou, Loo Wan, shalt be commander for Eta-shong; and thou, Biwawotha, shalt be commender for Damaya.

7. And to ye of heaven, I assign the care and protection of my kingdoms with your armies. And ye shall wall your places around, and fortify me on every side with angel warriors. Yet, menace not the angels of Budha, nor of Looeamong. Nevertheless, if they offend, or are disrespectful of me and my kingdoms, ye shall arrest them, and provide places of torment for them, and cast them in.

8. But as for thee, Ya'deth, thou and thy hosts shalt return again to the earth, to mortals,

948

and establish me as BRAHMA, which shall be my name on earth and in heaven from this time forth forever. And thou shalt possess the oracles, and by all possible means establish me amongst mortals, as well as in Vind'yu and Chine'ya. And all who profess Brahma hereafter, shall be my subjects on their entrance into heaven. 9. And if it come to pass that Budha's mortal warriors fall upon the mortal Brahmins, to destroy them, then shalt thou consider that Budha is my enemy.

10. And thou and thy angel warriors shall obsess every Brahmin to take up arms, and war to the death every aggressing Budha. For Budha shall learn that I, Brahma, rule these heavens in mine own way.

11. So it came to pass, the four thousand million warriors of Ennochissa (now falsely named Brahma), were selected, and apportioned and marched off to their several places in great pomp and glory. To describe even one of these armies, with their music and their implements of war, their manual and procession, would require a large book. Then their vessels of war; their implements of fire and water; their banners and flags; and, above all, their enthusiasm. For many of them had been warriors in earth-life, and knew no other trade, and now exulted in the prospect of mortal blood and death.

12. Of the sub-Gods of Vind'yu and Chine'ya, Jehovih said: For this, alone, these things are good. For, in time to come, man of the earth will look abroad over the earth and say: How came the Vind'yu Gods in Roma? How came the Chine'ya Gods in Athena?

13. For, since they will not be able to answer their own questions, they will perceive, there must have been a heavenly cause that mortals knew not of.

14. For in time of the fulfillment of My revelations, it will not be sufficient unto either heaven or earth to re-establish spiritual communion; but it shall also be shown unto them that there are kingdoms and principalities in heaven. And they are ruled over by both good and bad Gods. Moreover, they shall understand that of a truth whoso worshippeth Budha shall go to Budha to be his slaves; and whoso worshippeth Brahma shall go to Brahma, and be his slaves.

15. I will make it plain to them that to worship a spirit, though he be a God, is but the giving of their own souls into bondage. For they shall in that day understand that the Great Spirit, the Ever Present, is not an idol in the figure of a man, sitting on a throne.

16. Moreover, spirits and mortals shall perceive that to deny My Person, will, soon or late, bring the doer into a trap from which he can not escape. Give then to Ennochissa the name Brahma, for it is his choice. And thou shalt perceive that the time will come, when he will seek to throw aside even this name, and even his own person, in order to escape hell.

17. Thus was established the two false Gods, Budha and Brahma. And at once there was a war in heaven, as well as on earth. And this was virtually the end of the schools and colleges in these heavens, and also the beginning of the breaking up of the factories and places of industry in the two kingdoms, Eta-shong and Haractu, in atmospherea.

18. As to the earth regions, Vind'yu and Chine'ya, this is how they stood in that day:

19. Chine'ya was so well established in the doctrines of Chine and Ka'yu, that the people shunned war and idolatry. The Saviors had gained but little footing. And now, when the Gods sought to inspire the people to war, in order to establish themselves, Brahma and Budha, only the most barbarous regions could be influenced.

20. Brahma, the false God, now perceiving the potency of Ka'yu's books, sent his angel

warriors to inspire the Sun King, T'sin, to have all the books in Chine'ya destroyed, in order to reduce the empire to ignorance. Accordingly, the Sun King, T'sin, issued a decree, commanding all the books and tablets of Chine'ya to be destroyed.

21. Brahma said: I will have all, or destroy all. My angels shall not let sleep in peace, any king or governor in all this land, until he engage in the work of thus destroying mine enemy, Learning.

22. And there were destroyed, in one year, more than five million books, and one million tablets of stone and copper; being the destruction of the books of the ancients, for upward of twenty thousand years. Besides these, there were destroyed many of the books of Ka'yu, but not all of them.

23. In the meantime, the anti-war spirit of the people had cried out to the Creator: O Father, what shall we do to avert war, and to preserve the revelations of Thy holy ones of old?

24. And Jehovih answered them, through God of Paradise, Jehovih's Son, saying: Build ye walls against the barbarians. And your walls shall stand as a testimony of what ye are willing to do, rather than engage in war, even for self-preservation.

25. Because ye have faith in Me, I will be with you even unto the end.

26. And it came to pass that the Faithists of Chine'ya built stone walls, the greatest buildings in all the world. And they stand to this day.

27. Jehovih said: Behold the works of My chosen. As long as these walls stand, they shall be testimony of the struggle of My people, to maintain themselves, by means of peace instead of war. And the walls shall be monuments to the Faithists of this land, who have perished by the false Gods, Brahma and Budha.

28. Yea, the testimony of these walls shall be stronger, in time to come, against Brahma and Budha, than though every stone were a sword and spear. And the followers of My Son, Ka'yu, shall loathe them with pity and hate.

29. In Vind'yu also, did the machinations of Budha and Brahma work sore mischief on mortals. In this country both of these false Gods decreed the destruction of all books and tablets, save such as looked favorable to their own doctrines. And there were here destroyed more than two million books and one million tablets, of stone and copper.

30. And the schools and colleges of the people were well nigh destroyed, the whole length and breadth of the land.

31. And in both, Chine'ya and Vind'yu, were there slain in war, in order to establish the names of these Gods amongst mortals, more than one hundred and forty millions of people, men, women and children.

32. By the angel warriors of these two Gods were mortals thus inspired in the work of destruction. Not only against the Faithists were these Gods, but against each other also. And mortals were their victims, for the glory and exaltation of the two heavenly kingdoms, Haractu and Eta-shong.

CHAPTER XLI.

1. God said: Hear ye, O earth, and ye, O heaven, of Looeamong, the other of the Triunes, the founders of the doctrines of the Holy Ghost and Trinity.

2. My word is gone forth; the kingdoms of the spirit of the dead shall reveal through me unto all men; their libraries shall be as an open book to Jehovih's Sons and Daughters in

heaven and earth.

3. Because Looeamong pursued Ashtaroth in conjunction with Baal, and overthrew her and her kingdom, and cast them into hell, he became as a lion, savage at the taste of blood.

4. And I cried out unto him, saying: Hold, hold; enough! But he said: Nay, till I have Baal also cast into hell, I will not cease the carnage of mortal blood.

5. And he cast about in Hapsendi, his heavenly place, calling up angel warriors, tens of millions, hundreds of millions. But Baal, the self-God of Heleste, called his mighty legions in heaven, and sent them down to the earth, redoubled, to inspire mortals to bloody deeds.

6. Baal said: Mine is an easy doctrine to understand. All mortals that worship not Baal shall be put to death. The worshipers of the Trinity, the Father, Son and Holy Ghost, are my enemies. Such mortals shall die! Such angels shall go the way of hell.

7. The Faithists, the worshipers of Jehovih, are also my enemies. Such mortals shall be tortured and sawed in halves. Such angels shall be bound in knots in hell, and suffocated forever! I will have them know that Baal is the All Highest God of heaven and earth.

8. All the land of Arabin'ya, Heleste and part of Uropa, was as one great seat of anarchy and war.

9. Looeamong said: I come not to bring peace, but war! I come to set nation against nation, people against people, man against man. For righteousness sake will I purify the earth with human blood.

10. I will not have a half-way peace; I will destroy my enemies, east and west and north and south. By the Holy Ghost have I sworn it!

11. And the kingdoms of Egupt, and of Media, of Armenia, and Phrygia, and Argos, and Scythia and Noamedia, and of all the regions of Arabin'ya and the west, shall know no peace till I have destroyed the worship of all Gods but the Triunes.

12. And it came to pass, that there was no peace in any of those lands. Neither was there system to the warfare, looking to any important result.

13. Jehovih hath said: Let this stand as a testimony unto coming generations. For they shall look back to these times, and behold, that the wars raged without purpose on the part of any king. And that mortals were the instruments in the hands of the angels, who ruled over them. And it shall be testimony unto them of what cometh upon peoples, who deny My Person. For they shall compare the peace and rejoicing of My people, whilst they had no king, but kept My commandments, with such as put Me away, and tried to make themselves strong in kings and standing armies.

14. Baal now established two more heavenly kingdoms, one over Jerusalem, and one above the Apennine mountains, off from Roma. And in the latter kingdom, which he called Arkoli, he made an alliance with the Vind'yu Gods that escaped from their own heavenly regions and fled to the mortal city, Roma. And near Athena, he founded a sub-kingdom of five hundred million angels, and made an alliance with the Gods that escaped from the Brahmin kingdoms.

15. In this emergency, Looeamong, the Triune God of the Holy Ghost, beheld, with fear and trembling, his formidable enemy, Baal. And so he determined, to send to Buddha for assistance. Thus he solicited, to wit:

16. To the Triune, the Holy Budha, Son of the Holy Ghost, greeting in love and majesty.

17. By the power of the Triunes are we sworn to each other, to establish the Holy Ghost in heaven and earth. By which confederacy are we three Gods powerful above all other Gods.

18. Now behold, Baal, the most fiendish of all Gods, wageth war against our holy doctrines in all the regions of my heavenly kingdoms and on my dominions of the earth also. But my forces in heaven and earth need re-enforcement. And I come to thee, according to our original compact, asking thee for a thousand million angel warriors.

19. By messengers Looeamong sent this to Budha, who answered him as followeth, to wit:

20. It is said that great trials are the making of angels and mortals. I need my hosts for mine own purposes. Nevertheless, if thou wilt cede Egupt to me, thou shalt have the army thou asketh for, for the space of one hundred years.

21. Insulting as was this proposal, Looeamong was obliged to accede to it, or to have his kingdom destroyed by Baal.

22. Accordingly, such an alliance was entered into; and so, Looeamong removed his heavenly city, Hapsendi, westward, and cast it over Naomedia. And immediately thereafter, Budha established a heavenly kingdom in Egupt, and called it, Celonia, giving its management into the keeping of Thoth, the Bertian, an angel, so named, because he was cunning, like a fox.

23. With these additional forces, Looeamong now renewed the assault on Baal on every side, even more violently in his heavenly places than on the earth.

24. And it came to pass, that Looeamong routed Baal from his heavenly kingdom, and from his sub-kingdoms also, but he did not capture him, or subdue him. And the angels of Looeamong obtained Jerusalem and Athena, besides two hundred small cities with their oracle-houses and temples also. And Looeamong's angel warriors took possession of them, so they could answer the oracles, the magicians and priests, in their own way.

25. Baal still maintained an army of three thousand million angel warriors; and he established himself in the city of Roma and Hieadas, that is, Bizantium, but used most of his army as rambling marauders.

26. Now, when Looeamong beheld, that the other two Triunes had taken new names falsely, and that they had gained power thereby, he resolved to adopt for himself the names, Lord and God.

27. Thoth, his chief warrior angel, fighting against Baal, had said: Most Holy Triune, I must give mortals a name to fight for. The term, Holy Ghost, is not potent.

28. So, Looeamong falsely assumed to be God, the Lord of heaven and earth.

29. He said to Thoth: Go tell mortals I am the same, who wrought wonders for the Israelites. And, forsooth, the Israelites will fight for me.

30. Thoth did this. And furthermore Looeamong inspired one, Ezra, to gather all the records he could, to be proof of his labors for the Israelites.

31. To accomplish this, Thoth employed seven hundred thousand angels, to be with Ezra and the numerous scribes whom Ezra employed. And by their inspiration were the books of the Ezra Bible written and compiled, according to the commandments of Looeamong. And there were thus collected seventy-two books, and they were put on file in the king's library in Jerusalem, after the manner in which the ancients preserved important records of events, and these books were named by Ezra, The Holy Library, of which number fifty-four remain to this day.

32. But, of all these, not one book was inspired of Jehovih, or His Son, God of heaven and earth. Nevertheless, there are many things within them, that were of Jehovih and His angels. Howbeit, though they were put on record by men, and interpreted by men.

33. Looeamong, in these things sinneth not against Jehovih, for he did not cause his own name, Looeamong, to be made worshipful.

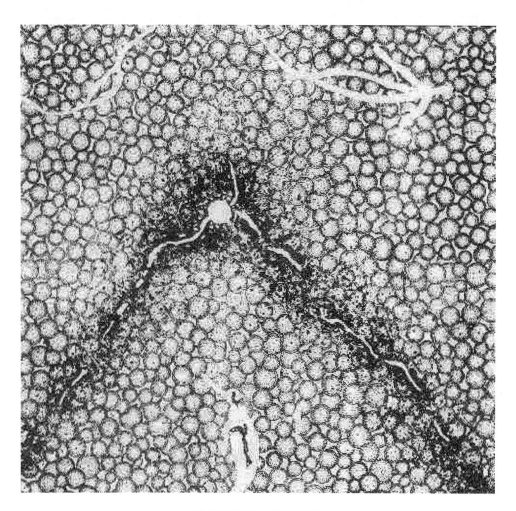

PLATE 35. LO'IASK.

The position of the earth that led to the building of the Chinese Wall. It came to pass, in those days, that the spirit of the Father dwelt in mortals, and they were turned away from the shedding of blood. And when the earth came into Lo'iask, in etherea, His etherean angels penetrated the darkness and inspired the chosen of China to build a wall to protect themselves from destruction. And a wall was so built, the greatest on the whole earth. Jehovih said: Since these, My chosen people, have achieved the age of peace on earth, let them shut themselves in, away from the barbarians without, and they shall endure as a secluded people till the coming of kosmon. And it was so.

CHAPTER XLII.

1. God, Jehovih's Son, was wise above all these trials, for he had the light of Jehovih's kingdoms with him.

2. And it will be shown, presently, how much further ahead are the plans laid out by Jehovih's Sons, than by His enemies.

3. Because Pharaoh persecuted the Israelites, Moses put a curse upon Pharaoh. Now, after hundreds of years in the lower heavens, behold, Pharaoh was cast into hell, and then into chaos, and none but Moses could deliver him, as hath been previously described.

4. So, Moses descended from the higher heavens, and delivered Pharaoh, and he provided Pharaoh a new name, Illaes, and sent him back to earth to labor with the Israelites, in order to fulfill his shortness in righteous works. Illaes, therefore, became a willing volunteer, and many angels with him.

5. And these angels inspired seven hundred Israelites to separate themselves from all other people, and to go and live by direction of the angels of Jehovih. Moreover, the angels inspired these people to call themselves Es'eans, as commanded by Moses in heaven.

6. These Es'eans were, therefore, a separate people, pledged to Jehovih, to have no king nor earth-ruler, save their rab'bahs. And they dwelt in communities and families of tens and twenties and hundreds, holding all things in common. But in marriage, they were monagamic; neither would they have more than one suit of clothes each; and they lived on fruit and herbs only; nor ate they fish nor flesh of anything that had ever breathed the breath of life. And they bathed every morning at sunrise, and worshipped before the altar of Jehovih, doing, in all things, after the manner of the ancient Faithists. By virtue of the angel hosts, who were with them, did they these things. And they held communion with the angels of heaven, every night before going to sleep.

7. Illaes had said: Because I persecuted the Faithists, and raised up my hands against them and against Jehovih, I was instrumental, in part for their fall. Now will I labor with them, to re-establish them in purity and love. And he so labored.

8. And Illaes and his angel hosts made the camps of the Es'eans their dwelling places, watching over these few Israelites, day and night for hundreds of years. Yea, without leaving them, these faithful angels guarded them from all the warring hosts of angels, belonging to the armies of Baal and Ashtaroth, and to the Triune God, Looeamong, and his hosts.

9. And, though the Es'eans lived in great purity of body and soul, yet they were evilly slandered by the world's people around about them on every side.

10. But Jehovih prospered the seed of the Es'eans, in holiness and love, for many generations.

11. Then came Gafonaya, chief of the loo'is, according to the command of God, to raise up an heir to the Voice of Jehovih. And, in four generations more, an heir was born, and named, Joshu, and he was the child of Joseph and his wife, Mara, devout worshippers of Jehovih, who stood aloof from all other people, save the Es'eans.

12. And, because of the extreme youth of Mara, the child was of doubtful sex, whereupon the rab'bahs said, the child was an iesu, signifying neutral.

13. The time of the birth of the child, was three days after the descent of a heavenly ship from the throne of God. And many of the Es'eans looked up and beheld the star, and they felt the cold wind of the higher heavens fall upon the place and around about the tent, where the child was born. And they said, one to another: Jehovih, remembers us.

14. Gafonaya, the chief angel of the loo'is, knew beforehand what the birth would be, and he sent out around about the Es'ean encampments extra guardian angels; and these notified the descending hosts of heaven of what was near at hand.

15. So the messengers from heaven tarried until after the child was born, acquainting Illaes of the time ahead when Moses and Elias, with their hosts would come to complete the deliverance of the spirits of the Eguptians, whom Moses had colonized in atmospherea.

16. Illaes said: Thank Jehovih, I shall once more look upon Moses' face.

17. When the birth was completed, the angels of heaven re-entered their star-ship and hastened back to Paradise, God's heavenly seat.

CHAPTER XLIII.

1. When Joshu was grown up, and ready for his labor, God provided a host of one hundred million angels to make a line of light from his Holy Council down to the earth; and they so made it.

2. And God provided a guardian host of two thousand million angels to protect the line of communications; for it was war times in heaven and earth.

3. Then came Moses from his etherean realms, accompanied by Elias and a sufficient host. And he came to Paradise, to God on the throne, where due preparation had been made for them. For the heavenly kingdoms of God were stirred from center to circumference, when it was heralded abroad that Moses and Elias were coming.

4. And Paradise was like a new heavenly city, being acceded by an influx of more than a thousand million visitors for the occasion.

5. And heralds and receivers and marshals and musicians extended every way.

6. A whole book might be written on the glory of the occasion, when that etherean ship descended from the higher heavens. Suffice it, Moses was received according to the custom of Gods. And God said to Moses and Elias: Come ye, and honor my throne; and I will proclaim a file before the throne, to be followed by two days' recreation.

7. Then Moses and Elias went up, and sat on the throne of God, that they might look upon Moses' face. And Moses stood up before them. Moses said: I remember standing on the earth whilst the hosts that came out of Egupt passed before me! Great Jehovih, what symbols of things Thou givest. And ever with a new thrill of joy to the soul. O Thou Almighty!

8. That was all he said; but so great was the love and glory in his face as he stood on the throne of God that every soul that passed said: Moses, blessed Son of Jehovih!

9. And God granted two days' recreation, during which time the ethereans mingled with the atmosphereans in great delight. After that, Moses, with his hosts, went to Elaban, his colony of Eguptians, who were now raised high in the grades. And Moses had them removed to Aroqu, where they were duly prepared and adorned as Brides and Bridegrooms of Jehovih. And, after suitable preparation, Moses provided for their ascent

to the Nirvanian fields of Metapotamas, in etherea, sending them in charge of his own hosts.

10. After that, Moses and his remaining hosts descended to the earth, to Kanna'yan, to the tribes of Es'eans, which had been raised up by Illaes (Pharaoh). And great was the meeting betwixt Illaes and Moses. The former broke down with emotion. He said: All praise to Thee, O Jehovih! Thou has remembered me at last.

11. Moses came to him, and said: I have come for thee, O Nu'ghan! I have a place prepared for thee and thy hosts in my etherean kingdoms! Thou hast done well!

12. Then Moses and his hosts drew their otevan down to the angel camp, which was near the camp of the mortals, the Es'eans, and they made the light to fall upon the boat; and it came to pass that many of the Es'eans looked up and beheld the otevan, calling it a chariot.

13. And Moses and Elias went and stood before Joshu, and he saw them.

14. Moses said unto him: My son! my son! The light of Eloih is upon thee. Israel, through thee, shall regain the All One, which was lost.

15. Thereupon, Moses and his hosts, together with Illaes and his hosts, went into the otevan, and immediately took course for Paradise, God's heavenly seat, where they arrived in due season. And, after three days, they again entered the fire-ship, and took course for Moses' etherean realms.

CHAPTER XLIV.
DOCTRINES OF JOSHU AND HIS DEATH.

1. God said: These were my doctrines, as I taught through Joshu:

2. Thou shalt keep the ten commandments of Moses.

3. Thou shalt not engage in war, nor abet war.

4. Thou shalt eat no flesh of any animal, or fish, or bird, or fowl, or creeping thing which Jehovih created alive.

5. Thou shalt dwell in families, after the manner of the ancient Israelites, who held all things in common.

6. Thou shalt have no king nor queen, nor bow down in worship to any, save thy Creator.

7. Thou shalt not call on the name of angels to worship them, nor to counsel with them on the affairs of earth.

8. Thou shalt love thy neighbor as thyself, and do unto thy fellow man as thou wouldst have him do unto thee.

9. Thou shalt return good for evil, and pity to them that sin.

10. It hath been said: An eye for an eye, a tooth for a tooth; but I say, return good for evil.

11. And if a man smite thee on one cheek, turn the other unto him also.

12. The man shall have but one wife, and the woman but one husband.

13. As the children honor the father, so will the family be blest with peace and plenty.

14. Remember, that all things are of Jehovih, and ye are His servants, to help one another.

15. And as much as ye do these services to one another, so serve ye Jehovih.

16. Behold only the virtues and wisdom in thy neighbor; his faults thou shalt not discover.

17. His matters are with his Creator.

18. Call not on the name of any God or Lord in worship; but worship Jehovih only.

19. And when thou prayest, let it be after this manner:

20. Jehovih, who rulest in heaven and earth, hallowed be Thy name, and reverent amongst men. Sufficient unto me is my daily bread; and, as much as I forgive those that trespass against me, forgive Thou me, and make me steadfast, to shun temptation, for all honor and glory are Thine, worlds without end. Amen!

21. To visit the sick and distressed, the helpless and blind, and to relieve them; to provide for the widow and orphan, and keep thyself unspotted before men; these are the way of redemption.

22. Thou shalt take no part in the governments of men, but observe the will of Jehovih, being obedient unto all governments for His sake.

23. All men are the children of One Father, who is Jehovih; and whosoever chooseth Him, and keepeth His commandments, is His chosen.

24. To preserve the seed of His chosen, thou shalt not wed but with the chosen.

25. Contend not with any man for opinion's sake, nor for any earthly thing.

26. And let thy speech be for other's joy; nor open not thy mouth, if thy words will give pain.

27. Therefore, be considerate of thy speech; teaching others by gentleness and love, to be respectful toward all men.

28. Preserve the sacred days of the rab'bahs; and the rites and ceremonies of emethachavah.

29. For three years, Joshu traveled amongst the Israelites, preaching, and restoring the ancient doctrines.

30. And there were gathered in groups, of tens and twenties and fifties, more than two thousand Israelites, of the ancient Order of Moses, who became steadfast followers of the teachings of Joshu.

31. But, because of persecution, by the apostate Jews, they kept themselves aloof from the world, having signs and pass-words, whereby they knew one another.

32. First, the God, Baal, and after him, Thoth, inspired the kings and rulers, against these Faithists.

33. And they proved them by commanding them to eat flesh, even swine's flesh, the which, if they refused, was testimony sufficient before the laws, to convict them of being enemies against the Gods.

34. So, they were scourged, and put to death, whenever found.

35. Now, it came to pass, that Joshu went into Jerusalem to preach, and in not many days thereafter, he was accused of preaching Jehovih.

36. And he was arrested, and whilst being carried to prison, he said:

37. Ye are hypocrites and blasphemers! Ye practice none of the commandments, but all the evils of satan.

38. Behold, the temple shall be rent in twain, and ye shall become vagabonds on the earth.

39. At that, the multitude cast stones upon him, and killed him!

40. And Jehovih sent a chariot of fire, and bore his soul to Paradise.

CHAPTER XLV.

1. The Lord said: Now, behold, Looeamong stood no longer upon the practice of righteousness, but upon might.

2. Neither considered he more the resurrection of mortals or angels.

3. The craft and wisdom of Baal baffled Looeamong, in both his heavenly battles and his battles for mortals.

4. Behold, the whole of the countries of Egupt, Parsi'e, Heleste and Uropa were in war; and the heavens of these countries were also in war, with hundreds of hells within them.

5. Looeamong fought no longer for the Trinity nor the Holy Ghost, but to save his heavenly kingdom, lest he be captured, and cast into hell.

6. And even more desperately was Baal situated against him.

7. In the meantime, the other two Triunes began to war against each other in their heavenly kingdoms, contending for boundaries and subjects.

8. Thoth sent the following message to Looeamong, to wit: Greeting to thee, thou Most High Triune, in the name of the Holy Ghost.

9. Wherein I am embarrassed, I pray thee, give me leniency. My suit is not without due deliberation and through prayers to the Holy Ghost. Long have I fought thy battles, and I have gained great power and authority in many kingdoms, in heaven and earth.

10. But, behold, I labor against Gods who have the advantage of me. The Chine'ya rebel Gods and the Vind'yu rebel Gods, that fled from the Triune kingdoms in the east, have taken upon themselves names popular with mortals. Witness these names: Nestor, alias Puith; Neptune, alias Poseidon; Oileus, alias Pendre; Priam, alias Hogath; Phoebus, alias Onewakax, alias Apollo; Pales, alias Shugansitha; Pelides, alias Peleus; Saturn, alias Kronos; Thaleia, alias Musae; Thestor, alias Suko, alias Bayrith, alias Calchas; Thetis, alias Arama, alias Mi, alias Mara, alias Achill'ya, alias Argos; Venus, alias Seinalt, alias Vishnu, alias Mira, alias Thor, alias Theo; Vulcan, alias Anawahah, alias Ir, alias Agni, alias Hefaste'yan; Calianessa, alias Vritta; Hecla, alias Jah, alias Tyronia, alias Nileus; Nemertis, alias Itra, alias Prometh'ya, alias Ari, alias Mithra; Opsendes, alias Miletus, alias Brahma, alias Ishaka, alias Davetat, alias Sakaya, alias Morototha; Pherna, alias Holasa, alias Iao, alias Crite, alias Thammus; Spieo, alias Pelides, alias Hecla, alias Vulcan; Thor, alias Padua, alias Hermes, alias Belus, alias Hiroth, alias Yossammis; Thoa, alias Thor, alias Neptune, alias Orion, alias Aph, alias Thulis; Quiurnus, alias Vishnu, alias Ahambre, alias I'isna, alias Atys, alias Etus.

11. Thoth continued: And yet these are not all. For these Gods have no fear of the Holy Ghost, and they choose any name that will be flattering to mortals. And the magicians and priests, and such others as have power to hear the voices of spirits, are led to believe that they hear the very Gods whose names are given.

12. This, then, is my misfortune, thou most Holy God of the Triune: I am commanded to give but one name, even the Holy Ghost, or the Father, to mortals. Or, whether my angel hosts speak to the oracles or to persons capable of hearing spirits, and say to them: Fight ye for the Holy Ghost, or fight ye for the Creative element, mortals heed us not. Or, they irreverently mock us, saying: What care we for a God that is but a ghost, a shadow, a creative element? Give us Gods that talk, and of themselves. We want no angels from the Holy Ghost. Bring your Gods, and let the oracles tell us what they say.

13. Looeamong then sent messengers and a suitable escort to Jerusalem, on the earth, where Thoth was stationed at the time, with an angel host of warriors, commanding his presence before his Holy Council in Hapsendi, Looeamong's heavenly city and kingdom.

14. Now, after Thoth went thither, and they held a Council of many days, a disturbance arose in the Council in consequence of the heat of the debates.

15. For the Gods of the Council, for the most part, said: What better are we than the Jehovians? What greater power have we than the Jehovians? Who can answer the philosophy of Thoth? It is a truth, mortals have never been satisfied with AN ANGEL FROM THE GODS. . They want the God himself.

16. Was not this forever the weakness of the Jehovians? Such angels could give no name that mortals knew, save they falsely assumed a name. Hence their weakness, compared to such angels as unscrupulously assumed to be Gods.

17. We all knew these things before our Holy Confederacy was formed. Yea, one of the chief reasons for forming a confederacy in heaven was that we might more effectually overcome the power of evil spirits over mortals.

18. In that day, we said: The three persons, the Son, the Father and the Holy Ghost, would enable us to appear in person and with authority unto mortals.

19. Behold, it hath now come to pass mortals desire a more definite God, one known unto them. We can not truthfully take the name of any God Thoth hath named, nor of any other God worshipped by mortals.

20. Looeamong then drove hence from the palace his Holy Council, that he might have an opportunity to reason with himself, as to what he should do.

CHAPTER XLVI.
SATAN ENTERETH THE HOLY COUNCIL OF HAPSENDI, AND SPEAKETH UNTO LOOAMONG, THE TRIUNE.

1. Hear me, O thou most upright of Gods. Mine is a tale of pity and of horrors for thy people.

2. Behold, thy one-time brother Triunes have had great advantage of thee from the start.

3. They had more populous kingdoms and subjects of higher grades.

4. Nevertheless, wherein they have prospered thou shalt be wise.

5. They also found it necessary to have a name, that mortals could call unto.

6. And they took upon themselves the names, Brahma and Budha, both of which signify knowledge, no more nor less.

7. This hath satisfied mortals.

8. Now, thou shalt chose the name, Kriste, which is the Ahamic word for knowledge also.

9. In this, then, thou shalt have truth on thy side in heaven before thy Holy Council, and on earth thou shalt have a personal embodiment.

CHAPTER XLVII.
LOOEAMONG FALSELY ANNOUNCETH HIMSELF THE KRIST (CHRIST)

1. The Lord said: Behold, it came to pass as had been foretold by God, Jehovih's Son: The Triunes will all become false Gods, because they have denied the Almighty.

2. God said: There is but One, who is All Knowledge. Whatsoever angel or God

959

announceth himself to be All Knowledge, is false in presence of Jehovih.

3. Nevertheless, Looeamong had it proclaimed in heaven and earth that he was The Kriste, which is the Ahamic expression for All Knowledge.

4. The Lord said: Now, therefore, Looeamong was from this time forth a false God in heaven and on earth.

5. And Looeamong commanded Thoth, his angel warrior in command of his earthly dominions, to raise up tribes of warriors amongst mortals.

6. And, by the inspiration of said Thoth, these warriors were induced to call themselves Kriste'yans (Christians).

7. God said: That man may know, this is true, behold, the followers of Jehovih are not warriors, nor have they ever been.

8. Jehovih said: This mark put I upon man from the time of Cain to the present day, that whoso raiseth his hand against his brother, raiseth his hand against Me also. And this mark shall distinguish My servants to the end of the world. Behold, I alone, am All Knowledge.

9. Now, it came to pass, that from this time forth great success attended the wars of Looeamong for the glory of his heavenly kingdoms.

10. And, for the space of three hundred years, Looeamong gradually gained on Baal and his alliances, both on earth and in heaven.

11. And Looeamong captured and cast out of his dominions more than seven hundred false Gods and false Lords.

12. And he broke up six hundred and eighty oracle-houses and temples, used for consulting the spirits, who called themselves Gods, whose only service was to advise on war, conquest and destruction.

13. So, that, even in Looeamong's falsity to himself, he rendered a great service to Jehovih, against whom he was doing battle.

14. For three hundred years more, Looeamong, with upward of six thousand million angel warriors, pursued war in heaven and on earth; and he had captured mostly all the earthly strong-holds of other false Gods. Baal, however, still maintained himself in Roma, and as God of the Roman empire, but under many names.

15. God, Son of Jehovih, said: Now, behold, even Looeamong, the false God, bewailed the wars, and he also bewailed his own doctrines.

16. Looeamong cried out in his despair, saying: To whom shall I pray, O thou Holy Ghost? Thou shadow, thou nothing, thou void?

17. Shall I say: O thou all nothing? Thou inconceivable? Thou unknowable? Thou all hidden?

18. Or shall I say: O thou nature? Thou God of nature? Thou senseless? Thou scattered?

19. Thou that hearest not? Thou that knowest not? Thou that seest not?

20. Thou essence? Thou fountain, that is dumb? Thou accident? Thou shapeless?

21. Thou imperson? Thou shortness in all? That beguileth us to come hither, to find thee? Or to go thither to find thee?

22. And find of a truth, that we find thee not? Yea, to understand that thou art the waste and desolate of all that is?

23. And, as for the Father, which we three built up, is He not dead? A divided kingdom, with three astrayed sons? And every one for himself?

24. O thou Brahma, thou hadst a peaceful division. And thou Budha, a place of great profit.

25. But I, your equal, with an unprofitable division of these western heavens. Mine are warriors in heaven and on earth. Yours, peace and profit. How can I embellish Hapsendi, my heavenly seat? And make it a place of grandeur, like unto yours?

26. Behold, my thousands of millions of angels are needed for warriors. How have I time to embellish my throne, and my heavenly city? No wonder, ye twain point the finger of mockery at me, for the poverty of my heavenly kingdom.

27. Have I not been fighting battles with satan all these hundreds and hundreds of years? Did I not find heaven, even from the first, a place of war?

28. Shall these things continue forever? Who shall I inquire of? Have I not declared, I am one with the Father, and one with the Holy Ghost?

29. Why, then, shall I not look to myself? And is this not the sum of all? Every one for himself? Was not myself a self from the first? And to continue a self for itself forever?

30. Henceforth, I go not down to send peace on earth; I go not to send peace, but a sword.

31. I go to set man at variance against his brother and father, and woman against her sister and mother, and a daughter-in-law against her mother-in-law.

32. I will make the foes of a man, they of his own household.

33. He that loveth father or mother more than me, is not worthy of me; and he that loveth son or daughter more than me, is not worthy of me.

34. And he that will not take up his sword and proclaim me, is not worthy of me.

35. My signs shall be a sword, a skull and cross-bones, and a bull.

36. My edicts shall be bulls; by these shall mine enemies be destroyed.

37. Before me shall every knee bow down, and every tongue confess me, Lord of all.

38. Behold, I will give them a book and a guide, whereby they shall know me; in blood will I seal them to the end of the world.

CHAPTER XLVIII.

1. The Lord said: Whilst Looeamong, the false God, was yet bewailing, behold, Thoth, his chief warrior God, came upon him, saying:

2. Alas, O master, thy followers have no king or queen on earth to protect them.

3. Thy mortal Kriste'yan warriors, who drew the sword to establish thee, have been slaughtered in Cardalia, Cyprus, Aitina, Thessalonica, Dalmatia, Lacaonia, Napla, Selucia, Macedon, Galati and Scythia.

4. In Thebes, six thousand Kriste'yan warriors were massacred by the armies of the emperor Maximum, inspired by Baal.

5. In Eocla, the Gods Jupiter and Ira inspired the king Hoethus to slaughter three thousand seven hundred Kriste'yan soldiers.

6. In Utica, the God Jupiter, with seven thousand angels caused three hundred of thy soldiers to be burned in a lime kiln. And they were soldiers battling for thee.

7. In Damascus, two thousand seven hundred of thy warriors were cut to pieces with the sword. And the only charge against them was their fighting for thee. Yea, their sacred bull was taken from them and roasted alive. And their bloody cross, which thou gavest them as a sign of the battle-cry, was broken and burnt.

8. In Crete, one thousand eight hundred of thy warriors, who had served thee well in slaughtering pagans, were walled around with fire, and roasted alive.

9. On the plains of Agatha, where thy soldiers, three hundred and eighty of them, were returning with their booty, having done thee great service in destroying heathen temples, they were set upon by the Gath'yans and destroyed, and for no other cause than that they served thee.

10. Looeamong cried out: Enough! Enough, O Thoth! I, too, will have a mortal emperor.

11. Descend thou again to the earth, to Hatuas (Constantine), and inspire thou him to raise a mortal army of forty thousand men, and move upon Roma.

12. Behold, I will prove myself before Hatuas, and he shall covenant unto me. Through him will I drive Baal out of Roma. And, as I make myself Kriste of heaven, so will I make Hatuas (Constantine) emperor of the whole earth.

13.Thoth then descended to the earth, to Hatuas, who was a su'is, and could both see angels and hear them talk; and Thoth induced Hatuas to raise an army of forty thousand soldiers, and set out for conquest.

14. And when they had come to the plains of Agatha, even where the Kriste'yans had been massacred many years before, behold, Looeamong and his angel hosts appeared in the heavens above Hatuas' army, so that all the soldiers thereof beheld the heavenly visitors.

15. And Looeamong showed unto Hatuas, in the air of heaven, a true cross, on which was written in letters of blood: IL'KRISTE.

16. Nevertheless, there was no man present who could read the inscription; and many were the conjectures thereon. In the evening, Looeamong descended to Hatuas, and said unto him: This is the interpretation of the sign and the cross I showed thee:

17. IN THIS THOU SHALT CONQUER! And when thou arisest in the morning thou shalt cause to be made a cross, of most excellent workmanship; and thou shalt have it inscribed: THE KRISTE, OUR LORD, SON OF THE HOLY GHOST.

18. And this cross shalt thou cause to be carried at the head of thy army. And thy edicts shalt thou call, bulls, and they shall be written with lamb's blood, in remembrance of the sacrifice of the Jews in Egupt, through which sacrifice the Father in heaven delivered them. For I am Lord of heaven and earth.

19. Accordingly, a cross was made, and highly decorated, and inscribed as commanded, and Hatuas and his soldiers went forth with renewed courage. And so great was their zeal, that everything fell before them.

20. And now, that Looeamong's angels had an anchorage on earth, they were in all respects the equals of angels of the pagan Gods. So that, whilst Hatuas was victorious on earth, Gabriel, otherwise Thoth, was victorious in heaven.

21. And it came to pass in not many years, that Looeamong, through Gabriel, captured Baal and all the false Gods in all the regions far and near. And Gabriel took, along with the captured Gods, seven million and six hundred thousand warring angels, and carried them altogether to Makavishtu, in hada, and cast them into hell, where there were already more than ten millions who were in chaos and madness.

22. And Gabriel had the place walled around with fire and noxious gases, so that none could escape.

23. Such was the end of the earthly dominion of Baal, who had ruled over mortals for

evil, for upward of three thousand years. And, in fact, it was the final termination of the earthly Gods that ruled over mortals through oracles and pagan practices.

24. The earth was now clear of evil Gods, whose chief labor had been for thousands of years to capture the spirits of the recent dead, and make slaves of them for the glory of the hadan kingdoms.

25. Thus had Looeamong done a good service; for the earth and lower heavens had now nothing to suffer from any Gods, save the Triunes.

26. Looeamong inspired Hatuas, the mortal emperor, to call together a council of wise men from all the kingdoms of Arabin'ya, Heleste, Parsi'e and Uropa, to select from all the religious doctrines in the world, that which was the wisest and best, that it might be established by kings, emperors and governors by the sword and spear, so there should never more be but one religion.

27. And, in course of time, there assembled a council of seventeen hundred and eighty-six learned men from all the regions named, and they placed themselves under the rules and presence of Hatuas. And he selected from them one hundred and forty-four speakers.

28. As for the others, they were divided into groups of twelves, besides a goodly number being appointed scribes and translators. But many, having the appearance of Jews, were rejected altogether.

29. Now, the council had brought with them, in all, two thousand two hundred and thirty-one books and legendary tales of Gods and Saviors and great men, together with a record of the doctrines taught by them.

30. Hatuas, being under the inspiration of Looeamong, through Gabriel, alias Thoth, thus spake:

31. Search ye these books, and whatsoever is good in them, that retain; but, whatsoever is evil, that cast away. What is good in one book, unite ye with that which is good in another book. And whatsoever is thus brought together shall be called, THE BOOK OF BOOKS. And it shall be the doctrine of my people, which I will recommend unto all nations, that there shall be no more war for religions' sake.

32. Thoth (Gabriel) and his angel hosts formed a circle around about the mortal council, a thousand angels deep on every side, and extending upward densely for a long way, and thence, by a line of light, extending to Looeamong's throne, in Hapsendi, his heavenly kingdom.

33. By day and by night, Thoth and his hosts watched over the mortal council, over-shadowing their every thought and word.

34. For four years and seven months the council thus deliberated, and selected from the two thousand two hundred and thirty-one books and legendary tales.

35. And, at the end of that time, there had been selected and combined much that was good and great, and worded so as to be well-remembered by mortals.

36. As yet, no God had been selected by the council, and so they balloted, in order to determine that matter. And the first ballot gave prominence to the following Gods: Jove, Jupiter, Salenus, Baal, Thor, Gade, Apollo, Juno, Aries, Taurus, Minerva, Rhets, Mithra, Theo, Fragapatti, Atys, Durga, Indra, Neptune, Vulcan, Kriste, Agni, Croesus, Pelides, Huit, Hermes, Thulis, Thammus, Eguptus, Iao, Aph, Saturn, Gitchens, Minos, Maximo, Hecla and Phernes.

37. Besides these, there were twenty-two other Gods and Goddesses, that received a small

number of votes each.

38. In seven days thereafter, another ballot was taken, and the number of Gods was reduced to twenty-seven.

39. In seven days thereafter, another ballot was taken, and the number of Gods was reduced to twenty-one.

40. Thus was the number reduced each ballot, but slower and slower. Six days in the week were allotted to discuss the merits and demerits of the Gods. But many weeks elapsed towards the last, when the number was not reduced.

41. For one year and five months the balloting lasted, and at that time the ballot rested nearly equally on five Gods, namely: Jove, Kriste, Mars, Crite and Siva. And here the ballot changed not for yet seven time more, which was seven weeks.

42. Hatuas spake before the council, saying: Ours is a labor for all the nations of the earth, and for all time. I know the angels of heaven are with us in this matter. We have found five Gods, good and acceptable before the world. What say the council, that the angels give us a sign? For we all do know the angels' signs of these Gods.

43. The council said: Well said, thou wisest of men! Such a God shall be ours, now and forever.

44. And immediately, there and then, LOOEAMONG AND HIS ANGELS GAVE A SIGN IN FIRE, OF A CROSS SMEARED WITH BLOOD, AND IT RESTED ON A BULL'S HORN, even as a cloud of fire on a cloud of fire!

45. Whereupon Kriste was declared GOD AND LORD OF ALL NATIONS OF THE EARTH.

46. And the council agreed thereto, unanimously, and, moreover, to reject all the other Gods.

47. The next question was, what mortal representative should be chosen?

48. The first ballot brought out the following men: Zarasthustra, Thothma, Abraham, Brahma, Atys, Thammus, Joshu, Sakaya, Habron, Bali, Crite, Chrisna, Thulis, Witoba and Speio. Besides these, there were included in the ballot, forty-six other men, who received a small number of ballots each.

49. God, Son of Jehovih, said: Behold, the Council of Nice balloted for a twelve-month, as to what man heard the Voice? Sayest thou, Jehovih sendeth His matters to a council of men?

50. Hatuas said: The Gods will not let us choose any man. Now, therefore, hear me: All the law-givers chosen by the Gods, have been iesu. Now, since we can not make preference as to a man, let us say: THE MAN, IESU?

51. Thereupon, the name, Iesu, was adopted, and the sacred books were written accordingly.

52. God, Son of Jehovih, said: The Council of Nice sinned not, for the doctrines set forth, as Iesu's, were for Jehovih.

53. But, wherein their words made worshipful the names of Kriste and the Holy Ghost, behold, that matter was with Looeamong.

54. God said: My testimonies were previously with Abraham and Brahma and Moses, and I spake not of Kriste nor of the Holy Ghost, I spake of God and of the I AM.

55. They have said: Whosoever speaketh a word against the son of man, it shall be forgiven him; but, whosoever speaketh against the Holy Ghost, it shall not be forgiven him.

56. Therefore, suffer ye Looeamong to bear his own testimony to the kingdom whence it sprang. The Holy Ghost was his labor.

57. Jehovih said: Had I weakened since the time of Moses, that I need to incarnate Myself, in order to make man understand Me?

58. God said: Sufficient unto a time is the work of Jehovih; because the Triunes over threw the oracles and hundreds of false Gods and hundreds of sacred books full of error and evil, behold they fulfilled their time.

59. Sufficient unto another time, even the present, is another work of Jehovih, which is to establish His Presence with the living generation.

60. Jehovih said: Behold, I created; and I am sufficient unto all men.

61. In the olden times, man worshipped all the spirits of the dead, and I cut him short, giving him many Gods; and, again, I cut him short, and gave him three Gods, and then, three Gods in one.

62. This day, I cut him short of all, save his Creator. Behold the signs of My times, My preachers are legions.

CHAPTER XLIX.
ORIGIN OF MOHAMMEDANISM.

1. The Lord said: After Looeamong had cast out all other false Gods in his earth dominions, he set to work enriching his heavenly home, employing no less than seven thousand million angel slaves for that purpose.

2. Now, the place and extent of his heavenly capital was from Hasetus to Roma, and thence northward to the Aquarian Mountains.

3. His palace was modeled after Ennochissa's, at Eta-shong, and of equal magnificence.

4. His greatest warriors were now exalted as Lords, generals, marshals, and so on. And he provided rites and ceremonies, and tournaments, and all manner of heavenly diversities.

5. But he made the rules of entrance to his palace so rigid, that only his highest officers and visiting Gods could gain access to him.

6. Now, for upward of a thousand years, the angel warrior, Gabriel, alias Thoth, had been to Looeamong his most faithful sub-God.

7. And Looeamong had promised Gabriel that, when he overthrew Baal, and cast him in hell, he would give to Gabriel a great heavenly kingdom, with an earthly base.

8. Accordingly, Gabriel applied for Jerusalem (his station), and for the heavens thereunto, and for one thousand million slaves.

9. But Looeamong postponed the matter from time to time, for more than six hundred years.

10. Thoth, alias Gabriel, then sent this message to Looeamong, to wit:

11. By virtue of mine own worth before the Gods of heaven, I greet thee in peace and love. First, in remembrance of thy many promises to me, in which thou hast kept no part thereof faithfully.

12. Second, that thou art not Kriste, which is All Knowledge, but a usurper and pretender.

13. Third, that I made thee what thou art; and by mine own hand helped thee to cast out Baal and Ashtaroth, and all the Roman'yan and Argos'yan Gods. Of which matters it is known in these three great heavens, thou didst promise me for more

than seven hundred years, to give me a kingdom of a thousand million subjects.

14. And, fourth, since thou art safely raised up above all Gods within these regions, thou hast affected to not know me. Yea, and in thy great heavenly recreations and tournaments and receptions, thou hast not commanded my presence, or in any way shown more remembrance of me than as if I were an es'yan.

15. And, fifth, thou didst long promise me that, if thou shouldst succeed in establishing a sub-kingdom on the earth, or in hada, near the earth, thou wouldst hand the same over to me, to rank thee in all things. But thou hast greedily kept both kingdoms to thyself, making either place thy residence, according to the times and seasons most propitious to thine own glory and ease.

16. And, lastly, that thou sacrificest the liberty of thy subjects, making them thy laborers to embellish thy kingdom, and making them little better than slaves, in forever parading in the ceremonies given in thy applause.

17. These things have I often desired to speak to thee about; but thou ever affectedst to be overrun with other matters, so as to put me off from my opportunity. Whereupon I have prayed to the Holy Ghost, for hundreds of years, to have my suit just and honorable and holy.

18. But I shall search no further. Hundreds of millions of thy highest grades, who went down to the earth with me to fight thy battles, and who know the justness of my cause, will, at a word from me, withdraw from thy kingdom, and join me in an enterprise of my own.

19. I shall await patiently for thy reply.

20. But Gabriel received no reply to his message. And so, in course of time, he called together ten thousand angel warriors, and they assembled in a place called, Kalla-Hored, the place of seven steps, in hada. Gabriel spake before them, saying:

21. Here will I establish my kingdom of heaven, and forever. I will show this false Kriste, what I can do. Mark ye, the great power of a God is to establish a good foothold on the earth. The natural increase will soon populate a heavenly kingdom.

22. I will raise me up a prophet and seer of mine own on the earth, and establish a new doctrine amongst mortals. Behold, I have a sword that will cut to pieces Looeamong's kingdom on earth. For, listen! In the old Eguptian libraries are books and tablets and manuscripts, that will show the perversity of the Constantine bible.

23. Now, when I have established my prophet, I will cause mortal legions of Arabin'yans to possess these libraries, especially Alexandria's. And I will raise up mortal scholars, who shall establish the truth of my prophet's doctrines, and the falsity of this false Kriste's doctrines; and I will thus overturn his earthly kingdom, and possess all these mortal regions myself, to be mine forever!

24. After that manner, the angel, Gabriel, boasted. And he made the ten thousand his Holy Council, and from amongst them he appointed marshals, captains, generals, heralds and officers in general. And they built a throne in heaven unto Gabriel, and called it, the THRONE OF KALLA-HORED; and he went and sat thereon, and then crowned himself, GABRIEL, GOD OF HEAVEN AND EARTH.

25. And then he crowned ten Lords, to wit: Ateiniv, Le Chung, Tudol, Raim, Hakaya, Wochorf, Yademis, Stu'born, Wolf and Gussak. And Gabriel thereafter commenced the initiation of members to his kingdom. And there thus acceded to his heavenly place

upward of five hundred thousand angels every day, and this continued until Kalla contained more than eight hundred million angel subjects.

26. Of these, certain selections were made, according to grade, who were appointed as officers over the rest; and immediately they were put to work, building heavenly mansions, and constructing streets and roads, and all things required in an exalted heaven, and in the meantime Gabriel's palace and throne were extended and beautified beyond description.

27. Gabriel knew the power of rites and ceremonies, and he provided unto his heavenly kingdom accordingly, so that his people were kept in a constant state of excitement, because of his wonderful inventions. So that millions and millions of them truly believed he was the veritable Creator of heaven and earth, thus in form of an angel.

28. Gabriel perceived this, and for these he provided places of trust and nearness to him, that his miraculous power might be the better strengthened with the unbelieving.

29. Now, the time came when Gabriel's kingdom was sufficiently established, and he began to provide for his great scheme to establish himself with mortals, that their spirits after death might be brought to his kingdom. For such is the order of Jehovih's creation, that whosoever man worshippeth whilst he is on earth, to that God will his spirit float after death; and without resistance become a dutiful slave, not knowing there be other Gods and other heavens.

30. And Gabriel made Ateiniv Chief Lord of Lords to go down to the earth, and find a mortal capable of the required inspiration. And he gave to Ateiniv to be his co-laborers, Yademis, Stu'born, and Wolf, and with them, at their call, three hundred million warrior angels.

31. And with this host, Ateiniv departed for the earth, for Arabin'ya; and as he went forth he dropped of his hosts, at certain distances, groups of angels, which formed the line of light from Gabriel down to the earth.

CHAPTER L.

1. The Lord said: Gabriel raised upon the earth one Mohammed, and inspired him through his angel hosts. And the angels inspired Mohammed to go once every month in the year into the cave of Hara; on which occasions, Gabriel came in person, and talked with Mohammed, who had su'is in great perfection.

2. Twelve years in peace did Gabriel inspire mortals through Mohammed. But, at the end of thirteen years, Mohammed attained to sufficient strength to draw the sword for Gabriel's doctrines. And Gabriel, through inspiration, caused the Mohammedans to commemorate this as the beginning of his kingdoms on earth. And they, therefore, consecrated the said period of time.

3. And, on this first meeting of the faithful in Gabriel, Mohammed, being under inspiration, spake before the multitude, saying:

4. There is but one God, and he is God. Heaven is his. The earth is the Lord's, through the angel, Gabriel. This is the sum and substance of all things. This was the doctrine of Abraham and of Moses, our forefathers.

5. But evil men have invented other Gods, which have no existence. They are idols, which exist only in superstition and ignorance.

6. Revere me not, nor call me wise. I am not wise; I have little learning. Knowledge cometh to me from the Unseen. My eyes are open, my ears are open. I see and hear spiritual things. The angels of heaven tell me things of wisdom.

7. I do but repeat them. Therefore, I am not wise, nor great. I strive to be honest and upright before God, but I am weaker than a child in these respects. Therefore, worship not me, nor bow down before me. I am nothing.

8. As I am an instrument in the hands of God, through his angel, Gabriel, so also were Abraham and Moses and many of the prophets. They could work miracles. I can not. Therefore, I am the least of God's prophets.

9. That ye may become exalted before God, I am sent into the world. Shall I reveal what Gabriel hath told me? Or do ye believe God is dead, or gone afar off? Believe ye, that he can not raise up a prophet in this day? Is God weak? or hath he forgotten the world he created?

10. Why hath this thing come at this time? No man can answer that. Gabriel saith: There is a false God in heaven, and he hath falsely called himself, Kriste. Gabriel saith, that he himself, Gabriel, provided the way for the gathering of the lost sheep of Israel, through an iesu.

11. Brothers, I will tell you why I am chosen of God: It is to circumvent the Kriste'yan's idolatry from coming into Arabin'ya and the countries north and south and east.

12. These countries were given by God to our forefathers, Abraham, Isaac and Jacob, and thence down to Moses, and thence down to us.

13. There is but one God, and Gabriel is his angel of all the world.

14. And God raiseth up a prophet from time to time, to bless his chosen people.

15. He put this matter upon me; I know only to serve God.

16. The Kriste'yans are merciless warriors. This false Kriste and his worshipers are working for the Romans, and not for salvation. Wherever they go, they destroy the libraries and all manner of learning.

17. Will ye submit, like slaves, to have them despoil you? Is there no Arabin'yan blood in your veins?

18. When asked to state the Mohammedan doctrines, he said: To tell no lies; to not commit fornication; to preserve the ceremonies; to give to the poor freely; to observe the sacred days; to aggress not; but to war for the innocent and oppressed; to maintain the liberty of the people; to steal not, and to deceive no man.

19. Mohammed, being under inspiration of the God, Gabriel, and his angels, collected together thousands and tens of thousands of warriors, and went forth to conquer. And the angel hosts of Gabriel went forth with Mohammed's army, and inspired them to such degree that they were without fear or hesitation. And Gabriel's hosts of angels went into the armies that fought against Mohammed, and inspired them with fear and cowardice and panic.

20. And it came to pass, that wherever Mohammed went, there was sure victory, the like of which had not been for many centuries.

21. Now, Looeamong, the false Kriste, had previously destroyed, for the most part, the Alexandrian library, having inspired a mortal priest, Coatulius, to do the work.

22. And Looeamong, now perceiving the triumph of Mohammed, inspired three hundred monks and priests to go throughout Heleste and Arabin'ya, and destroy the ancient state

records and libraries. And they went thither, and accomplished the destruction.

23. Mohammed was shown this by Gabriel, and he used it as a battle-cry for his soldiers.

24. Looeamong now declared war in heaven against the false God-Gabriel; and, in not many years they both carried their war down to earth, contending for certain localities on the earth.

25. As for the other two false Gods, Kabalactes, alias Budha, and Ennochissa, alias Brahma, they had been in war against each other for over six hundred years.

26. Now had these four false Gods possession of the whole earth, at least, wherever there were mortal kingdoms and empires.

27. Now, in reference to the Faithists: In Chine'ya and Vind'yu, they were no longer identified with the kingdoms or governments, but lived about in scattered families. In Arabin'ya, Heleste and Uropa, they were scattered in all directions. From the time of Joshu's death, in Jerusalem, they began to migrate, mostly toward the west.

28. And these called themselves, Israelites and Jews.

29. Nevertheless, many of the Israelites and Jews, so-called, were apostates in fact; eating flesh, and marrying with other peoples.

30. Now, after the fall of the great empire, Egupt, her people migrated westward, hundreds of thousands of them, and they settled in western Uropa, where these people married with the aborigines. Their offspring were called Druids, Picts, Gales (Gaelic), Wales (Welsh), Galls (Gauls), and Yohans (Johns), all of which are Eguptian names, preserved to this day.

31. Now, when the Faithists were moved by the inspiration of God to have no more kings, and to flee away from the Kriste'yan warriors, they came amongst the people above mentioned. (The apostate Faithists married with them, and their offspring were the forefathers of those now called, French, German, Russian and English.)

32. God, Son of Jehovih, had said: Suffer the apostates to so marry, for here will I find a way to raise up disbelievers in the false Kriste; and they shall ultimately become believers in Jehovih only.

33. For, inasmuch as I have suffered them to become scattered, so will I appropriate them as seed to quicken all the races of men to comprehend the All One.

CHAPTER LI.

1. For five hundred years more, the wars lasted between the four false Gods, Looeamong, Thoth, Ennochissa and Kabalactes. And then they came to terms, and ratified a division of the earth and her heavens into four great parts, with fixed boundaries.

2. And it was stipulated by them, that the spirits of all mortals at time of death, should go to the heaven which reigned on the portion of earth where they had lived. (Unless carried away by God, Son of Jehovih, to Paradise.)

3. So comparative peace reigned in the heavens of the earth. And after this, there was nothing in common between them. Their respective heavens and their earth possessions were under each one in his own way.

4. And they now fell to work in earnest to adorn and glorify their heavenly kingdoms, their cities, their palaces, and thrones. And each of them exalted their great war captains who had fought so long for them, and they all had councils of millions and millions; and

marshals and heralds, and masters of ceremonies, and musicians, hundreds of millions.

5. And they all had thousands of millions of subjects; but as for themselves, they kept aloof from their people. The private palaces of these Gods, and their private heavenly seats of splendor were exclusive to themselves and their favorite Lords and high officers.

6. And all angels else, who desired to see these Gods, were obliged to pass through rigid examinations, and solemnly bind themselves in oaths and castigations before they were permitted to pass the outer columns of fire. After this, they were permitted to walk on their knees to the second columns of fire.

7. Here they were obliged to repeat a thousand prayers and a thousand anthems ere they could pass within. And now, when within the arena, they were obliged to crawl on their bellies; and, for every length crawled, they had to repeat seven new prayers. And it was a thousand lengths from the inner pillars of fire to the arches of the palace, especially of Kabalactes' and Looeamong's. Of these arches, there were three million three hundred and thirty-three thousand three hundred and thirty-three in number. And there were four marshals for each arch, and these four had two relief watches for each twenty-four hours.

8. To pass the arches, another examination had to be undergone; and, after this, the person must again crawl on the belly till merging into the under arch, where stairs began, of which there were seven steps. On each of these steps he must lay one day, repeating prayers and praises to his God. On the upper step, however, he was not required to pray, but might look in silence at the throne, on which, at times, his God came and sat, his Holy Council sitting to the west, facing to the east, to the throne.

9. From the place of the person on the upper step to the throne, was five hundred lengths, nearer than which none were permitted to come, save by the God's special decree.

10. And, if the God was not on his throne, and his Holy Council sitting, then the person must wait, not moving from his place, perhaps for a day, or more.

11. But, after he had observed his God, he was not permitted to remain longer than to say seven prayers. After this he must return, and depart in the same way he came.

12. Now, as to the throne and its brilliancy and grandeur, no mortal words can convey a knowledge thereof to mortal understanding; for it was so vast, and withal adorned with elements not found on the earth. Thousands of millions of which gems had been captured from the dispossessed false Gods of centuries before, and even from heavens from other star worlds.

13. And equally astonishing and overwhelming were the seats and places and robes of the Holy Council, which also baffleth mortal words to convey an idea of. Only to look on, to be overcome with emotion, to remember what great effects can be accomplished by concentrated labor, and to feel the insignificance of isolation, one's wonder was swallowed up in silent awe before the scene.

14. Such was the magnificence of each of the four heavenly places of the four hadan Gods, and not differing but little from one another.

15. In order to obtain the privilege of thus going to look upon the throne and the God thereof, one had to first serve a hundred years in the labors of that heaven, and to have his record good during all the while.

16. If, in the mortal life, a man had served his God, by preaching and praying, or by fighting battles for him, and had thus attained a good record, one hundred years' servitude in heaven entitled him to visit his God on the throne, at the distance named above.

17. But if the mortal had been an enemy to the God during his earth-life, he could not attain to approach the throne in less than three hundred years' servitude. Which servitude consisted in laboring in building mansions, or in paving roads in heaven, or in bringing produce up from the earth, or in bringing up other atmospherean elements for the gratification and glory of the God and his tens of millions of high officers.

18. So great and grand and far-reaching were these four kingdoms, that angels dwelt therein, hundreds of millions of them, never even hearing of any other heaven than the one they were in.

19. Now, for the most part, the Brahmins of the earth, on entering the es world, went to the Brahmin heavens (Eta-shong), ruled over by the false Brahma, alias Ennochissa.

20. And the Budhists of the earth, on entering the es world, went to the Budhist heavens, ruled over by the false Budha, alias Kabalactes.

21. The Kriste'yans of earth, on entering the es world, went to the heavens of Looeamong, the false Kriste.

22. The Mohammedans went to Gabriel's heavens.

23. God, Jehovih's Son, said: Behold the stubbornness of the angels of the heavens! To whom they bound themselves on earth, they were bound in heaven. Neither would they admit they were bound, though they were slaves. Their priests and monks and bishops, arch-bishops and popes, marched in the processions of heaven, praying, singing, and even carrying burdens, hundreds of years, for the privilege of ultimately approaching the throne of Ennochissa, or Kabalactes, or Looeamong, or Thoth, honestly believing they were to look upon the very Creator.

24. God said: Their minds were in bondage to so great an extent, that even after they had attained to view their God (at such a distance and in such artificial splendor), they could not receive truth.

25. And when an angel of Jehovih came to the, and said: Behold, this is only one heaven, of which there are millions, they would not believe. And when he said to them: Behold, this heaven, with all its magnificence, is only one of the lowest of heavens, they would not believe. And when he said to them: Behold, this God, with all his glory, is only one God, of which there are many, they would not believe. And when he said to them: Behold, there are higher Gods than this, they would not believe. And when he said to them: Behold, the All Highest God is not thus, but One not in shape of man, they would not believe.

26. These subjects would say: I want not your Jehovih! Behold, I can see my God; he is the Creative element personified. This is the all highest heaven; here is the place and person of the Lord!

27. God said: Man sinned not in this; neither sinned the angels of the heavens.

28. The fault was with these false Gods.

29. Because they had taught men that the Creator was in the image of a man, and sitting on a throne, behold, their subjects would not believe otherwise.

30. And it came to pass, on earth, when a man died, his neighbors said: Behold, he hath gone to see the Lord, who sitteth on the right hand of God.

CHAPTER LII.

GOD JUDGETH THE FOUR FALSE GODS.

1. The Lord said: Hear, O ye of earth, and ye of the heavens thereof; hear ye of the labor of God, Son of Jehovih.

2. For what was given me by Jehovih, to be in my keeping for the resurrection of men and angels, was gone away from me.

3. My kingdoms in heaven were scattered and broken up.

4. I, the God of the heavens of the earth, sent my appeal unto the four false Gods, saying:

5. In the name of Jehovih, greeting unto you. Behold, what ye have done, and also what hath come to pass!

6. Wherein ye have copied after my ways, ye have gained dominion; but of what profit unto mortals or angels?

7. Because ye knew that Jehovih's God appointed ashars unto mortals, ye have also appointed ashars unto them, though not for their resurrection, but to raise up mortals with faith in yourselves.

8. Ye have thus built on the earth for the glory of your own kingdoms; for your ashars teach mortals not of eternal resurrection, but of attaining unto your heavens only.

9. Where and when I send angels to inspire mortals to obtain education and knowledge, ye send contravening angels, and they incite mortals to destroy their own libraries and places of learning.

10. Ye persuade mortals that the only good and necessary knowledge is contained in your sacred books; for ye desire to prevent mortals from knowing there are other heavens than your own, and other Gods than yourselves.

11. When I have gathered together wandering spirits and chaotic spirits, and provided ways for their resurrection, ye have sent angel emissaries to thwart my labors.

12. Ye have provided wicked heavenly pastimes, and disgusting tournaments, within your heavenly places, in order to win subjects for your dominions.

13. Ye provide excursions from your heavenly places down to mortals, for your angels to witness battles between mortal warriors, that these angels may satiate their own evil curiosity.

14. Ye thus degrade your own angel subjects by causing them to rejoice in the havoc of mortal flesh and flowing blood.

15. Ye thus call away from my heavenly schools and colleges angels who had begun resurrection, flattering yourselves that you are thus augmenting your heavenly kingdoms by additional subjects.

16. On mortal battle-fields, where there are hosts of chaotic angels, the spirits of the slain, I send my angels with heavenly ships to gather them up and restore them. But your emissaries come and destroy my ships for wickedness' sake, calling it glorious sport.

17. Of these great evils ye have been notified times and times again, but ye put not forth your hands to remedy the wickedness.

18. Ye sell indulgencies to your angels to engage in wicked practices; and ye suffer your ashars to inspire mortal priests to sell indulgences to their followers in the same way.

19. Thus do ye compound sin.

20. Ye profess to confess the sins of your angels in your heavens, exacting servitude of

them as a purchase of your excuse.

21. And your ashars inspire mortal priests to do the same things for their mortal followers, for stipulated prices in money.

22. Thus do your ashars prepare mortals to become slaves in your heavenly kingdoms, that they build unto your own personal glory.

23. For ye take advantage of the infant mind, to bend it away from Jehovih, and away from eternal progress, that ye may inherit it as your dutiful subject.

CHAPTER LIII.

GOD CONTNUETH TO JUDGE THE FOUR FALSE GODS.

1. In the name of the Almighty, greeting unto you.

2. A thousand years ago, the grades of your heavenly subjects were from thirty to fifty; now, they are fallen to fifteen.

3. As ye have declined the grades of the angels in your heavens, even so have ye declined the grades of mortals within your dominions.

4. Instead of well-tilled fields and good orchards, ye have given them war, widows, orphans, paupers, debauchees, thieves and murderers.

5. Instead of giving them good harvests, ye have given them famines and pestilences.

6. For your ashars inspire the priests, and they in turn entice their followers away from the fields, to come and dwell in the cities, where they can be conveniently absolved from neglect in not confessing you.

7. Thus have ye set aside good works and instruction and the desire for the knowledge, both within your heavenly kingdoms and on the earth also; and, instead thereof, ye have given them rites and ceremonies, leading angels and mortals as if they were cattle for your markets.

8. Instead of teaching angels and mortals to think for themselves, ye have prohibited them from thinking, save as your leaders think for them.

9. Thus have ye thwarted, with all your might, the cultivations of the talents Jehovih created with all.

10. Say not, that I, Jehovih's Son, desire subjects or worshipers; behold, I prohibit both angels and mortals from worshipping me, or announcing me or my kingdoms, as the all highest.

11. I teach them, One only is the All Highest, even Jehovih.

12. I teach them, that I am but Jehovih's servant, working for the resurrection of mortals and angels.

13. I teach both angels and mortals, they shall not worship any one born of woman.

14. And behold, my foot-prints can not be mistaken; I raised up Zarathustra, and the man Brahma, and Abraham and Moses and Po and Chine and Capilya.

15. Yet, not one of these, with all the wonders they accomplished, was worshipped by their followers

16. Yet, who was greater than Moses? that stretched forth his hand, and said: Come! Come!

17. And four millions of people, in bondage, marched out of Egupt!

18. Yet none worshipped Moses.

19. Behold, the seventy colonies founded by Zarathustra, and yet they worshipped not him.

20. Behold Chine, who named the empire, who turned three hundred millions of warriors to a people of peace.

21. Behold Capilya, who overturned the laws of thirteen kingdoms in Vind'yu, and gave peace and plenty to a hundred millions of people.

22. Yet, not Chine nor Capilya were worshipped.

23. But ye harp on the idle tales of obscure magicians, and teach mortals to worship them.

24. Nevertheless, ye have caused to be preached, in your heavens, that I am a God like unto yourselves, working for mine own glory.

25. Now, behold, I prepare my angel hosts in wisdom and virtue, that they may go away from me, and inherit the etherean heavens above.

26. For this was my labor for which Jehovih, through His exalted Gods, made me God of the earth and her heavens.

27. And I have sent thus away, as Brides and Bridegrooms to Jehovih, thousands of millions of angels, whom I had raised to grade ninety-nine.

28. Yet, in all the time of your dominions ye have not raised one angel to the emancipated grades.

29. Such as are wise within your dominions, tire of your pomp and splendor, and, in course of time, come to my heavens, and renounce all Lords and Gods, and betroth themselves to Jehovih only.

30. And I give them places in my schools, colleges, hospitals and factories, and thus educate them, that they may, indeed, in time, become fit companions to Gods and Goddesses.

31. Thus are your kingdoms forever depleted of your highest grades. So that your heavenly kingdoms and your earthly dominions have chiefly the ignorant and depraved as your idolaters.

CHAPTER LIV.
GOD CHASTISETH THE FOUR GODS SEPARATELY.

1. In Jehovih's name, greeting unto thee, Looeamong.

2. Thou hadst a warrior angel, Thoth, alias Gabriel, who labored for thee more than a thousand years, in order to make thee under thy false names worshipful on earth.

3. And thou didst promise Thoth, that when he overcame Dagon, Ashtaroth, Baal and other false Gods, thou wouldst give to him a heavenly sub-kingdom, with a thousand million subjects.

4. And Thoth did thus accomplish thy desire, but thou didst not give him anything.

5. But thou didst further exact of him the destroying of idol worship amongst mortals, and the destroying of the oracle-temples for consulting spirits, re-promising him, that when he had fulfilled these things, thou wouldst give unto him the promised heavenly kingdom.

6. And Thoth did accomplish these things also; but thou didst refuse again to fulfill thy promise.

7. Whereby Thoth rebelled against thee, and set up his present heavenly dominions, inspiring his followers under the name of Mohammed.

8. And now, behold, thou hast since that day tried to destroy him in heaven and on earth.

9. But Thoth was anchored in earthly possessions, in Jerusalem and Te-theas and Egupt.

10. And thou didst inspire mortals in western Uropa to made crusades against Thoth, in order to possess Jerusalem and Te-theas, whereby millions of mortals were slain, and vast regions of country laid desolate.

11. Behold, thou hadst pretended thou wert the all highest God, and yet thou wert unable to take a small earthly kingdom.

12. Thou didst also inflict dire punishment and torturing of the flesh on Jehovih's worshipers and on infidels, against thy doctrines. With red-hot pincers pulled the flesh from the bones; or in boiling oil slowly dipped them; or from precipices hurled them; or in boxes lined with pricking spikes of iron bound them, thus to blot all knowledge and learning and opposition. Millions and millions hast thou thus cast in death in thy earthly regions.

13. In Es'pan (Spain) and Itius (Italy), thou hast thus put to death more than seven million mortals.

14. Nevertheless, these angels will come home to thee in after-time, with vengeance in their souls.

15. Behold, thy false promises to Thoth are already visited upon thy kingdoms.

16. But, as for Thoth, who became thy willing tool to do destruction for thy glory, what merit hath he?

17. How shall I judge thee, O Thoth?

18. Because thou hast a heavenly kingdom, and withal art master on earth, of Jerusalem and Te-theas and Egupt and Punjaub, thou flatterest thyself thou art a great God.

19. But thy heavenly kingdom hath become a place for lusters and foul-smelling spirits in the lowest of grades.

20. And thy heaven is surely and steadily declining in grade.

21. Now, as to thee, Kabalactes, though thou hast destroyed a thousand mortal libraries, and put to death sixty millions of people, in order to establish thyself as Budha, still thou hast steadily declined in grade, and thy kingdoms with thee.

22. Thou has fashioned many sacred cities, and framed many tales as to who thou wert in mortal life.

23. Thou hast falsely called thyself, Budha; and doubly false hast thou taken the name, Sakaya Muni.

24. Thou hast tortured to death millions of mortals who rejected thee.

25. And when my heavenly ships rescued their distracted and chaotic spirits, thou didst wantonly connive with thy drujas to despoil my ships, and cast these helpless spirits into darkness.

26. Thou hast done these things for pastimes and diversities for thy falling heavens.

27. And even so hath it been with thee, Ennochissa.

28. Never had a Lord a fairer opportunity in all the earth's heavens to do a good and great work, than what fell into thy hands.

29. But, behold how thou hast harvested thy heavens!

30. A thousand years ago, thy grades were from forty to sixty-five; and this day, they average but ten.

31. It needeth no prophet to foretell that thy declension will lead to destruction in the end.

32. Now, lastly: O ye false Gods, ye deceivers and hypocrites, ye have divided the earth and the heavens thereof between yourselves, and re-confederated together for a balance of power.

33. Ye have also persuaded mortal kingdoms to divide the earth into sections and regions, and to clamor for a balance of power between different kingdoms.

34. Ye have thus caused mortals to provide standing armies to protect themselves, kingdom against kingdom, after the manner ye protect your own kingdoms in the heavens.

35. Kriste'yans against Kriste'yans; Brahmins against Brahmins; Budhists against Budhists; Mohammedans against Mohammedans; yet all of these four have ye arrayed against one another. In very likeness of your heavens, have ye built on the earth.

36. Ye have inspired mortals to keep, as standing armies, forty million soldiers.

37. Ye have inspired mortals to build military schools and colleges, where the young may be trained in the art of war and destruction.

38. Ye have inspired mortals to build monuments to their generals and captains, because of their courage to destroy.

39. Ye have inspired the wickedest of mortals to believe that, if they would read your sacred books, and call on your names, ye would surely save them, and, after death, take them to the highest of heavens.

40. And, yet, when they die, your hosts are not there to receive them.

41. And when they call out for you, your emissaries kick them, and beat them,

42. And they return with vengeance, to afflict mortals.

CHAPTER LV.

GOD CONTINUETH HIS CHASTISEMENT AGAINST THE FOUR FALSE GODS.

1. God said: In the name of Jehovih, wherein shall I find an excuse for your behavior?

2. When my angels taught man how to make a capstan and a screw and a telescope and a compass, behold, your emissaries inspired my chosen to be tortured, or put to death.

3. When my angels inspired man to comprehend and announce the glory of the stars and planets, ye put my chosen to death; through your vindictive angels against Jehovih were these things accomplished.

4. When my angels taught man by inspiration that the earth was round instead of flat, ye sent spirits of darkness to inspire the death of my philosophers.

5. Because, forsooth, my inspiration agreed not with the sacred books which ye compounded for your own glory.

6. Yea, ye palmed off your compilations from other false Gods as being Jehovih's; and ye played upon the honest innocence of man's understanding, contrary to the will of the Almighty.

7. Ye have holden your sacred books up, and said: Here is the ultimate; beyond this, no man shall go!

8. And ye knew, the while, that any fixed revelation could not be true, because all the universe is in constant progress.

9. Ye have holden up your own sacred books, and said: Here are rules and a sure guide to reach the all highest heavens!

10. Knowing the while that your heavens were the lowest of the bound heavens of the earth.

11. Now, behold, the same rules apply unto you as to the least of Jehovih's children; which are, that whoso setteth up a mark, with himself as the highest, and he, the interpreter thereof, is already on the downward grade.

12. And whoso seeketh to glorify himself by his kingdoms, or by the magnificence of his possessions, taketh a burden upon his shoulders, that will, soon or late, fall upon him, and crush him.

13. And whoso fortifieth himself by armies, whether in the heavens or on the earth, bindeth himself therewith for his ultimate sorrow.

14. And whoso turneth away from Jehovih, and saith: I will go not after Him, nor search to find Him more; but I will build unto myself, planneth an edifice that will tumble down upon him in time to come.

CHAPTER LVI.
GOD CONTINUETH HIS CHASTISEMENT OF THE FOUR FALSE GODS.

1. In the name of the Almighty, my brothers, look at the glory ye boast of!

2. Ye say: Behold, we have scattered Jehovih's Faithists into all the places of the earth; they are without a kingdom; they have not left one community to themselves on the whole earth!

3. Think ye, Jehovih hath appropriated them?

4. Behold, it is true, ye have despoiled them, and scattered them abroad.

5. Ye have hunted them down in Chine'ya, Vind'yu, Arabin'ya, Parsi'e, Heleste and Uropa.

6. Ye have denied them the right to own lands, the right to follow their choice of avocations.

7. Ye have denied them justice, and even a hearing, in courts of trial.

8. And your accusation against them was: They worship not Gods born of woman.

9. But behold the wisdom of Jehovih; because ye thus dispossessed His people, and they were scattered abroad, they have sown the doctrine of the All One over all the earth and in the heavens thereof.

10. They have been as a leaven, to work in the foundations of mighty kingdoms and empires.

11. They have given learning unto all peoples, to show the magnificence of Jehovih's universe.

12. Behold, inhabitants of the earth now look upward, and ask: May there not be other worlds? How long hath been the earth standing? Could the Creator of thousands of millions of worlds, which have stood for thousands of millions of years, be so young as any one of these pretended Gods? And descend to earth, and do a work so imperfectly that only one small kingdom heard of him?

CHAPTER LVII.

GOD PROPHESIETH OF THE FOUR FALSE GODS, LOOEAMONG, ENNOCHISSA, KABALACTES AND GABRIEL.

1. God said: In the name of the All Highest, greeting, my brothers.

2. When ye first established your Holy Confederacy, behold, ye professed to be in service of Jehovih, and that your confederation was to raise up sons and daughters for the etherean heavens.

3. But, even before ye had completed your organization, ye modified the name, Jehovih, signifying the All Person, to the name, Holy Ghost, signifying no person, but a principle only.

4. Thus, in the very outset, ye prepared your kingdoms without distinctive purpose, and resurrection guided toward unity:

5. For, to declare, all things are not parts and principles comprising one universal All is to found a base for discord.

6. (As the players, when each one turneth away from the tune, playing a strain on his own account.)

7. Whereas, what ye declared of Jehovih, will also be declared of you, as ye denied His Person, substituting that which was void; and, as an incomprehensible state, so shall the same judgment come upon you all.

8. As ye put away Jehovih, so will mortals put you away.

9. As ye declare the Creator to be but a principle, a nonentity, without sense or unity of purpose, so shall mortals declare of you all.

10. They will say: Behold, Brahma is not a person, but a principle; Budha is not a person, but a principle; Kriste is not a person, but a principle; God-Gabriel is not a person, but a principle.

11. Because ye labored to pull down Jehovih's name, behold, the names which ye falsely assumed, will be pulled down, and cast out also, both on earth and in heaven.

12. Because ye have sought to confine in Jehovih's firmament the spirits that rise up from the earth, your kingdoms are falling lower and lower.

13. Because ye sought to confine the talents of mortals to your sacred books, your sacred books have become worthless before Jehovih.

14. Mortals, as well as angels, will repudiate you and your books. Only druks and drujas will be your followers.

15. And thou, Thoth, shalt be the first to be cast down, and thy heavenly kingdoms with thee.

16. And thou, Ennochissa, shalt be next, and thy heavenly kingdoms with thee.

17. And thou, Kabalactes, shalt be third, and thy heavenly kingdoms with thee.

18. And, last of all, thou, Looeamong, shalt go down, and thy heavenly kingdoms with thee.

19. Nevertheless, thou shalt conquer all the earth, and trail it round with mortal blood. And, after that, thou shalt be hated above all other false Gods, that have ever been.

CHAPTER LVIII.

GOD PLEADETH WITH THE FOUR FALSE GODS.

1. God said: In the name of Jehovih, greeting unto you.

2. Hear the plea of God, Jehovih's Son.

3. Like one that is whipped and beaten in a great contest, I cry out, because of the Almighty, whom I serve.

4. What is the fault of Jehovih, that ye have turned away from Him?

5. Behold, I will plead for Him. Was not His name good enough? What name is greater than the word, Creator?

6. If ye rejoice that ye live, then are ye not beholden to Him?

7. Why have ye substituted other names? Who was to be the gainer thereby?

8. Certainly not Jehovih.

9. What excuse can ye assign, that ye have made other names than Jehovih's worshipful on earth and in heaven?

10. Mortals will ask these questions in time to come.

11. Did not the Almighty, before your times, find a way to reveal Himself and his commandments?

12. Why have ye persecuted, abused and put to death mortals for worshipping Jehovih?

13. Behold, all ye four profess to be the Prince of Peace; but ye carry concealed daggers, and ye strike to death those who glorify the Creator.

14. I run after my children, as a father would, to snatch them away from a serpent; but ye slaughter them before my eyes.

15. I weep for them.

16. In shame, I look upon the earth and the heavens thereof, and I say unto myself: O thou God, to whom these were given in charge, how incompetent thou art against the flood of evil!

17. And I pray unto Jehovih, that your hearts may be turned to pity. I see, before you all, certain ruin and terrible hells; and I cry out to Jehovih, to give me the means to save you.

18. I pray, that I may be even unmolested in rescuing and saving the helpless and distressed, but ye frustrate all my inventions.

19. I am weary with my labor, and with the great kingdoms given into my keeping.

20. Alas, I am shut off on all sides from doing good, and yet, that is all I desire to do.

21. Now, I beseech you, O ye false Gods, make ye concessions unto Jehovih.

22. Save yourself from certain destruction, and Jehovih's Son from humiliation, before the high-raised Gods of other worlds.

CHAPTER LIX.

THE FOUR FALSE GODS' REPLY TO GOD, JEHOVIH'S SON.

1. In the names of the Son, the Father and the Holy Ghost, greeting unto Thee, God, Jehovih's Son.

2. In confederation assembled, we reply unto thee, with patience and mercy.

3. We sat not up our kingdoms for self-glorification, but righteousness and good works.

4. Behold, the firmament was overcast with falling a'ji, and our former Lord-doms were

broken up and gone.

5. And we chose our several places in uninhabited heavenly regions; therefore, we took nothing from thee.

6. We admit the goodness of thy heart and the honesty of thy purpose, but we do not acknowledge thy wisdom a sufficient guide unto heavens like our own.

7. The wise and exalted may rise in wisdom, purity and power, by the policy of love and non-resistance and by the example of good works.

8. But where such inhabitants, either on earth, or in the heavens thereof, comprise but a small per cent of the population, they become the victims of the lawless.

9. And this is the reason thy followers, both on earth and in heaven, are persecuted and abused.

10. We admit the declension of our grades, as thou hast said; but, behold, thy emissaries carry off our highest grades.

11. If thou would carry away our drujas only, we would not interdict the travel of thy ships in our heavenly dominions. But, as soon as thy ships come, behold, our highest grades rush for them.

12. For which reason, we have been obliged to prohibit thy laborers within our midsts.

13. Touching our slaves, of whom we have more than eighteen thousand millions, without slavery they would do nothing in heaven, and, for the most part, would inhabit mortals as vampires, familiars, demons, engrafters (re-incarnaters) and familiars.

14. Only by holding them as our slaves can we restrain them from these vices.

15. Forget not, that ere our heavenly kingdoms were established, the earth was covered over in many places with oracles and temples used to consult the spirits.

16. And these spirits were in darkness, holding mortals down in darkness.

17. We broke them all up, and thus cleared the earth from innumerable self-Gods and self-Lords.

18. Touching the matter of the name, Holy Ghost, have we not freedom, as well as thou, to choose a name to please ourselves?

19. Thou hast prophesied our downfall, and yet pleadst for us to prevent it. If we are to be overthrown, how, then, could we avert it; then thy prophecy would not realize truth.

20. Nevertheless, we propose unto thee, if thou wilt renounce the Person of the Creator, and style it, the Holy Ghost, we are prepared to treat with thee.

21. Otherwise, no more!

CHAPTER LX.

1. The Lord said: In the same hour, when God, in Paradise, received the epistle from the four false Gods, a light appeared in the firmament above, descending from the etherean heavens.

2. It was a star-ship from the Nirvanian heavens of Chia'hakad, only four hundred years from the dawn of the arc of kosmon, of the era of kosmon.

3. Like a crescent, made of stars, with a sun betwixt the horns, it came, a very world of light, swiftly coming toward Paradise.

4. Down came the ship of fire far below the moon's orbit, and then halted. For two whole days it halted, as if to warn the false Gods, the pretended Saviors of angels and mortals,

that Jehovih had spoken in the higher heavens.

5. Then came again the star-ship, till it anchored near the throne of God.

6. And the lights and the etherean waves of higher worlds were opened, and there came out of the midst of the arches of ships, a million angels, well trained in the management of worlds, and they were headed by Hyaponitissa, Goddess of Vaigonataj, in the plains of Myagoth.

7. And God of Paradise raised the lights of his heavens, and opened his palace and throne to the approaching Goddess and her hosts. God's Holy Council made way, and Hyaponitissa and her hosts entered the palace of God.

8. God said: Hail, Daughter of Jehovih! in His name, welcome to my throne!

9. And God saluted on the sign, THE CIRCLE AND TRIANGLE. Hyaponitissa answered in the sign, CHAIN OF THE CIRCUIT, saying: All honor and praise to thee, O God, Jehovih's Son.

10. Then she went up, and sat on the throne of God; and her hosts filed in front in a crescent, maintaining the chain of etherean light to the ships, and thence to the worlds above.

11. The es'enaurs chanted an anthem to Jehovih, and, after that, the Goddess rose up on the throne of God, and said:

12. Praise be unto Thee, Jehovih; mine eyes have beholden a Son of Thy love; the glory of the red star and her heavens, Thou hast uncovered before me.

13. The toils and trials of thy God, Thou has opened as a book is opened. And the dark ages of hundreds of years Thou hast made transparent by the light of Thy countenance.

14. Thou hast appropriated those, that labored for their own glory, to sweep from off the earth and her heavens, oracle worship and idolatry; and these curses shall return not again forever.

15. The prayer of Thy God reached up to the heavens Chia'hakad; the Gods of other worlds hearkened unto his voice.

16. And Thy Voice, Jehovih, came upon me, saying: Daughter of Vaigonataj, haste thou quickly to the red star; My God is calling!

17. And Thou gavest into my hands a million of Thy Holy Sons and Daughters, with a great ship of fire.

18. And I sped through Thy etherean seas and wide roadways, glorying in the work Thou gavest me.

19. Now, behold, I am honored before Thee and before Thy God and his Holy Council.

20. My love is to them, like a sister's, who had found a long lost brother; the glory of Thy handiwork, Thou hast manifested in them.

21. Thereupon, the Goddess gave the sign, LOVE TO ALL, and she sat down. Then, God rose up, and said:

22. Because Thou hast blest my people, O Jehovih, I am abashed before Thy Goddess, who hath come so far to see me.

23. Behold, in the last hour of my trials, Thou sent unto me; in the time I was heartbroken, Thou thrust into my kingdom the chain of Thy etherean light.

24. How can I be unmindful of Thee, Jehovih; how can I doubt the triumph of the Almighty. Thou hast dwellers in Thy Orian realms, whose presence are as a power to overturn a world.

25. And Thou hast found one that rusheth forth at Thy command to show me the way of succor.

26. Thereupon, God gave the sign, A GRATEFUL HEART, and he also sat down.

27. Again the es'enaurs chanted; and, presently, a ray of light passed over the head of Hyaponitissa, the Goddess, and it formed above the throne like a brilliant star.

28. And the Voice came out of the star, saying: My Son, God of the red star and her heavens, all honor and glory be unto thee.

29. The measure of thy labor is known to My Sons and Daughters in the higher worlds.

30. From this time forth, concern not thyself more about the four false Gods; sufficient unto them is the work they have undertaken.

31. Behold, they have appropriated four great divisions of the earth unto themselves; and the heavens thereof have become their dominions. Suffer them, therefore, to keep what they have taken.

32. Because they have bound mortals by their religions, and established themselves by mortal laws, and by force of their standing armies, thou shalt give unto them even all they have bound on earth and in the heavens.

33. But, behold, I have another continent, laying beyond the ocean, Guatama, where My people know Me, and worship Me.

34. Thither shalt thou inspire mortals to go from the east and find Guatama, and inhabit it.

35. And thither, it shall come to pass, none of the false Gods shall establish their doctrines by mortal laws, and bind My people.

36. And, as for the spirits of such mortals as the false Gods caused to be slain in the inquisitions, leave them to those Gods that took them.

37. And, though such spirits have vengeance in their hearts, and will be the means of ultimately casting the false Gods into hell, yet thou shalt not go near them.

38. But thou shalt look to the mortals whom thou shalt take over to inhabit the western continent.

39. And thou shalt send loo'is thither, and raise up, by birth, certain mortals, who shall ignore the doctrine of enforced worship for any God or Lord or Savior.

40. For the people of that land shall be free, not only in body, but in spirit also.

41. And it shall be guaranteed unto them to worship in My way, that their conscience may dictate.

42. And, when the dawn of the arc of kosmon cometh, behold, I will open up My heavens unto mortals, and prepare the foundation of My kingdom on earth.

43. The Voice ceased, and now God declared a day of recreation, that the ethereans and atm25atmosphereans might mingle together, and rejoice before Jehovih. And this was done also. And on the next day Hyaponitissa departed, leaving the requisite etherean laborers with God.

END OF GOD'S BOOK OF ESKRA.

BOOK OF ES, DAUGHTER OF JEHOVIH.

BEING A HEAVENLY HISTORY OF THE EARTH AND HER HEAVENS AND OF ETHEREA, SINCE FOUR HUNDRED YEARS AGO, DOWN TO THE DAWN OF THE KOSMON ERA.

CHAPTER I.

1. When Jehovih brought the great serpent (solar phalanx) along the road of Vorkum, in etherea, behold, the earth passed into the light of the Arc of Kosmon, rising upward, higher and higher in the dawn thereof.

2. To His etherean Gods and Goddesses, Jehovih said: As ye have founded arcs of light in my etherean heavens, to determine the travel of My corporeal worlds, so shall My God of the earth inspire mortals to build light-houses for man's ships that travel on the oceans. And they that travel in the ships, and they on the land shall know when a ship neareth the port, even as ye behold My traveling earth approaching the place of kosmon.

3. For this shall be an illustration unto mortals that I have appointed cycles of times and dawns of times, with Gods and Goddesses to superintend My creations in tenderness and love. (Lest peradventure man become despondent, saying: Alas, Jehovih provided not in wisdom commensurate with the magnificence of His creations.)

4. Behold, the time draweth near when the nations of the earth shall course around the whole earth in ships, crossing the seas and oceans, to all the places I created.

5. And those that have built in one place shall no longer say: This is our country.

6. For I will no more have the nations of the earth locked up unto themselves; nor one continent exclusive to one people; nor one ocean, nor sea, nor port, nor river, for any nation or tribe of men.

7. They shall know that the whole earth is Mine, and all the waters of the earth, and the air of the firmament; and that I created them for all My people, to receive them, and enjoy them unto Mine own glory.

8. They shall throw open their places, and say to one another: Welcome, my brother. Wheresoever Jehovih prompteth thee to dwell, be it so with thee, and I will give unto thee also.

9. Now, it shall come to pass, when the different nations and peoples begin to travel from one country to another, they will scornfully say of each other: Thou heathen; thou outside barbarian!

10. For they will judge with men's eyes, and with men's understanding; not comprehending the magnificence of the plans of My resurrections, which I provided unto them through My Gods and Goddesses.

11. As in former cycles, I sent unto the nations separately; so in kosmon, I shall not send separately, but unto the whole world. As in former cycles, I sent leaders and commanding Gods; so in kosmon, I shall not send either earthly leaders or a worshipful God or Lord.

12. When man was in great darkness, I sent Saviors and deliverers unto him. And My Saviors taught man, by certain commandments and by prayers, how he should live, to be saved from sin.

13. But in kosmon I shall send nor Savior, nor archangel, with a loud-sounding trumpet; but I will come to man's understanding through the light of Mine own wisdom. And man shall interpret My words as I speak to his own soul; and such shall be his sacred words.

14. Man shall pray to Me, and speak to Me in his own way, and not according to the dictation of any man, nor priest, nor sacred book, save the book of My creations.

15. Neither shall man longer accept any of the former revelations, and bow down unto them; for, as I was sufficient unto the ancients to speak to them things that were good for them, even so will I speak to My chosen of the kosmon era that which is good for them also.

16. My heavens shall be revealed unto them, as promised by My prophets of old, and man shall be taught how to see and comprehend My heavens with his own judgment, and not according to what any other man saith My revelations are.

17. Behold, in the ancient days, I provided Saviors and rab'bahs and priests to pray for man, and confess him of his sins; but these things will I put away, and no one shall pray for the living, nor confess him of his sins, by words or signs or ceremonies.

18. But every man shall pray for himself, in his own way, and confess his sins unto Me for forgiveness.

19. And instead of praying in words for his brother, saying: Jehovih, help him, he shall go in person, and help him with his own hands.

20. Neither shall man sit idly and say: O Jehovih, help Thou me; come and save me!

21. But he shall rise up in the majesty I created him, saying: Behold me, Jehovih! I will save myself. Guide Thou me, O Father!

22. And he shall walk forth, proudly in My sight, scorning evil and sin, doing with all his might for his own salvation. And I will come unto him, for of such shall be My chosen.

23. In kosmon, I shall not come to make a servant of man unto man; nor to make him afraid, when the priest speaketh. I will make man hold up his head fearlessly before men, in remembrance of his daily covenant unto Me, his Creator, in the practice of righteousness.

24. In that day, the preacher and the priest shall be of little avail; My standard shall be of good works, and not of words.

25. Neither shall My hand be unto individuals only, but unto nations, kingdoms and empires.

26. Whatsoever people embrace Me, the same will I embrace also. And a sign shall be unto them: their ports and lands and waters shall be thrown open unto all other people.

27. And they shall prosper, and become numerous, thriving in peace and plenty. And My Holy angels from My exalted heavens shall minister unto them, and they shall grow in wisdom, good works and in learning and in inventions and discoveries.

28. But whatsoever people will not embrace Me, the same will I not embrace. Their ports shall be bound up, and their lands and waters shall not be opened unto others. Verily, shall they attempt to be an exclusive people; and I will withdraw My exalted angels away from them, and they shall be encompassed with darkness.

29. These signs shall be before the world as My living testimony; and My prophets shall use these signs in determining which nations and peoples My hand covereth over to protect, and save them.

30. My prophets shall remember the countries of old which strove against Me and My chosen, how they went down in darkness.

31. When My dawn of a cycle cometh, I ever put away the ancient doctrines, and the established Gods and Saviors; none have ever stayed My hand. Now, behold, man shall

look about in the kosmon era and see My foot-prints in the ancient times, how I ministered unto the races of men. And he shall apply with judgment the history of other days.

32. This also will I accomplish: Kingdoms and nations shall judge their own strength by their rigid laws and standing armies.

33. And they shall look upon My people, and say: Alas, they are weak; they have neither kings, nor armies, nor rigid laws!

34. But My prophets shall remember My chosen of old, who had faith in Me. And My prophets shall say to the kings with mighty armies: Behold, ye are the weakest; and those that have no armies are the strongest. And their prophecies shall not fail.

35. That which applieth in My heavens of the earth, shall apply on the earth; that, which applieth on the earth, shall apply in the heavens thereof.

36. The bondage of kings and queens and emperors and rich men and leaders of men, shall be with them in the heavens of this earth. Until they have undone the tyranny they had over others, their heavens shall be without liberty to them. Whom they sought to lead on earth, they shall lead in heaven; neither shall there be exalted resurrection for them, until the lowest of their subjects have risen before them.

37. And they that live isolated and alone on the earth, shall be isolated and alone in the heavens of the earth. Man shall learn that affiliation and brotherhood unto others on earth, shall find affiliation and brotherhood in the heavens of the earth.

38. Whosoever openeth his soul in love and harmony unto others on earth, shall find love and harmony in heaven.

39. And the same rule shall apply to nations and peoples: according to their love and harmony and the breadth of their liberality unto other nations and peoples, even so shall be the heavens of the earth, whither they shall migrate after death.

40. All these things of heaven and earth shall be made plain to man in kosmon; with his own eyes he shall behold the justice of his Creator.

CHAPTER II.

1. To His etherean Gods and Goddesses, Jehovih said: Behold, in twelve generations My dawn of kosmon will reach the earth.

2. Go ye down to the earth, and provide mortals and angels unto the work of My cycle.

3. In other times, My Gods and Goddesses said unto man: Thou shalt, and thou shalt not. Behold, in kosmon, ye shall declare the glory of My works and the plans of My heavens unto the nations of the earth. In all My fullness shall ye declare the glories of My creations.

4. But ye shall not say to this man nor to that man: Thou shalt believe, nor that thou shalt not believe.

5. Neither shall ye say to man: Thou shalt do this, and thou shalt not do that.

6. Such were the ancient cycles and the custom of My revelators; but such shall not be the custom of My revelators in this day.

7. But man, having heard and seen, shall judge what he will do; he shall believe, or not believe; and do, or not do, according to his own judgment.

8. Because I hold man responsible, even so should he have liberty to choose.

9. And if he strive to choose Me, by doing righteously, he shall not fail.

10. Though he accept none of the ancient doctrines, nor rites, nor ceremonies, nor Gods, nor Lords, nor Saviors, but strive for Me in doing good unto others, he shall be My chosen, even though he accept not My name.

11. Liberty, first of all, unto all people; then discipline and harmony, and then the improvement of all the talents I created with all.

12. Next to this, to have no leader, nor any one to think for another; nor to abandon one's own judgment contrary to wisdom and truth.

13. But to contend not, nor to be stubborn and positive as to the righteousness of one's own opinion. For I created no two men to see alike the same thing on earth or in heaven.

14. As to which matters, the highest wisdom is to suffer all men to have full liberty to think on all subjects in their own way.

15. In the olden times, they had inquisitors, to watch as to what another did, or said, or intimated; now, behold, in kosmon, exactly the opposite of this shall be the behavior of My chosen.

16. Though man seeth his neighbor do differently from what he himself would, he shall look the other way; or, if he speak to him of the matter, it shall be with respect, even as he would to his own mother or father.

17. And for any shortness of speech, or error, or evil expression, man shall not reprove his neighbor, nor find fault with him, more than he would with his own mother, or father, or sister, or brother. Rather shall he strive, not to see, nor hear the shortness of any man.

18. They shall be taught to see the good that is in others; to speak of the delights of all My living creatures.

19. To reprove with words, to circumspect the doings of one's neighbors, their opinions and behavior, these shall I put away in kosmon.

20. Neither shall one man advise another without becoming bound to him that followeth his advice. This, also, shall man be made to understand in kosmon.

21. In other cycles, I sent My loo'is to raise up certain mortals, through whom I could reveal My commandments unto others. In kosmon, behold, I shall not raise up any great leader-forth; My light shall fall upon thousands and thousands. Of many varieties of talents shall be My chosen in that day.

22. For which reason, when ye have descended to the earth, ye shall appoint loo'is unto millions of mortals, and they shall raise up a numerous offspring unto Me.

23. And it shall be born with them to see and feel, that a new era is at hand; and they shall be born skeptical to the ancient doctrines, Gods, Lords and Saviors.

24. Nevertheless, they shall be the best of men, and wise and charitable and most considerate of the opinions of others.

25. And it shall come to pass, that when the western continent is inhabited across from east to west, all the earth will be circumscribed with men of wisdom and learning.

26. And the year of the circumscribing shall be the beginning of kosmon.

27. And the heavens of the earth shall be opened, and the angels thereof shall descend to the earth, and make themselves known to mortals; even through them which your loo'is shall have born unto the work.

28. And from that time forth, the old order shall decline, to be put away forever; and the new order shall take its place, to triumph over all the earth.

29. Thereafter, shall the virtue of preaching come to an end; but practice, in fulfilling good works and living up to My commandments, shall be all that will avail for the establishing of My kingdom on earth.

30. Go ye forth, My beloved; fulfill the seasons of the earth, that My people may rejoice in their lives, in peace and love, for the glory of My heavens, which I created for them.

CHAPTER III.

1. Es said: Far up in the vault of the firmament, in the etherean realms of Jehovih, the Voice of the Almighty had spoken. The Orian Chief of Huamat and Balis called unto the Gods and Goddesses on the plains of Thessalona and Nadab and Vraghaoma, called for ten million volunteers.

2. Chonling, Son of Jehovih, Chief of Fabi'wotch'osi and Balis, said: Come, O ye Gods and Goddesses; come with me down to the red star; the earth is near the arc of kosmon, era of kosmon. Come and think for mortals; inspire them with holier thoughts; make them comprehend the light of Jehovih.

3. Then spake Thetchaya, Chieftainess of Huamat and Dikaddonas, saying: Come, O ye Gods and Goddesses, I will lead you yonder to the rising red star, the little traveling earth. Behold, she cometh our way; she will cross the Arc of Kosmon in four hundred years.

4. Litabakathrava, Orian Chief of Yohamma, of two hundred thousand years, God of Ithwan, forty thousand years, said: Come, O ye Gods and Goddesses, come to the red star. Behold, my otevan, my fire-ship, goeth that way on her cruise of ten thousand years. Come with me, my otevan will carry a thousand millions; I will halt and leave you on the earth with mortals.

5. Che Sin, Chief of Ahwentaba, of sixty thousand years, called a host of his swift messengers, ten thousand. Unto them he said: Provide an arrow-ship of great velocity, and go ye in the former roadway of the earth, in the regions whither she traveled thousands of years; proclaim it in the etherean heavens, another corporeal world, the earth, near the time of kosmon.

6. Mortals on the earth are to be illumed and, like Gods, made to comprehend the glorious plans of the heavens of the Almighty. In four hundred years, the Father's kingdom is to be founded on the red star.

7. Bornothetes, Chief of Guaga, called his Holy Council, in the palace of Nu, gardens of Lasanitizi. And they looked across the firmament, far off, to see the slow rolling earth, where mortals still groped in darkness; whose people could not read the unseen heavens.

8. Here they deliberated; some to wonder how it was, that the earth, in all the time of her being, had only sent a few hundred thousand million angels into the etherean heavens; and as to where they dwelt, that they had as yet never been heard of in these fruitful gardens, in etherea. Others surmised the lowness of her grades.

9. Then spake Atavia, Goddess of Peronitus. She said: O, I remember the earth! Her side was crushed, and the form of her lands changed by Aph, in the Arc of Noe, twenty four thousand years ago. Hi'ata, Goddess of the Flying Wing, was there, and I with her, in her airavagna. O, it is a glorious world. I will be one, a volunteer, to go thither, for the four hundred years.

10. Atavia was the first volunteer; but now, the names enrolled like sparks of fire,

flashing in the firmament.

11. Presently the numerators sent up rockets, the signals, that the ten millions had responded to Jehovih's call.

12. These, then, were the etherean kingdoms who contributed: Jaison, in the swamps of Loe; Rodus, of the mountains of Kembak; Tisain and Carwa, of the plains of Tassahacha; Amos, the Chosone Resort, and Sagamma, the kingdom of Methiasi, Goddess of Tuesta.

13. Bornothetes sent swift messengers to these kingdoms; some were half a million miles distant, and some lay on crooked lanes, and hid amidst nebulous forests, and yet others over and beyond mountains, thousand of miles high and broad. And he called them, to assemble in Piatyu, the port of Nabrokaxax, under the arches of Geddis, to consult together, and prepare for the journey.

14. So, when the hosts were assembled in Piatya, Jehovih appointed Thotagawawa as God of the cruise and mission.

15. And Litabakathrava ordered his fire-ship to be brought to Piatya, where it no sooner arrived than the hosts of the mission, the ten millions, went aboard, as guests and companions to Litabakathrava's fifty million traveling visitors to worlds, ten thousand times further on.

16. And now began the trumpeters and the es'enaurs in songs of praise, the two bands of musicians, a million performers.

17. Then upward, outward, rose the airavagna, the ship of fire, whose photosphere, as to size, was like a world; rose up higher and higher, heading for the far-off red star, that coursed in the serpent's coil, a million and a half miles a day.

18. Two thousand million miles off, lay the red star, the earth, seen by the magnifying instruments of the Gods, seen in its little orbit round the sun, of half a thousand million miles.

19. Four hundred million miles a day, sped the airavagna through the etherean worlds; like a flash of light shot forth the ship of Litabakathrava, Orian Chief of thousands of years, coursing the etherean heavens of Jehovih! A God that, but to look on a corporeal world, knew the grade of her mortals and angels, even as in his flight he passed on.

20. Five days and nights traveled the hosts of the emancipated heavens, to reach the earth; traveled through thousands and thousands of etherean worlds, of forests and swamps of ji'ay, and of nebula, and a'ji, and regions of light, and mountains and rivers and plains; countless places, inhabited and uninhabited in the great expanse of Jehovih's kingdoms.

21. Then, they came to Chinvat, the bridge of the boundary of the earth's vortex, and there halted to survey the earth and her unruly heavens, where the four false Gods proclaimed themselves monarchs of the universe! A day they rested, in a day they measured the grade and standing of the earth's mortals and angels, and then, they descended straight to Paradise, the place of God, Jehovih's Son.

CHAPTER IV.

THE ALARM IN HARACTU, HEAVENLY PLACE OF KABALACTES, THE FALSE, BUT REIGNING BUDHA.

1. Kabalactes said: My most high Holy Council, Lords of heaven and earth, give ear. This day, my scouts on the borders of Vridat, my suburban kingdom in Tua, saw a light descending, like a world on fire. Consternation came upon my dutiful subjects, fearing

some foreign God menaced their liberties. To appease them, Hathav, my Lord in command, dispatched hither messengers, to know my will.

2. But when they arrived, others came also, but from the heavenly plateau, Itussak, my northern kingdom, with the same ominous tale. Then others, from other kingdoms in my heavenly regions. Some have seen the light but faintly, some have seen it brilliant as a pillar of fire. Whilst here, within our well secured heavenly seat, it hath been only as a falling meteor.

3. Speak, my Lords, know ye more of this?

4. Maithivi, Lordess, said: All Highest of Gods, be considerate of womanly fears, and detract accordingly from my magnified expressions. To me, this descended star is some far-off ally with God, Jehovih's worshiper in Paradise. For by the course of the falling light, it landed thither. Is not this some stratagem to re-establish Jehovih, whom we have chased from earth and heaven?

5. Fiebowh, Lord, said: It is not a year since some other foreign God descended to Paradise. Behold, this last one cometh from the same angle beyond Chinvat. Peradventure, the former was but a scout sent from some realm, which hath now answered this mighty airavagna?

6. Sin Loo, Lord, said: It was said of old: When the heavens clear, look out for Jehovih's worshipers, the infidels against the reigning Gods. Now, behold, in the very season when a'ji flieth away, and our souls are on the eve of rejoicing, here cometh an ominous meddler with our slaves, to do us mischief.

7. Thus spake many Lords, alarmed; for a secret sin, as slavery, justified by the master's conscience, being held down, is easily tormented with suspected griefs, not yet come to pass.

8. And more than this; in Kabalactes' Holy Council of one million members, were many who had been long promised preferment and higher dominion than to legislate for another's kingdom; and they had received nothing worthy of the name, for more than a thousand years.

9. And these had a small spark of hope left, that some external disaster to Kabalactes' extensive kingdoms would open the way for rich adventures in their own behalf, with millions of slaves to do them reverence.

10. So, even whilst their tongues upheld their monstrous idol, Budha (the false), their own souls were equally perfidious.

11. When many of the Holy Council had spoken, then again Kabalactes went on: My marshal in chief shall select a host a million strong, and provide them an arrow-boat; to which command I appoint, Teanvettas, general, to go to Paradise in my name, greeting, to learn the will and pleasure of this adventurous God that cometh to the vanquished kingdom of Jehovih's Son; to offer him the freedom of my kingdom for a monthly visit. Perchance, he hath never seen a city built of gems and precious stones; and the palace and throne of the all highest God. The which to look on may abash him from undertaking some foolish scheme.

12. Now, accordingly, from the false Budha's magnificent heavenly kingdom, there went out an arrow-boat, the most precious gem ever built in these heavens. And in it a million hosts, arrayed as very Gods and Goddesses in splendor. Whilst Teanvettas, with his shining crown and blazing jewels, bespake his general-ship as from a rich kingdom.

13. Two hundred thousand slaves worked the boat, and many of these had been in earth-life Budhist priests, and were now serving their apprentice-ship of two hundred years, in order to have the privilege in future time of crawling on their bellies to see the throne of Budha (the false), and see their all highest ideal God.

14. Thus, then, went the arrow-boat, in all its glory, to Paradise, seat of Jehovih's Son.

CHAPTER V.

THE ALARM IN ETA-SHONG, HEAVENLY KINGDOM OF
ENNOCHISSA, THE FALSE, BUT REIGNING GOD, BRAHAMA.

1. Whilst Ennochissa and his Holy Council were assembled in the palace of Eta-shong, there came messengers from no less than thirty and six of Ennochissa's sub-kingdoms, alarmed, and with magnified accounts of the fire-ship seen descending to Paradise.

2. And each and all of these messengers told his tale before the throne; expressing the fear of the sub-kingdoms' Lords, and praying to know Ennochissa's will and pleasure.

3. Now, here, even as at Haractu, the Lords of the Holy Council spake expressive of their hopes and fears. And here also were many Lords, who had long been promised exaltation, but never received it. And they pretended heart-felt loyalty to Ennochissa, the false Brahma, even whilst with secretive hope they prayed some adventurous God might come and break up Ennochissa's kingdom, feeling, that in the spoil they would profit in heavenly kingdoms of their own.

4. Then spake Ennochissa, saying: In the name of the Holy Ghost, I thank you all. And for your loyalty make myself your humble God to do your wills and pleasure.

5. First, then, that our unapproachable kingdom shall ever remain the all highest heaven, where ye shall rest secure forever, I will prove most alert to learn the designs of this visiting God.

6. Behold, I will send thither an arrow-boat, with a million Lords, arrayed in splendor, and every one crowned; and over them, Kosimathara, Lord in chief.

7. In my name and in the name of the Holy Ghost, my hosts shall greet this God, and invite him hither on a monthly visit. Perchance he hath no knowledge, as to what the all highest God is.

8. So, it came to pass, an arrow-boat was made, the most magnificent ever seen in Eta-shong; and in it the million Lords with jeweled crowns embarked, commanded by Kosimathara, Lord in chief, and they sped off for Paradise also.

CHAPTER VI.

THE ALARM IN KELLA-HORED, THE HEAVENLY KINGDOM OF
GOD-GABRIEL, ALIAS THOTH, THE MOHAMMEDAN HEAVEN.

1. When the Lords of the Holy Council of Kalla-Hored, the heaven of the false Mohammed, had expressed their hopes and fears as to the fire-ship descending to Paradise, Thoth, alias Gabriel, said:

2. Who here feareth, let him speak; who here feareth not, let him speak also. I will know my Lords and Holy Council.

3. Behold, I am a warrior God. I profess not peace, like the Triunes, and practice war. I

profess war, and I practice it.

4. I made Looeamong. When he chose to have himself established as Kriste, I established him. When he denied me justice, I exposed him in heaven and on the earth as the false Kriste. When he refused me the heavenly kingdom which he promised, I took it, and established myself.

5. I made ye Lords of my Holy Council; I drove away from the earth a thousand false Lords, and broke up the oracle-houses of mortals.

6. What, then, have I to fear from a foreign God, coming to the heavens of the earth? Behold, these heavens belong to such as are born of the earth. Let the foreign Gods return to worlds where they were native born.

7. If this God hath come to battle me, in behalf of Jehovih's God, let him come. Till he or I shall be cast into hell, let the battle wage.

8. Did I not the daring Goddess, Ashtaroth, send to hell? and the mighty Baal after her? And all the Argos'yan Gods; and the Gods of Roma silence and cast into torments?

9. Now, behold, I will send an arrow-boat, a million strong, to Paradise, and banter this adventurous God to give me battle. Better try our respective powers, as to who shall go down, than to live in uncertain surmises as to such a God's business in another God's heavens.

10. Then let my marshal provide an arrow-boat, armed with shafts of fire and water, and choose a million warriors for this adventure. Over them, my warrior Lord, Justin, shall hold command.

11. And he shall go to Paradise, greeting, in the name of God-Gabriel, to know of the coming God by what right he hath ventured near my holy kingdoms.

12. So, it came to pass, Thoth dispatched a boat to Paradise, as he had commanded.

CHAPTER VII.

THE ALARM IN HAPSENDI, HEAVENLY KINGDOM OF LOOEAMONG, THE FALSE KRISTE.

1. Even as at the heavenly kingdoms of the other three false Gods, so was the alarm in Hapsendi, capital of the heavenly kingdom of Looeamong, who had falsely assumed to be Kriste.

2. After Looeamong's hundreds of messengers, from his various sub-kingdoms, had made their reports as to the appearance of the great light that had descended to Paradise, and of the consternation of the sub-Lords, then spake the Holy Council before the throne of Looeamong. Some magnified the omen as a menace; some suggested doubling the number of the standing armies of Looeamong's heavenly kingdoms, and yet others suggested numerous other things.

3. After thousands of them had spoken, then spake Looeamong, saying:

4. Wise and Holy Lords and Gods of the all highest heavenly kingdom, great have been your wisdom and suggestions. Now, therefore, by the light of the Holy Ghost, hear ye of my decrees:

5. I will send unto this stranger God, who hath come to Paradise, a fire-boat a million strong, and every one shall go crowned and arrayed with jewels and diadems, and weapons of warfare; and they shall have shields and figure-heads of tau (bull) and aires (lamb), as symbols of my attributes.

6. Behold, I send unto him as a lamb of peace, but I send also the spear and sword.

7. In command of the fire-boat and the hosts thereof I appoint, Ajudus, whom I will crown with the miter and the triangle and the cut ring.

8. And this shall be my message to the stranger God, to wit: In the name of the Holy Ghost and of the Son, greeting and love. Behold the kingdom of Hapsendi, the all highest holy heaven, is open, and free unto thee. The all highest God and ruler of the greatest heavenly kingdom would know thy will and pleasure. And if it be thy purpose to engage in a good and holy work, behold, I have employment for thee, for thy profit and honor and glory. And, for whatsoever thou canst accomplish for the resurrection of my people, shall receive a just reward from my hand.

9. Accordingly, a fire-boat of excellent workmanship was provided, and equipped in gorgeousness and splendor. And into it the million hosts, crowned as Lords, and commanded by Ajudus and Justin, embarked, and set sail for Paradise, the heavenly place of God, Jehovih's Son.

10. To work the fire-boat there were four hundred thousand slaves, composed of the spirits of such as had been on earth, popes, archbishops, bishops, cardinals, priests, and others who were serving their bondage of two hundred years (as they verily believed in purgatory), for the privilege of ultimately crawling on their bellies through the arena of the palace, and to approach near enough to look upon Looeamong, their supposed all highest God and Savior.

11. Such, then, was the magnificence and the object of the fire-boat sent to Paradise.

CHAPTER VIII.

OF GOD IN PARADISE.

1. Es said: After the Light of Jehovih came to God, saying: Go, provide mortals to cross the ocean, to build up the western continent, God ceased striving to redeem the four heavenly kingdoms of the four false Gods, but directed his energies, to regain a broader earth-anchorage, for sake of Jehovih's kingdom.

2. So, God sent down from Paradise, one Melkazad, crowned as Lord, with ten thousand angels in his command to inspire migration to Guatama, and to make the country known to the eastern peoples.

3. And Melkazad, with his hosts, came and ascertained the grade and choice of mortals for such purpose. And Melkazad and his hosts did raise up Columbo (Columbus), a mortal from Genoa, together with crews, sufficient in number, whom they inspired to go with ships to the westward, across the ocean, in search of the lay and plan of the world.

4. And it came to pass, that Columbo, thus inspired of God, through his holy angels, did discover the western continent, not knowing, he was under inspiration.

5. It was shortly after this, that the angel hosts from etherea came down to the throne of God in Paradise, to labor with him in providing for the approach of the kosmon era.

6. Now, whilst God and his angels in the heavenly kingdom of Paradise were rejoicing because of the success of Columbo, which had been reported by Melkazad to God, behold, in that same time it was, that the etherean ship of Litabakathrava arrived.

7. And God received the ethereans with great rejoicing; and, after due ceremonies, God declared a recreation of three days, that the angels of Paradise might rejoice, before

Jehovih, because the a'ji of so many hundreds of years was breaking away, and because of Columbo's success, and because of the coming of the ethereans.

8. Great, indeed, were the rejoicings, the praise, the music and glee of the thousand million angels of Paradise.

9. At the end of three days, the trumpet called the Holy Council of God, to resume labor before the throne. Then, the marshals from various places in Gods kingdoms called their students and laborers, and withdrew to their several departments. The Holy Council resumed their places before God, and God ascended the throne, and order was.

10. Then, God called the ethereans, Chonling, Thetchaya, Che Sin, Bornothetes, Atavia and Thotagawawa to come and honor the throne. Whereupon, these visiting Gods did as commanded.

11. Then spake God, saying: What tribute, O Jehovih, can I pay to Thy Son, Litabakathrava? For the light and glory of his presence provide Thou unto me and my Holy Council.

12. Thereupon, all the Holy Council, one million, rose to their feet, and then all the Gods rose up also. God said: Come thou, honor my throne.

13. Then, Litabakathrava walked up, and sat on the throne of God. When he was seated, God commanded all the rest to be seated. And thereupon, Litabakathrava rose up, and said:

14. Thou hast given me great honor, O God of the earth and her heavens. May be light of the Person of Jehovih dawn upon all the kingdoms of heaven and earth.

15. Yet, O God, be not puffed up with the hope of sudden success. I have seen many corporeal worlds arrive at the kosmon era. But it is like a new birth, brought forth in pain, and with much labor.

16. Thou hast yet several generations of mortals to be born ere kosmon come. The four dark corners of the lodge will bound upon thee, to destroy the work of thy hand and of Jehovih's.

17. The four false Gods will fight thee to the death; only till they go down in hell, can Jehovih's kingdom come.

18. On all the planetary worlds it is ever the same; certain four false Gods rise up to possess the corporeal worlds and her heavens.

19. They will profess truth, but practice falsehood; profess peace, but practice war. They will incite mortals and angels to all manner of evil for sake of thwarting Jehovih's Person and proceedings. Yea, they will even yet assume that they themselves are Jehovih, the veritable Creator. And they will inspire mortals, to consider them as such.

20. And when thy people profess Jehovih and not them, behold, they will inspire others to fall upon thy people to destroy them, or to torture them with great suffering.

21. Nevertheless, it shall come to pass with thee, Jehovih shall triumph over all the earth and in the heavens of the earth. Men and angels shall be free, and none shall make them afraid.

22. Litabakathrava ceased, and sat down, and suddenly a great shining light gathered above his head, and a Voice spake out of the light saying:

23. All the earth is Mine, and the waters, and the air above the earth. These are members of My body and Person. Man I created not to possess them, but to dwell thereon and therein. Unto all men alike gave I of these inheritances; nor to any man a part, nor to any

nation or people a part.

24. But with liberty and privilege unto these, gave I man the right to draw sustenance and support.

25. All men are My children; into conscious being created I them alike, privileged unto all the earth, and the waters of the earth, and the air in the firmament above the earth.

26. Brothers and sisters created I them; of various tribes and races and colors and sizes, but nevertheless, in Mine own way I created them, every one for a glory in the way I made them.

27. In the early days, behold, I kept man on certain continents and places, that I might unfold him in the glory for which I designed him.

28. But in kosmon, I open the gates of the oceans, and the seas, and the rivers, and I say unto all My people: Come forth, behold your brethren; go ye into this country, and into that, and learn wisdom from that which I have proved in the family of My house. Be ye profitable unto one another, in the experience and practice of My hand upon all peoples.

29. In one, tallness; in another, shortness; in one, sound teeth and bones and well-formed limbs; in another, sagacity; in one, a dense population and well-tilled lands; in another, plain food and long life; for in kosmon, man shall go abroad into all countries, one nation with another; and they shall profit by wisdom, to bring forth a new race with all the glories selected from the whole.

30. Neither shall man be bound more by the doctrines of this God or that God, or by this Savior or that Savior, nor by any of the ancient books, nor by inspirations of the olden times. But he shall know how to obtain inspirations from My Gods, and My heavens for his own good, and for his own wisdom.

31. Neither shall one nation judge another, and cry out, heathen; nor one people judge another and cry out, pagan.

32. Behold, I alone shall judge; My mark is upon all those that engage in war, or who keep warriors; or who keep forts and arsenals, and use weapons of death; and upon all who kill, and eat the flesh of anything I created alive; for all such are pagan and heathen in My sight.

33. Neither shall they go from nation to nation to find evil, but to find goodness and wisdom and virtue.

34. My Gods shall minister unto all nations and peoples to these ends, to bring them together in peace and harmony, to open the ports of those that have been seclusive nations and peoples, to persuade them to put away war and the glory of destruction, to make nations and peoples acceptable to one another.

35. The Voice of the Light ceased, and all about the throne of God was like a sea of golden fire.

36. The time for the departure of Litabakathrava and his hosts had arrived. Accordingly, he went down, and sat on the foot of the throne, and then, God descended, and took his hand, saying: Arise, Orian Chief, Jehovih's Son, and go thy way. The Father calleth thee and thy people.

37. So Litabakathrava passed down into the arena, and saluted on the sign, DAWN OF KOSMON, and God answered in the sign, FORTIFIED IN JEHOVIH'S NAME!

38. Litabakathrava and his hosts then went into the otevan, the monster ship, with its photosphere, large as a continent. And presently, whilst the es'enaurs and the trumpeters

chanted, Praise to the Almighty, the vessel started from its foundation, and rose slowly upward, applauded by the thousands of millions assembled in Paradise.

CHAPTER IX.

1. Es said: Now, behold, just as the ship of Litabakathrava had risen upward, and was on its way starting forth, the fire-boats of the four false Gods arrived in Paradise.

2. And the hosts, in the boats, were discomfited and angry withal, because their boasted audacity was thwarted from having an interview with the Orian Chief and his hosts.

3. And they of the fire-boats saw one another, and were incensed and jealous, and puzzled to know what to do. Neither would any of them confer with God, Jehovih's Son, for they had been thus commanded by the respective false Gods.

4. Now, therefore, after the fire-boats had cruised about awhile, displaying their splendor, three of them departed, leaving only the fire-boat of Looeamong's hosts remaining.

5. The captain of this boat had said: It is not sufficient that I come hither, and find the foreign God departed. I will ascertain what hath been said and done, and what these Jehovih worshipers are up to.

6. So, he went aside, and made his boat fast and he and his hosts, arrayed in splendor, went and talked with the inhabitants of Paradise, inquiring, amongst other things, the cause of such great rejoicing amongst the people.

7. And one of the people, being unguarded, said: Behold, it is well with us that we rejoice; God, Jehovih's Son, hath inspired a new mortal anchorage. He hath taken Columbo, across the ocean, and showed him a new country, where only the Great Spirit, Jehovih, is worshipped.

8. The captain of the fire-boat thus discovered one of the plans of God for redeeming the world; but the captain disclosed not his joy, though presently, he and his hosts went aboard and departed, making all haste to Hapsendi, the heaven of Looeamong, the false Kriste.

9. On the day after Looeamong learned this matter, he sent a war-ship with seven million warring angels to stir up a mutiny amongst mortals in countries whence Columbo sailed.

10. And, by inspiration, Looeamong's warrior angels did set the rulers of Spain against Columbo, and had him cast in prison, thus breaking the chain of inspiration betwixt Columbo and the throne of God.

11. In the meantime, Looeamong's angels made all haste to have mortal ships and ship-masters of their own kind cross the ocean to the countries Columbo had discovered.

12. Thus did Looeamong's mortal worshipers cross over to Guatama, and, with them, Looeamong landed and stationed in Guatama one thousand million angel warriors, sworn laborers to the false Kriste, to establish him in these great lands.

13. When God saw how evil had already taken root in these countries, behold, he was doubly resolved to obey Jehovih's commandment, in regard to the inquisitions, in which Jehovih had said:

14. Suffer Looeamong to carry out the inquisitions, to put to death whosoever he will. For it shall come to pass that the spirits of those he slayeth in Roma and Venice and Napla and all other cities and countries will remain in their places with vengeance on their souls. And the time shall come when thou shalt withdraw thy protecting angel hosts from these

cities; and, behold, these angels of vengeance will come forth and visit their wrath upon this false God and his kingdoms.

15. So, God was strong in resolution to let evil take its course; and, so, in all countries where the false Kriste had been afflicting mortals, God withdrew his protecting hosts, leaving those countries and those heavens to take their course.

16. And it came to pass, the angels of vengeance came forth for battle; to battle other angels, and to obsess mortals unto battle also, and all against the false Kriste.

17. Thus was opened the door for the split in Looeamong's doctrines, which was to ultimate in the entire overthrow of the Trinity, and of the Holy Ghost, and of Looeamong also, under his false name.

18. Thus did war begin again on earth, and in Looeamong's heavens, about himself and his doctrines.

19. To make matters worse for himself, he established angel emissaries in his earthly kingdom, in Roma, to inspire the popes to cause mortals to be scourged, imprisoned and put to death for heresy, and these things were done in the name of Kriste and the Holy Ghost.

20. And it came to pass that no man could express a word, or thought, reflecting upon Looeamong's earthly doctrines or government, without falling a victim to mortal and angel emissaries of this false Kriste. Verily were many of these mortal cities obsessed by angels of darkness and evil.

21. In course of time, behold, mortals, inspired by vengeance-loving spirits, rose up against Looeamong's popes and cardinals, and protested against the abnegation of man's right to think for himself; and these people called themselves, protestants, professing that there were two Kristes, a true one and a false one, and, moreover, that they themselves were worshipers of the true Kriste.

22. Nevertheless, they were also under the inspiration of evil angels, for they fell to work burning and flaying their opponents also.

23. And God foresaw that now was the time to inspire the western nations of Uropa to great learning and to science and to philosophy and to western migration.

24. So, God sent angels to teach man once more the telescope and the art of printing; and to inspire man to question the spiritual powers of kings.

25. Thus was Looeamong's power in great measure locked up in managing his disrupted kingdoms, whilst God's holy angels pursued the road of righteous development for the coming era of kosmon.

CHAPTER X.

1. Es said: When God saw that Looeamong's warrior angels had come upon the earth regions, discovered by Columbo, God withdrew, saying:

2. Behold, I will use this as a testimony unto Jehovih and against this false Kriste, in time to come. For I will withdraw my angel hosts and give up, for a season, the central lands of Guatama.

3. And it shall come to pass, that mortals in these lands shall not prosper in peace, nor righteousness, nor in learning, nor in science, nor in inventions, nor in anything good under the sun. For Looeamong's warrior angels shall obsess them, and they shall build up, and then destroy, and the people of Aliattes, the Yodopans, shall be destroyed, and the

I'tuans and their cities shall be ruined.

4. Now it did come to pass, as spoken by God, the central lands of Guatama, from sea to sea, fell under the dominion of the warrior angels of Looeamong, the false Kriste, and they became warriors and destroyers; nor rose they in peace, nor wisdom, nor in anything good under the sun. But they lived as pilferers, debauchees, warriors, murderers and idolaters of the false Kriste.

5. God had said: I will go to the northward, to the western coast of Uropa, and my angel hosts shall inspire another people to migrate to Guatama for conscience sake (Jehovih's sake).

6. And it shall be proved, in time to come, that they whom I shall take across the ocean, shall inherit Guatama; and they shall prosper in peace and virtue and wisdom and learning and inventions. And man, in after time, shall witness the difference betwixt the people of Looeamong's possessions as compared with mine own in the northern regions.

7. And so, God sent his angel hosts amongst the factions of western Uropa, and inspired mortals to rise up, and depart out of that country for conscience sake. And they that were inspired of God crossed over the ocean, and landed in Guatama, and they named the place of their landing Plymouth Rock, saying: For God's sake and for liberty, help us, O Thou, our Creator.

8. But they said not: For Kriste's sake, nor for sake of the Holy Ghost.

9. Nevertheless, Looeamong's angel warriors had accompanied them across the ocean; and, when they beheld what mortals had done, they departed, by means of the mortal ships returning to Uropa, for these angels were too low in grade to cross the ocean without the presence of mortals.

10. And, when they had come to the other side, they reported to Looeamong's angel generals what had been done by mortals, in Guatama, and these angel generals sent a dispatch to Hapsendi, Looeamong's heavenly kingdom, to learn his will and pleasure.

11. Looeamong sent back word as followeth, to wit: Send thou a sufficient inspiring host to obsess all mortals who have thus possessed Guatama, lest the country fall into Jehovih's hands. Spare them not; possess all, or ruin all, in the name of Kriste and the Holy Ghost.

12. And thus it came to pass, as regardeth this false Kriste and his affairs with God:

13. The latter had inspired, for sake of Jehovih, certain other people in north-western Uropa, who were Faithists in heart, but not practisers of the rites and ceremonies, who called themselves Quakers, to migrate to Guatama, to shape the destiny of the inhabitants to peace and virtue and wisdom; and these Quakers were covenanted to Jehovih, to never engage in war, nor to quarrel, nor to contend with any man for opinion's sake.

14. So Looeamong's obsssessing angels did fall upon the colonies of settlers in Guatama, and obsess them to flay and to burn and to exterminate the Quakers, for Kriste's sake, as mortals said.

15. And the angels of Looeamong inspired mortals to lay in wait for any such other Faithists as might migrate to Guatama.

16. God had said: Suffer these hardships to my people to be recorded, for in kosmon, they shall be testimony of the power of heaven on mortals.

17. To the end, that these things might become historical, God suffered Looeamong's angels to raise up, and obsess one, Cotton Mather, who devoted his time and labor to the

establishing of this false God.

18. And the said Cotton Mather not only accomplished these wicked deeds, but he put himself on record as a worshiper of Kriste. Thus, as followeth, were his words, to wit:

"To ye aged and beloved John Higginson:

There be now at sea a shippe (for our friend Esias Holdcraft, of London, did advise me by the last packet that it would sail sometime in August), called ye 'Welcome,' R. Greenwas, master, which has aboard a hundred or more of ye heretics and malignants called Quakers, with W. Penn, who is ye scamp at ye head of them. Ye General Court has accordingly given secret orders to Master Malachi Huxtett, of ye brig 'Porpoise,' to waylaye ye said 'Welcome,' as near ye coast of Codd, as may be, and make captives of ye Penn and his ungodly crew, so that ye Lord may be glorified and not mocked on ye soil of this new country with ye heathen worshippers of these people. Much spoil can be made by selling ye whole lot to Barbadoes, where slaves fetch good prices in rumme and sugar; and we shall not only do ye Lord great service by punishing ye wicked, but shall make gayne for his ministers and people. Yours, in ye bowels of Christ, Cotton Mather."

19. Such then were the trials of God in establishing Jehovih in Guatama. And yet, the bitterest struggle had not begun.

CHAPTER XI.

1. Es said: Hear ye, O earth, and ye, heavens of the earth, of the ways of Jehovih, through his God, in this, His kingdom. Understand ye how all things are accomplished for the ultimate triumph of righteousness.

2. Now, after the etherean angels came to Paradise, in answer to God's prayer for help, God divided his hosts unto all the earth and the heavens thereof, not for sudden triumph by violent means, but to the end that man should, in after years, comprehend the wisdom and glory of Jehovih.

3. So, God made eleven divisions of his hosts, four divisions for the earth, and seven for the heavens of the earth.

4. And as chiefs of the four divisions for the earth, he appointed, Eezen, Khan, Ah Cho and Lakash, to go to hada, the heavenly kingdoms of the four false Gods, to establish a guard, thence to the earth.

5. And God gave to each of them one thousand million hosts to labor with them. And when these were all selected, and had come before the throne of God, he said unto them:

6. Because the four false Gods have accomplished all the good they can accomplish, and are now only leading mortals and angels down into darkness, I shall presently cut them and their supplies off from the earth. In that day and hour there will be danger in heaven.

7. For there are more than three hundred million spirits in the hadan heavens, who were put to untimely deaths, in order to establish the false Brahma, the false Budha, the false Kriste, and the false God-Gabriel.

8. Go ye, then, to your places, and provide yourselves in wisdom and strength. Guard well these spirits, for once they congregate for vengeance sake, they will cast their Gods in hell.

9. They answered with one voice: Jehovih's will and thine be done! And they saluted, and departed.

10. God then called up the other seven of the Holy Eleven, to wit: Yopes Loe, Likar, Vadhuan, Ardolfus, Yutemis, Zahawe and Yedna, together with their seven thousand million hosts, and he said unto them:

11. Behold, the eleven kingdoms which have been preparing for more than two thousand years shall now be opened up, and established, with roadways to the kingdoms of the four false Gods. For the time is near at hand when I shall cast them out, and remove them and their kingdoms away from the earth, and forever.

12. That a revolt may be prevented, ye shall provide places and vessels for the removal of their drujas, of which there are more than twenty thousand millions. Go, then, to your respective places, and be ye ready by the time of my command.

13. They answered unanimously: Jehovih's will and thine be done! And they saluted, and departed also.

14. After this, God appointed twelve of the etherean Gods and Goddesses as a Severing Host, and he allotted to them six thousand million angels to work with them, when the time should require them.

15. To these twelve Gods and Goddesses, God said: When the time is at hand, behold, ye shall take your six thousand million hosts, and cut off all the earth supplies on which the four false Gods and their kingdoms subsist.

16. And their kingdoms shall fall in anarchy and ruin. Their drujas shall be liberated; none shall stay them; and they shall fall upon their Gods' kingdoms, and despoil them utterly, and cast their false Gods into hell (anarchy).

17. Go, therefore, to the places whither I have provided, as my messengers will show you, and make ready in all things, for the time and the signal of my hand.

18. So, these twelve Gods and Goddesses saluted and departed for their labor also.

19. Now, as yet, none but the Holy Council and the Gods and Goddesses knew the plans of God, Jehovih's Son, nor the object and labor provided unto the hosts sent thus forth to all parts of the earth and the hadan (lowest) heavens.

20. Nevertheless, God had commanded the officers to maintain lines of light with his throne in Paradise, so that concert of action would manifest all around the earth, in the same moment of time.

21. Now, therefore, be it known, that of the fire-boats and crews sent by the false Gods to Paradise, only one, Looeamong's, returned to tell the tale of chagrin and disappointment in not meeting the etherean God, Litabakathrava.

22. As for the other three, fitted out so extravagantly, with a million hosts, crowned and adorned in such magnificence, they concluded to go away, each into a different heavenly region, and establish three independent kingdoms of their own.

23. Many of these angel hosts had been promised, for hundreds of years, that they should have sub-kingdoms, with millions of slaves, but had ever been put off, until they were discouraged.

24. Accordingly, they resolved to appropriate their outfits in founding thrones and capitals.

25. So, the fire-boat sent out by Ennochissa, returned to his heavenly regions, but not to Ennochissa. And that of Kabalactes went to his regions, but not to Kabalactes. And that

of Gabriel (Thoth) returned to his regions, but not to him.

26. And they all proceeded much after the same manner, which was, after having found a place, to go about in the fire-boat, enticing subjects to come to their places.

27. And it came to pass, ere their respective masters were aware of it, they had heavenly kingdoms, with hundreds of millions of slaves.

28. When the three false Gods, Ennochissa, Kabalactes, and Gabriel-God, heard of the proceedings of their traitorous subjects, they, separately, declared war against the pretenders.

29. In not many years, therefore, from this small beginning, great wars engrossed these three false Gods' kingdoms on every side, but wholly interior to each one's kingdom.

30. Which enabled God, Jehovih's Son, to pursue the two great plans for the redemption of mortals and angels. These plans were, to provide protection to the Ka'yuans (Confucians) of Chine'ya, the worshipers of Jehovih, and to found the country of Guatama free from the grasp of Looeamong.

31. So, as soon as God had provided a sufficient protecting host of angels for the Ka'yuans, he devoted his energies to Guatama and her heavens.

CHAPTER XII.

1. Whilst the heavens of the earth were thus stirred up with war and with anticipated misfortunes and strange doctrines, there came to Paradise, before the throne of God, a host of seven thousand angels who had been victims of the inquisitions under the inspiration of the false Kriste, Looeamong, praying an audience with God.

2. Accordingly, after the chief marshal had announced this before the throne and Holy Council, God commanded them to approach, and speak.

3. And those who were leaders then came, and spake. These were: Rochus, Estella, Coceicas, Martin, Ajedio, Burton, Gardener, Oguier, Isagades, Thornton, Wincelaus, Hepburn, Autonus, Hague, Bothna, Hijas, Sedasius, Prague, Septullus, Thilinae, Portia, Fuessa, Barm, Donia, Sarekka, Solomon, Jolif, Gallileo, Sega, Spinola, Sutton, Jinuthes, Sirach, Obenaes, Pelachon, Berttimo, Feirdonas, Puberttas, Quidonatus, Paglia, Suzarathga, Wotchganheim, Givier, Dospastonitus, Leiberanz, Jasman, Orolf, Meyer, Litz, Herman, Dolche, Mogan, Ruchtevolt, Yokamsteimer, Bolch, Calas, Radby, Yan'tos, Le'chaim, Fetch, Bliney, Catherine (queen), Lambert, Holt, Renn, Savicht, John, Barnes, Sanwalt, Biers, Drumfoldt, Nekairo, Hemsted, Wight, Thuce, Kerby, Askew, Wolfe, Bartholf, Brown, Wishartd, Mille, Sadarak, Gaepon, Hutton, Somerset, Railif, Bedford, Wehlen, Gaison, Darcy, Wallace, Tudon, Taylor, Farrar, Jones, White, Myers, Henry, Atino, Percy, Alies, Flower, Joseph, Milne, Warne, Simpson, Latimer, Ridley, Cranmer, Lang, Pesth, Bradbridge, Walstein, Allin, Jesse, Ormes, Staveson and Donald. And this is the substance of what they said:

4. Most Holy God, Jehovih's Son, greeting in love, in pity and in anger!

5. We are not Gods, nor pure, nor holy. Therefore pity us.

6. We are not happy, and feel that in our struggles to find the truth we have been unfairly used. Therefore, pity us.

7. We were born in mud-holes, and have soiled garments. Therefore, have compassion upon us.

8. We are in search of clean water, that we may go wash ourselves. Therefore, guide us.

9. We have such strength as a mad wolf might be proud of. Therefore, use us.

10. We have not such mercy and forgiveness as becometh Gods. Therefore, give us rough work to do.

11. Such work, in fact, as would require no one to split a hair to discern right or wrong.

12. Not that we desire to glut ourselves in vengeance against the false Kriste. One step higher, O God.

13. As such a matter, if an innocent lamb were pursued by a wolf, give us to rush in, and save the lamb.

14. Now, behold, the rumor hath come to us, that thou wilt establish Guatama free from the dominion of Gods and Saviors.

15. And it cometh to this: we are so far on the road to purification, that we can no longer catch the false Kriste's angels, and hurl them into hell.

16. Nevertheless, we are not so fastidiously pure, but we would seize his evil-working angels, and hold them by the throats till thou hadst thy great country founded safely for Jehovih's kingdom.

17. If, therefore, thou canst appropriate seven thousand angels in some loose and unscrupulous corner, to do thee good service against the tyrant and remorseless Looeamong, behold, we stand before Jehovih and thee, to do thy will as thou mayest command.

18. God said unto them: My brothers and sisters, in the name of Jehovih, I welcome you.

19. What ye can do, that shall ye do; nor shall any but yourselves judge yourselves.

20. As far as ye have the light of the Father, so shall ye serve Him.

21. To Him only are ye responsible; for His triumph shall be the redemption of heaven and earth.

22. Behold, Looeamong will surely inspire a war, both in Guatama, with mortals, and in the heavens thereof, with the angels.

23. My angel hosts shall inspire the mortals of Guatama to found a government free from the dominion of Gods and Saviors.

24. War will follow. Now, behold, I have appointed Yotahiza, as my Lord for those regions. Repair ye thither with my messengers who know the way, and Yotahiza will receive you in my name, and give you work in justice, truth and wisdom.

25. The army of the inquisition then saluted, and departed, and they came to Yotahiza's heavenly station with the colonists in Guatama.

CHAPTER XIII.
THE REPUBLIC ESTABLISHED.

1. Es said: Since three hundred years, the loo'is of God's allotment to the earth, had been providing the generations of men unto the coming work of God.

2. And through these had God, Jehovih's Son, raised up one thousand two hundred men, to be directly under the inspiration of the second resurrection, for establishing an emancipated government for mortals.

3. And these one thousand two hundred men were raised to grades above sixty, and some of them to eighty.

4. Chief of these men raised up by God, to establish the foundation of Jehovih's kingdom with mortals, were the following, all of whom stood above grade eighty, to wit:

5. Paine, Jefferson, Adams, Franklin, Caroll, Hancock and Washington.

6. Into the hands of these seven men did Jehovih, through God, His Son, place the leadership of the mortal hosts; and they were under the guidance of Jehovih's Lord, Yotahiza.

7. And the Lord caused Paine, to proclaim the new doctrines, as against Looeamong and the sacred books, on which the inquisitions had been carried out.

8. These, then, were the doctrines of Paine, inspired by the Lord, Jehovih's Son, to wit:

9. One, the Creator, who is Almighty, matchless in wisdom, truth, power and unity of purpose; the author of all things, on the earth and on all other worlds, seen and unseen.

10. That the soul of man is immortal and everlasting, and shall ultimately attain to peace and joy in the heavens of the Almighty.

11. That, according to man's good or evil deeds, words, thoughts and actions whilst on earth, even so shall he inherit in heaven, light or darkness, joy or unhappiness.

12. That all the world is my country, and the same right alike to all men.

13. To do good, with all of one's wisdom and strength, is the highest religion.

14. That man hath a natural right, above all kings, priests and sacred writings, to serve his Creator in his own way.

15. That this is an age of reason, in which all men should be inspired, to read and think, and judge with their own judgment and not through any priest or church or Savior.

16. That the doctrine of a Savior is unjust; that no honest man should accept another's dying for him.

17. That the so-called sacred books are not the writings of the Creator; that their multiplicity of defects prove them to have been manufactured by corruptible authors.

18. That, in practice, the said sacred books have been used by unprincipled priests to promote wars, inquisitions, tyranny and destruction.

19. That man should rise up in his might to embrace his Creator, by the practice of good works, and by promoting brotherly love toward all men; and by charity and independence elicit the protection, the pride and the glory of the Almighty.

20. The doctrines of God, Paine proclaimed publicly; and they were printed, and circulated amongst the inhabitants of Guatama.

21. And it came to pass, that they fell into the hands of such men and women as had been previously prepared by God to receive them. And these people applauded the new doctrines to so great an extent that the colonies repudiated the Divine right (Divan laws) of kings to govern without the consent of the governed.

22. Looeamong, the false Kriste, perceived the design of God, Jehovih's Son, and immediately sent down to the earth, to Guatama, two thousand angel warriors, to overthrow Paine's doctrines, and to precipitate the colonies into war against the home government in western Uropa.

23. So, war in Guatama, on earth, and in the heavens thereof, set in, mortals against mortals and angels against angels.

24. The Lord, Yotahiza, now assigned the army of the inquisition, the seven thousand angels sent of God, to be the protecting hosts to the seven leaders of the Guatama revolt.

25. Besides these angels, who were generals and captains of the hosts, there were of non-

commissioned angel officers, two thousand seven hundred and eighty-four, who had also been martyred as to earth-life, by scourging, and by the rack, and by being pulled in quarters, and by being burnt, who were distributed amongst the mortal armies of soldiers. And these angel officers had angel armies and companies, disciplined and quartered in the camps of the mortals with the soldiers.

26. Such, then, were the inspiring hosts, varying in number from six millions to twelve millions, who remained with the soldiers of the republic during the war, day and night, inspiring them to fortitude, and manipulating them to give them health and strength and endurance.

27. God spake to the angel commander of these hosts, saying: Though thy hosts inspire these mortals to liberty as to earthly things, yet thou shalt also take advantage of this opportunity to sow the seed of higher spiritual light amongst them. Remember, then, the sermon of the All High: There is but one Great Spirit, Jehovih. And this shall thy hosts forever inspire the mortals with.

28. For seven years the war lasted, and during all the while, the earthly commander, Washington, was under the guardianship of the commander of the angel hosts. And there were detailed to guard Washington, day and night, one thousand angels. And though he was shot at, and in many ways sought for to be destroyed, these angels saved him, even catching in their hands the bullets that were fired at him.

29. And in like manner were many other mortal leaders and privates in the war protected and saved from harm by the angels.

30. And yet all this while the angels of Looeamong fought on the other side, endeavoring to pull away the guardian angels, and so make the mortal leaders vulnerable.

31. But these angels were lower in grade and less potent, and, withal, not so enthusiastic, for they had not suffered martyrdom.

32. Jehovih hath said: Rather let a man glory in martyrdom for righteousness' sake; for herein he taketh high resolves against evil; which resolves are a great power to the soul when it entereth heaven.

33. And it came to pass that the republic was established.

34. And God caused the commander of the angels who had accomplished this work, to call his hosts together, that they might hear the voice of Jehovih. And there thus assembled eighteen million three hundred and forty thousand in number, in an extemporized heaven above the Haguan mountains, where the chiefs of Paradise had already prepared an altar to Jehovih for the occasion.

35. Of the higher grades from other plateaux, were here assembled in the sacred circle, seventy million angels, to promote the Voice. Of which matters God had previously sent word to Aroqu, that a chain of light might be made to the upper heavens.

36. Now, when the angels of the inquisition were thus assembled before God, and duly placed by the marshals, God caused the light to be lowered, so that they might rejoice rather than suffer because of its brilliancy.

37. And when God sat on the throne, and the es'enaurs had chanted unto Jehovih glory for having founded the republic of mortals, a ray of light was seen descending from the upper realms, and it extended down to the throne of God, where now, on all sides, the illumination was in splendor. Presently, just above the throne, a single star of light was formed, and out of this came the Voice of Jehovih, saying:

38. Peace, My beloved. The way is open: liberty to the conscience of mortals is founded on earth. Ye have lifted them above the bondage of Gods.

39. Because ye were cut down before ye had finished your labor on earth, I suffered ye to come back to mortals to complete your own aspirations.

40. Because ye united with one another in companies and phalanxes for a good work, instead of working single-handed, ye are now admitted into the second resurrection of My kingdoms.

41. By the light of My throne are ye this day absolved from the bondage of earth and first resurrection.

42. The Voice ceased; but God spake unto his marshals, saying: Provide ye an avalanza sufficient for the ascension of these my beloved angels, and take them to the fields and forests of Attusasabak, in the Ortheon plateau, where I have already provided them ample residences.

43. And, after they are delivered, grade them, and give unto them suitable instructors and companions, that in due time they may become Brides and Bridegrooms to Jehovih, and ascend to the emancipated kingdoms in the etherean worlds.

44. Suffer them now to pass before the throne, that they may receive badges from the Most High! For these will be to them a connection with the exalted kingdoms.

45. The marshals then filed them past the throne, and there fell, from the heavens above, upon them, badges of immortal light, unchangeable.

46. And the builders in Yutis brought them an avalanza, and they went therein, to the sound of the singing of three millions of voices in Jehovih's praise. And when they were within, God again spake to them, saying:

47. Ye go now far off from the earth. But as ye freed this land unto itself, and now go away, behold, I will call ye back again before another hundred years, to free the people from the doctrines and creeds of the ancients. No God nor Lord nor Savior shall be enforced in this land! Till then, Jehovih be with you all, and give you joy and happiness!

48. Thereupon, the officers of the avalanza set it in motion, rising upward. And the musicians, they that remained and they that ascended, sang and trumpeted until the fire-ship ascended out of sight.

CHAPTER XIV.

1. For three hundred years prior to the above transactions, the four false Gods had been in war to a limited extent in their heavens, and for certain earth possessions also.

2. In Chine'ya, the Ka'yuans (Confucians) had made great progress, to the injury of the false Brahma, Ennochissa. But the latter had pushed his people into Vind'yu and Parsi'e.

3. On the part of Kabalactes, the false Budha, he had pushed his people into Chine'ya and Parsi'e also. And in many parts of Vind'yu, these Budhists had treated the Brahmins with great slaughter.

4. But neither of the above false Gods was a match for Thoth, alias God-Gabriel. Under the name and doctrines of Mohammed, he had made great inroads upon the possessions of the other two false Gods, both as to the earth and the heavens thereof.

5. And yet, on the other hand, Looeamong, the false Kriste, had taken advantage of all the other three false Gods. He had found mortal emissaries in Britain (western Uropa) whom

he had inspired under the name, East India Company. To these he had said: Come, I will lead you where there is great wealth and most luxurious enjoyment. Behold, ye shall possess the place, and overcome the heathen of a rich country.

6. So, Looeamong led them, and they took with them missionaries and bibles and swords and cannons and war-ships. And when they arrived at Vind'yu, Looeamong, through his angel hosts, said unto them: Tell these heathen, ye are worshipers of the Lamb of Peace; that ye have come in love and for righteousness' sake. And, behold, they will receive you. And it shall come to pass, when ye are once within, ye shall fall upon them, and destroy them by the million, men, women and children. And ye shall fall upon their aqueducts, which irrigate the lands, and ye shall destroy them also; and, behold, millions of these heathen shall starve every year, because of the famines that shall surely come upon them.

7. Now, all these came to pass; the idolaters of Looeamong did fall upon the Budhists' earthly possessions, and did possess the land of Vind'yu, and, in the name of Kriste and the Holy Ghost, did kill seven million men, women and children.

8. And they also destroyed the aqueducts, whereby famines came upon the Vind'yuans, so that, in course of time, thirty millions more perished of starvation.

9. Now, although Kabalactes thus lost, in a great measure, his earthly possessions, he still maintained the heavens of Vind'yu, so that Looeamong really gained but few souls, in heaven, after all his destructions.

10. Looeamong had also led his mortal emissaries into Chine'ya, in hope to possess that country also. He had said to them: Go thither, and enforce upon them the opium trade. And it shall come to pass, they will become a drunken and worthless people, and ye shall fall upon them, and overcome them, and possess all their country, wherein there are stored great riches.

11. And the idolaters of the false Kriste did fall upon the Chine'yans and enforce the opium trade, and did also make many of them a drunken and worthless people. And after they were thus drunk, the idolaters of the false Kriste raised the cry: Behold, the drunken heathen! The indulgers in opium!

12. Nevertheless, the Ka'yuans of Chine'ya were a mighty power, and they baffled Looeamong's emissaries in all further encroachments.

13. Now, although Looeamong had been beaten by the wisdom of God, in possessing the colonies of Guatama, nevertheless, Looeamong still hoped to regain the country to himself. And to carry out his designs, he sent two thousand million angel warriors to accomplish the destruction of the Algonquin tribes that inhabited the country.

14. And this also came to pass, the idolaters of Looeamong did fall upon the Algonquins, and caused three millions of them to be put to death, men, women and children.

CHAPTER XV.

GOD, JEHOVIH'S SON, CASTETH OUT THE FOUR FALSE GODS.

1. When the right time came, Jehovih spake to God, saying: My Son, behold, the kosmon era is near, and the light of the arc of su'is entereth the fields of Paradise. Stretch forth thy hand over the nations of the earth and over the heavens thereof, and sweep clean thy kingdoms for My everlasting light.

2. The four false Gods, the perpetuators of the beast, will call out in agony, but thou shalt

heed them not in My judgments.

3. Then God sent forth his disciplined hosts, twelve thousand millions, to cut off the supplies of the earth. Even as a mortal general cutteth off the supplies of a wicked city to subdue it, so was the accumulated power of the All Light upon the four kingdoms of the four false Gods, they that had proclaimed themselves the Saviors of mortals and angels.

4. And the angels of God spread around about the whole earth! In armies of millions and tens of millions, well disciplined, they gathered together in the mortal cities, and in the country places, amongst all nations, tribes and peoples.

5. And these angel armies were officered and drilled to work in concert, with lines of light extending to the throne of God.

6. And God spake in Paradise, by means of the lines of light, and his voice went into all the mighty armies of his hosts, the twelve thousand million, saying:

7. Cut off the earth supplies of the four beasts of the earth. They and their countless legions of followers have become profitless in the resurrection of mortals and angels.

8. Their names have become a stench upon the earth. Their mortal followers are grovelers in all manner of uncleanness. Their spirits have become as vagabonds on the earth and in the heavens thereof.

9. My hosts have tried to persuade them, but they will not hear; the light of the upper kingdoms, they will not receive.

10. But I will make them look up. Like beasts that are untamed, they shall cry out for sustenance, but they shall not find it in the places of their old haunts.

11. Then, the hosts of God marched in betwixt the drujas, the worshipers of the four false Gods, and their mortal harvests.

12. And the drujas turned to their respective Gods, the false Brahma, the false Budha, and Gabriel of Kalla, and the false Kriste, crying out: Behold, our supplies are cut off! Is not the earth thy kingdom, and the place of thy footstool. Saidst thou not that thou wert the Almighty? How, then, hath another God come between? If thou art, indeed, our Savior, now save us! But if thou hast been all this while deceiving, then shall hell by thy portion!

13. The four false Gods heard the cry of anger and suspicion in their mighty kingdoms; heard the wailings of the sixty thousand millions. And they feared, and trembled.

14. Most of all in fear was the false Kriste, for, for sake of aggrandizing his own kingdom, he had had it proclaimed on the earth that: Whosoever believeth in me, shall be saved; but whosoever believeth not in me, shall be in danger of hell-fire!

15. And countless millions of mortals had taken no thought as to self-resurrection, but taken him at his word; and so had lived and died and become his slaves for hundreds of years. Millions of these angels had heavenly banners made, with the promises of this false Lord inscribed thereon, and with these went in processions in heaven, crying out: Bread or blood! Bread or blood! We come not to bring peace in heaven; we come to bring a sword! We come to set angel against angel! Give unto us, O thou, our God, or hell shall be thy portion!

16. Thus, it came to pass, as had been foretold by God, whereof he had said: Anarchy shall encompass your heavenly kingdoms, and ye shall yet own that ye are false before Jehovih.

17. And the four false Gods, fearing the fires of hell, went about, crying out: I am not the true Brahma! I am not the true Budah! I am not the true God! I am not the true Kriste!

18. For they hoped thereby to save themselves. But, alas, for them. Their thousands of millions fell upon their heavenly cities, palaces and thrones, and robbed them.

19. And, when their fury was started, behold, the vast multitudes rushed for the false Gods, and fell upon them, beat them, suffocated them with foul smells, covered them up with suffocating gases, walled them in with sulfurous fires.

20. And they brought the officers and priests and monks and high officers, and cast them into hells also, millions and millions of high-ruling angels of the false Gods.

21. Thus were these four false Gods hemmed in, even within their own dissolute kingdoms, and every day and every hour grew more terrible. It was the infuriated madness of sixty thousand millions of deceived angels, broken loose from slavery, turned upon them.

22. Then Jehovih's God, from Paradise, went forth in a ship of fire, brilliant, past the endurance of drujas; went forth with ten millions high in the grades; ten millions against sixty thousand millions. God brought these from the realms of Aroqu and Harivya, well disciplined for the purpose.

23. And on the ship, and on the banners thereof, were inscribed these words: THERE IS BUT ONE GREAT SPIRIT, JEHOVIH,. TO ASSIMILATE WITH HIM, IS THE SALVATION OF MORTALS AND ANGELS.

24. He crieth out: Come unto Me; My kingdoms are ample unto all the living. Be ye strong in resurrection, for I am come to deliver.

25. And God gathered in from the highest grades of the disrupted heavenly kingdoms thirteen thousand million homeless angels, who had been worshipers of the four false Gods. And God had them sent to Luana, on the plateau, Hivestos, where he officered them in colonies, with places for education and labor.

26. God said unto them: Ye hoped to ascend to Jehovih's highest kingdoms by prayers and confessions to false Gods. Behold, I say unto you, there is no resurrection but by developing the talents Jehovih created unto all men. Go ye to work, therefore, and to places of education, that ye may become fit companions to Jehovih's exalted angels.

CHAPTER XVI.

GOD DELIVERETH THE FOUR FALSE GODS OUT OF THE FOUR HELLS.

1. Es said: Now, was God, Jehovih's Son, master of the whole earth and her heavens.

2. And, behold, the era of kosmon was at hand.

3. The light of the arc had fallen on the throne of God. Jehovih's Orian Chiefs from the emancipated heavens had come!

4. Paradise was like a new kingdom. A thousand million ethereans had arrived to labor with God, in clearing away the hells of the lower heavens, and in providing for opening the gates of the heavens for the angels to appear unto mortals.

5. Metahazi, Goddess of Alefad, in the roads of Loo, in etherea, had brought back the armies of the inquisitions. Hativi, Goddess of the Lutian swamps, in Wessatow plains, in etherea, was there, with Massecred of Bow-gan-ghad. Monetzian, Goddess of Tuissa, was there, with the persecutors of Zarathustra. Norwoth-chissa, Goddess of the forest of Nidea, in etherea, was there with the persecutors of Brahma (the pure and true) and the persecutors of Moses and Capilya.

6. Besides these, there were forty-six other Goddesses, each with a host of angels who

had in the ancient times striven against Jehovih, in favor of some false God.

7. But now, in the coming of kosmon, behold they returned as pure and exalted Gods and Goddesses.

8. And God, Jehovih's Son, called forth all these one-time persecutors, and he said unto them:

9. Behold, there are four great hells and six smaller hells and fourteen still smaller hells, still existing in these lower heavens.

10. Since ye were once cast into hells, and afterward delivered by the angels of Jehovih, go ye now, and deliver the hells of these heavens. And bring ye the chief false Gods before me. My marshal will allot you to the respective places, I have appointed unto you.

11. Then went forth the Gods and Goddesses as appointed by God to deliver the twenty-four hells of the heavens of the earth. And they took with them unto this labor six thousand million angel laborers well skilled in such matters.

12. And, in thirty-four days, the hells were delivered, broken up and gone. And from these hells, there were thus delivered more than seventy thousand million angels; who were carried to the plateaux, prepared for them by God, Jehovih's Son.

13. And God had also provided unto them, in their new heavenly places, divisions and sub-divisions, with generals, captains, overseers and other such officers, necessary to prevent them running into knots and hells again.

14. Of the false Gods and Goddesses thus delivered and brought before God, in Paradise, for judgment, the chiefs of them were: Ashtaroth, Dagon, Ashdod, Yotemas, Sathias, Goluth, Plutoya, Itis, Hamgad, Moak, Hoar, Baal, Ennochissa, Kabalactes, Gabriel and Looeamong. Besides these, there were seventy other false Gods and Goddesses delivered, but who were not brought before the throne of God, but were sent to hospitals, because they were in chaos.

15. God had previously provided Paradise, through his Holy Council, for the time of the judgment of the false Gods, that were brought before him.

16. So the Holy Councils were formed in crescent, so that the throne of God laid betwixt the horns thereof, in order to promote the Voice.

17. The marshals, then, brought the false Gods and Goddesses into the arena of circle where the light should fall upon them.

CHAPTER XVII.

JEHOVIH JUDGETH THE FALSE GODS AND GODDESSES.

1. Es said: The Voice spake out of the light over the throne of God, saying:

2. Because, I admonished both, earth and heaven, saying: Whoso setteth up more than the I AM, shall be bound: And whoso hearkeneth unto them, and runneth after them, shall be bound unto them. And they heeded not my commandments, but made worshipful other Gods than Me, so shall they reap the harvest they have sown.

3. Because they drew the sword to establish themselves, they were bound by the sword.

4. Because they took upon themselves heavenly kingdoms, I bound them thereunto.

5. Because they professed salvation in the names of false Gods, I let them run their course; and, lo and behold, they have shown no salvation in heaven or earth.

6. They have built up kingdom against kingdom, standing army against standing army.

Verily, they have brought judgment upon themselves.

7. Hear the words of Jehovih, O ye false Gods and Goddesses, who set up heavenly kingdoms against Me.

8. Who slew hundreds of millions of mortals, in order to make other names than Mine worshipful on earth and in the heavens thereof.

9. Ye, who cried out falsely: Behold me; I am the light and the life; through me is the way of salvation.

10. Ye, who have used your names to lead mortals and angels away from the Creator; saying of yourselves: Behold me, I am the Lord; I am God; my heavenly place is the all highest.

11. Behold, I had spoken in the olden times; I had said:

12. Whoso aspireth to be a king of the earth, or queen, or emperor, or ruler over a nation or people, and I give to him his desire, he shall be bound with the people of his administration. Neither shall he rise to My emancipated heavens, till he hath carried up with him every soul that he had dominion over. But he shall be bound unto that people in the first and second resurrection, until even the lowest of them are raised in wisdom and virtue and good works, sufficient for the grade of Brides and Bridegrooms to My etherean realms.

13. And if a king stretch forth his arm to subdue and annex other countries unto his own, suffer thou him to do so, for he is magnifying his bondage for the resurrection of the low.

14. And, thou shalt apply these rules unto all earthly rulers, be they kings, or queens, or emperors, or presidents, or governors, or legislators, or judges, or popes, or priests, or preachers, or whosoever presumeth to rule over, or to lead, or to exact servitude from others. And the term of the bondage unto them in the lower heavens shall be in proportion to the magnitude of their dominions.

15. But, to whomsoever attaineth dominion by the sword, or extendeth dominion by the sword, and by blood and death, his bondage shall be a hundred-fold.

16. And whosoever maintaineth his dominion by standing armies, thou shalt compute the number thereof, and to him and his high officers, the bondage in the lowest heaven shall be equal to ten times the number of soldiers thereof, and ten times the number of years of the servitude of the multitude of his armies.

17. For, whosoever taketh from My people for his own glory or dominion, shall render unto Me the just value.

18. Whosoever engageth in war, or leadeth in war, or is a captain, or a general, and causeth the death of whom I created alive, he shall not rise to inherit My emancipated heavens as long as there remaineth war upon the earth. But he shall toil in the lowest heavens of the earth to educate and raise up the drujas thereof, which shall be his labor.

19. And whoso hath great riches, and many servants, his resurrection shall be no faster than the resurrection of those that serve him.

20. And whoso hath great riches and yet no servants, but liveth for himself, thou shalt apportion his place in the first resurrection even according to the good he might have done, had he obeyed My commandments; and he shall do in heaven, what he neglected to do on earth. And he shall not rise to My emancipated heavens, until he hath appropriated according to that which I gave him into his keeping.

21. God said: The words that come out of man's mouth, even though they profess prayers

and repentance, are of little avail before Jehovih. But the words that come out of good works done unto others to raise them up, are as the sound of a trumpet that reacheth beyond the stars.

22. For, in all ages of the world, there have been deceivers and hypocrites, with temples and churches to worship in, professing to serve the Creator, but, in fact, serving an idol.

23. And their priests and preachers speak good doctrines, but they practice them not, save a little, as a blind to lead the multitude astray.

24. And they live in fine houses, and fare sumptuously every day; and are skilled in oratory and in doctrinal precepts; but they will not go, and serve the poor, teaching them how to live. Again the Voice spake, saying:

25. My judgments are upon those that profess Me, dealing out their pittance to the poor, whilst they themselves live above want. When such men die, and enter the first resurrection, they shall be handed over to those that are in darkness, and their bondage shall be a hundred-fold. For they preached words of righteousness with the mouth, but, in their behavior, they laid their foundation for the kingdom of hypocrisy. Verily, I give unto them the harvest that cometh of their own sowing.

26. These, then, have been My doctrines since thousands of years, and known unto you before ye deserted My kingdoms.

27. If such, then, by My judgments unto mortals who serve false Gods, how much greater, then, must be the penalty upon the false Gods, who set themselves up to establish these iniquities?

28. Hear ye, then, the judgment of Jehovih: Whosoever hath established the name of any God but the Creator, and made it worshipful on earth or in heaven, shall be bound on earth or in heaven, shall be bound in the first resurrection till that name is no longer worshipful on earth or in heaven.

29. And whatever God or Goddess hath said: Come unto me, ye that are heavily laden, and I will give you rest, for I am the way of salvation and of light and of everlasting life, then, that God or Goddess shall be bound in the first resurrection as long as mortals or angels go unto him or her.

30. Behold, as such a God called, and they answered unto him, so do I give unto both, the God that calleth, and the subject that runneth unto him. (For I give liberty even unto Mine enemies.)

31. But, when a subject goeth to a God, and saith: Behold, thou hast said: Whither I go, I will call all men unto me, and I believed in thee,--then that God shall not put him away.

32. Whilst Osiris was worshipped, I gave unto Osiris (the false).

33. Whilst Ashtaroth was worshipped, I gave unto her.

34. Whilst Baal was worshipped, I gave unto Baal.

35. But, when any of these Gods were no longer worshipped, behold, I gave them no more subjects.

36. As long as Brahma is worshipped, I will give unto him, who is before me.

37. As long as Budha is worshipped, I will give unto him, who is before me.

38. As long as Kriste is worshipped, I will give unto him, who is before me.

39. As long as Mohammedans are upheld on the earth, I will give unto him, who built up Mohammed.

40. And, when all of you have purified, and raised up all those who idolize you, in that

same time, will I raise you up to higher heavens also.

41. Es said: And now, when the Voice ceased, and all was still, the false Gods and Goddesses raised up their heads, and they spake with one voice, saying:

42. Thou art just, O Jehovih. Unto thee do I now covenant that I will serve thee forever. Neither will I aspire to rise to higher heavens till I have raised up all whom I have led astray.

43. Make me strong, O Jehovih, in this my everlasting covenant!

44. Teach me, O Father, the labor I should do, that Thou shalt be glorified forever!

45. Thus ended the judgment. God's marshals removed them to the places allotted for them, and they went to work.

CHAPTER XVIII.

1. Es said: Such, then, was the fate of the chief false Gods in the lower heavens.

2. But, during the last three or four hundred years, many of the officers of these false Gods had seceded from them, and had set up small heavenly kingdoms of their own. And their mortal followers were called, sects.

3. These little heavens were, for the most part, situated on the earth, and usually these small Gods inhabited the churches where mortals came to worship.

4. And the preachers within these churches fell under the inspiration of these itinerant Gods and their gangs of wandering spirits.

5. In Guatama, these inspirations were carried to such an extent, by these drujan Gods, that the mortals of one sect were made hostile, one sect against another.

6. An enmity, therefore, existed betwixt protestants and catholics, and betwixt protestants themselves, and betwixt all of these and the Jews. And, not only on earth, betwixt mortals, did these things take place, but these petty Gods had small kingdoms of their won; as a presbyterian heaven; a methodist heaven; a baptist heaven, and so on. And, when a mortal member died, his spirit fell into his heaven, where he had lived, becoming a servant to these drujas. And, when he cried out: I want to go to Jesus, I want to go to Kriste, he was shown the drujan God, and told: That is he! The which he would believe to be true. For what is bound on earth, is bound in heaven.

7. A drujan God, Piad, established a sect, and named it, Mormon, and he located his kingdom on earth with his mortal followers, and he became master over the spirits of his mortal followers in the same way, calling himself, the True Kriste.

8. Piad taught, that all good Mormons would ultimately attain to rule over some planet and her heavens. But, he never permitted the angels of his kingdom to go out of his reach. He also taught mortals, that the more numerous progeny a man begot, the greater would be his heavenly kingdom, in time to come. For this was Piad's scheme, to make his own heavenly kingdom large and powerful.

9. Another drujan God, Lowgannus, established a kingdom on earth, and named it, Shaker Heaven, pretending, he was the True Kriste. And his place became a heavenly bondage unto himself.

10. Another drujan God, Sayawan, established a heavenly kingdom on earth, and called it, The All Highest Heaven.

11. This Lord called himself, The Lord. He raised up a mortal, Swedenborg, whom he

took in spirit, subjectively, into many of the lowest heavens and hells, saying to him:

12. Behold, they that serve not THE LORD! How hard it is with them! And he further said: This place of darkness is the Brahmin heaven; that place of darkness is the Budhist heaven! But this place of light is my heaven, I, THE LORD.

13. Thus did this drujan God establish a Swedenborg heaven, and mortals looked upon him as the true Kriste, and, after death, their souls went thither.

14. So, it came to pass, as had been prophesied of old: Lo, Kriste, here! Lo, Kriste, there!

15. And, as it was with Looeamong's heavenly kingdoms, thus split into hundreds of remnants, even so was it with the heavenly kingdoms of the other false Gods, Brahma, the false, and Budha, the false, so that there were on the earth thousands of petty Gods' heavenly kingdoms of darkness and misery.

16. Now, all of these drujan Gods, whether of Chine'ya, or Vind'yu, or Arabin'ya, or Uropa, or Guatama, rejected Jehovih, but took the name of some one of the four false Gods, and protested that he himself, was the real and true God and Savior.

17. And mortal sects, that followed them, did the same thing. The presbyterian professed the true Kriste, but denounced all others as false; the methodist professed the true Kriste, but denounced all others as false; the Mormon professed the true Kriste, but denounced all others; the Roman catholics also professed the true Kriste, but denounced all others as false. Even so was it with all of them, and none of them practiced righteousness and good works, but were warriors and money-getters, for self sake.

18. God had said: Behold, I give a new testimony unto the nations of the earth: In the time I overcame, and cast out the four heads of the beast, the acrimony existing between different sects began, suddenly, to die out, and they spake friendly to one another.

19. And it was so.

CHAPTER XIX.

THE DAWN OF KOSMON.

1. Es said: Now, whilst the Holy Council were still sitting in Paradise, a light, like a star, came, and stood above the throne of God. And the Voice came out of the light, saying:

2. Behold, the false Gods are cast out, and sent unto their places.

3. Never more shall there be any other false God, or Lord, or Savior, to lead my people away.

4. I am sufficient unto Mine own creations.

5. Let this, therefore, be the beginning of the kosmon era.

6. My people have settled the whole earth around, from east to west; the lands on the western borders of Guatama have become inhabited.

7. Go, then, My God, My Son, open the gates of heaven unto mortals.

8. Let My angels meet them, and talk with them, face to face.

9. Behold, My etherean embassadress, Che'sivi'anathaotes, cometh in a sea of fire!

10. The ships of the etherean Goddess were seen descending from the higher heavens, coming as an open ring, to embrace the whole earth.

11. Again, the Voice spake out of the light, saying:

12. I know no distinctions of men, of races, or sects, or doctrines, or past revelations. All people are My people!

13. Open the gates of heaven; let my angels speak to mortals!

14. Swifter and swifter came the etherean archangels, till all the heavens of Paradise were encircled in the love of the Almighty.

15. Then, God called out the legions who had the matter in charge, where mortals had been born for the work of Jehovih's kingdom. And God said:

16. Open the gates of heaven; let the angels of heaven speak with mortals; the time of the Father's kingdom is at hand!

17. Open the gates of heaven! Let the angels come forth in power!

18. And in Hidesville, in Guatama, on the earth, the angels opened the door in Jehovih's name, to be not closed again forever, forever!

Plate 91. ARC OF KOSMON.

Showing the earth in the thirty-second year of the kosmon era. Jehovih said: When the world approacheth dan'ha in Sabea, the nations shall be quickened with new light; for kosmon cometh out of the midst. And my etherean hosts shall press upon the understanding of men, and they shall fill all the nations and kingdoms with new discoveries and inventions and books of learning. And men shall be conceited of themselves above all the ages past, and they shall deny Me and quarrel with My name, and cast Me out. But I will come upon them as a Father, in love and mercy; and My hosts of heaven shall cause babes and fools to confound the wise, by signs and miracles. My hosts from heaven shall cause chairs to speak; and inanimate things to walk and dance. The dead

1013

shall re-appear to the living, and talk with them face to face, and eat and drink, and prove themselves to the children of earth, and make My kingdoms known. Yea, they shall encompass the whole earth around about with signs and wonders, and set at naught the philosophy of men and the idolatries of the ancients. For both, the living and dead, shall know that I, Jehovih, live and reign over heaven and earth. This shall be a new era, and it shall be called, kosmon, because it embraceth the present and all the past. Then will I reveal Myself; and they that deny Me shall accept Me; of their own accord will they put away their Lords and their Gods and their Saviors; nor shall they more have idols of Me, either on earth or in heaven, for I am sufficient unto all.

CHAPTER XX.
JEHOVIH OVERTHROWETH SLAVERY IN GUATAMA.

1. Es said: In the olden times, and in the eastern countries, Jehovih began His revelations. The western continent He left for the finishing thereof.

2. Now, when God looked abroad over Guatama, he saw four millions of people in bondage, as slaves; and he saw that they must be liberated. And so, God inquired of the chief mathematician in the Holy Council, one Arak, saying: Who, of all the kings of earth, hath had the greatest number of slaves?

3. And Arak said: Xerxes, who dwelleth in Yope'gah, in atmospherea.

4. God said: Send thou a heavenly ship for him, and for a thousand million of his angels. And send also for the Argos'yan, Leonidas, and for a thousand million of his angels. And, when they are brought here, they shall descend to the earth, to these barbarians, and liberate their slaves.

5. Arak saluted, and departed, giving his instructions to the heavenly marshals, who at once sent ships and messengers as directed.

6. God, then, said: I will now recall the ashars, who hold guard over these mortals; and, for a season, they shall dwell in drujan darkness.

7. And this was accomplished, and straightway a war ensued betwixt the owners of the slaves and the neighboring states.

8. Then, came the Gods and angels, high in the grades, to witness the play of mortal death, and to determine how best to win to liberty and to Jehovih, the inhabitants of this great land.

9. God had said: It is an easy matter to win in war; but to make mortals see the triumph of righteousness, is not so easy. Therefore, be discreet in appropriating testimony unto Jehovih.

10. And, there rose up two million men in arms, pushing on in war on every side, coursing the rich soil in mortal blood. And yet, neither side had defined its principles, or taken stand for righteousness sake. But went on in fearful destruction, laying in death tens of thousands, and tens of thousands!

11. Jehovih said: Send thou, thy Parsi'e'an and Argos'yan angels, down to these mortals, and, by inspiration and by dreams and by visions, thy angels shall say to them: Whoso professeth the earth, shall battle in vain; but whoso professeth righteousness in My name, shall win. And millions of angels descended, and tried to persuade them.

12. But mortals would not hear. Even the chief general, on liberty's side, closed his soul against Jehovih. Aye, himself, enforced slavery with his mighty army.

13. And years went on, and all the people began to perceive that, without righteousness, there would be no end to the war.

14. Jehovih had said: Only death can reach these people, or make them behold my hand. Yet, thou shalt send thy angel hosts over all the north regions and inspire them, to call out for liberty.

15. Then went forth Xerxes and Leonidas, with their two thousand million angels, to overspread the north, to inspire mortals to a more heavenly stand, to make them see justice and liberty.

16. And, for a hundred days, these angels dwelt with mortals; but many mortals were too gross in the earth to comprehend. Then, Xerxes came to New York, and took hence the guardian angels, those of holiness, and he left the city in the hand of drujas. And, at once, the city was plunged in hell, and the people were as a mad people, wild and fearful.

17. Again, Jehovih spake in the Holy Council in heaven, saying: Let My angels go once more, and inspire mortals to rise to the light of My will.

18. Again, the angels overrun the land, inspiring mortals day and night to demand freedom for the slaves. And the Embassadress of Jehovih said to her inspiring hosts of angels: Number ye the mortals, north and south, as to their majority voice for freedom.

19. Now, when the Gods numbered the mortals and graded them, they discovered the majority had turned to freedom's side.

20. Jehovih said to his Embassadress: Take thine own inspiring host, and go down to the earth, to Washington, to Lincoln, the president, and hold this matter up to him, that he may understand Me. For he is not bound in doctrines. For which reason My angels made him president, and for this purpose which I have in hand.

21. And it shall come to pass that Lincoln will hear thee, and he shall resolve in his own mind freedom for the slaves. But he will seek for some external sign, fearing he may have mistaken the angels that minister unto him. But I will provide a way for this end also.

22. And the angels of Jehovih went to Lincoln in a vision, like a dream, and they said unto him: Lincoln! Lincoln! And he answered and said: Who art thou?

23. And the angels said: Such as come in Jehovih's name for freedom's sake. Behold, millions of his angels look down from heaven, and would come to thy armies, if thou wouldst but proclaim freedom to the slaves. Jehovih's hand is in this matter.

24. Lincoln awoke, and was troubled with his dream.

25. The next night, the angels came again, and re-told their words, and added thereunto: The great majority of the country is ripe for this matter. Thou fearest this is but a foolish dream. Behold, we will give thee proof tomorrow.

26. Lincoln awoke more troubled than before, but remembered, the angels said: We will give thee proof to-morrow.

27. Jehovih said: I will make this matter a testimony to this nation, so that no man may gainsay it. And I will show also how My angels work singly and in mighty legions.

28. Now, at that time, there was living in Washington, a seeress, Nettie Mainard, through whom spirits spake in her entrancement. And on the day mentioned, the angels spake through her, saying to one Kase: Go thou, and fetch the president into the presence of this woman.

29. And Kase went to Lincoln, and told him what was said. And when Lincoln was before the seeress, the angel of Jehovih entranced her, and said unto him: We said, we would give thee proof to-morrow. Behold, we repeat unto thee, Jehovih is in this matter. Save, thou proclaimest the freedom of the slaves thou shalt not succeed. Do thou this, and the enemy's armies shall melt away like snow in the sun.

30. Lincoln's eyes were opened, and he went straight away, and proclaimed freedom to the whole four million slaves.

31. Xerxes said to Leonidas: Thou, great conquerer, thou shalt conquer me again. Take thy thousand million angels, and go with the armies of the north, and inspire them on to victory. Give them such strength and courage as they have not before manifested. And, as for myself and my hosts, we will go to the armies of the south, and we will inspire them to believe they are conquered, and so make them flee before thy soldiers.

32. Thus, these great angel warriors allotted themselves to the work. And, lo and behold, the northern armies ran forth over the enemy's country as if war were but play; and the southern armies vanished, disarming themselves, and returning to their homes.

33. The slaves were free!

34. Jehovih said: Let this be a testimony, that this land is the place of the beginning of the kosmon era. There shall be no caste amongst my people.

35. Behold, I went to the Israelites, and in that day, I said: Keep yourselves as a separate people! For I had work for them, which was to travel westward, and establish Me, the All One. And they came westward, and fulfilled My commandments. Wherefore I have blessed them.

36. And I went to Chine'ya, and I said: Let the followers of Chine keep themselves as an exclusive people; for I have a work for them; which was to establish Me, the All One, and to demonstrate the most numerous people in all the world united as one people, peacefully. And they have accomplished their work. And I blessed them. And I went to Vind'yu also, and established a mighty people with a multiplicity of Gods and languages. For I had a work for them to do, which was to preserve My revelations of some of the divisions in My heavens above; and to prove, in after-time, things which I had revealed to the ancients. They have accomplished their work also, and I have blessed them.

37. But, in this era, I come not to an exclusive people, but to the combination of all peoples commingled together as one people. Hence, I have called this, the KOSMON ERA.

38. Henceforth, my chosen shall be of the amalgamated races, who choose Me. And these shall become the best, most perfect of all peoples on the earth.

39. And they shall not consider race or color, but health and nobleness as to the mortal part; and as to spirit, peace, love, wisdom and good works, and one Great Spirit only.

40. Leonidas said to Xerxes: It will be revealed ere long that we have been here with our angel hosts. As a testimony of this, let us allot a number of our angels to remain a season with mortals. And they shall inspire them to athletic sports peculiar to the Argos'yans and Parsi'e'ans.

41. To this, Xerxes consented, and they asked for six hundred thousand angel volunteers; and they received them, and officered them, and distributed them in such way that their inspiration should develop mortals in health, strength and endurance, by means of athletic games.

42. And it came to pass that the angels of heaven established athletic games amongst this

people, far and near. Jehovih said: Even in this shall man behold the Cause of causes which lieth behind all things done on the earth.

43. And man searched as to the Cause of these things, and tried to persuade himself of any cause but the true one!

44. Jehovih said: I will show these people, that the chief causes of great affairs amongst mortals come from the angels of My heavens.

45. I come in kosmon not to free only the corporeal man, but the spiritual man. I raised My hand against a God being founded in their constitution; neither will I have them to fight battles for Me. The past is past; angels and mortals shall be free!

CHAPTER XXI.
ASCENT OF THE ETHEREAN HOSTS.

1. Es said: God, Jehovih's Son, was relieved of his arduous toils over the earth and her heavens; and his successor, and the Lords were duly crowned.

2. Then, the Chieftainesses and high Gods and Goddesses, from the etherean heavens, prepared for the marriage of Jehovih's Brides and Bridegrooms.

3. And God and his Lords and high officers called in all heavenly grades prepared for the third resurrection; and there were, in all, twenty-seven thousand million Brides and Bridegrooms.

4. Beside these, there were in Paradise, to witness the ceremonies, more than thirty thousand million angels of lower grades.

5. So, accordingly, the ceremonies were accomplished in the usual form; and the Brides and Bridegrooms were conducted into the avalanzas, of which there were eleven in number. Then went in the etherean hosts, who had brought forth the birth of kosmon. And, after them, God and his Lords and high officers.

6. In the meantime, the es'enaurs and trumpeters, two thousand millions, chanted and played before the hosts in glory to Jehovih.

7. After that, the Chieftainess gave the signal for the ascent, and, with one voice, the mighty hosts said: Arise! To Thee, Jehovih! Nearer, nearer to Thee, Thou Almighty.

8. And the fire-ships started upward, turning and rising. With more than forty thousand million angels aboard, rose the avalanzas above the pillars of fire, above the throne of God, higher and higher, turned and rose the ships of the hosts of Jehovih.

9. And the angels arising, and the angels below, clapped their hands and shouted in glee and exalted glory, because of the overwhelming scene.

10. Thus rose up, and departed to the higher heavens, those thousands of millions of worshipers of the Creator, who had witnessed the birth of the kosmon era, for the angels and mortals of this world.

END OF THE BOOK OF ES, DAUGHTER OF JEHOVIH.

THE BOOK OF JUDGMENT.

BEING THE GRADES AND RATES OF MORTALS AND ANGELS IN THE
LIGHT OF GOD, AS THE WORD CAME TO ES, DAUGHTER OF JEHOVIH.

CHAPTER I.

1. These are the words of Judgment by the will of God, Jehovih's Son, as rendered by Es, for the resurrection of man:

2. Hear the words of thy God, O man! I am thy elder brother of tens of thousands of years experience. Profit thou in my wisdom, and learn the discourse of thy God.

3. Jehovih, Creator of all things, spake to me, thy God, saying: Give ear unto Me, O God, My embassador of the earth and her heavens for this thy season. Obey My mandates, and teach mortals and the angels of thy lower heavens to know Me and to rejoice in My creations. The time is now come when the light of thy inspiration and thy angels shall extend around the whole earth and in her heavens also.

4. In all former cycles, My Gods had to deal with separate divisions of the earth; My revelations were unto each, for a special time, which is now at hand. I have prepared this land untrammeled with Gods and Saviors and Lords, enforced by the sword, so that My revelations of this day shall be published and not suppressed. And thou shalt reveal to mortals the plan of My worlds; and, as to who thou art, and the method of thy inspiration and dominion on the earth and her heavenly kingdoms.

5. Thou shalt keep open the gates of heaven for a season, and the spirits of the dead shall commune with mortals, good and evil, wise and foolish. And mortals shall see them, and talk with them, face to face; and they shall recognize their own kin, sons and daughters, fathers and mothers, brothers and sisters, the dead and the living.

6. And the angels shall demonstrate the subtlety of corporeal things, and the capacity of one solid to pass through another solid uninjured.

7. Yea, the angels shall bring forth from great distances heavy substances, and cast them down in the presence of mortals, who shall see these things done, and testify thereto.

8. And man shall understand, that, even as plants and trees and fish and serpents can be wielded by My angels, so also can virus and pestilence be carried by angels of darkness to cast mortals in death.

9. And thou shalt suffer evil spirits and all manner of drujas, and vampires and engrafters, to come, and manifest unto mortals, that they may know, whereof My revelations unfold the matters of earth and heaven.

10. For man shall understand what I mean by the words: As ye live on the earth, so shall ye reap in heaven.

11. And thou shalt suffer to fall in darkness such mortals as consult the angels in regard to riches, or to marriage, or to self, or for curiosity, or frivolity, or for anything of an earthly nature for profit's sake. They shall prosper for a season, but end in being confronted with folly and falsehood.

12. And whoso asketh for the spirits of great men, suffer ye him, to be deceived by drujas and all manner of lying spirits.

13. And whoso asketh of the sar'gis for great men, or for Moses, or Jesus, or Kriste, or for any well-known name, as applied to ancient times, suffer him to be answered by evil spirits and deceivers.

14. Whoso desireth the angels for profit's sake, and he have power in sar'gis, give unto him a band of drujas and vampires, and give them great power in signs and miracles.

15. And whoso consulteth the angels, without regard to becoming a better man himself, suffer him also, to become captive to lying spirits.

16. And to all men that feed on fish or flesh, suffer thou vampires to inhabit them.

17. And to such as drink to drunkenness, and smoke or take narcotics, suffer thou fetals and engrafters, to come upon them.

18. And in families, whose heirs are born from parents, wed for earthly considerations, suffer thou spirits of obsession, to enter and drive them mad.

19. For they shall be made to know the meaning of the word, hell, as applied to the lower heavens.

20. And to whomsoever worshippeth Gods or Saviors because of miracles, give thou them plentifully of miracles and signs through unclean spirits, and through mortal sar'gis (mediums) of low grade. Yea, thou shalt let spirits of darkness assume to be these very Gods, that mortals may be made to know what manner of evil spirits dwell in their churches and temples.

21. And to the rich man, who maketh pretence to righteousness, but who doeth not toward the poor as to himself, give thou him a host of spirits of hypocrisy and lying, that he may realize the company he is preparing his own spirit for in heaven.

22. Give thou signs and miracles to the unclean seer as well as to the clean; to the liar and deceiver, as well as to the truthful man.

23. For I will destroy the worship of all Gods and Lords and Saviors on the ground of miracles.

24. And thou shalt take great liars, and give them lying spirits to speak through them by inspiration and entrancement. And these spirits shall profess the names of great persons long since dead. And they shall manifest great oratory and wisdom and truth; but, nevertheless, their preaching shall be of little avail for righteousness sake, or for good works.

25. And their applauding audiences will not contribute to the poor, nor found any improvement on the doctrines of the ancients.

26. For the spirits, who speak through them, shall be the first resurrection, and know not Me nor the higher kingdoms. Verily shall they be of the same order as the spirits who minister in the churches and temples, being such spirits as have not yet been delivered up from the earth.

27. And some shall say: Hear thou me, for I am God! Some shall say: Hear thou me, for I am the Lord! Some shall say: Hear thou me, for I am Jehovih! And others shall profess the names of mortals who had great power on the earth. Suffer thou them to do these things.

28. For I will make man understand that he shall accept nothing from angels or men because of the name professed. On the merit only of wisdom and truth, and such good doctrines as raise men up out of darkness and poverty and crime, shall they accept either spoken or written words.

29. And they shall try to organize to carry out good works, but they shall fail. For many will desire to be leaders, being under the influence of selfish considerations, desiring the applause of men.

30. And they will profess freedom, but they will not pledge themselves to any sacrifice, either of money or opinion for sake of the public good.

31. And little good shall come out of their works, and even less peace of soul shall come unto them. For they shall dispute and quarrel, being divided in all their ideas and philosophies and sentiments and in their understanding of My kingdoms.

32. For, by this means, shalt thou show them they are under the inspiration of the unorganized es world; and of spirits who have not yet entered into My resurrections, which I created for them. But in the time of the light of My revelations, thou shalt raise up a few, here and there, capable of the All Light. And these, thou shalt cause to form a basis for My kingdom on earth.

33. And they shall forswear all Gods and Lords and Saviors, but profess Me, the Great Spirit, Jehovih.

34. And they shall pledge themselves unto one another in fullness, as brothers and sisters, holding their possessions in common.

35. To live for sake of perfecting themselves and others in spirit, and for good works.

36. They shall not eat fish nor flesh of any creature that breathed the breath of life.

37. And keep the seventh day as a day of communion with Me and My angel hosts.

38. With rites and ceremonies explanatory of all the doctrines in the world.

39. Practicing good for evil; non-resistance to persecution and abuse.

40. And abjure war; even, if necessary, by submitting to death rather than take part therein.

41. And they shall become an organic body in communities of tens and twenties and hundreds and thousands.

42. But they shall have no leaders, only their Creator; but be organic, for sake of good works.

43. But they shall not go about preaching for sinners to go to repentance.

44. Nor preaching for charity to the poor.

45. But they shall go themselves about gathering up sinners, and the poor and helpless and orphans; and bring them into comfortable homes, teaching them how to live, to be a glory unto Me and My kingdoms.

46. To such persons shall My angels from the second resurrection come, and minister in My name for the joy of the earth.

47. And when such people die, they shall be received into the second resurrection, escaping the first.

48. Neither shall any other people in all the world escape the place of the first resurrection.

49. Be they kings, or queens, or beggars, or Brahmins, or Budhists, or Kriste'yans, or Mohammedans, or any other pretenders in heaven or earth.

50. Behold, the day of preaching and professions is at an end. I will have practice only.

51. Whoso is not in My organic kingdoms on earth, shall go into My inorganic kingdoms in heaven.

52. Like unto like, created I the heavens and the earth, and all things therein.

CHAPTER II.

1. God, embassador of Jehovih, saith: Ye shall assemble for the communion of angels, regularly, and maintain intercourse with them. For in no other way can ye demonstrate the immortality of the soul.

2. Doing this in the name of Jehovih, and for spiritual light in regard to spiritual things.

3. Whoso consulteth the spirits for earthly things, shall fall in darkness.

4. But when ye assemble, let no man nor spirit be as a spectacle to others. But as all men labor in the field to gather the harvest, so shall all members in the assembly, by prayer or by music, contribute a glory unto the Father.

5. Remembering that the humblest prayer, even with weak words, if given with a full heart, is as strong unto Jehovih as the best oratory.

6. From all men the spirit shall pour forth unto the Father in praise, according to what hath been created unto it. Neither is more required of any man.

7. But this shall happen unto many: Learning to speak by entrancement or by inspiration, they shall imagine themselves controlled by certain angels, when, in fact, it is only their own spirit, eliminated from the corporeal senses.

8. Others, being influenced, shall imagine it is themselves and not an angel, whereas it is an angel speaking through them. This was the case of Ka'yu. Both are good, and shall be practiced.

9. Let no man concern himself as to whether it be the spirit of himself or an angel; for it is only the subject uttered which is of value. In this day, all things shall stand on their own merit, and not on a supposed authority.

10. And let not him, who speaketh with his own spirit, judge others to be the same; nor yet the reverse of this; for no two in all the world are alike.

11. To them, that have not experienced elimination of the spirit-self from the corporeal self (trance), all speech is believed to be of the corporeal senses only, or of a diseased condition. Such men are not to be blamed for their interpretation; rather shall ye pity them, and not answer them.

12. For many such, even after death, will not admit they are dead, because of the darkness upon them.

13. It is wiser for the spiritual-minded to keep to themselves, especially when communing with Jehovih and His angels. For a greater wonder than these will follow: Some will enter the trance of the first resurrection, and go in spirit out of the body, but only subjectively; others will enter the trance of the second resurrection, and go in spirit out of the body objectively. And the first shall not believe but the second was like himself, going only subjectively. No two men in all the world have I created alike, saith Jehovih. Even many, after death, are not capable of entering the second resurrection objectively. He, that is in subjective state, speaketh and writeth from the earth, looking upward; he, that cometh of the objective heavens, speaketh and writeth as one come down from My kingdoms to the earth.

14. Two conditions will manifest: Subjective spiritualists will affiliate with the world's people, being deniers of the Ever Present Person, and they will pursue earthly avocations for self sake; but objective spiritualists, being such as live for the spirit's sake, will be Faithists, believers in the Ever Present Person, Jehovih, Whom they will worship not only

in words, but by abjuring self, and uniting themselves in brotherhoods, for sake of doing good unto others. These latter are the chosen people of the Father of the kosmon era, and they will become supreme in all the world.

15. These three peoples, the world's people, the believers and the Faithists, have been in all ages of the world. The latter only of them all practiceth harmony and good works. Both of the others are resistants, quarrelers and warriors and disintegrators and breakers-down of all things.

16. Yet, the Faithists, having faith in the All Person, shall ultimately possess the whole earth, and make it a paradise of peace and love.

17. As the first is bound in the flesh, and as the second is bound by the hadan spirits, so is the Faithist bound unto Jehovih, which is emancipation. As the second can commune with the spirits of the first resurrection, so can the Faithist commune with the Father through the second resurrection.

18. Nevertheless, this shall happen: The second shall say: My angels are high, thine are low! Or they shall ask: How know ye your light is higher than ours?

19. And the Faithists shall answer them, saying: We know no high, no low. We give up all things, in order to serve Jehovih by doing good works unto our fellows.

20. And Jehovih shall judge betwixt them, as to which is high or low, not by their words, but by their works.

21. And the signs of good works and self-abnegation shall be as a witness before the world, whence cometh the inspiration of each.

22. Let no man say, that only seers and prophets and such persons as work signs and miracles are under the influence of spirits; for even as much as these, so are other mortals under the dominion of spirits. Yea, the infidel, the disbeliever, the philosopher, the lawyer, the judge, the preacher, the fanatic, and all others, are more controlled by the spirits of the dead than by their own personal spirit. And the more a man's spirit is wrapped up in his own corporeality, the more is he subject to vampires and spirits of darkness.

23. Neither knoweth the philosopher whether his ideas come from Jehovih or from the spirits of the dead.

24. Whosoever hath witnessed and knoweth of a truth, that he hath seen the spirits of the dead, that knowledge is impregnable. And whoso hath entered the second resurrection, even though in mortality, that knowledge is impregnable.

25. But, whoso hath found the All Person, his knowledge is greater than all. And none below him can judge him. Neither can any man attain to this knowledge, till he hath passed through the other two conditions.

26. No man knoweth the Creator, unless he hath proven the communion of spirits. Neither can any man rise to the second resurrection, till he hath arisen to faith in the All One, Jehovih.

27. Neither shall the Brahmin, nor Mohammedan, nor Budhist, nor Kriste'yan join in the second resurrection on earth or in heaven.

28. For they have not the doctrine of unit; they are as a house divided against itself. Their colonies and communities shall fail in all cases.

29. There shall be but one doctrine, which is Jehovih, the All Person, who is Ever Present; with good works done unto others, with all of one's wisdom and strength.

30. And this shall prevail with the young; whom, as orphans and castaways, ye shall gather up in infancy, founding them in the light of Jehovih, teaching them from the start to sing and pray unto Him, in reverence and fear and joy, that He may be glorified in their purity and good works.

31. And they shall grow up of all nationalities, and races, knowing not: This is mine, or that is mine, or that is thine, but understanding, that they own nothing, and that all things are Jehovih's.

CHAPTER III.

THE JUDGMENT UPON THE BRAHMINS, THE BUDHISTS, THE KRISTE'YANS, THE MOHAMMEDANS, THE CONFUCIANS, THE JEWS AND ALL OTHER PEOPLES ON THE EARTH, IN THE WORDS OF GOD.

1. Think not, O man, that I am insufficient to the times and seasons. Or say thou that God spake in the dark days of the earth, but latterly holdeth his tongue.

2. Behold, I am thy elder brother, even as a captain of the earth and her heavens for a season. As I am, even so were my predecessors in the time of the ancients:

3. Embassadors of the Most High, Jehovih!

4. Whose power and wisdom are given unto me, even after the same manner as are thy earthly kingdoms governed and disciplined.

5. Whereby order may contribute to the resurrection of all of His created beings.

6. First, I charge thee that whoso saith: GOD, GOD! calleth in vain.

7. I am not come to establish, but to abolish all Gods and Lords and Saviors amongst mortals.

8. For what is past, is past.

9. But whosoever, henceforth, heareth my word and the decree of my commandment, and continueth to make an idol of any name, save the Great Spirit, blasphemeth against his Creator.

10. But whoso cryeth out in fullness of heart, saying: GOD, GOD! meaning thereby the Ever Present, the Creator, is not a blasphemer before me.

11. And whoso saith: ORMAZD, ORMAZD! meaning thereby the Ever Present, the Creator, is not a blasphemer before me.

12. And whoso calleth any name in any language that signifieth the Ever Present, the Creator, is not a blasphemer before me.

13. And whoso saith: BRAHMA, BRAHMA! signifying a God in figure and shape of a man, sitting on a throne in heaven, is a blasphemer against Jehovih, the Ever Present, the Creator.

14. And whoso saith: BUDAH, BUDAH! signifying a God in figure and shape of a man, sitting on a throne in heaven, is a blasphemer against Jehovih, the Ever Present, the Creator.

15. And whoso saith: KRISTE, KRISTE! signifying a God in the figure and shape of a man, sitting on a throne in heaven, is a blasphemer against Jehovih, the Creator, the All Person.

16. And whoso calleth on the name of any other man or angel, worshipping such as a God, is an idolater in my sight.

17. Nor do I judge them less idolatrous than though they worshipped stone idols or graven images.

18. And whosoever saith: DEITY, DEITY! and DIVINITY, DIVINITY! and DIVINE LAW and

NATURAL LAW, are adjudged in darkness.

19. For I proclaim my heavens open, and the way of understanding clear.

20. Jehovih is Ever Present, and doeth by virtue of his Presence, and not by any law.

21. And whoso saith that which will lead men to believe He is not Present, or that he hath gone away, leaving certain laws after Him in His stead, the same is adjudged a blasphemer against Jehovih.

22. And whoso saith: CALL THOU ON THIS SAVIOR, OR CALL THOU ON THAT SAVIOR, AND THY SINS WILL BE FORGIVEN THEE; AND, IN THE HOUR OF THY DEATH, BECAUSE THOU HAST SO CALLED ON HIM, THOU SHALT ASCEND INTO A HEAVENLY PARADISE, the same is a falsifier of my kingdoms and a blasphemer against Jehovih.

23. And whoso saith: COME THOU BEFORE THE CHURCH, AND BEFORE THE PRIEST, AND MAKE PRAYERS AND CONFESSIONS, AND THOU SHALT BE ABSOLVED AND FORGIVEN THY SINS, the same are falsifiers of my kingdoms and blasphemers against Jehovih, the Creator.

24. Nor have I provided resurrection in this world, nor in my heavens above, save by good works done unto others; and this is serving Jehovih, the All Person; and not because of any worship or confessions done before any of the idols on earth or in heaven.

25. Nor is there any redemptions in heaven to the Brahmins, nor to the Budhists, nor to the Kriste'yans, because of their prayers and confessions.

26. But wherein good works have resulted in affiliation; and in lifting the people up out of misery and crime, the same is adjudged as worship of the Great Spirit, Jehovih.

27. Wherein the Brahmins have suffered a people to fall from knowledge into ignorance, or from virtue into vice, my judgment is against them.

28. Wherein the Budhists have suffered a people to fall from knowledge into ignorance, or from virtue into vice, my judgment is against them.

29. Wherein the Ka'yuans have suffered a people to fall from knowledge into ignorance, or from virtue into vice, my judgment is against them.

30. Wherein the Kriste'yans have suffered a people to fall from knowledge into ignorance, or from virtue into vice, my judgment is against them.

31. Wherein the Mohammedans have suffered a people to fall from knowledge into ignorance, or from virtue into vice, my judgment is against them.

32. Where beggary and vagrancy and all manner of darkness have increased in any of the cities or countries of any of these idolaters, my judgment is against them.

33. They shall not excuse themselves, nor escape my judgment, by saying: O the true Brahmin, or the true Budhist, or the true Mohammedan hath not fallen. These, that fell, were such as embraced not our doctrine in fullness of heart.

34. Because my judgment is also against impotency. They have tried their respective religions hundreds of years. And they have not raised up one city of righteous people.

35. Wherefore, I have come to put these doctrines away, and give them that which shall prove itself potent in all the world.

36. That, which I proclaim, shall be proclaimed by the angels of the second resurrection, unto all nations and peoples.

37. My light is not to one people only, save to the righteous, who serve the Creator by doing good unto all men. In my sight, the nations of the divisions of the earth are as one people only, brothers and sisters.

38. I take from all of them their idols, their Gods; but I give them a greater, even the

Creator.

39. I say to them: I suffered my children to have idols; but now, that ye are men, put away your idols, and accept Jehovih, Who is the Creator of all.

40. Nor shall any man more say: I worship the Brahmin principle, or the Budhist principle, or the Ka'yuan principle, or the Kriste'yan principle, or the Mohammedan principle. For all of these have proved themselves to result in war and destruction.

41. None of them have faith in Jehovih, but faith in their armies of soldiers, and in their weapons of death.

42. But I give unto all people one principle only, which is to serve Jehovih. This is broad enough for the redemption and resurrection of all men. And I will have none other.

43. Seek, thou, O man, to believe in the All Person, Who is Ever Present, Whose eye is upon thee, Whose ear heareth thee; for He is the All One, Who is the pass-word to the highest of heavens.

44. And thou mayest call on thy idol at the gates of my heavens, but the gates shall not be opened unto thee. For I will have no quarrel in my exalted kingdoms in heaven as to Gods and Lords and Saviors.

45. Till thou art washed clean of them; coming in spotless white, a servant of the Most High, thou canst not withstand the light of my kingdoms in heaven.

46. But thou shalt return in spirit to the earth, and abide in the church and temple of thy chosen God, wandering about, in stubbornness of heart, a prey to drujas and vampires and other angels of darkness.

47. Have faith, O man, in Him, Who created thee alive; about Him there can be no mistake. Glorify Him by righteous works, having faith, that even as He brought thee into life, so will He provide unto thee, according to thy just deserts.

CHAPTER IV.

THE NUMBERS OF THE JUDGMENT, IN THE WORDS OF GOD.

1. Hear the words of thy God, O man; I am thy elder brother, the captain of heaven and earth.

2. Wherefore, declare I unto thee in this day, the same shall be testified to by millions of angels unto mortals ere one generation pass away.

3. Of Brahmin angels in the lowest of heavens, as wanderers on the earth, there are this day more than four thousand millions.

4. Of Budhist angels in the lowest of heavens, as wanderers on the earth, there are this day more than seven thousand millions.

5. Of Ka'yuan angels in the lowest heavens, as wanderers on the earth, there are this day more than a thousand millions.

6. Of Kriste'yan angels in the lowest heavens, as wanderers on the earth, there are this day more than three thousand millions.

7. Of Mohammedan angels in the lowest heavens, as wanderers on the earth, there are this day more than two thousand millions.

8. Of Jewish angels in the lowest heavens, as wanderers on the earth, there are this day more than thirty millions.

9. And of other angels, idolatrous and otherwise, even on the earth, more than twelve

thousand millions.

10. And of all these angels not one is above grade five, in the first resurrection.

11. But of such as are below grade one, there are more than six thousand millions, which compriseth such angels as know nothing more than babes, though, for the most part, they were full grown adults as to earth-life. Some are fetals, some engrafters (professional re-incarnaters), who dwell with one mortal during his life-time, and then engraft themselves on another mortal during his life time, and so on, calling themselves re-incarnated, and, in fact, knowing no other heavens, being disbelievers in the All Person and in my exalted kingdoms.

12. Such as are below grade one, I have classed this day as drujas, because they have not left the earth and entered the first resurrection.

13. They inhabit mostly the oldest cities, and places of filth and indecency; nevertheless, they also inhabit the palaces of kings and queens and emperors and popes and priests and rich men.

14. Of grade one, there are hundreds of millions of angels strolling about on the earth, crying out: I want to go to Brahma, I want to go to Budha, I want to go to Jesus, I want to go to Kriste.

15. And I send my hosts of high-raised angels to them, saying: Come ye to the kingdoms of Jehovih, and be clothed and fed, and learn to clothe and feed others, for this is the way of resurrection.

16. But they will not believe, but turn away in stubbornness of heart, even as ye of the earth, saying: Nay, I will rise only by prayers and confessions. I want to be changed in a moment, in the twinkling of an eye, and rise and sit on the right hand of God.

17. And there are hundreds of millions who, being dead, know not anything; but, through belief in a judgment day, went to sleep, and are waiting for the trumpet of Gabriel to call them forth.

18. And I send my exalted ones to them to awake them up, and call them up; but they are drunk with their faith, and they relapse again and again, for years and years, for hundreds of years!

19. Fulfilling Jehovih's mandate, that whatsoever is bound on earth shall be bound in heaven.

20. And, even as one drunken man on earth enticeth another to drunkenness, so are there hundreds of millions of idolatrous angels, who return to mortals and persuade them to their same doctrines and to their same debaucheries.

21. Hear the words of thy God, O man, and be wise in thy judgment: He Who created thee alive, gave to thee of His Own Being. Be thou steadfast unto Him, and thou shalt not err, but eliminate thyself from the chance of error.

22. He alone is unmistakably thy sure foundation, in Whom thou shalt not be tript up.

23. Sufficient unto thee and thy resurrection is thy Creator. Wherefore, in thy soul thou shalt abjure all Gods and Lords and Saviors.

24. Neither shalt thou try to exalt His name by adding thereunto any name in the shape and figure of man, nor by any one of woman born.

25. Seek thou to attain to His voice in all things, and to obey Him for righteousness sake. Be not stubborn in thy conceit.

26. In thy singleness of purpose thou shalt be ministered unto by the spirits of the

first resurrection; but, as thou unitest thyself in a brotherhood on earth, in the name of Jehovih, so shalt thou be ministered unto by the light of my second resurrection.

27. But it hath been proved, and it shall be proved again, that all brotherhoods on earth founded on any of the idols in heaven, shall not stand.

28. Because, there is no second resurrection to minister unto them.

29. And all societies and constitutions and by-laws founded by men, not capable of the second resurrection, shall fail.

30. But whosoever establisheth, in the second resurrection; which is the abnegation of self to serve Jehovih, shall not fail.

CHAPTER V.
OF THE JEWS.

1. Hear the words of thy God, O Israel. Shut not thyself up against the wisdom of thy elder brother, God of heaven and earth.

2. Nor magnify thou the ancient days above the present; nor feign and say, thy God is gone away to come no more forever.

3. Behold, thou hast gone forth as a little man to battle against a giant. With thy sling thou hast smitten him with thy *one* stone, Jehovih!

4. Thou was encompassed on all sides by a multiplicity of Gods; one by one, thou hast overcome them, and cast them out.

5. The giant of the great beast, the false Gods, lieth dead and cold at thy feet.

6. The nations of the earth cry out: There is but one Great Spirit, Jehovih!

7. And I declare unto thee, O Israel, the Voice of the I Am is not gone from the earth.

8. Through the seed of the Faithists have I held up the Father's kingdom; by the voice of my beloved founded Him in all the nations of the earth.

9. Thy enemy exulted, saying: Behold, they are a scattered people!

10. But thy God profited in thy footsteps, and in the words of thy mouth: There is but one Great Spirit, Jehovih!

11. And I have provided unto thee, after the manner of thy forefathers, a place to inhabit, where thou shalt not longer pay tribute to the Gods of the idolaters.

12. Come thou out of the darkness of despotism, and inherit the wilderness of this land. And they shall bloom as a new paradise before thy hand.

13. But, because thou hast accomplished the One Ever Present, behold, thou shalt no longer be an exclusive people; but shalt suffer thy sons and daughters to commingle with the Faithists of all the races and tribes of men.

14. And thou shalt forsake the ways of the world, and go, and live after the manner of thy forefathers, in colonies, without kings or rulers; serving none, but Jehovih.

15. And thy people shall hold all things in common, being neither rich nor poor; master nor servant. And thou shalt call out to the idolater, saying: Come into my house, and be one with me. Behold, there is but one Creator; thou art my brother.

16. And it shall come to pass unto thee, O Israel, the way of thy people shall be open, and they shall be delivered out of the bound kingdoms of the east.

17. Because, for two thousand years, thou hast not gone forth with the sword to possess any new country, and establish thyself, thou art glorified before thy God.

18. Because of thy long suffering, thou shalt find peace through the light of my kingdoms. Behold, a new cycle is upon the earth; thy people shall find proof of these my words.

19. My angels will come into the houses of my people, and they shall talk with them, face to face.

20. Think not that this book is mine only revelation in this day; within thine house, O Israel, thou shalt prepare unto the voice of thy God.

21. For I will raise up many seers and prophets amongst thy people. And they shall testify to my words, on all sides.

22. Judge thou not, O Israel, who are apostates before thy God. I say unto thee: He, that forsaketh Jehovih and worshipeth mammon and the ways of the world, is an apostate in my sight. For, even though they maintain the rites and ceremonies, they have forsaken the spirit and truth of my commandments.

23. Whereas, many who have forsaken the rites and ceremonies in search of higher light, are more to the way of Jehovih.

24. Do they not, indeed, keep the rites and ceremonies, but drink to drunkenness, and eat to gluttony, feasting on flesh, wherefrom they have taken life?

25. And they engage in selling wine, and in dealing in stocks, after the manner of the idolater. Whilst thy forefathers were scrupulous to labor, and bring forth out of the earth, wherewith to feed and clothe man.

26. And they say: God prospered me!

27. Wherein they falsify me, and blaspheme Jehovih and His kingdoms. I say unto thee, they are prospered by satan; and their prosperity is the wages of bondage in heaven.

28. And because of their wickedness, they have led my people to disbelieve in my justice and the plans of my kingdoms.

29. For which reason, more are they apostatized in my sight, than such as are good, who say: There is no God.

30. Throw open thy doors, O Israel; my angels stand at the threshold. These, my words, which I have told to thee beforehand, shall be corroborated by hundreds of thousands of witnesses from my heavens.

31. Seek for the resurrection of thy soul, O Israel, that Jehovih may be glorified in thee, forever and ever!

CHAPTER VI.

OF RESURRECTION, IN THE WORDS OF GOD.

1. Whether on earth or in heaven, the same rules apply unto both:

2. He that serveth himself one-half, and serveth others one-half, shall stand grade fifty.

3. He that serveth himself three-quarters, and others one quarter, shall stand grade twenty-five.

4. He that serveth himself one-quarter, and others three-quarters, shall stand grade seventy-five.

5. He that serveth himself only, shall stand grade one.

6. He that serveth others wholly, shall stand grade ninety-nine.

7. And whoso serveth accordingly, himself or others, shall stand in grade even as his works manifest.

8. To serve one's self is to work for one's self; to strive for one's self, to think of one's own self, as to what will profit one's own self only.

9. To serve others, is to do good unto others; to help them; to teach them; to give them joy and comfort. This is the service of Jehovih.

10. But there are some who are below the grades; who seek to do evil; who seek to make others unhappy; who delight in crime and pollution. These, if mortal, shall be called druks, and if spirits, shall be called drujas.

11. After such manner, in general, are the grades of my heavens of the earth, atmospherea.

12. Grade one is on the earth; grade fifty, midway betwixt the earth and the emancipated heavens, etherea.

13. Grade twenty-five is one-quarter way up from the earth, toward etherea; but grade seventy-five is three-quarters way upward, toward etherea. And so on, relatively, grade and place of ascent intermediately.

14. But grade ninety-nine is the highest atmospherean grade, preparatory to entrance into the company of the all pure in spirit.

15. But good works alone are not sufficient to attain the highest grades, for they require knowledge and capacity to unfold others.

16. To accomplish which, those of the higher grades shall oft return to the lower, and learn to lift them up. For this is that which calleth the ethereans in the times of resurrections.

17. Wherein the righteous, who are yet mortal, begin at once lifting up their fellows.

18. Which labor is to the spirit as exercise is to the mortal body, that which giveth strength.

19. Judge, then, thyself, O man of the earth, as to the place thy spirit will rise in the time of thy death.

CHAPTER VII.

1. A man may be wise as to books and philosophy and mathematics and poetry and great learning, and yet be low in grade as to spirit.

2. A man may know little of all such knowledge, and may be poor withal, but by hardship and experience, developed in sympathy and good works done unto others, and be high in grade as to spirit.

3. So also may it be with spirits that manifest through you as great orators, who stand even in the lowest grade in heaven.

4. Let not thyself deceive thyself, O man, as to thy knowledge, or thy speech or professions.

5. Thou hast the scales in thine own hands, and shall, soon or late, weigh thyself justly, and take thy place, even as thou hast prepared thyself.

6. Nor flatter thyself that thou canst cheat heaven, or change the ways thereof.

7. Nor hide thyself behind doctrines, or behind the promises of Gods or Saviors.

8. Old things are done away, and none of these things shall avail thee on earth or in heaven.

9. Be thou king or queen or judge or servant, the same judgment shall stand upon all.

10. When the garment is gone, and the diadem and riches and the flesh withal, consider thou the grade of thy spirit and the bondage upon thee.

11. Thou shalt take that for which thou hast fitted thyself, according to what thou hast done.

CHAPTER VIII.

1. Hear my words, O man, and be considerate of the justice of thy Creator.

2. These are my exhibits which I place before thee, that thou shalt not err:

3. And thou be a rich man, and adorn a city by donating unto it a park, with statuary and pleasure-walks, hoping to glorify thyself thereby, and be praised by men; therein thyself burieth thyself in the first resurrection. And the act lowereth thy grade instead of raising it.

4. For in whatsoever thou givest, thou shalt consider, first, the lowest of the low, whether they have bread to eat, and a place to sleep: And the sick, whether they have attendance and good provision.

5. And thou be a rich man and contribute a house for the orphans or for the helpless and aged who cannot help themselves, it raiseth thee in grade.

6. But so far as thou doeth this for the applause of men, thou detracteth from the rate of thy beneficence.

7. Neither doth such a good work help thee more than the poor man helpeth his own grade by assisting one poor orphan.

8. For thy resurrection dependeth not on the quantity thou givest, but as to whether thou givest according to what thou hast. Of which matter thou shalt judge thyself.

9. For he who giveth a penny may be raised up more by so doing, than he that giveth ten times ten thousand.

10. A certain rich man, being converted from the desires of earth, went about casting his money freely in the streets, and in giving to whosoever asked him therefore.

11. And some gathered it up, and fed and clothed themselves; others took of it, and went and got drunk, and became worse than before.

12. The measure of righteousness of that man's behavior was not in giving what he had to the poor, but in the good and evil that came of it, being weighed, as to which outbalanced the other.

13. And where he lowered the grade of them that received this money, or where he lowered a greater number than he raised, there his act of casting the money away was a judgment against him.

14. He who giveth, saying: Here, thou beggar! doeth a good corporeal act, but an evil spiritual act. He lifteth up with one hand, but knocketh down with the other. Such an act detracteth from the grade of that man.

15. A certain rich man, being converted to do good works, went and built a score of soup-houses to feed the poor gratuitously.

16. And all the poor people of that town went therein and were fed. But the next year, behold, there were twice as many poor. And the rich man built another score of soup-houses, and they were all fed.

17. But the next year, there were still twice as many poor people to feed; but the rich man

had exhausted his means, and could feed none at all.

18. Judgment is therefore rendered against that man for his supposed beneficence.

19. For, whilst he did a little corporeal good, he did a great spiritual wrong, because he lowered the grade of manhood and womanhood in those that he fed. His benevolence promoted dependence.

20. A rich man founded a place of labor for the poor, who had nothing to eat and nowhere to sleep. And he said unto them:

21. The Creator hath given you hands to work with; come ye, be men and women.

22. And they went and worked and earned their living.

23. Judgment is rendered in favor of that man, for he raised the spiritual grade of the poor. This is a beneficence that extendeth into heaven.

24. Let thy charity be to the sick and helpless, but be thou wise in directing the able-bodied to help themselves.

25. For all charity tendeth to lower the self-respect of the receiver, and casteth him lower in the grades in heaven.

26. Certain ones depend on alms, not having either sickness nor yet strong bodies. Nevertheless, were they aroused, they could support themselves.

27. When thou givest them regularly, they depend on thee. These become beggars in the lowest grades in heaven.

28. That which thou givest them accounteth against thine own grade. Better is it for thee and for them, that thou arouse them from their degradation.

29. To do this tenderly and mercifully, is a great virtue; to do it cruelly, is a great crime.

30. Consider not so much what thou shalt do to raise thine own grade, but what thou canst do to raise the grade of those within thy reach.

31. Remember, all men and women are thy brothers and sisters, and thou shalt labor to make them make themselves a glory unto the Creator.

CHAPTER IX.

1. Remember thy Creator and the magnitude of his creations. Before Him thou art but an atom, and as only one small creature.

2. Nevertheless, a multitude of people make a nation, with cities and hamlets.

3. These are also graded by thy God, according to the ascendancy or the declension of the whole.

4. If a city, then the grades of all the people shall be summed together in a scale of one hundred.

5. And if a nation, then the grades of the cities and hamlets, and of people of isolation, shall be summed together in a scale of a hundred.

6. And if half the people are above grade fifty, and half below fifty, the grade of that people shall be fifty.

7. If one quarter only, then the grade of that people shall be twenty-five.

8. On the basis of individual grades, shall be the grades of a city and of a nation.

9. And the behavior of a city or a nation shall be graded in the same way, after the manner of an individual.

10. A certain nation built alms-houses and asylums sufficient for the needy, and, by its

tyranny, made an equal number of needy ones. That nation raised not its grade for the good it had done.

11. Another nation built no alms-houses, but, by its wholesome laws, there were none needed. That nation raised its grade many-fold.

12. And yet another nation maintained a standing army, in order to maintain itself. That nation stood in grade one only.

13. The place of this last nation, in entrance into the es world, shall be grade one, which is the animal region, which is on the earth.

14. Whoso dwelleth in such a land, though he have a good individual grade, shall suffer deduction in the ratio of the grades of different nations of the earth.

15. But whoso dwelleth in a nation, high in grade, shall be ascended in his own individual grade.

16. As these grades are on earth, so have I made them in the heavens thereof. In all cases depending on what one doeth for the resurrection of others.

17. If a city, or nation, or a kingdom in heaven do unto others in resurrection, then shall that nation be graded accordingly.

18. But, if there be no gain in the good than any of these do, they shall receive no grade.

19. But, if they increase in raising individual grade, then are such cities and nations rising in grade.

20. Consider thy nation, O man, one generation with another; and as the relative proportion of individual grades rise or fall, so shalt thou determine whether thy nation is ascending or falling in grade. Number its paupers and criminals as to increase or decrease.

21. Consider not its wealth, nor its ships, nor its armies, nor its great buildings. These all together are only one grade, and are of no value as to the spiritual grade of its people.

22. For the strength and life of thy nation depend on its spiritual grade. Pursue this, and thou shalt prophesy truly as to the growth or the downfall of a nation.

23. Pursue this also with regard to the nations of the earth, and thou shalt determine the relative place of thine own nation in the es world.

CHAPTER X.

1. Thou art remembered, O man, by thy God, and admonished and instructed for thy soul's sake that thou mayest become a glory to thy Creator and to thyself.

2. Hear then, thy responsibility and the extent thereof, and consider the magnitude of thine own grade on earth and in heaven.

3. Which is in proportion to the power and the distance of thy reach. Which I have also graded unto all men on earth and in heaven.

4. If thy Creator give thee strength to carry four men on thy back, and thou wilt carry but one, thou shalt be one-quarter grade. But, if thou carriest the whole four, thou shalt be full grade.

5. One man hath wherewithal to feed one man; another hath sufficient for a thousand; and another for a hundred thousand. These are the distances of the reach and power of these men, which is the extent beyond which nothing more can be exacted of them, on earth or in heaven.

6. Yet, when they have all fulfilled these to the utmost, they shall be therein only equal in

grade.

7. But, if they fail in their parts, the responsibility of one shall be a hundred thousand; and another shall be ten thousand, and the least shall be only one. These are the debts men owe the people of the nation, the city and the hamlet.

8. Consider, therefore, the darkness of the people of thy nation; the poverty and the crime; and judge thyself as to thine own responsibility.

9. And this rule shall apply both, on earth and in heaven. And thy grade of responsibility in heaven shall begin even in the same place thou established it on the earth. Wherein thou wert short, thou shalt labor; wherein thou didst fulfill, thou shalt rejoice, and be without compunctions.

10. Also shall this rule be with the king and queen and emperor, and all rulers who have means and power; and the responsibility shall extend to all the people of the kingdom or empire.

11. Nor shall this responsibility be escaped by death; but the bondage in heaven shall be according to the avoidance of the trust imposed.

12. Consider, then, what thou shalt be encumbered with in the es world.

13. Pursue this philosophy, and thou shalt determine what shall be the labor of the king and the queen and the great ruler, after they have died, and entered the es world.

14. Find the grade of their respective dominions, and thou shalt determine, by the ascension thereof, the duration of their bondage in the first resurrection, whether it be fifty years or five hundred years.

15. But if such emperor's dominions be in declension instead of resurrection, then, on his entrance into heaven, he shall be at the mercy of the spirits of his kingdom, who shall be in wait for him, and he shall not escape them.

16. Some other heavenly kingdom shall deliver them; otherwise, they fall into anarchy and madness (hell).

CHAPTER XI.

1. Remember thy Creator and the comprehension of His kingdoms; and be considerate of the words of thy God:

2. All men profess to desire resurrection; they hope to ascend to exalted heavenly spheres.

3. Yet, many will not even try to exalt themselves.

4. He saith in one breath: To not eat the flesh of anything created alive, is the highest.

5. But, straightway, he filleth his belly with flesh.

6. He saith: To return good for evil is the highest.

7. But he doeth evil even before the sound of his voice is hushed.

8. And yet, he will find fault with his Creator, if holy angels promise him not a high seat in heaven.

9. And there are others who constantly profess to have the higher light; but they go about tattling, and making evil remarks of their neighbors.

10. Yet, many of these do good unto others, giving to the helpless; verily are they both rising and falling, in regard to the resurrection.

11. The measure of the grade of such shall be by weighing the whole behavior as to its result in the community where he abideth. And this rule shall apply, both on earth and in

heaven, to all such people.

12. There are men who do great good unto others, and are talented withal, but who are great liars; and much prone to exaggeration. So, that their good works are outbalanced by the shame of their tongues.

13. The grade of resurrection of such shall not be modified or benefited but little by their good works. But they shall be weighed as to such evil habit, whether it be increasing or decreasing; and the grade of such man shall be accordingly, and shall come under the rank of spiritual disease. Because it will be entailed upon them into the es world, and shut them out from the grade which they manifested.

14. When thou searchest for the grade of a city, therefore, all such persons shall stand as grade one.

15. There be some who say: I care not for the spiritual man nor the es worlds. One world at a time is sufficient for me.

16. And they may be good as to the way of the city, contributing alms to the helpless, and visiting the sick. Nevertheless, they utter truthfully their own resurrection, which shall stand grade one.

17. There is no crime in them, but a misfortunate imbecility of spirit. When such persons die, their knowledge, for the most part, dieth with them. And the enter the es world even as if they had died in infancy.

18. They shall stand grade one, because owing to their weakness of spirit, they must need be inhabited on the earth for many years.

19. There be others, who are forever talking of heaven, and consulting the spirits of the dead, who are, nevertheless, low as to good works, and low in holiness of heart. These shall be graded the same as liars and hypocrites.

20. For in prophecy, thou shalt estimate the sum of all the virtues and vices of thyself, and of thy neighbor, and of the whole city, or state, or even the world; and accredit the grade in ascension or declension, and thou shalt compare one generation with another, as to the increase or decrease of its spirituality.

21. And thou shalt know of a truth the standing of the whole world.

22. And from this, thou shalt also determine the time, when man came on the earth; how long the race will survive and bring forh; and the time he shall become extinct as to the earth.

CHAPTER XII.

1. O man, remember thy Creator and praise Him. In this, thou art graded by thy God.

2. Who see not Him, are weak in spirit; who see Him in all things, and hear His voice in the leaves, and in every herb, are strong in spirit.

3. These are the grades of the resurrection of the souls of men.

4. For what is the earth but a foaling nest, and the possessions of the earth but chains of bondage.

5. My heavens rest upon the earth; the place of the es'yan is in my keeping. And the places of the grades of my heavens have I adjusted, according to the inhabitants thereof.

6. I people the heavens of the earth with the spirits of the dead; according to their grade in their corporeal lives, so do I arrange them.

7. To provide them unto everlasting resurrection, and make them to rejoice in their being.

These are the labors of thy God.

8. For the beasts of the field and the birds and fowls of the air, and for many animals that are companions to man, made I a place in heaven, where their spirits should survive for a season.

9. And this animal heaven I graded, one, in the order of my heavens.

10. For I saw that man on the earth had delight in them; and I provided unto him for his es'yan period, that he might rejoice in remembrance of finding his loves.

11. And I made the animal heaven to rest on the face of the lands of the earth even the same as the place of the es'yan in grade one.

12. Remember, O man, thy Creator gave to every animal a season on the earth; but He limited them to a time to become extinct. Even so, and of like duration made I a heavenly period for the spirits of animals companionable to man.

13. But for man I provided heavens above, where he should rise as to place, even as he riseth, as to goodness and knowledge.

14. Magnify thy perception, O man, that thou mayst comprehend the kingdoms of thy God. Behold the example thy Creator sat before thee in the fashion of the earth.

15. In large bodies, He placed the lands; in large bodies, He placed the oceans. Not in little hillocks of land and little puddles of water.

16. Even larger than these are the divisions (plateaux) of the heavens of thy God; the heavens of the earth are separated by atmospherean oceans.

17. I fill not the air of the firmament with angels scattered about; but I give unto them regions habitable and home-like. And I grade them suitable to the resurrection of the spirits of the dead.

18. Consider the work of thy Creator, and the knowledge and symbols He placeth before thee. Thou holdest up a lump of salt, and it is solid and of dimensions; but cast it into water, and it is seen not, but dissolved and lost as to thy perception.

19. And thou beholdest the earth, which hath dimensions also; but the ethe, thou seest not. As water is to salt the solvent, so is ethe to corporeal things the solvent. By slow velocity holdeth the solid earth its form; yet, in ethe, external to the body of the earth, the swift velocity of corpor is magnified into dissolution. By vortices in ethe are these things accomplished.

20. In the atmosphere of the earth, there is sufficient corpor to make many worlds like this habitable earth. And this corpor, which is in solution (as to a mortal's eyes), floateth in the firmament of the earth, in continents wide as the earth, and deep as the earth; and there are thousands of them.

21. And yet, O man, these are but the atmospherean heavens. These are the dominions given into the keeping of thy God. These are my kingdoms and my heavens for a season.

22. As thou, O man of the earth, sailest thy ships abroad over the ocean, and coming to a new land, going ashore, dost settle thy people thereon, and it becometh a new kingdom, even so doth thy God in the heavens of the earth, in the plateaux of this vortex.

23. Remember the magnitude of thy Creator's works and the symbols He sat before thee: Where the clouds float high, it raineth not; where they drag on the face of the earth, it raineth daily.

24. Consider the habitations of the resurrections of the dead which are in the keeping of thy God.

25. Even as to the square of the distance away from the earth, so are the grades of my resurrections.

26. According to the exaltation of man's soul, so shall he inhabit the places I have made.

27. According to his own soul's growth and development, so shall he ascend in my kingdoms, outward away from the earth; grade unto grade adapted I them.

CHAPTER XIII.

1. O man, to know the creations of thy Creator, and the things He hath placed in thy reach!

2. To apply thy knowledge and understand with reverence the work of His hand!

3. How considerate of thy little wisdom, and thy love of liberty, which He gave unto thee.

4. Even before He had perfected thee, He called out unto thee to behold His creations. And thou tarriedst not to learn, but ran away, half completed, to vent the exuberance of thy soul, which He gave unto thee.

5. Behold me, thy God; I am thy elder brother which He sent after thee. Come thou, and learn wisdom of thy God.

6. Thou tarriest in the grade; thou art not aroused to know thy Creator. Thou turnest thy back to me, and sayest: Behold, there is no God!

7. I beseech thee, turn about, and hear the wisdom of my words: I will teach thee to know thy Creator; to hear His voice, and to see His hand.

8. And thou shalt rejoice in thy life, and teach thy brethren to rejoice also.

9. Thou hast a corporeal body and a spiritual body: Hear me, and I will open thy understanding.

10. Thy spirit hath eyes and ears and judgment. Nevertheless, the beginning of thy two parts was, at the same time, quickened into a one person, because of the presence of thy Creator.

11. O man of the earth, would that thy spirit and thy corpor stood even in wisdom and power all the days of thy life!

12. But thou art so delighted in the earth, thou hast left thy spirit unfed. And it standeth within thee, as a spear of grass covered with a stone.

13. And thou seest not spiritual things; nor hearest the Unseen. For a stone lieth upon thy soul.

14. Yet, thou hast great learning as to corporeal knowledge; and great vigor as to corporeal judgment.

15. And thou ratest thy neighbor a fool, because, forsooth, in contradistinction to thee, he heareth and seeth spiritually.

16. And thy God weepeth for thee; because, in the time of thy death, thou shalt stand in heaven in grade one, even as the spirits of the beasts of the field.

17. Thy present knowledge shall be void, and thy vigor, only as a newborn child. And my angels who are wise and strong shall take thee about, in hada, the heavenly plateaux that rest on the earth, and divert thee with things proximating betwixt the two worlds, that thou mayest be made to comprehend thyself and thy Creator's work.

18. As thy corpor was fed on corporeal substances, so, then, shall thy young spirit be fed on atmospherean substances, which thy guardians shall provide unto thee.

19. Consider the wisdom of thy Creator, Who sent me to fetch thee into places of delight.

20. O that I could take thee to the highest heavenly places! That thou couldst stand before me, and talk face to face!

21. But even as a newborn child is unsuited to feed on corn and nuts, thy spirit is as a starveling in high heaven. And I take thee to the nurseries where I have provided for thee according to thy weakness.

22. Thy mother was provided unto thee before thou wert born; and my heavens arranged before thy spirit entered therein. Thou shapedst not thyself in thy mother's womb; and, behold the perfection of thine every part.

23. Trust thou in thy Creator, but seek thou also to go with Him, and thou shalt attain easily to the highest mountains He created for thy glory.

24. O that thou hadst not contaminated thy corporeal part by the flesh of the beast and the meat of His living creatures! This is as one of the stones that covereth up thy soul, and blockadeth thy way to the upper grades.

25. Thy young spirit must remain within the atmosphere of the animal creation for a long season; like unto like, hast thou fashioned thy spirit to the flesh of thy body.

26. According to the atmosphere of things, as to the purity and sweetness, behold, thy Creator hath fashioned them in relative ascent above the earth. That which stinketh, resteth on the earth; that which is pure, is upward and high.

27. Consider the place of the hells of the spirits of the dead, and the weapons of warfare in their hands. As the corporean is to corpor, so is the spirit as to the atmosphere of the earth.

28. O man of the earth, consider what thou puttest into thy mouth, for the atmosphere thereof is the food of thy spirit. And the habit thereof will be entailed on thy spirit for a long season after thy mortal death.

29. If thou hast been a gross feeder on flesh, thy spirit will seek to linger in the atmosphere of gross feeders still dwelling on the earth. The slaughter-house and the cook-house and the eating-house shall be the places of thy spirit's resort.

30. And thy spirit shall feed therein and thereon; and thy companions shall be millions and millions of drujas; like vultures that flock to a dead carcass, and thou can not away; like a loadstone, are these haunts to the spirits of darkness.

31. O man, I have heard thee, in thy fullness, say: I must have my flesh-food; I must have my wine and beer and tobacco and opium.

32. I say unto thee, if thou hast not strength in this day, neither shalt thou have strength tomorrow. What strength shall thou gain by the loss of thy corporeal body?

33. Consider thy corporeal body as a ship, in which thy spirit is sailing across a wide sea of water. Better that thy spirit learn to acquire strength whilst it hath a corporeal body to ride in. After death, it floateth in the direction thou hast shaped it. Neither hast thou power to go against the current.

34. Remember, O man, these are the lessons of thy Creator, which he gave unto thee, to learn to master the elements of thy surrounding.

35. Stretch forth thy hand unto thy Creator, and swear thou unto Him, thou wilt conquer every passion that is unclean, and every habit not conducive to the purity of the growth of thy spirit.

36. This is the beginning of thy resurrection; and thou shalt be thine own judge and

master.

37. Neither shalt thou call out: God, God, exalt my soul! or, O Lord, save me and raise me up! -- until thou hast first begun to do something for thyself.

38. O, that thou knew where the virtue of prayer beginneth! And that he that practiceth the All Highest he knoweth, hath the ear and the hand of his God! Wherein the prayers of the righteous accomplish, whilst the prayer of the ungodlike is void as the wind.

39. Certain men were down in a deep well, and they laid flat down on their bellies, and prayed to be taken up, yet, they would not even raise their eyes to look upward. And others, at the top of the well, let down ropes, and they called down to them beneath to look up, and catch the ropes, but they would not. And, in course of time, they at the bottom said: Alas! our prayers are not answered!

40. O man, that thou wouldst put thyself in the way of thy God! To put away the uncleanness of the body first, and the uncleanness of thy spirit afterward.

41. To seek for things that are pure and good, instead of criticisms and philosophies, that rise up out of thy contaminated flesh-house.

42. Whoso desireth resurrection, let him begin to resurrect himself.

43. Make not thy confessions, which are betwixt thee and thy Creator, before men; but covenant thou with Him, within thine own soul, saying nothing of this for the laudation of men.

44. Thy spirit is as a seed of a beautiful tree, which thy Creator planted; give thou it good light and a clean soil, that the blossoms and the fruit thereon may glorify thy Creator and thee.

45. Such is the resurrection of the spirit of men. Wait not for a Savior to save thee; nor depend thou on words or prayers; nor on hearkening to good sermons, flattering thyself, thou hast done well; but begin to save thyself.

46. By purifying thy flesh, by purifying thy thoughts, and by the practice of good works done unto others, with all thy wisdom, love and strength.

47. For through these only is there any resurrection for thee, either in this world or the next.

CHAPTER XIV.

1. Of the foundations of the resurrections of thy God, there are two kinds; one, which dealeth with those already born, and the other, with such as are not yet born.

2. For, after thou hast purified thyself as to flesh and spirit, two conditions are open to thee, celibacy and marriage.

3. To such as are by nature inclined to celibacy, let them rejoice; for, in not having offspring, they shall have less bondage after death to remain in the lower heavens, and to return to the earth, to their kindred.

4. It is a great glory for them to make themselves Brides and Bridegrooms to the Great Spirit, to be His for righteousness sake.

5. But, as to thee, who desireth marriage, pursue thou the same course as to purity and holiness of person, as to thine own resurrection.

6. For, in this, thou shalt be graded also, according to what thou dost.

7. The delight of thy God, who hath dominion over both, the earth and her heavens,

is to witness the birth as such as come from the pure in flesh and pure in spirit.

8. In likeness of the father and mother are all children born into the world; and every child is a new creation, quickened into life by the presence of the Creator, Who is the All Life.

9. If thou art pure in flesh, thy child shall be pure; and, if thou art pure in spirit, thy child shall be pure in spirit.

10. If thou art a flesh-eater, a drinker of strong drink, and a user of narcotics, thy child shall come forth with thy contaminations upon it.

11. Consider, then, what thy grade shall be, which shall be according to thy heirs, as to their grade in the place where they are born. As to whether thou encumberest the world with progeny lower in grade, or liftest up the world by progeny of an exalted grade.

12. Be wise as to the selection of thy partner, as to purity and righteousness. But be not deceived by such as eat not flesh merely, for the purification of the corporeal body is but half the matter. Look for one who is pure in spirit.

13. Whoso is pure in flesh and in spirit shall bring forth heirs unto resurrection, which shall be little or no bondage to the spirit, after death.

14. But, whoso marrieth for the earth only, shall bring forth heirs of bondage. And profligacy and debauchery and sin shall come upon the heirs of that marriage.

15. The spirits of such fathers and mothers shall fall in the grades in heaven; and long will be their bondage in hada.

16. Flesh-eaters seek their partners according to the impulse of the flesh, as to the temptation thereof, or according to riches, or caste, all of which are earthly considerations and for themselves only, and in no regard as to what their heirs will be.

17. And their offspring come forth in darkness; they are void of su'is, void of heavenly aspiration, and dumb as to the voice of the Creator.

18. They go about, saying: I see no All Person! I hear not the Unseen! Nay, I believe not that any man hath seen or heard Him!

19. Herein was it revealed to thee of old: Some are born of the beast, and some are born of the spirit. Which I declare unto thee, O man, is the interpretation of all the poverty and crime and war and licentiousness there is in the world.

20. This is the fountain-head, which thy God would bring to the understanding of all people. But there are many, even hundreds of millions, that can not be made to appreciate this.

21. Nevertheless, the kingdom of peace and righteousness shall not cover the earth over until this is understood by all men and women.

22. Whoso understandeth this, let him wed accordingly; and let such people be as societies to themselves. In this day, no mark of circumcision is required; but men and women shall converse on the ways of the Creator understandingly.

23. And, when thou hast children born unto thee, thou shalt more consider the place of thy habitation, as to temptation, than thy dominion over them.

24. To dwell in a city, which is full of iniquity, thou shalt be a tyrant over thy heirs, restraining them from liberty, in order to keep them from vice.

25. And in this, thou wilt be a sinner also.

26. But dwell thou in a place of purity, and give unto them liberty and nobleness. They shall not be thy slaves.

27. In this matter, thou takest upon thyself a new grade, according to thy heirs and thy God-ship over them.

28. Be cautious in thy proceedings. He, who created thee alive, gave thee no sinful desires.

29. Because thou art not yet a completed man, these things are.

30. Thou shalt find joy in thy talents, and profit in the wisdom of thy God.

31. To perfect thyself is a great glory; to raise up sons and daughters who are also perfect, is a ten-fold greater glory.

32. For, it is the fullness of the life thy Creator gave into thy keeping; which is the glory of heaven and earth.

CHAPTER XV.

1. Of the abundance of thy Creator's creations be thou appalled, O man!

2. Consider the inhabitants of the whole earth, and the number of a thousand millions brought into life every thirty-three years.

3. Compute thou the number for a thousand years, and for ten thousand years.

4. And, yet, the earth is not full.

5. And the heavens of the earth are yet even as if scarcely habited. Thousands of plateaux there are, with no angels to dwell thereon.

6. But to induce the spirits of the dead to rise up from the earth, this is the work and the glory of thy God.

7. To make them put away earthly desires, to become pure and wise and strong and adapted to the sublimated spheres, what an endless labor for thy God and his exalted angels.

8. As thou, O man of the earth, holdest to the desire for earthly things, thou entailest thyself in heaven, and canst not rise upward. Even so is it with the great harvest, the thousands of millions of angels born of the earth.

9. If thou stand a pyramid before thee, wide at the base, equal to the height, such is the manner of the proportions of the spirits of the dead on their entrance into the es world.

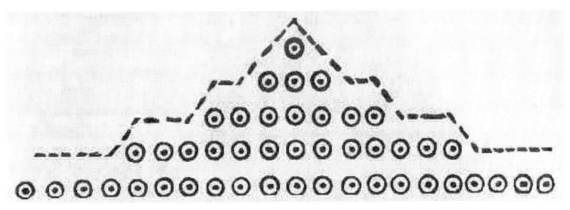

Plate 94. GRADES.

10. Consider, then, O man, how sparse are the settlements in the upper kingdoms of the earth's heavens, compared to the numbers in the lowest grade. And remember thou, the

percentage of inspiration that cometh to thee, from this grade, which is doubly degraded in the cities and great capitals.

11. Know thou, O man, that all cities built by men, soon or late, fall into destruction. Search into the generations, as to the grade of mortals, and thou hast a type of the spirits of that city, chiefly as to the lowest grades. But, remember, the highest grades of angels go away, whilst the lowest remain. As the spirits of one generation are to the form of a pyramid, so, not so will be the spirits of that city in the next generation.

12. But, in proportion to the increase of the mortal city, and in proportion to the raising up of the second, third, fourth and fifth grades, so will be the relative increase in the proportion of drujas that dwell in that city.

13. And, in time, all holiness passeth away therefrom; and, when thy God abandoneth that city for a day, taking hence his holy angels, the people fall into anarchy, or run with brands of fire, and burn down the city.

14. And the hundreds of millions of drujas lose their anchorage on the earth, and thy God and his exalted ones march them away.

15. Find thou the grade and the rate of declension of the mortals of a city, and, when the whole number, with the spirits therein, hath fallen to one per cent, thou shalt prophecy the time of the fall of that city.

16. Be thou fearful of the abundance of drujas about thee; and search out thine own imperfections and uncleanness and thy passions, lest drujas fasten upon thee in a way thou knowest not of.

17. Call not upon the spirits of the dead to come to thee; but call thou on thy Creator for wisdom and light and truth and purity; and, if it will be well for thee, He will send unto thee such spirits as are best adapted to thee for thy resurrection.

18. Whoso consulteth the spirits as to earthly things, or profit, or great undertakings, or marriage, or war, or riches, is already in the hands of drujas. Woe be unto him in the hour of death.

19. When thou sittest in communion with angels, do so reverently to thy Creator; and the members of thy circle shall pray unto Him, or sing songs of praise and glory unto Him and His works. Nor shalt thou habit thyself to sit with such as do not this reverence to Jehovih. And, when the angels appear and converse with thee, remember thou that even the least of them hath passed the bars of death.

20. Be not long-faced or melancholy with doleful songs; but rather cheerful, like the birds that sing unto the Creator. And let thy speech be respectful, and relating to spiritual things. Learn thou from them of the places they inhabit in heaven, and the manner of their occupations.

21. And if thou inquire of them as to earthly things, let it be as to how thou mayst help the poor and distressed.

22. For, if the angel that talketh with thee be a druj only, thy discourse shall, in this way, awake him to see his own shortness.

23. And if they be high-raised angels, they shall understand the working of thy soul, and they will provide unto thee for thy everlasting exaltation.

24. Be upright before thy Creator and thy God, who know thy weakness. Emulate them in all thy doings, for this is the way of resurrection, worlds without end.

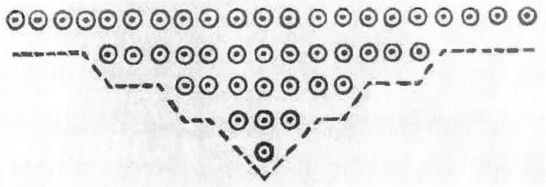

Plate 93. RATES.

CHAPTER XVI.

1. O man, weigh the words of thy God, thy elder brother, of tens of thousands of years experience.

2. Wherein thy soul perceiveth a ray of light, follow it in truth, and not in words merely.

3. It hath been said of old: Thou canst not serve both, God and self. And many go about preaching this, but they themselves, labor for self every day.

4. To serve thy God, is to work for others, especially the sick and helpless, and not for thyself. Thy prayers and confessions to me are but the waste of thy breath.

5. There be such as preach for money, and withal are graduated from the colleges and called, learned priests; but they have not yet learned not to serve mammon, save in words.

6. I say unto thee, that a poor man, who can not read a line, that goeth into the house of the afflicted, giving what little he hath, and, with a willing heart, cleaneth the floor and garments of the bed-ridden, is more learned in my kingdoms than are these graduated preachers.

7. The word, labor, or work, is easily understood.

8. Suffer not thyself to be deceived by them whose trade is preaching and praying. They profess to be laboring for the spiritual man; and, according to the number of their converts, who are also taught words and prayers and confessions, instead of works, so are they called, great workers unto the Lord.

9. But I say unto thee, all these are but the subterfuges of satan (self), to palm off words for works.

10. All such preachers and priests and converts are still tarrying in the mire of grade one.

11. Hear thou thy God, and weigh his words in the balance, and be not blinded by the tricks of satan.

12. A preacher, receiving a good salary, giveth half his money to the poor, and the other half to the church; and his people say: O what a good man!

13. And straightway they raise his salary, and they present him a good house, where he feasteth sumptuously every day, laughing in his sleeve.

14. Now, I say unto thee, that that preacher contributed nothing to the poor. The money, he gave away, was not his, but the fruit of hypocrisy.

15. Because he practiced not labor; but as a beggar and a vampire obtained his money, not for work, but for words, he was false before Jehovih.

16. To serve thy God, or to preach and practice the words of thy God, require not great

oratory or education. I require not colleges to brace me up; nor preachers, that serve not the Creator.

17. One crieth out: Come to God! or: Make thy peace with the Lord! But he himself would not give up his bed to a poor sick woman.

18. I say unto thee: All such are either hypocrites, or deceivers of their own souls.

19. Except thou usest thy hands, and bendest thy back in practice, and in producing something in the world, and contributing it unto others, thou art none of mine, nor knowest the way to come to me, nor to make peace with me.

20. It hath been said of old: Do unto others, as thou desirest should be done unto thee; also, to return good for evil, and to sell all thou hast, and give to the poor, and love thy neighbor as thyself.

21. And these words are well known; but who is there, that practiceth them?

22. Wherein the words are impotent and of non-effect.

23. To remedy which, many practice serving themselves by their labor; but in Jehovih's service, their practice is by prayers and confessions: words, words, words!

24. Saying: It is not possible, in the present condition of society, to do these things!

25. Did thy God limit thee, saying: Do thou this, in the present condition of society? The way was open for another condition; but thou soughtst not to find it. Thou wouldst not give up thyself, and live in a brotherhood. Under the name of liberty, thou held fast to satan and his haunts, saying: I am willing to serve the Creator, but I will not sacrifice my liberty.

26. And thou sellest thyself to self, which shall follow thee into hada.

27. Know then, O man, that whoso would rise into my organic kingdoms in heaven, shall teach himself the first lesson of liberty, which is to free himself from self.

28. He shall not say: I want this; or I must have that; or, I cannot have self abridged; or, I will suffer no dictation.

29. I say unto thee, all such men are already in the bonds of drujas and the throes of hell.

30. But thou shalt say: Here I am, O Jehovih, Thy servant! Appropriate Thou me whichever way I can do the most good unto others! Myself is no longer any consideration.

31. This it is, to be a Faithist in the Father.

32. If an exalted man marry a woman beneath him, he can lift her up.

33. But if an exalted woman marry a man beneath her, he will pull her down.

34. Even so is it with the righteous man, that weddeth to the world and liveth therein; soon or late, it will pull him down.

35. But, if the righteous man go with his fellows into a separate place, and wed himself to Jehovih and His ways, then shall that righteous man be lifted up. And, moreover, he shall be a power to lift up the world.

36. Shall a bride not live with her husband? And they that chose the Creator, live with him?

37. I say unto thee. If thou do not live in a brotherhood on earth, thou shalt not soon find one in heaven.

38. But thou shalt unite thyself with such as are compatible with thee; with whom thou shalt live equal in all things, wherein thou canst do unto them as thou wouldst be done by, loving them as thyself, returning them good constantly.

39. Being willing to make any sacrifice of thine own self's desires for sake of founding

the Father's kingdom on earth.

40. Remembering, thou wert born in darkness, and art not the same as will be the generations who come after thee, who shall be born in these communities, His kingdoms.

41. Even for them that are yet unborn shalt thy sacrifice be.

42. In which shalt thou consider that it is for the resurrection of others, and not for thyself, that thou art chosen of Jehovih.

43. For herein lieth the key of all resurrections; which is to labor for others; to induce them to assimilate unto Jehovih, and with one another.

44. The words of thy God are not for the glory of any man under the sun, or for any angel in heaven, but for Jehovih.

45. Thou hast had revelation sufficient since thousands of years; and sacred books with most holy doctrines. And, yet, many that know these well, come into the es world as low as drujas, and as wandering spirits.

46. Thou shalt judge thyself; thy spirit is as a manuscript in thine own handwriting; thou art daily writing thy grade and the place of thy abode in heaven.

CHAPTER XVII.

1. Remember the words of thy God, O man, and be reasonable in thy understanding.

2. Whithersoever thou buildest a city, and it increase in inhabitants, it equally increaseth in pauperism and crime. Neither hast thou any doctrine under the sun to provide against this.

3. But I have now opened the book of knowledge before thee. The place of my habitation and of the line of my light and of my holy angels I have made plain.

4. Thou mayest travel a thousand other roads, but none other shall be blessed with the light of my countenance.

5. As thou sayest at the door of the college: Young man, neither prayers nor confessions shall graduate thee in my house, to be companion to such as have passed on before thee.

6. So I say at the gates of my exalted heavens, unto the inhabitants of the earth: Only by knowledge and righteous works, done unto one another, shall ye be able to endure the light of my kingdoms.

7. Now, it shall come to pass, early in the kosmon era, that many shall be gifted to heal by laying on of hands. And they shall say: Behold, the lost gift is returned! Have I not done a good thing in the world?

8. But I say unto thee, O man, that these also mistake the coming of Jehovih's kingdom.

9. The healing of the sick may be compared unto giving alms to the poor, and saying: Have I not done a good work?

10. I say unto thee, these things were of the past cycles. They shall now consider what shall be done to prevent sickness. This is better than to heal. They shall now consider what shall be done to prevent poverty. This is better than giving to the poor.

11. I have not come to heal and treat the diseased in flesh or spirit; nor to re-establish any of the ancient doctrine or revelations.

12. I am not a patcher-up of old garments.

13. I am not an apologizer for ancient revelations, nor have I anything in common with what is past.

14. Neither their doctrines, nor sacred books, nor their Gods, nor Lords, nor Saviors are anything before me.

15. I am not come to captivate the ignorant and unlearned. Nor am I come to call sinners to repentance. Nor to convert the debauchee, nor to convert the profane man, nor to convert the harlot.

16. Sufficient have been other revelations unto all these.

17. Nor have I come to say: Behold, this is my book! And there shall be none other!

18. But, behold, I come to found Jehovih's kingdom on earth. I come to the wise and learned. And not to one man only; but to thousands.

19. That which I am uttering in these words, in this place, I am also uttering in the souls of thousands, and I will bring them together.

20. I do not command, saying: Thou shalt believe, because I, thy God, hath said it, or revealed it in this book.

21. I come as thy elder brother, in the name of Jehovih. I show thee how thou canst live without the governments of man. And how thou shalt live, in order to join in my resurrections.

22. Let not the Faithist of this day say: I will purity the government! I will leaven the whole mass!

23. But I say unto thee, thy God laboreth not in such method. The cure is, come thou out of Uz, and be thou clean.

24. Whoso hath more faith in Uz, let him remain in Uz; whoso hath faith in Jehovih, let him come into His kingdoms.

25. To know thy Father in heaven, O man, who hath learned this? They profess Him in words, but they belie Him in their behavior.

26. Renounce them, O my beloved; gather up thy household, and follow my voice, which I speak into thy soul from the Almighty. Follow thou thy highest knowledge, and make thyself a glory in Jehovih's kingdoms, forever and ever.

CHAPTER XVIII.

1. Hear the words of your God, O ye priests and preachers and rab'bahs, and all ye that set yourselves up before men, professing to hold the key to salvation and the places of my resurrections in heaven.

2. Hearken to the words of your elder brother, God of these heavens and the earth; behold, I will set you in judgment over yourselves; and the powers of Jehovih within you shall cry out for truth and justice.

3. Take your chosen of the congregation of your church, and make manifest whereof ye preach.

4. And prove that you have a good and sufficient doctrine for the salvation of your souls.

5. Choose ye the best of your flock, and show before your God an example of all such as serve not mammon, but Jehovih. Seal up their mouths; for ye shall judge them, not by words, but by what cometh of the soul.

6. And ye shall divide with one another your earthly possessions, being as brethren. And ye shall cast it upon the altar of your church, saying: We give it to the poor!

7. Or, if ye have houses, ye shall say to the poor: Come and dwell herein!

8. Persuade not yourselves, O men of darkness, that ye are not graded by the angels above; or, say to yourselves: Jehovih seeth not, nor heareth.

9. Nor say: When we are dead, our souls shall turn suddenly good, and ascend to the right hand of God.

10. Nor flatter yourselves, saying: We did the best we could under the circumstances.

11. Verily, I say unto you: Ye have not fulfilled the first law, which is to make clean your own corporeal bodies. Because ye have stuffed yourselves with carnal food, my holy angels can not approach you; neither can your understanding approach the place of my kingdoms.

12. How much less, then, have ye purified your souls? Wherein ye will not put away flesh, because ye love flesh, even so will ye not put away self-righteousness. Because ye shun the practice of labor, showing to the world, ye love words, and the renown of men and caste, making preferences in your churches, having rich and poor therein, which is itself your condemnation. For ye should divide with one another; putting in practice your doctrines.

13. What one of you hath a congregation who have given up all, and who make themselves alike and like, rich and poor?

14. Say ye, my kingdoms in heaven are after such manner.

15. I say unto you: Ye shall be bound in the first resurrection, in hada, to all these whom ye have professed to lead; neither shall ye ascend until the lowest of your congregations of spirits have put away uncleanness and selfishness; which is the first labor. And, after this, they shall learn to practice fellowship in union, for the resurrection of others.

16. Flatter not yourselves, that, because ye wear fine cloth, and ye preach, that ye are not responsible also. Nor hope, that when ye become spirits, ye shall ascend suddenly into places of delight. Ye are marked by your God!

17. Your souls are written all over with your deeds and works and words; and ye shall see yourselves as in a mirror, and of your own accord shun my kingdoms of light.

18. Because ye have learned words, and practiced only in words, behold, I come in this day to command practice in works. Not for a pittance, but for all ye have.

19. I am not come to destroy your religions; ye have done that already.

20. I come to give ye a religion wherein all men can be as brethren.

21. Even the infidel shall accept the Creator and good works. For he, being the fruit of your behavior, is even in the foreground in the march of my armies.

CHAPTER XIX.

GOD GIVETH A NEW RELIGION.

1. God said: Hear the words of your God, O ye preachers, priests and rab'bahs; seek not to gainsay my words.

2. In times past, I had such representatives, and I said unto them: Go ye, preach my doctrines unto the inhabitants of the earth; make them understand the way of the Almighty.

3. And ye shall take neither money, nor scrip for your labor, but be an example of faith in the promises of God.

4. So, your predecessors went forth fulfilling my commandments.

5. But, behold what ye are doing in this day! Ye patronize the man of wealth; ye boast of the riches of your congregations!

6. Ye receive salaries, and ye dwell in fine houses; my doctrines ye sell as merchandise! Ye have fine temples and fashionable audiences, and ye curry favor with those who are in affluence.

7. Ye go not to the drunkard's den, nor to the unfortunate woman; these ye take not in your arms, saying: My brother, my sister, come with me, I will show you the kingdom of God!

8. Behold, I have come to you in spirit and in truth, but ye put me off, saying: Is not the first duty to one's own household? Is not self-preservation the first law?

9. Now, I answer you: These questions spring from the beast, and not from the spirit.

10. Neither availeth it you one jot or tittle, to rise at break of day and recite prayers all day, nor to say: God help the poor! or: Blessed art thou, my God!

11. When ye can not purchase one another by flattery, how hope ye for the favor of the Almighty, by praise and prayers and flattery?

12. Behold, the selfishness of man hath made the world like a house on fire! My little ones are in pain and suffocation.

13. Go, then, quickly, to them, and provide a remedy. This is the new religion I give unto you: Demanding sacrifice of you, and your congregations, of all ye have, that is not in use and actual need.

14. And ye shall judge the limit thereof, remembering that whosoever is bound on earth, is bound in heaven.

15. I have drawn aside the veil of death, your sons and daughters, your fathers and mothers, the dead and the living, stand face to face.

16. And the angels are testimony unto you, that your doctrines, as ye practice them, are a blasphemy against the Almighty.

17. Ye persuade yourselves and your congregations, that, after death, the soul shall go far away, and to an exalted heaven. But, behold, they that are dead are with you. They testify unto you by the thousands, and by tens of thousands, that ye led them astray.

18. The evidence of the work of heaven is at your door. Ye stand accused before Jehovih, that ye practice not what ye preach; that ye fare sumptuously, and connive at sin; that ye preach what ye can not prove; by the angels of your own blood and kin, are ye accused.

19. Ye have no personal knowledge of heaven, and, in stubbornness of heart, ye dispute with my seers and prophets, who can prove before you, they have power to see unseen things, and to hear that which ye can not hear.

20. Ye study spiritual things with your corporeal senses; neither have ye capacity to see and hear the spirits of the dead. How much less, then, shall ye presume to interpret Jehovih and his kingdoms?

21. Now, behold, I come in this era, not only to declare to you, that the time of preaching is at an end, save wherein it is practiced in deed as it is spoken in word, but also to prophesy to you, that many of you will give up your calling, and preach no more.

22. And your temples and churches and meeting-houses shall be turned into consultation chambers, to find remedies against poverty, crime and debauchery.

23. And the congregations shall be enrolled, and, at the meetings, they shall be inquired after, to see if they are in need. And they shall have volunteers, who shall go about

seeking out the helpless and distressed.

24. So, that, instead of the congregations sitting to hear your sermons, they shall come as co-workers for Jehovih's children.

25. This is the new religion, which I give unto you; and, moreover, let it be a prophecy to you of the words of your God. For there is no such congregation this day in all the world; and yet, ere this generation pass away, this shall be proven before you.

CHAPTER XX.

GOD DECLARETH A DAY OF JUDGMENT, AND ALSO HE BEQUEATHETH LIBERTY UNTO ALL MEN.

1. God said: There shall be a day of judgment unto thee, O man. Soon or late, thou shalt take the matter into thine own hand; and thou shalt look into thine own soul to judge thyself. This is unto all men; none can escape it.

2. Such, then, is the judgment day. Let no man complain against the judge; thou shalt be thine own judge.

3. And every one judgeth against himself, and, soon or late, crieth out: O Jehovih, I have sinned against thee; in my youth I tried to find excuses for my behavior, but now I am broken down utterly.

4. After judgment, reformation and resurrection within man begin as a new tree of life.

5. But, whether thou shalt judge thyself in this life, or wait till thou art dead and risen in spirit, the matter is in thine own hands.

6. Yet, better would it be for thee, if thou wouldst sit in judgment on thyself every day of thy life.

7. But touching the matter, as to how thou shalt judge thyself, hear thou the wisdom of thy God, thy elder brother, and profit thou accordingly.

8. Because of the Ever Presence of Jehovih, thou wert quickened into a conscious being. As thy earth-body is of the earth, so is thy spirit of Jehovih. Nevertheless, spirit is the opposite of corporeal life; for the latter cometh to an end; but the spirit of man is a tree of everlasting life.

9. Thy spirit groweth by cultivation, which is by the practice of wisdom, truth, virtue, benevolence and affiliation unto others.

10. Think not, that the soul groweth by prayers or confessions unto this God, or that God; for, in whatsoever God thou firmly believest, him shalt thou worship, for he is thy choice. Nor shall any man prevent thee in this thy liberty. But, remember, the same rule holdeth unto all in this day: Thou shalt never see the God thou worshippest, save, indeed, it be an idol, or an image of wood or stone or some corporeal substance.

11. For, behold, I have cast out all Gods, Lords and Saviors on the earth and in the heavens of the earth.

12. And, when the spirits of the dead come to thee in sar'gis, saying: Behold me! I am thy Savior! I am thy Lord! I say unto thee: All such spirits are drujas.

13. Nevertheless, if thou worship a God, or Lord, let it be as a figure unto thee to cast thine eyes into thine own soul, to purify thyself in the sight of thy Creator, whom thou canst not doubt.

14. In such respect, it is no sin for thee to worship any good ideal, whom thou shalt emulate in thy behavior.

15. Yet this also shalt thou prove: That, whosoever of the ancients was great, or whatever Gods was well known, that thou settest thy soul on to love, behold, familiar spirits will come to thee to deceive thee, professing to be that ancient or that God.

16. And, when thou art dead, and thy soul risen from the dead, behold, some deceiving spirit will come to thee to use thee; neither shalt thou discover for a long season that thou hast been the dupe and slave of an unscrupulous master.

17. This day in the lower heavens there are millions of false Brahmas, millions of false Budhas, millions of false Kristes and millions of false Gabriel-Gods.

18. Whosoever bindeth himself to these names whilst on earth, becometh a fit subject for drujas to fall upon when he entereth heaven.

19. Think not that great wisdom cometh suddenly by dying; in thy early entrance into the es world, thou shalt be easily deceived.

20. For which reason thou shalt school thyself every day of thy life, that thy Creator only is thy God; and that Him thou shalt never see as thou seest a man or an angel; but that Him also thou canst see every day in the glory of His works.

21. With this faith in thy soul, thou shalt die and enter heaven fearlessly; and, when a pretended God or Savior cometh to thee asking tribute, thou shalt know of a truth he is false.

22. Now, therefore, when thou judgest thyself, to determine the balance of thy good and evil deeds, and thy good and evil thoughts, let thy Creator stand as the light of thy soul, and, through Him, judge thou thyself, but not as to thy worship, but as to thy works.

23. Neither shalt thou judge thyself by any God, or Lord, or Savior, or by any idol, or by any man or woman; for thou standest thyself second to Jehovih in thy attributes. It behooveth thee to make a God of thyself, in thy behavior and in thy words and deeds.

24. Neither shalt thou judge thyself by any sacred book, or any bible, in all the world; nor by the words within them purporting to be my words, or the words of any God, Lord or Savior.

25. For I have abolished all such sacred books and bibles and words and sayings contained in them, purporting to be my words and the words of any God, Lord or Savior.

26. Neither shalt thou bind thyself by them, nor judge thyself by anything that is written or printed in them.

27. But, behold, I declare a greater glory and judge unto thee in place thereof, which is Jehovih, thy Creator.

28. By Him and through Him shalt thou judge, and be judged.

29. Books are maculate; but Jehovih, never.

30. Neither shalt thou, henceforth, swear by any book under the sun; nor by any God, nor Lord, nor Savior, nor spirit, nor idol, nor image. But thou shalt swear by Jehovih, thy Creator.

31. To Jehovih only shalt thou covenant thyself, and this shalt thou do in thine own way only, and not according to any book, or bible, or priest, or church, or spirit.

32. Behold, the olden times are past away; and thy God setteth aside the bondages of the olden times also.

33. Sufficient were they for the times they were created. A man shall not be bound as a child; neither shall the judgment of man be bound by the things that were intended for man before he attained judgment.

34. Hast thou not beholden the signs of the times? What I here give in words, Jehovih manifesteth over all the length and breadth of the world.

35. None can stay the hand of the Almighty.

CHAPTER XXI.
GOD DECREETH AGAINST INFIDELITY.

1. God said: Hear the words of thy God, O man. In the ancient times, I came as a father to a child, dictating unto man.

2. Now, that thou hast attained to comprehensive judgment, Jehovih hath inspired thee to liberty, and to think for thyself, and to consider what is best for thee.

3. And thy God cometh not now as a dictator, but as thy elder brother, with ample experience.

4. And I say unto thee, after the manner of thy professors in the college to their graduated classes: Behold, thou art free; go thy way, and no longer hope to hold thy God accountable for thy behavior.

5. For, with thy freedom, thou also attainest to responsibility.

6. Think not, because I emancipate thee from the God and Lords and Saviors of the ancients:

7. And from the bibles and sacred books of the ancients; and from the ancient commandments and injunctions, that, as a consequence, thou art not bound in fidelity to thy Creator.

8. More art thou bound now than before; for thou shalt not, henceforth, throw the responsibility of thy conduct on to this man, nor that man, nor this God, nor Lord, nor Savior, nor holy book, nor bible, nor priest, nor church decree.

9. So, that thy fidelity to thy Creator and to thy fellow-man, in righteousness, love and good works, shall be the most sacred study of thy life.

10. And thy example from day to day shall be a perpetual register of thy accountability; verily shalt thou be a living sermon before men and before Jehovih.

11. And, wherein thy behavior detracteth from the grades of thy fellow-men, thou shalt be bound in the behavior of those that copy after thee, and, for the shortness thou bringest them into, thou shalt suffer for them in time to come.

12. Beware, O man, for this rule applieth unto all the generations of men: That, by sudden emancipation from an old condition, man runneth into another extreme, from which spring libertinism and licentiousness.

13. For which reason, rather shall thou proclaim before the multitude the responsibilities of the new condition, than try to win their applause by proclaiming their emancipation from the old.

14. Because I have opened the heavens, the spirits of the dead return to thee, and commune in thy household; flatter not thyself that the whole of the Father's kingdoms are revealed to thee, and that the angels who converse with thee, can make plain the dominions of the higher heavens.

15. Many of these shall return to thee, saying: There is no hell, no satan, no God, or Lord, nor anything in this world to make thee afraid. For, of a truth, the hell they looked for, they found not; nor found they a God, nor Lord, nor Savior, such as they

had hoped to find. And, for this reason, such angels are jubilant for the time being.

16. Nevertheless, a time shall come to them also, when they shall tire of dwelling on the earth, in the places of their mortal kin; and they shall seek resurrection into more exalted places, where wisdom and purity dwell. Then, indeed, shall they begin to comprehend the ways of the kingdoms of the Almighty.

17. And they will cry out in pain; pleading for pity, compassion and help. And after that, when they come to thee, they will also proclaim, even as thy God now doth: That the commandments must be fulfilled:

18. To love the Creator above all else;

19. And thy neighbor as thyself;

20. Sell all thou hast, and give to the poor;

21. Return good for evil;

22. Do good unto others, with all thy wisdom and strength;

23. Abnegate self in all respects;

24. Making thyself a servant to thy Creator;

25. Owning or possessing nothing under the sun;

26. And look into thy soul, to judge thyself constantly, to discover where and how thou shalt do the most good;

27. Complaining not against Jehovih for anything that happeneth;

28. Making thy neighbor rejoice in thee;

29. Making thyself affiliative;

30. Without self-righteousness above any one;

31. Being a producer of something good;

32. And learn to rejoice in thine own life, with singing and dancing and with a jovial heart, paying due respect to rites and ceremonies, that all things may be orderly before Jehovih.

33. Remember the words of thy God, O man, when angels or men advise thee against these commandments, they have little to offer thee that will promote the harmony of the state.

34. Consider, therefore, that whatsoever promoteth the greatest harmony and wisdom within the state, hath also been discovered and is in practice in the higher heavens.

35. And, wherein it hath been proven to thee, that a state divided against itself can not stand, even so are the heavens above not divided, but as a unit.

36. Judge, then, O man, when one spirit cometh to thee preaching one thing, and another spirit cometh to thee preaching another thing, their words are proof that they have not yet entered the harmonious heavens of thy God.

37. And it is because of the inharmony of thine own soul, that thou art open to these conflicting messengers. This is infidelity against the All Person, Jehovih. And such conflicting spirits deny the Person and the Unity of the Almighty.

38. Let not thy emancipation from the bondage of the doctrines of the ancients lead thee into infidelity against Jehovih.

CHAPTER XXII.

THE FATHER'S KINGDOM ON EARTH.

1. God said: I have heard thy prayer, O man: Thy kingdom come on earth, as it is in

heaven.

2. Hast thou considered thy words? And art thou prepared for it? Hast thou fulfilled the commandments? And lovest thou thy neighbor as thyself? And hast thou done unto the least, as thou desirest thy Creator to do unto thee?

3. Now, behold, Jehovih hath sent me, thy God, to answer thy prayer.

4. I demand of thee, that thou hast no favorite doctrine above thy neighbor;

5. And that thou art servant to no God, nor Lord, nor Savior, nor church, unacceptable to any man in all the world.

6. But, that thou servest Jehovih with all thy wisdom and strength, by doing good unto thy fellow-men with all thy might.

7. That, because thou art strong, or wise, or rich, thou understandest, that thou shalt use these excellencies for raising up such as have them not, believing, that Jehovih so provided thee to that end.

8. Consider, O man! Thou hast a kingdom already. Wouldst thou have two kingdoms?

9. Behold, the kingdom of man hath its power in armies and ships of war.

10. The kingdoms of thy Father have not these, but love, wisdom, righteousness and peace.

11. I demand of thee, that thou shalt give up thy army and navy. Art thou prepared to say: To whom smiteth me on one cheek, I turn the other to be smitten also?

12. Is thy faith still more in weapons of death, than in the Voice of Everlasting Life? Esteemest thou thy army and navy more to be depended on, than Jehovih?

13. Art thou willing to sacrifice thy time and money and self-interest for sake of Jehovih's kingdom?

14. Use thy judgment, O man. Since the time of the ancients till now, the only progress towards the Father's kingdom hath been through sacrifice.

15. What less canst thou expect?

16. If thou sellest what thou hast, and givest to the poor, behold thy neighbors will imprison thee for a madman.

17. If thou abnegate thyself and labor for others, they will persecute thee, and revile thee.

18. If thou shouldst profess to love thy neighbor as thyself, they would mock at thee.

19. Therefore, I declare unto thee, O man, in the land of Uz the Father's kingdom can not be.

20. But thou shalt go hence; and, behold, I will go with thee, and with thy neighbor, and show thee how to build, even as a kingdom in heaven.

CHAPTER XXIII.

GOD JUDGETH UZ, COMMONLY CALLED THE WORLD'S PEOPLE.

1. God said: I am not come in this era to judge the drunkard, the harlot and thieves and murderers; these are known unto thee, O man.

2. I am not come to repeat former judgments against whom all men understand to be sinful; for, behold, I gave governments into the hands of men, to deal unto such themselves.

3. But I am come to the leaders of men; to kings, queens, emperors and presidents; and to philosophers and men of learning, priests, rab'bahs, cardinals and popes; and to

merchants, bankers, manufacturers, farmers, shippers, and hucksters.

4. Such as pass unscathed before the laws and government of man, and are reckoned passably wise and good before the world.

5. And not even to such of these as are bad men in disguise, who escape condemnation before the courts, by cunning and stratagem.

6. But I am come to the best of all of them, be they true Brahmins, true Ka'yuans, true Budhists, true Kriste'yans, or true Mohammedans.

7. Therefore, O man, hear the judgment of thy God against them: They are not united and affiliated as brothers.

8. But the best of all of them are as so many individual entities pulling in different ways, every one for himself.

9. The Brahmins are not communal; the Ka'yuans are not communal; neither are the Budhists, nor the Kriste'yans, nor the Mohammedans; neither the philosophers, priests, merchants, nor any one people in all the world.

10. There is no fullness of heaven amongst any of them. They are divided into thousands of ideas and projects.

11. Now, hear me, O man, and consider the wisdom of thy God: Satan is wiser than any of these I have named.

12. For satan hath made armies of soldiers communal. He hath discovered the power of affiliation and discipline.

13. Behold, a thousand soldiers are more efficient than ten thousand men, unorganized.

14. Judgment is rendered against the best of men in all the world, because they are inorganic for righteousness, and for establishing the Father's kingdom.

15. This, then, is what befalleth the nations and peoples of the earth: Alike and like the angels of heaven minister unto mortals (save wherein thy God and his Lords provide especially otherwise), the inorganic heavenly regions to the inorganic inhabitants of the earth.

16. Now, behold, I said unto thee, in the olden times, try the spirits, and see, if they be of God.

17. For the angels who wander about on the earth know not my kingdoms, and they deny me, and deny all order and system and discipline in heaven and earth.

18. And each and all such angels, coming to mortals, do so on their own account, assuming any form and name they may find acceptable unto men.

19. Such angels have not yet entered the first resurrection; nor belong they to any disciplined kingdom in heaven.

20. And all mortals, such as I have named to thee as the best and highest of mortals, enter the es world (after death), only into the inorganic regions of heaven.

21. Neither can they enter into the lowest of my kingdoms until they abnegate self and learn affiliation.

22. Therefore, after death, they remain, for the most part, in their former places: The merchant in his counting-house, the banker in his bank, the shipper in his place, the philosopher in his place, the pope in his place, the king in his, the farmer in his.

23. Neither have they power or wisdom to go to any other place; and they stroll about, like one that hath lost his master. Neither will they affiliate with other angels; but, in stubbornness and moroseness, persist in working out an individual identity, until they are

broken down in sorrow and darkness, which may be in a few years, or it may be hundreds of years.

24. And, then, my holy ones come to them, and carry them away to my es'yan schools.

CHAPTER XXIV.

GOD SHOWETH HOW TO KNOW THE KIND OF ANGELS THAT MINISTER UNTO MORTALS.

1. God said: One rule have I given unto all men, whereby it may be known what kind of angels minister unto them; that rule is a mortal's own manifestations and behavior.

2. Whoso manifesteth serving himself chiefly, hath little light from my organic kingdoms; but whoso serveth Jehovih by laboring for others, with all his wisdom and strength, is attended by the light of my organic kingdoms.

3. Judge thyself, O man, as to thyself, who and what angels attend thee.

4. Behold, one man will say to thee: I have a band of wise and most ancient angels who attend me! Another will say: I have very Gods who attend me!

5. Judge them not by their words, nor by the names professed; but judge them by the work they accomplish. Nevertheless, hold thy peace in regard to them.

6. This rule do I also give unto thee, in regard to the angels who attend mortals.

7. As, for example, thou knowest that a soldier is not permitted to go away from his regiment, and pursue other employment.

8. The soldier belongeth to his regiment; he is one with the regiment; he moveth therewith; the affairs and business of the regiment are his affairs and business also.

9. Even so is it with my organic heavens, wherein es'yans become volunteers to accomplish resurrection.

10. And, thereafter, they apply themselves not to isolated development, but to affiliation, for attaining to the higher kingdoms.

11. The least of my organic kingdoms containeth half a thousand million angels; and many of them contain five thousand millions.

12. These are composed of thousands of branches, suited to the various talents created with all; so, that all who enter find a delightful adaptation.

13. When thou wert taught of old, to say: May thy kingdom come on earth as it is in heaven, it was instruction given thee to lead thee in the method of my dominions.

14. As to wandering spirits, they have not yet entered the first resurrection; but, such as have enlisted in my organic kingdoms, are called es'yans, whilst learning the rites and discipline, and are said to be in the first resurrection. And such as have become organic workers are in the second resurrection, and this is a kingdom of heavens.

15. This rule is also uniform in all my heavenly kingdoms: That, after the entrance to the first resurrection, none of the angels return as individuals, to commune with mortals, save as hereinafter mentioned, or save when especially commissioned by me or my Lords.

16. Think not, that my discipline is less systematic than that of a mortal general's army, or that the heavens of thy God are permitted to run at loose ends, and without order or concert of action.

17. Be reasonable, O man, weigh these things according to thine own observation and judgment, for there is not, in all the heavens, any wide departure from what thou hast in some form a counterpart-resemblance on earth.

CHAPTER XXV.

GOD SHOWETH HOW AND WHEN THE SECOND RESURRECTION MANIFESTEH UNTO MORTALS.

1. God said: In the cities and country places, I have innumerable Lords, apportioned to districts and to the mortals and angels thereof.

2. And my Lords know the rates and grades of their people, their occupations, their aspirations, their labor, their behavior, private and public.

3. Now, behold, I have said unto my Lords: The era of dictation is past; man hath arrived at kosmon. Declare ye the light of my heavens unto man; but let man judge himself, and labor to save himself, that he may have honor and glory thereby.

4. And I further said unto my Lords: Man hath prayed, saying: Thy kingdom come on earth as it is in heaven. Now, this I give unto you: That, where men abnegate self, and affiliate into a communal brotherhood, after the manner of my heavenly kingdoms, then shall ye affiliate my organic angels with such mortals, and make them one with my second resurrections.

5. And ye shall surround such communal brotherhoods with the light of my kingdoms, thereby controlling the angelic intercourse with mortals, so that drujas and vampire spirits cannot molest them.

6. And these brotherhoods shall be taught to question not the spirits and oracles on personal matters, but for light and truth as to what will contribute to meliorating the condition of man, and as to light and truth, regarding the higher and lower heavens; and as to attaining spiritual gifts and great wisdom.

7. And such mortals shall have times and places for worshipful matters; and these times shall be in concert with my Lord of that district; and the light of his throne shall be given unto such a brotherhood.

8. The members of such a brotherhood shall not desire a leader; neither will any one of them desire to be a leader. For, if one should so desire, he would not be of the Godhead, but of himself.

9. Moreover, none of the members of such a brotherhood shall go off, of his own accord, to minister as an individual to the inhabitants of Uz. But each and all in the brotherhood shall concentrate their profits and force unto one end and object.

10. Even so, O man, are my organic heavens; all the members of each heaven being as a unit with the whole, they waste not their strength and time in isolated endeavors.

11. Whereby, when a prophet foolishly boasteth to thee, as to having some high-raised angel, with a loud-sounding name, as his special guardian and guide, know thou such prophet is in the hands of drujas, who have not entered my heavenly kingdoms.

12. Neither hath it ever happened on the earth with any individual man, raised up by me or my Lords for a specific work, like Moses, or Ka'yu, or Sakaya, or any other, that they knew of or boasted of any especial angel over them; but all of them experienced the light, which was as a pillar of fire.

13. Even such is the manifestation of the second resurrection through my Lord and his Holy Council.

14. And the manifestations are not like those of a mere magician; but the accomplishment of something that embraceth nations, empires and mighty peoples.

15. For this reason, O man, I declare unto thee that the Father's kingdom is now being founded on earth, and the mortal manifestation thereof is near at hand.

16. But it shall not come in this era, as in the past, through any one great leader-forth; but it shall appear as a spontaneous light, permeating the soul of thousands; and they shall come forth, establishing Jehovih in truth and fullness.

17. Now, therefore, O man, consider the judgment of God against all such as are called the best of men, the wisest of men, the greatest of kings or queens or popes; for none of these have even entered the first resurrection in their own practice.

CHAPTER XXVI.
GOD JUDGETH THE ASCETIC.

1. God said: There are such as shut themselves up in colleges (convents and nunneries), and such as retire to the forests, devoting their lives to prayers, confessions and rites and ceremonies, being most systematic in routine, and in being shut away from the Uzians.

2. And they allot certain ones as leaders and overseers, making themselves inquisitors over one another, in hope of purifying their thoughts and aspirations, constantly trapping one another for shortness, and, then, submitting to petty punishment and inflictions, hoping thereby to check evil thoughts, words and actions.

3. Judgment is rendered against all such people, be they mortals or angels.

4. For these are the methods of the imprisonment of mind. All such mortals are preparing themselves for the bondage of drujas on their entrance into the es world.

5. Yea, even in that same college (convent and nunnery), shall they be immured after death, by thousands of drujas who inhabit the place, who profess to have some scheme of projected salvation.

6. All such people are the manifestation of darkness instead of light. Jehovih created man with capacity for developing talent to do good unto others.

7. Now, behold, these ascetics labor for themselves in these foolish proceedings; they do not these things in order to meliorate the condition of their neighbors. Neither have they shown, in a single instance, where a benefit resulted to the state in consequence of their practices.

8. They call their initiations sacred, but I declare unto thee, they are a blasphemy against Jehovih. They are as a snare for the imprisonment of the mind and the soul.

9. And, after death, these people are prevented by their drujan masters from entering heavenly places of resurrection, becoming, instead, slaves in the es world, to pursue such calling and practice as may be put upon them.

10. For the same rule holdeth on earth and in heaven, as regardeth the bondage of the mind. If, by imposing rites and ceremonies, and by the stratagems and cunning of mortal priests, they can be captured on earth, even so can they be retained in bondage in heaven.

11. And it happeneth with them, that even as they honestly believe they are right on earth, so will they persist they are right in heaven, even willingly submitting to cruelty and to torture, in order to prove their fidelity.

12. Be considerate, O man, of the words of thy God: He, who created thee, gave to thee one star of light whereby thou mayst determine truth and wisdom.

13. Whatever doctrine showeth self as the chief consideration, even if it be for obtaining wisdom or supposed purity for self sake, is not of Jehovih.

14. The aborigine, that roveth foolishly in the forest, standeth higher, therefore, before thy God, than doth the nun or the ascetic. For though the former liveth for self only, yet he is not bound in spirit.

15. In all things, thou shalt weigh the object and end aimed at, and the final result; and, wherein self standeth as a part, or whole consideration, know thou such matter is not of Jehovih, but of satan.

16. It is not sufficient for the apologist of satan to say: O we dwell in the colleges (nunneries and convents), in order to pray for Uzians.

17. But thou shalt weigh their prayers also, and thou shalt estimate the value thereof by what is accomplished. And thou shalt prove whether their prayers provided harvests of wheat and corn, and food and clothing for the poor, and education for the unlearned, or any other thing that was good.

18. Be thou not put off by the cunning of satan's words in the mouths of priests or popes; but look matters in the face, and be thou a God thyself in discerning things that meliorate the condition of man.

CHAPTER XXVII.
GOD JUDGETH CHARITIES.

1. God said: A certain man built a dam across a river, using only stones, but no cement. And the water ran through the crevices, rendering the dam worthless.

2. Then came certain neighbors to him, saying: Thou shalt apply cement to the crevices.

3. So, the man went to the lower side, and applied cement; but, lo and behold, the result was only temporary, for the water washed the cement away.

4. Again his neighbors said unto him: Apply thou the cement at the upper side, and the water will carry it into the crevices, where it will remain with good effect.

5. And the man did so, and, behold, the dam was a complete structure.

6. After such manner, O man, consider all charities. Thou mayst apply thy riches, and thy estates for charity's sake, but of no profit under the sun.

7. When the man applied the cement, where it was not self-sustaining, the waters washed it away.

8. Wherein thou appliest charity, and it be not self-sustaining, judgment is rendered against thee.

9. When the man applied the cement toward the fountain, it became self-sustaining.

10. Wherein thou appliest charity, and it be self-sustaining, judgment is rendered in thy favor.

11. When thou meetest thy neighbor on the road, and he hath fallen down, and broken his legs, and can not stand, consider how foolish it would be, to lift him up, and, then, let him fall again. Flatter not thyself, that such would be charity.

12. And yet, how much of the so-called charity of the world is of that kind.

13. Thou mayst feed three drunkards' families, and flatter thyself thou hast done charity worthily; but, if thou hast not done that which will make them no longer in need of charity, thou hast done little.

14. Another man may not feed them, but he may reform them, and put them in the way to be self-sustaining. Such a man will have done a hundred-fold greater charity.

15. To open the way for employment and industry, this is the greatest of all charity. For, by these avenues, charity will not be needed, even for the aged, nor for orphans.

16. Consider, then, how little any people have to boast of for charity's sake. Even their asylums and poor-houses and homes for the aged and helpless are so many witnesses of condemnation against the people who built them; because some great wrongs and evils existing within the state were also built by the people in the first place.

17. They are as paint and plaster, hiding and redeeming them, in some measure, for the sins of a wicked people.

18. And, when such a city saith: Behold us! what a charitable people we are! I say unto thee, that that city understandeth not the kingdom of thy God.

19. Yet, thou shalt avoid going to the other extreme, doing nothing, which is worst of all. But thou shalt go to the root of the matter; thy charity shall be directed to prevent the causes of such ill-fortunes.

CHAPTER XXVIII.

GOD SHOWETH HOW TO DO CHARITY.

1. God said: O man, consider the folly of individual effort! One will say: I help my family and my neighbors; let others do so, and all will be well.

2. This is his philosophy and doctrine! Now, I say unto thee, this is just what hath been tried for thousands of years, and it hath resulted in impotency all the while.

3. It hath been said: Sell all thou hast and give it to the poor; but I say unto thee, thou shalt not do this.

4. Though that opened the way to salvation in the ancient days, it is not sufficient in this day. Neither shalt thou hope, that, by giving to the poor, thou shalt escape condemnation.

5. But thou shalt go to the foundation of things, and go systematically.

6. Thy efforts shall not be single-handed, but thou shalt unite with others; and, together, ye shall provide a remedy against poverty.

7. Remembering, it is wiser to accomplish with the young than with the aged. For the mature will be dead in a few years; and, in that day, those that are children will be mature.

8. Better is it, that ye provide a way unto ten fatherless children, than for forty people that are grown.

9. But, even in this, ye may err toward the children. For, to provide them an asylum in infancy, saying: Behold, what a good work we have done! showeth that ye measure not as your God measureth.

10. For it is not sufficient that ye feed and clothe little ones; but ye shall teach them a trade, and occupations, and give them learning, so that, when they are grown, they can sustain themselves.

11. But, even yet, your work is not the highest; but ye shall so provide them, they will not only be self-supporting, but that they shall be willing and capable of rescuing others, as they were rescued.

12. After this, ye shall see to it, that all things are so provided, that, after your death, your institution be not liable to fall into disuse or perversion.

13. This is founding the Father's kingdom on earth; and whoso laboreth thus, shall be ministered unto by my heavenly kingdoms for the glory of Jehovih.

14. Therefore, let your charity be not for a year, nor for a hundred years; but, be ye the corner-stones, founding places on earth where shall rest perpetually a system that will provide a new race, where poverty and crime and helplessness cannot enter.

15. Ye thus become, even in mortality, members of my second resurrection in heaven.

CHAPTER XXIX.

GOD JUDGETH THE MISSIONARIES.

1. God said: In the olden time, I commanded thee, saying: Go forth into all the world, preaching my doctrines, chief of which was: There is but ONE, even the I AM; Him shalt thou love with all thy heart and thy mind and thy soul, and love thy neighbor as thyself, having faith in Jehovih through righteousness and good works.

2. Moreover, I declared unto thee, that whosoever fulfilled my commandments, believing in Jehovih, certain signs should be given unto them, whereby they might be known unto men.

3. And thou wentst forth, and, behold, my signs went with thee, and thou didst accomplish service unto Jehovih.

4. But it came to pass, in course of time, thou didst forsake thy Creator, setting up Lords and Saviors of thine own, worshipping them instead of Jehovih.

5. And I looked down upon thee from my holy place in heaven, and I saw that thou hadst become obsessed with evil spirits, thousands and millions of them, who professed to be the Lords and Saviors whom thou worshippedst.

6. And I said unto my Lords: Behold, man hath erected an idol in heaven, go ye to them that preach in my name, and take from them the signs and miracles which I gave.

7. And my Lords came unto thee, finding thou wert gone abroad over all the world. And my Lords cut thee short of signs and miracles.

8. For this was the judgment of thy God against thee, because thou hadst turned against the I AM, teaching another God than Jehovih.

9. And I made this, my edict, manifest on the earth; for I withdrew my holy angels from thee, and, from that time forth, withersoever thou hast gone, behold, I have given thee none of the signs whereof I had been liberal before.

10. And I measured the work of thy hand in the places of thy mission, and I found that thou wert impotent to establish good works.

11. And, following in thy path, whithersoever thou hadst gone, thousands and millions of drujas followed thee; and thy people went with weapons of destruction, slaughtering those Jehovih had created alive, in order to establish thy idol-God.

12. And my Lords numbered all the places of thy missionaries in all the earth, and behold, there was not one place, which thou hadst established, which was not given up to sin and blasphemy against Jehovih.

13. Neither hadst thou raised up any member, or members in all of them, that practiced even the first commandments.

14. And I said unto thee: Behold, thou hast not the signs and miracles; give up thy preaching, and go thou amongst the barbarians teaching them how to plant, to sow and reap and clothe themselves, and to live in houses.

15. But this was untasteful to thee in thy hypocrisy; and thou madest of thy occupation a

scheme to live in worthlessness on the contributions of thy neighbors.

16. And, behold, thy doctrines have not prospered in any place in all the world to work righteousness for the glory of the Almighty.

17. Flatter not thyself that thou hast done a good work, because thou hast taught the ignorant to say: Brahma, Brahma! or Budha, Budha! or Lord, Lord! or to sing anthems in praise of thy idol-God.

18. Thy God measureth thee and thy converts according to such purification as addeth to the glory of everlasting life, as well in heaven as on earth. And such purification manifesteth not only in words, but in good works for the glory of the Father.

19. And when it hath come to pass that thy mission brought about a war afterward, behold, that war is also upon thy head.

20. I measure not a little good that happeneth for a moment, and there an end. I comprehend the lapse of scores of years and hundreds of years; and I weigh the whole matter, and render judgment in the aggregate.

21. Neither judge I by man's inventions or mechanical contrivances. My judgments are in reference to man's comfort and joy in life, and to his resurrection in my heavens.

22. According to a man's, or a people's, ascending grade in approximating Jehovih, so shall a man and a people be judged.

CHAPTER XXX.
GOD JUDGETH DOMINIONS.

1. God said: Now, behold, a certain rich man coveted his neighbors' children, and he went about and captured many of them. And withal he was mighty above his neighbors, and none of them could regain their offspring.

2. And a certain rab'bah inquired of Jehovih concerning the matter. And Jehovih answered him, saying: Whatsoever he coveted and hath taken, suffer him to keep. What he hath taken exultingly shall be a bondage unto him in sorrow, in time to come; for he shall provide according to law.

3. And it so happened that a famine came upon that land, and, according to the laws, the rich had to provide unto the kin of their own households.

4. And, behold, the rich man's possessions were consumed by the neighbors whom he had robbed, and great sorrow came upon him.

5. Such, O man, is the way of the dominions of men. A mighty king stretcheth forth his hand to possess his neighbor's kingdom, and Jehovih giveth it unto him.

6. And that king exulteth, saying: Behold my possessions and my power!

7. Hear, now, the judgment of thy God, O man: Soon or late, all things answer unto Jehovih in a way man imagineth not. Whoso coveteth and receiveth, is bound unto Jehovih.

8. And, when a king possesseth himself of a new country, he not only receiveth its riches but its misfortunes also. The profits and losses are all his.

9. And the sins of the people are his, and are henceforth upon his head.

10. And, when a famine cometh upon that country, the king shall be responsible therefore.

11. And he shall supply every want of the people, or judgment shall be upon his head.

12. And for all of the newly acquired subjects, who may be in sickness or distress, the king shall be judged.

13. Moreover, judgment shall pursue that king into the es world; and the subjects he took unto himself on earth shall be his in heaven to redeem, and provide for, and educate.

14. Neither shall he have exaltation in my heavens faster than the lowest of his subjects.

15. Behold, I not only bequeath the glory and joy of the Father's kingdom on earth, but I reveal also the responsibilities which shall be hereafter known to mortals.

16. Man shall not only perceive the justice of my judgments, but he shall realize the power of my hand upon kingdoms and empires.

17. I show man not only the way of liberty, but the way of bondage. He shall know understandingly the ways of my dominions, and the judgment that is upon him.

18. For every one whom the king causeth to be slain, in order to possess a new country, the king shall mete out retribution until all his enemies do pardon and forgive him.

19. Behold, I have revealed the grades and rates; and such king shall perceive, that his bondage can not be less than six generations, but may be twenty or forty generations, ere he reacheth beyond the second resurrection.

20. And the same rules shall apply to every king and queen and emperor, and every other ruler in all the world.

21. The resurrection in heaven of each and every one of them shall be with, and no faster than those they ruled over on earth.

22. And they shall be responsible to all their subjects for deaths resulting from wars, wherein the subjects were used for the glory and power of the king. And for all famines, pestilences, and all other injuries that come upon the multitude through any shortness in the king's government.

23. And for the poverty of the people, and for their ignorance and crime; nor shall the king escape retribution for any good thing he might have done, but did not accomplish.

24. And for all the profit and service the king receiveth on earth from his subjects, he shall render back to them an equivalent profit and service, either on earth, or in heaven.

25. Let not the king or other ruler, any longer flatter himself that death effaceth the bondage of man unto his subject and neighbor.

26. Behold, by opening the gates of heaven, I have also given you the glory thereof; and, with it, I also give you the responsibilities.

27. I have brought the angels to your door; they bring you news of great joy, and bring you also the afflictions ye cast upon them.

28. I told those of the olden time, that sword should answer sword; war should answer war; and peace receive in peace.

29. Such, then, is the judgment of thy God upon dominion; and this shall be ratified in time to come by every ruler on the face of the earth.

CHAPTER XXXI.
GOD JUDGETH THE MAN OF PROMISE.

1. God said: Consider the judgments of God, O thou man of many promises.

2. Behold, I have heard thee say: O God, if I were rich; or, if this undertaking hold good; or, if I am spared, then will I do something handsome for the Father's kingdom!

3. And thy vows have been registered in heaven, over and over again.

4. And my angels have labored with thee to fulfill thy promise. And, yet, thou dost not regard thy word. But thou holdest to thy earthly possessions, saying: Wait yet a little while.

5. Hear thou, then, the judgment of thy God, for it is that which thou shalt put upon thyself after thine entrance into the es world.

6. Which is, that thou shalt be bound in heaven till thou shalt accomplish what thou mightst have done, but failed to do.

7. And this is the penalty for neglecting, on earth, to fulfill the light that was given unto thee: Thou shalt, in heaven, accomplish without money, what thou couldst have done with money. And the difference it requireth to do a thing without means, as compared to what might be done by one with means, is the extra bondage and duration that shall be upon thy head and soul.

8. To all men, who set out with a promise to accomplish charity, or any good for the resurrection or melioration of man, and fail to do it, the same judgment shall be upon them in heaven. Nor shall they rise above the first resurrection until they have fulfilled the same in all particulars. Thus shall they judge themselves in heaven.

9. It is not sufficient for thee, O man, to say: I saw not my way clear as to the best method of doing a thing, and so I waited.

10. The commandment of Jehovih is upon thee, to do what thou canst, according to thy highest light and ability to accomplish. In this respect, then, thou shalt find no excuse, because thou knew not the best way.

11. Neither mattereth it, the amount of thy riches being less than another man's riches.

12. Nor shalt thou find an excuse, in saying: I did more according to my means than did my neighbor.

13. One man shall not be judged by another; but all shall be judged according to the light of Jehovih in them, and according to what He hath given unto them.

CHAPTER XXXII.

GOD JUDGETH AGAINST WAR.

1. God said: Now, behold, O man, I have declared my first and second resurrections unto thee. And in like manner is the third resurrection, but still higher. And so on are all the heavens of Jehovih, higher and higher, until the inhabitants thereof and therein become very Lords and Gods.

2. Nevertheless, hear thou, O man, the wisdom of thy God, and be appreciative of the way of resurrection being opened up unto thee.

3. Now, I declare unto thee, there are angels lower than the first resurrection; being incapacitated, from various causes, from knowing who they are, whence they came, or whither they are going. Yea, many of them know not words of speech, nor signs, nor tokens; but are as destitute of knowledge as young babes.

4. Many of them died in infancy; some of them were killed by abortion; some of them were idiots, and some of them deranged.

5. Many of these live by fetal. And that thou mayst know, what fetal is, behold. Jehovih hath given thee testimony in mortality, whereby, when a young child sleepeth with a very old person, that child is devoured of its substance. In such case, the old person is fetaled on the young child; the old person is said to live by fetal.

6. Now, hear thou, O man, the judgment of thy God: Half the people, born into the world, including still-births and abortions, die in infancy. Therefore, there are a thousand million angel infants fetaled on the earth every thirty years.

7. These angels never obtain objective knowledge of the corporeal earth, but are compelled to learn subjectively earthly things through mortals upon whom they are fetaled.

8. Judgment is rendered against all nations and peoples on the earth for this great darkness, these early deaths. And, because these angels are thus bound to mortals, and can not go away from them until such time as mortals die, mortals are responsible, and bound to train them up by examples of righteousness and good works.

9. Now, aside from such angels, there are such as are slain in war, whose minds are in chaos, who, dying in the heat of passion and fear and anger, become wild and bound on battle-fields, or, mayhap, stroll away into deserted houses and castles, and are lost, bewildered and unapproachable.

10. Of these, there are hundreds of millions; and they are in all countries and amongst all peoples in the world.

11. They are distracted and tormented with their own fears and bewilderment.

12. Judgment is rendered against all nations and peoples in the world who engage in war, thus bringing these afflictions upon the angels of heaven.

13. Judgment is rendered against every nation and all people in the world who carry on war, or who are accessory to war, whereby any man, created alive by Jehovih, is slain, in defense of any king or other ruler, or in defense of any country or government in all the world.

14. And, whether war be offensive or defensive, my judgment is against its aiders and abettors, and against the kings and queens, or other rulers who are parties to war, willingly, knowingly, or otherwise.

15. And I judge him guilty also who is general, commodore, captain, sergeant or private that engageth in war or taketh part therein, aiding, abetting, or otherwise, whereby any man, created alive by Jehovih, is slain or caused to suffer death.

16. And yet, aside from angels who are in chaos, there are hundreds of millions who are in declension, instead of resurrection. Such angels are those who in mortal life were whipped and tortured in prisons, or, mayhap, were hanged, or otherwise put to death.

17. These angels take delight in evil instead of good. Sometimes they go about singly, and sometimes in gangs of hundreds and even thousands.

18. In olden times, the false Gods used such angels to fulfill curses on mortals; and to carry poison in the air, and inoculate mortals with foul diseases.

19. Behold, in this day, my angels have shown thee that they can bring flowers and ponderous bodies; even so could the false Gods with their trained warrior angels, who delighted in evil, cast mortals in death by poisons and suffocation.

20. Judgment is rendered against all nations and peoples who use prisons as places for whipping and torturing prisoners; and against all nations and peoples who put to death, by hanging, shooting, or in any way whatsoever, any prisoner, or any person whom Jehovih created alive.

21. Judgment is rendered against the judge and the jury who condemn to death any man; and against the law-makers who make, or have left in force, a law authorizing death as a

penalty against any person whom Jehovih created alive.

22. And this is the bondage I put upon all such as obey not my judgments, and conform thereto: They shall not rise above the first resurrection in heaven, whilst war remaineth upon the earth. Even though their bondage be a hundred years, or a thousand years, yet this, my judgment against them, shall not be put aside.

23. Neither shall any king, nor queen, nor any other ruler in all the world, impress as a soldier, any man who is unwilling to engage in war. And whosoever obeyeth not this my judgment shall not rise above the first resurrection in heaven whilst war remaineth on the earth.

24. Neither will I more consider the prayers of any king, or queen, or any other ruler, or any nation or people in all the world who engage in war, offensive or defensive, or who aid or abet war in any way whatsoever.

25. But I will abandon all such people; and my Lords shall abandon them; and my holy angels shall abandon them.

26. And they shall be left as a prey to their own harvest of evil spirits, and to all manner of drujas.

27. And they shall be afflicted with assassinations, and intriguers and despoilers, and with anarchy and riots and destruction.

28. For they shall be made to understand that whosoever Jehovih created alive is sacred upon the earth; and that whosoever heedeth not these, my judgments, sinneth against the Almighty.

29. Behold, it is not sufficient apology for them to say: O, an evil king will come upon my country and possess it!

30. I say unto thee, O man: All countries are Jehovih's. Be thou His servant unto peace and righteousness, having faith in Him.

31. Behold, thy God hath come to put away old things, and to give unto you the kingdoms of Jehovih, as they are in His exalted heavens.

32. Heed thou the judgments of thy God; thou canst not stay the hand of the Almighty.

CHAPTER XXXIII.

GOD JUDGETH AGAINST EXCLUSIVENESS.

1. God said: Hear the judgments of thy God, O man; look thou upon all the world with the eye of a God.

2. Be thou comprehensive in judgment over all nations and peoples upon the earth.

3. Jehovih hath said: Out of My very self created I all the living; brothers and sisters made I them, from the members of My body.

4. Jehovih hath said: In the early days of a world, behold, I provided unto man different continents and islands, separated by mighty waters, that man, in one division of the earth, might not interfere with man in another division of the earth.

5. Jehovih hath said: Behold, one nation and people I allot to one civilization, and another nation and people I allot to another civilization. Separately, on the different divisions of the earth and on the islands in the seas, situated I the different peoples I created.

6. Jehovih hath said: But, when the world groweth older, and man attaineth to wisdom, I say unto him: Build thou ships, and sail across the waters I created; go visit thy brothers

and sisters in the different divisions of the earth.

7. Jehovih hath said: As man mastereth the ocean, and cometh to his brothers and sisters, afar off, and I say unto man: Because thou hast mastered the ocean, let this be a testimony unto thee, that there shall be no barrier, henceforth, between all the nations and peoples I created.

8. Jehovih hath said: In kosmon I come, saying: Be ye brethren upon the face of the earth and upon the waters of the earth; these are the legacies I bequeath unto My children.

9. Jehovih hath said: Be ye a help and a profit unto one another, judging wisely of the differences which circumstances and places of habitation have developed in the races of man.

10. Now, I, thy God, O man, declare this judgment unto thee: Inasmuch as thy wisdom hath surmounted the corporeal barrier, the ocean, betwixt thee and thy brother, it is meet and proper, that thy soul surmount the barrier of prejudice against thy brother.

11. And that, instead of making laws against him, thou shalt do the opposite of this, and throw open the place of thy habitation, and thy soul, and thy love, to receive thy brother, godlike, and with open arms.

12. Flatter not thyself, that thou canst turn aside, or set backward, the seasons of the Almighty.

13. Wherein thou dost this, affliction shall surely come upon thee.

14. Behold, I have made the heavens of the earth universal; and established heavenly roadways around about the earth, that the angels of the different nations and peoples may be as angels of universal heavens, to help one another.

15. Wilt thou make a law to incite the enmity of the spirits of the dead against thee? And open the door for still more aggressive wars?

16. Shall the laws of man interdict the march of Jehovih?

17. Now, behold, when kosmon came, I said unto thee: Come with thy God; peacefully shalt thou knock at the doors of Chine'ya and Japan, and they shall open unto thee.

18. This, thou accomplished; and those who had been exclusive hundreds of years, turned from the olden ways to welcome Jehovih's hand in thy promises.

19. Now, I declare unto thee, I will not more have exclusiveness in any of the nations and peoples in all the world.

20. Neither shall there be taxes and duties of one nation or people against another.

21. Behold, thou hast asked for the Father's kingdom to come on earth as it is in heaven, and I will give unto thee. As thou hast prayed, so will I answer thee, in the name of Jehovih.

22. Thou shalt not serve both, Jehovih and mammon. Neither shall the light of my heavens be with thee, save thou heedest my judgments.

23. I will have all the ports open and free, nor shall there be partisan taxation, in favor of one nation against another, nor of one people against another people.

24. It is not excusable for thee to say: Lo, the poor foreigner will come and consume my riches!

25. Thou shalt say the opposite: Welcome, my poor brothers and sisters! Whatsoever is mine, is yours also. Come ye, and dwell within my country; it is ample, and Jehovih will provide unto us.

CHAPTER XXXIV.

GOD JUDGETH THE GOVERNMENTS OF MAN.

1. God said: When a man hath young children, he maketh just laws, in order to teach them discretion, justice, harmony and consideration, in regard to one another.

2. But, when his children attain to be men and women, man no longer holdeth a law over them, for they become his equals, as brothers and sisters.

3. Even so, in the ancient times, provided I thee, O man, with governments and laws for different nations and peoples.

4. Nevertheless, I said unto thee: Let thy government be as a father over the people, and not as a separate matter against them.

5. But thou hast disobeyed my commandments; thy government is as one thing, and thy people as another thing. That which should be one entity, thou hast made into two.

6. Thy government hath become a separate self from the people; and the people are as servants, supporting the law-makers, who trade in projects and schemes for their own profit and glory.

7. Since the earliest days, all the governments of man have drifted into this.

8. When a government no longer filleth the grade, according to the advancement of the people, behold, thy God withdraweth his heavenly protection from that government. And, straightway, the people run into anarchy.

9. Lay not the blame of anarchy and revolution and assassinations on the people; my judgment is against the government in all cases. These conditions of vengeance are but the fruit resulting from the government's divergence from the will of Jehovih, and the march of His light.

10. As, for example, the offspring of inharmonious parents, or of parents wrapt up in selfishness, are lower in grade than their predecessors, even so do the subjects of a king decline in grade in proportion to the prevention of liberty and the neglect of general instruction.

11. Judgment is rendered against government wherein it provideth not liberty to the people, and neglecteth providing means for the development of the talents created with all.

12. In these respects, O man, governments are measured and graded by thy God. And, whenever a government setteth up itself to enforce and strengthen itself by violence against justice unto the multitude, behold, I turn away from that government; and I call away my Lords and holy angels.

13. And, thereupon, drujas come upon that people, and the people fall upon their government, and destroy it.

14. If a government be a king only, and he have no holy council, then the responsibility of the shortness is wholly his.

15. But, if the king have a holy council, then the responsibility for shortness lieth partly with the king and partly with the council.

16. Judgment is rendered against them, not only in this world, but in the es world. And each and every member of such council shall be bound in the first resurrection until he hath made amends unto all his people for the shortness he manifested on the earth.

17. Hear the wisdom of thy God, O man, and consider the way of righteousness in the

governments of mortals:

18. The nearer the twain are to being one, that is, the government and the people, the nearer they are like unto my heavenly kingdoms.

19. The more diverse the government is from the people, the farther it is from the kingdom of thy God.

20. Let this be a guide unto thee, O man, in prophesying the change and the overthrow of governments: According to the square of the distance a government is from Jehovih (which is Righteousness) so is the quickness of its coming change or destruction.

21. Think not these matters are governed by chance or accident: Jehovih is Perfect Righteousness: the all Everlasting.

22. He is All One. For a people and their government to attain to be all one with each other, this is great strength, with a long existence and internal peace.

23. This, also, shalt thou consider, O man: All governments are tending toward oneness with one another. This is the march of Jehovih. None can stay Him.

24. Consider, then, what is wisdom between governments: To make themselves reciprocal toward one another.

25. A government that setteth up itself for itself, and against other governments, is a selfish government. And thy God rateth it the same as a selfish man, being diverse from Jehovih and his kingdoms.

26. Judgment is rendered against such a government. Neither my Lords nor my holy angels shall bless that government.

27. Governments that practice affiliation, to bring about reciprocal brotherhoods between governments, are on the right road toward the Father's everlasting kingdoms.

28. Flatter not thyself, O man, that these matters can escape the observation of thy God. The affairs, legislations, laws, treaties, and all things whatsoever that governments accomplish, are known and recorded in the heavens of the earth. And the leaders, kings and councils, shall, soon or late, face them; and they shall judge of their own fullness or shortness in serving Jehovih in righteousness and wisdom.

CHAPTER XXXV.
GOD DECLARETH AGAINST THE GOVERNMENTS OF MAN.

1. God said: Whoso liveth with Jehovih is free from Jehovih. These need no man's government; for they practice righteousness, peace, love, industry and wisdom, with due regard to one another.

2. Such is the Father's kingdom on earth. In which there shall be no laws made by man; neither shall there be leaders or rulers.

3. The progress of man is toward this; the progress of the governments of man should shape toward such a consummation.

4. The time was, when laws were requisite unto all things, even to the manner of a man coming in and going out of a house; and to every occupation that man followed; with licenses and taxes regulating them; the time of apprenticeship to a barber, to a weaver, to a lawyer, to a preacher, to a physician, to a smith, and to all other trades and occupations, with examinations and passports to practice within the king's dominions; with rates for fees and rights and privileges.

5. But these laws and governments were for the past eras; they were righteous in the first place, for they shaped man's judgment, toward perfecting himself.

6. But, behold, a new time is in the world; from the acquisition of knowledge a new liberty hath been born into the world. And it crieth out on every side: Throw open the doors unto all trades and occupations; behold, the multitude are sufficiently wise to judge themselves as to who they shall patronize.

7. Judgment is rendered against the laws and governments of man in all cases where they prevent the liberty and choice of man to his avocation and knowledge.

8. It is not sufficient for thee to say: Behold, the public will be taken advantage of by ignorant pretenders. Thou hast no right to say what the public will suffer, and thus base a law on prospective damage.

9. When the public have suffered, and when they, themselves, demand protection by such laws, then shall such laws be made. To make such laws beforehand, is to sin against Jehovih.

10. It was said of old: Thou shalt keep holy the Sabbath day. And it was defined what a man should not do on that day.

11. Judgment is rendered against that law; nevertheless, I put not aside the practice.

12. But the time hath now come when man shall judge himself as to whether he will or will not keep any day sacred.

13. Moreover, man shall not, henceforth, be accountable as to whether he keep or not keep any day as a sacred day. Yet, this accountability shall be unto all men, whether they fulfill in wisdom and righteousness their utmost capacities.

14. There was a law of circumcision; but I render judgment against that law also, for it hath fulfilled its time. This law, I put aside in practice. But I give it as a permission to the adult, that he may or may not fulfill the circumcision according to his own judgment.

15. Judgment is also rendered against infant baptism; and I put aside this law also, and I make it an abomination before Jehovih.

16. Nevertheless, when a child hath attained to fourteen years of age, and it choose of its own accord to be sprinkled with water, to conform to the rites and ceremonies, then that child shall be thus baptized in the name of Jehovih, but not in the name of God, nor any Lord, nor a Savior, nor an angel.

17. This is wisdom, O man, to have no law or government between man and wife.

18. This is ignorance, to have a law between man and wife.

19. Yet, because there are bad men and bad women who do marry, it hath been found necessary to have a law between man and wife, as regardeth their duties.

20. But consider how wrong it is to have a law between a good man and a good wife, as regardeth her duties. Better is it for them to be thrown upon their own love and judgment.

21. After such manner gave I governments and laws unto all peoples. To the bad and evil-minded, rigid laws, with many details; but to the wise and good, I come now as an emancipator, saying: Go ye, without laws and government, fulfill your destinies according to your own judgment, that ye may be an honor and glory to Jehovih.

22. In kosmon, man shall not be longer driven in yoke and harness, but shall stand upright before Jehovih, practicing his highest light with rejoicing, being a free man, and a brother to his God!

23. Behold, the Uzians have a custom of eating bread, and drinking wine, saying, after the

manner of the worshipers of Baugh-ghan-ghad of old: Eat of this, for it is my flesh; and, drink of this, for it is my blood, signifying, that that they do, was commanded by me, God of heaven and earth.

24. Judgment is rendered against this custom, with abhorrence; moreover, it shall be, henceforth, known as blasphemy against Jehovih.

25. Thy God never commanded man to eat flesh and blood, nor pretended that bread and wine were flesh and blood, nor commanded them to be eaten in remembrance of the flesh and blood of any man born of woman.

26. Also have they a custom of decorating and draping themselves in crepe, and characterizing the same as a sign of mourning for the dead.

27. Judgment is rendered against such custom, but without prohibition.

28. Jehovih created alive, and Jehovih taketh life away, for all things are His.

29. Remember thy Creator with wisdom; and neither in thy dress nor habit shalt thou censure Him for what hath been.

30. Neither curb thou the full sorrow of thy heart and thy soul, because thy brother or sister, son or daughter, or father, or mother hath passed away.

31. But remember, Jehovih is over all His works, and provideth wisely unto the living and the dead.

32. Jehovih hath said: To man I gave an earthly body that he might learn earthly things; but death I gave to man that he might rise to the inheritance of My heavenly kingdoms.

33. He appointeth a time unto all; to some an hour, to some a year, and to some a hundred years; every one fulfilleth to result in wisdom and happiness, and for the glory of the Almighty.

CHAPTER XXXVI.
GOD SHOWETH HOW HE HATH WROUGHT.

1. God saith: Behold, the work of my hand, O man: As thou findest an old house, no longer habitable, thou sendest workmen to pull it down, and then, thou sendest laborers to clear away the rubbish.

2. And, afterward, thou bringest builders, and they lay a new foundation, larger and broader than the old one, and, thereon, they build thee a new edifice, adapted with new improvements unto the increase and requirements of thy family.

3. Even so, hath thy God labored, for hundreds of years, to prepare unto the generations of this day.

4. For I saw, beforehand, that man would circumscribe the earth, and that all the nations and peoples thereof would become known to one another.

5. And I beheld also, that, in the coming time, which is now at hand, the old edifices of doctrines and creeds and religions, as of the Brahmins, Buddhists, Jews, Ka'yuans, Kriste'yans and Mohammedans would not fulfill the requirements of man.

6. And now, behold, O man, the wisdom of Jehovih previously: He had permitted corruptions and contradictions to creep into the sacred books of all of the said great religions, purposely and with design, so as to make easy the work of thy God.

7. And when I saw that the coming together of nations and peoples would require a new religious edifice, I perceived, also, that the old ones must be cleared away.

8. And, behold, I, thy God, went to work systematically, inspiring man to accomplish even what man hath accomplished.

9. I raised up scholars and infidels against these religions; inspiring them to attack the corruptions and contradictions in the sacred books of all these peoples.

10. And, in the same time, that I sent infidels against the Jewish bible, I sent infidels against the Hindoo bibles, and against the doctrines of Brahma and Budha and Ka'yu, and against the Kriste'yans and Mohammedans.

11. And I made the beginning of the work of these infidels and scholars to correspond with the discovery of Guatama by Columbo, and I kept them at their work for three hundred years, which was up to the time of the establishment of the republic of Guatama, which I, thy God, provided to be untrammeled by an established religion.

12. After my workmen, the scholars and infidels, had thus undermined the old edifice, behold, I sent laborers, under the name of merchants and traders, to commence clearing away the rubbish.

13. And, because of their desires in money-getting, they considered not the religious edifice of any people, and they provided comity relations withersoever they went.

14. For a hundred years, these, my laborers, have been at their work, stripping off and clearing away the prejudice of nations and peoples against one another.

15. And then, behold, I came with my builders, and I prepared a new foundation, broader and wider and firmer, for an edifice adapted to all the nations and peoples in the world.

16. First, I sent my miracle-workers forth into every quarter, saying unto them: Whatsoever was done by the ancient Gods and Saviors, do ye even so, and greater. For I will show, unto all the world, that no man nor God is worthy to be worshipped because of miracles.

17. And they went forth at my command, and my angels went with them, doing wonders.

18. They healed the sick, by the laying on of hands; they restored the blind to sight, and made the deaf to hear, and have brought the supposed dead to life.

19. They have caused writing to come on stone tablets, and on paper, in the light of day, by unseen hands.

20. They have caused ponderous bodies, without mortal contact to move, and to beat time to music.

21. A child hath lifted eight full-grown men with her little finger.

22. They have passed full-blown flowers and plants through boards and tables, unbruised and uninjured, and, yet, there was neither hole, nor opening in the boards and tables.

23. They have made stars of light that spake with audible voices; they have made pillars of fire by night, and pillars of cloud by day.

24. They have caused the spirits of the dead to appear as if in flesh and blood; and whilst thus appearing, talking face to face with their mortal kin, who saw them, heard them, and, by the subject of the discourse, proved them to be the very angels of heaven returned to their earth-kin and friends.

25. For the time of one generation thy God hath thus kept open the gates of heaven; working through mortals, by the angels of heaven.

26. My testimony and my witnesses are hundreds of thousands. I hide not the work of my hand and of my angels in a corner; I extend them abroad over the earth; I manifest in the cities and country places; I prove unto all peoples, that common men and women can do

the miracles for which Gods and Saviors have been worshipped.

27. Yea, I give these powers unto good and bad men, and unto good and bad women.

28. For I show miracles in order to break down the worship of miracle-workers.

29. For I will have none worshipped but Jehovih. And I have inspired angels to this end, and to the end that good works and wisdom shall be, henceforth, the means of resurrection in heaven.

30. And I have shown also, that only by harmony and the union of many, can any great good come unto the generations of men.

CHAPTER XXXVII.
GOD REVEALETH HIS METHOD OF WORK.

1. God said: Think not, O man, that thy God goeth about a work without a system and order.

2. Verily these are the first of my considerations.

3. First, I send my loo'is, my masters of generations, down to the earth, to the nations and peoples where I design to build my edifice.

4. And my loo'is, by inspiration, control the marriages of certain mortals, that heirs may be born into the world suited to the work I have on hand.

5. For many generations, my loo'is labor to this end, raising up thousands and tens of thousands of mortal heirs according to my commandments.

6. So, O man, since four hundred years my loo'is shaped mortal births to bring about the armies of thy God.

7. And now, when the time of kosmon had come, behold, I sent my Lords and my numerators, to receive the harvest and the records of my loo'is.

8. Thus, O man, thy God knew beforehand what part and what place each and every one of his mortal laborers was adapted to.

9. And through my Lords and generals and captains of my angel hosts, I commanded man to fall to work on my building.

10. Some to heal the sick, some to work signs and miracles, some to lecture, some to write, and so on, every one according to the work of his adaptation.

11. And all of this is to one purpose; not to build up or exalt any man, nor God, nor religion, but to found Jehovih's kingdom on earth.

12. To give man the system of universal peace, love, harmony and kosmon, adapted to all nations and peoples in all the world.

13. And I commanded my Lords and angels, generals and captains to this end; and I, furthermore, commanded certain angel registers to accompany and be with mortals in this, the kosmon era, to observe them at the work I provided them.

14. And to whoso doeth a good work in truth, righteousness, wisdom and love, my holy angels are commanded to extend their sphere of usefulness and light.

15. I said unto my angels: Go ye with these proofs, before mortals, with signs and miracles; go to the rich and the poor, to the learned and to the unlearned. And ye shall observe them, as to what use they make of the new revelations.

16. For some shall appropriate these things to money-making; some, to personal fame; some, to evil purposes; but a few, to the glory of the Almighty, and the exaltation of

mankind.

17. Try ye all mortals, and make a register of them and their behavior, and preserve the same in my heavens.

18. And it shall come to pass that many of my seers shall have great poverty and great hardships, for they will be unsuited to serve mammon. Nevertheless, they shall convert the rich, proving my truths unto them. And my seers shall go to them in distress, and the rich shall deny them, and refuse them.

19. Make a record of these also. For, in course of time, and, because of the hardness of their hearts, I shall withdraw my holy angels away from such rich people, and they shall be left to fall into the obsession of drujas.

20. And their families shall be obsessed, their wives, or husbands, or sons, or daughters.

21. And the drujas shall divide the families, turning a man against his father, and a daughter against a mother, and a daughter-in-law against her mother-in-law.

22. For, whoever goeth away from me, paying tribute to satan (self), I will not follow after.

23. And the drujas shall say: Think not we are come to send peace on earth, we come not to bring peace, but to bring a sword.

24. And families of the unrighteous, being obsessed with drujas, shall keep secret their convictions, and they shall say: This is lunacy, meaning derangement.

25. Others, being asked if they belong to the new dispensation, shall say: Nay, we know nothing of it; behold, we are good members of the church!

26. And now, accordingly, all such matters were recorded in my heavens, and such mortals became known to me.

27. And such as consulteth the spirits in regard to money-making, or to earthly matters for self sake, also became known to me.

28. And I commanded my holy angels to withdraw from all mortals who were not working for Jehovih's new kingdom, who were of no profit in the resurrection of man; and, behold, this was also done.

29. And it came to pass, that many whom I had designed for exalted work, fell into the hands of drujas. And they held conferences, and were divided, man against man, and woman against woman; full of boasting and short-sighted wisdom, seeking the applause of the multitude.

30. And, so, my angels sifted them and sorted them, in order to find such as were willing to sacrifice self for the sake of the Father's kingdom.

31. These I drew aside, and I said unto them: Ye, that choose to serve Jehovih, behold, Jehovih hath chosen you also.

CHAPTER XXXVIII.

GOD SHOWETH THE MISTAKES OF MAN'S JUDGMENT.

1. God said: I said unto thee, O man, pursue thy wisdom after the manner of thy God.

2. I go to the beginning; I labor not so much to convert adults, as to prepare the minds of the young.

3. Now, behold, because I told thee this, thou sought to have children born unto thee after the manner of Gods.

4. Thou saidst: I understand the new kingdom; I have the solution for raising up a new generation on the earth. I have chosen me my women, who also comprehend, and, behold, our offspring will be very Gods!

5. But I admonished thee, saying: Thou openst the door for adultery; thou shalt surely go down.

6. Thou wouldst not profit by the wisdom of the ages. I had holden up my hand, and said: One wife, one husband!

7. Now, hear me, O man: In a new cycle man ever runneth to the extreme opposite of the old errors, and thus bringeth upon himself new ones, that he knew not of.

8. I say unto thee: The new edifice shall be of all that was good of the past, of things proven in heaven and on earth.

9. Also, I say unto thee, it shall be of the young, and not of the adult.

10. Because thou hast attempted to beget offspring for the new kingdom, thou, of all men, art the most unfit.

11. My laborers shall not have desire to be either fathers or mothers. Nor shall they seek in any way things that belong on the earth; nor have passions that belong only to the earth.

12. Nevertheless, they shall be the founders of the Father's kingdom on earth, and with the young.

13. They shall gather up orphans and castaways in infancy, and take them into colonies, hundreds and thousands of them.

14. And these infants shall be fed and clothed and raised up, not after any man's whim or conceit, but according to the accumulated wisdom collected from all the different nations and peoples in all the world, as to how to make the best corporeal and spiritual men and women.

15. Behold, it hath been proven in the warrior and pugilist how to raise a savage man, by flesh diet and inharmonious surroundings; and in nations and tribes of peace, how to raise a virtuous and industrious man, on herbs and fruit diet.

16. These are things for thee to learn, O man, going at the subject systematically, to find the best way to make the best man and woman out of the infants entrusted to thee.

17. Not only as to diet, but as to clothing, and as to comfort and cleanliness; and to avoid disease; and as to strength and suppleness and swiftness; and as to virtue and modesty; and as to education, practical and theoretical; and as to industry and quick perception; and as to willingness to work for one another; and to trades and occupations; and as to pastimes, amusements and recreations, singing, dancing, and playing with great joy and delight; and as to worship, to rites and ceremonies; and as to acquiring seership and prophecy and signs and miracles, in su'is and sar'gis; as to communing with angels, and as to the value of angels as teachers and instructors by tangible presence and audible voices.

18. And yet, above all things, thou shalt preserve liberty unto all, with pleasant and enjoyable discipline for everything, after the manner of my heavenly kingdoms.

19. Remembering, that every faculty in every one shall be cultivated to the utmost.

20. Teaching them, from the first, that the eye of Jehovih is upon them, and that His hand is stretched over them, to bless them, according to their goodness, purity, love, gentleness and wisdom.

21. And that they shall not own nor possess individually; but that all things are Jehovih's,

and they, themselves, are angels in mortal form, created by Jehovih to rejoice and to help one another forever.

CHAPTER XXXIX.
GOD PROVIDETH FOR INCREASE.

1. God said: When thy educational colony of infants shall have grown up to manhood and womanhood, they shall understand that, as they were once homeless and fatherless, and ye gathered them up, and provided unto them, even so shall they go, and do likewise, gathering up from the Uzians other orphans and castaways, and raising them in other colonies, after the same manner.

2. And it shall come to pass, that many will desire to marry, and it shall be granted unto them to choose amongst their own people, and marry whom they will.

3. But it shall be a law that no man nor woman shall marry more than one time.

4. Whether the partner die, or whether they divorce themselves, yet, to none other shall either ever wed more.

5. And it shall be a law, that, at maturity, if any one desireth to leave the colony, he shall do so without hindrance or prejudice.

6. Though it shall be inculcated into them, during their youth, that, at maturity, they are supposed to swarm out, after the fashion of bees, becoming too numerous for one hive, and go and form a new colony; that in all things they shall be taught not to do anything for self sake, but for the good of man and for the honor and glory of Jehovih.

7. And these things shall come to pass with these people:

8. They shall abjure war;

9. They shall be non-resistants;

10. They shall have su'is, and shall see without their mortal eyes, and hear without their mortal ears.

11. My angels shall appear before them, and walk with them, talking to them, and teaching them of my kingdoms.

12. And angels of the I'hin race will come to them; and of the I'huans, and of all other peoples whereof mention is made in this OAHSPE.

13. And mortals shall recover, from the libraries in heaven, things that have been lost on the earth, as to languages and histories of tens of thousands of years ago.

14. And mortals shall prophesy truly of things in heaven and on the earth.

15. And many shall attain adeptism, and, in spirit, go out of their mortal bodies, and appear hundreds of miles away, and there make themselves known; and they will return again to their mortal bodies, unharmed.

16. All these, and even greater things, shall my angels teach them.

17. Flatter not thyself, O man, that these things can come in Uz, or that they can come suddenly. They can neither come to Uzians, nor can they come suddenly.

18. It is not the work of thy God in this cycle to raise up any man to become worshipful because of such wonders; it is my work to show man how he shall attain to these things himself.

19. For this reason, I come not, in this day, to call sinners to repentance, nor to gather up the lost sheep of Israel.

20. I come now to the wise and pure, who have fulfilled the former commandments.

21. I come to give them a new lesson, which is, to show them how to build the Father's kingdom on earth.

22. I come to raise up a new people in the world, greater than hath ever been.

23. Those that I sent have cleared away the old edifice. I come not as a destroyer; I come as a builder.

24. Into thy hands, O man, I give the key to the heavenly kingdoms. Remember, the password which admitteth the to the all highest kingdoms is, JEHOVIH, THE I AM.

END OF THE BOOK OF JUDGMENT.

BOOK OF INSPIRATION.

CHAPTER I.

1. These are the words of Tae, in kosmon: I am Light; I am Central, but Boundless, saith Jehovih.

2. I give thee of My Light; and when thou hast received, thou criest out: Behold, I am wise!

3. Thy corpor I made, in which to localize thee; to mature thy entity.

4. Without Me, thou hadst not come to life. Thou art as the end of a ray of light from My Person.

5. And thou art focalized in thy corporeal body.

6. I am to thy spirit, as is the sun to a ray of light. I am the Light that illuminateth thy soul.

7. The ray of light that goeth out of Me, taketh root in mortality, and thou art the product, the tree.

8. Thou wert nothing; though all things that constitute thee, were before.

9. These I drove together, and quickened.

10. Thus I made thee.

11. After the manner I made thee corporeally, so made I thee spiritually, intellectually.

12. As out of corpor I made thy corporeal body, so, out of My Light, which is My Very Self, I built thee up in spirit, with consciousness that thou art.

13. Thou canst not add one jot or tittle to thy corporeal self, of thine own will and exertion.

14. It is by and through Me, that the process of absorption by the blood addeth unto thee.

15. Thy blood floweth in thy veins because of My quickening power upon thee.

16. When I withdraw My hand, thou diest. Life and death are of Me.

17. All thy corporeal part is, therefore, of Me and through Me.

18. Even so is thy spirit of Me also.

19. And as thou canst not add a fraction to thy corporeal self, neither canst thou add a fraction to thy spiritual self.

20. Out of Myself groweth thy spirit.

21. Neither canst thou, of thine own self, manufacture or acquire or take unto thyself, one new thought, nor idea, nor invention.

22. All thought and knowledge and judgment which thou hast, I gave unto thee.

23. As the whirlwind gathereth up dust, and driveth it toward a center, so is the plan of My universe.

24. Thou art as a center; all things come to thee from without.

25. Thy knowledge, as well as thy corporeality, came to thee from without, from that which was external to thyself.

CHAPTER II.

1. Thou art of inspiration made, saith Jehovih.

2. I made thee a corporeal body, and I wrote upon it. The result thou art.

3. And I made thee susceptible, so all things external to thyself could write upon thee.

4. The sum of these is thy knowledge.

5. As it is with thee, so is it with all men, and with all the living which I created.

6. Nor is there any knowledge in the world, but what I gave.

7. All of it is My inspiration.

8. Man said: By certain measurements I teach my son mathematics.

9. I am back of all, saith Jehovih.

10. I taught thy father's father and all who were before him. The sum of all of man's knowledge is but man's capacity to perceive My Light.

11. I made thee My servant, to teach thy son by certain measurements. This was the road I made to reach thy son's soul.

12. Man said: I know more than did my father; and yet my father knew more than did his father. We reason, we digest, we compound from one another.

13. I am the All External; from Me are smaller lights focalized, saith Jehovih.

14. A man holdeth a condensing lens to the sun, and he lighteth a fire thereby, but yet the lens contained not the heat.

15. After such manner hast thou accumulated knowledge; yet, no knowledge was of thine own begetting, but all came from Me. I gave it all.

16. The increase in knowledge now upon the earth, with all the races of men, is only the increase I gave. Man of himself created none of it.

17. Neither canst thou create one thought, nor idea, nor impulse.

18. Thou canst only gather together from My harvests, or from Me in Person.

CHAPTER III.

1. The eye of man I made to obtain knowledge by light; but the ear of man I made to obtain knowledge from darkness, and within darkness, saith Jehovih.

2. The power of touch I gave to man, whereby he might learn of things their adaptability and compatibility and incompatibility with himself.

3. These are the corporeal doorways I gave unto thee, O man, whereby thou mightst receive knowledge from Me and My creations, consciously to thyself.

4. Through these, thou art constantly impregnated; through these, thy soul accumulateth knowledge of My works.

5. Whatsoever is charged upon these doorways of my soul, is inspiration.

6. When thou seest bread, thou art inspired to eat; when thou seest a horse, thou art inspired to ride; when thou touchest a nettle, thou art inspired with pain.

7. Yet, in all cases, thou must have practice before thou canst comprehend the inspiration that cometh to thee from these external things.

8. Man saith: To-day, I remember my friend whom I saw not for many a year.

9. Jehovih saith: I made thee as a storehouse, and as a book that was written before.

10. And I gave to thee power to re-read thy stores and thy book, within thy soul.

11. This was the accumulated inspiration which I had previously given thee.

12. When thou art fevered, or entranced, or in diverse action from thy usual bent, thy soul turneth into these stores, and thy memory cometh forth wonderfully.

13. This is the manifestation of inspiration which I had previously given thee.

14. I made thee that thou shouldst receive inspiration, not only from the world external to thyself, but inspiration from the members of thy body.

15. My impression upon thee is inspiration; but thou must realize My inspiration, in order to know Me.

16. An idiot holdeth fire in his hand, and it giveth him pain, but yet, he knoweth not the cause, nor whence the origin of the pain.

17. So, also, I come to thee, and give thee inspiration, but thou discernest not Me.

18. Another man discerneth My Presence, and My inspiration. He heareth Me speak; he seeth My Person.

19. Yet, I am with both alike.

20. One man openeth his mouth to speak, and, behold My words come forth.

21. And yet another saith: No man know Jehovih; none have heard Him.

22. One man is sensitive, as a plate for a picture, and he catcheth My Light instantly, and knoweth it is from Me.

23. Another one saith: A sudden thought struck me! But he discerneth not whence it came.

CHAPTER IV.

1. When the infant is young, My Light is its first knowledge, saith Jehovih.

2. It seeth Me and heareth Me; and it seeth and heareth My angels.

3. By the pressure of My Light upon its corporeal eyes and ears, it learneth to see and hear corporeally.

4. This is the beginning of two senses, which I created to grow parallel to each other, and equal in strength.

5. But the infant, being in the corporeal world, heedeth more the things that appeal to the corporeal senses than such as appeal to the spiritual senses.

6. So that one person groweth up, forgetting Me and My angels. He is a skeptic.

7. But another person groweth up, remembering Me, and My angels. He is a believer.

8. And, behold, thou, O man, inquirest of them: Whence came the idea of a Creator, an All Person?

9. And one of them answereth thee: It is inherent; it is natural.

10. But the other answereth: It is folly; it came from darkness.

11. But I say unto thee, O man: Darkness can not create an idea; not even darkness would be known but for the light I make beside it.

12. Thou canst not imagine any animal under the sun which I have not created.

13. Man said: I imagine a horse with a fish's head and fins.

14. Whatsoever thou inventest, saith Jehovih, thou but taketh the parts of one of My creations, and puttest them to another.

15. Let this prove unto thee, if thou canst not invent a new living creature, that thy forefathers did not do so either in regard to Me.

16. Nevertheless, thou hast a thought, and an idea of Me and My Person.

17. And thou hast a thought, and an idea of the spirits of the dead.

18. By My Presence and inspiration upon thee, I taught thee I am the I AM, a Person.

19. By the inspiration and presence of My angels, I taught thee of them also.

20. My inspiration upon the bird causeth it to sing; by My Presence I teach it to build its nest.

21. By My Presence I color one rose red, and another white.

22. Proof of My Person is in the harmony of the whole, and of every one being a person of itself, perfect in its order.

CHAPTER V.

1. Two kinds of voices have I, saith Jehovih: The silent voice and the audible voice.

2. All men I created susceptible to one or the other of My voices, and many to both.

3. One man heareth My voice in the breeze, and in thunder, and in music.

4. One man heareth My voice in the flowers of the field, and in the scenery of the mountains.

5. And yet another feeleth My inspiration; and he skippeth up the mountain side, and tireth not on the way.

6. He that neither seeth nor feeleth My inspiration, goeth up the mountain in great labor.

7. In proportion as man is clear in his corporeality and in his spirit, so discerneth he My inspiration.

8. And if he have great purity as well, then he shapeth my Light into corporeal words.

9. These I taught man to call My revealed words.

10. Nevertheless, no corporeal man created I perfect; neither can any man reveal My words perfectly.

11. But I created the way open unto all men, to try to reveal Me.

12. According to man's approximation to perfect manhood, so reveal I unto him, by My Presence and My words.

13. According to man's imperfection in manhood, so doth not My inspiration manifest on his senses.

14. Perfect manhood created I possible, in equal corporeal and spiritual senses.

15. Strong corporeal senses and weak spiritual senses detract man from My Presence, and make him infidel to My Person.

16. Such a man denieth My inspiration and the inspiration of My angels. He is little more than a forest tree, which hath a trunk and many branches, but moveth not from its place.

CHAPTER VI.

1. I am One Spirit, saith Jehovih.

2. My quickening power is upon all the living; because of this, they live and move.

3. According to the different structure of the living, so is My inspiration manifested by them.

4. One, as the hare, runneth away in cowardice; another, as a lion, is ferocious; another, without judgment, as the serpent.

5. And as to man: One is inspired to music; another to mathematics; another to seership, and so on.

6. To all of these I am the One, the Universal Inspirer that moveth all of them.

7. According to their organic structure, so do they manifest My inspiration.

8. The lowest of living creatures made I the serpent, for I gave to him an element capable of destroying himself.

9. When the earth was encircled with poisonous gases, I created poisonous vines and weeds and trees and all kinds of herbs, rich-growing upon the earth.

10. Thus, from destroying gases and from earth-substance created I the vegetable world. And, in that day, all growing things upon the earth which I had created were poison as to animal life.

11. Then, I created the serpents; of all sizes created I them. And they were poison also.

12. And the serpents I created were carniverous, feeding upon one another. Self-impregnating created I them.

13. Thus drove I the poison of the air down into vegetation, and thence into the animal world; thus I purified the air of heaven.

14. This was the first creation I created on this world.

15. Then I overcast the earth with falling nebulae, and covered up the poisons growing upon the earth, and they were turned to oil and coal.

16. Then, I made a new creation; giving feet and legs and bones to the animals I designed for the earth.

17. And when the earth was ripe for man, then I created him; male and female created I those of the second creation.

18. And man was dumb, like other animals; without speech and without understanding, even less than any other creature which I had created.

19. Nevertheless, I had given to man, and thus made him, out of the dissolved elements of every living thing that had preceded him.

20. And man partook of the first and the second creations. After the manner of every animal on the earth, so created I man; with all the characteristics of all of them, so created I him, male and female created I them.

21. And man was unconscious of his creation, not knowing whence he came; nor knew he which was his own species.

22. And I sent angels to man, to teach him who he was, and to rouse him up to his capabilities, for which I created him.

23. And my angels drew, from man's side, substance, and thus took on corporeal forms; and the angels dwelt with man as helpmates, to make man understand.

CHAPTER VII.

1. I created man, even from the first, that he should learn to be an independent being, saith Jehovih.

2. And when My angels had taught man speech, making man name all the animals in the world, after the names the animals called themselves, I commanded My angels to come away from man, for a season.

3. To My angels I said: Behold, of all the animals I created in the world, to man only gave I capacity to transmit knowledge to his brethren by words.

4. And to man only gave I capacity to comprehend an idea of Me, his Creator.

5. Nevertheless, I inspire all living animals which I created; but they know it not.

6. I inspire the spider to make its net; the bird to build her nest; the wild goose to fly to the south, before the winter cometh; the mare to neigh for her colt; the ant to lay in its stores; the bees to dwell in a queendom; and so on, every living creature do I move and

control by My inspiration upon them.

7. Males and females I inspire to come together at times and seasons; and then to live apart during gestation. These I keep before man as a lesson of the wisdom of My inspiration.

8. To man I give liberty to acquire wisdom by observing the method of My work, as I manifest in other living creatures.

9. I have also given man capacity to attain to know My inspiration in contradistinction from the inspiration he receiveth from his surroundings.

10. To no other creature gave I this capacity.

11. What cometh of Me, is without pain or injury to any one, and with liberty unto all. Such are My inspirations.

12. When man witnesseth a battle, he is inspired to battle; when he witnesseth peace and love, he is inspired to peace and love.

13. What moveth man in consonance and wisdom, and to life, is My inspiration.

14. What moveth man in disconsonance and folly, and to death, is inspiration from man's surroundings.

15. I inspire the serpent to bite to death; for thus created I it. This is no sin, for it fulfilleth its labor; it is the remnant of poison of other eras.

16. Man I created not to destruction, but to life, wisdom, peace and love toward all.

17. When man practiceth virtue, wisdom, truth and love unto all, his inspiration is from Me direct.

18. When man practiceth destruction and selfishness, his inspiration is indirectly from Me, through the conflict of his surroundings.

19. And thus becometh he evil, instead of good.

20. By direct inspiration do I move upon all the animals I created.

21. This I also created possible unto men, separate from indirect inspiration.

CHAPTER VIII.

1. Although all inspiration goeth from Me to all the living, directly, yet I also created man susceptible to indirect inspiration from all My creations.

2. Whatsoever receiveth from Me direct, is in harmony with Me.

3. The lily and the rose I created perfect in their order; the female bird I inspire to build her nest in season, perfect in her order.

4. Even so is it with all My created beings, save man. All the rest err not, in the order I made them; and they all fulfill the glory for which I made them.

5. But because I made man capacitated to receive inspiration from all things, he manifesteth both, evil and good; according to his birth and surroundings, so is man good or bad.

6. Nevertheless, I created man with capacity to comprehend this also; for, I designed him, from the first, to work his way up to the Godhead, understanding all below him.

7. And I sent my angels to man, teaching him how to distinguish the difference in the inspirations upon him, that he might govern himself accordingly.

8. And My angels said unto man: Become thou one with thy Creator; these are His direct inspirations:

9. To love thy Creator above all else, and thy neighbor as thyself.

10. To give delights only, and not pain.

11. To kill not.

12. To do not violently against His creatures.

13. To be considerate of the liberty of all the living.

14. To interdict not the happiness and hope of others, only where thou canst return a transcendent glory and hope in place thereof.

15. For these are direct inspirations from thy Creator.

16. But these are thy evil inspirations, O man, these come from thy birth and surroundings, formerly called, satan:

17. To kill.

18. To slander.

19. To punish.

20. To destroy Jehovih's created beings.

21. To strive for thyself, above another.

22. To gratify thy flesh at the expense of purity or wisdom.

23. To be false to Jehovih.

24. To be false to thyself.

25. To speak falsely.

26. To covet another's.

27. To cohabit in the gestative period.

28. To engage in strife, or to aid and abet conflicts, which are the fruit of carnivorous food, transmitted in birth.

CHAPTER IX.

1. Man I created with capacity to distinguish My direct from My indirect inspirations, saith Jehovih.

2. And My angels gave him rules, whereby he might make manifest the difference betwixt the two.

3. Man has said: Behold, any man may say: Thus saith Jehovih! One killeth his neighbor, saying: I was thus inspired of Jehovih. Another practiseth all goodness, and his words are wisdom and comprehension, and he saith: I was inspired by Jehovih!

4. I say unto thee, O man: In this I also gave thee liberty; therefore, judge thou, thyself, which came from Me, and which from his surroundings (satan).

5. Thou shalt be thine own judge in all things.

6. Behold, I sent My God to judge thee; but thou shalt also judge the judgments of thy God; and, afterward, thou shalt judge thyself in the same way.

7. A perpetual judge created I thee, not only to judge thyself and all the world beside, but thou shalt judge Me, thy Creator.

8. I have given thee many sacred books, and I said to thee:

9. Save thou judgest them, thou shalt be caught in a snare; I charge thee, thou shalt accept nothing from men, nor angels, nor Gods.

10. But thou shalt rely on thine own inspiration from thy Creator.

11. Such is My word which I speak to thine own soul.

12. What cometh to thee from a man is indirect inspiration; what cometh from an angel is indirect; and what cometh from the Gods is indirect.

13. No direct inspiration of Me can come to thee from a book, nor a sermon, nor from anything in all My creations, but only from Me, thy Creator.

14. Though one man receive direct inspiration from Me, and he write it in a book, yet, when it cometh to thee, it is indirect inspiration, and is not binding upon thee, only so far as My direct inspiration upon thee moveth thee to receive it.

15. Yet, not all men created I with the same clearness to perceive Me, and to frame My wisdom in words.

16. Few only will turn away from the inspiration of the world, and come unto Me.

17. Many profess Me in words, but they do not fulfill My inspiration in practice.

18. My words come easily to the pure in heart; and My wisdom showeth itself in the frame of their speech.

19. For I give them words, even as I give to the animal inspiration to do perfectly and wisely the parts for which I created them.

20. Behold, I show the dumb spider how to weave its geometrical net; is it greater wonder for Me, to give words of wisdom to a righteous man?

21. Or to put him in the way of receiving My revelations?

22. Or to show him the harmony and glory of My creations?

CHAPTER X.

1. In the first creation none heard Me, or saw Me, saith Jehovih.

2. And, even to this day, many men deny Me and My Person.

3. To teach thee, O man, that thou shouldst be considerate of thy brother's talents, behold, what a labor for My Gods and ministering angels!

4. To show thee that no two men see alike anything I created;

5. To make thee cautious, that, because thou canst not hear Me, thou shalt not judge thy brother who can hear Me;

6. To induce thee thus and thus, without interfering with thy liberty;

7. To make thee watchful, to learn by thine own inspiration from Me;

8. To make thee skeptical to others' versions of My words, and yet make thee try to discover My words and My Person, of thine own self, to see Me and hear Me.

9. Now, behold, in the olden times, only here and there one, in all the world, could be made to comprehend Me.

10. As thou mayst say to the beast in the field, or to the dog, the most knowing of animals; Jehovih! Jehovih!

11. And they will not hear thee understandingly;

12. So was it with nearly all the world, in the olden time.

13. To-day, I have quickened many.

14. To-morrow, the whole of the people in all the world shall know Me.

15. This is the progress I created possible unto thee; this road shalt thou travel.

16. Thou hast blockaded the way against Me on every side.

17. Thou hast put Me away, and said: Natural law! Moral law! Divine law! Instinct! Reflection! Intuition! Second sight!

18. I say unto thee: I have abolished all these things. I will have them no more, forever!

19. I have no laws; I do by virtue of Mine own Presence.

20. I am not far away; behold, I am with thee.

21. I gave no instinct to any creature under the sun. By My Presence they do what they do.

22. I give no tuition by intuition; I am the Cause to all, and for all.

23. I am the most easily understood of all things.

24. My Hand is ready to whosoever will reach forth unto Me.

25. My Voice is ready and clear to whosoever will turn away from other things, and away from philosophies and ambiguous words, serving Me in good works.

26. My Light is present, and answereth unto all who follow their all highest knowledge.

CHAPTER XI.

1. Seek not to spread My gospels, and entice followers unto this, or that, saith Jehovih.

2. Neither go about preaching, saying: Thus saith Jehovih!

3. Let all men hear Me in their own way.

4. No man shall follow another.

5. I will have no sect.

6. I will have no creed.

7. I am not exclusive; but I am with all My living creatures.

8. To those who choose Me, practicing their all highest light, I am a shield and fortification against all darkness, and against all evil and contention.

9. Thou shalt not establish Me by man's laws, nor by the government of man, saith Jehovih.

10. Nor establish by man's laws or government any book or revelation, saying: Behold, this is Jehovih's book.

11. To keep man from interfering with man, this hath been great labor.

12. To teach man to comprehend liberty, especially as to thought and as to knowledge, this hath been a great labor.

13. For he falleth easily under the inspiration of his surroundings, and falleth under the teachings and persuasions of his brother.

14. Because he cometh from My hand into the world in innocence, a helpless infant.

15. And his elder brothers take advantage of his innocence, and teach him their own knowledge, instead of directing him to Me.

16. And his elder brothers were in darkness themselves, and their elder brothers before them.

17. I said unto man: Be free! Learn to know liberty! Think for thyself! Study thy Creator in all things, and in thyself in particular!

18. Turn thou away from thy elder brothers; come thou to the All Highest Fountain.

19. Be not confounded with abstruse reasonings; cut all things short, Godlike; learn thou of the Creator and His creations, there is nothing more.

20. Thou art one of the seeds of Jehovih, and wert planted by His Hand. Be thou free from all the world.

CHAPTER XII.

1. Man only, of all My created animals, created I not perfect in his order, saith Jehovih.

2. The most devoid of knowledge, and the most helpless of animals, created I man.

3. I gave not to the bird to improve her feathers; nor yet to improve her species; nor gave I her a book as to the manner of building her nest, nor as to her behavior with other birds.

4. Nor said I to the hare: Beware of foxes, or go thou, teach thy young to depend on their fleetness.

5. And yet, both, birds and beasts, move by My inspiration, perfectly in the order I made them; the bird doeth her work, and the hare fleeth from the fox.

6. But the child of man will put its finger in a serpent's mouth, and the child will also eat any deadly poison.

7. Thus differently created I man from all other things on earth; but I gave him the foundation whereon he might attain to perfection in all the attributes of My other living creatures.

8. And I said to man: Be thou observant of what thou shalt eat and drink, and where thou shalt dwell by day, and sleep by night.

9. For all things shall write upon thy soul the character and kind whereof they are made.

10. If thou wilt be gentle, like a lamb, and non-resistant and docile, so thou mayst obtain great knowledge, feed thou upon herbs and fruits and cereals.

11. And thy blood shall be pure and cool, and charged with food for thy spirit, in peace and love.

12. But if thou wilt be ferocious, like a carnivorous beast, then thou shalt feed upon flesh and fish, and thy blood shall be hot, and thy spirit shall be stirred with passion and anger and contention and tattling and war and jealousy and love of vengeance.

13. For whatsoever thou chargest thy blood with, shall be charged upon thy spirit.

14. Because thou canst not feed on fish nor flesh but through destruction unto death, even so, destruction unto death shall come upon thy soul.

15. From thine own blood shall thy spirit be inspired, even according to what thy blood containeth.

16. As through corpor thy corporeal part is nurtured, so through the gaseous, atmospherean part is thy spirit nurtured.

17. Woman said: Behold, I kill not any lamb, nor bird, nor fish. Others kill them, but I eat them.

18. To kill My lambs and birds, and whatsoever I created alive, is a simple act, saith Jehovih. Let no man waste much speech because of such destructions.

19. It is the contamination of the blood of man by carnivorous food, whereon thou shalt ponder.

20. Like unto like created I all the living. Whosoever maketh himself carnivorous, can not escape conflict and contention within his own members, soul and body.

21. Until the earth was circumscribed, I gave man carnivorous food; to-day, I make it poison to him.

22. And man shall turn away from it; and the smell of it shall sicken him; and the sight of blood shall fill him with horror.

23. The butcher shall be ashamed of his avocation; his neighbors shall say to him: Thou

stinkest of blood!

24. Because thou gavest us flesh, we also drank to drunkenness.

25. Because thou gavest flesh, we also did smoke and take narcotics.

26. Because thou gavest us flesh, we are rotten with catarrh, and wasted in the lungs.

27. Because we feasted on flesh, Jehovih answered us in corruptible flesh.

28. Lo, we stink from the sole of our feet to the crown of our heads.

29. And our offspring are born into the world so helpless and corrupt that half of them die in infancy.

30. Jehovih said: When I command the nations of the earth to peace, behold I raise My hand above the carnivorant's head.

31. As there was a time when I created every animal perfect in its order; so also shall such a time come unto man.

32. And now is the dawn thereof. Hence, I named it kosmon.

33. As the spider learneth to build her net without a book, and the bees to dwell in a queendom in peace and industry without books and written laws and instructions as how to do this and that, even so, now is a new birth to the generations of My people.

34. By My direct inspiration upon them shall they learn to do all things perfect, in the order of man for which I created him.

35. Man shall know how to do things easily, and without the long labor of books, and without showing, or explanations.

36. As of old, I commanded thee to have dominion over every living thing I created; so, now, I command thee to take the earth and the waters of the earth and the air above the earth into thy dominion also.

37. And thou shalt rule over them; to drive away the heat, and bring the cold; to drive away the cold, and bring the heat, as thou wilt, for the benefit of all the living.

38. To accomplish which, thou shalt now, first of all, adapt thyself to thy Creator, according to My highest Light upon thee:

39. To put away thine own inharmony in thy blood and flesh, and in thy soul.

40. Opening the way for My inspiration to come direct to thee, that thou mayst be one with Me.

CHAPTER XIII.

1. Man saith: If I can not add one jot or tittle to my corporeal body, and it is all built up by Jehovih, then, indeed, it is His.

2. Neither am I accountable whether it be well made, or well preserved.

3. And if I can not make one new thought nor idea, then, indeed are all my thoughts and ideas Jehovih's, given to me by inspiration, either directly by Jehovih, or by His creations.

4. Neither, then, am I accountable for my thoughts, nor ideas, nor behavior, whether they be good or bad. Verily, then, I am not responsible for anything, neither what I am, nor what I do, nor for what becometh of me. I am but an automation; I, myself, am nothing.

5. Jehovih saith: Because I gave thee liberty, thou art responsible for all thou art, and for all thou makest thyself, and for all that shall come to thee, and for thy peace and happiness, both in this world and the next.

6. Liberty I gave thee as to what thou shouldst eat, and shouldst wear to cover thyself, and

where thou shouldst abide.

7. I gave thee liberty to build thy house in thine own way; but, behold, such liberty I gave not to the bird, as to her nest, nor to the beaver, nor to the ant, nor to any other living creature.

8. Liberty I gave thee as to whether thou should eat herbs or flesh. But such liberty I gave not to any other living creature.

9. To the sheep and the horse I said: Eat ye of herbs; to the tiger and lion: Eat ye of flesh.

10. To thee I gave liberty to make thyself carnivorous, or herbivorous, or omnivorous.

11. Whatsoever thou didst put in thy mouth, and it united with thy blood, and entered thy body, behold, it was by My labor and by My power it was accomplished.

12. Verily was I thy workman.

13. All that thou didst in the matter was to choose. Thou wert, in that respect, the master, and I thy servant. And, behold, I made not the servant responsible for the master's behavior.

14. Because thou madst thyself carnivorous, the fault is thine own. I placed before thee the herbivorous animals and the carnivorous animals; and I gave thee eyes to look upon them as to their behavior, whether ferocious and destructive, or peaceful, patient and docile.

15. And I spake unto thy soul, saying: Look, judge for thyself as to what thou shalt eat; behold the order of My creations and the result upon all My living creatures.

16. Hence, thou art accountable unto thyself, and responsible unto all the world for having made thy corporeal body as thou hast.

17. Even so, in regard to thy spirit, thy soul, thy mind, thy ideas and thy thoughts, I gave thee liberty in the same way.

18. I gave thee liberty to receive thy inspiration from drunkards and harlots and fighters; or from men of wisdom, or the innocence of childhood, or the virtue of a virgin.

19. Or from a city of corruption, or from the country, with pure air and trees, and flowers and mountains and valleys.

20. And I spake unto thy soul, saying: Choose thou what thou wilt to be the inspiration of thy mind and spirit and soul; behold, I, thy Creator, am thy servant to impregnate thee with thoughts and ideas and disposition. All thou hast to do, is to choose.

21. Yea, I said: I will even take thee to whichever place and condition thou mayst choose.

22. And, now, because I gave unto thee this extreme liberty, and thou hast chosen, behold, thou art accountable unto thyself for thine every thought and idea; and for thy spirit and soul, and in thy behavior thou art responsible to all the world.

23. With liberty I bestowed responsibility also.

24. I am the Power, the Light and the Life.

25. In one thing, chiefly, thou art not an automaton, and that is thine own entity, thine own self, thine own whatsoever thou art.

26. Thyself I gave to thyself, and even at the zero of thy entity, I said unto thee: Go thou, make thyself. All other animals I created perfectly with Mine own hands, but to thee I gave liberty to make thyself, even as thou hast. Yea, even in this, I said: Choose thou, and I will do for thee thy labor Myself.

27. So that, choice and liberty were the sum total which I gave to thee.

28. Now, therefore, O man, as I gave choice and liberty unto thee, so shalt thou give the

same unto thy neighbor and associate.

29. Without these, there is no responsibility; with these, all responsibility.

30. Choose thou thine own food, and thine own raiment and thine house; and choose thou the place, and provide thou the way for whatever inspiration thou mayst, still thou shalt be responsible in all; and the result shall be to thee according to thine own choice, whether thou fawn upon satan, or emulate thy Creator.

CHAPTER XIV.

1. These are Tae's revelations of Jehovih's times and seasons, appointed unto the chosen:

2. The northern line of the sun shall be the end of the year, and it shall be called the last day of the old year, saith Jehovih.

3. And the first day thereafter, when the sun starteth on his southern course, shall be the beginning of the year, and it shall be called the new year's day.

4. These are My times of the end and the beginning of a year, which I created; and I made the earth and the sun as My written testimony thereof.

5. And I blessed and sanctified the old year's day and the new year's day, and I appointed them to be holy days, that men might remember the order and the system of My works.

6. And I said unto man: From one new year's day until the succeeding one shall be called one year, for it is one completed oscillation of the earth, and of her revolution in the orbit where I placed her.

7. Therefore, what thou hast completed within a year shall be remembered by thee, that thou mayst judge thyself therein.

8. And, on the old year's day, thou shalt render up in full forgiveness in all things against all people.

9. And with the setting of the sun on that day, thou shalt be purged of all animosity and claims against every man, woman and child, in all the world.

10. And thou shalt make acknowledgement of this in words and songs and prayers, and in tokens, of no intrinsic value, to whomsoever thou shalt have offended during the past year.

11. Tae said: For which reason the old year's day shall be named, the Most Holy Sabbath Day. Behold, it is in accord with His heavenly kingdoms. And it shall be with thee a day of spiritual communion, and of praise to Jehovih and His creations; with music and oratory, and ceremonies, and processions of thy youth, orderly and well disciplined.

12. And, on the new year's day, thou shalt rejoice and sing and dance; mingling together, old and young, even as the old year and the new year are joined together, side by side.

13. The seventh day of the new year shall be thy next sabbath day, and it shall be a day of rest and of spiritual communion and praise to Jehovih and His creations, with singing and oratory.

14. So also shall every seventh day be a sabbath day; for which reason seven days shall be one week, being six days for labor, and one for rest and worship.

15. For this hath been proven in all the world to be good for man.

16. These, then, shall be the moon's days (months):

17. The first new moon's day after new year's day shall be the beginning of the first month; and the completion of the fourth quarter of the moon shall be the completion of

the first month, and it shall be named, First month.

18. The next four quarters of the moon shall be the second month, and it shall be named, Second month.

19. And the next completed four quarters of the moon shall be named, Third month. And so on, to the completion of the year.

20. Such, then, shall be the month in any and every year, for these are the moon's times as Jehovih created them.

21. Neither shall it matter or not whether the months overlap a new year's day; as they are created and moved by the Almighty, even so shall man compute and register them.

22. (For example, a new year's day may come upon the twentieth day of the Twelfth moon or on another moon's day, still, as they fall, so shall they be numbered in truth.)

23. As the moon's time differeth to different continents, so shall the months' times of the inhabitants of different continents be locally unto them.

24. But, in the intercourse between different nations on different continents, the month times shall not be enumerated.

25. But, in all such cases, the year and the days thereof shall be named.

26. (As, for example, the seventieth year and the ninety-sixth day.)

27. And it shall come to pass that the sabbath days all around the world shall be the same day unto all people, even with the travel of the sun.

28. Whereby, Jehovih's heavenly kingdoms shall be in concert with mortals, as to times and seasons in all things.

CHAPTER XV.
HOLY COMPACT DAY.

1. As Jehovih, through His God, bequeathed to the children of Guatama a government unfettered by the name of God or Lord or Savior, so Jehovih sanctified the day of the ratification and the signing and sealing of His compact (American Constitution), as the DAY OF THE HOLY SEAL.

2. And the sign thereof He made, A HAND HOLDING A QUILL.

3. Which shall be the master's sign of salutation in the lodge on the day and evening commemorating the same.

4. And Jehovih made the answer to the master's sign, THE HOLDING UP (by the member of the lodge) OF A PIECE OF PAPER, signifying, CONSTITUTION.

5. Therefore it was said: The master saluted on the sign, DAY OF THE HOLY SEAL, and the lodge answered in the sign, CONSTITUTION.

6. And Jehovih said: Remember this day, and keep it holy, to the end of the world, for hereat was the beginning of the liberty of man!

CHAPTER XVI.
HOLY VEIL DAY.

1. As Jehovih, through His God, pulled aside the veil of heaven, saying:

2. Let My angels forth; together shall converse the living and the dead.

3. So santified He the day when the angels of heaven were made known to mortals.

(March 31, 1848.)

4. And He gave the sign, A HAND HOLDING ASIDE A VEIL, signifying, HEAVEN REVEALED, as the master's sign in the lodge on the day and evening commemorating the same.

5. And Jehovih gave to the members of the lodge to answer in the sign, THREE CLAPPINGS, signifying, ENDLESS JOY!

6. And Jehovih said: Remember this day, and keep it holy, to the end of the world. For, without books and without arguments, behold, I have proven unto you the immortality of the soul of man!

CHAPTER XVII.
THE FALLEN SWORD'S DAY.

1. As Jehovih, through His God, delivered into freedom Guatama's slaves, and, thus, to general slavery dealt the final blow, so Jehovih blessed that day, and sanctified it.

2. And He gave to man, as the master's sign in the lodge, A HAND POINTING TOWARD A PEN, signifying, I HAVE PROVED THIS MIGHTIER THAN THE SWORD.

3. And Jehovih gave to the members in the lodge to answer in the sign, CLASPED HANDS, AND LOOKING UPWARD. signifying, IN THY PRAISE, JEHOVIH!

4. Jehovih said: Remember the day of proclamation of freedom, for it is My day, which I bequeath unto you as a day of freedom in all righteous jollification, which ye shall keep every year, and commemorate, to the end of the world.

CHAPTER XVIII.
HOLY KOSMON DAY.

1. Beside the above, Jehovih gave one more holy day, Kosmon Day, which He also commanded to be kept in commemoration of another matter, which Jehovih commanded to be secret with the Faithists for a certain period of time, the which time hath not expired to this day. Therefore, the day of kosmon is still a secret with the Faithists.

2. And Jehovih said: That mortals and angels may live and labor in concert, behold, I have given certain days, whereby large congregations on earth may be met by My organic heavens, in re-union, mortals and angels, for the happiness of both, and for the glory of My works.

3. Now, behold also, as by My Presence I inspire thee, when thou laborest with Me, and thou art doing righteously, and with purity and love, so also is it with thee, in regard to My angels.

4. When thou makest and keepest thy corporeal body pure and clean, My angels, who are pure and clean, come to thee to aid thee, and to enlighten thee.

5. And when thou puttest away all unclean thoughts and all unselfish desires, and seekest to obtain wisdom, and to learn how best thou canst help thy fellow-man, behold, My angels of light and wisdom come to thee, and, by virtue of their presence, which thou seest not, they inspire thy soul in the light of thy Creator.

6. Man hath said: I will not be a seer, or a prophet, nor a su'is, nor sar'gis; verily, I will not have angels with me to teach me, or to give me any light or knowledge under the sun.

7. Whatever I can attain, it shall be mine own. Wiser is it for me to obtain to know, and to

do things of myself, than have angels come and give to me, or manifest through me.

8. Verily, I will not be used, by man nor angel, for it would be prostituting my flesh and my spirit to others.

9. Behold, my body was given to me for mine own use and profit, to establish and develop mine own soul unto eternal happiness in individuality.

10. Alike unto all people is My Presence, saith Jehovih. I am unto the just and the unjust; I am everywhere, both, in darkness and in light.

11. Because thou art in darkness, thou beholdest not Me.

12. Because thou art imperfect in flesh and spirit, thou deniest Me.

13. Because thou art confounded with inharmony, thou believest not in Me.

14. He, who hath not an ear for music, discovereth not a tune; even as he that is discordant denieth My Person.

15. To the pure there is no selfishness, neither for earthly things, nor for their own flesh and spirit.

16. A pure man is as a clear glass; he can see out of himself, and, so, perceive My angels and Me.

17. Through the pure man, pure angels can see mortality as well as spirituality. Their presence inspireth him to understand all things.

18. As much with the man that is not a seer, or a su'is, are the angels, as with those that are seer, or su'is, or sar'gis.

19. Because thou seest not, nor hearest angels, only proveth thy darkness, but proveth not the absence of angels.

20. To the dark, come the dark; with the dark, abide the dark, both, angels and mortals. 21. More is the man of darkness ruled by angels, than is the man of light.

22. Behold, I created thee not to fill any place in all the world for thine own self's sake.

23. Neither gave I thy flesh nor thy spirit to be thine only.

24. These, also, shalt thou relinquish, saying: To Thee, O Jehovih, I give all; my flesh, my spirit, mind, and all my service; to be Thine forever.

25. Thou shalt say: Appropriate Thou me, soul and body, in whatsoever way Thou canst, that I may do the most good unto others, mortals and angels.

26. Until thou attainest this, thou shalt not hear My Voice, nor see My Hand.

27. As I gave away Myself, and thus created all things, so shalt thou follow in My footsteps, in order to become one with Me.

28. Herein lieth the secret of wisdom, truth, love and power, time without end.

END OF THE BOOK OF INSPIRATION.

BOOK OF JEHOVIH'S KINGDOM ON EARTH,

WHICH CONTAINETH WITHIN IT

THE BOOK OF SHALEM.

ALL OF WHICH IS ANTE-SCRIPT.

CHAPTER I.

1. In the early days of the kosmon era, after the revelations of the Father's kingdom on earth had been published, and was known abroad over all the world, there went forth many, in Jehovih's name, to accomplish unto the resurrection of man, and for the glory of the Almighty, the new kingdom.

2. Foremost, amongst the many, there came out of Uz one who was esteemed wise and good above all others; and because he was a representative man, the people named him, Tae.

3. And Tae prayed unto Jehovih for light and knowledge as to how best he could accomplish good unto the resurrection of the race of man.

4. And Jehovih answered Tae, saying: Go, bring My people out of Uz, and found them in a place by themselves; for now is the beginning of the founding of My kingdom on earth.

5. Tae answered, saying: Behold, O Jehovih, I have gathered together many men and many women, and they all profess a desire to found Thy kingdom.

6. One desireth to be a teacher; another, to be a superintendent; another, an overseer; another, an adviser.

7. And they are all learned and wise and good in their own way; but, also, they are neither workers nor capitalists, the two chief of all that I require.

8. Now, I pray to Thee, O Father, what shall thy servant do?

9. Jehovih answered Tae, saying: Go, seek, and bring out of Uz orphan babes and castaway infants and foundlings.

10. And these shall by thy colony, which shall be My new kingdom on earth.

11. Tae inquired: What can a man do with babes? How shall I feed them? Moreover I have not money to hire nurses.

12. Jehovih said: Have faith in thy Creator; in a good work done unto My little ones, behold, I will provide.

13. Whatsoever thou dost unto them, even so dost thou unto Me, wherein thou shalt not fail.

14. Neither shalt thou have anything to do with any adult man or woman who is without faith in Me. Behold, My people are infants in this era.

15. Deal thou with them, and with such only as are willing to serve them; for as much as they are served, so am I served also.

CHAPTER II.

1. So, Tae gathered together orphan babes and castaway infants and foundlings, a great number.

2. And a woman named, Es, heard of Tae and his work, and she came to him, inquiring:

3. How can a man attend babes? Now, because I have heard of thy work, behold, I have come to thee to labor for our Father in heaven.

4. Tae said: Whoso would labor for our Father in heaven, let her do unto these little ones. 5. Es said: Even for that I am before thee; I beseech thee, put me to work. 6. Tae inquired: Knowest thou the care of infants? And she answered him, saying:

7. In such labor, alas, I have had no experience, but I know Jehovih will guide me aright; otherwise, He had not inspired my soul unto the work. All wisdom is possible through Jehovih.

8. Tae said: Such being thy faith, thou art the first chosen woman in the Father's new kingdom. Go, therefore, and fulfill thy part, and may the Father be with thee.

9. So, Es went to work, accomplishing what was required unto the infants.

10. And Tae went again unto Uz, and brought hence more infants; many more than were possible unto the care of one woman.

11. So Tae issued a call, to wit:

12. Wanted, fifty men and women, who are Faithists in Jehovih, and are willing to take part in founding the Father's kingdom on earth as it is in heaven!

13. And there came in answer to Tae's call thousands and thousands of men and women.

14. And Tae cried out: O Jehovih, what shall Thy servant do? Behold, I asked for fifty men and women, and here are come thousands and thousands.

15. Jehovih answered Tae, saying: Try them My Son, and see if they be worthy. As many as are prepared, thou shalt accept; as many as are not prepared, thou shalt not accept. Behold, there is room for millions!

16. And Tae spake unto the multitude, saying: I called for fifty men and women and, lo, here are thousands, willing to take part in founding the Father's kingdom on earth.

17. Now, behold, when I saw your great number, I cried out: O Jehovih, what shall Thy servant do? I did ask for but fifty, and there are come here thousands and thousands.

18. And Jehovih answered, saying: Try them, my Son; as many as are prepared, accept; as many as are not prepared, accept not. Behold, there is room for millions.

19. Now, therefore, how say ye: What is the founding of the Fathers kingdom? Who here knoweth the way, and how to take part therein?

CHAPTER III.

1. It came to pass that many of the multitude answered Tae; and of all that thus spake, the following were the chief words, to wit:

2. Sutta said: To do what I am willing to do, is to take part in founding the Father's kingdom; therefore, hear me:

3. To adjust capital and labor, that each shall contribute to the advantage and glory of both.

4. That the capitalist shall receive good profit on his capital; and the laborer high and uniform wages.

5. To adjust them that they can live side by side, equally, and neither above or under the other.

6. That they may have extensive domains and beautiful parks; excellent factories;

virtuous and industrious people.

7. The part that I am capacitated to fill in this great work, is to reveal the key and the plans; to explain all things to both, the capitalists and laborers.

8. After that manner, Sutta went on at great length, and he was followed by several others, who had similar plans, but each one doubted the other's capacity, as being qualified for the work.

9. Aborn spake next. He said: I have heard Sutta's project. It is a farce. Capital and labor can not harmonize.

10. And even if they could, it would be a worldly basis. It would not be the Father's kingdom.

11. In His kingdom there shall be neither buying nor selling; neither servant nor master.

12. Now, behold, I say to you all, men and women, as such, can not harmonize together. They are diverse in all their ideas and general knowledge.

13. The only way to accomplish the Father's kingdom is through infants, to raise them up in the way they should go.

14. But, even with these, failure will result, save their pre-natal condition is provided for.

15. Therefore, the part I am capacitated to accomplish is, to become father to innumerable offspring, by most exalted and enlightened women.

16. Also, I have great knowledge of physiology, mentology and psychology, and I would be willing to be examiner and dictator as to prospective parents.

17. Thus spake Aborn at great length; and others spake in like manner, but each one preferred himself as the prospective father of the offspring.

18. Next spake Thurtis. She said: This it is, to found the Father's kingdom on earth; hear me, that ye may understand.

19. Behold, all things shall be possible through woman, especially as to raising up a new generation on the earth.

20. During the period of gestation, man should not approach woman.

21. Nay, in that period, woman should be treated as a very Goddess.

22. Her every want and whim and notion should be gratified to the utmost.

23. When she spake, or raised her finger, during the gestative period, every man and woman and child should run to do her service.

24. And she should be surrounded by cultured and exalted companions and charmed with sweet music and delightful entertainments.

25. Yea, as a very Goddess should all men do her reverence.

26. When such a woman hath a child born, behold, there will be one child for the Father's kingdom.

27. Now, behold, give me the choice as to who shall father my children, and such a part shall be my part, to help found the Father's kingdom.

28. After Thurtis, then spake many of the women after the same manner, and each one doubted the other's capacity to fill the place, but recommended herself.

29. Amos spake next. He said: I have heard all these beautiful systems; I am ready for any of them. Behold, I am a landscape gardener.

30. The part I can do is to lay out the grounds; for plots of flowers and grass and ornamental trees.

31. But ye shall provide laborers for me. I work not with mine own hands; I plan and

design; my capacity is in my talent and in my education.

32. After Amos, then spake the five hundred physicians, each one offering himself, to be the physician for the Father's kingdom. Then spake an equal number of lawyers in the same way.

33. Next spake a thousand teachers of the piano, each one offering to teach the young for the Father's kingdom.

34. And now, with slow and solemn aspect, rose up and spake five hundred priests of Brahma.

35. They said: We have heard; we have seen. Behold, the Father's kingdom is none of these.

36. It is the second coming of Brahma. He shall come in flames of fire, from the east and west and north and south.

37. By the magic touch of his wand, the different castes of men shall be sorted; and the dead shall come forth from their graves, and Brahma shall judge them.

38. The sky shall be filled with holy angels, the spirits of the saints, with wings of fire and with tails a mile in length.

39. And the elect of the earth shall rise in glory, and be immersed in nirvana forever, even at the feet of Ormazd.

40. This it is, to found the Father's kingdom on earth. After which, all flesh shall come into life free from sin; the corruptible shall turn incorruptible forever.

41. Now, behold, our part, in founding His kingdom is to preach unto you Brahma's everlasting gospels.

42. Next to speak, were five hundred Buddhist priests. They said:

43. We have heard and seen also. Our learning, no man may gainsay. As for Brahma and his second coming, for that matter, he never came once.

44. None have seen him, nor found his dwelling-place. Therefore he is but a superstition, a relic of the dark ages.

45. Hear us, then, as to the founding of the Father's kingdom on earth:

46. It is the second coming of Buddha, when every knee shall bow down, and own him Lord of all the world.

47. Behold, Budha shall come with two swords and twelve spears, and he shall have ten thousand brides!

48. When Budha shall blow his breath upon the earth, the graves shall be opened, and the dead shall come forth, and speak.

49. And Budha shall judge them; according to case, so will he separate them.

50. And ten hundred times ten thousand million angels, with fiery wings and with tails two miles in length, shall overspread the earth.

51. And all flesh shall become incorruptible; the lion shall eat straw, and the lamb shall rejoice in its kin without fear.

52. Next spake five hundred Kriste'yan priests. They said:

53. What profanity we have heard! Behold, as for Brahma and Budha, they are but myths. It is the second coming of Kriste, which is the founding of the Father's kingdom.

54. Kriste said: Think not I came to send peace on earth; I came not to send peace, but a sword.

55. It is he that shall subdue all the world, and make men bow down, and own him Lord

of all.

56. He shall come in a sea of fire, with millions of archangels. And when his servant, Gabriel, bloweth his horn upon the earth, the graves shall open, and the dead shall come forth, and speak to the living.

57. And he shall judge them; separating them, the bad to everlasting torments, and the good, who have worshipped Him, shall rise and inherit everlasting bliss.

58. Now, behold, the part we can do in founding the Father's kingdom, is to preach and explain the beautiful doctrines of our blessed Lord.

59. When many others had thus spoken, Tae said unto them: I called for such as had faith in Jehovih. I am not in the labor of founding a kingdom for Brahma, nor Budha, nor Kriste, nor for any one but the Creator, our heavenly Father.

60. As for the graves opening, I have nothing to do with that; though, for the spirits of the dead appearing face to face with the living, behold, that hath been accomplished now for more than thirty years, to hundreds of thousands of good people. So with that I have nothing to do either.

61. But since ye have not proved the communion of angels during all these years, how hope ye to labor for the Father's kingdom? To all such I say, go your ways; I have no use for you.

62. At once, one-half of the multitude rose up, and departed; mocking, saying: The spirits of the dead! We will have none such, but angels with wings, and with fleecy tails a mile in length.

63. Tae inquired once more: Who, here, hath faith in Jehovih, and, if we labor together in His name, living our all highest light, that His kingdom will be founded?

64. Hundreds and hundreds said: It depends on having plenty of money and a good plantation. With money, it can be accomplished; without money, it can not be.

65. Tae said: Your faith being in money, I have no use for you. I called for those with faith in Jehovih! Therefore, go your ways also. So, many more of the multitude departed, returning to Uz also, even as had the others.

66. Tae asked again: Who here are capable and desirous of being leaders, let them speak?

67. More than a thousand cried out: Here! That is my part. I am suited to it by nature and by experience and by great wisdom.

68. Tae said unto them: Behold the spirit of the age in which we live! No man desireth a leader or dictator over him. For that reason, go your ways also; I have no use for you.

69. Tae asked again: Who here have made a study of this subject, and are prepared to be lecturers and teachers and advisers, let them speak?

70. And, behold, another thousand cried out: That is my strength. I can explain all subjects; of diet, clothing, social intercourse, health, marriage and worship!

71. Others cried out: I am a trance speaker; I have angel guides two thousand years old!

72. Others said: I am inspirational; the ancient prophets are my spirit guides! St. John, the revelator! Confucius! Hosea! King Solomon! Daniel!

73. Tae interrupted them, saying: Behold, the signs of the times show us that, as to founding the Father's kingdom by words, sermons and lectures, they are worthless.

74. See here; I have gathered together hundreds of helpless orphan babes. They care for none of the things that have been offered; they need washing and feeding, and their clothes are to wash and mend.

75. Who, so believing in the Father, that he will give up self, in all respects, and work for these little ones, having faith that Jehovih will provide justly and sufficiently unto all, let him come.

76. You all do know how the farmers go about gathering up calves and colts and the young of all sorts; and they take them to a good place and feed them; and when they are grown up, they are the choice in market.

77. Now, behold, there are thousands of fatherless and destitute children in Uz, which, left to themselves, either die or grow up to be thieves, robbers and murderers.

78. These are cheaper than calves and young colts. And they may be raised to be of more profit to themselves and to the state, than ten times as many cattle.

79. Who, then, is ready to join in this labor without money and without price, devoting his life to training them up to practical knowledge, not only of books, but to use their hands in trades and factories, that these little ones may become useful citizens, and a joy to themselves and glory to the Father. Let such speak.

80. And, now, behold, fifty men and women spake, saying: Take us, in Jehovih's name. We have neither whim or conceit to carry out.

81. We are willing and anxious to go to this labor, and we know Jehovih will provide unto us. From day to day His Light will shine upon us, and we shall know what to do.

82. Thy children shall be our children; thy hardships our hardships. We come not for rest, nor glory, nor for comforts; but we come to serve Jehovih in whatsoever He may give us to do for His kingdom.

83. Tae said: In Jehovih's name, I accept you. Whatsoever is mine shall be yours also.

84. Thus it came to pass, out of all the thousands and thousands who came, only fifty were accepted.

85. And the others went their way, mocking, saying: A most beautiful Father's kingdom on earth!

CHAPTER IV.

HISTORY OF SHALEM, FORMERLY CALLED "BOOK OF SHALEM."

1. The Voice of Jehovih came to Tae, saying: Take thy people and go whither I will lead thee, and ye all shall be blessed. Quite sufficient are these, to begin the founding of My kingdom on earth.

2. And Tae and his people went away to an unoccupied country, by the river Shalam, so-called because Tae had said:

3. I take the babes the Uzians would not have, and I come to a place where the Uzians would not live, and yet I will make it a place of peace and plenty; therefore, it shall be called Shalam.

4. And when they had pitched their tents and fed the children, Tae called them together that he might speak before them.

5. Tae said: By and through Jehovih, are all things accomplished, either directly or indirectly.

6. If directly, by His inspiration, then are all things well done, and in peace and righteousness and love and wisdom.

7. If indirectly, and through other inspiration, then, indeed, is man answered in disaster

and unhappiness.

8. Foremost of all, must it be man's aim to receive light directly from Jehovih in regard to all things.

9. To do which, man must approach his Creator, in words and conduct, doing in practice the right which he perceiveth in judgment.

10. Now, therefore, from our youth up we have repeated the prayer: Thy kingdom come on earth as it is in heaven.

11. Yet, not one of us put forth a hand to accomplish what we prayed for.

12. In which our prayers profaned the Almighty.

13. For had we been true in heart, we had taken hold in practice, according to our best ability.

14. In not doing which, we were false before Jehovih, and He could not answer our prayers in truth.

15. Moreover, we had said to one another from our youth up: As ye would that others should do unto you, do ye even so unto them.

16. Nevertheless, we served ourselves only.

17. We visited not the fatherless and motherless.

18. We sold not what we might, and gave to to poor.

19. We professed faith in Jehovih, but we manifested faith in money and in soldiers and warfare.

20. We had said: Love the Creator with all thy soul and heart and mind, and thy neighbor as thyself.

21. Neither of which we fulfilled.

22. Now, therefore, we were unrighteous toward man, and false before Jehovih.

23. In repentance and shame have we come out of Uz; because we could not fulfill the commandments whilst dwelling in Uz. Behold, we have come thence, to begin a new life upon the earth.

24. That our labor and our lives may be given unto Jehovih, with profit for the raising up of the race of man, and for the glory of the Almighty, let us covenant ourselves unto Him in fullness of heart and of soul and with all our mind, to practice all the commandments in fullness. What say ye?

25. The multitude answered with one voice: We desire to covenant with Jehovih, that our labor and our growth may contribute to the founding of His kingdom on earth.

26. Make thou, therefore, thy covenant with the Creator, and, that we may be in unison, behold, we will repeat with thee thy words, that Jehovih may be glorified therein.

27. Tae said: Hear me, then, ere we make the covenant to Jehovih: In the heavens, the angels surround the heavenly throne with columns of fire and water; and all the space within the circuit is named, the PLACE OF THE HOLY COVENANT, and it is appropriated to worship and to sacred rites and ceremonies.

28. But places of amusement and of all other kinds of entertainments, not sacred in rites and ceremonies, are situated external to the Place of the Holy Covenant.

29. Now, therefore, in remembrance of Jehovih's heavenly kingdoms, let us mark a circular line around about this place, and march in procession, dedicating the enclosure to the Holy Covenant.

30. The multitude said: This is wise; by system and order and a place for all things,

harmony will answer unto us. Lead thou, therefore, the way, and we will march with thee.

31. Then Tae marched, DRAWING THE LINE OF THE SACRED CIRCLE, and the multitude, two abreast, marched after him.

32. Tae said: I draw the LINE OF THE SACRED CIRCLE unto Thee, Jehovih. In Thy name I dedicate and enclose this, Thy PLACE OF THE HOLY COVENANT, to be Thine forever!

33. The multitude responded: May I remember Thy LINE OF THE SACRED CIRCLE, Jehovih, and comport myself within it for Thine honor and glory forever!

34. Within this place am I about to covenant myself to Thee forever, as a laborer to fulfill Thy kingdom on earth for the resurrection of man.

35. Response: May I remember the little ones within this SACRED CIRCLE, whom Thou hast given into my charge, for whose welfare on earth and in heaven, I am about to covenant myself unto Thee, to make myself an example and sacrifice before them during all my life.

36. Together: In remembrance of the pillars of light in heaven, that surround the throne of Thy Son, God of earth and heaven, we build here a hedge and a fence, as a lasting testimony that we dedicated to Thee, Jehovih, the enclosed PLACE OF THE SACRED COVENANT.

CHAPTER V.
THE HOLY COVENANT.

1. Then Tae and his hosts went into the midst of the Place of the Holy Covenant; and the hosts formed in a crescent, and Tae stood betwixt the horns thereof.

2. And, whilst thus standing, Tae, being moved by the Light of Jehovih upon him, uttered the covenant, and his hosts, in concert, uttered the words after him.

3. And these words were called, THE HOLY COVENANT, even as they are to this day, to wit:

4. Thou, O Jehovih! As Thou hast declared Thyself in the Book of Jehovih!

5. To Thee I covenant myself, to be Thine forever! And to Thee only, O Jehovih!

6. And I abjure all Gods but Thee.

7. And I abjure all Lords but Thee.

8. And I abjure all Saviors but Thee.

9. In this, Thy Place of the Holy Covenant, do I covenant myself unto Thee, to be only Thine, and forever!

10. My corporeal body, I dedicate and covenant unto Thee, to be in Thy service during all my life.

11. Because Thou madest it out of Thine own material, behold, it is Thine.

12. The workmanship is Thine; the material is Thine also.

13. I have no claim upon it; unto Thee, and for Thy service, do I resign it forever.

14. Into my charge Thou gavest it unto me, as the habitation of my spirit.

15. Because it is Thy gift, I will care for it, and keep it clean and pure, before Thee, that it may be acceptable to Thee, and to the presence of Thy holy angels.

16. My spirit I also dedicate and covenant unto Thee, to be in Thy service, henceforth forever.

17. My mind and soul, I dedicate and covenant unto Thee, to be in Thy service, henceforth forever.

18. My whole self, whereof I am made, soul and body, dedicate and covenant I unto Thee,

to be in Thy service forever.

19. Out of Thine own self madest Thou me, soul and body, and they are Thine only, to be used by Thee forever.

20. Appropriate Thou me, O Jehovih, my corporeal body, and my spirit, my mind, my behavior and thoughts, to be of profit to Thee, for founding Thy kingdom on earth.

21. And I covenant unto Thee, Jehovih, I will search constantly into mine own every act and deed and word and thought, to make myself true in the practice of Thy highest Light upon me.

22. That henceforth, forever, I will search to find the highest Light, and I will practice the same toward all men, women and children.

23. Unto them will I not only do as I would be done by, but more; I will do for them, with all my wisdom and strength, all my life.

24. I covenant unto Thee, Jehovih, that, since all things are Thine, I will not own nor possess, exclusively unto myself, anything under the sun, which may be entrusted to me, which any other person or persons may covet or desire, or stand in need of.

25. Neither more will I talk of myself, either in laudation of what I am, nor of what I have done; but Thou shalt judge me, and hold me accountable for shortness in word and behavior, wherein, by any means, I may manifest self-esteem or covetousness for fame, or the applause of men, even for any good I may have done unto others.

26. Neither more will I censure, nor criticize, nor blame, any man, or woman, nor any child over fourteen years of age, as an individual, in all the world, for any shortness in word or deed they manifest.

27. For they are Thine, Jehovih, and not mine, to be led or driven by me.

28. To all these Faithists, my brothers and sisters in Thy kingdom, will I deal and think and behave, in affiliation, as gentle and truly as were they my own blood and kin, brothers and sisters, or father and mother.

29. And over these babes, which Thou hast entrusted to me, will I be as loving and true as were they mine own blood and kin, sons and daughters.

30. According to Thy Light, which Thou mayst bestow upon me, will I raise them up to know Thee, and to be a glory in Thy kingdom.

31. First of my teaching unto them shall be, to make them know Thee, and to remember that Thy eye is upon them, and Thy hand above them, to bless them according to their wisdom, truth, love and purity.

32. And I will teach them the way of the communion of Thy angels; to develop them in su'is and sar'gis.

33. Teaching them to live for the spirit within, rather than for corpor.

34. Teaching them by books and instruments.

35. Teaching them useful trades and occupations.

36. Teaching them music and worship.

37. Teaching them dancing and gymnastics.

38. And, in all things, developing in them all the talents Thou hast created in them, that they may grow up to be an honor and a glory on the earth, and to rejoice because Thou hast created them alive.

39. And I will emancipate them from infancy at fourteen years of age; and bestow upon them the rights of man and woman, in their thoughts, words, deeds, choice and actions.

40. Throwing upon them, at that age, their responsibility unto Thee, for their thoughts, words, ideas, behavior, as fully as I claim the same unto mine own self.

41. And now, O Jehovih, that this, Thy kingdom on earth, may be known and distinguished from the habitations of the Uzians, we make this our solemn oath unto Thee:

42. We will not, now, nor forever, make war, nor engage in war, nor take any part in war, for any God, nor Lord, nor Savior, nor country, nor king or other ruler on earth; nor will we aid nor abet war in any way whatever.

43. Neither will we now, nor forever, eat fish nor flesh of any creature Thou didst create alive.

44. And we swear unto Thee, Jehovih, in regard to these our babes, which Thou hast given unto our keeping, to found Thy kingdom on earth, we will raise them up to abjure war, like unto this our oath unto Thee, and to practice not the carnivorous habit belonging to the Uzians.

45. Neither will we use, nor permit to be used, in Shalam, any intoxicating drink, nor weed, nor root, nor gum, nor any other drug, for the contamination of human flesh by intoxication or for stimulation unnaturally.

46. Make us strong and wise, O Jehovih, in this our covenant and oath unto Thee, for Thine are the honor and the glory of all things, time without end. Amen.

CHAPTER VI.
THE COVENANT OF THE BROTHERHOOD.

1. Now, when Tae and his hosts had made the covenant with Jehovih, behold, the Voice descended upon Tae by entrancement, with the holy angels of the God of heaven and earth, and he said:

2. Whosoever Choose Me, I choose in return.

3. Whosoever serve Me, I serve in return.

4. Alike unto like, created I the adaptation of angels and mortals.

5. As ye have drawn a corporeal circle around My kingdom, behold, My holy angels have drawn a spiritual circle around you.

6. As ye have dedicated to Me, so do I dedicate to you, to serve you in holiness and wisdom, by angels from the throne of My God.

7. As much as ye have come to raise up My little ones, I will come to you, through My angels, and raise you up also.

8. As ye make My little ones wise, and useful, and to rejoice in their lives, so will I minister unto you.

9. As ye are covenanted unto Me against war, and to establish the practice of peace on earth, so will My hand be over you in this My kingdom, both on earth and in heaven.

10. And as much as ye are come to found My kingdom on earth, even so have I opened the kingdoms of the second resurrection in heaven unto you.

11. Proclaim it in the east and west and north and south, My kingdom is founded on earth.

12. The Voice departed, and then Tae, in his own wisdom, faced to the east, and he said:

13. Hear ye, hear ye, O mortals and angels, Jehovih's kingdom is founded on earth!

14. Then Tae faced to the west, saying: Hear ye, hear ye, O mortals and angels, Jehovih's

kingdom is founded on earth!

15. Then Tae faced to the north, and said: Hear ye, hear ye, O mortals and angels, Jehovih's kingdom is founded on earth!

16. Next, Tae faced to the south, saying: Hear ye, hear ye, O mortals and angels, Jehovih's kingdom is founded on earth!

17. And Tae made the SIGN OF THE CIRCLE TWICE CUT, and his hosts answered under the sign, JEHOVIH'S DAWN.

18. And, now, the Light of Jehovih came upon Tae, and, of his own accord, he said:

19. Without a covenant of brotherhood, behold, we are like an unorganized school without a teacher.

20. As satan, in the management of his soldiers for war purposes, hath demonstrated the advantage of power through discipline, let us be wise in the Father's kingdom, by discipline also, but in peace and righteousness.

21. Unity can not be achieved but through order and discipline and rites and ceremonies and words.

22. Power is obtained more by concerted oneness of purpose than by anything else under the sun.

23. For which purposes, let us become organic for the founding of Jehovih's kingdom on earth.

24. So that, henceforth, we shall be a unit before the world, guided by Jehovih to the single end of establishing a community that can practice His commandments in full.

25. And, though we may fail in some measure, let us remember the generation we are raising up shall have more advantages and practice; and their successors shall also advance still higher.

26. Ultimately, all the world shall attain to peace, virtue, plenty and wisdom.

27. Already are we covenanted to live our all highest light, and to practice it.

28. How, then, shall we become organic, and still have no leader or overseer?

29. The highest wisdom in the state, or in a community, is not with the majority, but with a small minority.

30. The highest wisdom, which is the highest light, should guide the individual and the family and the community and the state.

31. Now, therefore, let us divide ourselves into groups of tens.

32. And each group shall select its wisest man, as speaker, and his title shall be Chief.

33. And let the chiefs be a group also, and they shall select a speaker, whose title shall be C'chief.

34. Let the business within the colony be divided into as many departments as there are groups, one to each.

35. But let the united business of the colony, in its relations to the world, and to sister colonies, be in the care of the C'chief and the other chiefs.

36. Now, behold, in the kingdoms of heaven, when a matter is announced, requiring the Holy Council's action, each and all the members who desire, speak thereon, giving their highest light.

37. And, after that, the chief giveth his highest light, which is the decree.

38. So let it be with us.

39. And it shall be discovered in a short time who is the highest light, not only of each

group, but of all the groups.

40. And whosoever is chief, shall be held responsible for the errors or shortness of his group; and whosoever is C'chief shall be held responsible for the shortness or errors of the whole colony as such.

41. Who, then, knowing that what is bound on earth is also bound in heaven, is willing to bind himself unto these heavenly laws for the sake of Jehovih's kingdom on earth?

42. When Tae asked this, the whole of the multitude answered: In Jehovih's name, I bind myself in this also.

43. Tae said: Then, in Jehovih's name, repeat after me:

44. In the name of Jehovih, I bind myself to the C'chief's decree; and I bind myself to the chief's decree also, and I bind myself in the brotherhood of groups.

45. When they had thus repeated the words of brotherhood, Tae said: Let the hosts form in circle, facing the center.

46. When they were thus formed, Tae went round the circle on the inside, going with the sun, shaking hands with each one as he passed, saying: Welcome, my brother (sister), in the Brotherhood of Faithists; with thee, I covenant to be thine equal and obedient servant, to whom I wed myself both in this world and in the next, for the resurrection of man and the establishing of Jehovih's kingdom with mortals.

47. Then, after Tae, the next one on his left went round the circle also, shaking hands, and repeating the marriage words of the brotherhood.

48. And so on, they went, until all of them had completed the Covenant of the Brotherhood.

49. Tae said: I salute you all under the sign, Jehovih's Name.

50. And they answered, by his instruction, in the sign, Many in One.

51. The Voice spake through Tae, saying: Whoever, hereafter, shall join my kingdom, shall repeat My Covenant and the Covenant of My Brotherhood, before the C'chief and the chiefs and before My chosen, in the manner ye have done before Me and My holy angels.

CHAPTER VII.
FOUNDING THE GROUPS.

1. The Light of Jehovih being upon Tae, he said: Let the examples of Uz be not lost upon you. But where ye have learned, and what ye have acquired, these shall ye appropriate wisely in Shalam.

2. For which purpose, it is wise that we appoint our groups as now required, to be added unto afterward, when more is required.

3. How say ye, then, shall we appoint groups this day?

4. Thereupon, different persons spake, and the sum of their wisdom was that there should be:

5. A group of architects;

6. A group of clothiers;

7. A group of dieticians;

8. A group of engineers;

9. A group of manufacturers;

10. A group of horticulturists;

11. A group of agriculturists;

12. A group of botanists;

13. A group of nurses;

14. A group of physicians;

15. A group of artists (sculpture, painting and gardening);

16. A group of musicians.

17. And these were all the groups required at that time. Accordingly, Tae proclaimed them, and called for volunteers for each and every group.

18. And these were filled, though, because there were but fifty-two members, some of them took membership in two or three groups, so that all were filled.

19. The Light still being upon Tae, he said: Since ye have made the groups, let each group now select a chief.

20. Now, many of them spake up, saying: I neither wish fame for being chief, nor do I wish the responsibility of the position.

21. Tae said: Suffer me, then, to declare the Light that is upon me; which is, that ye are here to fulfill whatsoever Jehovih may put upon you, with all your wisdom and strength.

22. Whether ye be made chiefs or not made chiefs, it is Jehovih's work ye are here to fulfill, without any regard as to your personal selves.

23. To covet chieftainship would be selfish; to refuse chieftainship would be selfish.

24. We can not found the Father's kingdom with any other members than such as say, with all their hearts, and mind and soul: Whatsoever Thou puttest upon me, O Jehovih, that will I do with all my wisdom and strength.

25. To have faith in this way, is to have faith with practice; such a one is a Faithist in fact.

26. Now, those who had spoken before relented, saying: O Jehovih, what have I done? Behold, I tript myself up even in the start. Make this a rebuke to me, O Father, and heap Thou upon me whatsoever Thou wilt.

27. Tae said: What any one can do, it is well done; wherein he faileth, because of incapacity, behold, it is not his fault, but his misfortune.

28. So, it came to pass, chiefs were selected for every group, men and women.

29. And Tae was made C'chief. And so, Tae delivered to each of the chiefs a synopsis of his duties.

CHAPTER VIII.

1. To the chief of architecture, Tae said: Thy duties shall be one with thy group, and what I say to thee shall apply to them also. Thou shalt not only build houses for Shalam, providing them comfortably with rooms and with wholesome conveniences, but thou shalt teach our adopted infants, by models and otherwise, the art and science of architecture.

2. At a very early age thou shalt explain to them, by blocks and with tools, the science and measurements of architecture, as to the names and kinds thereof, to the place and use of braces, beams and roofs.

3. Moreover, as soon as they are capable of holding a pencil, thou shalt teach them to make drafts of houses, and the parts thereof. And when they are old enough to handle

tools, thou shalt teach them to make models of houses, and to estimate the strength of the parts required.

4. To the chief of clothiers, Tae said: Thy duties shall be one with thy group, and what I say to thee is to them also. Thou shalt not only provide clothing for Shalam, in wisdom as to comfort, pattern and beauty, but thou shalt prepare the way to teach these, our adopted infants, the art and workmanship of clothing the human form in the way most conducive to health and comfort.

5. At an early age thou shalt teach them the art of sewing and cutting, providing for them models in human form, so they may learn everything from a hat to a shoe, as to the material used, the strength required, and how to determine the same.

6. To the chief of dieticians, Tae said: Thou and thy group shall be one; what I say to thee is to them also. Thou shalt determine and provide diet for Shalam; as to the best herbivorous foods, and how to prepare them, and how to preserve such as shall be kept over.

7. In this matter thou shalt determine and explain the constituent parts of the human body, and shalt find and provide herbivorous elements adapted to development and purity, so that the best and strongest and healthiest of men and women may be made out of these, our adopted infants. Neither shalt thou follow whims or fancies; but thou shalt support thyself by facts collected from the different nations of the earth.

8. And in the preparation of food, thou shalt teach these infants the art and the properties and all things pertaining to food and diet. And explain to them the blood-thirsty character of carnivorous animals, and carnivorous people, giving them facts and figures, so that in all thou teachest them they shall be learned wisely, and not in conceit merely.

9. Thus spake Tae to all the chiefs, explaining to them their parts. And after he had finished with them individually, then he spake to them collectively, saying:

10. The greatest of all learning is to learn how to live in the best way, that we may be happy here and hereafter. There is no other learning so important as this.

11. To man, Jehovih provided neither wool nor hair nor feathers to cover his body; and yet He created him too tender to live without covering.

12. In sexual relation, man and woman alone, of all the animal world, can be taught shame.

13. Whatever dress attracteth the least thought to sex is the most modest dress; whatever dress giveth the fullest, best development to all parts of the body, with adaptation to comfort for the seasons, is the best dress.

14. Next to dress is diet. As to what is best to eat, for the best, healthiest corporeal man, and the best for the wisest, holiest spiritual man, is the best diet.

15. These, with houses to live in, comprise the chief requirements for the corporeal life of man.

16. And yet, to produce these, and prepare them up unto man's service, many trades and sciences have been developed on the earth.

17. Now, behold, in this day Jehovih hath provided amply unto us. He hath opened up unto us the nations of the earth, where we can go and witness many things, especially as to the habits and dispositions of man; as to his mode of life, in food and clothes and houses.

18. Now, behold, ye have taken a great work upon yourselves; which is to raise up these

little ones according to your highest light.

19. Ye have bound yourselves to follow your own highest light. And ye know that all light is progressive. Ye can not settle down, saying: I know enough!

20. But ye are bound to investigate. And how can ye do this without acquainting yourselves with what hath been proved amongst other peoples?

21. In some countries, infants are whipped for crying; in other countries, they are held up by the heels; and, in some countries, infants cry not at all.

22. The chief of nurses shall discover these facts, and appropriate them.

23. In like manner, shall every chief take his part, and develop the highest proven and possible standard.

24. As much as ye thus fulfill your places, so shall be your satisfaction and happiness afterward. As much as ye neglect your parts, so will ye censure and accuse yourselves afterward.

25. As Faithists, ye accept all people as angels; mortals are simply undelivered.

26. All mortals are in an embryonic state, preparing for birth (commonly called, death).

27. Heaven is now, and is near, even within all who will accept it.

28. At an early age, infants can be taught that to serve Jehovih bringeth happiness; to serve mortal inspirations and surroundings (satan) bringeth unhappiness.

29. Therefore, though ye teach our infants about diet and architecture and clothing and all other things, ye will still be but little improvement on Uz, save ye teach them that the chief aim of life should be to develop the spiritual man that is within.

30. By this system of education in Shalam, there shall be two branches, one relating to corporeal things and one to spiritual things.

CHAPTER IX.

1. Tae said: Behold, the Uzians have schools, and they teach their young by and in books. But when their youth are thus educated, as to their brains, their hands are useless for providing food and clothes and habitations.

2. Education, in regard to corporeal things, must embrace the manipulation and handling of corporeal things for useful purposes. And, foremost of all problems is: How to provide the necessities of life with one's own hands, that he may not be rendered a dependent on others.

3. This shall be one of the first problems ye shall make our infants understand.

4. Young children not only ask questions, but they desire illustrations, with the privilege of trying to do something themselves.

5. Their questions must be answered by their nurses and their teachers.

6. It is not sufficient unto Jehovih's requirements of you, that ye put off His children with elusive answers, or with incomprehensible explanations.

7. Education must be accompanied with practice. As, for example, ye show the child certain seeds, explaining what will grow therefrom; ye shall plant and illustrate. And when the vine hath come up out of the ground, ye shall not only illustrate its corporeality, but shall display the life therein as a manifestation of Jehovih's Presence.

8. To simply teach the child the botany, without reference to the spirituality that underlieth all living things, would have little effect in turning the child's thoughts to its

own life and growth in spirit.

9. At an early age, these infants shall be thus put to work in gratification of their own desires to do something; and their work shall be educational, corporeally and spiritually.

10. And when they are large enough to handle tools, they shall be permitted to work at trades, or in art; and full and sufficient explanations shall be given to all their questions.

11. And this shall come to pass in Shalam; without tiresome study and without tiresome labor, these infants, at fourteen years, shall be wiser and better learned than Uzians at twenty.

12. For they shall not be limited to one trade each, or one occupation each; but, to a great extent, all of them shall know all trades and occupations.

13. For botany, they shall have a garden; and for astronomy, an observatory; for chemistry, a laboratory; for clothing, a factory; for horticulture and agriculture, they shall have orchards, fields and gardens.

14. Such, then, shall be the method of teaching our infants.

15. Now, as to Jehovih and His creations, in magnitude and perfection, they shall be ever kept before the child's mind, to exalt its gratitude and adoration, and to make it rejoice in its own life.

16. For there is not, in all the philosophies in all the world, wherewith to restrain the private life and habits from secret vice, save through belief in Jehovih's eye being ever upon us.

17. Nevertheless, a child that is raised up without learning angel communion is but half raised.

18. By the actual presence of angels, and by children seeing them and conversing with them, the proximity of heaven to earth becometh firmly established in the child's mind, and it beholdeth the fitness of one world to the other.

19. For which education the infants shall, at an early age, be made familiar with the unseen world, by training in the crescent.

20. And their teachers shall try them to discover su'is and sar'gis in them; and, finding these talents, shall cultivate them in righteousness and wisdom for the glory of the Father.

21. And it shall come to pass that many of these infants shall not only see without their corporeal eyes, and hear without their corporeal ears, but they will attain to adeptism.

22. And the angels of heaven shall descend amongst us, appearing so as to be seen, and talking with us so as to be heard.

23. And, because of such exceeding great light amongst us, no one shall practice deception; for the minds and souls of all shall become as an open book.

24. These are the promises Jehovih hath given us; by the signs of the times they are proven probable. Through faith in Him we shall make these things true.

25. In faith He will bless you all.

CHAPTER X.

1. Now, whilst the organization of Shalam had been going on, Tae and his hosts had interspersed the same in laboring; some in building houses, some in digging and planting, and others in clearing the ground from stones and rubbish, whilst the women were busy with the infants.

2. And it so happened that amongst the hosts, Jehovih had provided a goodly number of musicians, players and singers, who furnished spiritual entertainment in response to the prayers and sermons of such as supplicated the Almighty.

3. In addition to these occupations, the groups were cast into responsible positions for the future; so that the members of all the groups found it necessary to begin and pursue a special line of education, themselves, so as to become teachers.

4. Consequently, each group became as a school in its specialty; for whoso had taken it upon himself to live and practice his highest light was bound also to admit an increase of light.

5. Jehovih hath said: Two conditions have I placed before all men, ascension and declension; let no man stand still, for so I did not create him.

6. Such as will not ascend, shall be in declension; such as desire not declension, let them not stand still.

7. And I have given to My Gods and Lords of heaven, and to wise men on earth, knowledge to provide unto the multitude something to do constantly, that satan (mischief) may not enter in amongst them to their injury.

8. Tae said: Now is kosmon; men and women know of their own knowledge a way to provide unto self-development in wisdom, virtue, truth and affiliation.

9. And it was so; the hosts of Shalam had been chosen and provided by Jehovih as an example of self-purifiers and self-instructors for founding His kingdom on earth.

10. Jehovih hath said: In kosmon, purification shall not come by baptism with either water or fire. But each one shall turn his thoughts inward, to himself, to becoming a constant magistrate, sitting in judgment upon himself as to his thoughts, works and behavior.

11. To perfect himself in his part, in the family of My kingdom, is My new commandment unto My chosen.

12. For no man perfecteth himself unto full requitement whilst he leaveth undone that which he might have done.

13. After awhile, Tae and his hosts divided and apportioned the hours of the day; so many to labor, so many to rest, so many to study, thus to one thing and another, that the groups might be orderly. Nevertheless, entire freedom was given to all the members to come and go, to labor or rest, as they might elect.

14. Now, it so happened that more than half of the people were celibates, and they reasoned, and said, inquiring: Is it not better that the teachers and nurses be celibates? And this question extended throughout the colony, so it became necessary to determine which should be . And though the question was not weighty of itself, yet, in order to provide an understanding for similar questions, the chiefs of the nurses and the chiefs of the teachers appealed to Tae, who was C'chief.

15. And the Light of Jehovih came upon Tae, and he said unto them: Did either one shirk from service it would be plain what should be judged for righteousness' sake. But because ye are ambitious to do good work, which is tedious, with many trials, ye all deserve great honor.

16. Because ye are ambitious to serve the Father, by serving these little ones, your aspirations are noble. Because ye are willing to yield to one another any preference, ye are an example of holiness.

17. The question ye have asked, which is simply: Who can be the highest best teacher of an orphan child, a celibate who has never raised a child, or a married person who hath raised a child? is not a question, therefore, of self-interest or self-gratification, but one of knowledge.

18. If I decide this matter, behold, it would be simply one man's decision. Why should I make myself responsible in a matter that can be determined by yourselves?

19. Take ye, therefore, sufficient time to inquire as to the facts that have been demonstrated. Go, find of married people who have raised up children of their own in the right way, and number their proportion to those who have raised up their children in the wrong way.

20. The chiefs took the matter in hand, and they not only examined those in Shalam, but hundreds of families of Uzians, and again they came before Tae, to report.

21. And this was the sum of their report, namely: Every one accuseth all others, that no married people have raised up their children in the right way, and, yet, each one accrediteth himself as having raised his own in nearly the right way.

22. Tae asked: But how found ye the children they had raised?

23. They answered: They were all raised in the wrong way. Though they were good enough in their own parents' eyes, yet, to others, they were far short of the mark of either wisdom or righteousness.

24. Tae said: Why, then, since those who have raised children have been failures, ye shall surely not choose them. The celibates have made no failures, for they have not tried.

25. Let this, then, be our rule and guide: Since every mortal life should be made ripe with experience in all things, and since celibates have no children of their own, and since these children are orphans and castaways, let it be testimony that Jehovih hath thus provided the celibates as substitutes for natural parents.

26. So, let the nurses and teachers, in their youngest infancy, be celibates.

27. And this was carried out in practice.

CHAPTER XI.

1. Jehovih had prospered Shalam in every way, more than had been possible to any other people in all the world.

2. Whilst the nurses and teachers were providing for the infants, the rest of the people were providing habitations, factories and educational workshops, and also tilling the ground and ornamenting it with fields, gardens and orchards, and with walks and terraces.

3. In regard to the houses, the temple of Jehovih, the temple of Apollo and the gymnasium were the most important, and, yet, none of these were like unto the buildings of the ancients.

4. Jehovih had said: Behold, the ancients built their temples so durable that succeeding generations forgot the art of building. Better is it for man's talent to remain, than for stones and pillars of iron.

5. For which reason, in kosmon, thou shalt not build imperishably in corporeal things; but rather leave the way open for succeeding generations to build also.

6. The temple of Jehovih, which was devoted to public worship on every seventh day of the week, was provided with fountains in the north-east and south-west, and with the four

lights of the square, and with the four dark corners of evil and temptation, and with a throne of Light in the east, with time-bells, a gau and sacred wheel. The ceiling represented the stars and planets, interblended with plateaux of the heavenly kingdoms. The east was adorned with the rising sun, the south with the sun at noon, and the west with the setting sun. The north was adorned with the pole-star and aurora borealis. The belt of the zodiac, colored in cream-yellow, crossed over the ceiling and faded down the east and west walls. On the south wall was the coil and travel of the great serpent (solar phalanx), from the time of the Arc of Bon (of Moses, Capilya and Chine) down to the Arc of Kosmon, in the etherean heavens. Flags of golden colors were provided for the four lights, and were mounted on silver-colored staffs inclining toward the altar of the Covenant; and this was in the place Tae stood, betwixt the crescent horns, when they had, on the first day, made the covenant. And in the place of the crescent, where the fifty-one stood, was laid a stone crescent, provided with seats and gate-ways for successive affiliations to Jehovih's kingdom. The outside of the temple was of wood, and was surrounded by posts made of native trees, surmounted with a roof of cement.

7. When the temple was completed, Tae said: Who but Gods could have made anything so beautiful with such cheap material! And if it perish in two generations, two things man shall gain; the third generation can build another; and, moreover, we shall not have left a temple on earth that will call us back from the higher heavens for more than two generations of time, to look after mortals who might applaud us.

8. In regard to worship in the temple, Jehovih had said:

9. As, in the olden times, I provided a preacher to stand at the altar in the east, and speak unto the multitude, behold, in kosmon, the multitude shall render an account before My altar of their fulfillment of My commandments, and My C'chief shall respond in My name.

10. And such, indeed, it was; instead of a preacher denouncing people for their sins, it was a place where the people returned thanks and praises to Jehovih, with rejoicing, in anthems and songs of praise, with pleadings in Jehovih's name for the Uzians to learn the lessons of the new kingdom.

11. And it came to pass that Uzians did come, and listen, and look on, and examine, saying and inquiring:

12. Why was not this tried before? A people without a leader!

13. And whilst they thus pondered, they looked upon the meadows and lawns, the orchards and hot-houses and the rich-growing fields, saying: Is not this the garden of Paradise?

14. The temple of Apollo was devoted to music, dancing, calisthenics, initiative processions, rites and ceremonies of amusement. The interior was finished illustrative of proportions and figures of symmetry and beauty. The decorations illustrated attitudes, posings and groupings. On the east summit was a figurative illustration of the God Apollo with his heavenly hosts, descended to the lower heavens, in past ages, looking down on to earth at a group of druks (ill-formed mortals) with long arms, who were squatting on their haunches. Apollo was illustrating, on a well-formed model, to his angels, how the druks of earth were to be changed into shapeliness and beauty.

15. In its external structure, the temple of Apollo illustrated a combination of one thousand designs of architecture, arches, curves, columns, pillars and so on. And yet all of

this was made of the forest trees of Shalam and without cost.

16. Next to these was the gymnasium, which contained also two swimming baths and one hundred single bath-rooms.

17. Here were all kinds of places for developing muscular action, with swings, ropes to walk, places for leaping, places for tumbling and climbing. This was under the charge of the group of physicians. The temple of Apollo was under the charge of the group of musicians. The temple of Jehovih was under the charge of the C'chief and his group of chiefs.

18. Besides these, were the houses of Architecture, the house of Mechanics, the house of Horticulture, which adjoined the hothouses on the north and west. Here were grown all kinds of fruit and herbs for food, and many beautiful flowers, rich-growing all the year around.

19. Then the Agricultural house; then the factories, for hats, clothing, shoes, cutlery, and, in fact, all conceivable places required by man.

20. And not the least interesting of all was the house of Nurseries.

21. Here were the heart and kernel of the whole colony, the orphans and castaways gathered up from amongst the Uzians.

22. Now, from the first of the inhabitation of Shalam, the Voice had constantly urged Tae and Es to make continual additions of infants to the colony.

23. The Voice had said: Give thy people plenty to do. Keep the nurses busy; give them little to mourn for coming out of Egypt (Uz); keep them at work; keep them in the rites and ceremonies.

24. Then Tae said to Es: Take thou one of the women with thee, and go back to Uz; gather in more infants.

25. And that ye may be known and respected by the Uzians as to your occupation, go in plain black dress, without oddity, and I will give to each of you a wooden triangle, which shall be suspended on your bosoms by a cord over the neck; for this is the symbol of earth, sky and spirit, the three entities which constitute the universe, being emblematical of Jehovih.

26. So, Es took Hamarias, a young woman of Thessagowan, and went back to Uz, and in the cities gathered up infant waifs and brought them to Shalam.

27. And thus, every year, they brought from twenty to fifty additional infants, and adopted them in the nurseries.

28. So that, in not many years, there were more than a thousand orphans in the colony.

29. It so happened, in the second year of Shalam, that a disease came amongst the cows, and the physicians forbade the babes being fed on their milk.

30. So, for some days, they were in straits as to how to support the infants till other milk could be supplied.

31. And one Abbayith, an elderly woman, said unto them: Why worry yourselves? Behold, the corn is in ear. Go, gather it, and press out the milk and cook it, and give to the babes; for this also is good milk.

32. So, they gathered the corn and scraped it and pressed out the milk which, on being boiled a little, was found to be excellent food for infants.

33. Thus was discovered artificial milk, even as it is bottled and sold to this day. And the chemists also made water extracts from slippery elm bark, and from flax seed, combined

with rice milk, and this also made an excellent liquid food for infants.

34. Jehovih had said: Whether flesh or milk or cheese that man useth for food, behold, in the herbs and plants and trees I created, I gave the same things. Let man discover them, and understand the fruit of My inventions.

CHAPTER XII.

1. Es, the chief nurse, had said: I must tell you of the wonderful Light of Jehovih, that always cometh to us in time of emergency. Even at the moment despair is about to reach us, lo, His Light provideth unto us.

2. I had undertaken to nurse, with bottles, ever so many babes, more than was possible for one woman to attend, taking one at a time on my lap, but I could not get round in time. So, also, I had had observation that babes should be held in somebody's arms, and that when they cried they should be taken up, held upright, and diverted by walking with them or by tossing them.

3. To do these things for many babes was not possible for one nurse; so, after I had prayed for strength and light as to what was best to be done, the Voice came to me, plainly, as if I had read it in a book, saying:

4. My Daughter, why thwartest thou the way of My creations? Had I designed My little ones to be upright, I should have provided a way for them.

5. Thou shalt permit them to lie down, and to roll about. Neither shalt thou encumber them with pillows and cushions. Permit them to exercise themselves by crawling in their own way.

6. And when the proper time cometh for them to stand upright, and to jump, behold, I will be with them.

7. Es said: Now, thereupon, I began a new system. I not only searched to know myself, but to develop these little ones. And when I took away the pillows and cushions, giving them double blankets to lie on, and opportunity to exercise by rolling about, behold, they grew in strength daily, and not only soon ceased to cry, but began to sing songs (to me they were songs) and to laugh and amuse themselves with their hands and toes and whatever they got hold of.

8. From this little light, of applying the law of development unto babes, I applied myself to make them understand that they should divert themselves, without depending on their nurses. For many of the orphans we had received were little tyrants, having been spoiled by former nurses, and they screamed constantly, to make some one carry them about and divert them.

9. Now, therefore, I perceived that Jehovih required more of me than merely to feed and clean these little ones; the minds of the spoiled ones had to be remodeled; they should be made to comprehend that no one was slave unto them; and, moreover, that they themselves should cultivate patience, gentleness and love, as better attributes than fretfulness and authority.

10. For, let no one be surprised, even babes can be spoiled to think themselves an authority, with power to command obedience from adults. And they discover, at an early age, that to give vent to peevishness and passion bringeth the nurse to do them service.

11. And I saw, too, that some, even such as could merely hold up their heads, became

jealous, to be the first fed, or the first washed, and answered my negligence with fearful screams.

12. Now, it came to pass, when I ceased taking them up to feed them, and did away with the pillow-props, and laid them all down alike, and gave them food at the same time (according to their groups), I had not only provided unto them better corporeal development, but better spiritual development.

13. Such as had been peevish and jealous ceased their former habits, and began to look with respect to the other babes, rolling beside them.

14. Not many months passed by till they began to be interested in one another, examining their feet and hands, and evidently trying to comprehend who they were, and whence they came. And they also saw in one another a representation of themselves, appreciating a fellowship that was surpassingly beautiful.

CHAPTER XIII.

1. Tae said: Never grew such straight and handsome children as those of Shalam.

2. And it was so. And, moreover, they were of all shades of color, and of all nations and peoples on the earth.

3. And they were timed and disciplined from the very first; a time to be fed, a time for bathing, a time for dressing and a time for sleeping.

4. Besides these times, the nurses provided music twice a day for them, and at regular hours. And many of the babes began to sing and to beat time to the music, even before they could stand upright.

5. And when the children were able to walk, the nurses provided them, in processions, with music to their steps; and a time was also set apart for these.

6. Soon after this, they were given simple calisthenics; and, in time after this, calisthenics proper, for the development of the arms, limbs and person.

7. Thus were they trained to keep time with music; to carry themselves erect; to control the motions of their feet, limbs, arms and hands, and, also, made to develop the full use of their joints. And they were taught the names of the bones, joints and muscles, by repeating the words in time to the music, being in songs and semi-songs.

8. Great were the delight and interest these little ones took in these exercises; and it came to pass, that even whilst they were little more than babes, they had mastered the names and uses of the bones and muscles of the body.

9. And they were timed and limited in exercise, adapted to the most delicate and slender, and to the most robust; and every one learned simply by diversion, and not by talk or labor.

10. After this, they were taught marching, slow and fast, even running in time to music; and, after this, simple tournaments.

11. Simple tournaments embraced games of hunting and chasing; some of them taking the part of foxes or wolves, and others, the part of hunters. Yet, in all these games, the teachers and musicians took part, directing and cautioning, guarding and supervising the games, teaching the little ones the oneness of teachers and pupils. Teaching the stronger children to be observant and gentle toward the weaker ones, illustrating to them how Jehovih had made them all as brothers and sisters.

12. Es said: Never was I so reproved for the shortness of my former life, and for my belief in the depravity of man, as now, when these little ones demonstrated love and respect toward one another, as if they had indeed been begotten by the angels of heaven. They were like little saints, and more of a lesson to their teachers of the glorious creation of Jehovih, than the teachers were to them of the wisdom of man.

13. Amongst their first lessons of labor were those in the gardens, teaching them how to plant; teaching them the names of seeds, flowers, plants, trees and all growing things; explaining to them how Jehovih, by His Ever Presence, giveth life and growth and form unto all things.

14. And they listened, heeded, and, with delight, sought their turns and privileges to do some little work.

15. Now, with the beginning of labor, with them, was also the beginning of times and seasons for recreation (play), which, for the first six years, occupied the principal part of the day. And, yet, every day they took lessons of a few minutes in painting or drawing, or demonstrating with blocks, cords, squares and angles.

16. At six years of age, they were entered as apprentices to labor, devoting half an hour daily to knitting, or sewing, or working with tools, giving them an opportunity of manifesting their best adaptation.

17. At six years of age, they were also taught for half an hour one evening in the week to sit in the sacred circle for angel communion, that they might become conversant with angels, seeing them, and hearing them discourse on heavenly things. Here they were taught praying in concert, and the order of praise to Jehovih and His creations.

18. And the angels appeared amongst them, oft carrying them in their arms, and otherwise demonstrating the tangibility of the presence of the spirits of the dead.

19. And the children were delighted, often ejaculating thanks unto Jehovih and praise for His everlasting heavens.

20. Now was also the time that many of them began to manifest su'is, being capable of seeing and hearing angels whilst in normal condition, and also of seeing and hearing corporeal things miles away, and without their corporeal eyes and ears.

CHAPTER XIV.

1. This, then, is after the manner of their angel communion, to wit: The sacred circles were composed of sixty-six children, seven teachers and one chieftainess.

2. The chieftainess sat in the midst, and was representative of the Light, repeating from the words of Jehovih or His Embassadors. And the responses were by the children, and by the angels, and many of them were after this manner, to wit:

3. Chieftainess: I am the Light and the Life; My creations are for the joy and glory of My Sons and Daughters.

4. Response: All Light is Jehovih; let His Sons and Daughters rejoice in Him.

5. Proclaim Him with great joy; shout with glee in the house of the Almighty!

6. C.: To show them the glory of My love, and the wide dominions I created for their everlasting inheritance, I send My holy angels from My kingdoms on high.

7. R.: Who shall fathom the inventions of Jehovih, and the foundation of His love! He provided His holy angels to come down from the skies, the light and joy of His

everlasting heavens.

8. He fashioned a way for the soul of man to live forever; from the resting-place of the spirits of the dead, He bringeth them in the Voices of His love.

9. C.: I have swallowed up death in victory; the pain of the parting, betwixt the living and the dead, I have bridged over with Mine own hand, for the joy of My chosen.

10. R.: Greater than life, greater than death, is the Almighty; with His own hand He handleth them as toys; by His breath bloweth He away all terrors.

11. He provided us a life on the earth to learn earthly things; death was His invention to adapt us to His imperishable heavens.

12. Glory be to Jehovih on high; glory for His beloved angels who come to bless us.

13. Sing unto the Almighty, O ye little ones; His eye guardeth over you; His hand reacheth to the uttermost places.

14. C.: The earth is My paradise; the songs of My beloved reach up to My realms in the skies.

15. R.: Proclaim the Creator to the ends of the world; to His children He gave the earth as a paradise.

16. Sing a song of gladness unto the Almighty; with the harp and the horn, and with the voices of His beloved, mete out praise forever!

17. Let us praise Him; let us adore Him; the Almighty hath given us loves on the earth and loves in heaven.

18. Shout unto Him in love; be outspoken to the Almighty; He answereth in fair fields and plenteous harvests. He filleth the air with sweet perfumes; the color of the fields and forests are records of His skill.

19. Now, during the chanting, the angels came and joined audibly in the response, and often took on the semblance of corporeal forms and walked about within and without the sacred circle, and, at times, spake a few words of greeting and joy in Jehovih's name.

CHAPTER XV.

1. At six years of age, the children were entered in the school of oratory, and also given the signs and graces of unspoken words by means of gestures. And, now, they began to take part in theatricals and operatic performances.

2. For such purposes these two houses were provided with angel chambers adjoining the stages, and during the performances the angels came in sar'gis, also taking parts in the operas, ascending and descending before the audiences, singing and speaking audibly, so all could hear them.

3. Many of the plays and operas were composed and prepared by the angels, who also gave directions how to put the pieces on the stage. And in some of the pieces there were, of the children and angels combined, more than three hundred performers on the stage at one time.

4. Instead of the crude and loud-sounding horns and hideous instruments, as used by the Uzians for their operas, the opera here was provided with an organ of full power, and with instruments of delicacy and sweetness, so that the most refined ear should not be shocked or pained by any crude or disgusting noise, so common in the Uzian orchestras.

5. Now, as to the plays, whether in the opera or in the theatre, they varied on different

nights, as to being adapted to young children, or to older ones, or to adults. But, for the most part, the plays and operas pertained to illustrations embracing a life on earth and an entrance into the lower heavens, showing also the part in real life which angels of purity take in guarding and advising mortals, by inspiration, to righteousness, and also showing how drujas inspire mortals to sensual things and to wickedness.

6. So, that the plays required the presence of angels, to illustrate their parts in the affairs of mortal; and every play was made a lesson and sermon on life, so simple a child could understand them and apply the instructions to its own soul.

7. Herein, then, was the difference betwixt the plays and operas in Shalam, as compared with plays and operas with the Uzians: With the latter, they apply to the lives and adventures of mortals, and to histories of mortal affairs and occurrences wrapt up in inexplicable causes; but the plays and operas with the Faithists, in Shalam, illustrated the same things by showing the causes that govern and control mortals by spirit-presence.

8. So that (for example), were it necessary to exhibit a drunkard on the stage, it was also shown how the drunkard was surrounded by dark spirits (drujas), who inspired him to his course; and also was exhibited the struggle of his guardian angels to save him, showing thus how the choice lay with himself as to who he would serve, satan or Jehovih.

9. In the simple plays, where the children took their parts at first, they were taught without books, by repeating after their teachers.

10. And here was a new school, not known amongst the Uzians; which was, to learn by hearing words spoken, to repeat them. First, they practiced with half a dozen words, then with a dozen words, then with two dozen, then four dozen, and so on. And it came to pass, in a little while, many of the children could repeat whole chapters, by simply hearing the words spoken once.

11. Tae said: Here, first of all, began to manifest that clearness of mind resulting from an herbivorous diet which was and is wholly unknown amongst the Uzians.

12. Tae said: And Jehovih further blessed our children in su'is, so that many of them who had not yet been taught to read, could lay a hand on a printed page, and repeat it word for word.

13. Tae said: And their little playmates, hearing them, could repeat the same things. And some of them would hold a sealed letter in their hands, and read it word by word; so that dissemblance and secrecy were become as a farce before Jehovih's children.

CHAPTER XVI.

1. Jehovih said: Let the order of the labor of My little ones be increasive; one half hour a day at six years of age, one hour a day at eight years, two hours at twelve, and three hours at fourteen.

2. Nevertheless, these thou shalt temper according to their strength and inclination, making labor itself a delightful pastime.

3. And it was so; all avocations were as a change from one amusement to another. And so great were their capacities to comprehend all things, that, at the age of fourteen, they were master of all trades and occupations.

4. And, of the first thousand children that reached fourteen years, scarce one could be found but was master of horticulture, agriculture (with botany), engineering, surveying,

landscape gardening, architecture and general mechanics. They knew how to make shoes, hats, clothing (also spinning and weaving cloth), the mathematics of musical instruments; and they were musicians as well.

5. Tae said: Though they lacked the age and strength of full-grown men and women, yet they had attained to practical knowledge, the like of which had never been known to any adults in all the world. Scarcely anything was known that they could not make, or describe how it should be made.

6. And yet, in all things, scarcely any part had been taught them by means of books, but by practical observations and by illustrations and actual measurements.

7. Jehovih hath said: By My spirit, I move infants to ask questions; answer ye them, and, behold, they shall become as Gods. For this is a door I opened with Mine own hand; whoso answereth them not, shutteth the door against knowledge, and ill-useth My loves.

8. Tae said: With all that our children knew, behold, we still rebuked ourselves because we had not answered half the questions they had asked us.

9. Now, from twelve to fourteen, they were initiated into the religious rites and ceremonies of the ancients, after the manner as set forth in the Book of Saphah, with explanations of signs, symbols, emblems and the sacred implements; with the ranks of Gods and Lords and Saviors and archangels; with the divisions of the higher and lower heavens; with the first, second and third resurrections in atmospherea, as set forth in the Book of Ben; and with the cosmogony of the corporeal worlds; the position and travel of the solar phalanx; with actual observations of the stars, planets and satellites, with their times and seasons, as set forth in the Book of Cosmogony and Prophecy.

10. And they could point out the constellations; describe the distances and revolutions of planets; explain the zodiac, the polar lights, and the use of telescopes and the spectrum. And, yet, not one of them had been tired or wearied in learning all these things.

CHAPTER XVII.

1. The Voice came to Tae, saying: The fourteenth year is My year. Behold, the harvest of My laborers, who came first out of Uz, is ripe unto deliverance.

2. In the heavens of My Gods, I bequeath a time to labor unto them also; and when their angel hosts are prepared for a new resurrection to a higher heaven, I come and deliver them.

3. For fourteen years, thou and thine hosts have labored with My infants; those which I gave into your keeping have prospered, and shall be now emancipated from all further responsibility over them, save such as ye may take upon yourselves.

4. Call them together, old and young, and, with suitable rites and ceremonies, fulfill My commandments unto them, and bequeath unto My children the titles, brides and bridegrooms of liberty.

5. So, Tae appointed a day of emancipation, and had it proclaimed before all the people of the colony.

6. And, on the day named, there came into the temple of Jehovih one thousand of the infants who had attained to fourteen years of age. And they were clothed in white, with uncovered heads, boys and girls, each carrying a sprig of acacia, and they marched in from the west, two and two, but separated one to either side, forming a crescent, with the

horns to the east.

7. The fifty-two founders sat in the east, and were thus betwixt the horns of the crescent, and they were clothed in black, with white aprons, but with Zarathustrian hats on the men's, and with sky-crescents on the women's heads.

8. Back of the founders, were stationed another thousand children of younger years, and they bore the flower-wreaths intended for the brides and bridegrooms of liberty.

9. But within the midst of the crescent stood Es, facing the east. Still outside of the crescent, were stationed the next younger class of a thousand infants. And, beyond these, were the members of Shalam; and beyond them, were the visiting Uzians.

10. On the north and south were stationed the musicians, and betwixt them and the crescent horns, on the exterior, were the marshals of Shalam.

11. Tae represented the Voice of Jehovih, and Es the voice of the young brides and bridegrooms who were to speak in concert with her. After prayer and suitable music,

12. Tae said: In the name of Jehovih, and by His Light upon me, I declare the place of the Holy Covenant open to the voice of mortals. Who here knoweth the times of Jehovih, and the day and year in the place of His kingdom?

13. Es and the brides and bridegrooms of liberty: In Jehovih's name, greeting from the west. Behold, this is the brides' and bridegrooms' day of liberty. We stand before thee and thy hosts to answer our love for the benefits ye have bestowed upon us in the Father's kingdom. We bring to ye sprigs of acacia as memorials of the everlasting life ye have shown unto us.

14. Tae said: The east answereth in love and sorrow, but receiveth your memorials with great joy.

15. Es: Before the Almighty, all things move onward; to His decrees we bow in reverence.

16. Tae: Are ye not satisfied?

17. Es: We are more than satisfied with the love and blessings we have received.

18. We were fatherless and motherless, and ye gathered us up and fed us and clothed us. But, greater than all, ye have taught us to love and honor you in our Father's name.

19. Tae: We went forth in duty, but Jehovih hath answered us with love. We found you helpless, with none to care for you, or to save you from destruction. We brought you hither and provided unto you without price and without hope of reward.

20. Es: But ye have bound us; how can we ever repay? None can know the fullness of our gratitude.

21. Tae: We have watched you since before ye stood upright; your every little step hath been both a responsibility and a joy unto us. O, why will you leave us? Who knoweth the love of the aged for the young, whom they have watched from day to day?

22. Es: We will not leave you; but, behold, we are no longer babes, we are strong and learned.

23. As ye saved us, so let us go forth in our might to save others. Who can teach the aged that those they raised up are not always babes? O, give us our liberty! Behold, we are clothed as brides and bridegrooms!

24. Tae: And turn you loose without anyone over you to guard and bless you?

25. Es: Jehovih will guard and bless the righteous who serve Him. We are His!

26. Tae: Who is Jehovih? and where?

27. Es: He is the Life and the Knowledge, Who is everywhere present, the All Person, Who created us alive, Who, by giving, created all things. He is our shield.

28. Tae: Your faith being in Jehovih, it is well; but ye have bound us with your love. What is bound on earth shall remain bound in heaven. Though we give you the form of liberty, yet our hearts will ever go out in love to you.

29. Though we emancipate you here on earth, remember, we are growing old. Ere long, we shall join our fathers in heaven. Whither we go, we shall again prepare unto you.

30. And, when ye come again to us for a season, behold, we shall again go on for a time and a season.

31. Es: O Jehovih, preserve Thou us ever pure and wise, that Thy hosts may continue this love in our travel in Thy everlasting kingdoms!

32. Tae: Such is ever the beginning of a kingdom of the Father: Where a few gather together in His name, fulfilling the commandments, there is the starting-place unto them.

33. Pity those that live and die in this world, not having found and lived within a kingdom of the Father.

34. Es: To remain true to Jehovih's heaven, what a glory, time without end! Make us strong and wise, O Father, to bring them into Thy kingdom on earth. Help us to make them comprehend.

35. Tae, in the Voice: With liberty I give also responsibility.

36. Es, in the Voice: Thy chosen comprehend; as Thou givest them liberty, even so do they emancipate those who saved them.

37. Tae: To the helpless, I provide saviors; to the wise and strong, I say: Save yourselves.

38. Es: We want none but Thee, Jehovih, to save us. We bind ourselves unto Thee from this time forth, forever!

39. Tae: Whosoever striveth to save himself, shall not fail before Me.

40. We covenant unto Thee, Jehovih, to strive hereafter, forever, to save ourselves from all sin and righteousness, in thoughts, words and deeds, and to serve Thee with all our wisdom and strength, by doing good unto others as long as we may live.

41. Tae, of himself: Then, in Jehovih's name, and by His authority vested in me, I bequeath you liberty forever. Jehovih be with you all. Amen.

42. In Jehovih's name we release our saviors from all responsibility for us forevermore. Jehovih be with you all. Amen!

43. Tae: Draw unto Me, and receive from My hand, saith Jehovih. Whoso covenanteth unto Me, I covenant unto him.

44. Whoso registereth unto Me, shall be registered in My heavenly kingdoms. Upon the entrance in heaven of My chosen, behold, My holy angels are there to receive them.

45. The brides and bridegrooms: We covenant unto Thee, O Jehovih, to be Thine forever.

46. Register us in thy everlasting kingdoms; make us acceptable associates for Thy holy ones in heaven.

47. Teach Thou us, O Jehovih, to look down into our thoughts, words and behavior, every day and hour, with swift remembrance to do all the good we can unto others that we may be an honor and glory in Thy works.

48. Tae: Come unto Me, My beloved; receive from My altar the token of liberty in My name!

49. The marshals then brought the points of the crescent together, in front of Tae, leaving

a space between. The guards, then, brought the children with wreaths forward, filed to pass betwixt Tae and Es, who had advanced to the apex of the horns. The saviors (the founders) drew up in single file, facing the west.

50. And, now, at a signal from the chief marshal, the brides and bridegrooms turned in at the crescent, two and two, and, as they did so, they gave the acacia to the founders, whilst the wreaths were placed on their heads by Tae and Es, the bearers passing the other way. And, as they did so, Tae said:

51. Receive thou this token of liberty in the name of the Almighty. It was grown by Him, gathered by His loves, and is bestowed by thy benefactor as a crown of Jehovih's kingdom on earth.

52. Es, in response: More precious is this than the crown of any king or queen on earth. In Jehovih's praise I receive it; it is an emblem of a new beginning in my life, a wreath of liberty. The saviors (founders) said: This acacia shall be my register before the Almighty of your love.

53. After this, the musicians sang and chanted whilst the audience resumed seats.

54. Tae said: A new life is before you. Heretofore, you have been directed and criticized, and told what to do and what not to do. Hereafter, ye shall not be thus disciplined, but shall discipline yourselves.

55. As much as ye are thus bestowed by us, so shall ye bestow one another. And, henceforth, ye shall not criticize or direct or dictate to one another. As much as ye are free from us, ye are free from one another.

56. Heretofore, ye reproved one another for various trifling faults; hereafter, ye shall not reprove one another, nor reprove any person above fourteen years of age; remember constantly that ye are not keepers or supervisors over your equals or your elders.

57. And for such faults or shortness ye may perceive in others, save infants, turn away, behold them not, nor mention them. Such matters are betwixt Jehovih and the doers.

58. And, now, behold, it is proper for you to go into Uz, and see them, and observe how they live, both in splendor and in misery.

59. For which purpose, ye shall be provided in groups of dozens or more, and accompanied to the cities of Uz to sojourn there for a season.

60. And, if it so happen that ye desire to remain in Uz, then be it so; ye shall remain.

61. And, if ye desire to return hither, then shall ye return.

62. But ye shall not return here as before, as helpless babes, but as workers.

63. And, if ye elect to remain with us, then shall ye make the covenant of brotherhood with us, being one with us in all things, and this place, or its sister colonies, shall be your home as long as ye may desire.

CHAPTER XVIII.

1. When the groups were prepared to visit Uz, Tae himself took charge of one dozen, going with them. As the incidents of these visiting groups were similar, the following account of Tae's group sufficeth here, to wit:

2. Tae took them to the city of Meig, to the most fashionable hotels, and had them provided with every luxury, so-called.

3. Hardly had he them located, when they came before him, saying: Our rooms are small;

the air of the city smells foul.

4. Tell us, what is the meaning, so many people strolling about in idleness? Why do they sit reading papers? Which are the masters, and which the servants? How do they know? Why do the servants not be masters, and have the others serve them? What beautiful wagons! What beautiful mirrors! What do the women have their clothes stuffed for? What are those bells ringing for? Are they in the temples of Jehovih? Take us thither! What causeth these disagreeable smells? See that old woman with a half naked babe, and leading that dirty child! Why holdeth she out her hand as we pass? Is she a servant or a master? Why hath not some one told the rich, it is wrong to pass that poor woman by without helping her to a home? Why does she not come into our hotel, and have a room? What do the people mean about rights and privileges? Can one person in Uz have more rights and privileges than another? And why so?

5. What is that sour smell, down yonder, in that cellar, where they talk so loud? What is sour beer? See, behold, a man with a bloody face! Fighting? What with, a tiger? Are those the flesh-eaters? Why do they smoke? Why hath not some one told them they should rather seek to purify themselves, than to do in the opposite way? O, here is the temple of worship, take us in!

6. Tae took them in, and they heard the sermon, and afterward, they said:

7. O the mystery of mysteries! How can these things be? The chief preached most excellently; he knoweth all the doctrines for right-doing; but why is it that his people heed him not? Why doth he not gather up little children, and raise them up to observe the commandments? He must be the best of men. Take us to see him.

8. Tae took them, but a servant met them at the gate, and demanded to know their business.

9. They answered: We have come to consult about the poor. Then the gate-keeper withdrew a while, but returned, saying: The preacher is not at home!

10. From an upper window, behind the lattices, they saw his face; not at home!

11. They said: Can these things be? O, take us to the poor; to the streets of misery! Let us see them.

12. Tae took them, and when they looked about, they asked: Why do the poor live in the dirty streets? Why do they not go away, and dwell in the beautiful places? Who gave these different allotments to the rich and poor? Why do the poor not clean themselves, and clean their clothes, and clean their houses? Why do the poor remain in the cities? And huddle together in such little rooms?

13. What is that large house? A theological college? What is that for? What is the meaning of, teaching religion? Can it be learned with words? What is the reason they do not live religion? Why hath not some one explained to the professors that religion is a thing of practice? Could not they understand? Why do they not love their neighbors as themselves? Dividing up what they have, with the poor? Why do these children go without shoes, and so ragged and dirty? Why do not the professors and students in the theological college go, and wash them and clothe them?

14. Thus, Tae took them amongst the fashion and splendor and amongst the poverty and shame of Uz; showing them the banks and great merchant houses, and the fleets of ships; and then to the prisons and poor-houses, and to the houses for the insane, and to the hospitals.

15. Now, since their infancy up, many of them possessed su'is, and could see the spirits of the dead, even as they saw mortals. And they inquired of Tae concerning such spirits, saying and inquiring:

16. Who are these restless, sullen spirits, strolling about the banking houses?

17. Tae answered them: These were bankers; these were the founders of great banking houses. As they bound their minds and thoughts to earthly gain whilst they were mortal, so drift they now, even as they bound themselves on earth. They can not go hence.

18. Again, they asked: Tell us, then, what spirits are these strolling sulkily in merchant houses and on the docks?

19. Tae said: These were great merchants and their ship-masters; behold, they float also into the places they bound themselves.

20. Tell us, then, who are these drunken, foul-smelling spirits in the saloons?

21. Tae said: These were tipplers, drunkards, gormandizers; these were their mortal resorts. They can not go hence.

22. Thus, Tae explained the tens of thousands of spirits that huddled around about the different places in the city of Meig, in the land of Uz.

23. Now, after the time of the visit was completed, Tae said unto them: What will you, remain in Uz, or return to Shalam?

24. And they answered: O, take us back; give us clear air to breathe; let us be where we can see and hear Jehovih!

25. But since thou and thy people gathered us up in Uz, and bore us hence, let us go and gather up infants also, and take them with us. We will raise them up in the Light of our Father in heaven.

26. So, in fact, did they; and they returned to Shalam, taking with them a great number of waifs and castaways and orphan babes.

CHAPTER XIX.

1. When the multitude returned to Shalam, the place was more than filled, and the Voice came to Tae, saying:

2. Thou hast now fulfilled the first part of My kingdom on earth, but, behold, it is yet but a small branch of that which will overspread this great land.

3. Moreover, let the lessons of Uz be a profit unto thee and thy people.

4. Because the Uzians build large cities, their would-be reformers are powerless to work righteousness amongst the people.

5. Let not the cities of My chosen be large nor more numerous than Shalam is already. Sufficient is such a size to all that is required for the fulfillment of mortal life.

6. Therefore, thou shalt proclaim it unto My chosen, that no city shall contain more than three thousand people.

7. Suffice it, then, as I have placed the example of bees before thee, showing how they swarm, and go hence and establish a new hive, according to their numbers, even so shall My people go hence, and establish a new place, after the manner of Shalam.

8. This, also, shalt thou proclaim unto them; and thou shalt ask for volunteers in My name to accomplish these things righteously, as an example to coming generations.

9. So Tae called the people together, and proclaimed Jehovih's words, adding also:

10. Whoso volunteereth to go hence shall not find the fullness of Shalam, but, instead, shall find discomforts and hard work!

11. Beware of disappointments and trials and hardships. For is it not the way with all men to desire to reap too quickly the harvest, and to consider its fullness, rather than to contemplate the labor of tilling the ground and of sowing?

12. For the spirit of man conceiveth the result of perfection; but the judgment looketh to the labor required to bring it about.

13. Who, then, having the joys and fullness of Shalam, will turn away from them, in order to build another place, and yet, the while, not repine for his choice?

14. A colony shall stand as an individual before Jehovih. A colony may thwart its own righteousness by living for itself only.

15. The whole world is to be redeemed. It is not sufficient for Shalam to say: Behold, I am the fullness of the Father's kingdom. Let others go and do as I have done!

16. The selfishness of a colony shall be, therefore, guarded against, even as the selfishness of an individual.

17. Discipline, as regardeth the means and power of a colony, shall manifest in directing to the given purpose of founding the Father's kingdom.

18. Shalam might appropriate her excess of production, by sending into Uz, and giving to the poor.

19. Jehovih forbid that this should be done. The business of Shalam is not to distribute charity where it would thwart its own purpose.

20. Shalam shall use her excess of means to extending the Father's kingdom, in building new colonies.

21. Jehovih is with us, and we shall draw Uz unto us, to make them know Jehovih. To feed Uz in his debauchery is to send him in the way of destruction.

22. Guard ye, therefore, the appropriations of Shalam to such as labor for Jehovih's kingdom. As we have drawn a few away from Uz, let us prepare to draw more.

23. The way is open for any to go hence to found a new colony. Neither shall it be a branch of Shalam, nor a dependent. But it shall be in independent sister colony.

24. Neither shall it copy after Shalam, saying: Shalam shall be our example.

25. This would be following an earthly light.

26. Neither shall its people copy after Tae, saying: Tae did so and so, let us also.

27. For this would be following a lower light.

28. But it shall follow the Light of Jehovih as it cometh unto you who found it.

29. Save Jehovih found it, they shall fail who attempt it.

30. Jehovih designed not that man should build his house exactly like his neighbor's. The misfortune of man is to copy after others, instead of following Jehovih's Light as it cometh to himself.

31. Let not this misfortune come unto Shalam's sister colony. Another locality will call for other things. Be mindful of these, and adapt yourselves accordingly.

CHAPTER XX.

1. And there volunteered, and went out of Shalam, two hundred adults and more than three hundred children, of whom more than a hundred were infants.

2. And they went into another part of the country, and came to a place called Busiris, which was unoccupied. And they purchased the country there, and settled, and called the colony Illaem, signifying, healing waters, for there were mineral springs on the place, said to contain great virtue in healing the sick.

3. Now, in a similar manner to Shalam, so did Illaem, building and improving the place. But the people of Illaem had less hardship, for they drew supplies and assistance from Shalam.

4. Nevertheless, they had also many hardships and trials, for several years.

5. And Jehovih prospered Illaem also; so that it came to pass, that it was established in great perfection.

6. As to Shalam, after the first swarm departed, the inhabitants sent back to Uz, of their women, whose allotment it was, and collected yet more infants, castaways and orphans, and brought them to Shalam, and raised them in the same way.

7. From this time onward, every year, a goodly number reached the age of fourteen, and they were also liberated from infancy, and admitted as brothers and sisters. And, nearly every year, a swarm departed out of Shalam.

8. In addition to the infants admitted into Shalam, there were also admitted many adults. But these were examined after the same manner as were those at the first founding of Shalam.

9. And none were accepted save those, who were Faithists in the All Person, Jehovih, and who were willing to work.

10. But there came many of the poor of Uz, seeking membership for charity's sake.

11. But none of them were admitted. Jehovih had said: The laborers, in establishing My kingdom, shall not do for charity's sake. Their labor shall be to provide a way to prevent poverty, not to alleviate it. Behold, I will have a new race of people in the world, and they shall not waste their substance on those that deny Me.

12. But the poor were fed and sent on their way.

13. Now, it happened that many lazy people from Uz, having heard of the beauty and peace in Shalam, sought also to become members, being willing to make any covenant and to swear any oath, for sake of living in idleness.

14. But the Light of Jehovih had also made this matter clear; so that they were suffered to remain a while in Shalam at work, and to attend the schools of discipline, that they might be judged; and, if found worthy, they were admitted, but if unworthy, they were rejected.

15. But it came to pass, that many who came with no thought of self-resurrection, but came for a home, to be cared for by others, were entirely changed in their habits in a few months, being converted in truth from worthlessness to industry and self-improvement.

16. And many of these became zealous in purification and in good works, even above the average.

17. But nearly all who applied for admittance were poor, or misfortunate, or discouraged with life, and with the ways of the world in particular.

18. Neither came many who were rich; hence the saying, the difficulty for a rich man to enter the kingdom of heaven.

19. For, having corporeal comforts, they took little concern as to the spirit, and especially as to affiliation.

CHAPTER XXI.

OF THE VOICE OF JEHOVIH.

1. This is the sermon of the Voice, as delivered in Shalam to such as were admitted on trial, to wit:

2. My Voice is with all men, saith Jehovih.

3. Whoso is admonished against wrong-doing hath heard Me. By that shall he know My Presence.

4 . The man of Uz crieth out in mockery: Who hath heard Jehovih? Do the Faithists say, they have heard the Creator's voice? How can empty space speak?

5. But I am sufficient unto all My creations. The ant heareth Me, and the bee, the bird and the spider and all manner of living things which I created.

6. How think ye they hear Me, learning to do My will? Go I to them with lips and tongue, or with a trumpet?

7. I am Spirit; I am the Soul of things. By way of the soul is My Voice unto every living creature that I created.

8. But man locketh up his soul, and will not hear Me.

9. He heedeth that which cometh upon his corporeal senses. And this darkness groweth upon him, generation after generation.

10. Then he crieth out: Where is Jehovih? Who hath heard Him? Perhaps the ancients; but none in this day.

11. Jehovih saith: I am as one on the top of a mountain, calling to all people to come up to Me. But they hearken to darkness at the foot of the mountain, calling them down in corpor.

12. Now, behold, whatsoever thou hearest, or seest or readest or any indulgence that riseth thee upward, the same is My Voice unto thee.

13. But, whatsoever thou hearest, or seest or readest that casteth thee downward, is the voice of darkness.

14. Whoso studieth to know the right, shall hear Me; whoso striveth to be all truth, to himself and to others, already heareth My Voice.

15. Whoso indulgeth in anger, or vengeance, or in wrong-doing, casteth a veil up betwixt Me and himself; he shutteth out My Voice.

16. It is a talent to hear Me; I bestowed it upon all the living; it is seated in the soul.

17. By cultivation, it groweth; yea, it becometh mighty above all other talents.

18. By its culture, man attaineth to all possibilities, for so I created him.

19. When My Voice is weak, because of the darkness of man, he calleth Me conscience, or setteth Me aside as a faint impression.

20. But, with culture, behold, My Voice cometh to man with words and with power.

21. And he knoweth Me, and is mighty in good works and wisdom.

22. And he becometh a proof before the world, that My Voice is with him.

23. Jehovih saith: Whoso hath not heard Me, is in darkness indeed. He hath not yet turned his thoughts inward to purify himself and seek wisdom.

24. Whoso hath heard Me, knoweth it, and all the world can not convince him to the contrary.

CHAPTER XXII.

1. This was commanded unto the inhabitants of Shalam, to wit:

2. Ye shall not persuade any adult to come into the Father's kingdom.

3. But ye shall say unto whoso cometh your way: Come and see us, and judge thou, in thine own way, what is best for thee and for the world.

4. Others shall come to Shalam, inquiring for curiosity's sake, and for the sake of relating mischievous falsehoods founded on a grain of truth.

5. Therefore, be ye guarded, saying to such: The time of word-doctrines is at an end; examine thou, and judge as thou wilt.

6. Others will seek to convict you of self-righteousness. Therefore, if they inquire after this manner, to wit: Say ye, the Faithists are immaculate? or, say ye, all others are wrong? then shall ye answer them, saying:

7. Nothing mortal is immaculate; and, as for others, we are not their judges. Go thou to Jehovih, and inquire of Him. Sufficient unto us is it to do all the good we can, having faith in Jehovih.

8. Some will seek to trap you on the subject of marriage, inquiring after this manner, to wit:

9. Say ye, celibacy is higher than marriage? or, is marriage the higher? What say ye of marriage and of divorce?

10. To these ye shall answer after this manner: We are no man's keeper; neither say we whether celibacy or marriage is the higher. We give liberty unto all to serve Jehovih, on that matter, in their own way. One marriage only do we permit to any man or woman. And, though one or the other die, yet the survivor can not marry again. And, as to such as are married, they can, at the option of either one, return to celibacy, by being publicly proclaimed in the temple of Jehovih.

11. And if they inquire of you as to leadership, saying:

12. Who is the leader? Who is the highest? Who is the head? Ye shall answer them, saying: Jehovih. We have no man-leader; no man who is higher than another. We are brothers and sisters.

13. They will press you, inquiring: Some men can do more work; some men are stronger; some men are wiser; now, therefore, how do ye grade them that excellence may be known and respected?

14. To these ye shall reply, saying: All men are Jehovih's. He designed the strong ones to carry heavier burdens than the weak; He designed the wise ones to teach the less wise. Why, then, shall we give any preference to one over another? They are not ours, but Jehovih's. Sufficient is it for us to do our own parts, with all our wisdom and strength.

CHAPTER XXIII.

1. In course of time, the first heirs of Shalam came to maturity and to marriageable ages. And since they had been guarded as to diet, and as to controlling their passions, they were unlike Uzians in their general characteristics.

2. Because they had never known to say: This is mine, and that is thine, they were without selfishness or selfish desires; looking upon all things as Jehovih's, and on themselves as laborers to render good unto others.

3. They said: We were created in order to help rescue the world from darkness, and to rejoice in our own lives, because of such good as we can do unto others.

4. Behold, we were orphans and castaways; Jehovih wedded us to all the world.

5. Having, therefore, wisdom and purity within themselves, and, withal, having sufficient association to choose from, they did choose and wed for love's sake.

6. Nor did any worldly ambition control their choice, or influence them in hope of any gain as to their wedded partners.

7. And it came to pass that the offspring begotten of these were indeed a new race in the world, as to wisdom, love, purity and spirituality, and new also as to beauty and shapeliness, the like of which had never been before in all the world.

8. And they were by birth so developed in su'is, that, when they were grown a little, education came to them without books. To see and to hear, either corporeally or spiritually, was all they required in order to accomplish wisely all things required unto mortals.

9. And, with them, the heavens were as an open book; the libraries of the heavens as the sound of voices full of wisdom.

10. And the angels of ancient and modern times came, and stood by them, and walked with them, revealing the past and the future.

11. And, now, the fame of Shalam and her people were spread abroad, and, lo and behold, colonies were springing up in the east, west, north and south.

12. Hundreds of forest places and unoccupied lands were purchased and put under cultivation.

13. The wisest and best people began to depart out of the cities of Uz. Many of the Uzians, lawyers, preachers and priests and physicians, gave up their callings. And they went forth, saying: Alas, what good have I produced in the world? O Jehovih, teach Thou me the way to work in one of Thy kingdoms.

14. And some of the rich gathered up their means, calling: Come, O all ye poor and helpless! Behold, I have purchased land; come hither, and build a colony unto Jehovih.

15. And judges and governors gave up their callings also, and went and joined the Faithists, founding and practicing Jehovih's kingdom on earth.

16. And kings and queens and emperors deserted their thrones, and went and dwelt with the poor.

17. So, colonies of Faithists in Jehovih spread in every direction, becoming the chief foundation of the state and of the world.

18. And, yet, none of these colonies were bound by written laws, nor had any of them leaders or masters, nor any government, save the Light of Jehovih.

19. Nor was one colony bound by the customs and commands of another colony; but all of them lived by the highest Light that came to them.

20. Nor owned any man, woman or child anything more than the clothes he or she wore; but all things were Jehovih's, in care of the keeping of the colony.

21. Nor was there buying or selling between the colonies; but they exchanged with one another according to production, and without any regard to value.

22. And whosoever came and joined a colony, bringing gold or silver or valuable goods of any kind, donated them to Jehovih, and not to the colony, to be distributed according to the light thereof for the Father's kingdoms.

23. Neither labored any one for the colony, but for Jehovih; nor did any colony hire any man nor woman nor child to work for them.

24. Such, then, was Shalam and her example before the world, of the Father's kingdom on earth.

END OF THE HISTORY OF SHALEM.

CHAPTER XXIV.

1. These are the records of the C'chiefs of the Faithists kingdoms:

2. Jehovih separated the people, the Uzians on one hand, and the Faithists on the other.

3. And He said unto the Uzians: Because I called, and ye came not;

4. Because ye said: Thy kingdom come on earth as it is in heaven, and ye put not forth a hand in My behalf;

5. Because ye saw the multitude going after intoxicating drink and smoke and opium;

6. Because ye rose not up, saying: Stay thy hand, satan!

7. But shirked, granting licenses unto these sins;

8. And ye have become a polluted people;

9. Given to drunkenness and to smoking and to all manner of dissipation;

10. Each one casting the blame on others, and hiding himself in self-righteousness;

11. Thus opening the doors of your houses of debauchery as a temptation to the young:

12. Behold, I am risen in judgment against you.

13. My holy angels I shall withdraw from your cities.

14. And from your places of worship;

15. And from your government, and your law-makers and rulers;

16. For they have profaned Me.

17. Making laws and granting licenses to carry on evils, knowingly and willfully, for policy's sake;

18. Hoping for personal favor and gain.

19. For they knew that what was not good for one person, was not good for a nation;

20. And that, whatever sin indulged in, would, soon or late, bring its own punishment.

21. And they said: We derive a large revenue from the duties and licenses for these iniquities!

22. Thus hoping to justify themselves by compounding themselves.

23. And I said unto them: A revenue thus received shall be expended in prisons and alms-houses, and shall not be sufficient.

24. Because ye granted licenses, and polluted the people, behold, the pollution shall more than balance the revenue.

25. The criminals and paupers shall be a greater burden than though ye received no revenue.

26. Behold, I showed unto you that, as an individual could not sin against Me without, soon or late, becoming answerable unto Me, I showed ye also that the same responsibility and result would befall a nation or a people in like manner.

27. For which reasons, and because of your evasions of My commandments, I called unto My God and Lords and My holy angels, saying: Waste not your time and labor more with

the Uzians.

28. Nor answer ye their prayers when they call on My name;

29. And, though their chief rulers and law-makers be in the throes of death, and they call, saying: O Jehovih, heal Thou or Chief Magistrate!

30. Yet, ye shall not go unto them, nor do them service more.

31. For they have become a conceited people, saying: There is no God, and Jehovih is void as the wind.

32. Behold, ye shall let them go their way; their cities shall become full of crime, for angels of darkness shall come amongst them, and no city shall be safe from theft, murder and arson.

33. And vagabonds shall travel in the country places, stealing and robbing and murdering.

34. And their great men shall take bribes, and their judges shall connive with sin; and the innocent shall be confined to mad-houses.

35. And justice shall depart away from them.

36. The employee shall pilfer and steal from his employer; and the employer shall hire others to look after those in his employ.

37. But all things shall fail them.

38. For I will make them understand, I am the First Principle in all things;

39. And that I am Justice;

40. And that I am Purity;

41. And that whoso raiseth a hand against justice, purity, virtue, wisdom and truth, also raiseth his hand against Me.

42. I made the way of life like going up a mountain; whoso turneth aside or goeth downward, shall ultimately repent of his course, and he shall retrace his steps.

43. To a nation and a people, and to a government of a people, I am the same.

44. Righteousness shall be first and foremost of all things.

45. Their governors and law-makers shall be made to know this.

46. When they were a monarchy, I held the king responsible.

47. But when I gave unto the multitude to govern themselves, behold, I gave also responsibility unto them.

48. And they sought not to make laws for righteous government unto the whole, but sought to favor certain cliques of iniquities, and to make laws to protect them in evil manufacturies, and for traffic in tobacco and opium and alcohol.

49. And no man more sought to be a governor or law-maker for the good of the people, or to serve Me;

50. But he sought office for profit's sake and vainglory.

51. Now, therefore, My holy angels went away from them, and no more answered their prayers.

52. And the righteous of the first days departed away from them.

53. And they became a nation of money-getters and servants of mammon.

54. And I blessed not their marriages nor their households.

55. And their sons and daughters respected not their fathers and mothers; for, as the fathers and mothers respected not Me, so came disrespect and misery upon them.

56. And their sons and daughters became profligates and idlers, growing up for no good under the sun, depending on their wits to work out a life of sin and luxury.

57. And whoso married, peace came not to them; but contention and jealousy and bitterness of heart.

58. And their offspring fell in the grades, becoming outcasts and paupers and criminals.

59. And husbands and wives cried out for divorcement on all hands.

60. And the law-makers granted them and favored them; but, lo and behold, the evil multiplied on the earth.

61. In pity I cried out unto them, saying: Ye may make laws forever, but My kingdom cometh not by the road of man's laws. Except ye turn about, and begin anew, there is no help for you under the sun.

62. But they would not hear Me.

63. Then I sent My angels unto them, teaching them the same things that were taught of old, amongst which were: As ye bind yourselves on earth, even so shall ye be bound in heaven; as ye live on earth, serving self only, even so, in a selfish heaven, shall ye enter My es worlds.

64. But they denied My angels, and abused My seers and prophets.

65. In their own self-esteem, sat they themselves up to judge Me, saying: There is no All Person; there is nothing, save certain natural and divine laws, and they are dumb, like the wind; they see not, nor do they hear.

66. Then I called out over the earth, saying: The time of My kingdom is come. Now is the time of My reign amongst mortals.

67. And those that had faith came; and, behold, they have built unto Me.

68. I have a new people on the earth.

69. Again I called to My God and to his angel hosts, saying: Behold, I have separated the wheat from the chaff; I have divided the sheep from the goats.

70. Go ye unto those that serve Me in the practice of My kingdom, for they shall become the chief people in all the world.

71. They shall rejoice and prosper in all things; they shall sing songs of gladness.

72. Their sons and daughters shall be an honor unto them and a glory in My household.

73. Because they seek to serve Me by practicing good works with all their wisdom and strength.

CHAPTER XXV.

1. This rule I made in all My works, saith Jehovih: When I separate the people, the good go away out from amongst the evil.

2. Even as I drew the Israelites out of Egupt.

3. And, whoso go out, prosper in My hand; I make them an everlasting people.

4. But those that remain, go down to destruction; and they become unknown upon the earth.

5. Their great men are forgotten, and their wisest men lose caste in the histories of a thousand years.

6. Behold, these things I had made known unto the generations of the earth.

7. Now, when I separated the Faithists and the Uzians, in the kosmon era, I sent angels, warning them. I said unto them:

8. Flatter not yourselves that man is all wisdom; I say unto you, I am with the righteous;

might shall not triumph through wrong-doing. Behold, a judgment shall come upon this people.

9. When I begin to call them, My chosen shall come and found My kingdom; and they shall come faster and faster every year.

10. And the Uzians shall fall into iniquity, more and more every year.

11. And, now, behold what hath been!

12. The prince of devils came upon the Uzians, saying:

13. Think not that I come to send peace on earth; I come not to send peace, but a sword.

14. I come to set man at variance against his father, and a daughter against her mother.

15. Now, therefore, when My angels went in behalf of My kingdom, behold, the prince of devils did invade the places of the ungodly.

16. And, whoso received My angels, and practiced righteousness, were fallen upon by the emissaries of the prince of devils, and unmercifully treated with curses and tortures.

17. But I called the righteous hence, and they built unto Me My kingdom.

18. And I said unto the Uzians: Let this be a testimony unto you of the power of the Almighty;

19. Ye go about building ships of war, and harbors for defense, with torpedoes, and with all manner of wicked inventions;

20. But I say unto you, this nation, this government and this people shall not be attacked in the places ye build.

21. It is within.

22. For I will draw away the righteous, and none but rogues shall accept your great offices.

23. And this matter shall grow upon you in the way of evil, declining in virtue more and more every year.

24. Look, therefore, at your grade; judge ye the words of the Almighty.

25. My hands fashioned the signs of the times.

26. As the hirer this day hireth one man to watch another, even so shall it come unto you in the great offices of your government.

27. By force and by might, ye shall hope to overcome the prince of devils, but ye shall fail.

28. And, in proportion as ye go down in corruption, even so shall the Faithists go away into My kingdoms.

CHAPTER XXVI.

1. The C'chiefs said: And Jehovih prospered the New Kingdoms, as they were called in mockery, for they were not kingdoms, but the opposite.

2. Jehovih had said: A republic can not follow the highest Light; it followeth the majority. And a majority is, and was, and ever shall be, the lesser light.

3. Therefore, a republic is not the all highest government; and, since only the All Highest can triumph in the end, behold, and interpret ye what shall come to pass.

4. The C'chiefs said: But many understood not. Nevertheless, the Faithists had little in common with the Uzians.

5. The Faithists established a reciprocity between different colonies.

6. For, some were suited to agriculture and some to manufactures.

7. And they exchanged produce, so there was neither buying nor selling between them.

8. And it came to pass also, that, as some of the colonies were situated to the south, where it was warm, and some to the north, where it was cold, so the people went and sojourned in any place suited unto them, continuing their membership wherever they went.

9. Now, thus it did come to pass, in Jehovih's kingdom on earth, man was without a government, such as man's government.

10. And this was the next higher condition that came up after republics.

11. The angels of Jehovih, perceiving this was coming to pass, said unto the Faithists:

12. Bother not your heads much about passing new laws for the Uzians; neither take ye any part in the government, whether it doth this or that.

13. For many men shall rise up, saying: If the government would make a law of peace; or, if the government would prohibit the traffic and the manufacture of this curse or that curse,--

14. But we say unto you, all these things shall fail. Trust ye not in the ungodly to do a godlike matter.

15. The societies shall fail; the Peace Society shall become a farce; the Prohibitory Society shall be lost sight of.

16. Even the churches that profess peace and temperance will not embrace peace and temperance. They will fraternize with liquor-traffickers and with colonels and generals of war, for sake of policy.

17. The boast of the Uzians shall be: This is a home for all peoples; but, nevertheless, even in the midst of their boastings they shall make prohibitory laws to the contrary.

18. For they are fallen under the lower light; none can turn them about the other way.

19. Under the name of liberty, they shall claim the right to practice ungodliness.

20. But ye shall come out from amongst them, and be as a separate people in the world.

21. Thus it came to pass; the people were admonished by God and his angels, and by Jehovih speaking in the souls of mortals.

22. And those that were of the Spirit believed; but those that were of the flesh disbelieved.

23. Wider and wider apart, these two people separated. And the believers, having faith in Jehovih, practiced righteousness, rising higher and higher in wisdom and purity. But the disbelievers went down in darkness; were scattered and lost from off the face of the earth.

24. Thus, Jehovih's kingdom swallowed up all things in victory; His dominion was over all, and all people dwelt in peace and liberty.

END OF THE BOOK OF JEHOVIH'S KINGDOM EARTH,

AND

END OF OAHSPE.

MORE OF

OAHSPE

(NEW ERA)
KOSMON REVELATION

IN

THE WORDS OF JEHOVIH

AND HIS

ANGEL EMBASSADORS.

INDEX

ADDENDUM

An explanation of the reasons for the photographic reproduction of the 1882 (first) edition of OAHSPE, plus reproductions of original oil paintings and photographs by John Ballou Newbrough excerpted from the 1891 (second and revised) edition.

John Ballou Newbrough was born on June 5, 1828, on a Springfield, Ohio farm. A college man, he specialized in medicine, particularly dentistry, which later became his profession. He was a big man, powerful and vigorous and adventurous. After college he went to the goldfields of California, and also to Australia. After becoming a dentist in New York City, he married, and became the father of a son and a daughter. A second marriage gave him another daughter. Part of his normal home life was an interest in spiritualism, and together with a dear friend, Edwin Augustus Davis, he interviewed many mediums, even entertained them in his home, in an effort to learn all he could of the occult. Davis was a photographer, and cooperated with Newbrough in taking pictures of spiritual phenomena, and many unusual pictures were secured. However, both men were dissatisfied with the caliber of spirit communications being received, and Newbrough particularly felt that there must be something more interesting and practical. The advent of the Fox sisters upon the New York scene brought matters to a head in Newbrough's mind, and he earnestly desired to know how the angels lived, the plan of the universe, and the true facts of spiritual existence. He believed that if he purified himself, he might establish higher contacts.

One morning in 1870, Newbrough went to the home of his friend Davis, who lived on Sixth Avenue, near the old Hay Market, and said: "I've come for your advice; I had quite an experience about 4 a.m. this morning. I was sleeping nicely when I felt a hand on my shoulder. A voice said: 'Wake up, doctor. Everything is all right. I only want to ask you a question and we will go.'

"I sat up and answered: 'Yes, if I can.' The voice said: 'Would you like to perform a mission for Jehovih?'

"I rubbed my eyes and saw that the room was lit up with pillars of a soft light so pleasing to the eyes that it was indescribable. I saw great numbers of beautiful spirits or angels. They did not have wings. I spoke: 'What is the mission, so that I may know whether to say yes or no?' The answer came back, 'Jehovih would like you to live spiritually for ten years, and at the end of that time we will come back and tell you what it is we desire, for your body and mind are not sufficiently perceptible now. You must be pure.'

"What do you mean by living spiritually?"

"We want you never to kill anything, or eat anything that breathes: meat, fish, birds, reptiles, etcetera. Live on nuts, fruit, vegetables. You don't need so much food, as you are too heavy now; you need to lose weight. One other thing is very important: you must help people; give your services to people who need dental help, without pay, if they cannot pay. Do charity work; by individual charity you change the person's thoughts. They will think of you as a good man, and will send out good thoughts to you. You will need all the good will you can get.'

I answered: 'This will be quite a change of living for me. I will let you know.'

"We already know your answer; it will be yes!' the voice said, and then the lights dimmed and went out, and the atmosphere changed back to its normal darkness. I got up and wrote down everything that had happened, then I drank a glass of milk and came over to talk to you."

Davis and Newbrough discussed the matter for hours, and during the conversation Newbrough revealed that he thought he had recognized three of the spirits, although he had not had a good look at them. He asked Davis if he thought the adventure was real, or only a dream.

"John," said Davis, "I don't believe it was a dream. I'd say, go ahead. I myself don't like meat or fish, and I would have no objection to going on the same diet so that you will have assistance in keeping to it, as it will certainly be hard on you to be so different in public eating habits. Perhaps the ten year wait will be worth it, when you find out what it is that you are to do."

At 4 a.m. one morning late in 1880, John Ballou Newbrough was awakened from his slumber to find the same mysterious and beautiful lights filling his room. He sat up and demanded: "Am I worthy?" The same voice spoke: "You have done well. You have passed our test. We know that you feel more healthy. Now we want you to buy a typewriter and place it on this table. We will thereafter awaken you one hour before dawn each morning, and you will sit in this chair before the typewriter and put your hands on the keys. You will buy plenty of paper and keep it always ready to use.

"I don't know how to use a typewriter."

"We will control your hands and arms, and perform the task for you, so don't worry. You must not look at what is written until it is finished."

There was further discussion and instruction, then the pillars of light dimmed and went out.

On the morning of January 1, 1881, having followed all instructions, the first writing session began at 4 a.m. As Newbrough later told it to his friend, Davis: "To my amazement as I sat in the chair, my hands went up and started to pound at the keys. It seemed to me that I was half asleep, but I saw everything I was doing. I saw no spirits, but I knew they were using my body and thought. I looked at my hands and fingers; they were going like mad. Then it occurred to me that it was fantastic.

"The papers seemed to pile up fast on the right side of the typewriter. As the days went by, I was doing more and more. At first I was thinking what am I writing about? My mind seemed blank, but I had never felt better in my life. I always locked my door after me, and it was locked when I came back. I noticed, though that there was a blank paper over the pile I had finished, and a paperweight on top. It was oblong in shape. As I left my room the next morning I took particular notice of how the paperweight lay on the stack of finished work. When I returned that evening, I wanted to see if it had been moved, but it had not. But to my surprise, my bed had been made. Everything had been dusted and cleaned. I said to myself: 'The spirits are certainly working hard around here!' I heard a loud laugh, and the voice said: 'We are! We don't want you to worry about a thing. We are taking care of you, and no harm can come to you, Remember this!'"

Every morning, before sunrise, until December 15, 1881, John Ballou Newbrough wrote at his Sholes typewriter, at a speed physically almost impossible considering the crudity of this first typewriter, and finally the manuscript was complete.

In 1882 the book was published. Newbrough kept the very first copy off the press, and presented the second copy to his friend Edwin Augustus Davis in appreciation for his assistance over the years.

The foregoing information (which it is significant to note is essentially the same as the account given by Newbrough himself in a letter written on January 1, 1883 to the editor of The Banner of Light in Boston, Massachusetts) comes from the diary of the grandson of Edwin Augustus Davis.

Although copies of the first edition of OAHSPE are reputed to exist in the possession of various individuals, only one copy has been located in fifteen years of diligent searching by the publisher of this photo-copied edition, and it is from this single copy that the photographic offset plates have been made. Inasmuch as there are considerable differences in the 1891 edition (and those subsequent) and the 1882 edition, it seems desirable to preserve the first edition in greater quantities for the purposes of those more erudite and concerned students of OAHSPE who, made aware that a "revision" was made, may wonder at the extent of the revision and the reasons for it.

The original manuscript, it is said, was destroyed in a flood in El Paso, Texas, after it had been carefully checked against the 1891 edition by Andrew M Howland, who aided Newbrough in the work of revising the 1882 edition. Destroyed also were the paintings from the 1891 edition reproduced in this photo-copied edition. Howland has written that the 1891 edition is identical with the manuscript; while Newbrough's daughter insists that the only differences in the two editions are a few typographical errors (which naturally reappear in this photo-copied edition). Aside from the incompatibility of these two statements, Wing Anderson, who has diligently and faithfully published OAHSPE since 1936, has stated that he has certain pages of the original manuscript (the VOICE OF MAN) and notes that they are perfectly typed, whereas a letter written by Newbrough on the original typewriter is a curious example of inept typing ability. Newbrough was unable to type a single line without error.

In view of the differences in the two editions, and the existence of some of the pages of the original manuscript, there is reason to wonder about the circumstances behind the destruction of the original manuscript. Howland, in a letter written in 1893, mentions that the BOOK OF PRAISE was nearly double its present size, and that quite likely this is also true of the BOOK OF BEN. The BOOK OF DISCIPLINE, which appears in the 1891 edition, does not appear in the 1882 edition, and unfortunately there is now no evidence that it appeared in the original manuscript. Other fragments of original proof sheets, including an introduction to the BOOK OF SAPHAH and an explanation of the TREE OF LANGUAGE, appeared only in very recent editions. Apparently it is true that the original OAHSPE manuscript has never actually been published in its entirety, and because the manuscript is destroyed, some considerable portions are now lost.

It is not surprising that some effort (on the part of the drujas of OAHSPE?) would have been made to destroy or at least render confused and subject to criticism through inconsistency a book as vital to understanding as is OAHSPE. Certainly the high-raised angels whom Newbrough says wrote OAHSPE through his hands, would not have performed so inefficiently that revision was later necessary by persons in no whit originally involved, such as Andrew Howland.

Little can be done today to remedy any lack, but certainly none of the published editions should be allowed to become unavailable, as is the original manuscript. Therefore, we humbly offer this photographed edition of the 1882 printing, which was the very first, together with all its typographical errors, its language key charts, its Commentary, and as an added feature reproductions of the paintings (also destroyed in the same flood that removed the original manuscript from the ken of man) of the key prophets in OAHSPE, to those students who will value the opportunity to debate in their own minds the reasons for any changes at all, and to evaluate the history of OAHSPE in its proper perspective.

The publication of the photo copy of the 1882 edition is not to say that subsequent editions are invalid, for in fact the doctrinal content is unchanged, and the bulk of the publication is materially the same, except for the omissions, additions and revision changes as will be noted. This photo copy of the 1882 edition is offered solely in the interests of completion, and in answer to those who ask questions concerning the first edition and the exact nature of the changes that were actually made, and what their total effect on the validity of OAHSPE has been. The paintings are also included from the 1891 edition, because that is also very rare.

In our humble opinion, the first edition should not be lost, as was the original manuscript. It is to prevent this loss that this work has been done, and because it has been done, OAHSPE cannot now be attacked as an expurgated and perverted book and summarily dismissed. In the light of present day science, the BOOK OF COSMOGONY alone is evidence of a superior fore-knowledge that stands as a sturdy sentinel over the doctrinal portions. And in the light of present day anthropology and archaeology, its historical portions stand as remarkable evidence of that same superior fore-knowledge. OAHSPE is truly a gateway to understanding.

Ray Palmer
June 2, 1960

The BOOK OF DISCIPLINE reproduced on the following pages, did not appear in the 1882 edition of OAHSPE, although it was a part of the original manuscript. It was, however, included in the revised 1891 edition, and it is from this edition that the photo-copied pages included in this volume were reproduced. They are the same as appear in all subsequent editions of OAHSPE, including the British edition, which is still being published in Great Britain. Because of its importance, and in the interest of completeness, the BOOK OF DISCIPLINE has been included for the first time in this photo-copy of the original 1882 edition.

Ray Palmer, Amherst, Wisconsin 55406
April 24, 1970

BOOK OF DISCIPLINE.

CHAPTER I.
GOD REVEALETH WHO HE IS.

1. This is the word from the organic heaven:

2. Hear the words of thy God, O man, I am thy brother, risen from mortality to a holy place in heaven; profit thou in my wisdom, and be admonished by my love.

3. For as I am thy elder brother, so shall it be with thee, to rise also in time to come, and look back to mortals and call them to the exalted heavens of the Almighty.

4. To Jehovih all adoration and glory, forever, Amen!

5. By and through Him is all life and motion, and power, things seen and unseen.

6. Nor is there an angel in heaven so high, or sufficiently wise to comprehend Jehovih in His entirety, nor to see Him as thou seest thy fellow man.

7. For He is within all; beyond and over all:

8. Being Ever Present in all places:

9. Doing by Virtue of His presence:

10. Quickening all the living:

11. Adorable above all things:

12. Even as the sun is to the light of day, so is Jehovih to the understanding of all the living:

13. Whereon to contemplate is the road of everlasting life, rising in wisdom, love and power forever.

14. Hear thy God, O man, and distinguish then that the twain, God and Jehovih, are not the same one; nor more is thy God than what thou shalt be in time to come.

15. First, mortality, then death, which is the first resurrection; such are the spirits of the dead, angels dwelling with mortals upon the earth, where they abide, some for a few years, some for a hundred and some for a thousand or more years.

16. Second, angel organization in heaven, and their abandonment of mortals, which is the second resurrection.

17. As a kingdom on earth hath a king, and the king is nevertheless a mortal, so in like manner is the heavenly place of thy God a kingdom of angels, and the chief over them is God, an angel also.

18. Howbeit the kingdom of thy God embraceth all the heavens of the earth. So is it also with all the corporeal worlds and their atmospherean heavens, a God and organic heavens belonging to each and all of them.

19. Nor is this all; for there is a third resurrection, in which the angels rise still higher in wisdom, love and power, and are sent by thy God into etherea, mid-way between the planets, the highest of all heavens, over which there are Chiefs, who are also Gods and Goddesses of still more comprehensive attributes.

20. Therefore I am as any other spirit of the dead, a one time man upon the earth, even as thou art in this day; but one within the organic heavens of the earth.

CHAPTER II.

GOD EXPLAINETH THE FIRST AND SECOND RESURRECTION, AND THE DIFFERENCE IN MANIFESTATIONS FROM THEM.

1. Hear me, O man, and consider the weight of the arguments of thy God. Thou hast communed with the spirits of the dead; thy father and mother and sister and brother who are gone from mortality have spoken to thee in spirit, and thou art convinced.

2. And thy kin and thy neighbor have done so likewise; yea, from east to west, and north to south the communion of angels and a multitude of miracles have stirred up thousands and millions, to know that the souls of the dead do live.

3. Moreover thou wert taught in thy youth to say: I believe in the holy communion of angels.

4. And of a truth this hath come to pass. And thou rejoicest with all thy heart and soul. Thou puttest aside the ancient scriptures, saying: Why shall I read them? Do I not converse with heaven itself? Behold, I have seen my father and mother and brother and sister who were dead; they have spoken to me; there is no devil nor place of hell.

5. For a season thy God hath suffered this also to come to pass, that the spirits say there is no God; that there is no higher heaven than to dwell upon the earth, to enjoy the things thereof; to be reincarnated, and to live over and over in mortality.

6. That the evidence of my words might be substantiated by thy experience, and thou be led to consider the testimonies, present and past, in order to comprehend the plan of Jehovih's works, and the glory and completeness thereof.

7. Consider then the result of angel communion as thou hast found it, and bear witness that Jehovih was wise in providing comfort to both the dead and the living by this proximity of spirit unto them, rather than a heaven far remote.

8. Nevertheless, this also hath been proved unto thee, that there are false angels and wise angels, as well as false seers and wise seers, and that out of the multitude of revelations from them, there hath come neither harmony nor good works.

9. They have been pullers down and clearers away of the ancient revelations, doctrines and religions; but they have built not an edifice of unity and glory to the Almighty.

10. And it hath been shown thee that not only the seer, prophet, su'is, and miracle worker, but that all people are subject to the influence of the spirits of the dead, even though unconsciously to themselves.

11. And it hath been shown that the spirits of the dead possess for a long period of time the same characteristics and prejudices as when in mortality; and since there is neither harmony nor community of life amongst mortals, neither is there harmony nor community of life nor of teaching amongst the angels who manifest unto them.

12. For the angels through one prophet teach one doctrine, and through another prophet another doctrine, after the manner of the doctrines of the prophets themselves.

13. Consider also the multitude of infants, that die without any knowledge of either earth or heaven. And the multitude of unlearned, and foolish, and depraved; for all of these as well as the wise and good enter the first resurrection.

14. And of the wise and good, who strive for continual elevation, how few, compared to the whole! Yet such is the relative proportions of angels of light and angels of darkness in proximity to mortals.

15. Thus hath it ever been. Nevertheless, in time long past, the minority, who were wise and good were moved by the spirit of Jehovih upon them, saying:

16. Come ye together, O all ye who desire to rise to a higher heaven; my heavens are for raising the soul upward for ever and ever.

17. And thy God gathered them together, and said unto them:

18. Behold, this darkness is more than we can bear; let us hence and inhabit a heaven by ourselves, where there shall be no wrangling, or falsehood, or malice, or blasphemy against our Creator.

19. And they responded: Yea, let us hence. And we will covenant ourselves unto Jehovih to return no more to these regions, nor to mortals on earth. For doth not the behavior of mortals invite darkness rather than light? Do they not want us for servants, to find lost treasures or riches, or social indulgence? or to entertain them with miracles?

20. Thus it came to pass that the wisest and best angels departed away from the earth; away from mortals, and away from the inharmonious presence of the legions of the spirits of the dead, and they inhabited a heavenly region by themselves.

21. And they covenanted themselves unto Jehovih not to return again single-handed to minister unto mortals; neither to return again to mortals save they came in phalanxes, and only when duly authorized and directed by their most Holy Council, and their chief, who was God.

22. Such then was the beginning of the second resurrection; and the condition of membership required the renunciation of all associations and conditions below it. And the rank of all such angels was, ANGELS OF GOD, or ANGELS OF JEHOVIH, in contradistinction from the angels of the first resurrection, who know no organization for righteousness' sake.

23. But that mortals be not left in darkness, behold thy God and his holy council prepared certain rules of discipline and conduct and commandments, whereby the angels of the second resurrection should be as a unit in their duties and teachings thereafter.

24. Chief of which rules was, that the angels of Jehovih should never manifest themselves as individuals unto mortals, lest mortals become servants to, and worshippers of the spirits instead of the All Highest, Jehovih.

25. Second to this, that when the angels of Jehovih should be appointed to mortals, it should be as guardians over infants, to inspire them by way of the natural consciousness within, as to what was right and good in reference to eternal life. And that such guardian angels be in phalanxes of millions and tens of millions (but still in close membership with thy God and his Holy Council) in order to relieve one another on guard.

26. For, by the inspirations of the angels of thy God, the individual entity of a mortal is directed in its normal growth; but by the angels of the first resurrection, mortals are used abnormally, by entrancement, by miracles, or by sar'gis, oracles or otherwise.

27. That the angels of God might inspire mortals with the same inspiration, behold, he and his Holy Council prepared certain instruction with rules, words and commandments adapted to the understanding of mortals for the good of their souls, pandering not to their earthly desires. Such words being designated as sacred writings in the original, though for the most part perverted or lost sight of afterward.

28. Chief angels over these phalanxes being Lords, Marshals, Captains, and so on, the second resurrection being orderly, disciplined and organized in its glorious work.

29. Thus my Lords have angels under them who are authorized and ordained in my name,

1141

and in the name of Jehovih to abide for times and seasons with mortals as guardians and inspirers; to provide dreams, thoughts and visions in the minds of mortals, and to otherwise labor in elevating them in purity, love and wisdom.

30. Such then are the angels of God and of Jehovih. And their teachings are the same as my Lord's and thy God's; nor doth one of them teach a matter in one way, and another teach it differently; howbeit there are different grades and systems adapted to the different degrees of intelligence of the different peoples on earth.

CHAPTER III.
GOD ILLUSTRATETH THE DIFFERENCE OF METHOD BETWIXT THE FIRST AND SECOND RESURRECTION.

1. Open thy understanding, O man, that thou mayest discern the beauty and glory of heavenly places prepared by thy God, Lords and guardian angels.

2. For as we came up out of the first resurrection, which may be likened to a great medley, a noise and confusion of a mighty multitude, so covenanted we with Jehovih to make ourselves orderly, and a unit in growth, manifestation, expression and future development, that the place of the second resurrection should do nothing in common with the first.

3. For alike and like Jehovih created mortals and angels to attract each other; and since the aspiration and desire of most mortals pertain to themselves as individuals, so the twain bound themselves in the same pursuits and earthly hopes.

4. For whoso on earth loved riches, or fame, or great learning, or even evil, such as dissipation, drunkenness, gluttony, sexual indulgence, or theft, gambling or arson, doing any or all of these things for self's sake, or for evil, attracted angel companions of a like order, who, by inspiration or otherwise, led him on to achieve his heart's desire.

5. And it came to pass when such mortals died and entered the first resurrection, their former inspirers became their companions and rulers, having shaped their thoughts whilst in mortality through their labors for self and earthly objects. And these in turn became angel inspirers unto other mortals of like characteristics, so that a long period of time passed away, before the spirits who were thus bound to earth could be persuaded there were other heavens open for them to come and inherit. And as it was so then, even so is it this day with the spirits of the dead.

6. As there are good lands on earth still unoccupied, whilst in other regions there are great cities with mortals crowded together, starving, and dwelling in misery, and they will not hence, even so is the great multitude of angels of darkness gathered together upon the face of the earth, and many of them will not hence into the higher heavens of Jehovih.

7. As cold metal in contact with hot metal changeth temperature, so by angel contact with the spirit of man, knowledge passeth from one to the other. So also is it of the passions, sentiments, desires and aspirations betwixt the twain.

8. Also, as where the sea breaketh upon the land, and the twain are ever in contact, so is the spirit world ever in contact with the mortal world (which place of contact was named by the ancients the intermediate world or place of purgation, wherefrom none could rise till made organically pure).

9. Now therefore thy God showeth thee certain signs characteristic of the difference

betwixt the angels of the first and the second resurrection:

10. Of the first, coming as individuals, whether professing names, signs or histories, and especially the ancients. Whose words are uttered from the standpoint of the earth looking upward.

11. But of the second, as light only. Whose words emanate from my holy places in heaven coming down to thee.

12. Of the first, flatterers, to win thy favor. Whose counsel pertaineth to thyself and to earthly things.

13. Of the second, to teach thee self-abnegation, and lead thee to do good unto others regardless of thine own profit, caring little whether thou art prosperous on the earth provided thou shalt be raised up in time to come.

14. For the revelations of the second resurrection come from the light of my Holy Council, who have abandoned their earthly habits and desires; knowing the way of raising up everlastingly is by constantly putting away the conditions below.

15. Thy God cometh not as an individual; neither do my Lords (nor holy angels though they come in my name). I come in legions of thousands and millions.

16. Neither varieth the inspiration from my kingdom one jot or tittle from what it hath ever been, save in greater fullness, according to the increase of capacity in mortals to receive knowledge.

17. The spirit of my heavens pervadeth my words; through my holy angels I have spoken unto thee from thy youth up; and in my revelations thou perceivest the touch of my hand.

18. I cry out Order, Purity, Discipline, Justice and Good Works, or, Retribution!

19. O man, beware of angels who say: In heaven there is no organization, nor God, nor Holy Council, nor discipline, nor order, nor teaching, nor self-denial, or,

20. Who say: There is no God, no Jehovih, no government in heaven, or,

21. Who say: There is no bondage after death; no place or condition of suffering, or,

22. Who say: When thou diest thy spirit shall enter paradise and dwell in perpetual ease and glory.

23. Who say: Heaven is an endless summer land, with silvery rivers and golden boats for all, or,

24. Who say: Eat, drink and enjoy thyself for the gratification of thine earthly passions, for when thou art dead thy path shall be straight to glory.

25. Who say: Heap up riches, for there is no punishment after death, or,

26. Who say: Turn not thy thoughts into thine own soul to discover thy ungodliness, for when thou art dead thy spirit shall revel in bliss, or,

27. Who say: The angel world is a place of progression without self-abnegation and good works, or,

28. Who saith: Behold me, I am from the highest, most exalted sphere, or from a far-off star, or,

29. Who saith: I have visited the planets, or,

30. Who saith: Resurrection cometh by reincarnation, first a stone, then lead, then silver, then gold, then a tree, then a worm, then an animal and then man, or that a spirit re-entereth the womb, and is born again in mortality, or,

31. Who saith: Blessed art thou; for a host of ancient spirits attend thee, thou hast a great mission.

32. For all of these are the utterances of the angels of the first resurrection. And though they may inspire great oratory and learned discourses, yet they are flatterers, and will surely lead thee into grief.

CHAPTER IV.

GOD ILLUSTRATETH THE CHARACTERISTICS OF MORTALS ACCORDINGLY AS THEY ARE UNDER THE INFLUENCE OF THE FIRST OR SECOND RESURRECTION.

1. Consider the words of thy God, O man, and profit thou in the application of thy judgment for the growth of thy soul everlastingly.

2. Of the first resurrection man saith: I know my rights and dare maintain them.

3. Of the second, he saith: I ask not for rights for my own self; whatsoever is put upon me, that will I bear.

4. Of the first: No man shall impose upon me.

5. Of the second: Impose upon me whatsoever thou wilt.

6. Of the first: Let me justify myself in what I have done; behold, I am falsely accused.

7. Of the second: Jehovih knoweth my case; neither will I plead in my own behalf. Whoso is falsely accused, let him wait; in time the Father will right all things.

8. Of the first: Let no man try to rule over me; I will maintain my liberty at all hazards.

9. Of the second: Since no man in all the world hath full liberty, why should I ask it?

10. Of the first: Make me a leader; let me be the head.

11. Of the second: Make me not a leader; lest I would feel responsible for those I led.

12. Of the first: I have done my share, let others do as well.

13. Of the second: Though I do all I can, yet I am short before Jehovih.

14. Of the first: O that I were rich as my neighbor, what a great good I would do!

15. Of the second: Take all I have, and at once.

16. Of the first: Myself, and then my family will I help; after that, others.

17. Of the second: We are all brothers and sisters; why shall we prefer one of Jehovih's children above another?

18. Of the first: I will not consider my shortcomings, lest I be dejected in spirit.

19. Of the second: Teach me, O Father, to look into my every act, word and thought, to purify myself in Thy sight.

20. Of the first: What might the world say? Ah! my reputation is at stake!

21. Of the second: What will Jehovih say? With Him must I preserve my reputation, more than with ten thousand worlds.

22. Of the first: Who injureth me shall suffer by my hand.

23. Of the second: Let us render good unto those that injure us.

CHAPTER V.

GOD SHOWETH HOW MORTALS MAY ATTAIN INSPIRATION FROM JEHOVIH AND FROM THE ANGELS OF THE SECOND RESURRECTION.

1. Whoso ruleth over his own earthly desires, passions, actions, words and thoughts, being constantly watchful for the highest light and greatest good, is on the right road.

2. And if he persist in this till it hath become a constitutional growth within him, then

shall he hear the Voice.

3. Who then can judge him, save they have also attained to the same high estate? Is it wise for the unlearned to dispute with the learned; or the unholy with the holy?

4. Shall the drunken man, reeking with foul smell, sign the pledge to drink no more, and straightway say: We temperance men! and presume to dwell with the pure?

5. I say unto thee, till that man is purified and grown to be constitutionally temperate he is not temperate.

6. Consider then the seers and prophets (who hear the angels) whether they have grown constitutionally to be one with Purity, Wisdom and Goodness.

7. For this is required of such as presume to hear me and my holy ones. And having attained to this, who can judge them, save they have attained unto the same?

8. Shall a man inquire of the magician as to the inspiration of the prophets of thy God? Or the angels of the first resurrection be consulted as to their opinions of my revelations, and their words taken for truth without substantiation?

9. Let all things be proved, or supported by corresponding testimony known to be true. As the holy man perceiveth how things should be in the heavens above, so they are. The unholy man seeth heavenly things but dimly; he bindeth himself in ancient revelations which have become corrupted.

10. Jehovih is as near this day as in time of the ancients; put thyself in order, becoming one with Him, and no book so easily read as His created universe.

11. Inspiration cometh less by books, than by what Jehovih wrote, His worlds. Read thou Him and His works. Frame thy speech and thy thoughts for Him; He will answer thee in thine own behavior, and in the happiness of thy soul.

12. Great wisdom cannot be attained in a day; nor purity, and strength, to overcome temptation, till the growth be from the foundation.

13. The fool will say: The sacred books are no more than man of his own knowledge might write; yet, he hath not imitated wisely the power of the words of thy God.

14. Let him do this well, and, behold, he will also declare my words are from me. Yea, he will recognize them wherever found.

15. It is the will and wish of thy God, that all men become constitutionally capable of receiving and comprehending the highest light, and that they shall no longer depend upon any priest, church, oracle or holy book, or upon consulting the spirits.

16. That their behavior may make the earth a place of peace, with long life unto all people, for the glory of Jehovih.

CHAPTER VI.

OF JEHOVIH AND HIS KINGDOM ON EARTH.

1. O man, apply thyself to understand the spirit of my discourse, for herein shalt thou find the key to the Father's kingdom.

2. These are the rules of the second resurrection: To become an interpreter and worker without a written formula:

3. That whatsoever giveth joy to thy fellow and rendereth peace and good will unto all, shall be called light:

4. That whatsoever giveth sorrow to thy fellow, or discouragement to others, shall be called darkness:

5. As to find fault with another, or to aggravate unto displeasure, shall be called darkness:

6. But to make another's burden light, to encourage him unto strength and happiness, shall be called light:

7. To be forever complaining about this or that, shall be called darkness:

8. To be forever imparting cheerfulness, shall be called light.

9. Now therefore whoso becometh a member of my kingdom shall practice light; but whoso practiceth darkness, will depart away from my kingdom of his own accord.

10. Neither shalt thou practice darkness upon thy fellow for any shortness he hath done.

11. Nor shalt thou reprove him for error, nor blame him, nor make thyself an inquisitor over him, nor assume to be a judge over him.

12. Nor ask him to apologize, nor otherwise seek to make him humble himself before thee.

13. Nor shalt thou boast over him because thou art wiser or stronger or more expert.

14. For all such inquisition cometh of darkness, and shall return upon him who uttereth it, in time to come.

15. Rather shalt thou discover the good that is in thy neighbor, and laud him therefore, for this is the method of raising him higher.

CHAPTER VII.
GOD SHOWETH THE DIFFERENCE BETWIXT THE RELIGION OF OLDEN TIME AND THAT OF THE PRESENT.

1. To the All One, Jehovih, now as in the olden time, and for all time to come, all honor and glory, worlds beyond number.

2. The Highest Ideal, the Nearest Perfect the mind can conceive of, let such be thy Jehovih, even as in the olden time, which is the Ever Present thou shalt set thy heart and mind and soul upon to love and glorify above all things, forever and ever.

3. The All Highest in thy neighbor which he manifested, that perceive and discourse upon, all else in him, see not nor mention.

4. The All Highest subject, that discourse upon, all else pass by.

5. The first lowest thoughts pertain to eating and drinking; and on these the man of darkness delighteth to discourse.

6. The second lowest thoughts pertain to sexual matters; and on these the man of darkness delighteth to discourse.

7. The third lowest thoughts pertain to man's selfishness, as bodily comforts and luxuries, as ease and riches, as to what he hopes and desires for himself; and on these the man of darkness delighteth to discourse.

8. The fourth lowest thoughts pertain to criticizing others, as to doctrine, religion, philosophy, behavior, and so on, forever pulling all things to pieces; and the man of darkness delighteth in such discourse.

9. To abandon such discourse, and to discourse on the highest subjects, in preference, such as teaching, imparting knowledge, suggesting remedies for the unfortunate and unlearned, for improving in excellence the homes of others, the agriculture, mechanics and such like; the man of light delighteth to apply himself to these, both in word and practice, forever building up.

10. Consider then what thy mind shall go in search of, that it may pursue the highest. This is serving the All Highest, instead of darkness.

11. Now all of these things were taught in the religion of the olden time, and were given to man by thy God to raise man up toward my heavenly kingdom.

12. Nevertheless this religion pertained to man's own entity, a religion that was to be answered either in reward or punishment upon himself personally. His own salvation being the subject paramount to all other considerations.

13. And even where they founded brotherhoods, as the brotherhood of Brahma; brotherhood of Budha, and brotherhood of Jesus, they were nevertheless but selfish brotherhoods, whose aim was the salvation of each one's own self.

14. Neither was it possible in the olden time to give man any other religion, it being necessary to appeal to his own advantages to make him heed thy God.

15. But now, behold, O man, I come to give a great religion, yet not to set aside the old; I come to such as do fulfill the old, and to give them the religion of Gods themselves!

16. Saying unto them: Go save others, and no longer concern yourselves about yourselves.

17. Go ye and provide a place of second resurrection on earth, where the people shall put away all low things and practice the all highest.

18. And call ye out unto the Uzians to come and inherit the place with you.

19. Nevertheless whosoever is only concerned as to the salvation of his own soul is not yet ready for the religion I give unto you.

20. Mine shall not concern themselves as to their own self's salvation; for having faith in Jehovih, that if they raise others up, with their own wisdom and strength, they are already saved, and without fear.

21. Compare then my second resurrection in heaven with that which thou wouldst found on earth for the glory and honor of thy Creator.

22. How chooseth thy God his initiates? Hath he censors? saying to all who come, hold, be ye examined and tried, to prove ye are worthy of the second resurrection?

23. Nay, verily, for this would imply inquisition, a court of darkness.

24. Now, behold, O man, after the second resurrection was established in heaven, I called out unto all the heavens of the earth, saying: Come, all ye of the first resurrection, also, let my guardians go down to mortals and proclaim unto all people, the kingdom of God is open to all who choose to come.

25. Now some, who were not strong in faith in Jehovih said: Will we not be overrun with angels of darkness?

26. But thy God answered them, saying: That is not our matter; ours is to serve Jehovih by working for all whom He inspireth to come unto us. Because any one desireth to come, that is sufficient testimony that the light of Jehovih is upon him.

27. Others said: What of the indolent and the shiftless? Will they not overrun us and thus set aside the good we aim at?

28. And thy God answered them, saying: When ye practice the all highest, behold, the others will depart away from you.

29. Then others questioned, saying: Suppose they who come shall practice darkness, such as slander, or tattling, what then shall be done?

30. And thy God answered them, saying: Answer them not, lest ye also practice darkness.

31. Again they questioned, saying: Suppose they are good, but indolent? Suppose they say: Let us rest and sleep, Jehovih will provide for His chosen, what sayest thou of them?

32. And thy God answered, saying: Censure them not, for they are weak or diseased. Let your example heal them. Is it not in the covenant to do good with all of one's wisdom and strength? Because they do little, the matter is betwixt them and Jehovih?

33. Lastly, O man, how can they, who live the all highest, cast the first stone at their neighbor?

34. For the act itself would be the committing of darkness.

35. Nevertheless, whoso hath strength and yet will not support himself, teach thou one such man to change his attributes, and thou shalt be honored amongst Gods.

36. Thy glory is to fulfill the all highest thyself. When all who can, will do this, thereon rest thy faith that the quickening power and wisdom of Jehovih will sustain His kingdom through His holy angels.

CHAPTER VIII.
GOD SHOWETH WHAT IS MEANT BY FOLLOWING THE HIGHEST LIGHT.

1. Be considerate of thy fellow man, and weigh his standing place in the sight of thy God.

2. For one man saith: My highest light is to get money; another, to get great learning; another, to enjoy earthly pleasure; another, to contemplate sexual relations; another, to serve Budha; another, to serve Brahma; another, to serve Christ; another, to be efficient in warfare, and so on, every one from his own standpoint.

3. Many are also under the prejudice of old things, or the influence of a neighbor, or a spirit or their surroundings, or the impulse of their own flesh, and say: I too follow my highest light.

4. Whereas they are in darkness altogether; neither know they what is meant by the term, highest light, often venturing an opinion or a vague surmise instead, and believing they are expressing their highest light.

5. For which reasons thou shalt explain that only facts well known, or comparatively proven, are light. An opinion is not light.

6. That whoso professeth light must know the matter of his own knowledge.

7. That facts, numbers, figures or axioms can demonstrate light; and that without these, then the supposed light is only darkness.

8. Pursue this philosophy and thou shalt easily discover who amongst you hath the highest light; and also what kind of judgment shall govern the chief's rulings.

9. Some will desire to consult the angels, as to which, in a given matter, is the highest light; but I say unto thee, thou shalt weigh the words of angels even as if they were mortals, exacting similar facts and substantiation.

10. Was it not the consulting of the oracles that destroyed Vind'yu (India), Socatta, Fonece (Phoenecia), Persia, Ghem and Greece? Such consultation of angels is answered from the first resurrection; and it ever will be so, save man exact from the angels facts and substantial proof.

11. These, then, are rules of light: That which is self-evident: That which is axiomatic: That which is substantiated by facts: That which hath a parallel in known things: Things that lead to peace, order, and the uplifting of thy neighbor and thyself.

12. Also to discipline thyself to be constantly on the alert to be pure, good, truthful and gentle in thy speech; to practice right-doing, these are following the highest light.

13. This though is darkness: to express fault finding, criticism, censure, or even an opinion unsupportable by facts.

CHAPTER IX.

GOD SHOWETH WHO HE IS AND WHO IS NOT PREPARED TO ENTER JEHOVIH'S KINGDOM ON EARTH.

1. Whoso hath said: I have searched my heart and mind, and, now before Jehovih I desire to live a higher life.

2. I desire to put away my selfishness, and passions, and sentiments of unrighteousness and unclean thoughts, and words.

3. I desire more to serve others than myself.

4. I desire no possessions, nor preference over another, nor to be a leader nor a chief.

5. I wish to discipline myself not to speak of myself.

6. I would learn to speak truth only.

7. I would that I were affiliative.

8. I desire to do good unto others continually.

9. I long for association.

10. I will not criticize any person, nor censure them, or find fault with them.

11. I will conform to the rites and discipline of the fraternity.

12. I will fulfill my covenants with Jehovih, with all my wisdom and strength.

13. I renounce isolated labor.

14. I renounce the unorganized world.

15. I renounce the Uzians.

16. I consecrate myself to Jehovih.

17. I give up all unto Him.

18. What I do henceforth shall be by and through the fraternity in His name.

19. Then that man is prepared to enter the Father's kingdom.

20. But these are not prepared to enter the kingdom, who say: I want a home for comfort's sake, and where I may lead an easy life.

21. I desire this because I shall have opportunity to improve myself.

22. I desire this because I cannot care for myself, and that I may be cared for.

23. Where I may shirk my responsibilities.

24. Weigh this matter, O man, and be thine own judge as to whether thou art prepared in heart and soul. Neither flatter thyself that thou canst come in unprepared and not be discovered. For soon or late thine inmost thoughts will become known, and the fraternity will not be thy place.

25. To put away flesh-food is easy, but to put away dark thoughts and words, who can do this in a day?

CHAPTER X.

GOD REVEALETH THE CURE FOR REMORSE.

1. Be patient, O man, with thy neighbor and thy brother.

2. Many men are far short in righteousness, and without strength to accomplish to the

extent the mind conceives;

3. And for having done wrong suffer lamentably, with none to relieve them;

4. For which reason thou shalt provide them honorable comfort.

5. In olden time, such ones confessed to a priest, and he pardoned them, whereby they were quieted and relieved of great distress.

6. In a later time, it was said: Confess ye one another.

7. But in this day neither of these is compatible with the intelligence of such as shall be of Jehovih's kingdom.

8. If then a man have remorse for having wronged a brother or neighbor, he shall so acknowledge it to that member, and this shall be restitution, even as if the wrong had not been committed.

9. But if he hath wronged the community, then he shall acknowledge it to the whole assembly, and that shall be restitution, even as if the wrong had not been committed.

10. And in either case he shall not take further sorrow or remorse, or shame, nor shall any member ever speak of the matter afterward, save to comfort him.

11. But in all cases confession shall be made in the name of Jehovih, and forgiveness likewise. But whoso seeketh to justify himself, or to make it appear that he was but partly culpable, or that another led him into it, that man shall not be forgiven.

12. If he were led into it--then he who led him knoweth it and shall exonerate him.

13. Whoso Jehovih hath created in proximity as to time, country, place and association, the same shall not be far distant on many occasions in the next world; and in time to come they shall be as if in a house of glass, and all the deeds done while in mortality shall be read as if in an open book.

14. For which reason thou shalt not tarry by the way when thou hast wronged any man or the community, but go quickly and confess, that thy spirit become pure in the sight of Jehovih.

15. Though thou grieve, saying: Shall I humble myself? I say unto thee, this is Godliness, for it is the purification of thyself, and the beginning of power. But if a man wrong himself, as by pollution, dissipation, or otherwise, this is sin against Jehovih; and to Him shall he confess privately, making a covenant with his Creator to do so no more, which if he keep., then the wrong is forgiven him, and he shall have peace of soul.

CHAPTER XI.

GOD SHOWETH THAT THE RENUNCIATION OF THE UZIANS IS NECESSARY.

1. Hearken, O man, to the discourse of thy God upon the second resurrection in heaven, and apply thou these principles to founding Jehovih's kingdom on earth.

2. Many come to my holy place, saying: Hear me, O God, I am weary of the first resurrection and of the earth. Open the gates of paradise unto thy servant.

3. And I say unto them: Whoso will put aside all that is below, shall dwell in this heaven; but whoso cannot in heart, and mind, and soul renounce all that is below is not prepared to enter.

4. Hath not Jehovih said on earth: Husband and wife shall be the model and key of My kingdom?

5. As woman forsaketh father, mother, brother and sister and becometh one with her

husband, so do they of the first resurrection forsake all the earth and the lowest heaven in order to become one with the kingdom of thy God.

6. For, save the mind and heart be one with my holy place, the love of improvement will also depart out of that man's soul.

7. Isolation belongeth below the second resurrection, but unity is within it.

8. He who hath disciplined himself to be honest in his own sight may be in error; he who striveth to do good on his own account may be in error as to an ultimate good; and in all cases man alone is weak.

9. Yet no man can practice the highest whilst living with those who are inclined downward.

10. In the second resurrection the angels are relieved of individual responsibility, all matters being under the wisdom of the Holy Council, whose head is thy God.

11. First on earth, monarchies, then republics, then fraternities, the latter of which is now in embryo, and shall follow after both the others.

12. Behold, how hard it is for an ignorant man to conceive of a state without a master, or for the people of a republic to understand a state without votes and majorities, and a chief ruler. Yet such shall be the fraternities.

13. Have they not resolved their colleges into teachers and pupils? By their superior knowledge do these heads receive their places, yet not as rulers, but teachers.

14. Have they not resolved jurisprudence so that testimony governs the rulings? According to evidence adduced and the knowledge of the judge, so shall he decide, and not according to his own volition.

15. Out of the wisdom of the college and the court shalt thou discover the rules of fraternity, and by relieve-watch preserve the brotherhood against caste and dictatorship.

16. See to it then, in departing out of Uz, that thou take with thee only things that have proved good, the rest leave behind.

17. As Jehovih gave woman to man, and the twain became one in their aspiration, hope and labor, and especially with reference to their offspring, so shall the members of the fraternity be such as having renounced all the world, can become one with one another, and especially for raising up the young to become the Father's edifice on earth.

18. As the husband is the representative head of the family, yet he shall not tyrannize over them, nor by his rulings make himself a separate entity from the rest.

CHAPTER XII.

GOD DISCOURSETH ON LOVE.

1. Many will come to thee, inquiring: How sayest thou of such as are married, having children of their own? Shall they so love the fraternity and the kingdom of Jehovih that they shall set aside their filial love, assigning their children wholly to the teachers, day and night?

2. Thou shalt answer them: Nay, in all the fullness of their love, let them manifest unto their little ones. And let this be a testimony unto those who have children, how hard it is for foundlings and orphan babes that have none to love or caress them, that such parents may add unto their household others also, showing no partiality. And this is the highest of all mortal attributes, to be impartial in love.

3. Not to abridge love but to extend it, God-like, embracing all people, so shall the members of the brotherhood labor with thy God and his holy angels, for the glory of Jehovih.

CHAPTER XIII.

OF DESTROYERS AND BUILDERS.

1. One goeth about preaching against heavenly revelations, and against the wisdom of Jehovih; and his daring speeches and good logic fall upon errors and blunders in the written words, and he draweth the populace, after the manner of a gladiator.
2. Yet one such man that hath organized a brotherhood for doing good, the world hath not found.
3. Another man goeth forth preaching in laudation of heavenly revelations, and on the glory of Jehovih. The errors in inspiration he heedeth not; the good he treasureth. He may draw but few unto him and his work may seem little.
4. But in time to come his work becometh mighty over all the world. He organizeth his people in love and fellowship.
5. The latter is a builder on Jehovih's edifice.
6. Let these two examples stand before thee; and when the speech of the vain man is directed against heavenly revelations, saying: This is not of God; this is not of Jehovih, or this is not of angels, know thou that that man is not a builder.
7. But when a man saith all things are of Jehovih, either directly or indirectly; whatsoever is good in them is my delight, know thou that that man is a builder.
8. To strive continually to comprehend the right, and to do it, this is excellent discipline.
9. To be capable of judging the right, and ever to practice it within a fraternity, this is Godliness.
10. In the day thou judgest thyself, as with the eye of thy Creator, thou art as one about to start on a long journey through a delightful country.
11. In the day thou hast rendered judgment against thyself for not practicing thy highest light, thou art as one departed from a coast of breakers toward mid-ocean, like one turned from mortality toward Jehovih! like one turned from perishable things toward the Ever Eternal, the Almighty.
12. And when thou hast joined with others in a fraternity to do these things, then thou hast begun the second resurrection.

CHAPTER XIV.

GOD DISCOURETH ON THE AUTHORITY OF HIS OWN WORDS.

1. First, freedom unto all people on earth, and to the angels of heaven, to think and to speak whatever they will.
2. Second, that since no man can acquire knowledge for another, but that each and all must acquire knowledge for themselves, thou shalt dispose of whatsoever is before thee in thine own way;
3. Remembering that one man seeth Jehovih in the leaves and flowers; in the mountains and skies; in the sun and stars; or heareth Him in the wind and all corporeal sounds; yea,

he knoweth his Creator in the presence of everything under the sun. And he is happy.

4. Another seeth not Jehovih, nor knoweth Him. Nay, he denieth there is any All Person in the universe. He is not happy.

5. One man distinguiseth the harmony of sounds, and he is delighted.

6. Another man cannot distinguish the harmony, and he findeth no delight therein.

7. So, of the words of thy God, one man can distinguish, and another cannot.

8. The revelations of thy God portray the harmony and glory of Jehovih's creations, and of the organic heavens of His holy angels.

9. Whether thyself, or thy brother, or thy neighbor, shall profess to reveal the words of thy God, it is well.

10. Strive thou in this, and thou shalt improve thyself thereby.

11. In the preservation of my words for thousands of years resteth the recognition of my authority.

12. I call all people unto me and my kingdom; happiness proclaim I as a result of right-doing and good works; whoever do these are one with me in the framing of words.

13. To be one with Jehovih, this is Godliness; to be one with thy God, the way is open to all men.

14. To be organic for love and good works, this is like the fraternities in heaven.

15. Whoever striveth for this hath my authority already; his words in time shall become one with me and my works.

16. To improve thyself in these holy things is to discipline thyself to become a glory to thy Creator.

17. Let any who will, say: Thus saith God, or thus saith Jehovih, or thus say I. Truth expounded shall never die; the discrepancy from truth is short-lived.

18. Improve thyself, O man, to be sincere in thyself and in all thou doest; and, when thou hast attained this, thy words shall be with power.

19. Remember thy Creator and seek to discover Him in the best perfections; remembering that darkness knoweth Him not, but Light proclaimeth Him forever.

20. For on the foundation of an All Person, and believing in Him, lie the beginning and the way of everlasting resurrection. Without Him, none have risen.

21. These are the words and discipline; in such direction shapeth thy God the thoughts of millions. The twain are the authority vested in me, thine elder brother, by Jehovih, Creator, Ruler and Dispenser, worlds without end. Amen!

END OF THE BOOK OF DISCIPLINE.

BOOK OF KNOWLEDGE.

[This Book (and the following book of Saphah) was not part of the original 1882 or 1891 published versions of OAHSPE. The Book of Knowledge was later found as fragments in the original proof sheets. It may have been a part of the Book of Ben.]

Part I.

1. Jehovih spake through His sons and daughters. His voice came up out of the marsh and down from the heavens above, and the children of men heard and saw, and raised up because of the spirit in them. And they answered to Him, Who is Almighty; and their voices were called Tae, because as it is the universal word of all children born, so doth it represent the universal prayer of man.

2. Tae said: Reveal, O Father, give me light! I behold the wide earth, the sun, moon and stars. But the great vault of heaven is as an empty sky. Where is the abode of the dead; the place of the souls of men?

3. In times past Thou hast quickened seers and prophets, and through them lifted up Thy children and proclaimed other worlds! Am I more dumb than those in past ages? All the while myself and forefathers have withstood Thy mighty Presence.

4. Thou hast quickened my members by thine own hand, to be dissatisfied by the old revelations, and made me to peer deeper into the cause and place of things, and to desire further light from Thy holy places.

5. By Thy Power hath my manhood been raised up. By Thy Power and Wisdom only will I be appeased.

6. When I was a child I believed as a child, because it was told me; but now that I am grown up, I would know who Thy prophets were, and how they attained their gifts, and wisdom of words.

7. The cosmogony Thou taughtest in the olden time was sufficient for that day; but I am raised up by Thee to perceive the sun and stars of other worlds, and their travel in Thy great firmament. Now, I cry out unto Thee, where is the promised heaven? Where is the proof of immortal life? By Thee was I quickened into life and made conscious that I am. To Thee I come in the majesty Thou madest me, Thou my Father! By Thee was I made determined to sift all things to the bottom. In Thee do I know there is magnitude to encompass all my holy desires, and answer me.

8. Give me of Thy Light! When I was a child I besought Thee as a child; now, I call out in the manhood Thou hast bestowed upon me! I will know Thy Lords, Thy Gods, and Thy Saviors, and Thy promised heaven.

9. I have scaled the mountain; Thy myriads of corporeal worlds that travel in the eternal sea of space! I have beholden that all the stars in heaven would not fill the hollow of Thy Hand; yea, that Thy breath moveth the universe! The glory of Thy works hath inspired me with madness to come to Thy Mighty Home!

10. Speak, O Jehovih! Thou alone canst assuage this soaring spirit that sprang forth from Thee, inspired. Give me light!

11. I have encompassed the earth around, and bridged the nations thereof with assimilative words. My geography is finished. Give me a book of heaven! I have

burrowed deep in corporeal knowledge, and seen the drift of all on earth. Where is the spirit world, and land of the dead? Give me light!

12. Kosmon said: Jehovih heard the voice of Tae, and answered him. He said: Let the angels of heaven go down to the earth. My blessed son called to me in wisdom and truth. And the angels of heaven descended to the earth, for it was in the time of danha in the firmament of heaven, and the angels manifested and proved the immortal life of men.

13. Jehovih said: Let this day be the beginning of the reign of Kosmon; for it is the beginning of the wisdom of the earth, being cojoined in My Name.

14. Tae said: The half is not yet answered, O my Father in heaven. Since Thou hast proved the immortal life, Thou hast stirred me to my soul's foundation. Whence come these inhabitants of the unseen world? Where lieth this footstool for Thy Majesty?

15. If when I am dead I shall see the place, is not the germ of that sight already in me? How am I made that I see, but see not this? Hear, but hear not this? If I am now dead to that which is to be, will I not then be dead to what now is? Give me light, O Father!

16. Jehovih said: Man I gave a corporeal body that he might learn corporeal things; but death I made that he might rise in spirit and inhabit My etherean worlds.

17. Two senses gave I to all men, corporeal and spiritual senses; nevertheless the twain are one person. A man with corporeal senses in the ascendancy, chooseth corporeal things; a man with spiritual senses chooseth spiritual things.

18. Two kinds of worlds have I made, corporeal and es worlds. He who desireth of corpor shall receive from corpor, for he is My son, in whom I am well pleased. He who desireth from es shall receive from es, for she is my daughter in whom I am well pleased.

19. Kosmon said: Because man liveth on corporeal worlds, corpor is called son; but because man in spirit liveth in the es world, es is called daughter.

20. Tae said: Because Thou hast sent angels to me, and I have seen them, and talked to them face to face; yea, of my own flesh and kin, and proved them to be the spirits of the dead, verily, I know this much is true. Yet I cannot see them nor hear them, save they manifest through corporeal things. How, then, shall I know that they know one another?

21. Hear me, O Jehovih! Am I still a child, and must needs fall back on angels' testimony? Hast thou not given me an inquiring spirit that I must prove things to mine own knowledge? Verily, have I seen an angel's face and stature change to look like another person, even whilst I talked therewith. If these things are thus so subtle, cannot even our own presence mold them to truth or falsehood? Such a witness is of no value. When then, O Jehovih, shall I find growth for mine own members, that I may know the es worlds and the inhabitants thereof? I will not be appeased by merely seeing the spirits of the dead, nor by their testimony. They may call themselves God, Christ, Buddha, Brahma or Confucius, yet I will not rest on them for their word. To Thee, only, O Jehovih, will I put forth my plea. I am Thy son.

22. Thou hast quickened me to know things of my own knowledge; and though it be told me: Thus said the Lord or thy God, yet will I raise my voice ever above them, and though a spirit say: I am thy Jehovih, believe thou me! I will deny him.

23. Thou hast quickened me to rise up above the tales of the ancients, and to demand knowledge from Thy throne. By Thee is my soul moved to this magnificence, and only Thy magnificence can satisfy Thy son.

24. Since I have seen the spirits of the dead, I will know their abiding place, how they

live, how they travel, their manner of growth, their food and clothes, and how they spend heir time; whether they labor or live idly, and above all how far, and in what manner their corporeal lives had to bear on their spiritual happiness in heaven.

25. Give me light, O Jehovih! Not by word of mouth. I will have my members quickened that I shall comprehend within myself. Yet not one alone! Rather waste me in annihilation than not to give it unto all men or teach the way. For if one alone, he would become a god amongst men. Jehovih, forbid this!

26. Jehovih spake, through His sons and daughters, and each of them gave voice to the Spirit of the Creator's Voice in turn.

27. Kosmon said: Hear me, O man, I will speak in wisdom. Follow thou my counsel and be wise. What, then, hast thou learned in all the time of earth? Canst thou tell why the grass is green, or why one rose is red and another white, or the mountains raised up, or the valleys sunken low?

28. Knowest thou how all the people of earth clothe themselves, or travel over; why a man was not to fly as a bird, or live in the water like a fish? Whence came the thought of shame? Even thyself thou dost not comprehend, nor know of thine own knowledge the time of thy beginning. Thou knowest three times three are nine; and even this thou canst not prove but by symbols and images. Nor is there aught in thy corporeal knowledge that thou canst prove otherwise, save it be thy presence; and even that that thou seest is not thy presence, but the symbol and image of it, for thyself art but as a seed, a germ of the Father.

29. Be wise, therefore, in knowing thine own knowledge, and of a surety right the matter from the side of the es world.

30. Tae said: I will reason with Thee, Jehovih, for all I know shall be based on science and truth. From Thine own perfection am I inspired to this end, and my talents shall be strengthened by pursuing the exact sciences of all the known truths. Neither will I put away mine own judgment, nor accept for truth that which is at variance with Thy established laws.

31. Thou madest both the seen and the unseen. Are they at war, or in harmony? My corporeal body is made of earth, and stone and water. Is the spiritual body, then, not made of air, oxygen and hydrogen, and imperceptible dust?

32. The angels Thou hast sent have feet and legs! Wherefore? Do they walk on the air, or wade through it? They have no wings, they cannot fly; they have not seen the illustrious angels who have been long dead. Must I also go into the es world simply to meet my neighbors, and never salute the wise of olden time? Give me light O Jehovih!

33. Something within me maketh me to anticipate the light and glory of what I have not seen; but I must have it tangible and demonstrated, the immaculate truth!

34. Then answered Jehovih, through His daughter Esfoma.

35. Esfoma said: Hear me, O Tae; I will speak words of wisdom and truth, and thou shall not depart from my word.

36. Science is that which the ignorant look up to, but seeth not. Is a ship, science, or a stone arch, or a machine? Verily not. Is the idea of these things, science? Can an idea be science, or a multitude of ideas?

37. Is it not said of the man who findeth the vertebra of an insect, he is scientific? But he who findeth the backbone of a horse, is a vulgar fellow. Another man findeth a

route over a mountain or through the forest, and he is scientific. Why, a dog can do this. 38. Another man findeth a new way to solve problems, and he is scientific! but the pupil after him who doeth the same thing is nothing. Who, then are the scientific? For have they not all borrowed, compiled, and only added a little? Verily, then, what is science? Is not the sand-glass more scientific than a clock? What, then, meanest thou by science? Is not the sum of it all but a figurehead, undesignable and without foundation? Yet all thy life thou hast heard of science. and so have thy neighbors, and ye understand one another, though not one understandeth himself.

39. Esfoma said: Hear me further, O man, for this, of all things, should stand high in thy soul. Take now, therefore, the chalk, and write thou ten for me. Tae took the chalk and wrote 10. saying, that is ten.

40. Esfoma said: Now will I convict thee before thine own face, that thou hast uttered falsely. Thou hast written but two strokes, and called them ten. Esfoma wrote I I I I I I I I I I. Yet, be not surprised, O Tae, for now will I convict myself, also, inasmuch as I have deceived thee. I said I would show thee ten, and straightway, I made ten marks; wherefore I should have written the word *ten.* Now thou art wise! Nay, hear me further, for all I have spoken is false; for have I not tried to persuade thee that the one uttered word TEN, was ten; wherefore I should have uttered ten utterances.

41. Pursue thy studies, O Tae, and thou shalt find that supposed exact science is nothing, and that supposed truth is only falsehood compounded and acquiesced in. Find thou the time the sun will rise tomorrow, and thou art scientific; but deviate thou the ten thousandth part of a second, and thou art not scientific; nay thou art a falsifier before Jehovih.

42. Yet be not discouraged of the exact sciences, or of finding the truth according to thy judgment. Thou art wise to desire to attain knowledge of thine own self, and not to accept, neither from man nor angels, on belief merely; but, wherein beginneth and endeth thyself?

43. Hast thou not robbed the tree of its fruit in order to feed the body? And the field of its wheat, and the young corn that was growing? Give to them their parts, and what hast thou left of thy corporeal body that is thine own?

44. Yet less than these hast thou of thine own judgment. Thou art but the fragment of an entity in all thou knowest of thine own judgment. Nine parts to ten are the gleanings of thy surrounding.

45. Wherefore, then, shalt thou expect to know the laws of earth or heaven! Give ear to my words, and be wise in thy proceedings.

46. Is it not a law of the earth that earth substance shall fall to it? Yet thou seest a tree come up out of the ground, ten thousand corporeal pounds, and stand erect in the air. Hast Jehovih made one law to pull one way, and another in another way? How knowest thou there is any law about the matter? Knowest thou of thine own knowledge?

Part II.

1. Tae said: Now I do perceive, O Jehovih, I am not wise, and that of myself I am nothing, having nothing. Neither is it possible for man to discern truth in abstract, nor Thy laws, whether Thou hast laws or hast not laws. Nay, he cannot adjust the scales for

his own self, and prove what part is his alone; nor in fact if he have an entity of self within himself.

2. How then shall I comprehend the magnitude of the laws of Thy universe? Yet in what time of my life have I not talked learnedly of these things, and the exact science?

3. Hear me, O Jehovih; I will not go back to the ancients to learn wisdom, nor will I shut up mine eyes against trying to understand. In Thee, only, have I faith. And since all other things in heaven and earth are Thine, there is none else to whom I can come justly. Give me light, O Jehovih! Thou, who gavest me myself shall answer me. What, then, is the true pursuit of man? Shall he be a beggar, and pray for light, and yet not receive it after all?

4. Jehovih answered Tae through His son, Corpor, saying:

5. Corpor said: Hear me, O man, for my wisdom shall be borne home to thee. Neither will I discourage thee in thy knowledge.

6. Know then, thou art, and that thy body is made from the corporeal earth. Jehovih is sufficient, for Jehovih so made thee. To thee he gave the desires of the earth. Is it wise, then, to defer corporeal happiness until thou hast risen in heaven? What mattereth it to thee, whether thou art built up out of wheat and fruits or flesh? Is it not sufficient that thou canst enjoy the building thereof?

7. What is science to thee? Or truth or laws of the universe? Is not thy earth life sufficient for the earth, and the earth for thee? If Jehovih made the earth in wisdom, has He not also wisely made heaven?

8. Leave off these abstract studies, O man, and be contented in the place thy Father has assigned thee. Thou that talkest of science understandeth not thyself and art without explanation. Neither canst thou define truth. How, then, canst thou judge, or even know what is before thee.

9. Thou talkest of laws, divine and natural, but knowest no law, no divinity, no nature. Is law a thing? Whither does it keep? Thou seeth a tree grow, but puttest Jehovih away, and sayest: Behold it groweth by natural laws! Art thou ashamed of Jehovih, that thou sayest not He groweth it? Is He not sufficient? Wherefore, then, sayest thou *law*, save but to put Him away? Wherefore sayest thou NATURE, save but to put Him away and deny His Person.

10. Corpor said: Is not the earth good, that thou turnest away, calling: Heaven! Give me light from thy far off worlds! Endow me with signs, and miracles and prophecies!

11. I will not discourage thee, but thou shalt be wise and happy in thy dwelling place. Are not these greater to be desired than all things else? To this end is the Kosmon era come; not to carry man up to heaven, but to found the Father's kingdom on earth.

12. Thou hast wisely asked: How shall a corporean's life affect his life in the next world? Hear me, then, and be wise in thy corporeal judgment. For am not I, Corpor, Jehovih's? Science is great; great learning is great; truth is great; but a greater than all is to know how to be happy. Thou shalt not put me away saying: All the earth is sin. I will not have it. For if thou profitest not in Jehovih's Person, how canst thou attain His spirit? For are not the twain His Person and His Spirit, the All One?

13. Teach thyself to be happy: and to perfect thyself in the way Jehovih hath created thee.

14. Tae said: Now I will be wise in thee, O Jehovih. Neither will I more talk of nature, nor of law; but when I mean Thee, I will speak of Thee, and to Thee.

15. Neither will I boast of science, nor of learning, nor of truth; nor will I deny them. For as Thy spirit is within and over all, what is science and learning, and truth but glimpses of Thy All Light?

16. Yet as a man proud in his estate, I come before Thee, saying: Give me light! I have looked over the broad earth, and found it full of sin and misery, and death.

17. I will not pray to Thee to remove these things. I will not meddle in Thy affairs. What more is it at best to pray than to beg? By thy spirit, I am no beggar! As Thou goest forth in majesty, so am I, Thy son, inspired to go forth in Thy behalf.

18. If Thou hast filled this world full of darkness and death, and sin, and misery, what more can I hope to find in heaven? Are they not both the work of Thy hands?

19. My hope hath ever looked ahead for the achievement of happiness, but when the time cometh I am sorely tried. My judgment teachest me, therefore, that heaven can be, at most, but little improvement on earth.

20. Then give me light, O Jehovih! For I would answer the children of darkness with good argument, and teach them to glorify Thee in Thy works.

21. Then answered Jehovih through His son, Uz, saying:

22. Uz said: Behold me in my power, O Tae. I am the fourth dimension, the vanishment of things unseen. Thou hast labored with Kosmon, but found not, and with Corpor, and found not. Hear thou me and be wise.

23. This, thy corporeal body is mine; thy flesh waiteth for me, and the moment thou relinquish thy hold, I will molder thee in dust. Yet I am not thy enemy, for whilst thou art master over thy flesh, I will touch it not.

24. Out of the darkness man is brought forth a blank, and his entity is a spark of Jehovih. His entity will never cease to grow. Yea, from the hour of conception it is a new star in the world, and it magnifieth itself forever.

25. The trials of the flesh to man are as nutriment to his spirit's growth. And yet, think not that thou shouldst rejoice in thy neighbor's trials, saying, it is good for his spirit's growth. But as Jehovih gave all He had, and thus made all things, be thou like unto Jehovih, and give to the man in trial, lest thou robbest thyself.

26. Thou knowest not how far thou hast been lifted up thyself. Can any man with his own hands lift himself up in the air? Flatter not thyself, then, that man alone can lift himself up in spirit, or that he hath power to evolve himself, one generation above another. Do not all nations perish? As they come up out of darkness, do they not go down in darkness?

27. Is it not unwise to say: O Jehovih, why didst Thou thus, or not thus? All thy questionings will not turn Jehovih or His plans one jot or tittle. Turn thine eyes inward, then, O Tae, and seek to adapt thyself to the Father and His kingdoms, of which this earth is one.

28. Tae said: How can I comprehend Thy wisdom, O my Father in heaven? I am tripped up at every corner; and yet I perceive that my generation is wiser than the ancients. Wherefore, then, didst Thou stir me up? The ancients found joy in an idol; were content to eat and sleep, their faith being equal to their wisdom.

29. But these that came after, cried out unto Thee for wisdom, and Thou gavest. Thus am I born above the faith of the ancients. I have grown beyond the measures of Thy olden revelations; my soul crieth out to Thee for more light.

30. I know that Thou hast sufficiency for all things. Give me wisdom, that I may help

myself. Had I been born in darkness, the idols of my forefathers would have sufficed.

31. Hear me, O Jehovih, in what I have done. I have measured the earth and high standing rocks, and the mountains Thou reardest up, and the valleys Thou has scooped out. Thy footstool hast shown me a record not written by man, and it proclaimeth the earth millions of years old.

32. Yea, I have measured the stars in Thy firmament, and the sun and moon, and weighed them, and they proclaimed a greater glory unto Thee. Their number is more than there are drops of water in the ocean; and many of them a thousand times larger than the earth. I have found them rich in air, and water, and heat and cold, and they proclaim themselves birth places for men, even as is the earth.

33. I have measured the light and computed the time of its coming, and lo, they also have existed for millions of years.

34. Wherein have I done wrong in this? Thou gavest me my talents, and Thou hast forever pressed me forward to search Thy glorious works.

35. A man cannot make himself a small child, neither can I compress my outbursting soul, which hath ripened on the magnitude and glory of Thy works.

36. How, then, shall I say that Thy worlds, which have run millions of years, were created by a man born two thousand years ago! Must I stoop myself to blaspheme against Thee for sake of swallowing the idols of men in darkness? Forbid Thou this, O Jehovih.

37. Now will I put my question to Thee plainly, and Thy voice shall not fail me. Wherefore, then, did not Thy angels of olden time reveal to man the truth about Thy works? Or if they revealed the truth, why permittedst Thou man to lose the truth? Give me light, O Jehovih!

38. Thou madest me! Thou art my Father; and I come to Thee in majesty, by the power Thou gavest me. None shall stand betwixt me and Thee; neither Thy Lords nor Thy angels from heaven, nor any man that is on the earth. I will know why Thou permittedst idols of stone and wood and graven images? Yea, I will know why man buildeth an idol on earth or imagineth one in heaven? I know Thou art sufficient unto the worship of all men. Wherefore, then, have men set up Zarathustra, and Brahma, and Buddha, and Christ, and the prophets of old? For, for these idols have they cursed the whole earth around about with war and destruction. Give me light, O Jehovih!

39. Jehovih heard the voice of Tae, and He answered him through His son, Seffas.

40. Seffas said: Hear me, O man, and be wise, for I will answer thee because of the justness of thy questions. Yea, I will answer thee, and also put thee in the way to prove all things to thine own judgment.

41. But be thou not puffed up with conceit; thou art little in advance of the ancients. They erected pyramids, and obelisks, and great temples, and they said: Behold, how greater and wiser we are than the ancients!

42. Thou also hast boasted, saying: Behold our ships of war! Behold our engines and railroads, and the telegraphs. How greater and wiser are we than the ancients!

43. I charge thee! The pyramids and temples did not raise up the poor, and cause them to glorify the Father because they were born into life. Neither do the warships in this day, nor the engines, nor railroads contribute but little to raise man up out of sorrow and poverty. Is not this the true scale to weigh the resurrection of men and nations?

44. Be considerate and wise in the Father's sight. Thou art prone to overlook all things;

thou beratest idols and graven images, without weighing thy speech. What more are the letters of a written word than graven images? Doth not all the wisdom in books hang on these? Nor canst thou prove a single problem in mathematics without graven images, and idols and symbols.

45. To a man who never saw a hat, without a sign, or image, or symbol or an idol of one, or by one itself, how wilt thou convince him? But, if thou hast none to show him, then wilt thou make something of some corporeal thing in order to convey to his mind that which is in your mind.

46. Why, then, complainest thou against the angels of old? Wert thou, then, with Asu, who could not talk? Bethink thee what stratagems thou wouldst have resorted to in order to teach him to think. For is it not the greatest of all wisdom to teach man to think for himself? Is this not better for man, than to reveal all things to him? For, in the latter case thou wouldst deprive him of the use of his own talents, and thus thwart the plan of Jehovih.

47. Thou hast portraits of thy wife and daughters, for they assist thy memory to recall their beauty to thy soul; but when thou desirest to convey to thy friend's mind a place he never saw, thou bringest him a landscape picture, saying: Behold, this is the place! Now, thou utterest a falsehood, for it is only a piece of cloth painted, whilst the place thou speakest of, is land, and trees, and water.

48. Bethink thee, now thou hast resorted to falsehood in order to convey a truth to thy friend's mind. Was such, a falsehood, if it really succeeded in conveying a truth, nor couldst thou convey the truth to thy friend, save thou wouldst have taken him to the place.

49. How, then, could the angels of Jehovih teach man of Jehovih, but by idols and graven images? Weigh the matter, and thou shalt perceive that knowledge is conveyed from man to man by idols and images. Even the sound of a spoken word, is an idol of an idea; and the idea is carried within that which is not the real thing itself, but merely wind.

50. Thy corporeal senses can only be reached by corporeal things. Spiritual things, of which ideas are a part, can be conveyed by es force, and without idols and images. Give heed to my words, and thou shalt find the way to thy Father's kingdom.

51. Having taught man of Jehovih through stone and wood, it was necessary, next, to teach him by means of spirit, that Jehovih was disassociated from the earth, otherwise man would not have desire to rise to the heavens in etherea. To this end man was taught that Jehovih's sons had ascended and were sitting at His right hand.

52. As thou speaketh not to the picture of thy wife, neither shalt thou worship the Lord, nor Buddha, nor Christ, but Jehovih alone. He is sufficient to all men and nations, and acceptable to them. Be not angry with the past but broad in thy perception; for all things, whether stones or wood or men, are from Jehovih for the ultimate resurrection of the souls of men to His etherean worlds, for their own happiness, and to glorify Jehovih forever.

Part III.

1. Tae said: How shall I come to Thee, O Jehovih? I have nothing more to stand upon.

2. My self-conceit hath been as a mountain before my vision. I have nothing to boast over the ancients; the things I gloried in, the inventions, and sciences, and discoveries of my time, I saw not from Thy standpoint, I exulted in myself, saying, have I not done great

things?

3. But I had not done a hand's turn with all my inventions and discoveries to better the poor and unlearned. What, then, is the measure of the good I have done more than the ancients?

4. Verily hast Thou turned my eyes inward and made me ashamed. The sciences I boasted of, hast Thou nailed down to the earth, and I perceive my spirit was burrowing into corporeal things only. And as to Thy Gods and saviors, and idols of all kinds, I was cursing Thee in cursing them. In my conceit I was demanding light from Thee, and straightway plunging my head into darkness.

5. Yet I come to Thee, O Jehovih! Thou alone art my theme. Thou my Love and my Glory. But I will not say: Give me light! Thine is the wisdom and the power to bestow whatever is for my own good.

6. When I called for light, it was for myself, and was void before Thee. I had raised up my voice against prayer lest I appear as a beggar in Thy presence. What, more, then, is any man, but a living prayer? One desireth riches, one power, one wisdom, one love, one food, and one rest. Henceforth, then, I will pray for nothing, but accept whatever Thou bestoweth. Yet how can I restrain myself? Do I not desire to know Thy heavens in the firmament? To find a way whereby I may come to the spirits of the wise men of olden time?

7. Can I restrain my desire to know all that hath been on the earth; to find the people who once lived in the buried cities; put myself in rapport with them in spirit, and hear them tell their earthly exploits of thousands of years ago?

8. Since thou hast put away words and become a worker in My behalf, I have drawn nearer thee in wisdom and power. Behold, then, thy reward!

9. Kosmon said: And Jehovih touched Tae on the forehead, and his spirit sense was opened. And Esfoma came and brought Tae a lava-stone, saying: Lay this on thy forehead. Tae laid the lava-stone on his forehead, but he saw it not.

10. Esfoma said: What now?

11. Tae said: I feel like a burning mountain. Lo, this stone has been hurled from a burning crater. Then Esfoma took a sealed record and gave it to Tae, saying: What of this, O man?

12. Tae said: I will lay it on my forehead, where the light cometh. And when he had done this he read the record without opening it.

13. Jehovih said: Unto all men I gave two senses, corpor and es. In the time of Seffas I allotted to man to mature corpor. But now is the time of Kosmon come, and man shall mature es.

14. It is well that thou shalt be believing toward men and angels; but it is better to develop thyself. Thou hast desired to know the mysteries of My unseen worlds, and the past histories of the earth. Behold, I give unto thee a new sense, the which will fulfill thy soul's desire. Yea, thou shalt read the books in the libraries of heaven!

15. Have I not said of old: All things shall be revealed! Think not that a messenger will come, loud speaking, for man would not believe; but I quickened the righteous with Mine own hand, and they will comprehend without belief.

16. The time of preaching and believing is at an end. Man shall know of his knowledge, and practice that which he knoweth. Herein is My light being manifested in this day.

17. Kosmon said: Tae called the new sense, suis, because it is spirit-seeing and spirit-

hearing. And Tae comprehended that approximate things leave an impression on each other, which impression can be read by the suis sense.

18. Tae said: Now will I cultivate this talent Jehovih hath given me, for I perceive it lieth closely to the es'ean worlds. Was it not for the cultivation of this sense that Samuel of old founded a college of prophecy? And did not Zarathustra do so also?

19. Jehovih spake through Kosmon: Whoever pursueth righteousness by this talent shall rise to receive not only the past, but the future also. But whosoever turneth suis down into the earth shall fall, and not rise. When danha is upon the earth, I give suis to as many as have risen in spirit above the flesh.

20. But many turned away from Me, using suis for riches, and they descended to darkness. Suis being a talent above the earth, shall not be used for earthly things, and in this respect, there are many dead who have not attained to suis.

21. Then went Tae forth, that he might comprehend unseen things; and the light of Jehovih went with him, and angels also.

22. And when he had come within a temple of worship where Christians were worshipping, Jehovih drew near, and the power and light of Jehovih's sons and daughters were upon him; and they said, what beholdest thou?

23. Tae said: Two peoples are before me, corporeans and es'eans (spirits) and they are alike, save one hath not corporeal bodies and the other hath, and they are clothed alike. As one worshippeth, so worshippeth the other, and the light that is upon them all is the same, no greater, no less.

24. Now, when Tae departed and came to a temple where Buddhans were worshipping, Kosmon said: What beholdest thou? And Tae answered, saying: Even as in the other place, mortals and spirits worshipping, and the same light is upon them both.

25. Jehovih led Tae forth again, saying: Since thou hast suis, thou shalt attain also to ethe, in after time. After that, Tae departed, and went into a saloon, where men were smoking and drinking, and Jehovih touched him and said: What beholdest thou?

26. Tae said: Corporeans and es'eans, and the same light is upon them both, and their habits are the same, and their avocations also. They are smoking and drinking, both mortals and spirits, neither is one above the other.

27. Jehovih caused Tae then to go to a place of pollution, and when Tae had beholden all, he said: Alas, what mine eyes have beholden this day! Both peoples are the same! And there came into the place the son of a rich man and the son of a king, and the spirits of darkness went and fondled them, but the young men saw them not. But their flesh was moved upon, for they lived for the flesh's sake, and they fell in sin. And when the young men departed out of the place of evil, lo and behold, many of the spirits of pollution went with them.

28. Jehovih said: Tae, My son, thou shalt follow them and bear testimony to what happeneth. And Tae did as commanded.

29. Presently the prince and the rich man's son came to a neighbor's house where assembled many young women, with their mothers and fathers. And the spirits of pollution went and fondled the women, yet the mothers urged their daughters to comply with the visitors' wishes, being desirous of wedding them. And whilst Tae was yet in the house a cloud of darkness came upon it, and he departed. But yet not many days elapsed when there went up from that house weeping and wailing because of the wickedness done

therein.

30. Tae said: Thou art just, O Jehovih! The gift of suis has made me strong in righteousness, and filled me with fear also. I perceive how Thou hast measured the lovers of earthly things, and meted to them the companions they have chosen. Herein doth it devolve on me to develop suis in my sons and daughters, and in all children whom I can raise up, and in time to come neither the good or evil that is in any man can escape their observation. Is not this the foundation of prophecy?

31. Kosmon said: By the light of Jehovih that dwelleth in me I declare unto thee, O Tae! Be thou wise not only in suis, but in thy corporeal judgment also. Thou hast perceived that all things leave an impression on all approximate things. To read these is suis.

32. Hath it not been written of old: save thou separatest thyself in body and spirit from the world, thou shalt not reach Nirvana? Put this and that together, learning from the past as well as the present.

33. Tae said: Now do I perceive, O Jehovih, I must avoid the imprint of evil things in order to attain Thy higher light. Is not this the true course to raise up my sons and daughters? For of what benefit in the world is suis if it remain amidst clouds. Tae withdrew from the world, taking his sons and daughters with him, besides orphans and infants without number. And he built a home in the country, and founded a college of suis, teaching the exercise of both the spiritual senses and the corporeal senses.

34. Tae said: Lo and behold, infants have suis at the first. In all the ages past hath man smothered it out by ministering to the corporeal senses alone. And Tae preserved to his sons and daughters, and to the infants, the power of suis.

35. Jehovih said: Fear not for them, O man, for in having suis, they will not depart away from Me. They shall be the founders of My kingdom on earth. Then Jehovih spake through Es.

26. Es said: For thy good works thou hast enlisted angels from the second heaven (etherea). Hear me, O Tae, and be wise in thy judgment. Whilst thou wert in the world and with it, thy voice of prayer rose not, but wasted itself amidst familiar spirits and mortals. The impressions of these being around about thee, transcend all other powers in thy soul. But now that thou hast freed thyself from the presence of them who live for earthly things alone, thou art open to receive the Father.

37. Remember that in this day Kosmon is bestowed on the earth; that is, the era in which man shall combine the wisdom of earth knowledge with the wisdom of spirit knowledge; the light of the hermit and recluse with the light of the city; the learning of the books of old with the spirit of making books of his own.

38. Give heed to my words: Jehovih giveth to one the power to heal by means of the spirit. Let such a person not fall back on spirit power alone, but diligently pursue all corporeal knowledge of healing. This is Kosmon.

39. Jehovih giveth to another oratory and music by means of spirit power. Let such a person not fall back on spirit alone, but diligently pursue also corporeal knowledge on oratory and music. This is Kosmon.

40. Did not the teacher of music under the reign of Seffas apply the corporeal notes and not the Spirit? And yet when he taught a bird to sing, he shut it up in a dark room and made it learn from es only. In this he was wiser with the bird than with his sons and daughters.

41. So also hath the man of much learning drowned his own spirit in darkness; nevertheless, the man of suis shall not neglect book learning; otherwise he is but as a clock without a regulator, or a ship without a rudder.

42. To attain to Kosmon is to find the secret of prophecy. Think not that prophecy can be attained without diligence in pursuing knowledge. As thou wouldst from corporeal knowledge foretell an eclipse, so from es knowledge shalt thou fore-tell and past-tell the nations of the earth. Yet all knowledge, corporeal or es'ean, is compatible with general principles, and one may lead to unfolding the other.

43. In olden times wise angels came to men and informed them of what was to happen, and these men were called prophets. but I tell thee, O Tae, such men were only instruments of revelation. In the time of Kosmon, men shall not be merely instruments of prophecy, but actual prophets themselves.

44. As man computeth motions of corporeal earth, and foretelleth an eclipse, so shalt thou compute the es of man and nations, and the vortices of the unseen worlds, and foretell coming events, and cause the hidden things of the earth to deliver up their long hidden secrets.

Part IV.

1. Tae said: Now will I apply myself to Thy works, O Jehovih. Thine is a book that never errs. The times Thou bestoweth shall be my sign-posts. Is this not the most exalted science under the sun?

2. Thereupon Tae collected histories from the arc of Bon to the coming of Kosmon; and the sons and daughters of Jehovih quickened him to remember all the knowledge that had come into the world from the revelations of that day. When Tae had completed his labors he made a tablet of events, and classified them, and he called the tablet Orachnebauhgalah, because it was of the line of the tree of Jehovih, being the last of the fruits of the Hebrew language. But the people called it the tablet of prophecy, signifying, the mathematics of both evil and good.

3. And Tae divided the time of the tablet according to the darkness and the light of the period, and for four hundred years prior, and it was in all, three thousand four hundred years.

4. Tae said: According to the light of my Father in heaven will I call the ends of the tablet dan'ha, for these are the quickened times mentioned by the prophets of old. Not only will I prove them whether they are true or not, but I will find the motion of the Great Serpent and this will determine the orbit thereof.

5. For since Jehovih hath made years, hath He not also made cycles, and will not the cycles comport with the rules of members?

6. Thus did Tae determine that an arc was three thousand years, but that the dan'ha varied from fifty to six hundred years.

7. Tae said: Though Thou, O Jehovih, hath made Thy arcs three thousand years, Thou hast wisely varied the heights thereof. Now will I compute the events within the cycle of Bon and find the members born into atmospherea, and the times of their abiding lights.

8. And Tae perceived that he could determine the dominions of the lower heaven, and from this revert to the earth and discover what had been in ages past. Thereupon Tae classified cycles at three thousand years, and the wave of the Great Serpent at two

hundred years and four hundred years. These again he subdivided, and he found that every thirty-third year was alike on the earth in heat and cold, and he discovered from these the nebulous regions within the vortex of the earth, and the cause of the variations in the times of falling meteors.

9. Again Tae subdivided the thirty-third year into eleven, and he found the variation one in ninety-nine years. Then sorrow came upon his soul, and he cried out unto the Father.

10. Tae said: O Jehovih, wherein have I done wrongfully? In all my computations I was puffed up with promised surety, but in my farthest research I am tripped up. The power betwixt the sun and the earth could not make this defect. Jehovih heard the voice of Tae, and answered him through His son Corpor.

11. Corpor said: Why repinest thou, O Tae. Thou hast taken for granted a power existeth betwixt the sun and earth, because, forsooth, philosophers have taught it. Did not the philosophers of old say the sun was the Creator?

12. Tae then cast aside the philosophy of this day, and proved the attraction of the corporeal worlds do not exceed seven diameters, each of its own, but many of them less than two. And he measured the satellites and their distances from their central corpor, and he perceived the diameters of the vortices could be determined by the loss or gain in the velocity of the satellites.

13. Where vortices had matured in form, he called them wark, as they had been called amongst the ancients, and the wark of the earth was one million five hundred and four miles in diameter, but the vortex of the sun in the places where the earth rideth, is three thousand years, which is to say, one year of the earth's wark is equal to one year of the sun's vortex, which is as one year to three thousand years in the trail of the serpent, and this again giveth the orbit of the Great Serpent four million seven hundred thousand years.

14. Tae said: All approximate things impress each other and to find the roadway in the earth's travel is to find what hath been and what will be. If, therefore, the past history of the earthly people for three thousand years were written truthfully it would disclose the roadways of one cycle of time, and this must be repeated each thirty-third cycle with one deviation in ninety-nine cycles, and half a deviation in eight cycles, which is equivalent to twenty-four thousand years.

15. And Tae measured the past cycles for twenty-four thousand years, and the sons and daughters of Jehovih were with him, contributing every one a part.

16. This, then, is the genesis of the cycles, i.e., first Jehovih and His times, and all the created things from without a beginning. And Jehovih was the Unseen, which is Spirit, and the Seen, which is His Person and Body.

17. By Jehovih in mastery over His Person created He countless worlds of which the corporeal earth is one, and He created the living thereon, and the time was one gadol, i.e., twenty-four thousand years.

18. Hak was second born, and then Semu, and they covered the earth abroad with Asu, till Hotu came, and Jehovih ceased creating new living things; and the second time of the earth was Hotu.

19. Jehovih sent Seffas, word-maker, with a sword; and in the seventh cycle of Seffas the continent of Pan was peopled over with men raised up to words and deeds of blood.

20. And yet in other cycles the earth had prospered only on one continent, and none could

be inspired to go abroad and live with Asu. So Jehovih saw wisdom in the arc of Suth, who held dominion for three thousand years; and He begat Iz, who was in dominion three thousand one hundred years, and He begat Aph, who reigned three thousand six hundred years; who begat Apollo, who reigned two thousand eight hundred years; who begat Osiris, the first, who reigned three thousand three hundred years; who begat Abraham and Brahma, who reigned two thousand four hundred years; who begat Moses and Capilya.

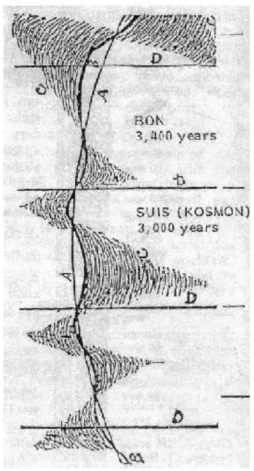

DEVIATION OF VORTICES
A = C'Vork'Um [orbit of the sun]
B = Deviation shown

21. It came to pass, that when the earth had entered into the thirty-third year of the arc of Kosmon in the etherean firmament, Jehovih spake out of the midst of heaven, and there were quickened up those whom His holy angels had prepared to hear the Father's voice.
22. Jehovih said: All who hear My voice shall know Me, and comprehend My Person. And as many as hear Me and behold My presence shall be called Tae, for they are the first-fruit of the resurrection in Kosmon. Of such were the Faithists in the arc of Bon and in the cycles prior to that period.
23. And Tae shall come forth in Me, for he is My word, speaking in his labor to that end, and not by books nor by the words of the mouth.
24. And I will quicken Tae and he shall be as a new race on the earth, practicing holiness

by good works, and by associative labor, dwelling in peace and love with one another, abnegating self in all things; for of such are My kingdoms; and Tae shall lay the foundation thereof upon the earth.

25. To the organic associations who labor in Me, I send representative angels from My etherean worlds; but to him who liveth for self, and by isolation and inorganically with neighbors, I permit the angels of atmospherea to minister. Neither shall My hosts of the second heaven (etherea) come to those who are wrapped up in the earth, for they are as a reservoir for the spirits of darkness.

26. And it came to pass that Tae was as one man, being attuned with the Father, and the light of the past and present came upon him. And the second heaven was let down to the earth, and the hosts of etherea ministered to Tae, and quickened him, that he might understand what it was to hear the voice of Jehovih, neither depending on the sacred books of the ancients, nor on the angels of heaven.

27. For Jehovih had said: In that day shall each and every one be as a covenant with Me, speaking and conversing with Me. They shall be as seers and prophets themselves, making their own sacred books, rites and ceremonies; and these shall stand above all else that have ever been.

28. When Tae pursued suis, which is the reading of unseen impressions, he was also developed in ethe, which is the overtaking of the vibrations of things long past. For as one may cast a stone in a lake, and it waveth the water, and the air above it, so also do all things vibrate to the uttermost places. He who hath developed in ethe, becometh as an unraveler of tangled threads; and things that are past are as an open book. To him the books of the libraries of heaven are open, for he not only seeth and heareth the spirits of the dead, but he goeth forth out of the corporeal body (for such have no longer sin and self in them) and he beholdeth the glories of heaven, and returneth again to his corporeal body unharmed.

29. Tae took the histories of men from the time of Moses to Kosmon, and for the periods of war and destruction he made one place, and for the periods of peace and good will amongst men, he made another place, for he saw that the actions and behaviors of nations were governed largely by the unseen worlds around about them. These formed a map of light and darkness, as it had been for three thousand four hundred years. And this became as a key to unlock the past, and a base to foretell the future.

30. So he made plates and tables of the firmament above, for even as they reveal the past, they also become as an index to what will happen on the earth for the next three thousand years, and they unfold the conditions of nations now on the earth and show what will be their places in heaven.

31. Tae said: To all peoples on earth, and to the spirits of the lower heaven do I declare in the name of Jehovih: Through Him and of His hand have I been lifted up. Hear me, O mortals! Give ear, O ye spirits of the dead! The Father has spoken. The secrets of His glory are in my keeping. By Him do I reveal; in Him am I mighty!

32. I was in darkness, but am now in light. His presence is upon me. Harken thee to my words, and be wise in your lives.

33. Seek not to disprove Him; seek not to prove that these things cannot be; seek not to deny His Person or Spirit. Of such was my bondage. In bitterness of heart was I bound in darkness. For those who deny, those who try to disprove His voice, are in darkness.

34. He is the same today and forever. The prophets of old found Him; so also can ye. But He cometh not to the denier, nor to the disprover.

35. He who will find His Person must look for Him. He who will hear His voice must harken.

36. Are there not those who hear and see the spirits of the dead? This is suis. But ethe lieth higher. This is hearing Jehovih, seeing His hand.

37. Who can believe, not knowing this? Who but His prophets have the just compounding of words? They do not utter and quibble as men, but give forth as Gods. Consider this: Seek to become one with Him, by proclaiming and practicing Him.

38. Go ye forth, saying: Now will I find Thee; now will I hear Thee, O Jehovih! Thy voice shall become my words.

39. This is the secret, O man! This is the attuning of thyself with Him. Seek, then, to make Him thine own holy book. Art thou as a servant coming to a master to read and write letters for thee? Such is not Kosmon.

40. Be a man in the presence of Jehovih. Build up thy kingdom at once. It shall be thine in heaven. Think not that thou canst sin by coming to Him. Sin lieth the other way.

KOSMON ARC IN ORIAN FIELD 'HUY'

Part V.

1. Tae then made a tablet of the nations of the earth, and of the people therein, rank and rank, caste and caste. And when it was completed, Jehovih spake to him through His sons and daughters.

2. Jehovih said: Separate thou all the people into four groups, and thou shalt determine the kingdoms of atmospherea. And thou shalt divide them after the manner of My judgment upon them. Remember, O man, that in all My kingdoms, like attracts like. According to their talents so do I prosper them.

3. He who desireth of the earth, I give of the earth. He who desireth of heaven, I give heavenly treasures.

4. Tae said: I perceive why the king desireth to be king, why the idler desireth to be idle,

1169

why the general desireth to rule, and the captain and leader of men, and why the rich man glorieth in riches. If they prosper in these things, is it not because the corporeal transcended the spirit?

5. And Tae brought all these together, and this he called the first division, saying: He who is farthest from Jehovih prospereth best in the corporeal world, for his desires show the direction of his soul.

6. Tae then called together all the laborers of the earth who were diligent but prospered not, and he found their spiritual judgment transcended their corporeal judgment. These he called the second division.

7. Tae then collected together all the infants in the world, and they were without judgment, and this he called the third division.

8. Tae then called together all the people who lived off the earnings and industry of others, and these were thieves, robbers, politicians, lawyers, judges, and preachers who live in fine houses. This he called the fourth division.

9. And when Tae looked abroad over the earth, lo and behold there was one man left, and he was alone of his kind on the earth.

10. Tae said: Who art thou? And the man answered, I know not, neither do I know whence I came, or whither I shall go.

11. Tae said: What is thy labor? The man answered: Whatsoever I can turn my hand to, that I do; and I give all I have, and my time to whosoever needeth me. Tae said: Shall I give thee gold? The man said: Nay, I need nothing. Tae said: Shall I make thee a leader of men? The man answered: Nay, to be a leader on earth is to be bound in heaven. Tae said: Then thou shalt have renown, for thou art the highest of men. But the man answered: Nay, I will not have renown, for when I am dead and gone to heaven I would be called back continually by the prayers of men. Naked I came into the world; permit me to depart when my time cometh as Jehovih directeth. Now when Tae found the man desired nothing of the earth for earth's sake, he cried out to the Father, saying:

12. Four divisions have I made of the people of the earth, but there is one man beside, and he fitteth none of the divisions. Where, then, shall I place him?

13. Jehovih said: Leave thou him alone, and when his death is at hand, My etherean angels shall carry his soul to the second heaven, for he is My son.

14. Then Jehovih questioned Tae, saying: How judgeth thou the children of men?

15. Tae said: The leaders, that is kings, queens, emperors, popes, and rich men, I have made into one division; producers into another division; idlers and babes another; and thieves, liars, robbers, politicians, judges, lawyers, and priests who live in fine houses, another division.

16. Then spake Jehovih, through His sons and daughters, saying: Thou hast done well, for what is one man more than another when stripped of his flesh body, save in the righteousness of his soul? And is not the labor of man the true basis to weigh the worth of his spirit? What is the king or the rich man, more in My sight than the most menial servant?

17. Then Tae counted the numbers of people whom he had collected in the four divisions, and they corresponded to the statistics of mortals.

18. Jehovih said: Of such, rank and rank, caste and caste, are My kingdoms in atmospherea. According to that which they have developed on the earth so do I assign

them in heaven. Let every man judge for himself and assign himself whithersoever he will. My kingdoms are open to all.

19. Thus did Tae discover the rank and grade of the lower heaven, and the numbers of people dwelling in each and every division thereof.

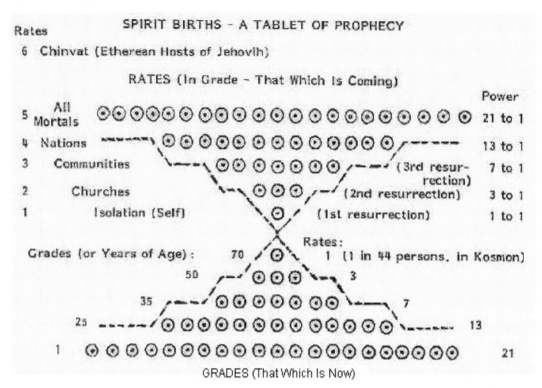

GRADES. (That which is now.) Abortions and premature births are included in rate 21. All below 50 years of age are considered minors (as to spirit). Familiar spirits come mostly from rate 21 (infants) and from rate 7 who were slain in war, and thrown into chaos, that is, spirits who know not who they are, and they anchor themselves on mortals, being in darkness (spirit obsession). At age 70 years of age some have outgrown all earthly desires, passions and abnegate self. Such a person stands in proportion of 1 to 44 in the average spirit births in the period of the world (beginning of Kosmon). In the Arc of Bon the proportion was 1 to 58, and in the ages long past it was 1 to a 1000 persons. And yet, O Jehovih, how many of thy sons and daughters attain the full age of 70 years, but in spirit have not risen above a newborn child.

RATES. (That which is coming.) 1 = Isolation, the sphere of the first resurrection: individual spirits manifesting. These are the es'yan order of spirits in heaven, belonging to no society or organization; strolling, playing, wandering about. 2 = Churches. The second sphere is the beginning of the second resurrection. Spirits of this order begin to have association in heaven, but limited. Christian, Buddhan, Braham and Mohammedan spirits belong to this grade. 3 = Communities. The third sphere is the beginning of the third resurrection in heaven. Spirits in this rate are risen above being followers. In fact, this is the beginning of the emancipation of the human soul. Spirits of this sphere only come to organic associations of mortals who practice doing good to one another with all their wisdom and strength. They cast aside all Gods and saviors, bowing to none but the Creator, Jehovih (they are Faithists in heaven). Their power is 7 to 1.

4 = Nations. This rate deals with nations, operating through the grades below them. Their power is 13 to 1.

5 = All Mortals. The fifth rate are the combined powers in heaven who control the inhabitants of

1171

the whole earth, through the rates below them (Atmospherean rule). Their power is 21 to 1 over mortals on the earth, and the spirits of the first resurrection.

6 = Ethereans. Spirits who have passed beyond all earthly attraction and powers and conditions. (As may be calculated from the forgoing rates, the power of ethereans over mortals and spirits is 31 to 1.)

In olden times, this tablet was called abracadabra, and written in triangular form. But it is incorrect, as it omitted infants.

EXAMPLE OF USING THIS TABLET. To calculate the bondage in heaven of any church or organization (second resurrection): GRADE = RATE = DESCENT + 3. For example, to calculate Christ's dominion: 3 = 7 + 13 + 21 equals 41 times the number of mortals professing him, say 200,000,000, equals 8,2000,000,000 spirits in Christ's kingdom in heaven at the beginning of Kosmon, which was the time his followers began to cast him out. The same holds true for all religions. Hence, the bondage signifies that the number shall rise in one resurrection, which cannot occur in less than two hundred years, the first dan, equivalent to 200 A.K. (2048); but full term is six hundred years, the second dan equivalent to 600 A.K. (2448) , which would be the longest limit of religious bondage. The periods of revolutions amongst mortals always corresponds to the resurrections in heaven of the order which has reference to the subject matter of the revolution. Hence, it will be observed that even the first grade is less bound in heaven than is the second.

20. Jehovih called His sons and daughters, and Tae stood upright before Him.

21. Jehovih said: What is thy wisdom, O man!

22. Tae then answered: I have learned by corporeal things, which are seen and heard. I have learned also of spiritual things, which are unseen and unheard.

23. Jehovih said: What thine eyes behold or what thine ears hear, is My Person; the others are of My spirit. When was the birth of this, thy Kosmon knowledge?

24. Tae said: When the inhabitants, who were descendants of Thy people, had circumscribed the earth and settled it around about, then Thy holy angels came and knocked on the walls of Rochester! They proclaimed Thee, and no other God or Lord.

25. Jehovih said: Before this I had searched the earth over, and selected and provided a place for My kingdom. By My angels did I inspire the founders of this new country to banish the dominion of Church with State, and to provide for the spirit of man to proclaim Me and My Person. They became a mighty nation, and the spirit of manhood was in them, for as I taught them to deny the divine right of kings, I foresaw they would also deny the same thing of Christ, and cast him out.

26. Tae perceived that these things were so, and that the time had come when all the people will bow to none save Jehovih, the Great Spirit.

27. Jehovih said: Hear Me, O Tae, for I speak through all the members of My family, and I will declare Myself to all My nations and peoples under the sun. Nor shall there be any more Gods or Lords or saviors on My footstool.

28. In the time of Kosmon, up to the thirty-third year thereof, these things have come to pass:

29. Thousands and thousands of men, women and children have been quickened by Jehovih to signs and miracles, even as in the time of the ancients, and many of them have attained to suis, seeing without corporeal eyes and hearing without corporeal hearing, knowing things far and near, by a sense not belonging to the corporeal organs.

30. And these people, being distinguished from others, are comprehended under the name

Tae, being the first-fruits of heaven on earth in this day. And many of them have foresense around about them of such kind that the spirits of the dead can come to them and openly commune, proving themselves unto all who are willing to receive truth, to be the spirits of friends and relatives deceased on the earth.

31. And the knowledge that cometh from the spirits of the dead proveth itself in many ways to transcend the knowledge of mortals, as is classed and distinguished from mortal knowledge by the word Es, because it cometh from the unseen, which is one of the kingdoms of Jehovih.

32. That, therefore, when Es speaketh, it signifieth the highest and the combined knowledge that hath come to mortals in the time of Kosmon, from the wisest of the spirits, who have communicated as aforesaid. And since all wisdom cometh from Jehovih, whether uttered by a mortal or a spirit, so is it said He speaketh through them.

33. Now when Tae had put away self, striving to come, by his behavior, to Jehovih, a new light dawned upon him, for as it was given to him to see the spirit of the recently dead, so by purification, did he attain to intercourse with associative bodies in the unseen worlds.

34. And these associative bodies being exalted angels in wisdom and purity, speak of the first elements and not of the instruments used, because it is their mode of language; that is to say, for example, Jehovih spake through Es saying: Whereas mortals, and spirits of the first heaven would say the same thing, thus: According to the accumulated testimony from the most advanced spirit world.

35. Let man be wise and perceive that the Father standeth behind all and within all; for as he riseth out of individualities, becoming comprehensive in expression, so riseth his spirit also.

36. These things Tae perceived. And the Father came to him through Es and unfolded the scroll of heaven.

37. Es said: Transversely, as seen by man, the worlds are: First the earth, then atmospherea, and then to the ether beyond.

38. Jehovih commanded man to be brought forth on the earth, and dwell thereon for a season; then to die and rise in spirit and dwell for a season in atmospherea, traveling with the earth, daily and yearly, even in its journey throughout the etherean heavens.

39. He who would know, therefore, the rank a man will inherit in heaven shall estimate the comparative strength of spirit and the purity of behavior. If a man live isolated on earth, laboring for self, he will be isolated in heaven and companionless.

40. It was said in olden time: Judge not, lest ye be judged; but I say unto thee, judge all men spiritually and corporeally, but hold thy tongue, looking to thyself to know how the Father judgeth thee by talents and by works. But above all things observe the unseen causes that play upon thee, quickening thy memory and thy perception, for herein lieth a great secret of acquiring spiritual knowledge.

41. Thou art a type of the world; thou hast a daily life, a yearly life, and a cyclic life; the latter of which, is first, infancy; second, puberty; third, maximus; fourth, old age; fifth, death. A corporeal world hath these, and she imparteth her periods to the people thereof.

42. Perceive, then, O man, to attune thyself to Jehovih is to become a prophet. To understand the kingdoms of the lower heaven is to know the appointments of familiar spirits and guardian spirits over mortals. Thus shalt thou perceive the first place allotted to them at the times of their death. But to understand the realms in etherea, thou shalt

discern the associative redemption of atmosphereans.

43. For as there are spirits who are captains over a star, or the earth, or sun, so are there generals over the etherean worlds; and yet beyond them, great commanders over the vortices in the wide universe. As thou hast felt the cold breeze of the spirit circle, made by the spirits in attendance, know there are those high raised in heaven in power and wisdom whose presence fashion the currents of the embryonic worlds, and propel them forth by a breath! They have others beneath them who are themselves Gods and Goddesses.

44. But remember, O man, that in all the glories there is still One who is higher than all, even the Person of All, who is Jehovih!

Part VI.

1. The light of the following truths will be manifest to him. Let him, on the other hand, shut himself up in denial; saying: I defy thee to prove the matter, and he shall not be enlightened.

2. In the testimony of Jehovih, speaking through Es, and by the spirit is man quickened.

3. As a man liveth on earth, acquiring perfections or imperfections in spirit, so will he enter the es world at death.

4. Death is the severing knife which separateth the corporeal man from the spiritual man. The former returneth to the earth, but the latter surviveth, and in time riseth upward.

5. By death man suffereth the loss of companionship of mortals, but is quickened and united with those he loved before.

6. A new world is open to him, full of light and splendor, having a fitness to his spirit, even more gloriously real than the corporeal world was to his mortal part.

7. As a corporeal man requireth corporeal food and clothes, with a habitable place to dwell, so in like manner requireth his spirit, and is so provided within atmospherea, but spiritually.

8. The first habitable place in es is on the earth, and near around the earth, and mostly within the same house wherein he dwelt in mortal form. But the spirit is subtle and moveth, but not as corporeal things move, having power and presence with friends and kin at remote distances, as if all was in one place; for of such nature is the es world.

9. Spirit existeth within corporea, and by this means are the dead enabled to manifest to the living. However, to such of the living who have no consciousness of their own spirit, the spirits of the dead cannot manifest intelligently.

10. For a mortal to be conscious of his own spirit, it must transcend his corporeal senses; he who knoweth not of his own spirit is weak indeed. Such a man born into the spirit world is as a newborn child, knowing nothing.

11. All men born into spirit life die imperfect and ignorant, and weak, depending on nurses, guardians and doctors. Many such who are slain in war, or in desperate madness, are born into spirit life in chaos. Some will not leave the battlefield.

12. To the long suffering and to the weary, who are upright of heart, death is a doorway to a world of bliss, of rest, and love.

13. To the captain and general, who were slayers of men, death is a doorway to them whence spring up at them ghastly wounds and frenzied maniacs, crying out for vengeance. And the slayers of men run away, but escape not; they cry out, but are mocked

at. The wailing of the widows and orphans is an increasing horror to them. Their nose is suffocated and their eyes appalled with gaping, bloody wounds.

14. The leader of men entereth the es world to meet an army of misled confidants; and his tricks and falsehoods are as garments soiled and spotted to hide a blackened heart. He turneth away, but the mirror of his past deeds hangeth up before him.

15. The rich man entereth the es world at the door of his bank. In the bank he tarrieth all day. At night he wandereth up and down. He meeteth another rich man; they shake hands but speak not. Then he goeth forth. In the morning he is in the door of his bank again, and all day he loitereth around about. He worrieth at the manner of the clerks; he feareth his widow will come to want, or that his bank will soon run low. He seeth the glory of the spirit world, but he cannot enter it. The servants that washed his clothes stand fairer than he. Yea, he is abashed for the whiteness of their raiment and the light of their souls; and so he turneth and hideth in his bank again.

16. But lo, the spirit of him who is dead sucketh out the spirit of the wine and leaveth him distracted still.

17. Another darker chamber openeth; a dealer in wines is dead; one with fashionable home, and wife and daughters, high aspiring. Confronted in his stores with the spirits of such as died from his temptations, bleary-eyed and boisterous, they come to welcome the newly dead, and with atmospherean potions sucked out of his plenteous barrels, greet him with rich applause. Then he flieth to wife and daughters in his mansion richly furnished. But lo, the drunken sots and spirits, foul smelling, fill his habitation! With terrible anger, helpless, beholdeth he the spirits of pollution fondling his daughter's person, and his widow a fountain for their revelry.

18. And yet the depth is not full. In a stately mansion a woman of high caste is dead. And it was said she was blessed, because since not having borne children, ease and glory were at her command. And now, with curious mirth and some envy, the spirits of other women who were outcasts come to behold the newborn spirit of the leader of fashion. And as they turn about, nurses come with children born from her body and her spirit, by abortion cast into heaven, even in Jehovih's face accursed! A curtain of black death that will not away, choketh her. To the left, the right, or up and down, there is nothing but the wail of sweet babes - Mother, why murderest thou me? Was I not Jehovih's gift? The woman of fashion hideth, but is not hidden. Even the soiled outcasts are white beside her; like a woman that is crushed but cannot die, she squirmeth and writheth in the kingdom she built with her own hands.

19. From the scene of horrors now opened Uz the door of the man of corporeal learning. His spirit wandereth in libraries and ancient tombs and hieroglyphs, and sigheth over problems never solved. Day by day, night by night, he restlessly peereth into the same paths, and over and over burroweth deep in darkness. Stripling youths and fairies pull his wig or upturn his spectacles, saying: O fool, knoweth thou not thou art dead? Turn from these corporeal tombs and behold Great Jehovih's light. In sorrow and pity he regardeth them, saying: I am not dead! When I am dead, there is the end. I am but sick, still dwelling in my corporeal body. And then he wandereth on, a living sepulcher.

20. A farmer is dead. It was his wont to rise early and toil all day; to ponder much on the fruit of his labor and to glory in his freedom. For himself and his family he lived; to himself and his family Jehovih giveth him. In his house and his fields his spirit walketh

about; he knoweth no heaven or hell. As a weed that is worthless to itself and the world, so is his spirit, and as the weed knoweth not the field that brought it forth, neither doth he know Jehovih's heaven. Nor can he go but from field to field, and back to his house, day and night. He liveth for nothing higher, and Jehovih gave him that which he desired.

21. What spirit is this that glutteth itself in the slaughter house? He was a gormandizer; he is dead. He goeth from saloon to saloon sniffing the air of roasted viands, and fat meats, and of wines; the smell of the fat man is his delight; and the woman that rejoiceth in sin, rare flesh and fat soups, is as a cushion for him to roll upon. One saith: I never come into this saloon but I recollect him that is dead; he so loved this place! And the other saith: I believe his spirit loitereth here still; else why do we so oft think of him? And thereupon they gorge themselves, even whilst the spirit of the dead feedeth on the atmospherean part. This is all the heaven he sought on earth, and Jehovih gave it to him.

22. And now cometh confusion in heaven. He that forever argued is dead. Scarce newborn in spirit life he setteth up to prove his position and enlighten all the world. The curious and the idler gather around to hear his speech again. He striveth to show that all the world is a fool; in endless ways he turneth his arguments, and repeateth them over, day by day, night by night. This was what he strove to build on earth, and Jehovih gave him the same.

23. And here, newborn in spirit, is the moderate man, who by industry earned a handsome house and raised up sons and daughters, creditable to the state. He is in his home still; heaven is too narrow for him. He saith: I would argue with Jehovih that I have not my share of heaven! Did I not give alms daily; the poor man a crust, and a poor woman a penny? When did I pass a blind man and not give? But none answer him. It is as if talking to the wind. Again and again he repeateth his complaint; but none take him by the hand, and he remaineth helplessly in his own home, which he asked Jehovih to help him build for his heirs.

24. The recluse, with a new philosophy and scheme of diet, but aimless and of little producing, to benefit anything under the sun, is dead. The breath of mortals was poison to him, and all human influence to be avoided as poison infecting his most holy spirit. Here again gather nymphs and fairies to see his spirit make its etherean flight. As mortals gather around a pretender that promises to sail a balloon around the world, so gather these jocose and mischief loving spirits in the house of the recluse, to see his promised ascent. He will show them how the higher spheres in heaven are reached; he would not deign even in mortal life to commune with the spirits of the dead. None so low for him! But now he is dead and his spirit limps and trembles in his hovel, still boasting. And as he produced nothing in the corporeal world, so produceth he nothing still; but boasteth and secludeth, secludeth and boasteth; and this is his heaven, day and night.

25. The light of Jehovih touched on the earth, and the heavens above were stirred to the foundation. Things past were moved forward. His voice was from the depth of darkness to the summit of All Light.

26. The nations that had not known Him, now knew Him. Acceptable, and with loud rejoicings, they shouted, Jehovih! Jehovih! Almighty and Everlasting! Glory be to Thee on High! Creator, Father! All praise to Thee forever!

27. And Jehovih went far and near swiftly, quickening with a new power, both the living and the dead. And the peoples raised up, and heard His voice from every corner, calling:

Come forth! Come forth! O My beloved! And it was not like any sound under the sun, for it reached deep into the souls of men.

28. And in the stirring up of things long past, it was as if a cloud of dust and darkness, foul and poisonous, overspread heaven and earth, was to be cleared away and make room for the immortal kingdom.

29. High above the clouds, and deep down in all the blackness, the All Light of Great Jehovih shone as the everlasting sun. The faith of men and angels rose up in increasing assurance to the Most High, that He in His matchless majesty, alone, would rise triumphant over all.

30. Jehovih said: Bring forth the legions of earth and heaven! Summon up the dead! Let the living rejoice! My kingdom is at hand! And the dead came forth as if out of their graves, but clothed in the raiment of heaven; and they walked upon the earth; yea, face to face talked with the living, proclaiming the fullness of Jehovih and His everlasting kingdoms.

31. Little infants that were long dead, returned to the living, full grown in heaven, singing in Jehovih's praise. Mothers returned from the unseen world with love and angel kisses for their mortal babes and sorrow-stricken husbands.

32. Then rose the cloud of darkness higher and higher and higher; the poisonous smell and damnable tricks of hades belched forth in blackness terrible. The spirits of those slain in war, delirious, mad, and full of vengeance; and those whose earth lives had bound them in torments; and those who lived on earth to glut themselves to the full in abhorrent lust, came assuming the names of Gods and Saviors.

33. And yet the voice of Jehovih called: Bring forth the legions of earth and heaven! Summon up the dead! Let the living rejoice! My kingdom is at hand.

34. And now the cloud reached all around the earth, and almost was the light of Jehovih obscured. Still the faith of angels and mortals rose up in one increasing voice: Jehovih is mighty! I know He will prevail!

35. And still the black giant arose, awful in gloom and blood-stained mantle, till the earth around became as a solemn night before a battle of death. Rattling bones and empty skulls, with gnashing teeth, all stained with human gore, made hideous by the portentous omen, caused angels and men to stand appalled.

36. Jehovih said: Bring forth the legions of earth and heaven! Summon up the dead! Let the living rejoice! My kingdom is at hand!

37. And now as the cloud of darkness stretched up out of the earth, girdling it all around, as a venomous reptile secureth his living food, lo and behold, the monster beast stretched forth four heads with flaming nostrils all on fire!

38. On each head were two horns, blood stained and fresh with human victims flesh macerated. Their tongues darted forth in menace, and their open mouths watered for human souls, and with suspicion mad, and much distrusted, their blood-shot eyes pierced the foul darkness, making many a mortal quake in fear.

39. And still the upraised of earth and heaven, with one voice, cried out: All hail, O Jehovih! Thou art mighty! Thou alone, shall prevail!

40. And Jehovih answered to His faithful sons and daughters, the living and the dead: Bring forth the legions of earth and heaven! Summon up the dead! Let the living rejoice! My kingdom is at hand!

Part VII.

1. And two heads of the beast stood in the east, and one stood in the midst, and one in the west. And the one that was oldest, and standing in the east, raised up his blood stained hands, trembling in miserly rage, and with a book tattered and torn and smutted with the foulness of glutted avarice, swore an oath saying: Down! Down! Jehovih! Unseen and godless! Down! Know thou this ancient lore! And the caste of men?

2. And rattling his hideous bones, even whilst with hissing breath he bated some to see the great awakening light.

3. But swift and terrible, the head of the beast that stood to the east and south, snorted loud, and with both hands black with clotted human blood, uplifted, cried out: Who art thou, of the north and east, that bellows out because thy tottering kingdom foresees its certain fall? Not only will I put Jehovih down, but thou, too, miscreant, deceiver of men! Know thou, O worthless Brahma, thy day is done. I, even I, great Buddha, will rule all the world. None but I shall save mortal souls.

4. Then with flashing sword raised high, and hungry for deeds of war, the head of the beast turned and shot forth his poisonous breath till all the world was foul. But ere he one stroke made, the head of the beast in the midst of the cloud, and more polluted than all the rest, and deep marked with lust, turned around to survey the scene, as if disturbed in amorous gluttony. And he shouted loud: Hold! You dogs of ancient! Only by me, Mohammed, shall man ascend to heaven! Behold my deeds of blood! By myself am I sworn! I will feast on your rotten carcasses, and banish Jehovih from the earth!

5. He raised himself upward, unwashed, and his head smoked with the fumes of mortal blood; he shook the mighty cloud of the beast far and near.

6. But now, horror arose afresh, for the head of the beast that lies to the west, stretched up his horns, and silently at first, always the most to fear, he felt around for his sword, and on the other heads of the beast contemplated, as one that knoweth his own power. Then toward great Jehovih he looked approvingly, but full of well-planned deceit.

7. Without more ado, he spake to the other three heads of the beast, saying: Think not I am come to send peace, but a sword. I come to set man at variance against his brother, and a daughter against her mother. Behold the millions I have slain! Behold how my mortals build torpedoes and ships of war! Behold the long trail of human gore where my banner goes forth! Know ye, too, I am the savior of men! Even great Jehovih shall bow the knee when I command! I will send my legions forth to rap on tables, and show the faces of the dead, and then proclaim through mortal tongues it is bolted loose, and thereon build my kingdom forever.

8. And then the head of the beast stood triumphant in the west, stripped of his bloody sleeves, and with one hand held high a banner whereon was written: I AM THE LAMB OF PEACE! And with the other swung high his mighty sword, like a whirlwind, it swung abroad over all the black clouds,

9. Then men and women of wealth and fashion cast aside their earthly goods and went and labored with the poor, teaching cleanliness, and wisdom and uprightness of heart. And those that preached were the spirits of the dead, who were ripe in experience in Jehovih's unseen worlds.

10. But the beast with his countless millions, was cast out from the earth. As a long black

cloud, riven and broken, floating, floating, floating, it passed away, and was seen no more! Nor was there more any God known upon the earth. But Jehovih rose supreme in every land; and all people under the sun sang anthems of glory to His name!

11. The voice of Jehovih came upon Es, saying:

12. Of the past, these things shalt thou comprehend, O Tae. The beast walked forth on the earth in every guise, and in the second sphere of atmospherea he became a living person, born out of the sins of men.

13. For one man worshipped science, and it was his beast; one worshipped riches, and it was his beast; one fashion, and it was her beast; another lust, and it was his; another worshipping nothing, and it was his beast; now all these and of such like order, continued to do the same things after death, for that which they had built up on earth became as a living entity within them, and they could not put it away. This was the first resurrection, being the birth of unclean man into the spirit world.

14. In the second sphere of atmospherea, which is the second resurrection, the condition was like unto the first but organic.

15. For one people worshipped Brahma, making a beast of him; another worshipped Buddha, making a beast of him; another worshipped Christ, making a beast of him; another Jesus, making a beast of him, and forever parading his crucifixion; and the beast that each one built up within his soul became an entity to him on his entrance into spirit life, and he became bound to the machinations of evil spirits professing to be that beast. And these evil spirits became as Gods, in fact, building kingdoms in the lower heavens, and making subjects and slaves of their worshippers, compelling them to contribute of their earnings and labor in spirit, even as mortal kings exact tribute on earth. Thousands and millions, and tens of millions of subjects and slaves had they, and their cities were even as represented to mortals, paved with comparative pearls and diamonds.

16. These things hast thou witnessed: that the spirits of the first birth discourse on the things of the earth, and of marriage and begetting; not having risen even to the second resurrection. Their hope and belief in heaven is to re-enter wombs and be born again, teaching reincarnation, and ministering to the proclivities of lust in mortals; inspiring visions of sexual desires and practices in heaven. For all such spirits have not risen up from the earth, and know no other abode, but to revel and glut themselves in corporeal debauchery. And many of them boastingly, and in darkness, teach falsely that spirits in heaven beget sons and daughters, and even that sons and daughters reincarnate themselves in mortal flesh, becoming children of the earth.

17. All such spirits shalt thou know by such teachings; for whatsoever seemeth the highest delight of a man on earth or a spirit in es, that will he exult in and proclaim.

18. And this sign hast thou witnessed of them in the second resurrection: they proclaim the beast they have made, whether it be an idol of Jesus or Christ, or Buddha, or Mohammed, or Brahma, and forever harp on him, knowing nothing higher; and he standeth as a figure of the beast, whereupon they hang their hopes of endless bliss.

19. By their preaching hast thou evidence of their place in heaven. Whosoever practiseth in them, receiveth his inspiration from the slaves of the beast he proclaimeth.

20. Yet the second is higher than the first, for the first is isolated, and the spirit or mortal belonging to the first, preacheth and practiseth on his own account, being wholly for self.

21. This sign hath the Father given: That in marriage, man and woman becometh the first

testimony before mortals, that self can be abnegated without loss of self experiencing a loss in fact. And this is the smallest possible number that can unite on earth or in heaven. Let the single man or the single woman stand, therefore, as a type of the lowest of the heavens, and let marriage stand as a type of the second resurrection; for those of the first are as individuals, but those of the second are as the beginning of association, and the committing of one's self to the combination of many.

22. Es said: A sign of the third resurrection hath Jehovih given to men whereby they shall be known, which is: that self shall not be maifest, save in the union of many. For as the first resurrection may have marriage between two persons who become as one, so do they of the third resurrection become Brides and Bridegrooms of Jehovih, manifesting in families of tens, and twenties, and hundreds, and thousands, who are also as one. Nor have they any other king, or chief ruler, or God, or Lord, or Christ.

23. Wherefore if a man say: I have no faith in these things, because they are impractical, ye may know he belongeth to one of the first two resurrections, and not to the third.

24. Es said: Nevertheless, it hath been proved in Israel that these things were for four hundred years, and these people attained to six millions of souls. Whoever then saith this day is void of righteousness like the ancients, is speaking from the first or second resurrection, denying the progress of man, and accusing Jehovih.

25. Judge not Jehovih's chosen by the standard of the worshippers of the beast, neither shall any man accuse Jehovih because man has set up natural law, putting Jehovih afar off; or because he hath set up Brahma, or Buddha, or Christ, putting Jehovih afar off, for all these idols were necessary to those who love the figure of a beast.

26. Those who have not attained to the third resurrection, must have, first, a mortal king or ruler; second, the sword; and third, the prison; for all of these were given to those who are begotten in sin and dwell in the beast.

27. Neither can he who preacheth any of the idols practice that which he preacheth. They are but as news vendors, proclaiming what Buddha did, or what is done by natural law, or divine law. Their mission is to preach and not to practice; for the practice of righteousness is not possible to them.

28. If a man come to thee and say: Behold, I am inspired by the angels of the third resurrection, see to it, and prove him, for if he be true, he is a practicer of Jehovih's kingdom, not in preaching, but in works.

29. But if he strive for himself in all things, then is he inspired of the first resurrection.

30. And yet if he be a proclaimer for one of the idols, then is he one of the second resurrection, asserting law, and even violence.

31. As one man alone cannot practice war, neither can one man alone practice the third resurrection. One man alone may giveth away all he hath, laboring for others all of his days, abjuring self before the world; yet he cannot thus be in the third resurrection. Because he hath not attained to the Father's kingdom, which is organic, and composed of a number.

32. Try them, therefore, before Jehovih, whether, for sake of Him they will become one with an army of brethren for righteousness. For such is a kingdom, and of it, Jehovih is king. All such will abjure war and violence, and contribute all they produce to the Father's kingdom, reserving nothing. This becometh power by virtue of righteousness and peace. These are ministered to by the spirits of the third resurrection, who have no Buddha or

Christ, but Jehovih only.

33. The proof of these things shall be manifest before all peoples. The Buddhan, or Brahman, or Mohammedan or Christian will not accept a brotherhood, either on earth or in heaven, because forsooth, he has his own idol. Neither will he abjure war, but declare it a necessary evil, even in the same breath he professeth peace. The charity he doeth is likewise vain and of little effect. It is like lifting water with a sieve. He buildeth asylums and houses for the poor, and places to feed the hungry, and in his places of worship raiseth money and provisions and raiments. But, lo and behold, the numbers who come to want, increase on his hands.

34. And yet worse than these are such as belong to the first resurrection. They worship nothing, and are without moral power before the world. Their charities are nothing, education nothing, and as for ideas of virtue, it is every one for himself.

PART VIII

1. Again Jehovih spake through Es, saying:

2. The first resurrection in heaven have I made to inspire the first resurrection on earth; the second resurrection in heaven have I made to inspire the second resurrection on earth. The third resurrection in heaven have I made to inspire the third resurrection on earth; the like to like, made I them.

3. Es said: Consider then, if a man on the earth strive for riches, or power, or self in any manner, whence he draweth his inspiration; and determine thou also by this what will be his rank in his birth into the es world.

4. And if a man be a preacher and not a practitioner, doing not the thing he knoweth to be the highest, thou shalt determine what will be his spirit birth.

5. On the other hand, he that liveth to the full, the highest of all he knoweth, by his own strength, producing for others all he can, thou shalt determine his place also.

6. These resurrections are possible, either on the earth or in heaven, but there are many so immersed in the earth, that only by death and by suffering hades, can they be aroused to strive for higher light in heaven.

7. Now, it will be said to thee: Such a man hath lived a good and exemplary life, giving to the poor, being temperate and respectable before the world. What will be his place in heaven?

8. Answer thou him, O Tae, saying: He that serveth himself, goeth to the lowest of bound heavens; he who serveth Jehovih with all his wisdom and strength, goeth to the third realm, but he who serveth betwixt these two goeth to the second lowest of the bound realms. Shall a man deceive Jehovih, saying: I did the best I knew, when he knoweth he did not?

9. Be thou wise in discerning Jehovih in all things, and seeing and judging as He would judge, for there are deceivers in heaven; and to him who would shelter his own deceit, these spirits come by thousands. But he of the third resurrection escapeth them.

10. And now, touching the prophecy of a nation, weigh thou the people and determine what resurrection they are already in, and the number of each division. Then determine the generation antecedent; and the one again antecedent to that, making tablets thereof.

11. They that are heavily laden, and dwell in Him, they are the type of My etherean

1181

worlds!

12. Forswear yourselves away from the world; she worshippeth the beast; the cloud of the second resurrection is upon her. Wash your hands and be clean. My hosts from the Most High heavens wait at your doors.

13. Behold, the spirits of darkness and of lies and deception have knocked, and ye opened unto them.

14. And now Tae looked abroad over the nations, and he said: What of the emperor, the queens, the king, and lords of the land?

15. Es said: Weigh thou them, O man, they and their peoples under them, and enumerate them according to the tablets, and thou shalt foretell the times that are set for them. As they were built up by the sword, they shall fall by the sword; as they stand by the strength of their standing armies, even by standing armies shall they be cut down.

16. By the sword shall Christ destroy Mohammed, and Brahma and Buddha; but he shall come against Confucius and fall. Then shall Christ destroy himself; for as his followers have cast him out of Rome, he will have no abiding place on the earth.

17. Search thou the road of Vishnu and Etau, and Ram, and Osiris, for all the idols of heaven run the same course, as thou shalt prove in Orachnebuahgalah, nor is here any help for them.

18. Jehovih is Omnipotent over all. He sendeth all Gods and saviors, by His Almighty command came they. They are books He bestoweth upon the generations of men, but when they are of no more use to man, behold, He taketh them away and giveth instead that which is suited to the progress of the world.

19. Be wise, and remember thy Creator all the days of thy life; be thou one with Him, and thou shalt live forever!

END OF THE BOOK OF KNOWLEDGE.

SAPHAH!

I am to perish. I, being SAPHAH, am of the perishable. I am of the earth perishable history. I am the dying history not dead; the legends; the skeleton of a one time giant. In my youth I was science and philosophy, religion. I reach into all the nations of the earth; distance with me is nothing; time nothing. I was as a tree of life in time long past, the devotedly loved SON OF LIGHT. The fruit I bore fed all the inhabitants of the earth. But the flesh of the fruit hath perished; the seed still liveth. My seed is in languages, in words, in rocks and ruined walls; in fallen temples and buried cities. These are the remnants of my corporeal body; in these my last days my remnants, that were once the living members of my body, shall forth and speak their parting words to the new born Kosmon. Hear ye these, my sons and daughters; O ye that search for the light of ages past, but find not. I am the book of the past, of the things that are past; of the corporeal world perishable.

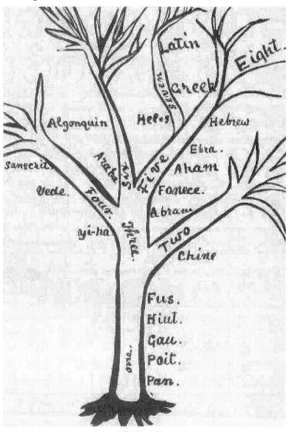

Plate 63.
The Tree of Language.

PAN, (of language) the first guttural sounds approximating words. POIT, beginning of labial word-sounds. HUIT, first acquiesced language. FUS, first written word-signs. CHINE, monosyllabic. YI-HA, combination words. ABRAM, first words; original text. FONECE, following the sound, but not the signs. (writing) AHAM, amalgamation. EBRA, the old; the sacred. SANSCRIT, mixture. ARABA, (first Egyptian also) 'Teeth and thorax.' ALGONQUIN, after the sacred name E-Go-Quin.

China, India, Europe and America, the four branches of the earth, languages from one root. What was the tree, and where grew it, that none can find it? Where lieth the submerged continent, the forgotten world? Whence escaped the struggling mortals, to float to far off continents, and tell the tale in all lands of a mighty flood?

PAN.

THE PRIMEVAL TONGUE.

1. Pan said: I am the earth; the first habitable place for man; I am beneath the water. Being submerged, my name survives. My words are man's first words. On the continent of Pan were words first used by man.

2. I am the 'Ah', signifying earth. I am earth words. I am the dispersed language. From me, Pan, came all earth languages. In all nations I am found. I deliver up; by me shall man know Him Who sent me. By His angels I was given to mortals; by them brought forth in this day.

3. Pan said: My steadfast lieth in the East. I founded the words of China and India. Fonecia and Ebra are my offspring. By the tribes of Faithists was I carried over. Egoquim founded me in Guatama. Egoquim became Algonquin. I am before all other languages; the first spoken words. Before me, man uttered as a beast, but made no words.

4. Pan said: The angels made some men as prophets and healers of the sick. By impression and by voice, taught they the prophets to utter words. These were Pan words; that is, earth words. The prophets taught their brethren. Many words were made sacred, that they might be well learned and sacred.

5. Pan said: I come not in a day, nor in a year, nor in a hundred years. I come not to one man only, but to many. I was uttered differently in different places on the 'Ah', the earth, according to the throats and tongues and lips and their development. Nevertheless, I was the same language.

6. Pan said: I am the key to unlock words. I make all things speak. Asu, the first men, were thus taught. As the camel uttered, so was he called; and the cat and dog and all the living. As the child called his father, so was the name 'man' made. This was in some places, Ghan, and Egan (China); Edam and Edan (Fonece); Adam (Ebra, Hebrew); Puam (Sanscrit); Pam (Vede); Sam (Kii); Ang (Algonquin); Anger (Poit); and Man (English).

7. Pan said: Think not that all the living uttered alike in all places. The wild dog spake not as the tame one; nor the small like the large one. Neither could all Asu utter the same sounds alike. Nevertheless, on the continent of Pan they were taught to name the living after their own speech. Thus was Asu taught of land animals and of the birds and all things whatsoever that utter.

8. Pan said: The wind spake but was seen not. Asu was taught that Corpor, the Seen, was ruled over by Es, the Unseen. In the leaves the wind said Ee; in the ocean surge and in the storm's roar, Oh; and in the winter's whistle, Ih; and he called the Unseen, E-O-Ih; Eolin (Poit); Eolih (Zerl); Eloih (Fonece); Jehovih (Ebra, Hebrew); Wenowin (Algonquin); Egoquim (Huit); Ze-jo-is (China). Nor were these all, for there were many imperfections of His name. He was the Unseen. What the Unseen spake, the Seen should not speak. E-O-IH was Almighty.

9. Pan said: I am language. I am two members, the utterance and the behavior. All things are embraced in my two members. The unmoving are dead; a stone has a name, but no behavior; it is unmoving; it is dead. It is the property of Uz.

10. Pan said: Two behaviors have things. If a man look toward Uz, it is downward; if toward Jehovih, it is upward. If a man march toward Uz, it is war and destruction; if toward Light, it is peace and wisdom. Whoever learneth these, my signs, shall read all languages.

SPEECH.

1. Jehovih said: As I caused man to grow, so I caused man's language to grow. Yea, even as the earth matureth in its place, so shall man look backward and judge what has been.

2. According to the time and place of the earth, so spake man. And it was so. And the deviation in the progress of speech was even as the deviation of the vortex of the earth.

3. Even the words of man in ages past shall be revealed by My seers in the time of Kosmon. And it was so.

The following, <u>Book of Gratiyus</u>, was written by J. B. Newbrough <u>after</u> he had built the Shalem Colony in New Mexico. Although it has merit... it was not written within in the same time period when the original OAHSPE Manuscript was written.

BOOK OF GRATIYUS,
OR THE
FOUNDING OF LEVITICA.

CHAPTER I.

1. Es, daughter of Jehovih, said: In the name of Jehovih, greeting unto all people. As by and through Him all things are accomplished, so shall we remember that through our own short-sightedness we oft interpret things wrongly, for in after time we discover that what happened was for the best, especially in extending the brotherhood of mankind.
2. In the founding of Jehovih's kingdom in Shalam, His chosen had many trials and difficulties, even as had been prophesied in the Oahspean Gospels. But their trials were different from what they had expected. People came amongst them who were unsuited to the work and to whom the work was not suited either. Some of these went away of their own accord, but some had to be sent away, yet much time elapsed before this resulted.
3. Finally, the chosen were separate and unmolested, and they began the work commanded by God, Jehovih's Son. Now, out of the aforesaid trials and difficulties, a new condition was born into the world, Levitica, the joy of man.
4. But before speaking of Levitica, a brief sketch of the condition of man should be made. He had been carnivorous for hundreds of generations. Passion, anger, disputation, opposition, and self-conceit were his strongest attributes. Even where gentleness and amiability manifested, they were generally cloaks to hide the selfishness within.
5. His antagonistic proclivities had become national, and nations themselves were comprehensive manifestations of the same selfish and antagonistic characteristics. Governments were organized on a basis of might, offensive and defensive. War and threatening standing armies were the pride and reliance of all nations. Faith in Jehovih had disappeared from nearly all the people of the earth. Neither could man be made to comprehend what was meant by the words, Faithist in Jehovih.
7. Carnivorous diet had reduced him to be little more than a carnivorous animal and a fighter in the struggle for life. The people were of four kinds: First, turbulent and quarrelsome; second, silently selfish; third, hypocritical, smooth-tongued; and, fourth, paupers and dependents. The dependents comprised the vast majority of the people.
8. The people justified war, offensive and defensive, wherever profit was promised. Their boast and glory was in invention of ships of war and weapons of death. This spirit reacted back again on the people, and manifested in their private and public transactions. Though the priests and preachers cried out peace, the example of all the world was against them. But these same expostulators for peace crippled their own efforts by telling the people any man should be called good and have salvation, no matter

what crime he committed, provided he called on the name of their Savior before death.

9. But it was not possible for so fixed a religion to keep pace with the growth of intelligence in man. And, as a consequence, many people revolted in heart against all religion, but hypocritically concealed their convictions. For their profit and success in the life struggle made this politic; thus the ignorant and dependent still remained as accessories to this mischievous religion.

10. Physiologically, flesh diet had made man foul from the sole of his feet to the crown of his head. Nearly all people had some ailments, as weak lungs, back, throat, chest, or rheumatism, catarrh, kidney weakness, prolapsus, decayed teeth, or deaf ears. Yea, the people smelt so of flesh and blood food they could only be compared to flesh-eating animals. They smoked tobacco, and to hide their smell they anointed themselves with various perfumes.

11. What wonder was it that man was intellectually and spiritually dumb as to the object and use of his creation? How was it possible to teach such a being a new religion and a new way of living? Who but very Gods could approach his stubbornness and self-conceit with good results? Three words: religion, goodness, and cleanliness, he could not understand. True he bathed himself, but, the while, he fed himself on the carcasses of animals and fish till he was like a pesthouse. Added to his grossness he wore close-fitting clothes, retaining dead and effete exudations of his skin as a perpetual poultice of filth. Not knowing what a clean corporeal body was, how was it possible to provide him with a knowledge of a spiritual body? Public opinion had also become a great bondage. When it happened, as it sometimes did, that a person awoke to a higher inspiration in regard to man's creation, prejudice was so against him he could not embrace what he wished without becoming a target for the unclean to shoot at. And if a man should sell all he had and give to the poor he was locked up in a lunatic prison as a madman.

12. Added to all the foregoing, a most corrupt competitive system of living prevailed. An undercurrent of warfare in the struggle for life lay down in the hearts of nearly all people.

13. Now, therefore, when God, Jehovih's Son, sent down from heaven the new Bible, Oahspe, commanding the chosen to come out of Uz and be clean, and be prepared to found the Father's kingdom on earth, many heard but they understood not. They thought they were prepared already.

14. And many came forth to Shalam hastily, forgetful of God's commandment, that they were to be constitutionally grown to the new life. As it had been said of a certain drunken man, who went and signed the pledge, and straightway said, "We temperance people," he was rebuked, for he had not yet grown to be constitutionally temperate. Now with many who came to Shalam, they had merely abstained from fish and flesh for a day or a month, and said, "We Faithists!" Yet the same corrupt body and contentious spirit was with them. Their habits were dissociative instead of associative, and when some of them perceived their own condition they said: If we go back to Uz, how can we prepare ourselves for Jehovih's work? We now perceive that we should live separate from the old conditions for several years before we can be prepared for the work Jehovih hath called His chosen to accomplish

15. It was to this kind of people that the thoughts and prayers of the chosen were turned, having faith that a condition could be provided for in time to come. So that it is not of the wicked, who came to Shalam to rule all or to ruin all, and who were sent

away, that contemplation is necessary. Sufficient was the judgment that came upon them.

16. Thus it came to pass that many felt the inspiration of our Father to help bring into the world a new and better condition, but were not constitutionally prepared for a Kosmon Home. And yet, many of these were not bad people under good circumstances. Perhaps extraordinarily good.

17. Many had isolated habits, desiring houses of isolation, where they could manage in their own way.

18. Others had children of their own, which required all their time and attention. The children were undisciplined, the parents were undisciplined, and knew not what discipline meant. Now the Arc of Kosmon had commanded that the Father's kingdom should be of orphans and foundlings, and other uncared children.

19. Others who came were so desirous of isolation that they could not work harmoniously in groups, as an association.

20. Nevertheless, it finally came to pass, as stated, Jehovih provided Shalam with the chosen alone, undisturbed by the presence of other people, and the work was fully begun.

21. Many who were sent away, and some who went away of their own accord, repeated the very words that had been prophesied years before, saying: A pretty Jehovih's kingdom.

22. Some who went away, and some who were sent away, obtained considerable sums of money by fraudulent representations; some goods and money was also stolen by the departers. And the world's people said: Why do not the Kosmons [A Kosmon is a non-owner of any and every thing. A Kosmon Home is a place for caring for and raising up foundling and orphan children.] arrest them, and send them to prison; but the Kosmons said: Nay, we came not here to live in the old way, but to build a home for little children, and to teach them to be non-resistants. Whoever will steal from us, stealeth from the Father's children.

23. Nor did the Kosmons take any action against the persons mentioned; but rested entirely in faith in Jehovih.

24. Now during the time of these trials, many slanderous tales were published in regard to the Kosmons, instigated by the persons who had been sent away. And because the Kosmons indulged not in strong drink and flesh diet, they were also derided and abused by the world's people of dissipated habits. And these entered more or less into an alliance with such as had been sent away for the circulation of slander. But the Kosmons retaliated not, saying: This is to be Jehovih's kingdom, not ours; we know not what is for the best in the long run. We suffer Him to manage these things in His own way. We are here to work, and to do what good we can, nor do we lament for anything that occurreth.

25. Now, then, of Levitica, which was sprung from what had happened in first founding Shalam. And as the latter was for unprotected and small children, their teachers and nurses, so was the former for adults, single and married, with their own children, and especially such as desired to live in isolated houses, and to work and to manage in their own way.

26. The Kosmons were strictly non-owners, as the name signifieth, whilst the Leviticans were non-owners of land and houses, but owners of household goods and other property. This, then, was the beginning of that doctrine, non-ownership of land by an individual, yet all these people were Faithists in fact.

CHAPTER II.

OF GRATIYUS.

THE PRAYER OF THE KOSMONS, AND THE ANSWER FROM HEAVEN.

1. All honor and glory to Thee, Jehovih, Creator and Dispenser, worlds without number. Thou art ever present, and mindful of such as serve Thee for righteousness' sake. Hear us, O Father! Thou hast commanded Thy chosen to come forth out of the world, where they may serve Thee by helping to raise up a new race, who may be taught how to live in plenty and peace. Now behold thy servants stand up before Thee in all holy works.

2. Behold, O Father, we have gathered together Thy little children, and allotted teachers and guardians to them, after the command of Thy Holy Arc. In which Thou hast blest us and them, for which we sing in Thy praise, and return thanks unto Thee.

3. But, behold, O Jehovih, the voice of many people cometh unto us, saying: I cannot come to Shalam, for I have children of my own. I am also bound in duty to my kindred, who are in need of my help. I have old habits to which I am bound, nor am I constitutionally grown up to live the life of the holy ones in Shalam, where ye live without animal food, even milk and butter, and eat not after noon; where ye speak not on personal matters, but strive to live after the manner of the adepts of the East, without idle gossip and trifling conversation. Now, hear me, O my brethren, for I worship not any God born of woman, but Jehovih alone. My surrounding in the world will not permit me to live in peace under reformed habits of dress, diet, and religion. In my neighborhood I am mocked and made as a target for the low and depraved. Nor can I do the little good I am inspired to do. As well clothe a pig with a lace gown, as preach a life of purity to these people. A new method of life is necessary. The competitive system must be abandoned. To help adults or try and elevate them is fruitless. The only good that I can perceive must come through the education of the young into a new mode of life. Now, therefore, O my beloved, tell me in what way I can lend a hand to so holy a work as that to which ye have committed your lives and fortunes? And may Jehovih's blessing rest upon you and His little children.

4. The Kosmons prayed: Now tell us, O Father, how shall we answer them? A way surely can be made for all Thy people!

5. Es, daughter of Jehovih, said: The light of the Father fell upon His people, and His blessing came also. For it came to pass that much land fell into the possession of the children, and when Shalam was portioned off, behold there was still left more than was possible to till in that day. All of this land was called Children's Land from that time onward. It was deeded to children in trust forever, and never could be sold to deprive them of an inheritance. The Kosmons decided to open and provide the settlement of this adjoining land by Faithists suited to the work. The wisdom grown out of these deliberations, being of Jehovih, was called Gratiyus, being the Es thereof.

CHAPTER III.

THE CALL OF GRATIYUS.

1. These are the words of Gratiyus. To the Faithists in Jehovih in all parts of the worlds: Hear me, O my brethren, and be willing to consider the light of our Father, come from

what source it may. The things of this era are not to be judged with the judgment which was suited to ages past. Be alive to the condition of the world as it now is. The inefficiency of governments and religions now existing are known to all learned people. Things are not now as in the olden times.

2. The time was when kings, emperors, pashas, and other rulers owned the people, and the people revolted not, nor knew they were entitled to any other privileges. And in times after that, even private citizens owned and possessed their fellow-men, bought and sold them at pleasure. And the slaves knew not that they were entitled to any other privileges.

3. But the doctrine finally obtained that man could not own and possess his fellow-man. And the uprising of the people gave liberty to man the world over.

4. Now is come a new doctrine also, which is that no man can own and possess land for his own individual use or profit, and certainly not for anyone else. That a greater liberty to man must extend, so he who will cultivate and use the land, shall have the use thereof. For it is now seen that great estates of land are lying waste and deserted, even whilst multitudes of people have no place to live upon. This is a great injustice. Jehovih is just. Let none thwart Him in the progress of man towards universal liberty.

5. Land is a natural inheritance for whomsoever will cultivate and use it, and to the extent thereof. No man shall countermand the Almighty!

6. Poor people shall not be forced to live in the cities because a few capitalists deprive them of homesteads in the country. For at present they are compelled to work for wages instead of working for themselves, glutting the market with laborers.

7. Nor shall the young man and the young woman fear to marry, lest they bring forth offspring with no place or home to dwell on. But they shall fulfill according to the inspiration of Jehovih, that moveth them to fulfill accordingly as He made them. To prevent the manifestation of this desire, behold great crimes have come into the world.

8. Nor shall farms be large and half tilled, as at present, with the people far apart, and no advantages like the people of the cities. But a new condition, with attractions and privileges, shall be added to the inhabitants of the country.

9. Nor shall young men and women, as at present, flee away from the country to the cities because their highest faculties are unappeased. But a new way of living shall be opened for them in the country for a higher and holier development. And the cares and fears of making a living shall pass away from them.

10. Nor shall mothers and fathers horde up money for their children, lest they should come to want; for a way is now opened for the children, yea, even for the yet unborn also.

11. The sons and daughters of the virtuous and good shall not be obliged, on coming to maturity, to migrate to some far off country to seek some way of living. But they may remain in their own neighborhood as a comfort to their aged parents. Nor shall young men rove around about in the cities, or over the world, looking for some employment, and find none. Nor the father say: "I know not what to put my son at."

12. Nor shall the land be given over as an inheritance to swine and beef, to feed the corrupt appetites of a polluted people. Nor shall man bestow, as at present, half his labor on the animal world, to the neglect of millions of people who have no place to live, and whose children cry out for bread.

13. Let no man imagine his own ideas of country life are correct. For he judgeth by what he hath seen, which are the old conditions, and which are all to be put away.

14. For the foundation in Children's Land is a new order and a new method of cultivating and subduing the earth, providing for the spiritual man as well as the corporeal man.

15. Let whosoever worshippeth Jehovih, and desireth to do good to His children, come.

16. Let all who are Samgwans and Sargwans, come.*

17. Let all who desire to take part in founding a world where poverty shall not come, and where all can do some good to help Jehovih's children, come. For all children are created alive by Him and are His. Before Him all are legitimate.

18. Unto all such, here are homes without money and without price. Come, O ye with faith in Jehovih, and inherit them.

19. But let not these come who worship any Lord, God, or Savior born of woman.

20. Let not these come who are disbelievers in the All Person, Jehovih.

21. Let not these come who eat fish or flesh, or drink or use stimulants and narcotics for exhilarating effects.

22. Let not these come who are not willing to support themselves.

23. Let not these come, the lawyer, doctor, preacher, and politician, who desire to live by their wits.

24. Let not these come who desire somebody else to support them.

25. Nor is here any distinction as to race or color, nor is here the abode of such as to desire to make money for money's sake.

The Philosophical Association in Shalam adopted from the Panic language the following words, in place of the words vegetarian, frugiverant, omnivorant, etc., to wit:

    1. *Eskgwa.* Fruits and nuts high growing.

    2. *Tekgwa.* Fruits, nuts high growing, annual herbs and their fruits.

    3. *Samgwa.* Fruits, nuts of all kinds, vegetables, roots, herbs of all kinds.

    4. *Sargwa.* Fruits, nuts of all kinds, vegetables, roots, herbs of all kinds, milk, butter, eggs, and cheese. Therefore the Kosmons of Shalam are Samgwans, and the Leviticans are Sargwans.

    5. *Unhgwa.* Omnivorous.

CHAPTER IV.
THE CALLING OF LEVITICA.

1. When the call of Gratiyus was sent abroad, many people came to Children's Land, and when they assembled together, they desired to learn more of the proposed life.

2. Gratiyus said: This is called Levitica, because it lieth between Shalam and the world's people. To build here a village and beautify it so all may be happy, is this not fulfilling a life in this world? And if man fulfill in the highest in this world, will he not be best prepared for the next? Where the greatest number of people can live together in peace, plenty, and happiness on the smallest piece of land is the highest civilization.

3. Whosoever desireth a house, let it be given him or her, and the land also shall be portioned to each and every one according to his or her capacity to cultivate and use it. But no more land shall be given to any one than he or she can cultivate or use. And the same shall be for life. But after death the trustees shall give it to another, and it shall be for that one during life also. For in that manner are all these lands held.

4. Whosoever desireth cattle for milk, let him have them, and a place for the cattle also.

But he shall not sell or dispose of the males to anybody to be slain for food. But where the males, as asses, oxen, or wool goats can be used, and not killed for food, suffer the people to keep them.

5. A common store-house for buying and selling goods shall be maintained, so that all who wish may obtain primary prices.

6. But no one shall keep a store for the sale of goods, or for buying goods, thereby living out of the profits.

7. Nor shall any lawyer, doctor, or preacher, or other professional person receive money or goods for his professional service. But a day's work for any one of these shall be equivalent to, and no more than a day's work at any labor. But for a preacher, as in preaching sermons, or marrying people, or saying service for the dead, no wages or pay shall be given.

8. Where certain men engage in some manufacture together, no wages shall be given, but the result of their production shall be according to the labor of each and all, and so divided.

9. Each and every household shall be under the dominion of the person or persons who dwell therein.

10. General schools shall be maintained for children, by an universal contribution in proportion to their incomes. But manual instruction shall be given to both boys and girls without regard to sex, in the various trades and occupations carried on in Levitica. All householders, even one for each occupied house, shall be entitled to one vote, without regard to sex.

11. Two worlds are bestowed by Jehovih, the adult world and the world of children under five years. The former is for man, the latter for woman, nor is one glory greater than the other. Men and women are in accord with Jehovih in proportion as they adapt themselves to their respective places.

12. The people desired to know about the government. Gratiyus said:

13. Where age is respected, discipline is esteemed. A young officer breedeth defiance. Respect to fathers and mothers, and to the aged, hath marked the highest and best civilizations. The want of such respect leadeth in the way of anarchy, dissipation, and misery. Therefore, the oldest inhabitant of the village shall be chief, and he shall be the executor of the majority voice. But where there are more than ten families, another chief shall be added for them, who shall be the second oldest inhabitant. And the first chief shall be called C'Chief. Each and all chiefs shall be officers for life if they choose, and if they comply with the rules of the village and the decrees of Tae.

14. And since it is an advantage to the virtue and good behavior of the people of one settlement to know one another, let not Levitica ever contain more than one thousand people.

CHAPTER V.
LAWS OF LEVITICA.

1. When the people saw the way to happy homes they remembered Jehovih, and returned thanks to him, because He had brought them out of cities of evil, and thus bestowed them.

2. With one voice they added: Shall we not manifest our gratitude for this new mode of

life, and of receiving homes without money or price, by extending a like benefit unto others? Let this be done: create a Children's Fund to be for ever.

3. And we will all pay into said fund one-tenth of our earnings, and the money shall go for the benefit of orphans, foundlings, and other little children, and for purchasing more land for children's sake. And all such lands shall be open for the Faithists and their children for ever.

4. To this the people universally agreed.

5. So the people entered into such a compact with one another, even as it remaineth to this day.

6. Gratiyus said unto them: A great evil existeth amongst the world's people--that is lawsuits, a greater tyranny and curse on the people than was ever exercised by any king or emperor in all the world. Amongst them any person can bring a suit at law, and inflict great hardships on a defendant without himself being at much expense, whilst the defendant is literally robbed and without any redress. For which reason the courts are used as a sort of blackmail for evil disposed people. See to it, O my brethren, that ye be circumspect in this. Make it a law amongst you that whoever bringeth a lawsuit must first pledge all he hath to the village, and if he lose the suit, then shall he forfeit his possessions and depart out of the place. But if he win the suit, then shall the one losing it depart out of Levitica. But in no case shall anyone bring a suit for wages or for debt of any kind. But if a man pay not his debts and agreements, a suit may be brought against him to make him leave the place, and if it be proved against him in more than one violation, then shall he depart away. But if a person complain against another, saying he oweth him money, or is in debt to him, then the man so complaining shall bring suit with like liabilities. For ye shall guard yourselves against evil and slanderous remarks made about one another.

7. Make these compacts in writing with all people who come amongst you, and have them sign them also.

8. Make it a law that ye shall settle all matters, if possible by arbitration before one of the chiefs, or before a representative of the Tae, the parties agreeing how many persons shall sit in arbitration, remembering that before Jehovih no contention should exist as to mortal things desired; and that to desire this or that of any one is not of Jehovih.

9. If any Levitican employ an Uzian he shall pay the wages of the Uzian, and also pay a like sum into the Children's Fund, but in no case shall an Uzian reside or dwell on Children's Land. And if any one slandereth another, the chief shall call a vote of the people of the village, and if more than half the people vote that the slander has been committed, then shall the slanderer depart out of the place, forfeiting all he hath.

10. Man-made laws are to guard against the evil which hath come into the world. In this, the Kosmon era, man must learn how to live without man-made laws. The virtuous and good have nothing to do in such matters in a place like this, but the opposite of this was the case in the world; for there they were even subject to more trials and tribulations than were the vicious.

11. Leave no place for politicians, lawyers, priests, and preachers, for these are more to be guarded against than thieves and robbers. Show less admiration for talent, but more for goodness of heart.

12. In a short time the Leviticans shall demonstrate to whom the most love and

admiration should belong.

13. Encourage the worship of Jehovih, and by your behavior teach the children that His eye is ever upon them, and that His ear heareth all; moreover that all deeds done in the mortal body leave their imprint on the spiritual body for ever.

CHAPTER VI.
THE BEAUTY OF THE NEW LIFE.

1. Es said: The founding of Levitica was like the beginning of a new world in fact.

2. The new method of living soon demonstrated that man needed not more than a tenth the amount of land as in the old way.

3. Dispensing with animals lessened the amount of labor nearly one-half. Dispensing with professional people and non-producers, and, moreover, all the people being producers, soon showed more prosperity and comfort than the people had ever before enjoyed.

4. And though the people were permitted to dress as they chose, yet the freedom and adaptation to the climate gave them health and buoyancy of spirits in the new costumes, such as could not be found in all the world beside.

5. The surety of food, clothes, and home comforts, gave them peace of mind, so that in a short time the care-worn expression, so painfully manifest in the Uzians was no more to be seen.

6. It was saying to the world: What need have we of riches? That happiness which Jehovih giveth to the rich He also giveth to us.

7. It was saying to Jehovih: Blessed is the sunshine; blessed is the mantle of night; blessed is quietness of spirit, for it knoweth no rent; blessed the songs of the birds and the romping and mirth of the children; blessed the security of old age; blessed are all Thy creations, O Jehovih!

8. The presence of all nationalities caused the children to make no distinction as to race or color, and they mingled together full of glee and gentleness.

9. The children grew not like other children as in the world at large; were not sulky and morose; nor sulky and secretive; nor self-conceited; nor seclusive; and with ideas of caste; nor awkward and lonely; but were gay and lively, yet respectful toward one another, and toward their elders.

10. Their advantage for manual instruction enabled even those who were quite young to work marvelously expertly at all kinds of vocations.

11. The entire freedom of the adults to work at whatever they choose, and to be communal or co-operative, or even isolated, gave them an opportunity to develop their talents as Jehovih had created them.

12. Some of the Leviticans worked for themselves, paying into the children's fund one-tenth of their earnings; some paid in all over and above their living. A few worked in Shalam, receiving merely their food, clothes, and necessary expenses. Some paid in their tenth in labor; some paid it in produce; and some paid it in money.

13. It soon came to pass that the Chiefs and C'Chief had little or nothing to do; such a thing as a government was scarcely more than a name. Everyone attended to his own business, and order and discipline reigned.

14. Soon the place became a place of beauty and comfort. Its gardens, walks, and places

of amusement abounded as never before in a village. The song of women and children and the mirth of men made Levitica seem as a place of holidays.

15. The one religion, to worship Jehovih and do good unto others, obliterated all arguments and discussions on such a subject. The silly gossips of atonement and free will, so disgusting in the world, found no place in Levitica.

CHAPTER VII.
THE LIFE OF A KOSMON.

1. It soon came to pass that the name of Levitica spread far and wide, and many people pleaded to be admitted for charity's sake.

2. To this it was answered unto them: If ye live the lives of a Faithist ye can come. To put away all uncleanliness, and to be upright before Jehovih, is the foundation whereon we build. But, remember, we do not these things for charity's sake but to develop a new way of living, and a higher race of people.

3. Others wrote, asking: Cannot I do missionary work where I am in the world for your benefit? And it was answered them: The time of missionary work with adults is past and gone.

4. They said: To provide the young with good surroundings, and comforts, and give them a moral education is the foundation of the Father's kingdom. These things cannot be done in the world, but a separate place must be provided.

5. To practice the covenants of Emethachavah; to slander not, nor practice the evil word; to do good unto others; to worship one All Person, Who is ever present, but no God, Lord, or Savior born of woman; to engage not in war, nor make, use, or sell war implements; to not use unclean food, but to bathe and be clean in body and spirit, thinking no evil of any man, woman, or child, with liberty of dress and thought unto all for righteousness sake, these are the works of a Faithist.

6. Thus was established Levitica; and it soon became conspicuous as a village of people who understood the meaning of the words salvation and religion.

CHAPTER VIII.
OF WOMAN'S WORLD.

1. The pride and glory of Levitica was more in woman's department than in any other opening that had ever been made for her.

2. With the world's people women had been led astray in regard to what ought to be done to elevate mankind and bring about a higher civilization. She, too, like other philosophers, had looked for some means of educating and raising up adults, and she hoped with her influence in public affairs a better result would manifest. But, alas, no. Being negative, the public place brought her down, instead of her helping others up. For with increasing fluency in argument and words her gentleness lost its force, and her words were as impotent as man's.

3. In Levitica a new field was open for her; a new kind of education. For as heretofore the word education meant book-learning merely, it now extended to practical manifestations of manual and moral behavior.

4. Prior to the age at which children here went to public school, they were formed in classes of three or more, even up to ten in a class, where they practiced objective lessons. Even the teaching of maxims for virtuous instruction in religious truths was done by signs, objects, and illustrations.

5. The teachers did not after the manner of the teachers in the world, dwelling and being with the children for a few hours only, and by making them repeat certain words, or by addressing them on their duties and obedience. But these teachers lived with their classes from early rising in the morning till they were put to bed at night; making themselves as one with the children in the plays and instructions, explaining such things as self-denial in the practice that came up before them, the non-ownership of everything; the doing to one another as one would be done by, selfishness and unselfishness, evil and good words and accusations; talking on personal matters, showing how anger and evil grow out of the same; the saying of pleasant things, showing how love is returned therefore; the presence of Jehovih with all children; the growth of the spirit, so it shall be strong on its road of everlasting life; teaching them of the life and resurrection of the great law-givers, Chine, Brahma, Capilla, Zarathrusta, Sakaya, Joshu, and others; teaching them spirit intercourse, and the difference betwixt spirits of the first and the second resurrection; teaching them of the dominion and homes of the Gods and Lords and other high angels; and, above all, making it plain to them who is Jehovih, the Creator, Who is over all.

6. Maxims suited to these and similar truths were formed by the teachers, and the answers were given sometimes in signs and gestures, and sometimes in both signs and words also. And the teachers took part therein, so that even mere babes played the parts of teachers in these most high and holy doctrines.

7. These small classes were numerous, and, of course, the teachers numerous also. And the teachers often conferred with one another, and made many inventions pertaining to their work. Here was manifest the craft and power of woman to bring a great good into the world, such as had never been before. They said: What care we for the affairs of the adult world. In a few years they will all be dead. Then will our little ones be the adults of a higher civilization; and it was so.

8. Added to the maxims were numerous marches, parades, and echo singing.

9. At the age of five years, and even less, the following results manifested:--A little boy being asked what was meant by self-denial, went and gave his toys to the others, and then sat down contented. Being asked if he did not wish to have them back again, said: "The triumph over selfishness is not to want a thing; but is it right to make a child talk about itself, as to whether it wishes this or that? All things are Jehovih's, and loaned but for a season."

10. Another boy being asked what was the best way to establish justice, answered: "For every one to give up all their wants." When asked what is the greatest cause of contention amongst men, answered: "The strife for earthly things. It is the animal man in ascendancy over the spiritual man. Flesh-eaters in the world are great contenders, I am told."

11. A little girl being asked what is the great cause of quarrels, pointed to her tongue, and then said: "With the tongue words are made. If quarrelers will let it rest, peace will result." Another girl being asked the meaning of doing to others as we desire others to do unto us, went and assisted one of her playmates to rise up. Then she said: "As we lift others up, so will our Heavenly Father lift us up." When asked what she meant by our

Heavenly Father lifting us up, she said: "To help us above all bondage in thought and desire, so we shall have higher happiness." Another girl being asked what was the best way to overcome selfishness in others, shut her eyes and stopped her ears for a moment, then said: "Answer selfishness by unselfishness, neither seeing or hearing the faults of others." A little boy was asked what is the worst of all conversation, answered: "Personal. When we speak evilly of any one, even behind their backs, the spirits of the dead go tell it to his soul, and he feeleth it, though he heard it not."

12. A four-year-old-girl being asked of what use is life to any one, answered, clapping her hands: "To be happy and rejoice in Jehovih and His beautiful creations." She was then asked why there is so much unhappiness in the world, she said: "People know not how to live as they ought." Another girl said: "They have not been taught how to make themselves happy." Still another one said: "They want the wrong things. Spiritual desires are unknown to them."

13. A four-year-old being asked what should be the highest consideration of man in regard to himself, answered: "To forget himself and all selfish things in striving to help others." He was then asked why people complain so much. He said: "To complain of one's lot is to acknowledge one's weakness of spirit."

14. But it is scarcely possible to describe an examination of one of these classes of mere babes. Often their answers were by signs and pantomimes, not possible to be written. The ingenuity of the teachers in thus construing maxims and religious training into pastimes and recreations so full of delight was a new field of education. With the utmost reverence did the little creatures pronounce the name Jehovih, and place their hands on their hearts, signifying His love and goodness. Every attitude was graceful and dignified. Yet amidst it all a vein of mirth and confidence in the Almighty was to be seen, expressive of love on their part also.

15. Their eyes were quickened by various devices. One was a large screen with a hole or doorway in the center. Behind this screen was a traveling panorama. On the face of the panorama were pinned printed objects, as dogs, cats, birds, or horses, and so on. These objects were in groups of three or more. Whilst the panorama moved past the hole in the curtain or screen, the little ones were to strive how many things they could distinguish. The objects were changed daily, so the children were obliged to observe the new arrangement every day. Some of the children could thus see and describe half a dozen objects at a mere glance. But in older classes some of the children could see and describe twenty objects discerned at one glance. In fact, the quickness of the sight of these babes was such as no one not having seen them could believe possible.

16. The memory of the children was strengthened by questioning them as to what was on the screen the previous day.

17. Besides the screen and panorama, they had large reels covered with cloth, on which objects were pinned also. The reel was then set in motion, turning rapidly, and the curtain raised. The children instantly made traverse motions of their fingers before their eyes, to change the rays of light, and thus decipher the objects on the reel, though it ran so swiftly that one not educated in it could scarcely distinguish any one object.

18. Their hearing was educated by beginning behind a screen, also striking first on an anvil or other iron, then on a piece of wood, then on a piece of cloth, then on the floor, and inducing the children to tell what was struck. After that, two objects were struck at

the same time, and again the children taught to tell what the two objects were. Then three objects were struck at the same time; then four, then five, then six, and so on, until it was really marvellous how quickly these young ears could detect every object struck. But a greater feat followed when the classes were older. A second teacher would read some very interesting story to the children whilst the objects were being struck. Then afterwards the children would relate the story that had been read, and also tell the objects struck the while. Then again, whilst another exhibition of reading and striking was going on, a third teacher came in and related some outside occurrence, and asked for some order to be executed. After the piece was thus read, the children would relate it, and tell the objects struck and the words and mission of the third teacher.

19. Then a teacher took a long, thin blade of steel behind the curtain, and balanced it, and whilst thus balanced, struck it with a hammer three or four times, till the children had it well fixed in mind. Then the teacher moved the blade from its axis nearer one end, and struck it again; and now asked the children how far, proportionately to its length, she had moved it; and they would tell by the sound alone. Next she had the children sing the sound note of the blade when balanced, and then she told them to strike up half an octave, the which they did. Then she called in one of the children, and said: Now move the blade so it will make half an octave sound, and the child moved it correctly according to its length.

20. Thus these little ones learned the philosophy of sound, and its measurement by the ear, whilst they were mere babies, and it was but an amusement and pastime full of delight.

21. In dancing the same remarkable expertness was displayed. Instead of merely the two or three dozen dances known to the world, these little ones were taught more than an hundred, and their ease and lightness was more like some dream of fairies than of mortal children.

22. The children's minds were thus constantly diverted, surprised, quickened, and filled with delight, but instead of having one teacher, as they do in the world for a dozen or more children, and drilling them monotonously through books and primers, they had in Levitica from one to three teachers for every group of children, or nearly half as many teachers as children; and these teachers were constantly on duty, inventing and devising an everlasting change and edification; for the object was to raise up a new race of a higher and purer order.

23. So that in fact from the time of waking in the morning till time to go to bed at night there was constant playing, singing, dancing, marching, swimming, praying, or training on the blackboard or behind the screens, and every day was different from every other day.

24. And when night came and the children had returned thanks to Jehovih for their creation, and covenanted themselves to be worthy before Him at all times, they quickly dropped to sleep, but even in their prayers they prayed not after the manner of the world's people, for ever asking for something, but they were taught that they must for ever offer something to Him and to His created beings, and be faithful in their covenants.

25. Here, then, was that new world for woman to apply herself accordingly as she had been created; and, strange enough, a short time in Levitica caused the place to be clear of that class that cried out so much in the world for the privilege of doing man's work. Yea,

even some of that class who come thither with such ideas, forsook their former inclinations when they saw the new way open, and they threw aside their bound up clothing, and dressed themselves in liberty, and went to work so entirely unlike what they had formerly been that one would hardly realize they were the same women. And, what was more, her talent in this direction soon showed what the next creation of Leviticans would be.

26. Thus, in a short time, in Levitica, there was no clamor for woman's rights or about her wrongs. Her new world was made plain before her, and she loved it, and embraced it naturally.

27. Her devices for moral and spiritual training of small children was thus unlimited, but at the age of five to seven years the children passed into the men's world, men's teaching, save in exceptions where women were assistants.

28. But to be a man teacher in Levitica was not like being a teacher in the schools of the world. To understand this, it must be borne in mind that the education of the children was so directed that the spiritual must ever transcend the intellectual.

29. In the primaries, woman had taught the children to use their fingers quickly and expertly, to use their eyes quickly, to hear and distinguish sounds clearly and quickly. In fact, she had not only sharpened them intellectually, but grounded them in spiritual and moral truths.

30. The men teachers had to begin where woman left off. They had to teach the children to apply their hands usefully. If at men's trade, then under a man assistant; but if at a woman's occupation, then under a woman assistant. Their quickened eyes, which had seen toys on the screen, now were turned to numeral and to various figures in geometry, also on the screens, and to multiply and add, and so on, with rapidity. Their ears, so well trained to hammers behind the screens, were now to be trained to sounds in music, also behind the screens, the scales, naturals, sharps, and flats, then to a number of sounds struck at one time. So that in a little practice one might strike ten notes on an instrument at one time, and the pupils would call every one by name. Now, they had in the world what was called lightning, phenomenal, mathematical, calculators; but here the ordinary children in a school could do the same things; for Jehovih hath from time to time raised up in the world phenomenal people to demonstrate what was possible for man. And even so was it with music. The so-called phenomenal musicians in the world were now equaled by even little children in Levitica. Here the teachers taught drawing and painting by new methods, ten times swifter than in the old way. The children illustrated the rise and fall of nations; the dark and light periods in the cycles of time; and laid the foundation of prophesy, to be taught in the next higher classes. Illustrations of light and magnetism were displayed before the pupils, and formed a pastime, even whilst they were instructive. These teachers had numerous assistants, nothing being left undone that would develop the children spiritually and intellectually; for it was really the first and chief aim of Leviticans to provide the next generation far in advance of anything that had ever before been on the earth. So, then, it was no trifling matter to find teachers competent to teach in Levitica.

31. Another unfortunate condition developed, which was that the world's people had been wrongly educated in regard to light and heat coming from the sun, and in regard to terrestrial magnetism and the motion of the heavenly bodies. After the revelation in

Oahspe, it was found that new books bearing on these subjects were necessary. And in these respects many so-called learned people who came to Levitica offering themselves as teachers were unprepared and uneducated for the work.

32. Nevertheless, Jehovih in time raised up such as were required.

33. In the idolatrous religion of Asia, Europe, and America, the children were early taught learning their signs, ceremonies, bowings before images, explaining their doctrines, sacred books, swords, and weapons of death. For the Faithists are not sectarians, nor did they from the first oppose or contend with any one of these great sects, as Brahmanism, Buddhism, and Christianity, but rather, as one might say vulgarly, swallow up all the religions in the world.

34. Such, then, was the pride and glory of Levitica. The people proved that only a small parcel of ground was necessary for existence, and that only a small amount of labour was necessary, and that much more time could be given to the education of children and developing a higher civilization. And such was soon made a demonstratable fact before all the world. It was a new religion and a new way of living.

35. And it came to pass that many men and women in the world, who had longed for some higher life, but being now old and unable to take part in the labour thereof, left their money to buy more land and to extend the new civilization. And it was done.

36. And the land thus bought was locked up for children, that it might never be sold, but forever kept to extend the Father's Kingdom.

37. And the Kosmon homes multiplied, and villages like unto Levitica multiplied also, and thousands and thousands of little children were brought out of the cities of Uz, and educated and provided with homes.

38. Thus did Jehovih, Who created all people alive, and Who is Father over all, bring a new blessing into the world, and He alone became the All One glorified over all the world.

END OF THE BOOK OF GRATIYUS.

BOOK OF OURANOTHEN.

CHAPTER I.

1. These are the words of Ouranothen: By Thy Light and Dominion, O Jehovih, peace and goodwill be unto all men, with faith in Thee, and forbearance toward one another for thy glory. Amen.

2. I come not to abridge liberty, but to give more unto you, with love and wisdom, that the resurrection of men be established on earth as it is in heaven.

3. Him that ye worship under diverse names, placing Him afar off, declare I unto you His actual presence. And accord to you much praise and thanks wherein ye worship in truth, fulfilling His commandments, acknowledging there is but one God, even Jehovih.

4. Whether ye say, Brahma, Brahma, or Buddha, Buddha, or Christ, Christ, doing so in reverence to the Almighty, our Creator, practicing good works with all your wisdom and strength--therein do I proclaim your good deeds in heaven.

5. For all of these are the Father's buildings, to bring His children into ultimate resurrection, for joy and glory within His kingdoms.

6. Therefore, I come not to take from you any of your Gods or Saviors, nor to abridge your field of righteousness, but rather to show you a greater glory in comprehending all of them in the plan of the Almighty, to reach the different peoples in all parts of the earth.

7. Pleading with you to be charitable to one another, and more comprehensive in your judgment, putting away egotism in professing amongst yourselves that such of you alone were the favored of Jehovih.

8. First, then His Living Presence declare I unto you: that He is now, always was, and ever shall be present in all places, worlds without end.

9. Doing by virtue of His Presence; quickening into life, and moving all things onward to a wise and definite purpose.

10. Whose Presence is everywhere and boundless.

11. That all the living are His sons and daughters.

12. That none are as orphans, but possessed of a Father, part and parcel of your flesh and spirit, even the Creator,

13. Into Whose harmony ye are as keys to one instrument, with Whom ye can become as one, by practicing His commandments;

14. That herein only is there peace and happiness to any man on earth or angel in heaven.

15. Second: this I also declare unto you, that wherein ye have put the Father afar off, saying such as: There is a divine law; there is a natural law, ye comprehend not the Living Presence of Jehovih, but profane Him and His works.

16. For there is no divine law, nor is there a natural law!

17. But all good things are accomplished by the living presence of the Creator;

18. Things commonly called evil being done by striving to go against Him.

19. Third, that Jehovih hath not finished His creations and retired from His works; that wherein ye have said: He tired, or He rested from His works, ye have suffered yourselves to fall, through the errors of language, into profanation of the Almighty.

20. For He is also Master over all weariness, and is His own everlasting rest and unrest, beyond the comprehension of mortals and angels.

21. For He is forever bringing together, and forever dissolving and dissipating, worlds without number.

22. Illimitable in Soul and Spirit, forever quickening into life from His own parts, without loss or waste, or lack of space, and without hindrance.

23. Fourth, that Jehovih is the soul of all, and that ye are as independent atoms of His Person.

24. Wherein then shall man say: Behold, my people are the chosen of the Almighty! He hath singled out my people to go forth and redeem the world!

25. I proclaim all people His People; and I say also, go forth and redeem the world. But not with words only, nor by the sword, nor by armies of destroyers but by peace and love, and providing remedies for the poor, the afflicted, the helpless and distressed.

CHAPTER II.

1. These are the words of Ouranothen: In the name of Jehovih, peace and love unto the angels and mortals of earth.

2. Because it hath been demonstrated unto you that the knowledge of man is but his own consciousness of the records that have been written on his body and spirit, so let it be testimony that the affairs of heaven and earth are registered everlastingly on the soul of man.

3. Whether by his own behavior or indulgence, or by the places of his resort, so is he the book of his own dominion in the hands of Jehovih, or else against Him.

4. Which shall also be testimony that the eye of the Father is ever upon all men, both in this world and the next.

5. For which reason no man shall say: God cut him off, meaning Jehovih turned away from the evil man,

6. Which is a profanation against the Father. For He turneth not away, nor cutteth He off any man.

7. Nevertheless many cut themselves off by denying Him and by not obeying His commandments.

8. And they bring darkness and misery upon themselves; and they cry out: Where is the justice of God, that He afflicteth me? or why cometh He not to those that are in distress?

9. And when they are in darkness, they marry and bring forth in darkness and with pre-disposition to misery and death;

10. For which reason it was said of old that the sins of a man are visited on the third and fourth generations of those that come after.

11. And then cryeth out the infidel: Behold the misery of the creatures of God!

12. But I say unto you, all these things were revealed long since, and ye are the testimonies of those that deny the wisdom and glory of Jehovih, your God.

13. What then is the register of the earth? Where shall the Father find an exemplary people?

14. Where ye love your neighbors as yourselves, practicing virtue and exaltation in righteousness above all else?

15. For I say unto you, they have cunningly interpreted the revelations of heaven so as to open the door to unrighteous teaching.

16. By saying such and such things are done by divine law instead of being done by the actual presence of the Creator,

17. Persuading themselves that their God had gone away, leaving certain laws to carry on His works.

18. And the ungodly interpreted them, that since God had gone afar off, He saw not the behavior of men, nor registered their deeds in truth as done in the body.

19. For they have been thus led to believe that sin and evil deeds are hid away, and not man, nor angels, nor God knoweth they have been done.

20. And they have grown up in disbelief, ignoring the person of the Almighty, even though the powers of life and death stand before them,

21. Being addicted to crimes and misdemeanors against one another, in no fear of God the Father, and only restrained by the laws and prisons of man.

22. Whom, therefore, ye ignorantly worship as being afar off, declare I unto you,

23. And that His eye is ever upon you; and that ye are a perpetual register of both the good and evil that ye practice toward one another and in the Father.

24. This is the foundation on which I proclaim Jehovih's kingdom on earth. Without this there is no resurrection, either in this world or the next.

25. And as much as ye establish this doctrine in the understanding of the young, so will ye have laid the corner-stone for the edifice of Jehovih, your Creator.

26. To which end, ye shall put away all such terms as DIVINE LAW and NATURAL LAW,

27. And henceforth teach them of the Living I AM, the JEHOVIH, Who is over all and within all His works, doing by virtue of His presence, call Him Lord or God as ye may.

CHAPTER III.

1. These are the words of Ouranothen: By the power and wisdom of Jehovih in me, I salute you in peace, love and reconciliation with the Father,

2. To make you magnanimous and of comprehensive judgment in discerning the dominion of Jehovih;

3. That ye be not puffed up with your knowledge of the ancient prophets and revelators of God, the Father, saying: His words were revealed of old; the ancient revelations were final.

4. Jehovih is the same today, yesterday and forever. His voice and His hands are with you; He changeth not as the wind bloweth.

5. Open your understanding to the Living Present, the I Am, in remembrance of the olden times, when the prophets of God were denied also;

6. For the same things come in every cycle in the travel of the world. And the same doctrines are revealed, embracing the same exalted commandments, proclaiming the actual presence of the Creator unto all men.

7. But they who love not Him with all their hearts and souls, and their neighbors as themselves, cry out: We will not have this; let us crucify him!

8. Now, behold, Jehovih's season is manifest amongst all nations and peoples. Do they not cry out against the skepticism of man? And are not their doctrines trembling on their foundation?

9. The enthusiasm they put forth is but for a day; with the death of the preacher his church becometh as the house of a stranger,

10. For they worship not the Father, but bow down before the oratory of man.

11. Wherefore in this day I say unto you the time is greater than of old, for the cycle embraceth the whole earth, becoming as one people around about it; so is the light of Jehovih being manifest amongst all nations and peoples.

12. And the skepticism and breaking to pieces in one region of the earth is but a type of the same manifestations in the others.

13. Think not then, with the circumscribing of the earth, Jehovih is not sufficient unto a universal doctrine, adapted to all the inhabitants of the earth.

14. For He plieth His angel hosts according to the work He hath at hand.

15. Raising up one man to one work, and another man to another work; appropriating all people to building His kingdom.

16. And He sendeth His angels to man to give him signs and omens; and man saith: I feel it coming; a new advent is at hand.

17. Of which matters the earth is stored with history,

18. As when in Egypt, in the great kingdom, the Pharaohs had fortified themselves with learning, and with monuments designed by man to be everlasting.

19. And both, angels of darkness, and angels of light, descended upon that land, and the people were overwhelmed with miracles and necromancy.

20. And the Father called unto the multitude to come out of Egypt; and as many as had faith in Him rose up and departed away from that land.

21. Then came darkness upon Egypt, and she went down to destruction. Her temples and places of great learning fell down, or became known no more.

22. Now this declare I unto you, that the same kinds of necromancy and angel manifestations appear in the beginning of every cycle.

23. For the Father suffereth even angels of darkness to appear before men to confound them in their unbelief, and to make them fearful in their unrighteous behavior.

24. And this also happeneth soon after the advent of a cycle--the angels of the second heaven come, calling sinners to repentance, and proclaiming the difference between the higher and lower heavens.

25. And such mortals as have faith in Jehovih, practicing righteousness, are led forth into a new place and holier condition. But such as heed not the voice of the angels of God, go down in darkness.

CHAPTER IV.

1. These are the words of Ouranothen: By the grace and power of the Creator, God of all peoples, faith be unto you and within you, for your own redemption.

2. First come signs and presentiments, then belief, and after that, faith, which is followed by works.

3. And this law is unto all the living, whether man, or bird, or beast, or creeping thing; there being signs and presentiments unto all the living, according to what concerneth them.

4. Behold the times of the heaven and earth are made of summers and winters unto all things: a time when the harvest of one revelation or one doctrine cometh to its ripening,

and a time afterward when it is gathered in by the Father, and is known no more.

5. To one age God bestoweth revelation on man, according to what is good for man, but when it hath fulfilled its work God gathereth it in, and bestoweth another revelation.

6. Such are the works of Jehovih, nor can man nor angels stay His Hand.

7. To Greece, and to Egypt and to India, He gave many gods. According to the necessities of the times and light of man, that man might be raised up through belief and faith, so gave He them gods and doctrines suited to them.

8. And man became tenacious of his gods, verily making idols of them, and depending on the gods and angels to accomplish, by intercession and otherwise, man's ultimate exaltation in heaven.

9. So man ceased to work out his own salvation, depending on his gods to save him, even in his crimes and blasphemy.

10. And Jehovih caused disbelievers and signs and miracles to overrun these peoples, and He raised up new prophets unto them, rebuking them for their unrighteous behavior.

11. The adherents of the past revelations rose up in might and slew the prophets of God, declaring them breakers of the laws of man.

12. Nevertheless, it came to pass with all of these peoples, their many gods went away from them, and the new revelations took root in the persecution and death of God's prophets.

13. Such are the cycles upon the earth; they are as the harvests of the Almighty, which He giveth unto the different periods of His creations.

14. Here is wisdom O man, to heed the signs of Jehovih's seasons and the march of His dominion on the earth;

15. Not suffering thyself to become bound by things of the past whilst the signs of the Almighty rise up before thee.

16. Nor judge thou the ways of God by the little that is done in a corner, nor by prejudices deep-rooted in thine own understanding, because of thy birth and surroundings.

17. But survey thou abroad over all the earth, considering what is good unto all people, as to whether the doctrines and revelations are powerful enough to abolish poverty and war and all manner of crimes amongst men.

18. This the guide thy Creator gave unto thee, that thou mightst learn to prophesy of the administration of thy God, Jehovih, being the only master of life and death (because whosoever He hath quickened into life is His, and death is His decree in His own time and way).

19. And whosoever cometh between man and his Creator, visiting death unto his brother, wageth war against his Creator.

20. Life and death are Mine, saith Jehovih.

21. Whoso then presumeth to engage in death no longer fulfilleth the righteousness of God.

22. In which sign thou shalt judge all people who engage in war, and know of a truth whether their doctrines and their gods be appropriate to establishing the Father's kingdom on earth.

23. Not suffering thyself to be blinded by their pretensions and professions of peace, but by their practice, observing if they have more faith in weapons of war and standing armies than in Jehovih.

24. This is one of the signs also, in addition to the infidelity and necromancy, wherefrom thou shalt surely prophesy that the doctrines and revelations have fulfilled their time unto mortals.

CHAPTER V.

1. These are the words of Ouranothen: In the love of God, peace and goodwill be unto you all, Amen.

2. In times past, the Almighty hath bestowed His signs and monuments and histories, whereby ye shall understand the dominion of His word.

3. Because the ancients were bound down by the doctrines and revelations of their predecessors, Jehovih suffered evil-disposed men to fall upon their libraries and destroy them.

4. And man mourned on the earth, saying the light of heaven was consumed.

5. But Jehovih comprehended what was good for man, desiring him not to be bound down to the ancients; but rather that man should be quickened to the ever present light of God.

6. For man had become like a drowning man, clinging to that which was taking him down under the water. So, only by the destruction of the ancient records could man be persuaded to turn to that which is Ever Present, even Jehovih.

7. And the like condition hath ever come unto all the ancient gods and men; for men fear to let go from that which is carrying them further and further away from their Creator.

8. This do I also declare unto you: the sum of revelation in each and every cycle hath been to bring man nearer and nearer to the comprehension of the Ever Present; to make man know that Jehovih now is, even as He was with the ancients.

9. That man might ultimately have his understanding open, so as to receive his own revelations from his Creator, and from the angels of God.

10. Such being, in fact, the founding of His kingdom on earth as it is in heaven.

11. Since, then, direct inspiration shall come from the Father unto all men, how hope ye not to be bound by the revelations of the prophets of old?

12. The same Creator now is, always was and ever shall be.

13. To be as near Him, and as much in Him, and as much one with Him, as were the ancient prophets, shall ye not also be one with the Father, to prophesy and to accomplish good works?

14. For if God, the Father, be ever the same, and ye fulfill His requirements as did the ancient prophets, the same result shall happen unto you as to them.

15. To quicken man, therefore, to enter into the living present, instead of leaving him as a follower of the ancient light, is the work of your God.

16. Whereto ye shall join in wisdom and earnestness regardless of self-sacrifice.

17. Now, therefore, when the signs of decadence in the old systems manifest themselves, as for example, when those who are of good mind and sound judgment, having been believers in the ancient doctrines and revelations, but afterward turn away from them because the doctrines are impotent, ye shall know of a truth a new cycle is at hand.

END OF THE BOOK OF OURANOTHEN.

JOHN BALLOU NEWBROUGH

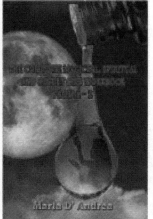

Made in the USA
Las Vegas, NV
07 March 2024

86839123R00334